5/96

EDWARD I

Michael Prestwich

Professor of History, University of Durham

UNIVERSITY OF CALIFORNIA PRESS

BERKELEY AND LOS ANGELES

First published in the United States in 1988
by University of California Press
Berkeley and Los Angeles, California
Copyright © 1988 Michael Prestwich

Printed in Great Britain

Library of Congress Cataloging-in-Publication Data

Prestwich, Michael.
Edward I.
Bibliography: p.
Includes index.
1. Edward I, King of England, 1239–1307.   2. Great
Britain – History – Edward I, 1272–1307.   3. Great
Britain – Kings and rulers – Biography.   I. Title.
II. Title: Edward the First.
DA229.P72   1989   942.03'5'0924   [B]   88–5759
ISBN 0–520–06266–3 (alk. paper)

For Robin, Chris and Kate

CONTENTS

LIST OF ILLUSTRATIONS

PLATES

GENEALOGICAL TABLES

Acknowledgements and thanks for permission to reproduce the photographs are due to the Ashmolean Museum, Oxford, for plates 21 and 22; to John Bethell for plates 8 and 9; to the Bodleian Library, Oxford, for plates 3 and 17; to the British Library for plates 5, 19, 24 and 25; to CADW: Welsh Historic Monuments for plate 12; to the Public Record Office for plates 18 and 20; to the Dean and Chapter of Westminster for plates 1, 2, 4 and 23; to the Pierpont Morgan Library, New York, for plate 7; and to the Pitkin Pictorial Archive for plates 10, 11 and 13. Plates 6 and 14 appear by gracious permission of Her Majesty the Queen.

The maps, plans and genealogical tables were redrawn from the author's roughs by Neil Hyslop.

PREFACE

In 1968, I decided not to write this book. The subject, Edward I, seemed altogether too large, and a book which concentrated on some aspects of his complex reign was, at that stage, a more attractive alternative. That book, *War, Politics and Finance under Edward I*, duly appeared in 1972, and the major task of writing a biography of Edward was taken on by Professor Harry Rothwell. He would undoubtedly have produced a superb volume, but sadly he died when it was still at an early stage. Thanks to the kindness of Mrs Rothwell, I was privileged to see his notes, from which I gained valuable insights. It was not possible, however, for me to produce the volume as he had envisaged it: he had not written much of it in final form. It would not have been fair to Professor Rothwell to try to write his book: my Edward is not his.

Edward I was sixty-seven when he died. He lived a full life, and the range of his activities presents the historian with considerable problems. He played a major part in the political troubles of the later years of his father's reign; went on crusade; governed England during a period particularly formative for legal and parliamentary development; conquered Wales, and came close, or so it seemed in 1304, to subjecting Scotland to his rule. He was not a purely English ruler. He held the duchy of Gascony in south-western France, and took a very considerable interest in its affairs. As befitted a ruler of his stature, he played a major part in European diplomacy and war. It would have been possible to adopt a narrative plan throughout this book, bringing out the chronological continuity of events, and stressing the many simultaneous pressures on the king. Some of the aspects of the reign can, however, be treated in an almost self-contained way, and in order to provide a clearer view of the problems that faced Edward, a thematic approach has been adopted for much of the book. This means that the reader may have to wait for a full explanation of some elements of the reign, such as parliament, until a later stage in the book; or that he or she may be faced, at an early point, with evidence taken from Edward's later years, as in the discussion of the royal household. I hope that the disadvantages of this approach are outweighed by the advantages, and that the constant inter-relationship of the various aspects of the king's career remains apparent.

Such a book as this owes a great deal to the help of others. Professor Lionel Stones took a great interest in it from the outset, and I owe him an immense debt. He made much manuscript material available to me in microfilm, saving me a great deal of time and trouble. He also undertook the labour of reading the entire typescript, correcting many infelicities of style, and, most importantly, putting right many mistakes and giving me much valuable advice. It is a matter of deep personal sadness that he did not live to see the book published. He was a most generous scholar, and his encouragement was heartening throughout. Dr Arnold Taylor has been extremely generous, providing me with transcripts of manuscripts in Turin and many references to items in the Public Record Office, London. Dr David d'Avray is another who most kindly provided me with copies of his transcripts. The various theses that I have consulted during the preparation of this book are all acknowledged in the footnotes, but I should make special mention of the work of Dr Robin Studd on Edward's *acta* prior to his accession, of that of Dr Huw Ridgeway on the aliens and their role in the court politics of the late 1250s and early 1260s, and of Dr P.C. Saunders on royal ecclesiastical patronage. Expert assistance in the selection of pictures from manuscript sources was given by Sally Dormer.

I have learned much from discussing Edward I with various friends, and would mention in particular Dr David Carpenter, Dr Robin Frame and Dr Paul Brand. The staff of all the libraries and record depositories I have used have all been most helpful: I have been most reliant upon the Public Record Office in London, and the University Library and the Library of the Dean and Chapter in Durham. The financial assistance of the Staff Travel and Research Fund of the University of Durham was essential. The immense labour of typing the whole book on to a word-processor was undertaken by Wendy Duery, with exemplary speed, accuracy and cheerfulness, which she maintained even when constant corrections were being made to the original text. I am very grateful to Professor Scott Waugh and the other anonymous academics who read this book for the publishers: their suggestions have removed many errors from the text, and have made for many improvements. At Methuen, Ann Wilson, Sarah Hannigan, Helen Everson and Ann Mansbridge have done all they could to make an author's life an easy one. The original genesis of this book probably lies in childhood visits to the great castles of north Wales, when I was first introduced to Edward I by my father: his influence on my work has been of central importance ever since. Finally, my wife's role has been invaluable. She has patiently read and criticized countless drafts, and her help with the proofs and index has also been essential. I could not have written this book without her help.

ABBREVIATED REFERENCES

The following abbreviations are used in the footnotes. For many works, the full title is given only for the first reference, and thereafter short titles are used. These are fully extended in the bibliography.

All manuscript references are to documents in the Public Record Office, London, unless otherwise stated.

Ann. Dunstable	'Annales Prioratus de Dunstaplia, A.D. 1–1297', *Annales Monastici*, ed. H.R. Luard (Rolls series, 1864–9), ii
Ann. London	'Annales Londonienses', *Chronicles of the Reigns of Edward I and Edward II*, ed. W. Stubbs (Rolls series, 1882–3), i
Ann. Osney	'Annales Monasterii de Oseneia, 1016–1347', *Annales Monastici*, ed. H.R. Luard (Rolls series, 1864–9), iv
Ann. Tewkesbury	'Annales Monasterii de Theokesburia', *Annales Monastici*, ed. H.R. Luard (Rolls series, 1864–9), i
Ann. Waverley	'Annales Monasterii de Waverleia, A.D. 1–1291', *Annales Monastici*, ed. H.R. Luard (Rolls series, 1864–9), ii
Ann. Winchester	'Annales Prioratus de Wintonia', 519–1277', *Annales Monastici*, ed. H.R. Luard (Rolls series, 1864–9), ii
Ann. Worcester	'Annales Prioratus de Wigornia, A.D. 1–1377', *Annales Monastici*, ed. H.R. Luard (Rolls series, 1864–9), iv
BIHR	*Bulletin of the Institute of Historical Research*
BL	British Library
Cal. Anc. Corr. Wales	*Calendar of Ancient Correspondence concerning Wales*, ed. J.G. Edwards (Cardiff, 1935)
Cal. Anc. Pet. Wales	*Calendar of Ancient Petitions relating to Wales*, ed. W. Rees (Cardiff, 1975)
CChR	*Calendar of Charter Rolls* (1903–)
CCR	*Calendar of Close Rolls* (1892–)

CDI	*Calendar of Documents relating to Ireland*, ed. H.S. Sweetman, 5 vols (1877–86)
CDS	*Calendar of Documents relating to Scotland*, i–iv, ed. J. Bain (1881–8); v, ed. G.G. Simpson and J.D. Galbraith (Edinburgh, 1986)
CFR	*Calendar of Fine Rolls* (1911–)
Chron. Bury St Edmunds	*The Chronicle of Bury St Edmunds, 1212–1301*, ed. A. Gransden (1964)
Chron. Lanercost	*Chronicon de Lanercost*, ed. J. Stevenson (Maitland Club, 1839)
CLR	*Calendar of Liberate Rolls* (1916–)
Cotton	*Bartholomaei de Cotton, Historia Anglicana (A.D. 449–1298)*, ed. H.R. Luard (Rolls series, 1859)
CPR	*Calendar of Patent Rolls* (1891–)
CWR	'Calendar of Welsh Rolls', *Calendar of Chancery Rolls Various, 1277–1326* (1912)
Documents 1297–8	*Documents Illustrating the Crisis of 1297–98 in England*, ed. M.C. Prestwich (Camden Society, 4th series, xxiv, 1980)
EHR	*English Historical Review*
Flores	*Flores Historiarum*, ed. H.R. Luard, 3 vols (Rolls series, 1890)
Foedera	*Foedera, Conventiones, Litterae et Acta Publica*, ed. T. Rymer (Record Commission ed., 4 vols, 1816–69)
Gervase of Canterbury	*Historical Works of Gervase of Canterbury*, ed. W. Stubbs, 2 vols (Rolls series, 1879–80)
Great Cause	*Edward I and the Throne of Scotland. An Edition of the Record Sources for the Great Cause*, ed. E.L.G. Stones and G.G. Simpson, 2 vols (Oxford, 1978)
Guisborough	*The Chronicle of Walter of Guisborough*, ed. H. Rothwell (Camden Society, 3rd series, lxxxix, 1957)
KW	*The History of the King's Works, i, ii, The Middle Ages*, ed. R.A. Brown, H.M. Colvin, A.J. Taylor (1963)
Langtoft	*The Chronicle of Pierre de Langtoft*, ed. T. Wright, 2 vols (Rolls series, 1886)

Liber Quotidianus	*Liber Quotidianus Contrarotulatoris Garderobiae, 1299–1300,* ed. J. Topham *et al* (1787)
Matthew Paris, *Chron. Maj.*	*Matthaei Parisiensis, Monachi Sancti Albani, Chronica Majora,* ed. H.R. Luard, 7 vols (Rolls series, 1872–83)
Oxenedes	*Chronica Johannis de Oxenedes,* ed. H. Ellis (Rolls series, 1859)
Parl. Writs	*Parliamentary Writs and Writs of Military Summons,* ed. F. Palgrave, 2 vols in 4 (Record Commission, 1827–34)
Reg. Peckham	*Registrum Epistolarum Johannis Peckham,* ed. C.T. Martin, 3 vols (Rolls series, 1882–4)
RH	*Rotuli Hundredorum,* 2 vols (Record Commission, 1812–18)
Rishanger	*Willelmi Rishanger, Chronica et Annales,* ed. H.T. Riley (Rolls series, 1865)
Rot. Parl.	*Rotuli Parliamentorum,* 7 vols (Record Commission, 1783–1832)
SHR	*Scottish Historical Review*
TRHS	*Transactions of the Royal Historical Society*
Wykes	'Chronicon vulgo dictum Chronicon Thomae Wykes, 1066–1289', *Annales Monastici,* ed. H.R. Luard (Rolls series, 1864–9), iv

NOTE ON MONEY

The monetary system of medieval England was based on that established by the emperor Charlemagne. The bulk of the currency consisted of silver pennies; under Edward I, half-pennies and farthings were also put into circulation. The usual method of accounting was in £ s d, with twelve pennies to the shilling, and twenty shillings to the pound. However, the mark was also used as a unit of account. It was worth 13s 4d, or two-thirds of a pound. Attempts to render medieval values in terms of modern prices are pointless, and soon become dated, with the seemingly inexorable inflation of today. As a very rough guide, a wealthy earl might expect an income of some £5,000 a year. A knight's wages in war amounted to 2s a day, a common infantryman's 2d. A good quality warhorse might be worth between £20 and £40. The value of sterling as against other currencies fluctuated, but until the great French debasements of the 1290s, the usual ratio of the English currency with the *livre tournois*, the main French coinage, was about 1:4.

PART I

The Heir to the Throne

Chapter 1

THE GREEN TREE, 1239–58

Matthew Paris, the most notable chronicler of the day, wrote in the late 1250s in despair as to what the future King Edward I would be like as king. He described a particularly unpleasant and wholly gratuitous attack by Edward and his followers on a young man, who at the prince's orders had an ear cut off and an eye gouged out. Matthew altered a quotation from St Luke to fit: 'If he does these things when the wood is green, what can be hoped for when it is seasoned?'[1] The chronicler's fears were not justified, to judge by reactions on Edward's death. The king was then described as a man of great goodness, a ruler who did more than any other for his country, and as the flower of chivalry.[2]

Was Edward a man whose personality was transformed by his accession to the throne in 1272, in the manner of Shakespeare's Henry V? In a strictly legal context it was indeed argued that as king Edward was 'as if another person' from the Edward who had been heir to the throne.[3] The great lawgiver, the conqueror of Wales, the constructive statesman, may seem to have little in common with the unruly youth described by Matthew Paris, or with the young man compared in the 1260s to the changeable and unreliable leopard.[4] Yet the trait of violence that alarmed Matthew can be shown by solid documentary evidence to have been present in maturity, with such incidents as the king's fierce assault on a squire at the wedding of one of the royal princesses, or his action in hurling the coronet belonging to another of his daughters into the fire.[5] The earls who in the late 1290s doubted, with considerable justification, the king's promises to confirm Magna Carta must have thought that there was still much of the leopard in Edward. The king's reign cannot be understood without looking first at the experiences of his early years. It is not only the king's violent and unreliable tendencies that can be detected in his youth: it was then also that he learned much that was to be put to constructive effect when he succeeded to the throne.

[1] Matthew Paris, *Chron. Maj.*, v, 598.
[2] *The Political Songs of England*, ed. T. Wright (Camden Soc., 1839), 241–2.
[3] *Placita de Quo Warranto* (Record Commission, 1811), 429–30.
[4] *Political Songs*, ed. Wright, 93.
[5] Below, 111.

Edward was born at Westminster on the night of 17 June 1239, the eldest child of Henry III and his young queen, Eleanor of Provence. The news was greeted with great joy. The citizens of London took to the streets and celebrated by torchlight: they felt that they could claim the young prince as one of their own number, a feeling that later events were not to justify. In the royal chapel the king's clerks sang *Christus Vincit* to mark the event. Earl Warenne's delight at the news proved highly profitable to the messenger who brought it, for he was promised land worth £10 a year. Not everyone shared this view, however. According to Matthew Paris, the general pleasure did not last long, for Henry III made it plain that the messengers sent out to announce the event were to bring back gifts. One courtier's sardonic comment was that 'God gave us this child, but the king is selling him to us'.[6] In the next year, when orders were given that all men should perform fealty to the young heir to the throne, there was trouble in Buckingham, where the hue and cry was raised against the officials appointed to perform the task.[7]

Baptism of the infant quickly followed birth: it was hardly wise to delay in an age of high infant mortality. The ceremony was conducted in Westminster Abbey by the papal legate Otto, in the presence of the archbishop of Canterbury, the bishops of London and Carlisle, the bishop-elect of Norwich, and a distinguished body of lay magnates including the king's brother, Richard earl of Cornwall, and his brother-in-law, Simon de Montfort, who had recently been invested with the earldom of Leicester.[8] The language of the court and nobility was French, yet the baby was given an English name. This was Henry III's personal choice, reflecting his devotion to the cult of Edward the Confessor, who had been canonized in 1161. The feast of the saintly king was always celebrated with great pomp by Henry: in 1263 he hoped to feed no less than 100,000 poor men on the occasion. In 1220 he had laid the foundation stone for a new Lady Chapel in the Confessor's church, Westminster Abbey, and in 1245 he was to begin a full-scale reconstruction of the whole building in the latest French style.[9] The cult was designed to add to the prestige of the monarchy, and to this extent the choice of the name Edward had political implications. Essentially, however, it was the product of Henry's personal piety. Similar motives, presumably, were to lead to the selection of another

[6] Matthew Paris, *Chron. Maj.*, iii, 539–40; *CLR 1226–40*, 406; *CPR 1232–47*, 417.

[7] *Close Rolls, 1237–42*, 182.

[8] Matthew Paris, *Chron. Maj.*, iii, 540. According to Guisborough, 177, Edward was baptized by the archbishop of Canterbury.

[9] *CPR 1258–66*, 282; *KW*, i, 130–1.

English name, Edmund, for Henry's second son, called after the Anglo-Saxon martyr king.[10]

Childhood, even when it was that of a probable future king, was not particularly well-recorded in the middle ages, and the early years of Edward I are no exception. The formal appointments of those put in charge of the boy are of course preserved, but the few personal details that survive give little idea of what Edward was like as a child. It is not known if the future builder of great fortresses in Wales had a toy castle to play with, as his own son Edward of Caernarfon did, nor are there accounts to show whether, like his youngest sons Thomas and Edmund, he broke not only his own drums, but also those of visiting minstrels.[11] More important, virtually nothing is known of Edward's education.

Royal children did not then stay for long in the company of their parents. Edward was very soon given his own household and his own staff. He was allocated a chamber at Windsor as early as August 1239, and was entrusted to the care of Hugh Giffard and his wife Sybil, who had acted as midwife at his birth. In March 1240 a clerk, Walter de Dya, was appointed to assist Giffard, and orders were given that the boy could only be visited with his knowledge. There were two wet-nurses, Alice and Sarah, of whom the former seems to have been the more important: the queen would hardly have been expected to feed her own children.[12] The young prince's household soon expanded, for it was decided that he should have the company of other children. The most important was his cousin Henry of Almain, son of Richard earl of Cornwall, probably sent to Windsor when his mother died in 1240. They were not all of exalted status: in 1243 the two sons of Ferrand, a former crossbowman in royal service, were with Edward. James, son of Nicholas de Molis, was another of the prince's companions.[13]

Various orders issued by the king testify to his concern for his son. In October 1242 he wrote to the constable of Windsor, saying that he had heard that the children had no good wine to drink, and instructing him to present them with two tuns of the best to be found in the castle. The age of three may seem remarkably young to drink wine, but at least it did not present the same health risks as water – not that this would have been realized at the time. In the same year the sheriff of Gloucester was asked to buy fifteen lampreys, and send them off one after the other to

[10] At the time of his usurpation Henry IV attempted to make use of the legend that Edmund was in fact Henry III's eldest son, but that he was passed over, because of a deformity, in favour of Edward. This legend has no basis in fact.

[11] KW, i, 202n; C. Bullock-Davies, Menestrallorum Multitudo (Cardiff, 1978), 136–7.

[12] CLR 1226–40, 409; Close Rolls, 1237–42, 236; CPR 1232–47, 247.

[13] Close Rolls, 1242–7, 30, 141; N. Denholm-Young, Richard of Cornwall (Oxford, 1947), 32.

Edward at Windsor. The king's chamberlain was asked to buy scarlet
robes with lavish fur trimmings for Edward and his sister Margaret,
younger by just over a year. Saddles were ordered for the two children,
each equipped with two seats, as they could not be expected to ride
unaided.[14]

The personnel of Edward's household did not remain stable. In 1245
William le Brun, who had taken over from Walter de Dya, was himself
replaced by Peter of Wakering. Hugh Giffard died in the next year, and
his place was taken by Bartholomew Pecche, who was given a grant of
£20 a year from the exchequer, for as long as he should remain
Edward's guardian.[15] The prince was to grow to be a tall, strong adult,
but his health in childhood seems to have been a constant worry. This was
hardly surprising in those days: he had at least four brothers and sisters
who died in infancy. He himself was seriously ill in 1246 when the royal
family was at Beaulieu for the consecration of the new abbey church.
Queen Eleanor, who seems to have been devoted to her son, insisted on
remaining in the abbey for some three weeks until he recovered, contrary
to the monastic rules. He was again ill in the next year, when the king
asked all the religious houses near London to pray for his recovery.
Another illness, this time in 1251, is attested by a licence for Bartholomew
Pecche and Eble des Montz to take kids in Windsor Forest in 1251, for
the prince to eat during convalescence.[16] These may have been no more
than the usual childhood ailments, but Edward's doctors, Thomas and
Alexander, would not have had any very effective remedies at their
disposal, and every illness must have been alarming.

Very little is known of Edward's education and early training, but it
probably took a conventional form.[17] None of those placed in charge of
him came to exercise a major influence in the way that Simon Burley
was to do over the young Richard II, though the friendships that
Edward made with his contemporaries, especially his cousin Henry of
Almain, were to be important. It is not known for certain whether
Edward learned to read and write: the first English king whose hand-
writing survives is Edward III. It is hard to imagine, however, that
Edward I was illiterate. His main language was of course French, more
specifically the Anglo-Norman dialect, but he had some understanding
of Latin, and could speak English. His mother possessed romances
written in French, and Edward may have gained a taste for such works
from her. Training in the knightly skills was more important for a
future king than scholastic attainments. Hunting was both a sport and

[14] *Close Rolls, 1237–42,* 476; *Close Rolls, 1242–7,* 45, 118; *CLR, 1240–5,* 174.
[15] *Close Rolls, 1242–7,* 326; *CPR 1232–47,* 495.
[16] Matthew Paris, *Chron. Maj.,* iv, 639; *Close Rolls 1247–51,* 27, 452; *CLR 1244–51,* 65.
[17] For a recent discussion of this topic, see N. Orme, *From Childhood to Chivalry*
(1984).

a training for war, and as early as the age of eight Edward had permission to hunt and disport himself in Windsor Forest. Horsemanship would have been learned early, and he must soon have been taught how to use sword and lance. The latter was a particularly difficult weapon to master. To hold the point of a long, heavy pole steady while galloping towards a target was no mean task, and acquisition of this skill must have involved many hours at the quintain. It was not until he was almost seventeen, in 1256, that he was equipped with suitable weapons and armour to try out his skills at a specially arranged tournament at Blyth. Many of those present were badly injured, but Edward, either through skill or the respect of the participants for the heir to the throne, seems not to have suffered. Travel was another part of Edward's education. Like all noble households, his was itinerant, and by the early 1250s Edward was travelling regularly from one royal residence to another. He possessed chambers in such places as Woodstock, Oxford, Silverstone, Guildford, Havering and Gillingham in Dorset, and was beginning the task of learning about the country he would one day govern.[18]

In his early years Edward's household was largely financed by means of grants from the exchequer. Administrative convenience, however, meant that it was simpler if the prince had his own sources of revenue, and in 1244 Edward was granted half of the lands which had recently been confiscated from the subjects of the king of France. The most important estate involved was the honour of Tickhill in Yorkshire, which had belonged to the countess of Eu. Edward also received at this time the revenues of the vacant bishopric of Chichester.[19] He was not given custody of any estates which might be regarded as forming part of the crown's patrimony. When he was ten, however, Edward received what must have seemed to be a lavish grant from his father. In September 1249 all of Gascony, the duchy in south-western France held by the English, together with the Isle of Oléron was bestowed upon him.[20] Henry had already shown that he did not regard the duchy of Gascony as inalienable, for in 1242 he had granted it to his brother Richard of Cornwall, but shortly afterwards the two men quarrelled, and at the suggestion of Queen Eleanor the deed was cancelled.[21] It is possible that even at this early stage she was anxious that Gascony should go to her son: she appears to have been far more concerned than Henry III that he should be properly provided for.

[18] H. Johnstone, *Edward of Caernarvon 1284–1307* (Manchester, 1946), 18; *Rôles Gascons*, i, no. 149; *Close Rolls 1247–51*, 18; Matthew Paris, *Chron. Maj.*, v, 557; *CLR 1251–60*, 3, 23, 92, 119, 193, 410.

[19] *CPR 1232–47*, 418, 420; *CLR 1245–51*, 28.

[20] *CChR 1226–57*, 345.

[21] Denholm-Young, *Richard of Cornwall*, 48–9.

The grant of 1249 proved to be little more than an empty formality.
The English position in south-western France at this period was not an
easy one. Henry III had an understandable desire to regain the lands
in France lost by his father John. Campaigns in 1230 and 1242 achieved
little: there was no prospect of regaining Normandy, and at Taillebourg
in 1242 Henry was ignominiously deserted by the Poitevin nobles.
However, Gascony, which had come to the English crown with the
marriage of Eleanor of Aquitaine to Henry II, remained in Henry's
hands, though after his military failures it was unlikely that the English
king would win the respect of his unruly subjects there. The duchy was
in a condition of near anarchy, with the most powerful noble, Gaston de
Béarn, in almost permanent rebellion. As English control of the duchy
weakened, so the kings of Castile and Aragon pressed their own claims
to it.[22]

In 1248 Henry III had appointed his brother-in-law, Simon de
Montfort, to act as royal lieutenant in Gascony for seven years. The
seriousness of the situation was reflected in the unprecedented powers
accorded to Montfort. His firm techniques, first making peace with
external enemies and then turning to the problems of internal order,
had considerable success, though they also provoked numerous complaints to Henry III in England. After an initial policy of neutrality
towards the two factions which dominated Bordeaux, the Colomb and
Soler families, Montfort sided with the former. The Soler protested to
the king, as did Gaston de Béarn, with whom Montfort had a private
dispute over the county of Bigorre. The story of Montfort's rule in
Gascony is a complex one: from Edward's point of view, the fact that
Earl Simon had been put in full control of the Gascon revenues meant
that the grant of 1249 amounted to virtually nothing in practical terms.
It is also relevant to note that there was little in Montfort's methods of
rule which presaged the role that he was to play in England as the
leader of the baronial reform movement in the 1260s.

Simon de Montfort's rule in Gascony did not last the intended seven
years. The volume of complaints reaching Henry III was such that in
1252, after royal commissioners had been sent to Gascony, the case
between Earl Simon and his Gascon opponents was heard at Westminster before the king. The trial was a dramatic one. Matthew Paris
described a bitter exchange between Henry III and his brother-in-
law, in which Montfort goaded the king, saying 'Who could believe that
you are a Christian? Have you ever been confessed?', a line of attack
which naturally infuriated the pious Henry.[23] An unsatisfactory

[22] For a recent brief account of Gascony in this period, see M.W. Labarge, *Gascony,
England's First Colony, 1204-1453* (1980), 17–28.
[23] Matthew Paris, *Chron. Maj.*, v, 290.

compromise led to Simon's return to Gascony and a truce with his opponents. A final settlement was to be made when Henry and his son Edward went to Gascony early in the next year. The Gascons seem to have been enthusiastic about the prospect of the grant to Edward being made a reality. The men of Bayonne and Bazas petitioned for the removal of Earl Simon and his replacement by Edward, and Henry III duly renewed the grant to his son of Gascony and Oléron, making a new condition that they should never be alienated from the English crown. But before this grant could be put into effect, Montfort had to be removed from office, as his appointment still had three years to run. An agreement was accordingly made between Edward and his uncle. In exchange for 7,000 marks, Montfort withdrew from Gascony.[24]

Edward was no more than a pawn in these events. He was only thirteen in 1252, and there was still no question of giving him anything more than a nominal position in Gascony. This was made very clear to him when Henry III eventually sailed for the duchy in August 1253, for Edward was left behind in England in the care of his mother and his uncle Richard of Cornwall. Matthew Paris painted an affecting picture of emotional farewells between father and son, with Edward finally left weeping on the shore as the ships set sail, refusing to leave until they were out of sight. It has been plausibly suggested that his tears may have been as much the result of his anger at the fact that he was not going to take over the duchy he had been promised, as of his sadness at being parted from his father.[25]

The situation in Gascony when Henry III arrived was still critical, and much was made by the English government of the dangers of imminent war. Gaston de Béarn was still in revolt, and there was a threat of invasion from Castile, whose ruler, Alphonso X, had a claim to the duchy through descent from Eleanor, daughter of Henry II. In fact, diplomacy triumphed and there was no war. Although in 1247 negotiations had taken place with Brabant for Edward's marriage, they had come to nothing, and the English diplomats were now free to offer Alphonso the prospect of a match between the heir to the throne and his sister Eleanor. There seem to have been few difficulties. Alphonso was understandably anxious to see Edward in person, to ensure that he was sufficiently handsome and accomplished, and suggested that he should knight him.[26] Henry III had intended that Edward should be knighted

[24] CChR 1226–57, 386; C. Bémont, Simon de Montfort, translated by E.F. Jacob (Oxford, 1930), 108, 321–4; CLR 1251–60, 167.

[25] Matthew Paris, Chron. Maj., v, 383; F.M. Powicke, Henry III and the Lord Edward (Oxford, 1947), i, 231.

[26] Matthew Paris, Chron. Maj., v, 397. For a discussion of Henry III's actions and policies during his stay in Gascony, see J.P. Trabut-Cussac, L'administration anglaise en Gascogne sous Henry III et Edouard I de 1254 à 1307 (Paris, 1972), xxxi-xli.

in England in a grand ceremony, along with a large number of other young men, but he was prepared to abandon this plan.[27] According to Matthew Paris, the English king was reluctant to entrust his son to a foreign ruler who might lead him astray, but he was persuaded by the Castilian envoys of the rectitude of Alphonso's character.[28] The Castilian's concerns were rather more practical than Henry's: Alphonso was clearly worried that his future son-in-law was insufficiently endowed with lands, and insisted that before marriage he should receive estates worth 15,000 marks a year. The negotiations proceeded slowly, but smoothly, and were concluded by the end of March 1254, although Henry still feared that there might be war.[29]

A week before his fifteenth birthday Edward finally set sail for Gascony, accompanied by his mother, his brother Edmund, and the archbishop of Canterbury. The men of Yarmouth had provided him with a fine ship, but when the sailors from Winchelsea who had been preparing vessels for the queen saw it, they were so angry that it was larger and better than theirs that they attacked it, killing many of the sailors.[30] This was one of many incidents in the long-running feud between the Cinque Ports and Yarmouth: Edward would experience the problem again in a more acute form in 1297. There were no further mishaps, and the fleet reached Bordeaux on about 10 June. The final negotiations for the marriage were concluded with no problems, and the fitting date of 13 October, the feast of the translation of Edward the Confessor, was set for the ceremony of Edward's knighting.[31]

Events did not quite go according to plan. Edward's entourage was not as large and splendid as had been intended, and his departure from Bayonne was late, so that the ceremonies at Burgos could not take place until 1 November, when both knighting and marriage took place in the church of the monastery of Las Huelgas. Three weeks later Edward and his bride were back in Gascony, at Bayonne. One of his clerks celebrated his master's position by describing him in a charter as 'now reigning in Gascony as prince and lord'. Henry III had not stayed in the south for his son's marriage: he was already on his way north, and received the news only on 20 November when he was at Marmoutier.[32]

This year 1254 was of prime importance in Edward's life. There was no formal attainment of an age of majority for him, but the grant of

[27] *Close Rolls 1251-3*, 37-8, 191, 442-3, 465, 471, 475, 508-9.

[28] Matthew Paris, *Chron. Maj.*, v, 397-8.

[29] Trabut-Cussac, *L'administration anglaise en Gascogne*, xxxvi-xxxviii.

[30] Matthew Paris, *Chron. Maj.*, v, 446-7. According to Paris, Henry III issued instructions at the last minute forbidding the queen to sail, but she wisely ignored his worries.

[31] Trabut-Cussac, *L'administration anglaise en Gascogne*, 7.

[32] Ibid., 7-8; *CPR 1247-58*, 382.

massive estates, his knighting and his marriage, all in the year of his fifteenth birthday, amounted to his achieving adult status. He owed a substantial debt of gratitude to Alphonso of Castile, for it was clearly through his insistence that Edward obtained so much when still so young. Knighting was perhaps little more than a formality due to Edward by right of birth, rather than because of any achievement, but it was an important initiation into chivalric society. Marriage was obviously very important, and although personal details are few, every indication is that this match with Eleanor proved to be a thoroughly satisfactory one. The grants made to Edward by his father, as a result of pressure from Alphonso, transformed Edward's wealth and position. The endowment was made on 14 February 1254, and was most impressive, at least on paper. It consisted of all Ireland, apart from the cities and counties of Dublin and Limerick, Athlone, and lands promised to Geoffrey de Lusignan and Robert Walerand. In Wales Edward was to receive the king's conquests in the north, the honour of the Three Castles (Skenfrith, Grosmont and White Castle) in south Wales, along with the castles of Montgomery, Carmarthen, Cardigan and Builth. Gascony, the Isle of Oléron and the Channel Isles were Edward's. In England he received the earldom of Chester, the town and castle of Bristol, Stamford and Grantham in Lincolnshire, the manor of Freemantle in Hampshire, and all the lands which the count of Eu had held. All were to be held on condition that they were not alienated from the English crown.[33]

Matthew Paris considered that having made such lavish grants, Henry III had turned himself into 'a mutilated kinglet'. Sir Maurice Powicke wrote that 'from this time Edward ruled his scattered fiefs in his own name'. Yet the reality of Edward's power has been forcefully questioned. J.R. Studd has pointed to the king's continued interference in his son's affairs, and to Edward's lack of a formal title, as evidence that the actual situation was very different from the apparent implications of the grant of 1245, and he argued that far from giving up vast estates, Henry III in practice reinforced his royal authority in areas where it was weak, by emphasizing his overriding rights of sovereignty.[34]

The first point to consider is Edward's lack of a title. In his charters he was simply termed 'Edward, first-born son and heir of lord Henry, illustrious king of England', or more simply 'Lord Edward, first-born son of the illustrious king of England'.[35] Henry III, despite the grant of

[33] CPR 1247–58, 382.

[34] Matthew Paris, Chron. Maj., v, 450; Powicke, Henry III and the Lord Edward, i, 233; J.R. Studd, 'The Lord Edward and Henry III', BIHR, xlx (1977), 4–19.

[35] See for example CChR 1226–57, 447–8.

1254 to his son, did not abandon his titles of lord of Ireland or duke
of Aquitaine. To contemporaries, Edward was simply *Dominus
Edwardus*, Lord Edward. The title Lord was a simple honorific, one
which the heir to the throne shared with magnates, bishops and even
academics.[36] Henry could have given his son a royal title: Henry II had
had his eldest son crowned king during his own lifetime, in 1170, and
there was also the precedent of Henry III's brother-in-law, the emperor Frederick II, who had organized the election of his son Henry as
king of the Romans (a title which gave him rule in Germany) in 1220.
Neither of these examples could be counted as successes, however, for
both young kings had rebelled against their fathers. Yet if Edward was
not to be given the rank of king, surely he could have been permitted to
use a lesser title? Richard I had been duke of Aquitaine prior to his
accession, and John lord of Ireland, although Richard and John had
received these titles before they became heirs to the throne. There was
no precedent for the heir using a territorial title in the way that was to
become usual in the fourteenth century. The fact that Edward did not
bear such a title should not, however, be taken as evidence that his
authority was limited. Rather, the English were following the example
of the French royal house, where the king's eldest son was always styled
'first-born (*primogenitus*) of the Lord King of France', or some variant on
that style.[37]

Edward's position in his various lands and estates needs to be
examined separately. The lands he received in England were not
long-standing parts of the royal demesne, but were relatively recent
acquisitions by the crown. Stamford and Grantham, for example, had
belonged to a Norman family until King John granted them to Earl
Warenne: it is not clear how the crown regained them. Bristol had been
the centre of the great honour of Gloucester, but in 1214 had been
retained by John when he gave his former wife, the countess of Gloucester, in marriage to the earl of Essex. On the death of the last earl of
Chester in 1237 Henry III bought out the four co-heiresses to the
estates, and obtained the right to the title in 1242.[38] In granting
Edward these estates in England Henry was not, therefore, diminishing
the crown's authority by abandoning control over long-standing royal
estates. Rather, in insisting that these lands should not be alienated

---

[36] As there is no definite article in Latin, there is no contemporary warrant for the
common modern usage of 'the lord Edward'. In contemporary French, Edward was
simply 'Sire Edward' (*Political Songs*, ed. Wright, 60).

[37] A.W. Lewis, *Royal Succession in Capetian France: Studies on Familiar Order and the State*
(Cambridge, Mass., 1981), 166 and note.

[38] S. Painter, *The Reign of King John* (Baltimore, 1949), 149, 283; Powicke, *Henry III
and the Lord Edward*, ii, 788–9; R. Stewart Brown, 'The End of the Norman Earldom of
Chester', *EHR*, xxxv (1920), 26–54.

from the crown, he was adding in the long term to the crown's demesnes. This provision can certainly be seen as a limitation on Edward's authority, though it was not one of which he took great notice, since he did in fact make various grants from his estates. Nor was Edward in a much weaker position than other major landowners as a result of this provision regarding alienation, for in 1256 a royal ordinance laid down that anyone who held land directly from the king could only grant it to another by special permission.[39] It should also be noted that Henry III did not attempt to limit Edward's powers in Cheshire: the prince retained the palatine authority that the earls of Chester had enjoyed, which provided for a remarkable degree of local autonomy, similar to that in the great episcopal palatinate of Durham.

In Ireland Edward's authority was not fully independent. The country was not an easy one to rule. Anglo-Norman conquest had begun in Henry II's reign, but was still not complete in the mid-thirteenth century. Some regions, such as the county of Dublin and the lordships of Leinster and Meath, were effectively colonized, but in others the Anglo-Norman aristocracy only exercised a very tenuous authority.[40] One royal official expressed himself very strongly in 1256, writing that he would rather go to prison than return to Ireland, where he had recently been attempting to raise money.[41]

Some of the initial limitations in the grant of Ireland to Edward did not last long: within four months Dublin, Limerick and Athlone were entrusted to him. Henry III, however, retained his rights over the church, and made it clear that Ireland still owed him allegiance.[42] It took a surprisingly long time for the grant to Edward to be fulfilled, probably because although it was intended that he should go in person to Ireland, he never in fact did so. He was prompt in appointing Richard de la Rochelle as his steward in Ireland, but it was not until 1256 that the royal justiciar, John FitzGeoffrey, relinquished his post. It is unlikely that there was any conflict between the two men, who were uncle and nephew. Henry III sometimes used his son's administration to implement or simply duplicate orders that he himself issued. Thus in late August he told the justiciar to restore Trim to Geoffrey de Geneville, and in mid-September Edward gave similar instructions to Richard de la Rochelle. Even after orders in May 1256 that Edward's seal should replace his own in the administration of Ireland, Henry still felt at liberty to intervene, on one occasion revoking a writ issued by his

<hr />

[39] J.M.W. Bean, *The Decline of English Feudalism* (Manchester, 1968), 66–79.

[40] The best recent brief account of Ireland in this period is R. Frame, *Colonial Ireland 1169–1369* (Dublin, 1981).

[41] *Royal and other historical letters illustrative of the reign of Henry III*, ed. W.W. Shirley (Rolls ser., 1866), ii, 119.

[42] *CDI 1252–1284*, no. 371.

son's chancery on the grounds that it was contrary to normal English legal form.[43] There were no major clashes over Irish policies between Henry III and his son. There were, however, considerable difficulties encountered in fulfilling the promise made by the king to his half-brother Geoffrey de Lusignan of £500 worth of land in Ireland, with Henry on one occasion angrily writing that, 'it is not just or fitting that the king's brother should be of worse condition than any other but rather of a better'.[44] The king failed to appreciate the problems involved in making over tracts of land in Connaught which were claimed by a local king, Felim O'Connor, to a French magnate, and eventually Geoffrey received instead estates in Louth and in England.[45] Edward's own main concern with Ireland was probably simply as a source of funds and supplies. His attitude, both at this time and later in his career, is exemplified by orders issued in 1254 for all the revenues of Ireland to be sent to him, and for 2,000 crannocks of wheat in addition, the cost of which was to be met out of future revenue.[46]

Gascony was always to be much more important to Edward than Ireland. He visited the duchy several times before his accession, was there from August 1273 until April 1274, and spent the period from 1286 to 1289 there as well. It was in Gascony that Edward had his first taste of power, to some extent, for when Henry III returned northwards in the autumn of 1254, he left his son there for a year. Edward had his own administration, headed by his chancellor, Michael de Fiennes.[47] A roll of letters issued in Edward's name while Henry was still in Gascony survives, and suggests that he had little real independence. He did, it seems, take the initiative in ordering the destruction of the church at La Réole, which rebels had earlier defended against the English. However, Henry III intervened, and after arbitration by two bishops only the recent fortifications were rased.[48]

Once Henry had left Gascony, Edward's administration was left in charge. The main concern was to continue the process of pacification by means of a complex combination of judicial judgement, negotiations of truces, and some military action, as when Edward besieged Gramont in July 1255. This must have been a formative period for the young prince, but details of his policies are not as full as might be wished. It is

---

[43] G.H. Orpen, *Ireland under the Normans 1216–1333* (Oxford, 1920), iii, 232; *CDI 1252–1284*, nos 391, 399, 457, 461, 529.

[44] *CPR 1247–58*, 384.

[45] Orpen, *Ireland under the Normans*, iii, 233–4.

[46] *CDI 1252–84*, nos 419, 446.

[47] G.P. Cuttino, 'A Chancellor of the Lord Edward', *BIHR*, xlx (1977), 229–32. Cuttino's assumption that he was the first to notice Fiennes' appointment is incorrect: see N. Denholm-Young, *Seigneurial Administration in England* (Oxford, 1937), 12, n.6.

[48] Trabut-Cussac, *L'administration anglaise en Gascogne*, 8–9.

interesting to see that already Edward was experiencing financial problems, for he borrowed extensively, and was compelled to levy a tax. This was, at least in part, presented by his officials as being a feudal aid that the Gascons were obliged to pay on the occasion of Edward's being knighted. Some of those now recruited into Edward's service were to form the nucleus of his administation in later years.[49]

In 1255 Edward returned to England, Eleanor of Castile preceding him by some weeks. He was still not his own master, for it was his father's decision that he should come home. It was only after the prince's return that signs of division between father and son over the question of Gascony began to appear. Matthew Paris provides a highly coloured account of a row between the two, resulting from the complaints put to Edward by Gascon merchants who objected to the exactions of royal officials. They stated that they would rather trade with Saracens than with England. Henry was furious that they should have complained to Edward, not him, and fulminated that there was still only one king in England who could do justice. When Edward put the Gascon case to his father, Henry produced a tirade about family ingratitude, recalling the way in which Henry I I's dearest sons turned against him. The dispute did not develop further, for Henry took sensible advice and met the grievances of the Gascons: in December 1255 he ordered his officials to take no more from them than was rightful and customary. According to Matthew Paris, Edward strengthened the size of his household at this time so that he had a force of two hundred horse, surely an exaggeration on the chronicler's part.[50]

The records reveal a much more serious split than this between Henry and his son over the question of Gascony. The king's instincts were all in favour of a policy of mediation between the two rival factions in Bordeaux, the Soler and Colomb. In contrast, Edward aimed to create a party in the city loyal to his interests, and with this in view determined on an alliance with the Soler family. On 9 September 1256 he made a treaty with Gaillard del Soler, of which Henry I I I was kept ignorant. Soler agreed to win control of the mayoralty of Bordeaux for Edward, to build a new castle in the town, not to make peace with his rivals without the prince's consent, and not to make marriage alliances prejudicial to his interests. For the time being little came of this, as Henry pursued his policies of reconciliation, giving the Soler and Colomb families permission to conclude marriage alliances, and compelling his son to confirm the status of the Bordeaux commune. Gaillard del Soler foolishly boasted, on his return to Gascony, about his alliance with Edward, and was duly arrested. Yet eventually it was

---

[49] Ibid., 8–15.
[50] Matthew Paris, *Chron. Maj.*, v, 538–9; *CPR 1247–58*, 453.

Edward's policy which was to triumph. In 1259 he renewed his treaty with Gaillard del Soler, and in the following year the Gascon was acquitted by the king of all charges made against him.[51]

Although there was evidently a major disagreement over policy in Gascony between Edward and his father, the prince had little real opportunity to act in this period from 1254 to 1258. He was ultimately subordinate to Henry's authority, and the seneschal of Gascony, Stephen Longespée, was the king's nominee. He had to conduct his policy of alliance with Gaillard del Soler in a secretive, underhand manner, and must have resented the position in which he had been placed.

The last element of the landed endowment that Edward received in 1254 which needs to be discussed is Wales. There is little in Edward's policies and experiences in this period to suggest that he was to be the conqueror of the principality. The mood when Edward received his grant of lands in 1254 was more one of post-war calm than of pre-war tension. The highly successful Welsh ruler Llywelyn the Great had died in 1240, and in the confused dynastic situation of the succeeding years the Welsh did not fare particularly well. Llywelyn's son Dafydd died in 1246, and the principality of Gwynedd was then placed under the rule of the two elder sons of Dafydd's half-brother Gruffydd, who had died when attempting to escape from the Tower of London in 1244. He had made a rope out of his bedclothes, but as one modern historian has put it, 'unfortunately, he did not allow for the weight of a particularly bulky body, made unwieldy by the torpor of a comfortable captivity'.[52] The two Welsh princes, Llywelyn and Owain, were forced to come to terms with the English at Woodstock in 1247. Henry I I I claimed the right to receive homage from all the Welsh nobility, and the princes had to abandon their claims to the lands of the Four Cantreds of Rhos, Rhufoniog, Dyffryn Clwyd and Tegeingl, land lying between the Dee and the Conwy. It seemed that the authority of Llywelyn the Great was shattered, with the authority of his descendants limited to Snowdonia and Anglesey. The laws of feudal inheritance, which kept an inheritance intact in the hands of the eldest son, did not apply in Wales, and Gwynedd appeared to be threatened with further fragmentation as lands were granted to another of Gruffydd's sons, Dafydd. It is only with hindsight that an alliance made in 1250 between Llywelyn and Gruffydd ap Madog of Bromfield, and another in the next year between Llywelyn and Owain on the one hand, and two princes of the south-west on the other, appear as pointers to the wide ambitions

---

[51] Trabut-Cussac, L'administration anglaise en Gascogne, 17–19; Gascon Register A, ed. G.P. Cuttino (Oxford, 1975), ii, 461, 544–5, 547–8.

[52] J.E. Lloyd, A History of Wales (2nd edn, 1912), ii, 701.

of the man who was to be Edward's greatest Welsh opponent, Prince Llywelyn.[53]

The combination of Llywelyn's ambitions, and the harsh manner in which Edward's lands in Wales were ruled, meant that the apparently peaceful situation of 1254 was rapidly shattered. The policy of Edward's officials was to try to impose English methods of administration and English law upon the Welsh, and also novel financial exactions. The policy was not new: the justice of Chester appointed in 1251, Alan la Zouche, was extremely unpopular in the Four Cantreds, but Henry III had been very willing to hear complaints against him. In 1252 a commission of two Welshmen and two Englishmen was appointed to look into the grievances of the Welsh against Zouche and his officials. However, under Edward's steward, Geoffrey de Langley, no concessions to the Welsh were made. The evidence of the substantial landed estate that Geoffrey built up for himself, largely at the expense of impoverished knightly families, strongly suggests that he was a corrupt and unscrupulous man.[54] He was not Edward's choice as steward: he had been one of the queen's officials, and was nominated for the post by the king, queen and royal council. William de Wilton was another of Edward's officials blamed by the chroniclers, along with Langley, for their harsh rule in Wales. According to Matthew Paris, Henry III in 1257 disclaimed all responsibility for Wales when his son appealed to him for help, saying 'What has this got to do with me? It is your land by gift.' Yet it was Henry who appointed justices in 1255 to hear cases between Llywelyn and his brother Owain, and in the next year various Welshmen came to see Henry on Llywelyn's business.[55] Edward himself paid only a brief visit to Wales, in the second half of July 1256, and there is no indication of his personal opinion of the policies being undertaken in his name, although his short-lived presence probably only made matters worse.

These policies, particularly those of anglicizing the law and administration of the Four Cantreds and linking them ever more closely to the lordship of Chester,[56] provoked rebellion in 1256, with appeal being made to Llywelyn for assistance. After a rapid and astonishing success

[53] *Littere Wallie*, ed. J.G. Edwards (Cardiff, 1940), xxxviii. A convenient brief account of Gwynedd's history is to be found in D. Stephenson, *The Governance of Gwynedd* (Cardiff, 1984), xxii–xv.

[54] A.J. Roderick, 'The Four Cantreds: a study in administration', *Bull. of the Board of Celtic Studies*, x (1940), 243–4; *CPR 1247–58*, 171; P.R. Coss, 'Sir Geoffrey de Langley and the Crisis of the Knightly Class in Thirteenth-Century England', *Past and Present*, lxviii (1975), 3–37.

[55] Matthew Paris, *Chron. Maj.*, v, 614; *CPR 1247–58*, 432, 470.

[56] J.R. Studd, 'The Lord Edward's Lordship of Chester, 1254–72', *Transactions of the Historic Society of Lancashire and Cheshire*, cxxvii (1979), 18.

in the north, Llywelyn attacked Meirionydd in December 1256 and
then advanced on Builth in mid-Wales. In the excitement of his triumphal progress Llywelyn did not confine his conquests to the lands
held by Edward and his rival Welsh princes: he also took estates from
Roger Mortimer, and early in 1257 advanced into South Wales, where
he achieved considerable success against the Marcher lords, including
the earl of Gloucester.[57]

The task of dealing with the rebellion was too much for the limited
forces at Edward's disposal. His accounts for this period show that his
official John le Bretun paid various small bodies of troops in South
Wales and the Marches. The largest force consisted of no more than 35
men-at-arms and 700 infantry, who were sent towards Llandovery.
Edward himself does not appear to have taken part in the operations
over the winter, which were largely directed by the earls of Gloucester
and Hereford. According to Matthew Paris the dreadful rain and
storms meant that little was achieved.[58] Henry III was not inclined to
offer his son much help, initially offering only a paltry 500 marks.
Edward's uncle Richard of Cornwall was of more use, with a loan of
4,000 marks. Richard's attempts at mediation were firmly rebuffed by
Llywelyn, who wrote of the injuries and oppression suffered by the
Welsh at the hands of Edward's men.

In the early summer of 1257 Edward's forces suffered a major defeat
in the Towy valley. Stephen Bauzan, who had also served Edward in
Gascony,[59] was in command of an operation intended to reinstate a
Welsh noble, Rhys Fychan, who had lost his lands. Rhys deserted the
English cause, and Bauzan was defeated. It was almost certainly this
news that impelled Henry III to change his policy, and propose direct
intervention in Wales. The English tenants-in-chief were summoned to
muster at Chester on 1 August. The instructions were later modified,
and some asked to go to Bristol.[60] Matthew Paris had it that Edward
was extremely reluctant to join his father for the campaign, even
suggesting that Wales should be left to the Welsh. Doubtless the young
prince deeply resented the fact that his father was now taking over an
enterprise which should have been his to conduct, and for which he
should have been provided with adequate resources.[61]

[57] Lloyd, *History of Wales*, ii, 717–22; M. Altschul, *A Baronial Family in Medieval
England: The Clares, 1217–1314* (Baltimore, 1965), 78–9.

[58] SC 6/1094/11; Matthew Paris, *Chron. Maj.*, v, 539.

[59] J.P. Trabut-Cussac, 'Un rôle de lettres patentes emanées du Prince Edouard',
Receuil de travaux offert à M. Clovis Brunel (Paris, 1955), ii, 604–5.

[60] *Close Rolls 1256–9*, 139. The date of the initial summons is not known. Matthew
Paris, *Chron. Maj.*, v, 639, 645–6, puts it before Bauzan's defeat, but there is no record
evidence to support this.

[61] Matthew Paris, *Chron. Maj.*, v, 640.

The dispute between father and son cannot have been too serious, as Edward did take part in the royal campaign. It proved to be as ineffective as most of Henry III's military exploits. The army advanced from Chester along the coast, reaching Deganwy in late August. Victualling arrangements were sadly deficient, an inevitable result of the haste with which the expedition was organized. The English troops were forced to make a dejected withdrawal, faced by famine and harassed by the triumphant Welsh. Promised supplies from Edward's Irish lordship failed to materialize.[62] The lessons of the campaign were obvious, and when, as king, Edward led expeditions along a very similar route, he showed that he had learned well from the mistakes of 1257.

By the end of 1257 the crisis in Wales was, for the English, very serious. It would be wrong to blame Edward for the situation. There is nothing to suggest that the harsh policies of his officials had been adopted at his prompting, and it is unreasonable to expect that one so inexperienced as Edward could have anticipated problems not foreseen by the officials acting in his name. Henry III must bear some of the blame, for failing to give his son sufficient support at an early stage in the Welsh rising. The English were, quite simply, not in a position in the late 1250s to deal with the rising star of Llywelyn ap Gruffydd, a man of immense ambition and considerable ability. It was to take Edward at the height of his powers to deal with him.

With his great estates in England, Ireland and Wales, Edward was a landowner of the first rank after 1254. There is unfortunately only one surviving account roll to show how the lands were administered. It is the record of an audit heard at Edward's exchequer at Bristol, and covers the year from Michaelmas 1256. It is far from being a complete record of Edward's finances, for it provides no details of the revenues received at the exchequers of Dublin, Chester or Bordeaux, and much of it is in a very summary form. It shows that Edward's estates were run in accordance with standard patterns of thirteenth-century estate management. The lands were grouped geographically: the Three Castles were linked with Abergavenny in South Wales: Stamford, Grantham and several minor properties were subordinate to Tickhill. The record shows how receipts were apportioned. Very little was retained by local bailiffs: of the total receipts at Grantham amounting to almost £148, all save £5 12s 4d was sent to the constable of Tickhill. From there, money was sent in all directions: £80 was sent to Ralph le Donjon, who was in charge of the wardrobe, the main household department; £133 went to William de Mohaut, constable of Chester; £229 was directed to the treasury at Bristol. At Abergavenny the constable, John le Bretun,

---

[62] Ibid., v, 633, 648–9; *Close Rolls 1256–9*, 90–1.

received a total of about £590: the situation in Wales required substantial resources.

It is hard to generalize about management methods from a single account roll, but it is striking that court profits were at a high level, suggesting that Edward's lordship was severe. At Tickhill, court pleas and other perquisites raised £22, roughly double the revenue from sales of grain. At Abergavenny, the honorial court produced an income of £113, as against grain sales of only £52. The indications are that the estates were efficiently run, with no substantial arrears, and with no signs that income was falling substantially behind expenditure.[63] However, the situation was probably deteriorating. John le Bretun's accounts for 1257–8 were never properly settled, and as late as 1274 his executors were dealing with the exchequer over this issue. By 1258, according to Matthew Paris, Edward was forced to hand over Stamford and Grantham to his uncle William de Valence.[64]

Medieval accounts were not drawn up to show profit and loss in the modern sense. Their prime purpose was to ensure that officials were not guilty of fraudulent practices. It is dangerous to try to calculate income from such documents as Edward's account for 1256–7. Denholm-Young used it as the basis for an estimate of £7,800 for Edward's income, excluding Gascon receipts, but this figure includes revenue from Ireland, Chester and Bristol, none of which featured in the document. There are considerable problems with Denholm-Young's calculations, and a better figure would probably be about £6,000.[65] It certainly seems most unlikely that Edward was ever in the position his father had intended him to be in, with an income from land of £10,000 a year. Edward's financial difficulties are apparent from the fact that in 1257 he sold the great wardship of Robert Ferrers, which the king had granted him, to his mother and Peter of Savoy for 6,000 marks. In the same year he borrowed £1,000 from the archbishop of Canterbury, and gave the citizens of Bristol the right to collect their own revenues for four years in return for 1,600 marks, of which 500 were paid immediately.[66] Political independence would be hard to achieve for a young man whose financial resources scarcely matched his status as the king's eldest born.

Edward's position in the years immediately following the grant of lands to him in 1254 was not easy. Most of his officials were chosen for

[63] SC 6/1094/11.

[64] E 159/50, m.16; Matthew Paris, *Chron. Maj.*, v, 679.

[65] N. Denholm-Young, *Seigneurial Administration in England*, 9. The figure of £3,000 for Irish income is much too high, and it is not clear where the figure of £1,500 for Tutbury comes from. Chester was farmed for 1,000 marks, not 700, as *CPR 1247–58*, 182, shows. Only a very rough estimate of Edward's income is possible from the surviving records.

[66] *CPR 1247–58*, 554, 569–70, 572.

him by the king or queen, and he was certainly not fully independent. His lands were his to hold, but not to grant away. He could make appointments, but they were subject to royal scrutiny. The resources which he had been promised were not fully forthcoming in financial terms. The seeds of friction between Henry III and his son were germinating, and in such incidents as the row over the complaints of the Gascon merchants the shoots of discord can be seen. The extent of conflict between Henry and Edward should not, however, be exaggerated. Edward was frequently present at meetings of the royal council,[67] and in popular estimation he was clearly regarded as being fully committed to a highly unpopular regime. There are no signs that anyone hoped that the heir to the throne might lend his support to those who hoped for reform.

The regime itself was hardly a united one, and Edward was bound to become involved in the struggles between the various factions of the court, even if he was not as yet a major figure in national politics. There were two major groupings at Henry's court, both of which were anxious to gain control of the heir to the throne. The queen's relations from Savoy were powerful, able and ambitious men. Peter of Savoy was given the honour of Richmond in 1240, and in the next year his brother Boniface was elected as archbishop of Canterbury. A third brother, William, bishop-elect of Valence, also played a significant role in English politics. In the wake of these men there came a number of lesser men, particularly in the course of the 1250s. The other important group of aliens at court was that of the Poitevin, or Lusignan, half-brothers of the king. They were the children of Henry III's mother Isabella's second marriage, to Hugh of Lusignan. One of them, William de Valence, was through marriage heir to the earldom of Pembroke. Guy and Geoffrey de Lusignan were not as fortunate as William, but received considerable favours from Henry III. The other brother, Aymer, was a cleric, and was elected to the see of Winchester in 1250, three years after the Lusignans came to England. The Poitevins were not so substantial a group at court as the Savoyards, nor were they so able, but their ambition and ruthlessness made them extremely dangerous.[68]

From 1254 until 1257 Edward appears to have been largely under the influence of the Savoyard faction, and of certain respected Englishmen.

---

[67] See for example *CPR 1247–58*, 500; *Close Rolls 1256–9*, 46.

[68] For a recent brief interpretation of Henry III's reign, which stresses the role of the aliens, see M.T. Clanchy, *England and its Rulers, 1066–1272* (1983), especially 210–40. The part played by the Savoyards and Poitevins has been analysed in detail by H.W. Ridgeway in his doctoral thesis, 'The Politics of the English Royal Court, 1247–65, with special reference to the role of the Aliens' (Oxford D.Phil thesis, 1984). I am very grateful to Dr Ridgeway for letting me read this work, to which I am deeply indebted for much of what follows.

Edward's marriage was negotiated by the royal clerk John Mansel and the Savoyard bishop of Hereford, Peter d'Aigueblanche. In 1255 it was Peter of Savoy who was sent to Gascony to assist Edward, and to organize his return to England.[69] Peter was a frequent witness of Edward's charters in this period, and must have been a major influence on him. A very important figure in the prince's entourage was Eble des Montz, while other Savoyards in his service included Imbert de Montferrand, Geoffrey de Geneville, and William de Salines.[70] The greatest of all the Savoyards who served Edward, Otto de Grandson, was, however, yet to appear on the English scene. One of the most important of Edward's English councillors was John FitzGeoffrey, a man of impeccable curial background whose father, Geoffrey FitzPeter, earl of Essex, had been justiciar under King John. He had himself served as justiciar in Ireland from 1245.[71] Peter de Montfort, a Marcher lord, was another important figure in Edward's entourage, as was the king's steward Robert Walerand. These men, along with officials such as Geoffrey de Langley, were clearly chosen for Edward by Henry III. William de Wilton was another of Edward's officials who had considerable experience in royal service, in his case largely as a justice.[72]

A young man such as Edward was bound to be resentful to some degree of the continued tutelage in which he was placed in these years. By 1258 he was clearly linking himself not with the Savoyard faction at court, but with the Lusignans. The fact that he handed Stamford and Grantham over to William de Valence in return for a loan is one indication of his changing alignment.[73] By June 1258 Edward was planning to make Geoffrey de Lusignan seneschal of Gascony, and his brother Guy keeper of Oléron and the Channel Isles, very probably in return for further loans.[74] Edward had perhaps found a common interest in Wales with William de Valence, who had substantial estates there, but the situation was also a reflection of the fact that Poitevin influence was resurgent at court in 1257. One indication of this was the return of the veteran Poitevin administrator Peter des Rivaux to the office of keeper of the wardrobe at Michaelmas 1257. Savoyard power was on the wane. Edward's changing position was not a reflection of increasing independence from his father, who had no reason to be suspicious of his son's friendship with the Lusignans, but was rather a

[69] Trabut-Cussac, *L'administration anglaise en Gascogne*, xxxvi, 13.

[70] Ridgeway, 'The Politics of the English Royal Court', 175–6.

[71] Orpen, *Ireland under the Normans*, iii, 230.

[72] H.W. Ridgeway, 'The Lord Edward and the Provisions of Oxford (1258): A Study in Faction', *Thirteenth Century England* I, ed. P.R. Coss and S.D. Lloyd (Woodbridge, 1986), 92–3.

[73] Matthew Paris, *Chron. Maj.*, v, 679.

[74] R.F. Treharne, *The Baronial Plan of Reform* (Manchester, 1932), 77.

natural consequence of the rise of one court faction at the expense of another.[75] What was important for the future, however, was the fact that by 1257 Edward was beginning to recruit men into his service who did not have a background in the royal court. Roger Clifford and Hamo Lestrange, both Marcher lords, emerged at this time in Edward's entourage, as did Earl Warenne and John de Vaux, and it was early in 1257 that Robert Burnell, who was to be Edward's greatest chancellor, first appeared in a witness-list along with other members of his council.[76]

It was Edward's links with the notoriously unruly Lusignans that help to explain the stories told by Matthew Paris about his misbehaviour at this period. They form part of a general criticism of the court circle, and show that Edward shared in the unpopularity of the king and his favourites. In addition to the unpleasant story of the attack on the young man mentioned at the start of this chapter, Matthew indignantly told of the outrages committed at the local priory by members of Edward's household while their master was visiting Richard of Cornwall at Wallingford. The monks were driven out, and an orgy of destruction followed. Some corroboration for such tales comes from the complaints put forward in 1258 by the men of Southwark, who objected in particular to the seizure of foodstuffs by Edward's men.[77] It would be wrong to make too much of the activities of a band of high-spirited young men, but there was certainly nothing in Edward's behaviour during these years of limited responsibility that suggested he would be a good king. He had not faced any severe test as yet. It was to be the next few years of political turmoil which were to provide him with the first real challenges of his life.

[75] Ridgeway, 'The Politics of the English Royal Court', 271–7, does see Edward's relationship with the Poitevins as an indication of political independence on the prince's part. Studd, 'The Lord Edward and Henry III', 8, argues that the appointments of Geoffrey and Guy de Lusignan were directly contrary to the king's wishes: but Henry's hostility to them only came after effective authority had been removed from the king at the Oxford parliament of 1258, and was in fact baronial rather than royal policy.

[76] *CDI 1252–84*, no. 564; *CPR 1247–58*, 589; Ridgeway, 'The Lord Edward and the Provisions of Oxford', 97.

[77] Matthew Paris, *Chron. Maj.*, v, 593–4, 598; JI 1/873, m.8d.

Chapter 2

THE LEOPARD, 1258–70

In a celebrated passage, the author of the *Song of Lewes* compared Edward to a leopard. On the one hand, he was a *leo*, a brave lion, proud and fierce. On the other hand, he was a *pard*, inconstant and unreliable, making promises when he was in a tight corner, and then forgetting them.[1] Edward's career from 1258 until his departure on crusade in 1270 is certainly full of contradictions. He can be seen as acting in a wilful way, changing sides in the civil conflict between king and baronage in an irresponsible fashion, and also as the man who did most to salvage the monarchy from an appallingly difficult situation. Whatever the truth, Edward during his twenties certainly served an extremely tough apprenticeship in politics and war, and there can be no doubt that he learned vital lessons from his experiences.

A biography of Edward I is not the place for a full exposition of the reasons for the great crisis of 1258. A combination of almost universal hatred for the king's half-brothers, the Lusignans; the fantastic folly of Henry's attempt to gain the Sicilian throne for his second son Edmund; the disasters in Wales; a widespread dissatisfaction with the conduct of local government in the shires; all these formed a potent mixture. In part the crisis reflected paradoxical divisions within the court, with curialists, such as Peter of Savoy and the earl of Gloucester, siding with the baronial opposition, and a former favourite of the king, the alien Simon de Montfort, eventually emerging as the leader of that opposition. At the same time, it was a crisis on a national scale, with political difficulties aggravated by the acute economic distress resulting from an extremely bad harvest in 1257.

A council was summoned by Henry III in April 1258 to discuss papal demands for money and men to support the Sicilian venture, the problem of Wales, and other urgent business. The magnates, lay and clerical, were unco-operative. The prelates withdrew from the discussions, and the lay magnates, threatening the use of force, demanded the expulsion of the hated alien favourites and the thorough reform of the realm. Seven major lords formed a sworn coalition for mutual assistance on 12 April. They were the earls of Gloucester, Leicester and

---

[1] *Political Songs*, ed. Wright, 93–4; *The Song of Lewes*, ed. C.L. Kingsford (1890), 14.

Norfolk, Hugh Bigod, John FitzGeoffrey, Peter de Montfort and Peter of Savoy. All save Norfolk had strong court connections, the last three being closely linked to Edward. Complaints against the king's Lusignan half-brothers were vehement: at the beginning of April men in the service of one of them, Aymer de Valence, had savagely attacked servants of John FitzGeoffrey, who duly protested to the king. The earls of Gloucester and Leicester were in bitter dispute with another of them, William de Valence. The king was forced to agree to the election of a committee of twenty-four, twelve chosen by himself and twelve by the barons, to meet in Oxford to begin the process of reform. On 30 April the king and his eldest son swore that they would accept what was decided. Although some of Edward's leading councillors were committed to the cause of reform, he undertook the oath with the greatest reluctance, for he was at this stage closely linked to the Lusignan faction at court.[2]

Matters proceeded rapidly after this. The Oxford parliament began on 11 June, after both sides had made some military preparations. A baronial petition, much of it dealing with technical legal matters, was presented as a basis for reform. Hugh Bigod, brother of the earl of Norfolk, was appointed justiciar. This had originally been a vice-regal post, but the position had become virtually that of a chief justice. There had been no justiciar since 1234, and revival of the post reflected discontent with the quality of Henry III's justice. New keepers of royal castles were appointed, making it hard for Henry to engage in armed resistance. A council of fifteen was selected by a complex electoral process, in which the royal and baronial twelves each chose two electors. The four electors then appointed the fifteen.

The attack on the king's half-brothers, the Lusignans, continued: among other things, they were said to have encouraged Edward, with others, to subvert the whole reform movement. The resumption of all lands and castles which had been granted out by the king was a move directed primarily at them: Henry of Almain, Richard of Cornwall's son and Edward's cousin, together with John de Warenne opposed this along with the Lusignans. There was no option save flight for the Lusignans, who went to take refuge at Winchester.[3] Edward provocatively made his support for them public, by appointing Geoffrey de Lusignan seneschal of Gascony, and granting the Isle of Oléron and the Channel Isles to his brother Guy. These grants were probably made

---

[2] *Documents of the Baronial Movement of Reform and Rebellion, 1258–1267*, selected R.F. Treharne, ed. I.J. Sanders (Oxford, 1973), 4, 72–4; D.A. Carpenter, 'What Happened in 1258', *War and Government in the Middle Ages*, ed. J. Gillingham and J.C. Holt (Woodbridge, 1984), 106–119.

[3] *Documents of the Baronial Movement*, ed. Sanders, 90–4; *Ann. Tewkesbury*, 165.

while negotiations were proceeding for the exile of the Lusignans, and on 28 June the council retaliated with orders forbidding the Gascons and the Irish to obey anyone appointed without royal consent.[4]

The pressure on the king's Lusignan half-brothers was great. Edward's support for them could not counterbalance Simon de Montfort's threats: 'You must know without a shadow of doubt that you will lose your castles or your life', were his words to William de Valence.[5] By 10 July Edward had abandoned his attempt to resist the barons, and two days later letters were issued in his name cancelling Geoffrey de Lusignan's appointment. Curiously, it was not until 26 October that Henry III wrote to the men of Oléron revoking the grant that had been made to Guy de Lusignan, and Edward did not cancel it himself until 4 November. Only by that time was he prepared to accept the nomination of Drogo de Barentin as seneschal of Gascony.[6]

The suggestion has been made that the row over the appointment of Geoffrey de Lusignan to Gascony was for Edward 'a bitter clash with his father'.[7] This seems unlikely. At the Oxford parliament all real power had been taken from the king, and letters written in his name were the work of the council, and do not provide evidence of the king's private attitude. He may very well have admired his son's attempt to resist the reformers, and the statement in the official correspondence that Edward had acted without consulting him is not one which should necessarily be believed.[8]

Edward's support of the Poitevins achieved little, but it did show the reformers that measures were needed to curb his activities. Accordingly, it was decided to provide him with four councillors, John Balliol, Roger de Mohaut, John de Grey and Stephen Longespée.[9] The first two were baronial supporters, the last two experienced servants of Edward, who had acted for him in Cheshire, Ireland and Gascony: this council was obviously intended to be a balanced body. Edward's chancellor had to swear a similar oath to that of the king's, and in particular he was not to seal any letters without the advice of the four councillors. Edward's household, like his father's, was to be reformed. It is far from clear how much was achieved in practice. The councillors do not

[4] Above, 22; *CPR 1247–58*, 639.
[5] Matthew Paris, *Chron. Maj.*, v, 697–8.
[6] *Documents of the Baronial Movement*, ed. Sanders, 94 n.10; *CPR 1247–58*, 664–5; *Gascon Register A*, ed. Cuttino, ii, 503–5; Trabut-Cussac, *L'administration Anglaise en Gascogne*, 16–17.
[7] Studd, 'The Lord Edward and Henry III', 10.
[8] *CPR 1247–58*, 641.
[9] *Documents of the Baronial Movement*, ed. Sanders, 95. This Balliol was the father of the future king of Scots.

appear to have been particularly effective, but the prince clearly abandoned any further attempts to block the work of the reformers. By the autumn of 1258 he was sufficiently in favour with the council for it to authorize an advance to him of 2,000 marks (£1,333) or failing that £1,000, so that he could prepare for a threatened war with the Welsh.[10]

In late July 1258, at Winchester, Edward breakfasted with the earl of Gloucester and his brother William, an indication that he was ready to co-operate with the reforming barons. The meal was a disastrous one, however, for both the de Clare brothers were extremely ill afterwards. William never recovered, and died shortly afterwards, and Earl Richard's hair fell out, as did his finger- and toe-nails. It was probably a simple case of food-poisoning, but in the excited atmosphere of the time rumours of plots abounded, and Gloucester's steward, Walter de Scoteny, was accused of poisoning his masters. He was duly found guilty, drawn and hanged. He was a tenant of Edward's, and in the following year the prince was granted the proceeds of his lands.[11]

The fateful breakfast did not, it seems, poison relations between Edward and the earl of Gloucester. An important document shows that on 14 March 1259 a formal alliance was made between Edward and his supporters on the one hand, and Richard de Clare with his on the other. Richard promised to counsel Edward, to aid him in recovering his lands, and to back his supporters. The list of these supporters shows that Edward had, in the later months of 1258 and early in 1259, become the focus of a new political grouping, whose creation was probably his work. Those concerned were Henry of Almain, Earl Warenne, Baldwin de Lisle, Philip Basset, Stephen Longespée, Robert Walerand, Roger Clifford, Roger Leyburn, John de Vaux, Warin de Bassingbourne, Hamo Lestrange and William la Zouche.[12] The fact that, of the councillors imposed on Edward in the previous year only Longespée was included, shows that the prince had effectively gained his independence, at least for a time.

Several of the names were of great significance. Henry of Almain, Edward's cousin and childhood companion, was clearly very close to him, and would undoubtedly have played a major part in Edward's career had it not been for his tragic murder at the hands of Guy de Montfort in 1271. Earl Warenne was a solidly royalist figure, who had been to Gascony with Edward in 1254, and had stood with him in 1258

[10] Ridgeway, 'The Politics of the English Royal Court', 339–40; *Close Rolls 1256–9*, 343.
[11] *Ann. Tewkesbury*, 165, 167; Guisborough, 186; Matthew Paris, *Chron. Maj.*, v, 747–8; *CPR 1258–67*, 32.
[12] Historical Manuscripts Commission, *Report on the Manuscripts of Lord Middleton* (1911), 67–9.

in resisting the reforming measures of the Oxford parliament. He was
to be a loyal, if unimaginative, supporter of the king until his death in
1304.[13] Roger Leyburn, a Kentish noble, was Edward's choice to
replace William de Wilton as his steward. Roger Clifford, a Welsh
Marcher lord, served Edward as his bailiff in the Three Castles, and
like Leyburn played a major role in the events of the 1260s. Hamo
Lestrange was another Marcher, who with Warin de Bassingbourne
was a close associate of Edward's at this time, accompanying him
abroad at tournaments.[14] Edward was very clearly surrounding himself with like-minded men, all laymen, whose prime loyalty was to
himself, in contrast to those who had served him before 1258 who owed
their position to the king. Not all of Edward's allies in the treaty with
Gloucester fitted this pattern, however. Robert Walerand was a former
royal steward, who co-operated with the reformers in 1258, and was
transferred to Edward's service. The council nominated him to be
constable of Bristol in July 1259, and when, in the following November,
Edward tried to replace him, he objected, as he had sworn not to leave
his post without royal consent.[15] Philip Basset was one of the baronial
twelve, and on the council of fifteen, but his allegiance shifted, and by
1261 he was appointed justiciar by the king. The group listed in the
treaty was, therefore, a heterogeneous one, but it is very striking how
many members of it were to prove loyal to Edward in the coming civil
war. Already the prince must have had the power to win and retain
loyalty.

Various explanations are possible for the deal between Edward and
the earl of Gloucester. One view has it that it was the result of a dispute
between the two men, but it is odd that if part of its purpose was to
resolve some question over the Welsh Marches, no mention was made
of this in the text.[16] There was provision for arbitration by Henry of
Almain and Hugh Bigod, but this was only to come into effect should
there be arguments over the fulfilment of the agreement, which appears
to have been primarily concerned with the question of Edward's lands
and his free enjoyment of them. It could be that the document had some
relation to the dispute of the earl of Gloucester with Simon de Montfort,
which resulted from Gloucester's reluctance to see his own estates
subjected to the same inquisitions as royal lands, but that quarrel was

---

[13] Warenne's career, like that of many others, is summarized in the *Dictionary of
National Biography* and G.E. Cockayne, *The Complete Peerage* (1910–59): see these works
for biographical details of Edward's supporters.

[14] *The Metrical Chronicle of Robert of Gloucester*, ed. W.A. Wright (Rolls ser, 1887), ii,
735.

[15] *CPR 1258–67*, 63–4; D.A. Carpenter, 'The Lord Edward's Oath to aid and
counsel Simon de Montfort, 15 October 1259', *BIHR*, lviii (1985), 234.

[16] Powicke, *Henry III and the Lord Edward*, i, 398 and n.

possibly settled by 22 February, although the ordinance dealing with the question was not formally issued until 22 March.[17]

The most plausible explanation is that Edward was trying to protect his overseas lands from being affected by the peace negotiations being conducted with the French. By 12 March arrangements had been finalized for the earls of Gloucester and Leicester, along with Peter of Savoy, to go to France. In February Edward's brother Edmund had given his formal consent to proposals that the king should renounce all his rights to Normandy, Maine, Touraine and Anjou, but he himself did not follow suit, though the treaty required the royal family do so.[18] It made good sense for Edward to win the support of at least one of the English negotiators. In fact, it was not Gloucester, but Simon de Montfort, earl of Leicester, who obstructed the course of negotiations, for his wife refused to abandon her claims in Normandy, a move which aroused Gloucester's anger.[19]

The work of reform was continuing all this time. After control of central government had been gained by the barons at the Oxford parliament of 1258, attention had turned to the question of maladministration in the counties. A full-scale process of inquiry was begun. In the autumn of 1258 detailed discussions took place about various legal questions. In February 1259 the council, acting with twelve barons elected to represent the community of the realm, promised that the wrongs committed by the magnates and their bailiffs would be corrected just like those done by royal officials. The document was confirmed by the king on 28 March. A further stage of reform was both needed and expected: it was necessary to provide proper legal remedies for the abuses which had been discovered, many of which were intended to provide protection for feudal sub-tenants, men of knightly rather than magnate status.[20]

In October 1259 Edward was brought directly into the arguments that were raging in the parliament then being held at Westminster. According to the annals of Burton abbey, a body calling itself the Community of the Bachelors of England told Edward, the earl of Gloucester and the others sworn as members of the council at Oxford that the king had done all that was required of him by the barons, but that the barons themselves had done nothing of what they had

[17] Matthew Paris, *Chron. Maj.*, v, 744; *Documents of the Baronial Movement*, ed. Sanders, 17–18; Powicke, *Henry III and the Lord Edward*, i, 406–7.

[18] *CPR 1258–66*, 14–15, 26.

[19] Matthew Paris, *Chron. Maj.*, v, 745. The countess of Leicester's claim was a complex matter relating to her dower rights and subsequent claims against Henry III: see *CPR 1258–66*, 25–7.

[20] The documents relating to these stages of the reform movement are given in *Documents of the Baronial Movement*, ed. Sanders, 97–137.

promised for the common good. If they did not fulfil their promises, then reform would have to be imposed by other methods. Edward promptly replied that although he had sworn the oath at Oxford unwillingly, he would stand by it, and was ready to expose himself to death on behalf of the community of the realm and the common good. He told the barons of the council that he was prepared to stand with the Bachelors, and make the barons carry out their promised reforms. This, according to the chronicle, led the council to publish the reforms known as the Provisions of Westminster.[21]

The passage raises many problems of interpretation, but as no other chronicler refers to the incident, it is not possible to reach any real certainty. The question of who the Bachelors were is an insoluble one. The common view that they were young men of knightly status attached to baronial households is not very plausible: on no other occasion did such men band together for a political purpose. The term bachelor was a fashionable one. Matthew Paris wrote that in 1249 at a tournament, 'many of the knights of the community of the realm, who wanted to be called bachelors, were defeated'. In 1262 Henry III was to describe the sheriffs as 'king's bachelors', and in 1263 bands of low-born townsmen termed themselves bachelors.[22] The nature of the group who made their protest to Edward and Gloucester in 1259 cannot be deduced from the label they gave themselves. Nor is it wholly clear what the Bachelors wanted. Although the Burton chronicler considered that it was publication of the promised reforms, it has been plausibly argued that it may have been the full extension of the reforming measures to baronial estates, the question which had been at issue earlier in the year.[23]

Why was the protest directed to Edward and Gloucester? One suggestion is that relations between the two had become increasingly strained in the summer of 1258, but it could be that the Bachelors recalled the alliance that the two men had made earlier in the year. By early 1260 the two were certainly in dispute, but there is little evidence to show that they were already at loggerheads at the time of the protest. Tension between them was likely, both over the question of the peace negotiations with the French, and their rival claims to Bristol.[24] It may

---

[21] 'Annales Monasterii de Burton', *Annales Monastici*, i, ed. H.R. Luard (Rolls ser., 1864), 471.

[22] T.F. Tout, 'The "Communitas bacheleriae Anglie"', *EHR*, xvii (1902), 89–95; Powicke, *Henry III and the Lord Edward*, i, 407n; Matthew Paris, *Chron. Maj.*, v, 83; *Close Rolls 1261–4*, 177; Wykes, 138.

[23] Treharne, *Baronial Plan of Reform*, 163.

[24] Ibid., 164; *Documents of the Baronial Movement*, ed. Sanders, 19; both stress the dispute between Edward and Gloucester, though the latter admits that 'there is little direct evidence to explain the estrangement'.

well be that the Burton annalist simply named Gloucester because he was the leading magnate among those of the council to whom the protest was directed: Simon de Montfort was probably abroad at the time. The fact that Edward was specifically mentioned is much more significant, however, for he was not a member of the council. It shows that he was considered to be an important political figure in his own right, and probably that he was now thought to be committed to the cause of reform. His answer to the Bachelors could be read as a cynical attempt to divide the ranks of the reformers, but it is more likely that it represented genuine, if temporary, conviction on the part of a young man of twenty who had been fired with enthusiasm.

Clearer evidence of Edward's changed political attitude in the autumn of 1259 is provided by letters patent he issued on 15 October. He announced that he had sworn to do all in his power to give aid and counsel to Simon de Montfort and his allies, and that he was bound with them to maintain the baronial enterprise, saving his fealty to the king. He would not attack anyone who supported the barons, provided that they accepted the judgements of the king's court, and he would do all he could to enforce such judgements. Along with Edward's seal, the document bore the seals of Henry of Almain, Earl Warenne and Roger Leyburn. The promise not to attack supporters of the baronial enterprise probably relates to Edward's response to the Bachelors' protest, for it amounted to a renunciation of the threat he had made to support the Bachelors in implementing reform by some other means. The emphasis on judgements of the king's court is ambiguous, but may refer to an expected verdict in favour of Simon de Montfort's wife against the other co-heirs of the Marshal inheritance. This was the case which caused her to obstruct the peace process with the French.[25] One problem with this formal alliance of Edward with Simon de Montfort is that it seems unlikely that Montfort was present at the time it was made, for he was certainly at Evreux in Normandy a mere four days later.[26] It may, therefore, have been a one-sided declaration by Edward of his position.

Edward had good reasons for this new alliance. Simon de Montfort was the husband of his aunt Eleanor, so there was a strong family link. Further, Simon was the one magnate who, although totally committed to the baronial reforms, was delaying the negotiations with France. If Edward was bitterly opposed to the peace plan as it threatened his interests in Gascony, then an alliance with Montfort made very good sense. Moreover, if Edward had quarrelled with Gloucester, then it was

[25] Carpenter, 'The Lord Edward's Oath to aid and counsel Simon de Montfort', 226–37.
[26] C. Bémont, *Simon de Montfort*, tr. E.F. Jacob (Oxford, 1930), 173.

natural for him to seek the support of Montfort, who had himself
exchanged bitter words with Gloucester.[27] Edward's new-found commitment to the baronial cause in the autumn of 1259 was not particularly surprising. The Poitevins had gone into exile, and no longer had
influence over him. Several of his other advisers, such as Peter of Savoy,
had given their support to the programme of reform set out at the
Oxford parliament of 1258. With the king apparently acquiescing in
what had taken place, there was no obvious future in opposing the
reformers. It must have seemed sensible to Edward to link himself with
the faction that was most likely to help preserve his interests in France,
that of Simon de Montfort. The link with Gloucester had not provided
Edward with the full independence he sought: the witness list of a
charter he issued in August 1259 suggests that he had not been able to
break free for long from the councillors imposed on him.[28] Their control
was still irksome in early November, when Edward was finding it
impossible to dismiss Robert Walerand from the custody of Bristol
castle.[29]

On 15 November 1259 Henry III crossed the Channel to negotiate
the final peace with the French. This gave Edward his chance. He was
now able to appoint his friend Roger Leyburn to Bristol castle, and
Roger Clifford received the Three Castles in south Wales.[30] Henry III
was kept short of detailed information on events in England. A letter he
wrote on 19 February shows that he had heard that the situation was
peaceful, but by 1 March a note of alarm can be detected in a letter to
Edward. He indicated that he was satisfied by the report he had
received from his confessor, John of Darlington, whom he had sent to
see Edward, but his conclusion that he intended to send another
emissary to see whether Edward's deeds matched his words shows that
he was worried.[31] According to the chronicler Thomas Wykes, when
Henry had reached St Omer on his return journey to England, at about
Easter, he was told that his son was plotting with various magnates to
capture and depose him. It was only the intervention of Richard of
Cornwall that persuaded Henry to return to England, for Richard
summoned the magnates to London and had letters sent to the king,
sealed by Edward and the magnates, promising safe-conduct.[32] The
extent of Henry's alarm at St Omer is indicated by the fact that he

---

[27] Above, 28–9.
[28] Ridgeway, 'The Politics of the English Royal Court', 343, citing BL Add. Ch.
20442.
[29] *CPR 1258–66*, 63–4.
[30] Ridgeway, op. cit., 345–6; J.R. Studd, 'A Catalogue of the Acts of the Lord
Edward, 1254–1272' (Leeds Ph.D., 1971), no. 742; C 61/4.
[31] *Documents of the Baronial Movement*, ed. Sanders, 170, 172, 174, 176.
[32] Wykes, 123–4.

issued orders to a considerable number of magnates to assemble at London with the military service which they owed.[33]

There was much alarm in London, as both Edward and the earl of Gloucester descended on the city with substantial armed retinues. The two men were at loggerheads, and Richard of Cornwall, after discussion with the civic authorities, prevented both from entering the city. When Henry appeared, late in April, he allowed Gloucester to enter, but refused to let his son through the gates, saying that if he were to see him, he would be unable to prevent himself from kissing him.[34] There were suggestions that Edward should undergo a formal trial, but he declared that the earls and barons were not his peers, and that he was not prepared to submit to their judgement. Instead, Richard of Cornwall, aided by the archbishop of Canterbury, succeeded in reconciling father and son. Edward and the earl of Gloucester then agreed to accept the arbitration of Henry III and Richard of Cornwall, and it was duly agreed that they should give up their claims against each other, and keep the terms of the agreements that they had made. Edward's friend and supporter Roger de Leyburn was pardoned for his part in the events. Charges against Simon de Montfort were not proceeded with.[35] The crisis was averted, and Henry III was able to begin the work of restoring royal authority. On 18 May Leyburn was ordered to give up Bristol, which was entrusted to Philip Basset, and Clifford was told to hand over the Three Castles to Gilbert Talbot. Edward's independence was at an end.[36]

Edward had not distinguished himself in his first major political venture, one which scarcely deserves to be called a rebellion. His alliance with Gloucester had broken down disastrously, and he and Montfort were quite unable to oppose the king once he returned to England. The Dunstable annalist commented bitterly on the lavish patronage by Edward in this period.[37] All the expenditure achieved little in the end. The prince did, however, manage to keep the loyalty of his immediate following: it is striking that Henry of Almain, John de Warenne and Roger de Leyburn all backed him both in the treaty with Gloucester, and in his declaration of support for Montfort. Edward should not be condemned too swiftly for his behaviour at this time. Politics was not a simple question of adherence to clear-cut principles: there was a welter of personal friendships and obligations to be considered, which were complicated by family and tenurial relationships,

[33] *Close Rolls, 1259–63*, 157.

[34] *Ann. Dunstable*, 215.

[35] Denholm-Young, *Richard of Cornwall*, 103; *Flores*, ii, 448; *Ann. London*, 55; *CPR 1258–66*, 79; *Ann. Dunstable*, 215.

[36] Studd, 'A Catalogue of the Acts of the Lord Edward', nos 790–2; C 61/4.

[37] *Ann. Dunstable*, 215.

all making up a complex pattern. While it is likely that Edward was attracted by the principles of the reformers, it is also striking that many of the disputes of the time were taking place within his own family. The Lusignans were his uncles, as was Richard of Cornwall, and Simon de Montfort was married to his aunt. The situation was obviously aggravated by rumour and gossip, notably when suggestions were made that Edward and Montfort intended to depose the king. The Dunstable annalist considered that the queen was a particularly evil influence in stirring up trouble.[38] To expect a young man to act consistently in such a situation is too much. In one respect, however, Edward was consistent. He was concerned over the question of the negotiations with the French, and clearly felt that his interests in the duchy of Gascony were being ignored, both by his father and by the majority of the baronial leaders.

However understandable Edward's actions in 1259 and early 1260 were, he had undoubtedly given a poor account of himself. He was duly sent abroad to exercise his talents at tournaments. One malicious account has it that he and the knights who were sent with him did very badly, and that he was often wounded, losing almost all his horses and armour.[39] By 8 October Edward was back in England, for he was present when arrangements were made for Henry of Almain to take Simon de Montfort's place as steward at a great feast held on St Edward's day. A grant of the wardship of the lands and heirs of William de Forz, earl of Aumale, showed that he had returned to favour: this act was 'by the counsel of the magnates of the council'. Edward's connection with Montfort was not broken, for it was now that he knighted the earl of Leicester's two elder sons.[40]

By early November 1260 Edward had returned to the continent, journeying to Gascony, and then once again taking part in tournaments in France early in the new year. Among those with him were Robert Burnell, his future chancellor, and some of his allies of 1259, notably John de Warenne, William la Zouche and Warin de Bassingbourne.[41] While abroad, Edward re-established his connection with the Lusignans. He met William de Valence and his brother Aymer in Paris late in November 1260, and appointed Guy de Lusignan as his lieutenant in Gascony. The government in England, still under strong baronial influence, was alarmed, and on 27 March orders were issued that Edward was not to bring William de Valence back to England with

[38] Ibid., 215.
[39] Ibid., 216–17.
[40] *CPR 1258–66*, 96–7; Powicke, *Henry III and the Lord Edward*, ii, 415.
[41] *CPR 1258–66*, 126, 181. *Close Rolls 1259–61*, 321, shows that on 28 December 1260 a royal writ was issued at Edward's instance, but this is not adequate evidence to suggest that the prince was in England at the time.

him.[42] Henry III, however, was plotting to seize power back from the baronial council, and when Valence did return, he was swiftly restored to favour.[43]

Edward's behaviour in returning with William de Valence suggests that he had lost all sympathy for the baronial cause. However, one account implies the reverse. The *Flores* states that when the king obtained letters of absolution from the pope, for himself and Edward, from the oath to observe the Provisions of Oxford, the prince in disgust renewed his own oath. It was this matter which brought Edward back to England, and on his return he fulminated against the king's royalist councillors, siding firmly with the barons. Edward, Montfort and the earl of Gloucester all put aside their differences, and united against the king, threatening civil war. Henry, however, made his way to Dover and secured control of the south-east. He then embarked on a strikingly successful campaign to restore his personal authority. As for Edward, his resistance did not last long: the persuasions of his mother led him to abandon the baronial cause very soon, according to the London Annals which makes this addition to the story given in the *Flores*.[44] No other chronicle has any mention of Edward's role in the political events of 1261, and one recent historian, Treharne, has dismissed the whole tale as a fabrication, 'an echo from the spring of 1260'.[45]

Certainly, if Edward did make common cause with the earls of Leicester and Gloucester in the spring of 1261, it was not for long. By 23 May Henry III was, at his son's request, pardoning Edward's associate Robert Ufford various debts owed to Jews, and on 4 June Edward received a grant of wardship from his father.[46] Indirect support, on the other hand, for the view that Edward did back the opposition for a time is provided by the fact that now for the first time Henry III raised the question of his son's behaviour in the arguments he put forward against the baronial councillors. One clause stated that the councillors had allowed Edward to squander the possessions given him by the king, which should not be alienated, with one text adding a complaint that Edward had appointed a seneschal in Gascony and other officials contrary to the king's wishes. A second clause had it that 'by the counsel of a certain man, Edward had been seduced from his father's friendship and obedience', with another version stating that it was 'by the counsel and assent of some members of the council' that he had been led astray. It is most unlikely that Henry III would have expressed

[42] Ridgeway, 'The Politics of the English Royal Court', 373; *Gascon Register A*, ed. Cuttino, ii, 419; *Close Rolls 1259–61*, 467.

[43] Treharne, *Baronial Plan of Reform*, 256–7; *CPR 1258–66*, 150.

[44] *Flores*, ii, 466–7; *Ann. London*, 57.

[45] Treharne, *Baronial Plan of Reform*, 258, n.1.

[46] *Close Rolls, 1259–61*, 381; *CPR 1258–66*, 156.

himself in such terms at a time when Edward was loyally supporting him, and the complaints therefore strongly suggest that the prince did indeed side with the barons for a time in the spring of 1261.[47]

The king's complaints are worth considering further. The squandering of Edward's possessions is surprisingly ill-documented, with commentators referring only to the grant of Stamford and Grantham to William de Valence in 1258, and to that of Elham in Kent to Roger Leyburn.[48] Grantham had in fact been recovered from Valence, and the complaint is more likely to have concerned the way in which Edward had pledged the estate to the abbot of Peterborough, who had acted as surety for a loan he had received from some Italian merchants. Edward certainly was in considerable financial difficulties at this time, partly as a result of the need to repay a loan of 4,000 *livres tournois* which he had received from the king of France. In June 1261 the king confirmed the sale of the wardship of Holderness by Edward for 3,000 marks. It is very likely that Edward had indeed been profligate with his lands, as the Dunstable annalist alleged. The question of Elham in Kent was certainly important, for Henry was to appear himself in the exchequer to announce, in connection with Leyburn's debts to Edward, that the prince had been granted his lands to sustain himself, and that they were not to be separated from the crown.[49] The charge relating to the appointment of a seneschal of Gascony could relate either to the appointment of Geoffrey de Lusignan back in 1258, or to the more recent authority given to Guy de Lusignan. Other contentious appointments were those of Leyburn and Clifford to Bristol and the Three Castles. As for the counsel by which Edward had been alienated from his father, this was surely a clear allusion to Simon de Montfort, though one version of the complaints wished to put the blame on several members of the council.

Edward's renewed sympathy for the baronial cause in the spring of

[47] The texts of these complaints present complex problems. That of one of the Latin versions, and that of the French, are printed conveniently in *Documents of the Baronial Movement*, ed. Sanders, 210–39. Another Latin version is in Durham, Muniments of the Dean and Chapter, Loc. I. 62. Both Powicke, *Henry III and the Lord Edward*, ii, 421 n. 3, and *Documents of the Baronial Movement*, 210, are incorrect in their statements about the Durham version, which is a separate text, related to the other two, but not identical to either. N. Denholm-Young, 'Documents of the Barons' Wars', *EHR*, xlviii (1933), has argued that the Latin version dates from 9 March 1260, not 1261, partly on the grounds that the references to Edward would fit his position in 1260, but if it is the case that the prince renewed his connections with the opposition in 1261, as the story in the *Flores*, ii, 466–7, has it, that argument is considerably weakened. The dating problems are discussed in detail in *Documents of the Baronial Movement*, 210–14.

[48] *Documents of the Baronial Movement*, ed. Sanders, 217, no. 9; Studd, 'The Lord Edward and Henry III', 11–12.

[49] *Close Rolls, 1259–61*, 448; *CPR 1258–66*, 161; *Ann. Dunstable*, 215; E 159/36, m.8d.

1261 should not receive too much emphasis. It did not last long, and did little to bolster the weakening position of Montfort and his allies in face of a determined and ingenious royalist counter-offensive. Earl Simon, indeed, was forced to leave the country, and Edward did the same. In July he left for Gascony. There his main concern was with the long-running saga of the feud between the Colomb and Soler families in Bordeaux. In October 1261 a new constitution for the city was promulgated, which gave Edward full control of the mayoralty, just as he had planned at the time of the secret treaty with Gaillard del Soler. His policies were succeeding. He reformed the coinage, did much to restore law and order, and gained some territory for the crown. There were problems: complaints over the violent seizure of the temporalities of the archbishopric of Bordeaux reached Henry III. Edward obviously did well, however, and a letter to the king in the autumn of 1261 reported that 'Our lord Edward is in a good and prosperous state, and by God's grace his affairs in Gascony are going well'.[50] He may have been fickle in his political alliances in England, but in Gascony Edward showed much more of the mettle of the future king.

Henry III expected his son to return to England in time for the Christmas festivities of 1261, but he did not in fact come back until late February. There was then much debate about the state of Edward's finances. The man who had been largely in charge of this aspect of the prince's affairs was Roger Leyburn. It was, according to one account, the malicious tongue of his mother which turned Edward against Leyburn, who was found guilty of misappropriating funds, and had all his lands taken from him. Exchequer records show that the sheriff of Kent was ordered to raise no less than £1,820 from Leyburn's lands, this being the sum for which he had failed to account properly. Leyburn was ordered to restore the manor of Elham in Kent to Edward, and accusations were levied against him regarding the destruction of woods there.[51] How far Edward was a willing participant in these proceedings is not clear. It may be that he was now simply in a position of tutelage once again, in which he could not resist the king, or he may have turned against Leyburn as he was later to turn against other men who served him loyally, but against whom corruption was alleged, such as Jean de Grailly and Ralph Hengham.

Leyburn's disgrace in the spring of 1262 meant that Edward parted company with Henry of Almain, John de Warenne, Roger Clifford and others of the group that had earlier provided him with his main

---

[50] Trabut-Cussac, *L'administration anglaise en Gascogne*, 22–7; *Royal and other Historical Letters illustrative of the Reign of Henry III*, ed. W.W. Shirley (Rolls ser., 1862–6), ii, 163.

[51] *The Historical Works of Gervase of Canterbury*, ed. W. Stubbs (1879–80), ii, 22–1; E 159/36, m.17; *Close Rolls 1261–4*, 117, 171; *CPR 1266–72*, 727.

backing. This did not mean, however, that the group lost coherence. A list of Simon de Montfort's supporters early in 1263, given by the Dunstable annalist, included the three men just named, along with John de Vaux and Hamo Lestrange.[52] This strongly suggests that it would be wrong to see Edward as the clear leader: Henry of Almain, or perhaps Earl Warenne, may have been responsible for holding the group together, and providing a political consistency which Edward himself lacked at this stage of his career.[53]

New arrangements had to be made for Edward's financing following Leyburn's fall. On 4 June a radical step was taken, with Henry III granting to his son the receipts from the Jewry in England for a three-year period, and Edward in return handing over to the king the bulk of his estates for the same period. The list of lands included Grantham, Tickhill, Abergavenny and the Three Castles, along with lands in Norfolk and Suffolk, obtained by exchange with Peter of Savoy, and the isles of Guernsey and Jersey. In addition, the deal covered the lands Edward held by wardship of the heirs of William de Cantilupe and John de Lungevilers. Such an arrangement severely limited Edward's freedom of action: he could no longer grant out lands in a profligate fashion to his supporters, although he was still provided with an income which the king and council considered adequate for him. Edward in fact entrusted the Jewry to some merchants from Cahors, presumably farming it out to them in return for a fixed annual render.[54]

In July 1262 Henry III went abroad, for further negotiations with the French over the treaty of Paris of 1259, and hoping for arbitration of his dispute with Simon de Montfort. Edward and his brother Edmund went as well, but little is known of their activities. It could be that it was now that he attended tournaments at Senlis and elsewhere, at which some of his followers incurred losses for which they only received compensation in 1285–6. The Dunstable annalist has it that Edward was himself badly wounded in a tournament.[55]

Edward returned to England early in 1263 to face major problems in Wales. Late in the previous year Llywelyn ap Gruffydd had achieved striking successes in the Marches. Letters from Peter de Montfort, in command at Abergavenny, reveal that the English felt their plight to be desperate. Despite some successes against Welsh foragers, Montfort thought that if he received no assistance, he would be forced to abandon

[52] *Ann. Dunstable*, 222.

[53] *Close Rolls 1261–4*, 133, has a list of men ordered not to participate in tournaments in a writ issued on 25 August, which is effectively of the same group of men. It includes Roger de Leyburn, Roger Clifford, Hamo Lestrange and John Giffard.

[54] *CPR 1258–66*, 233, 283.

[55] *Records of the Wardrobe and Household 1285–1286*, ed. B.F. and C.R. Byerley (1977), 63; *Ann. Dunstable*, 219.

his command. Accordingly, an expedition was prepared, under Edward's leadership. On 3 April, at Hereford, the prince made a treaty with Llywelyn's brother Dafydd. Yet little was achieved in the campaign which took place in April and May. The Burton annals attributed the failure to resentment on the part of the English magnates that Edward had brought a force of foreign knights with him; the *Flores* pointed to the successful Welsh tactics of withdrawal into the woods and mountains of Snowdonia, but reported that Edward had at least managed to revictual the castles of Dyserth and Deganwy before being recalled to England.[56]

The crisis in Wales was followed by a severe deterioration of the domestic situation. Simon de Montfort had left England in 1261, only returning very briefly in the next year. Now, in the spring of 1263, he came back to England, determined to re-establish the baronial reform movement, with himself as its undisputed leader. The widespread discontent in the Welsh Marches made it easy to recruit in that region. The death of Richard de Clare, earl of Gloucester, in 1262 had removed one major rival. The earl's heir, Gilbert, was more radical than his father, as was shown when he refused to take an oath of fealty to Edward when this was demanded by Henry III.[57] The situation in the spring and early summer of 1263 was confused. The Marchers followed up private feuds, rather than campaigning systematically: in particular they turned on the Savoyard bishop of Hereford, Peter of Aigueblanche. Simon de Montfort moved to Kent, where Roger Leyburn was active, for it was vital to prevent Henry III receiving help from abroad.

Attempts at mediation by Richard of Cornwall failed. Edward was in agressive mood, and Richard had to ask Henry III to order him not to attack the barons until the process of negotiation had been given a chance.[58] Henry III was forced to take refuge in the Tower, while his son occupied the hospital at Clerkenwell. The situation was desperate, not least because of a lack of funds. Edward determined on a desperate remedy, and went with Robert Walerand and others to the New Temple. They obtained entry by a trick, asking to see Queen Eleanor's jewels which were deposited there. Once inside, they broke open the treasure chests, and carried off large sums of cash.[59] This infuriated the

---

[56] *Royal and other Historical Letters, Henry III*, ed. Shirley, ii, 230–1; *CPR 1258–66*, 261; *Flores*, ii, 478; *Ann. Burton*, 500.

[57] *Ann. Dunstable*, 220.

[58] *Royal Letters, Henry III*, ii, 247.

[59] *Ann. Dunstable*, 222. Powicke, *Henry III and the Lord Edward*, ii, 439, tries to condone this act by stating that the chests contained royal treasure, but there is no evidence of this. Treharne, *Baronial Plan of Reform*, 304, argues on the basis of a later pardon to Robert Walerand that the action was ordered by Henry III, but the evidence is hardly strong.

Londoners, who rose in rebellion, sacking the residences of such royalist supporters as John de Grey. All Edward could do was to make his way to Windsor, which he garrisoned with his foreign mercenary knights, while Henry in London determined on capitulation. The queen, tougher minded by far, tried to join Edward, but her boat was pelted by the mob on London Bridge, and she had to turn back.[60]

On 16 July 1263 Henry III accepted the baronial terms, and four days later he ordered the mercenaries to leave Windsor, even asking the feudal host which had been summoned for a Welsh campaign to go to the castle.[61] Edward was not prepared to capitulate as his father had done. He moved to Bristol, where the conduct of his men caused the townspeople to rise in arms and besiege him in the castle. The bishop of Worcester managed to negotiate a truce, but Edward promptly ignored its terms, by returning to Windsor and his mercenaries. His position there was weak, and he was forced to agree to surrender the castle, with the mercenaries receiving safe-conduct to go to Staines.[62]

Simon de Montfort and his supporters appeared to be in an invincible position, but they were unable to force checkmate. In part this was because of the intervention of Louis IX of France, who summoned Henry III and baronial representatives to Boulogne, in a move which the English king had probably planned. Simon refused to accept the judgement of a French court, but the incident showed his weakness, and in the parliament which followed his and Henry's return from Boulogne, disputes were bitter, and the situation was evidently drifting into civil war.[63] The royalist position was greatly strengthened by Edward's successes during the summer.

One early sign of Edward's attempt to build up support came when on 15 July 1263 he gave Ulster to Walter de Burgh, lord of Connaught. This was a major grant of territory which had been in royal hands since 1242, and that such an alienation should take place ran counter to Henry III's policy. It made sense in Irish terms, for English authority in Ulster was distinctly fragile at this time, but the grant should largely be seen in an English context, of the lengths to which Edward was now prepared to go in order to obtain vitally needed help. He was not himself in a position to make Walter earl of Ulster: the title had come by 1266, and was perhaps conferred upon him by Henry III after the battle of Evesham.[64]

[60] *Ann. Dunstable*, 223; *Flores*, ii, 482.
[61] *CPR 1258–66*, 269–71; *Close Rolls, 1261–3*, 308–9.
[62] *Flores*, ii, 482–3; *CPR 1258–66*, 272.
[63] For a detailed analysis, see Treharne, *Baronial Plan of Reform*, 319–22.
[64] R.F. Frame, 'Ireland and the Barons' Wars', *Thirteenth Century England* I, 164–6: see also *Handbook of British Chronology*, 3rd edn, ed. E.B. Fryde, D.E. Greenway, S. Porter and I. Roy (1986), 497; *CDI 1252–84*, nos 860, 1458, 1520.

Most importantly, it was now that Edward succeeded in re-establishing his position with his former supporters. On 18 August 1263 Roger Leyburn, John de Vaux, Ralph Basset, Hamo Lestrange and John Giffard issued letters patent, which stated that they had agreed to give their full support to Edward, with such security as Henry of Almain and Earl Warenne should think fitting. They did not renounce their oaths to the Provisions of Oxford: there was a clause 'saving the common oath, which is to the honour of God and the fealty of the king and the profit of the realm'. What arguments Edward used to obtain the support of these men this time is not clear. Two chroniclers cynically considered that they were simply bribed by means of offers of lands, while the royalist Wykes wrote of Edward's persuasiveness. One possible reason for their change of heart may well have been the fact that Simon de Montfort intended to seek alliance with Llywelyn ap Gruffydd, a policy unacceptable to men with major interests in the Welsh March. The loss of Dyserth and Deganwy to Llywelyn must have demonstrated the dangers of such an alliance.[65] For his part, Edward must have agreed to abandon his reliance on foreign mercenaries, and may have made other promises.

The discussions in the October parliament of 1263 achieved nothing, and Edward withdrew, seizing Windsor castle. Henry III soon joined him, and early in December they tried unsuccessfully to take Dover castle from its baronial custodian.[66] Only the support of the Londoners enabled Simon de Montfort to escape capture by the king and prince.[67] Meanwhile, negotiations for a settlement had been proceeding, and both parties gave their consent to French arbitration. Among those who sealed the king's agreement were Edward's allies, Earl Warenne, Alan la Zouche, Roger Clifford, Hamo Lestrange, John de Vaux, Warin de Bassingbourne and Roger Leyburn.[68]

Edward accompanied his father to Amiens for the negotiations. The award, or *mise*, issued late in January by Louis IX was a firm justification of Henry III's position. The only concession to his baronial opponents was that Henry was to pardon them for any offences committed in defence of the Provisions of Oxford, but those provisions themselves were now wholly annulled.[69] There was little hope that such

---

[65] *Foedera*, i, 430; *Flores*, ii, 484–5; *Ann. Dunstable*, 225; Wykes, 137; Lloyd, *History of Wales*, ii, 732. For the importance of the Welsh Marcher lords in this period, see T.F. Tout, 'Wales and the March in the Barons' Wars', in his *Collected Papers* (Manchester, 1934), ii, 47–100.

[66] *CPR 1258–66*, 294, 300, suggest strongly that Edward was present on the expedition to Dover.

[67] *Ann. Dunstable*, 226; *Flores*, ii, 485.

[68] Treharne, *Baronial Plan of Reform*, 335.

[69] *Documents of the Baronial Movement*, ed. Sanders, 280–91.

terms would settle matters: the drift into civil war was becoming irresistible. Simon could hardly accept the Mise of Amiens, but quite as important was the widespread lawlessness in England, with a multiplicity of local conflicts. So many enmities had been aroused in the turbulent years since 1258 that the disorganized machinery of a disillusioned government had little hope of preventing major conflict.

Edward's allies were deeply involved in the deterioration of the situation. The seat of trouble was in the Welsh Marches, where, at Christmas, John Giffard attacked and ravaged the lands of Roger Mortimer. In January Clifford, Leyburn, de Vaux, Basset, Giffard, Lestrange and others were singled out as blameworthy for the 'injuries, damages and violences lately committed against the church' by them, and the king promised that they would make amends.[70] The troubles in the March became far more serious when Simon de Montfort, who was himself laid up with a broken leg, sent his sons Simon and Henry to join in the attack on Mortimer, in which Llywelyn ap Gruffydd also participated. Richard of Cornwall set out with Edward to try to pacify the region. Richard's approach was, no doubt, conciliatory, but Edward's was not. He took the Bohun castles of Hay and Huntingdon, and obtained the surrender of Brecon, handing these lands over to Mortimer.[71]

Meanwhile the rebels had gained the city of Gloucester, but not the castle, by a trick, entering disguised as Welsh wool traders. The castle held out, and Edward came to assist the garrison. He forced an entry by repairing a broken bridge over the Severn, and a good deal of fighting took place. Then with the appearance of Earl Robert Ferrers, of whom Edward was 'of no man so sore adread', the balance changed. Edward, with Henry of Almain and others, came out of the castle unarmed, and negotiated a truce, with the bishop of Worcester acting as intermediary. Ferrers and the baronial forces were satisfied and departed, whereupon Edward ignored the terms of the truce, imprisoned many of the citizens and imposed a heavy ransom on the city. He then went to join his father at Oxford, his skin safe and his reputation tarnished.[72]

On 6 March 1264 Henry III summoned the feudal host to meet him at Oxford for an expedition against Llywelyn of Wales. The list of those asked to attend ended with a curt note: 'those who are against the king are not written to', and it is clear that in reality this was intended to be an army to fight a civil war.[73] Further summonses on 18 March made

---

[70] *Ann. Tewkesbury*, 179; *CPR 1258–66*, 378.
[71] *Close Rolls 1261–64*, 334; *Flores*, ii, 486.
[72] *The Metrical Chronicle of Robert of Gloucester*, ii, 740–6; *Flores*, ii, 487; *Ann. Dunstable*, 227–8.
[73] *Close Rolls 1261–4*, 377–81.

this quite clear. Attempts at mediation failed, and early in April the host marched out. Henry made what amounted to a formal declaration of war by raising his dragon standard, a splendid device with jewelled eyes, made so that its tongue appeared to flicker constantly.[74] It had something of the symbolism of the French Oriflamme, and was only used for major campaigns. The army did not have to march far, for baronial forces, led by Simon de Montfort's son Simon and the un-related Peter de Montfort, had gathered at Northampton. The town walls were swiftly breached, and victory won. Edward played a leading part in the assault, displaying chivalric spirit in preventing the young Simon from being killed by the delighted royalist troops. The capture of many leading baronial supporters so early in the war was a major triumph, and it was swiftly followed up. Henry III and his son moved on to Leicester and Nottingham, which surrendered without a fight.

Edward then left the main army, and attacked the estates of Earl Ferrers, taking Tutbury castle and ravaging the lands.[75] These had, of course, been in his hands earlier, during the earl's minority, and it seems likely that it was as a result of that minority that a feud had developed between the two young men. Financing the campaign was obviously something of a problem for Edward, but he had few qualms about exacting protection money, taking, for example, £200 from the hundred of Wirksworth. He initially refused a bribe from the abbot of Peterborough, but this was at the request of his friend Warin de Bassingbourne, who had his own private feud with the abbey. Once Warin had been pacified with 60 marks, Edward willingly took his share of £114 paid to himself, the king and Richard of Cornwall.[76] The attack on Ferrers' estates suggests that Edward was pursuing his own ends rather than those of his father, but it perhaps made sense to try to pick off Simon de Montfort's supporters one by one.

The royalists, despite their initial triumph, did not have everything their own way. John Giffard captured the earl of Warwick, and the citizens of London were firm in their support for the cause of reform. Montfort and his ally the earl of Gloucester concentrated their attentions on the south-east, where they took the town of Rochester, along with the outer bailey of the great castle there. The keep, under the command of Earl Warenne, held out. Roger Leyburn was among those besieged: he was badly wounded in the fighting. The garrison was a large one, as is suggested by the fact that there were no less than 164

---

[74] *Close Rolls 1242–7*, 201.

[75] *Ann. Dunstable*, 230; *Flores*, ii, 489. The events of the war are described by Powicke, *Henry III and the Lord Edward*, ii, 460 ff., though in many ways W.H. Blaauw, *The Barons' War* (2nd edn, 1871) is still the best account.

[76] *Ann. Dunstable*, 230; Walter of Whytleseye in *Historiae Anglicanae Scriptores Varii*, ed. J. Sparke (1724), 135–6.

horses in the castle at the time of the siege. Supplies were reasonably ample: Edward had earlier sent twenty-five tuns of wine, so there was sufficient to drink. It was Lent, so the garrison's diet was confined to fish, and on the day the siege began they had mackerel, mullet, salmon and whiting.[77] In the event, the siege did not last long. Henry came to relieve the castle, and Montfort hurried back to London, where there were rumours of plots to hand the city over to Edward. Henry then moved to Tonbridge, where he took the earl of Gloucester's castle. By this time Edward had rejoined his father, and their combined forces moved on to receive the surrender of Winchelsea. From there they went to Lewes. Meanwhile Simon de Montfort had gathered his troops, and advanced from London, intent upon finally settling his dispute with the king. All was set for a decisive battle.

Contrary to popular belief, battles were rare in medieval warfare. It made more sense to ravage enemy territory, to reduce towns and castles by means of sieges, and to conduct raids and counter-raids, than it did to risk all on the field of battle. Edward I was to fight only three major battles in his life; Lewes, Evesham and Falkirk. Civil war, though, presented rather different problems from other forms of fighting. Here, battle offered a means of resolving the conflict, for it could be considered as a way of obtaining a divine verdict on the justice of a particular cause. Royal justice, in the form of Louis of France's decision at Amiens, had failed Earl Simon: it remained to be seen what the result of a trial by battle would be. The conflict at Lewes was certainly not the result of a chance encounter between two armies. Both sides went through formal preliminaries of issuing letters of defiance, and final, futile, attempts at compromise were made. Henry III wrote in very formal terms, announcing that he considered the barons now to be his enemies, not his subjects, while Edward and Richard of Cornwall in a joint letter expressed themselves more strongly, objecting to the baronial accusation that they had given the king false counsel, and challenging Montfort and the earl of Gloucester to justify themselves before their peers in the king's court. One chronicler considered that it was Edward and Richard who were responsible for the failure of the negotiations which preceded the battle.[78]

From a royalist point of view, to fight was a chance probably worth taking. The actual size of the armies is not known, but the estimate by one chronicler that the royalists had 1,500 cavalry as against Montfort's 500 is perhaps not far from the truth.[79] Montfort, however, was

[77] *Ann. Dunstable*, 230–1; Guisborough, 192; E 101/3/3.
[78] *The Chronicle of William de Rishanger of the Barons' Wars*, ed. J.O. Halliwell (Camden Soc., 1840), 28–30; *Flores*, ii, 493–4.
[79] Gervase of Canterbury, ii, 237.

undoubtedly a more experienced commander than anyone on the royalist side, though historians' estimates of his ability owe something to his own gifts for publicity. On this occasion he was hampered in that he had not recovered fully from his broken leg, as well as by the fact that many of his troops were untrained, if enthusiastic, Londoners.

Medieval battles are never easy to reconstruct. The participants themselves were in no position to judge events as a whole, in the noise and confusion, and chroniclers were not military experts. Lewes presents particular problems, with two divergent chronicle traditions of what actually happened.[80] The battle took place on 14 May, and Simon's army, no doubt encouraged by the pious exhortations of its leader, was probably better prepared than that of the royalists, though not too much credence should be given to the contrast, drawn by contemporaries, between the chaste manner in which the baronial forces spent the night before the battle, and the uproarious, sacrilegious and adulterous conduct of the royalists with their seven hundred whores.[81] Henry III's army was divided into three main battalions. That on the right was commanded by Edward, with Warenne and William de Valence, that on the left by Richard of Cornwall and his son Henry, with the king controlling the centre. Other troops had been left to guard Tonbridge.

Edward was in bellicose mood. An initial charge broke the line facing him: as they retreated, many knights were drowned in the river and marshy ground. The Londoners panicked and fled, with Edward in hot pursuit: he felt particularly vindictive towards them after the way they had treated his mother when she had attempted to join him at Windsor and had been pelted by the mob. It is possible that Edward was lured away from the main battlefield by a piece of low cunning. Montfort had come to Lewes in a cart, because of his injury, and this had been left, with a substantial guard and standard flying, in the rear of the army. Either at the start of the rout of the Londoners, or in returning from the chase, it was probably Edward and his men who seized the cart with delight, killing some unfortunate royalist Londoners who had been imprisoned in a sort of iron cage built into it.[82]

For Edward, the battle appeared to go splendidly: a magnificent charge, followed by a rout, with plenty of enemy casualties must have been just what he had hoped for. But when he returned to the main

---

[80] D.A. Carpenter, 'Simon de Montfort and the Mise of Lewes', *BIHR*, lviii (1985), 4–5.

[81] *Political Songs*, ed. Wright, 79; *Chronicon de Lanercost*, ed. J. Stevenson (Maitland Club, 1839), 74.

[82] Wykes, 150–1; Guisborough, 195. Rishanger, 27, does not attribute the attack on the cart to Edward's men.

battlefield, it was to find that the other elements of the royal army had fared very differently. Richard of Cornwall's battalion had been roundly defeated, and, after taking refuge in a windmill, Richard himself surrendered. The troops with the king also failed to resist the baronial charge, and Henry's own horse was slain. One tradition has it that he then surrendered to the earl of Gloucester; another that he took refuge in the nearby priory.[83] Edward was almost certainly unaware of what exactly had happened as he and his men circled the town after their return to the battlefield. They were attacked by baronial troops, and Earl Warenne with William de Valence and Guy de Lusignan fled. According to one account, Edward then went to look for his father in the castle, and when he failed to find him there, went to the priory. The barons besieged the castle, hoping to release the prisoners incarcerated there, and in the fighting much of the town was set on fire. They moved on to the priory, and Edward prepared to make a sortie and begin battle again. Wiser counsels prevailed, however, and the night was spent in negotiation. The king and his son were threatened that if they did not come to terms, then Richard of Cornwall, Philip Basset and other prisoners of the barons would be executed, and their heads stuck on the ends of lances.[84]

Though he had won the battle of Lewes, Simon de Montfort was not in a position of complete dominance, for the king and the heir to the throne were not in his hands. Precise details of the agreement, known as the Mise of Lewes, that was hammered out in the aftermath of the battle are not known, but it was evidently a complex affair.[85] The Provisions of Oxford were to stand, but there were procedures set up for modifying them in detail, and there was a separate arrangement for French arbitration of other outstanding questions. Importantly, the Marcher lords and some others were allowed to leave Lewes, promising that they would return to parliament to stand trial before their peers. Among these men were Roger Mortimer, Hamo Lestrange, Roger Clifford and Roger Leyburn. In order to guarantee this settlement, Edward and Henry of Almain gave themselves up as hostages, not to be released until a permanent settlement was achieved. From Simon's point of view, the two young men were not particularly good hostages, for he hardly dared threaten them with execution in view of their status.[86] From Edward's own position, the fact that his Marcher allies

---

[83] *Ann. Waverley*, 357; Wykes, 151; Guisborough, 195. For a more detailed analysis of the opinions of the chroniclers, see Carpenter, 'Simon de Montfort and the Mise of Lewes', 4–5.

[84] Guisborough, 195; *Flores*, iii, 260–1.

[85] For recent discussion, see J.R. Maddicott, 'The Mise of Lewes, 1264', *EHR*, xcviii (1983), 588–603, and Carpenter, 'Simon de Montfort and the Mise of Lewes', 1–11.

[86] Maddicott, op. cit., 600.

had gone free offered the best hope of a reversal of the defeat of Lewes.

The two hostages were not kept together. Henry of Almain was imprisoned at his father's castle of Berkhampstead, and Edward was taken first to Dover, then to Wallingford, and eventually Kenilworth. The royalist chronicler Wykes suggests that the conditions of imprisonment were harsher than was proper, but there is no solid evidence of this.[87] There was little hope of an early release. Louis IX and the papal legate prevaricated over the question of arbitration, the latter demanding as late as 12 August the release of the hostages, as the French had not received any copy of the agreement made at Lewes.[88] A temporary scheme of government was drawn up, without reference to the arbitrators proposed in the Mise of Lewes, but on 6 October it was made clear that this could not lead to the release of Edward and Henry of Almain while the Marcher lords were still fighting. An important group of Edward's men, including Warin de Bassingbourne, Robert Walerand and Robert de Tibetot, held Bristol for him. A bold attempt was made to rescue the prince from Wallingford, but the constable threatened to hurl him out of the castle by using a mangonel. Edward was then led up to the battlements, and instructed the attackers to go away, 'other he was dead'.[89]

Edward's supporters were few in number, and in the autumn of 1264 events drifted in Simon de Montfort's favour. The refusal of the Marchers to attend parliament was followed by a military expedition against them, and in December they were forced to come to terms, agreeing to go into exile in Ireland for a year. Mortimer, Clifford and Leyburn received safe-conducts to go to see Edward at Kenilworth, in the hope that he would order them to accept the terms. He requested that Bristol be given up, and as a further element in the settlement granted Simon de Montfort the earldom of Chester in exchange for other property of the same value – though when in May 1265 Earl Simon did make over some estates to Edward, they were certainly not equal to Chester.[90] The Marchers constantly prevaricated, and never did sail for Ireland, but negotiations continued for the release of Edward and Henry of Almain. This was the subject of much discussion in the celebrated parliament summoned by Montfort, which opened late in January 1265. An agreement was concluded on 11 March 1265. The terms were harsh for Edward. The agreement to hand over Chester, along with Newcastle-under-Lyme, was renewed. Bristol was to be

[87] Wykes, 153.
[88] Maddicott, op. cit., 595.
[89] *CPR 1258–66*, 374, 397; Robert of Gloucester, ii, 752.
[90] *CPR 1258–66*, 394–5, 397, 424. For a fuller discussion of the events of this period, see Powicke, *Henry III and the Lord Edward*, ii, 486–90.

retained by Earl Simon as a pledge for the full implementation of the agreement, and Edward promised to accept the new scheme of government. Five major royal castles were to be handed over by Henry III to Edward, and he was then to entrust them to Montfort as guarantees of his good conduct for the next five years.[91] Even then, Edward was still not free. He was kept under close surveillance, and Earl Simon's son Henry was given responsibility for watching his movements.[92]

The release of Edward from close custody might suggest that Simon de Montfort was in a strong position, but this was far from true. His strength was being fatally weakened by the defection of the young earl of Gloucester, Gilbert the Red.[93] Earl Gilbert had fought for Simon in 1264, although his commitment to him was probably never total. A propaganda letter written in his interest early in 1264 had emphasized his support for the principles of reform, but had expressed doubts about Montfort, because of the favour he showed to aliens, and because of his age. After Lewes there was a dispute over a prisoner, and in more general terms Gloucester challenged Earl Simon about the control he was demanding over royal castles, and even over the maintenance of the Provisions of Oxford and the terms of the Mise of Lewes.[94] When Montfort had Robert Earl Ferrers arrested and imprisoned, Gloucester felt threatened. By February 1265 there were clear signs of trouble when a tournament had to be cancelled because of fears of disturbances between Montfort's sons and the earl of Gloucester and his men. Another element in the growing tension was the alliance made with Llywelyn ap Gruffydd, which threatened Gloucester's massive interests in the Welsh Marches. In the spring of 1265 Gloucester, along with John Giffard, abandoned the baronial cause, and joined with the Marchers, who were still delaying their departure for Ireland. In May the baronial position was threatened still further, when Earl Warenne and William de Valence landed in Pembroke, ready to join forces with the Marchers.[95]

Simon de Montfort marched west to deal with this increasingly critical situation, and on 12 May reached a form of agreement with Gloucester. A few days later Stamford was restored to Edward and other lands were granted to him; presumably in an attempt to meet criticisms levelled by Gloucester. Optimistic Montfortian propaganda declared that there was no discord.[96] The situation was then

---

[91] CPR 1258–66, 414; Foedera, I.

[92] The Metrical Chronicle of Robert of Gloucester, ii, 755.

[93] Altschul, A Baronial Family, 107–10.

[94] Ann. Tewkesbury, 179–80; Ann. London, 65–6; The Metrical Chronicle of Robert of Gloucester, ii, 753; Liber de Antiquis Legibus, ed. T. Stapleton (Camden Soc., 1846), 73.

[95] Wykes, 166; Ann. London, 67; CPR 1258–66, 406, 409; Ann. Dunstable. 238.

[96] CPR 1258–66, 424.

transformed on Thursday 28 May, when Edward went out riding from Hereford in the company of a number of knights, including Gloucester's brother Thomas de Clare and Henry de Montfort. The classic account of what took place is that Edward asked to try all the horses in turn. Having found the swiftest, he dug in his spurs and rode off, shouting 'Lordings, I bid you good day. Greet my father well, and tell him that I hope to see him soon, and release him from custody.' One of many elaborations of the story is that the horse on which Edward escaped was sent to him in advance by Roger Mortimer. The official version, understandably reticent, has it that Edward escaped with two knights and four squires, which casts some doubt on the dramatic single-handed dash for freedom of the chronicle accounts.[97] The escape was clearly planned in advance by Edward and Gloucester, and its execution certainly demanded considerable bravery and some skill on Edward's part.

After making his escape, Edward rode to Roger Mortimer's castle of Wigmore, and then to Ludlow, where he joined forces with Gloucester. He promised the earl that, should they be successful in battle, he would ensure that the good old laws would be observed, evil customs abolished, aliens expelled from the realm and the council, and that the government would be entrusted to native-born Englishmen. This was the kind of programme that had been music to the ears of the baronage in 1258. Whatever Edward's private views were, his associates had not lost their commitment to the ideals of the reform movement. Gloucester certainly considered that Simon de Montfort, with his evident self-aggrandisement, the favours accorded to his own sons, and the lack of further progress in the process of legal and administrative reform, had failed, and that a new solution was required to resolve the problems of a deeply troubled country.

Once the news of Edward's release became known, men flocked to his standard. The Marchers predominated, of course, and Warenne and Valence were swift to join forces with Edward. The first success was the surrender of Worcester without a fight. The bridge across the Severn there was then broken, so that Simon de Montfort at Hereford would find it hard to join with forces mustered further east by his son Simon. From Worcester Edward moved to Gloucester. One section of the town wall was left undefended, and it was here that the attackers, headed by John Giffard, broke through. Grimbald Pauncefoot, who had earlier besieged Edward in Gloucester castle, now found the position reversed. The garrison were forced to surrender, and Grimbald was most favourably treated, being knighted by Edward, and joining

---

[97] *The Metrical Chronicle of Robert of Gloucester*, ii, 756–7; Guisborough, 198; *Close Rolls, 1264–8*, 124–5.

his forces. Edward was very ready to recognize the courage and ability of his opponents, and was often ready to welcome those who were prepared to change sides.[98]

The danger that Edward and Gloucester would be caught in a pincer movement by Earl Simon's troops from the west and the young Simon's men from the east was averted. More bridges across the Severn were destroyed, and ships in which Earl Simon hoped to reach Bristol were intercepted by three galleys provided by the earl of Gloucester.[99] Simon de Montfort then turned for support to Llywelyn ap Gruffydd, with whom he made a formal alliance on 19 June, an action which was highly unpopular in England. The Welsh were themselves most reluctant to fight for Montfort, whose troops were demoralized by the weeks they spent in Wales, where victualling arrangements were quite inadequate. Eventually Montfort and his men, still taking the captive Henry III with them, returned to Hereford. On 2 August he found a ford across the Severn that was still passable, and advanced eastwards.[100]

While the elder Montfort was wasting precious time in Wales, his son Simon advanced from the siege of Pevensey, which had gone on since the previous September, through Winchester, Oxford and Northampton, to Kenilworth. There his troops were billeted in the town and priory, as there was not room for so many in the castle. Edward and Gloucester had good intelligence, notably from a female transvestite spy called Margoth. They made a rapid night march from Worcester, and prepared for battle in a deep hollow from which they could not be seen. When a bell sounded in the morning, they thought they had been spotted, and quickly mounted and attacked. Their enemy was in fact totally unprepared: many were slaughtered, with the notables among them being captured. By one account, the young Simon escaped death because he was in the castle. A more dramatic account has him fleeing naked from his bed in the town, and rowing across the lake to take refuge within the castle walls. A slanderous tale, told many years later by an Irish magnate, had it that when Edward heard of the scale of the forces opposing him, he wanted to turn back, and was only dissuaded from doing so by Roger Clifford, who rode forward with his banner raised, giving him no option but to follow.[101] There is no evidence to support this, but it is probably the case that Edward's force was still not a large one.

---

[98] *The Metrical Chronicle of Robert of Gloucester*, ii, 758–9.

[99] Wykes, 167.

[100] *Royal Letters, Henry III*, ii, 284–7; Tout, 'Wales and the March', 117–18; Wykes, 168.

[101] *Rot. Parl.* i, 127; below, 354.

Meanwhile Earl Simon advanced towards Evesham, hoping to join forces with his son, and then go to London where he was sure of support. He did not move quickly, delaying at Evesham to hear mass. Henry III refused to go any further until he had eaten. Edward's intelligence was again good: Ralph de Ardern is said to have betrayed the Montfortian movements. Learning that the army was due to leave Evesham on 4 August, Edward and his men marched out of Worcester on the previous evening. They rode a few miles northwards, to deceive their enemies, and then doubled back to Evesham. Battle was joined next morning.[102]

Accounts of the battle of Evesham inevitably differ. Total surprise was not possible, but Edward resorted to a devious stratagem. He ordered the banners captured at Kenilworth to be carried in front of his army, so that Earl Simon's herald told his master that the advancing troops were Montfortian.[103] When they were properly recognized, Montfort with typical arrogance declared 'By the arm of St James, they are advancing well. They have not learned that for themselves, but were taught it by me.'[104] Simon's troops were drawn up in a defensive circular formation, but this was not strong enough to resist Edward and Gloucester's charges. The Welsh fled like sheep, but there was no repetition of the folly of Lewes with a chase by Edward. The Montfortian barons and knights fought with great bravery against an enemy consumed with blood-lust. In most medieval battles, casualties among the knightly class were low, as captured enemies were worth a substantial ransom, but at Evesham the casualty lists were long. Simon de Montfort himself fought bravely, but was eventually overcome and slain, as was his son Henry, though Guy de Montfort was taken prisoner. Henry III himself was in the midst of the battle, and was indeed slightly wounded, but he shouted out his name, and was duly recognized and reunited with his son. The mood of Edward's troops was one of savage revenge, epitomized by the crude mutilation of Simon de Montfort's corpse. His head and genitals were sent off in triumph to Roger Mortimer's wife at Wigmore, who was no doubt well pleased with the grisly parcel.[105]

The Evesham campaign had been a triumph for Edward. How far he was himself really responsible for the success is not clear: the impression given by the chroniclers is that Gloucester should share the

---

[102] Wykes, 171–2, is the fullest account, but the movements of the armies are hard to work out, and the sources not consistent. See Blaauw, *Barons' Wars*, 271–2.

[103] Guisborough, 200.

[104] *Chronicle of William de Rishanger*, ed. Halliwell, 45.

[105] Wykes, 172–5; Guisborough, 200–2; *The Metrical Chronicle of Robert of Gloucester*, ii, 764–5, all give some details of the battle.

credit with the future king. The chronicler Wykes commented on the way that Edward had learned from his earlier mistakes, and now acted with proper wisdom as well as courage. He and his allies were well served by their spies and scouts, and did well to seize their opportunities when they were presented. Although the campaign was as much lost by the Montfortians as won by Edward and Gloucester, the achievement was nonetheless considerable. In political terms, Edward's success was due above all to the links he had forged with the lords of the Welsh March. He was, of course, a major landowner himself in Wales, and he had connections there stretching back a long way. Roger Clifford and Hamo Lestrange had supported Edward at the time of his treaty with Gloucester in 1259. It was in 1263, however, that the real strength of the link with the Marchers was established. Particularly important was Mortimer's decision to back Edward, the consequence, according to the Dunstable annalist, of a promise of three of Simon de Montfort's manors.[106] The Marchers were not, of course, a united group, brought together by a common threat such as that which faced them in 1321 with the younger Despenser's ambitions. Many of their number did support Earl Simon, but by the time of Evesham Edward's supporters were dominant, and provided him with the experienced forces he needed for success in war.

Mention should also be made of the fact that as lord of Ireland Edward was able to summon several important Anglo-Irish magnates to his assistance.[107] Geoffrey de Geneville had very skilfully pacified Ireland. First he had raised an army against the pro-Montfortian Geraldines, then he had secured the release of the captured Richard de la Rochelle, Edward's representative in the country, and finally he won the support of all factions, by promising that all should hold their land on the same basis that they had held it before the war began. It was then possible for troops to be recruited in time to assist Edward's cause at the time of Evesham.[108]

It was rare, as Lewes had shown, for a single battle to be decisive. Evesham was a different matter, but although there can have been no real hope for the baronial cause after Simon de Montfort's death, resistance did not end on that day in early August 1265. There was still the younger Simon to be dealt with, along with the garrison of

---

[106] *Ann. Dunstable*, 226. Powicke, *Henry III and the Lord Edward*, 498 n.1, suggests that Edward escaped in 1265 into 'a family circle of Marchers, bound together by the Braose connection'. This is based on the fact that both Roger de Mortimer and Geoffrey de Geneville had married ladies called Matilda de Braose, but the argument is weak. One of Mortimer's sisters-in-law had married the earl of Hereford, who was killed at Evesham, and his family connection with Geneville's wife was not a strong one.

[107] *Ann. Waverley*, 365.

[108] Frame, 'Ireland and the Barons' Wars', 161–4.

Kenilworth, and many Montfortian supporters who had fought at Evesham. It was now obvious that Edward would play a major part in the pacification of England. As the victor of Evesham he had acquired the prestige appropriate to his status as heir to the throne, and it would no longer be possible for his father to deny him real power. Yet the evidence is not completely clear as to what Edward's own policies were in the years from 1265 until his departure on crusade in 1270, and it would certainly be dangerous to assume that his was throughout the dominant voice in the government of England.

After Evesham, Edward's first move was northwards to Chester to re-establish his authority there. Wider affairs than those of his own earldom concerned him, and an important letter sent from Chester on 24 August made arrangements for the security of the realm. Roger Leyburn and Nicholas de Lewknor, keeper of the royal wardrobe, were asked to see that Earl Warenne was properly empowered to receive the surrender of the Cinque Ports. He was to prevent piracy, and control the entry of foreigners to England. Edward then asked that letters be drafted inviting the garrison of Kenilworth to surrender, under threat of disinheritance and loss of life.[109] Powicke saw this as 'Edward's first recorded act of state, done by him as a responsible adviser of the crown'.[110] There is little reason, however, to suppose that this letter represents a considered statement of Edward's policy: the generous offer to the Kenilworth garrison was rather a device intended to induce them to surrender. The heir to the throne would not necessarily take so moderate a line with those who no longer represented any threat to him. Edward probably offered similar terms to the garrisons of Wallingford and Berkhampstead on his return from Chester, certainly promising at least four men that they could continue to hold their lands freely, but in more general terms he appears to have gone along willingly in the harsh policies that were adopted in the aftermath of Evesham.[111]

Immediately after the battle Henry gave permission for the seizure of rebel lands. Only two days later, the earl of Gloucester ordered his tenants in three counties to assist two knights he had commissioned to undertake this task.[112] Parliament was summoned to meet at Winchester in September; in addition to the prelates and lay magnates the wives of those captured or killed at Evesham were asked to attend. It was decided to disinherit all who had rebelled against the king: one chronicler noted that this was in spite of the fact that they had actually fought

[109] *Royal Letters, Henry III*, ed. Shirley, ii, 289-90.
[110] Powicke, *Henry III and the Lord Edward*, ii, 504.
[111] *Royal Letters, Henry III*, ii, 291; *Close Rolls 1264-8*, 131.
[112] E.F. Jacob, *Studies in the Period of Baronial Reform and Rebellion, 1258-1267* (Oxford, 1925), 406.

with Simon de Montfort under the king's banner. Commissioners were appointed to help the sheriffs in the seizure of lands, and the rents were to be collected. Limited provision was made for the wives and widows of the rebels.[113] The parliament was interrupted by news of incursions by Llywelyn ap Gruffydd into Cheshire. Hamo Lestrange and the Irish magnate Maurice FitzGerald were sent north, only to be roundly defeated by the Welsh.[114]

Initially, the attitude of the Montfortians had been reasonably con-ciliatory: they released the prisoners held since the battle of Lewes without condition. But no concessions were forthcoming in return. Henry III moved from Winchester to Windsor, where forces were gathered for an attack on London. The citizens, in terror, sent the mayor and forty others to Windsor, under royal safe-conduct, which had been negotiated with Roger Leyburn. In spite of the safe-conduct, they were arrested, and the mayor with four others was handed over to Edward's custody. Henry was then able to enter London, and an indiscriminate confiscation and redistribution of property began. Letters had been drawn up admitting the Londoners to the king's grace, but these were not handed over, and it was not until 5 December that new ones were issued. Only on 10 January 1266 was a pardon issued, in return for a fine of no less than 20,000 marks.[115]

Edward had his own reasons for wishing to take revenge on the Londoners: they had insulted his mother, and had opposed him at Lewes. In October 1265 a large number of grants of forfeited London property were made, and many of the recipients were close adher-ents and friends of Edward's. As well as such men as Warin de Bassingbourne, Hamo Lestrange, Roger Leyburn and John de Vaux, the list included Otto de Grandson, a Savoyard who was to prove one of Edward's most loyal and devoted supporters. Grimbald Pauncefoot now found his change of side well rewarded, and it is significant that the one major magnate to benefit was Earl Warenne. There was certainly no moderation in Edward's policy towards London: even in the pardon of 10 January it was specified that the hostages handed over to Edward were not to be released. It was also the case that the revenge taken upon London was indiscriminate, with many suffering who had in fact been loyal to Henry III and his son.[116]

[113] *Liber de Antiquis Legibus*, ed. Stapleton, 76; *CPR 1258–65*, 490–1; C.H. Knowles, 'Provision for the Families of the Montfortians disinherited after the Battle of Evesham', *Thirteenth Century England*, I, 124.

[114] *Ann. Waverley*, 366.

[115] The best account of events in London is provided by G.A. Williams, *Medieval London from Commune to Capital* (1963), 232–9. See also *Liber de Antiquis Legibus*, ed. Stapleton, 77–9; Wykes, 176–8; *CPR 1258–66*, 469, 519, 530–1.

[116] *CPR 1258–65*, 463–8, 531.

From London Edward went to Dover, towards the end of October, to greet his mother and the papal legate Ottobuono, and to obtain the surrender of Dover castle, where Simon de Montfort's widow, Edward's aunt Eleanor, was residing. Resistance did not last long: on 26 October Edward asked the chancellor to issue writs for the restoration of lands and goods to those who had surrendered. He had clearly made to the men in Dover a similar promise to that which he had suggested should be made to the Kenilworth garrison.[117] Edward then marched north, to deal with the problems posed by the younger Simon de Montfort, who had gathered his forces in the Isle of Axholme: John d'Eyville and Baldwin Wake were two of the more important of those with him. Royalist forces were recruited in Nottinghamshire and Derbyshire, and the isle, for all that it was surrounded by the dismal fens and marshes of north Lincolnshire, did not prove to be the safe redoubt its defenders had hoped. Edward had wooden bridges built so that he could advance on the rebels, and they came to terms at a place called Bickerdyke, or Bycarr's Dyke, at Christmas 1265.[118] The text of the agreement has not survived, but it promised that those who surrendered would not be imprisoned or executed, provided that they submitted to the king's judgement in parliament. Edward was perhaps too ready to accept the word of the rebels at Bickerdyke. The young de Montfort did come to parliament, but fled abroad rather than accept the terms set for him. Baldwin Wake delayed coming to court, and received a pardon only in November 1266, while John d'Eyville came to terms only in 1267.[119] Much further campaigning was to be needed.

After the brief Axholme campaign, the complex mopping-up operations continued. Edward joined Roger Leyburn in a campaign against the Cinque Ports, which culminated in a combined land and sea assault on Winchelsea. Capitulation soon followed, and in a peace concluded on 30 May the rebels were treated with moderation, being pardoned in return for promises of loyalty and obedient service in future. Edward received his reward with the custody of Dover castle, the wardenship of the Ports, and the chamberlainship of Sandwich. The latter appointment he then entrusted to Leyburn. Edward also received full authority over foreign merchants coming to England.[120]

Following the campaign in Kent, Edward and Leyburn divided their

---

[117] Wykes, 178; *Royal Letters, Henry III*, ii, 294–6. In fact, letters were enrolled only in favour of one former member of the garrison, John de la Haye: the evidence may be incomplete, or Edward may have gone back on his word.

[118] Powicke, *Henry III and the Lord Edward*, ii, 519n, discusses the location of Bicker-dyke: it was near Haxey, in Axholme.

[119] *CPR 1266–72*, 6, 8, 73.

[120] A Lewis, 'Roger Leyburn and the Pacification of England, 1265–7', *EHR*, liv (1939), 200–2; *CPR 1258–66*, 574–6, 578.

forces. The latter marched to Essex, while Edward's next direct encounter with the increasingly desperate rebels was in Hampshire, in an
incident which attracted much attention. Adam Gurdon had been an
important supporter of the baronial cause. Edward encountered him in
Alton forest, and boldy engaged him in single combat. Edward's men
were unable to assist him, as a ditch blocked their way. Despite Adam's
experience, Edward's skill and strength eventually prevailed. Several
of the rebels were slain, and others hanged after the skirmish, but Adam
himself was taken prisoner to Windsor castle, where he could provide
company for Robert Ferrers, earl of Derby, recently captured at
Chesterfield by royalist forces under Henry of Almain.[121] The tale of
Edward's fight with Adam Gurdon was later elaborated. One account
had it that Edward ordered his men to stand aside while he and Adam
exchanged blows, and so impressed was the prince with Adam's valour
that he promised him life and fortune if he surrendered, which he
promptly did. The record evidence, however, shows that Adam was in
fact given to the queen as a prisoner, and that he had to buy his estates
back for a stiff price. He was employed on various commissions by
Edward during his reign, but there is no evidence that he was ever
regarded with any special favour, though certainly his rebel past was
not held against him.[122]

The major problem for the crown in 1266 was that presented by the
rebel garrison in Kenilworth castle, one of the most powerful fortifications in the land. The siege was the largest such operation so far to take
place on English soil, and the way in which the garrison held out for
many months in face of the feudal host, and the mobilization of resources from some ten counties, was remarkable testimony to their
courage and the strength of the castle defences. Edward, however, was
not very much concerned in the siege. Initially, responsibility for
taming the Kenilworth defenders lay with his brother Edmund, and
not until the feudal host mustered in late May 1266 did Edward appear
on the scene, commanding one of the four battalions. The highly
provocative behaviour of the besieged, taunting and teasing their opponents, ensured that this was not to be an uneventful blockade. Various
attempts were made to bring machines up to bombard the castle, and
one assault was attempted across the lake, which formed an important
defence. Special barges were brought at great cost from Chester for this
purpose, but the ploy had no success.[123]

[121] Wykes, 189–90.
[122] *Nicholai Triveti Annales*, ed. T. Hog (1845), 269; F.M. Powicke, 'Edward I in Fact
and Fiction', *Fritz Saxl, Memorial Essays*, ed. D.J. Gordon (1957), 120–35.
[123] The best chronicle acounts of the siege are those in Wykes, 190–5; *Ann. Dunstable*,
242–3; *The Chronicle of William de Rishanger*, ed. Halliwell, 51–2. Details of the massive
supply operation are to be found in *CLR 1260–7*, 221–34.

It became clear that, given the immense strength of the defences, a straightforward military solution of the siege would take a long time. So at the end of August 1266 a committee of twelve was set up 'to provide for the state of the realm especially in the matter of the disinherited'. In the event of disagreements, Henry of Almain and the papal legate were to arbitrate. Edward was given no part in the drawing up of the proposals, and was not strongly represented on the committee, where only Warin de Bassingbourne and perhaps Robert Walerand could be relied upon to put his point of view. The indications are, in fact, that Edward had little to do with the debates and decisions that led to the promulgation of the Dictum of Kenilworth on 31 October 1266.[124] The central feature of this was the principle that former rebels should be allowed to buy back their lands from those who had received them in the orgy of confiscations after the battle of Evesham, the price varying according to their degree of involvement in the rebellion. The level set might vary from as little as the annual value of the land, to seven times as much. Some rebels had already been treated in this way: the system was now made general in a long and complex document. It did not win universal acceptance. Minor rebels accepted it, but the garrison at Kenilworth, along with those with John d'Eyville in the Isle of Ely, continued their resistance, so high were the levels at which they would have been able to buy back their lands.[125] In the end, cold and hunger forced surrender in mid-December 1266. So appalling were the conditions within the castle that the besiegers were almost overcome by the stench when they first entered the abandoned fortress.[126]

The final stages of the siege of Kenilworth had merely been a matter of time, and Edward left the royal camp at about the date that the Dictum was promulgated, or possibly even earlier. He went to deal with the rising in the north of John de Vescy. John had been captured at Evesham, and had rebelled again as a result of the policy of confiscation of lands adopted by the victors. Edward forced his surrender at Alnwick, and he had to pay 3,700 marks to redeem his lands. The chronicler Thomas Wykes commented on Edward's mercy, and John de Vescy certainly bore him no ill-will. Rather, he became one of Edward's most loyal associates.[127]

It was probably now that Edward took the opportunity of going further north, to Scotland, where he met his sister, the queen of Scots, at

[124] CPR 1258–66, 671–2; Documents of the Baronial Movement, ed. Sanders, 317–37.
[125] C.H. Knowles, 'The Resettlement of England after the Barons' War, 1264–67', TRHS, 5th ser., xxxii (1982), 28–31.
[126] Wykes, 195–6.
[127] Ibid., 197–8; Knowles, 'The Resettlement of England', 40–1.

Haddington. He also seems to have taken the opportunity of recruiting troops in Scotland, for there was still campaigning to be done in England.[128] The major remaining problem was that of the final rebel stronghold, the Isle of Ely, where John d'Eyville still held out. Discussions at a parliament held at Bury St Edmunds in February were inconclusive, and naval forces recruited from the East Anglian ports were driven back in confusion. In April 1267 the situation was transformed by the decision of the earl of Gloucester to lend his support to the cause of the disinherited rebels, and to centre resistance upon London.[129]

The earl of Gloucester had played a vital role in securing Edward's victory at Evesham, but he had good reasons to be resentful at the turn of events since then. He had received very little by way of royal grants in recognition of his services, and may have felt that Edward had not kept the bargain that had been made between the two men at Ludlow. Further, he was in dispute with Roger Mortimer over control of the Marcher estates of Humphrey de Bohun, the young heir to the earldom of Hereford, and he had a grievance against the crown which was preventing him from gaining control of some important dower lands held by his mother. There is no reason to doubt, however, that Gloucester's hostility to the government was primarily the result of his profound objections to the treatment of the former rebels.[130]

In April 1267 Earl Gilbert of Gloucester marched on London, where he joined forces with John d'Eyville, and a popular rising took place in the city in their support. There seemed a very real danger that civil war would break out again. Edward came rapidly south with troops to join the king, and it seems likely that he favoured a military solution of the problem. This was hardly practical, however. The siege of Kenilworth alone had exhausted the midland counties, and an attack on London was too vast a task to be undertaken at short notice. Some preparations were certainly made, though some were of a distinctly fraudulent character. The sheriff of Essex succeeded in a confidence trick when he took, among other supplies, chickens to feed the wounded, and forty or

---

[128] *Chron. Lanercost*, 81; *Flores*, iii, 15; *Ann. London*, 77. It is possible that these references do not all apply to the same visit to Scotland. Equally, it is likely that the story from the Barlings chronicle of Edward's collecting an army in 1269 so as to rescue his sister, who had been imprisoned by her husband, may have been misplaced chronologically. It is in any case highly implausible. The text is given in *Chronicles of the Reigns of Edward I and Edward II* ed. W. Stubbs (Rolls ser., 1883), ii, cxvi.

[129] Wykes, 197; *CPR 1266–72*, 44–5.

[130] Altschul, *A Baronial Family*, 110–21, provides a full discussion of Earl Gilbert's role in this period. See also Knowles, 'Resettlement of England after the Barons' War', 30.

more cocks, which, he said, were to be used as incendiaries, to be sent flying into London with combustibles tied to their feet.[131]

In the event, moderation prevailed. Gilbert de Clare, earl of Gloucester, for all his demands on behalf of the disinherited, was no Simon de Montfort, and there was strong pressure from the papal legate, immured in the Tower during the crisis, for a settlement. Richard of Cornwall, Henry of Almain and Philip Basset were all involved in the negotiations, as was Edward. By mid-June a settlement was reached, and Gloucester left London. He pledged himself not to engage in further hostilities, and to accept papal arbitration, offering 10,000 marks as security.[132] There was a return to the terms of the Dictum of Kenilworth, and the government began to adopt a distinctly more moderate attitude. On 1 July John d'Eyville, Nicholas Segrave, Norman d'Arcy and others were formally readmitted into the king's peace. Edward would later employ all three as bannerets in his household: indeed he bore few grudges as a result of what took place in the course of the Barons' Wars. It was now an easy matter to obtain the surrender of those who were still holding out in the Isle of Ely. The approach was much simpler in the dry summer months, and with skilled use of archers and crossbowmen Edward protected his main troops as they advanced. By threatening the rebels with execution if they did not surrender, Edward soon brought resistance to an end.[133] Peace was at long last achieved in England.

The next step towards achieving stability was the issue of the Statute of Marlborough in November 1267, a lengthy series of legal provisions which in many respects continued the work of legislative reform begun in 1259. This was technical work, and it was well done. In many ways it presaged the great legal reforms of Edward's reign, but there is no way of knowing what part he took in the debates at Marlborough, though it is impossible to imagine that the statute was promulgated without his approval.[134]

Welsh affairs must have been a major concern for Edward in 1267. On 29 September the Treaty of Montgomery was made with Llywelyn ap Gruffydd. In it, Llywelyn was recognized as prince of Wales, and as the feudal lord of the other Welsh princes, with the exception of Maredudd ap Rhys, who, like Llywelyn himself, owed homage directly to Henry III for his lands. The four Cantreds in the north were

---

[131] Williams, *Medieval London*, 239–40; H.M. Cam, *The Hundred and the Hundred Rolls*, (London, 1930), 101–2. Powicke, *Henry III and the Lord Edward*, ii, 544, is to be counted among those who fell for the sheriff's ruse. See below, 95.

[132] Denholm-Young, *Richard of Cornwall*, 143; *CPR 1266–72*, 73, 143–5. The pope raised Gloucester's security to 20,000 marks.

[133] Wykes, 207–10.

[134] *Statutes of the Realm*, i, 19–25.

formally conceded to Llywelyn. The English concessions were major ones, for until now the kings of England had claimed that all Welsh princes and nobles owed them homage. The loss of lands in the north was a major blow to Edward, but one he could for the present do little about.[135] He had already, in the autumn of 1265, granted Carmarthen and Cardigan to his brother Edmund, who also received the lordship of the Three Castles.[136] He was therefore largely abandoning his former interests in Wales, but it is hard to imagine that he was content with the Treaty of Montgomery, for all that his formal assent to it was recorded. The agreement was in fact largely the work of the papal legate Ottobuono, and it provides evidence that Edward's position at this time was not completely dominant.

In the relatively peaceful times that followed the agreement with the earl of Gloucester in 1267, Edward was able to devote some of his attention once again to the sport of tournaments. He, with his brother Edmund and his cousin Henry of Almain, was responsible for an edict allowing tournaments to be held, after years of prohibitions, and it is very probable that he took a leading part on many occasions. Tournaments were not at this time the gentlemanly, chivalric jousting competitions of the fifteenth and sixteenth centuries, but could be violent contests, barely distinguishable from battle. Much later, in 1292, Edward was to enact legislation in an attempt to control the armed supporters and servants who often caused much trouble at the tournaments, but if in the late 1260s he did anything to regulate what took place, the details of it are not recorded.[137]

The animosities of the period of civil war could not be completely forgotten. Edward's relations with the earl of Gloucester were not easy, and indeed were deteriorating in the late 1260s. There was the matter of Bristol. In 1268 Earl Gilbert asked Edward's permission to sue, reviving his old family claim to the city.[138] Edward agreed, only on condition that if the earl won, he would not actually receive Bristol, but other lands in compensation. The case was delayed, and did not in fact come to court until 1276, when, hardly surprisingly, it went against the earl. When Edward was sent in 1269 to hear disputes between Llywelyn, prince of Wales, and the Marcher lords, his decisions further antagonized Gloucester. Rumours, probably untrue, that Edward was paying

---

[135] *Littere Wallie*, xliii, 1–4.

[136] *CPR 1258–66*, 513; *CPR 1266–72*, 299.

[137] Wykes, 212; J.R.V. Barker, *The Tournament in England, 1100–1400* (Woodbridge, 1986), 56–9, 191–2. Dr Barker provides an important correction to N. Denholm-Young, 'The Tournament in the Thirteenth Century', *Studies in Medieval History presented to F.M. Powicke*, ed. R.W. Hunt, W.A. Pantin, R.W. Southern (Oxford, 1948), 257–62, for it was argued there that the legislation of 1292 in fact dated from 1267.

[138] Above, 30.

too much attention to the earl's wife cannot have helped the situation. Earl Gilbert also had reason to be angry with Henry III. In 1269 a commission was appointed to investigate his alleged usurpation of liberties in Kent during the civil war, and he was claiming, according to one chronicler, no less than £20,000 from the king to compensate him for losses incurred in the Evesham campaign.[139]

In 1269 there was also the problem of the earl of Derby, Robert Ferrers, who had played a violent if not a consistent role in the civil wars. Since the affair at Gloucester in 1264 he had been a bitter opponent of Edward, whose ward he had been. He was harshly treated under the terms of the Dictum of Kenilworth, being set a ransom of seven times the value of his lands if he wished to redeem them. He was kept in prison until he came before the king's council, in the early summer of 1269, and acknowledged a debt to Edward's younger brother Edmund of £50,000. This was in effect a fine for his release. Although Ferrers found guarantors, Edmund doubted that the money would be paid, and forced the earl under duress to agree to grant his lands over to the guarantors. If he did not make payment, then they were to make the estates over to Edmund. Inevitably, this is what took place. How far Edward was implicated in the affair is not clear, but it seems impossible that Edmund could have acted in this extremely unsavoury manner without his brother's connivance. Where Edward was really to blame was to be in the future, when he consistently denied Robert Ferrers and his son their rights. His sense of justice was considerably diminished when his family interests were at stake.[140]

How extensive was Edward's authority in England during these years? The Winchester annals contain an interesting story, that in parliament at Winchester in October 1268 Edward was made steward of England, and that at the following Christmas he was given custody of London and all royal castles in England. For one historian, Denholm-Young, this statement 'conceals the virtual abdication of Henry III'. Certainly, the stewardship had been claimed by Simon de Montfort, and the powers associated with the office threatened to give him great personal authority. The position should have gone to Edward's brother Edmund, along with the earldom of Leicester, but there must have been doubts about the wisdom of reviving the office in the immediate aftermath of Evesham. Yet in May 1269 Edmund did receive the stewardship, and this casts considerable doubt on the Winchester annalist's story. It seems very odd that it should have gone to Edward

---

[139] Altschul, *A Baronial Family*, 126–7; S.D. Lloyd, 'Gilbert de Clare, Richard of Cornwall and the Lord Edward's Crusade', *Nottingham Medieval Studies*, forthcoming.

[140] The story is given in most detail by R. Somerville, *History of the Duchy of Lancaster* (1953), i, 3–8. See also K.B. McFarlane, 'Did Edward I have a "policy" towards the earls?', *The Nobility of Later Medieval England* (Oxford, 1973), 254–5.

for some seven months, and the chronicler was perhaps confused both between the two brothers, and in his chronology.[141] London was certainly handed over to Edward, but in Lent 1269, not 1268. As for the castles, he certainly received Corfe, Devizes, Carlisle, Colchester, Oxford, Portchester and Scarborough, along with the counties of Lincoln, Norfolk, Suffolk, Oxford and Bedford, with Staffordshire, Shropshire and Hereford for a one-year period.[142] These grants, however, should probably be taken more as indicating Edward's financial needs than as demonstrating his political authority. The grant of the three counties for one year was specifically so that he could pay Roger Leyburn the debts he owed him, and the other grants were probably intended to assist Edward in meeting the enormous costs of his coming crusade.

Edward certainly took a leading role in the deliberations of the royal council in the late 1260s. The preamble to an ordinance made at Hilary 1269, which prevented Jews from selling debts that they were owed to any Christian, stated that it was made by the king, and by the counsel of Edward and other wise men.[143] Peter de Neville was ordered to appear at Westminster regarding various forest offences before the king and his eldest son. As they were unable to be present at the time, the case was postponed until it could be heard before the king, Edward, or the constable of the Tower. A writ, also from 1269, ordering a respite in a lawsuit between the countess of Devon and her daughter the countess of Aumale, was witnessed by the king, and drawn up on the advice of Edward, Henry of Almain and Philip Basset.[144] Such references as these show that Edward was playing a major part in the running of the government, but they certainly do not indicate that Henry III had abandoned all reality of power to his son. There is some evidence which shows that even at this period Edward had not fully escaped from the kind of control that was exercised over him in the 1250s.

There seems to have been disagreement between Edward and his father over an issue which had caused problems earlier: the inalienability of Edward's lands. In 1268 Henry of Almain was commissioned to go to Ireland to recover lands which Edward had granted out without royal licence, and in the following year Henry III rebuked his son for restoring the castle and lands of Belin in Gascony to Gaillard del Soler, so disinheriting the king and his heirs.[145] It would be wrong to make too

---

[141] Denholm-Young, *Richard of Cornwall*, 145; *Ann. Winton*, 106. The unreliability of this source is suggested by the statement that Henry III granted the earldom of Richmond to his son Edmund, when in fact it went to the duke of Brittany.

[142] *CPR 1266–72*, 397, 468, 470–1, 536, 616, 626, 642, 646.

[143] *CPR 1266–72*, 376; *Close Rolls 1268–72*, 101.

[144] *Close Rolls 1268–72*, 54–5, 105–6.

[145] Studd, 'The Lord Edward and King Henry III', 11; *CDI 1252–84*, no. 844; *CPR 1266–72*, 246.

much of this. Edward was not under any form of tutelage, and this question of the alienation of land and its recovery was not one which caused an open breach between father and son. Edward was simply having to adhere to a principle which had been firmly enunciated in the Dictum of Kenilworth regarding crown lands.[146]

Edward was not in any way thwarted in his policies in this period after the Barons' Wars, but his interests were increasingly directed away from England, and he was not anxious to establish himself as the de facto ruler at home. In 1268 he took the cross, and began to plan his crusading venture. It was increasingly this matter which dominated his actions, rather than the political troubles in England. He was not, of course, the only powerful figure in English politics. Until his departure in 1268, the papal legate Ottobuono was in many ways the dominant man in both lay and ecclesiastical affairs. Richard of Cornwall also left England in 1268, to attend to matters in Germany, but he returned in the following year bringing with him a new bride, Beatrice of Falkenburg, a woman of exceptional beauty to whom he was devoted. Richard's prestige was considerable. It was he who provided a settlement for the dispute between Edward and the earl of Gloucester in 1270, and by 1271, when the king was in ill-health, he was exercising effective authority in England in a way that Edward had not.[147]

These years, from 1258 to 1270, were surely the most testing that Edward faced in his long life. For the historian R.F. Treharne, Edward in the late 1250s and early 1260s was no more than 'an irresponsible, arrogant and headstrong boy, treacherously selfish in the heedless pursuit of his own ends, indulging every whim at his own pleasure, and incapable of self-discipline or obedience to external authority in anything that conflicted with the passions and hatreds of the moment'.[148] Such a view is understandable in view of Edward's changing allegiances in the early phases of the baronial movement. Initial hostility to the Provisions of Oxford and support of the king's Lusignan half-brothers was succeeded by agreement with the earl of Gloucester, then by support for the community of the Bachelors, and next by alliance with Simon de Montfort. The ease with which Edward was brought back to heel by Henry III in the spring of 1260 suggests that the young man's political convictions hardly ran deep. Some of Edward's actions in the civil war of the mid-1260s, notably those at Gloucester, suggest that he was a man whose word could not be trusted. Even in the years between the royalist triumph at Evesham and Edward's departure on

---

[146] *Documents of the Baronial Movement*, ed. Sanders, 320–2.
[147] Denholm-Young, *Richard of Cornwall*, 144–9.
[148] Treharne, *Baronial Plan of Reform*, 163–4.

crusade, his quarrel with the earl of Gloucester threatened the precarious stability of the land.

Yet to condemn Edward on such grounds is to fail to appreciate the difficulties in which he was placed, and to diminish his very considerable achievements. In the late 1250s there were deep divisions within the court circle, between those who supported moderate measures of reform and the Lusignan clique. The royal family was itself divided: Simon de Montfort was married to the king's sister, and for a time after returning from Germany in 1259 Richard of Cornwall, Henry III's brother, played a careful neutral role. In such circumstances it would have been remarkable had Edward been consistent throughout in his political alignment. His career after 1258 was not characterized by further acts of gratuitous violence, by either himself or his followers, such as those that had made him notorious earlier. Rather, it is possible to detect as early as 1259 a concern for justice which foreshadowed policies he would adopt after his accession to the throne. In a writ to the justiciar of Chester in August 1259 he stated in the preamble that if 'common justice is denied to any one of our subjects by us or by our bailiffs, we lose the favour both of God and man, and our lordship is belittled'.[149] In spite of his political inconsistencies, Edward built up a following of loyal supporters, and by 1263 he was showing considerable skill when he recruited the lords of the Welsh March to the royalist cause. At Lewes he was headstrong, but in 1265 he displayed strategic ability and powers of leadership in the campaign which culminated in the battle of Evesham. Simon de Montfort was a formidable enemy for a young man to face, and Edward acted with skill and courage.

Edward's role in the five years after Evesham is not easy to assess. He certainly showed statesmanlike moderation at times. He was always ready to offer rebels reasonable terms if they would surrender, and it is to his credit that he did not show much personal vindictiveness. Some former rebels, indeed, such as John de Vescy, became important friends and supporters of Edward. While Edward saw to it that his friends gained from the confiscations of lands that followed Evesham, he did not try to gain as much for himself as he might have done. It was his brother Edmund who profited from the fall of Robert Ferrers, earl of Derby, not Edward himself.

His role in these years was not, however, as dominant as might be expected. He was not involved in the final agreement of the Dictum of Kenilworth, and was not much concerned in the complex process by which the disinherited gradually recovered some of their lands. It was the active intervention of the earl of Gloucester that forced the

[149] Carpenter, 'The Lord Edward's Oath to aid and counsel Simon de Montfort', 235–7.

government to take a more conciliatory line, rather than any urgings from Edward. The Treaty of Montgomery was not a part of royal policy which met with Edward's approval. There is little evidence to show that Edward was deeply involved in the legislative work of this time. The only measures that can clearly be linked with him were not very notable: there was the provision for the holding of tournaments, and one dealing with Jewish debts. The latter proved unsatisfactory, and a fresh enactment was needed in 1271 to provide clarification.[150]

Edward learned much in these years from 1258 to 1270: few kings of England can have had such a testing apprenticeship. There was no sudden transformation in Edward's character, but he was forced to mature quickly. By the end of Henry III's reign there can have been few who were as pessimistic as Matthew Paris had been in 1259.[151] Yet it is only with hindsight that the indications of the great work of reform and of conquest that was to come can be detected. As king, Edward was to be much more considerable than he had been in his position as *primogenitus*.

[150] Denholm-Young, *Richard of Cornwall*, 143, 149.
[151] Above, 3.

Chapter 3

THE CRUSADER

Edward I occupies only a small place in the dramatic and often tragic history of the crusaders, but his crusade was an episode of great importance in his own career. In it he experienced problems which were to recur later, formed significant friendships and learned much. His reputation was greatly advanced by it. Although Edward went on only one expedition to the east, his ambition to lead a further crusade remained with him for the rest of his life. It was with some justice that his death was mourned with the words 'Jerusalem, you have lost the flower of all chivalry'.[1] Edward's crusade had little effect on the tenuous survival of the kingdom of Jerusalem, but the great efforts that were needed to finance it had considerable domestic implications in England, and in political terms the movement to take the cross played a part in the settlement of the issues raised by the civil war. The crusade is best remembered for the romantic tale of Eleanor of Castile sucking the poison from the wound inflicted on her husband by a Moslem assassin, but that is almost certainly apocryphal. The reality of Edward's stay in the east was one of discomfort and frustration, not of romance.

There was abundant need for a crusade in the 1260s. Under the rule of the powerful and able Mamluk sultan Baibars, Egyptian power was in the ascendant. The Mongols, seen by some as a possible ally for the crusader states, had been routed by Baibars shortly before the coup which gave him the sultanate in 1260. In 1265 Caesarea and Arsuf fell to the Mamluks, and the castle of Safad followed in 1266. Two years later Jaffa fell, and the principality of Antioch collapsed. The kingdom of Jerusalem was in a sorry state: the death of the last of the Hohenstaufen dynasty, Conradin, in 1268, put the throne nominally in the hands of the Lusignan king of Cyprus, Hugh, but he exercised little real authority. Nor did the kingdom possess the economic vitality of earlier periods. The merchants of Venice and Genoa were in bitter conflict. The Latin states of the eastern shore of the Mediterranean had always needed the assistance of crusading expeditions, but the story of the crusades of the thirteenth century is a dismal one of missed

[1] *Political Songs*, ed. Wright, 249.

opportunities, and of high motives applied all too often to base ends. In 1204 the fourth crusade had taken Constantinople, not Jerusalem. The fifth became bogged down in the Nile Delta. St Louis's first crusade, which began in 1248, was again directed against Damietta at the mouth of the Nile, and saw the western army forced to surrender. Louis himself was ransomed, and spent the years from 1250 to 1254 in what remained of the kingdom of Jerusalem, but he was able to do little to strengthen an enfeebled state.

Louis felt his failure deeply, and was determined on a further crusade. None was possible for many years, for the papacy was involved in its obsessive feud with the Hohenstaufen dynasty, and the French, under Louis's brother Charles of Anjou, were pursuing ambitions in southern Italy. French troops routed the illegitimate Hohenstaufen Manfred of Sicily in 1266, and two years later defeated Conradin. Once Charles's position in southern Italy was assured, a fresh crusade became a real possibility.

Crusades were, properly speaking, initiated by the papacy. Urban IV had begun to organize an expedition in 1263, but little was achieved, although in England the crusade was preached against the baronial rebels, in an attempt to assist Henry III. Only with the establishment of peace after the battle of Evesham was the possibility of an expedition to the east seriously raised. The legate Ottobuono was ordered to preach the crusade in the autumn of 1266: this was part of a European-wide movement, prompted by the news of the loss of Safad earlier in the year.[2] When St Louis decided, late in the year, that he would take part, and, with his sons, took the cross in March of the following year, it became evident that a new crusade would at long last take place.

Enthusiasm for the new crusade was not widespread. In France the royal council was said to have been unanimously opposed to the idea, and in England when Ottobuono raised the matter in parliament at Bury St Edmunds in February 1267 he found no support. It was even suspected by some that he wished to use the crusade as a means of removing Englishmen from the land, so that aliens could take their place.[3] Yet Ottobuono persisted, preaching through interpreters, and making much use of friars to arouse popular enthusiam. This was not, however, to be a crusade borne along by a tidal wave of popular emotion. It was, rather, a carefully planned expedition, largely aristocratic in composition. The decisive recruiting meeting took place at Midsummer in

---

[2] *Les registres de Clement IV (1265–68)*, ed. E. Jordan (Paris, 1945), nos. 1145, 1146; S. Lloyd, 'The Lord Edward's Crusade, 1270–2: its setting and significance', *War and Government in the Middle Ages*, ed. Gillingham and Holt, 121.

[3] Rishanger, 52–3.

1268, when, in parliament at Northampton, Edward, along with his brother Edmund, Henry of Almain, Earl Warenne, the earl of Gloucester, William de Valence and many others, agreed to go on crusade.[4]

Edward's motives in taking the cross can only be guessed at. It was hardly a prudent decision. In political terms, there was no case for his going: the country was not so settled that the leading royalist warrior could easily be dispensed with. Also, financial resources were scarcely adequate to meet the demands of the expedition. Edward had obviously been considering the matter for some time, and had sought papal advice: a letter from Clement IV in January 1268 showed that the pope was well aware of the problems in England. His view was that Edward should not go, and Henry III seems to have concurred in this. The English king had himself taken the cross in 1250, and had never fulfilled his vow, but it was not the case, as has sometimes been suggested, that he intended that Edward should act as his substitute. In 1268 he probably still hoped to go in person, while it was Edmund, not Edward, who was regarded by the pope as an acceptable substitute.[5]

The events of the crusade were to show that Edward was very strongly committed to the concept of a holy war in the east. His decision to take the cross was certainly not a cynical or self-interested one, as Charles of Anjou's almost certainly was, and it is perhaps a mistake to seek any more subtle motivation than that of the enthusiasm of a conventionally religious young man to prove himself in the greatest adventure of the day. Edward may well have welcomed the chance to escape from the preoccupations of domestic politics, and the opportunity to exercise his martial skills in a cause which had none of the complexities of the recent civil war in England. Admiration for St Louis may have played its part, and it is likely that Richard of Cornwall's advice was important. Edward certainly sought his counsel in 1269, and probably did so earlier, for Richard had first-hand experience of the east and its problems.[6] Edward may, too, have felt that honour demanded that he should go: if the sons of the king of France were to take part in the crusade, so too should those of the king of England.

Edward could not rely simply on the preaching of the crusade to provide him with an adequate force. The core of his expedition was provided by the members of his own household, and in July 1270 contracts were made with eighteen men to provide a total of 225 knights. Two such contracts survive, one with a Northumberland knight, Adam of Jesmond, and one with Payn de Chaworth and Robert Tibetot. The rate of pay was 100 marks for each knight for a year's

[4] Wykes, 217–18.
[5] Lloyd, 'The Lord Edward's Crusade', 122–3; *Registres de Clement IV*, nos 609, 1288.
[6] *Liber de Antiquis Legibus*, 110.

service, and in addition Edward promised to cover sea transport costs. Those who made such agreements included three great men, Edmund of Lancaster, William de Valence and Henry of Almain, who headed what must have amounted to virtually independent contingents. The others were mostly close associates of Edward's of some standing, men such as Roger Clifford, Roger Leyburn, Hamo Lestrange and Richard de la Rochelle. The list included Thomas de Clare, who for all that he was a younger brother of the earl of Gloucester, was a very close friend of Edward's.[7] Records of the grant of royal protections to those going on crusade reveal the names of many members of the household who went with Edward: clerks such as Anthony Bek and Philip de Willoughby, knights such as Hugh FitzOtho, soon to be steward, and the Savoyard Otto de Grandson, who had come to England in the 1250s. Others going on the crusade were members of the king's household, perhaps temporarily seconded to Edward's service. For a military expedition, there was nothing novel in the nucleus being provided by the household. There is, however, no earlier evidence for the use of contracts in the way Edward used them in 1270. It is dangerous to argue from silence, but it may be that their use was an innovation, adopted in imitation of techniques employed by St Louis, and perhaps intended as a means of guaranteeing that Edward's contingent would be as large as he promised the French king it would be.[8]

A crusading expedition differed from other wars by the way in which the status of the crusaders was carefully set out and defined in canon law. Not only were there the spiritual advantages of remission of sins to be gained, but the church also accorded protection to the lands and goods of those who went on crusade. It has been suggested that such crusader privileges were particularly important in the case of Edward's crusade. Royalists who had gained property in the aftermath of the civil war could expect their title to their gains to remain effectively unchallenged while they were absent in the east. Court proceedings against them would be dropped, and lands safely leased or sold. On the other hand, for former rebels, it is argued that crusading was hard to envisage, for not only was there a natural resentment against Edward and the papacy, but also there were the heavy costs of redemption of property under the terms of the Dictum of Kenilworth.[9]

Such arguments have some force, but it is hard to see that the

---

[7] Lloyd, 'The Lord Edward's Crusade', 126–7; H.G. Richardson and G.O. Sayles, *The Governance of Medieval England* (Edinburgh, 1963), 464–5.

[8] Lloyd, 'The Lord Edward's Crusade', 131–2; for lists of those who received protections to go on the crusade, see B. Beebe, 'The English Baronage and the Crusade of 1270', *BIHR*, xlviii (1975), 143–8.

[9] These arguments are strongly put by Beebe, 'The English Baronage and the Crusade', 136–9.

question of crusading privileges was any more important in the case of
Edward's expedition than in other crusades. In practice, the protections granted to the would-be crusaders by the crown were at least as
important as the privileges under canon law. Some royalists certainly
received important advantages. Edward's brother Edmund was quit of
any court actions brought against him, making it impossible for Robert
de Ferrers to take legal steps to recover his lands, and Luke de Tany
was given immunity from prosecution for the execution of various
former rebels. But it is hard to imagine that effective action could have
been taken against such men even had they not been crusaders, and
there is no evidence to show that protections were widely appealed to.
The bulk of crusaders did not receive such lavish grants as Edmund
of Lancaster: most protections excluded pleas of *novel disseisin* and
various other actions.[10] It has also been pointed out that only a dozen
crusaders were definitely still in full possession of rebel property when
they received their protections: the rest had all begun the process of
restitution.[11] It is difficult to imagine that anyone seriously considered
that there were real material advantages to be gained from going on
crusade. Some, such as Herbert de Boyvill, actually sold land in order
to finance themselves on the expedition, and many leased land to raise
funds.[12] Those who wished to retain gains made in and after the civil
war were surely better advised to stay at home.

It certainly was the case that royalists greatly outnumbered former
rebels in Edward's expedition. There was no technique used such as
that employed by St Louis for his first crusade, when he had insisted
that former opponents join him, in order to prevent them fomenting
trouble at home in his absence.[13] Yet the supporters of Simon de
Montfort could, arguably, have had much to gain from obtaining
crusader privileges, and for them the crusade could prove a route back
into royal favour. This was certainly true of John de Vescy, though he,
like John de Segrave, another former rebel who went on crusade, had
already established links with Edward before 1270.[14]

The main opponent of Edward's who agreed to go on crusade was
Gilbert de Clare, earl of Gloucester. He took the cross at Northampton
at the same time as Edward, and it may be that in this case there was a
real expectation that the dissension between the two men would be
ended if they could be brought together in a common cause. The earl,

---

[10] Ibid., 139; *CPR 1266–72*, 442; *Close Rolls 1268–72*, 571 (this is a case of use being
made of a writ of protection).

[11] S. Lloyd, 'English Society and the Crusades, 1216–1307' (Oxford D.Phil. thesis,
1983), 323.

[12] *CPR 1266–72*, 425.

[13] W.C. Jordan, *Louis IX and the Challenge of the Crusade* (Princeton, 1979), 17–19.

[14] Lloyd, 'English Society and the Crusades', 325–6.

however, became more and more obstinate, perhaps as it became increasingly clear that this was to be Edward's expedition, rather than a more general English crusade. Pressure was brought on him by St Louis, but this was in vain. It was only when Richard of Cornwall arbitrated between Edward and Gloucester at the Easter parliament of 1270 that agreement was reached. The earl was to follow Edward on crusade within six months. If he co-operated with Edward, he was to receive 8,000 marks; if not, only 2,000. Security was to be given, to ensure that the money was properly spent on the crusade. There were some problems over the arbitration, which was extremely one-sided. Gilbert was particularly worried lest the castles and manors he was to hand over as surety would, in practice, be lost to him. His arguments were strong ones, but the reply given by the earl of Cornwall, though conciliatory, did not yield on the question of giving sureties. In June, however, Gilbert appears to have come to terms, though some details still remained to be settled. In the event the earl did not go on crusade, nor did he hand over his castles. Welsh attacks on his lordship in South Wales made it impossible for him to set out, and provided an entirely adequate excuse for his failure to fulfil his crusading vow.[15] Although the agreement reached with him in June was not carried through, it was nevertheless important, for it cleared the final obstacle to Edward's departure.

There are no documents to show with any certainty how successful recruiting for the crusade had been. About 230 men received royal protections for the expedition, while the contractual arrangements suggest a force of 225 knights. Obviously, many lesser individuals would not trouble to obtain writs of protection, and the knights would have brought servants and others with them, but even so, the force was clearly not large. Walter of Guisborough has it that thirteen ships were needed to take Edward's men from Tunis to Sicily in the course of the crusade, while a contract to take them on to the Holy Land was made with a mere nine shipmasters. Even allowing for the large size of Mediterranean ships, it seems unlikely that the expedition numbered as many as the 1,000 men that Guisborough says arrived in the east with Edward.[16]

Recruitment of men was only one of the problems facing Edward in preparing for the crusade. Finance was a major difficulty. There was no hope of raising funds by means of papal taxation of the clergy, for

---

[15] Altschul, *A Baronial Family*, 128–9; Denholm-Young, *Richard of Cornwall*, 146–7; Gervase of Canterbury, ii, 249–50; Lloyd, 'Gilbert de Clare, Richard of Cornwall and the Lord Edward's Crusade', *Nottingham Medieval Studies*, xxxi (1986), 46–66.

[16] Guisborough, 207; R. Rohricht, 'Etudes sur les derniers temps du royaume de Jerusalem. C. Les combats du Sultan Baibars', *Archives de l'Orient Latin*, ii (1884), 407–9.

Clement IV had already imposed a clerical tenth for three years in 1266 in order to meet Henry III's debts and expenses.[17] Some funds were raised by the church, through such techniques as redemption of crusading vows for cash, sale of indulgences, and obtaining gifts and legacies, but the sums involved were not substantial. So, in 1268 the government began the business of negotiating a tax with both church and laity. The latter had not made a grant of taxation since 1237, and discussions did not go smoothly. The final lay grant was made in the spring of 1270, when the magnates and knights agreed reluctantly to the collection of a twentieth. It took even longer to obtain the consent of all the clergy. There were some difficulties in making the assessment, even though work on this had begun in 1269. Although it was hoped to have the bulk of the money in by Midsummer 1270, with the rest by Michaelmas, it is unlikely that Edward had actually received much of the total yield of some £31,000 by the time that he set out.[18] Another source of funds was the French monarchy. The crusade was throughout intended to be a French expedition, and Edward fully recognized St Louis's leadership. When Edward visited the French king, in the summer of 1269, he set out his financial difficulties, and succeeded in negotiating a loan of 70,000 *livres tournois* – about £17,500 – under severe terms. Edward promised to be at Aigues-Mortes, on the Mediterranean coast, ready to embark by 15 August 1270, and to hand over one of his sons as a hostage to Louis to guarantee the agreement. Repayment of the loan was to begin in 1274. 25,000 *livres* out of the total were to go to the Gascon magnate, Gaston de Béarn, though he did not, in the end, go on the crusade. Henry III, moved to the tears which were probably quite normal for him, gave his consent to the agreement. Edward was not in fact obliged to send one of his sons to Paris, and Louis made no difficulties when he failed to meet the deadline for his arrival at Aigues-Mortes.[19]

By the summer of 1270 all was at long last set. In parliament at Winchester in July Henry III finally gave his blessing to Edward's fulfilment, on his behalf, of his crusading vows. The proceeds of the twentieth were formally granted to the heir to the throne. At the beginning of August a committee was set up, headed by Richard of Cornwall, to look after Edward's interests while he was away, and to care for his children, for Eleanor was to accompany her husband on the

---

[17] W.E. Lunt, *Financial Relations of the Papacy with England to 1327* (Cambridge, Mass., 1939), 292–310.

[18] Powicke, *Henry III and the Lord Edward*, ii, 564–8; S.K. Mitchell, *Taxation in Medieval England* (Yale, 1951), 47–8.

[19] *Foedera*, I. i, 481; *Liber de Antiquis Legibus*, 111–14; J.P. Trabut-Cussac, 'Le financement de la croisade anglaise de 1270', *Bibl. de l'école des Chartes*, cxix (1961), 114, 123–4.

crusade. The other members of the committee were the archbishop of York, Philip Basset, Roger Mortimer, and Robert Walerand, though the last-named was soon replaced by Robert Burnell.[20]

Edward's plan was to sail from Portsmouth for Gascony, to visit his brother-in-law Alphonso of Castile, and then to go to Aigues-Mortes. However, while the fleet was held up by contrary winds news came through of the death of Boniface of Savoy, archbishop of Canterbury, while on a visit to his homeland. Edward wished to see his clerk Robert Burnell elected, and hurried to Canterbury, where his efforts at persuasion failed. For all Burnell's administrative skills, he was not, there is little doubt, an ideal candidate for the highest ecclesiastical office. From Canterbury Edward went to Dover, and probably crossed to France on 20 August, abandoning his plans to visit Gascony.[21] The journey through France took a little over a month. At about Michaelmas the expedition arrived at the walled seaport of Aigues-Mortes. The main expedition under St Louis had long since departed, and the news which Edward must have received of its progress cannot have pleased him.

King Louis's fleet had gathered in Sardinia for final instructions after sailing from Aigues–Mortes. Only then was the destination of the crusade announced: Tunis. Louis had been persuaded that an attack on Tunis would weaken Egypt, which was dependent on food supplies from North Africa, and there was a hope that the emir might be persuaded to convert to Christianity. Charles of Anjou had his own reasons for wishing to attack Tunis, for the emir had given some support to his Hohenstaufen enemies, and had ceased payment of annual tribute to Sicily since Charles's success there.[22] Edward was probably unaware of this new plan for the crusade: certainly his agreement with the French king had merely spoken in vague terms of a 'pilgrimage over the seas'.[23]

Hopes that Tunis would prove to be a soft target were in vain. The insanitary conditions of siege warfare, in the heat of a North African summer, led to the crippling of the crusading force by disease, with Louis himself succumbing and dying on 25 August. His successor, Philip III, was also stricken, though not fatally. Charles of Anjou arrived only after St Louis's death, and, realist that he was, promptly

[20] *Liber de Antiquis Legibus*, 125; *Foedera*, I. i, 484.
[21] *Ann. Winchester*, 109. This is the most plausible version of Edward's itinerary. Cotton, 145, has it that Edward had already reached Gascony when he heard of Boniface's death, and that he then returned to England. Wykes, 236, has Edward return to Portsmouth from Canterbury, and continue with his original plan.
[22] Wykes, 237–8; *Liber de Antiquis Legibus*, 111; J.R. Strayer, *Medieval Statecraft and the Perspectives of History* (Princeton, 1971), 189.
[23] Ibid., 190.

entered into negotiations with the Tunisian emir, reaching agreement on 1 November.[24] Edward arrived about a week later, and was appalled to discover what had happened, expressing his horror that the enemies of the cross were the subject of a treaty, to which he refused to give his consent. He rejected any share of the war indemnity to be paid by the Tunisian emir, though it is not clear that he was in fact entitled to one. Edward then accepted the decision of Charles of Anjou, and the other crusade leaders, to sail for Sicily where they would winter, prior to going on to Acre in the spring. English chroniclers tried to make the best of these events: Guisborough has a tale displaying Edward's chivalry. As the crusading fleet sailed from Tunis, over two hundred men were left behind, in great distress, and only Edward, of all the leaders, was prepared to turn his ships round to rescue them.[25]

Fortune appeared to smile on Edward when the fleet arrived in Sicily, for soon after making landfall, a violent storm wrecked most of the ships, still loaded with horses, victuals and treasure. Edward's vessels, however, had taken up a more secure anchorage than the rest, and were spared. The storm must have been the final disillusionment for most of the crusaders, and in discussions it was decided to postpone the expedition to the east for three years. Edward agreed to this, though qualifying his consent by stipulating that he might be excused if he showed sufficient cause to the king of France. He did not abandon his crusade plans, and unlike the other leaders, remained in Sicily. He set down four conditions which might prevent his going to the east: if a new pope was elected who forbad him to go; if he was ill; if his father died; or if civil war broke out in England.[26]

There were certainly good reasons why Edward should abandon the crusade. A letter sent to him by the government in England on 6 February 1271 informed him that his father had been gravely ill, and urged him to return home. Edward was not convinced, however, and merely appointed Henry of Almain to go to England via Gascony to see to affairs of state. He was obviously determined to fulfil his crusading vow: one chronicle records him as swearing by God's blood that he would go to Acre and carry out his oath even if all deserted him, save for his groom Fowyn.[27] Even the appalling news of the murder of Henry of Almain at Viterbo by Simon and Guy de Montfort, an act of revenge for the death of their father at Evesham, did not deter him from his objective. He had hired ships to take him to the

[24] Ibid., 190.
[25] Guisborough, 206.
[26] *Liber de Antiquis Legibus*, 131.
[27] *Close Rolls 1268–72*, 397–8; Rishanger, 68.

east in January, and at the beginning of May he sailed from Trapani.[28]

The fleet revictualled in Cyprus, where Edward was received with great honour and joy by the populace, who were presumably well aware of the deeds on the island of a greater English crusader, Richard I, some eighty years previously. Unlike Richard, Edward did not stay long on the island, and on 9 May, after a stormy voyage, he landed at the great crusading port of Acre.[29] A treatise written within the next twenty years, very possibly by Otto de Grandson, implies that all was not well with the English forces when they disembarked. With the knowledge of hindsight, the treatise argued that it was best for crusaders to arrive in autumn, preferably in Armenia, so that the army and in particular its horses could be ready to march on Jerusalem in the following spring. To land at Acre in early summer had major disadvantages, as the horses would be in bad condition after the sea voyage, and fodder was hard to obtain.[30]

According to the English sources, had Edward not arrived when he did, Acre would have been surrendered to Baibars' Mamluk troops. Baibars had certainly been conducting a most successful campaign, taking Chastel Blanc, Gibelacar, and the greatest of all crusader fortresses, Crac des Chevaliers. In May he had set out with a field army for Tripoli. It does not seem from the Arab sources that a major assault on either Acre or Tripoli was intended, as he had no siege train with him, but whatever his intentions, it does seem that the news of Edward's arrival caused him to change his plans, and to negotiate a ten-year truce with the ruler of Tripoli.[31]

Edward spent frustrating weeks in Acre before moving against the enemy. His men and horses had to be prepared, and diplomatic arrangements had to be made. An English embassy was sent to the Mongol Il-Khan Abagha, to try to organize concerted action against the redoubtable Baibars.[32] There were also matters in Acre itself that needed attention. Edward was appalled to find that Venetian

---

[28] Rohricht, 'Etudes sur les derniers temps du royaume de Jerusalem. C.', *Archives de l'Orient Latin*, ii (1884), 407–9. There may have been more than the nine ships mentioned in this contract in Edward's fleet. An Arab account, *Makrizi, Histoire des Sultans Mamlouks*, ed. M. Quatremère (Paris, 1837), i, 86, states that Edward had eight large ships, and galleys and other vessels making a total of thirty in all.

[29] 'Gestes des Chiprois'. *Receuil des Historiens des Croisades, Documents Arméniens*, ii (Paris, 1906), 777.

[30] C. Kohler, 'Deux projets de croisade en terre-sainte composée à la fin du xiiie siècle et au debut du xive', *Revue de l'Orient Latin*, x (1903–4), 407–8, 427–8.

[31] *Makrizi*, 86. *Ibn al-Furat, Ayyubids, Mamlukes and Crusaders*, ed. and tr. U. and M.C. Lyons, intr. J.S.C. Riley-Smith (Cambridge, 1971), 150, is derived from the same source.

[32] *Liber de Antiquis Legibus*, 143.

merchants there were trading with the Saracens in food and military supplies, though as their *bailli* was able to produce charters from the king of Jerusalem permitting this, he had to withdraw his objections. Traitors were found in the city, who were duly executed.[33] Edward's patience was sorely tried when on 12 June the Sultan Baibars himself rode right up to the gates of Acre, only to depart when no hostile moves were made against him.[34]

It was probably late in June that Edward decided he could wait no more, and launched his first raid on the enemy. This was against St Georges-de-Lebeyne, some fifteen miles east of Acre. The troops were ill used to the conditions, and the combined effects of heat and food-poisoning resulted in many casualties. All that was achieved was the destruction of some crops and houses.[35] The raid must have made it clear to Edward that he could not achieve anything effective without larger forces, and he spent much of the following months trying to organize concerted action in which he would be joined by Hugh of Cyprus and the forces of the military orders.

It was probably in the summer of 1271 that Edward became involved in a dispute between the king of Cyprus and his barons over the question of whether or not they owed military service in the kingdom of Jerusalem. Edward was called in to arbitrate, but unfortunately, although we have the cogent arguments put forward by the Cypriot barons, neither Hugh's case nor Edward's decision have survived. According to Walter of Guisborough, Edward appealed to the barons with success, for they agreed that they were bound to obey his orders, as his ancestors had ruled their land, and they were bound in fealty to the kings of England. This seems most implausible, and Edward's arbitration was probably along the lines of the eventual compromise, which provided that the Cypriots should serve the king on the mainland for four months at his expense. It was long ago noted by the great historian Stubbs that the case closely paralleled that which was to occur in

[33] *Flores*, iii, 21; Rohricht, 'Etudes sur les derniers temps du royaume de Jerusalem. A. La croisade du Prince Edouard d'Angleterre (1270–1274)', *Archives de l'Orient Latin*, i (1881), 622 n.33.

[34] *Ibn al-Furat*, 151–2; R. Rohricht, 'Annales de Terre Sainte', *Archives de l'Orient Latin*, ii (1884), 455.

[35] 'Annales de Terre Sainte', 455; Marino Sanudo, in *Gesta Dei per Francos*, ed. J. Bongars (Hannover, 1611), ii, 224. 'L'Estoire de Eracles Empereur', *Receuil des Historiens des Croisades, Historiens Occidentaux*, ii, 461, and *Ibn al-Furat*, 155, both place the raid in July. The main English source, Guisborough, 227, provides a very different account of Edward's raids from those of the crusading chronicles, with first an attack on Nazareth, then one on 24 June against Qaqun, and a third on 1 August against St Georges. It seems likely that his account is confused. *Flores*, iii, 23, is the only other chronicler to mention Nazareth, which, it states, Edward went through on the way to Qaqun.

England in 1297, over the overseas military obligations of the English baronage.[36]

In the autumn Edward's plans seemed to be succeeding. The Mongols advanced rapidly towards Syria, causing panic as they came. Much of the population of Damascus fled as they approached. In November Edward was able to launch a much larger raid than that against St Georges earlier in the year. Reinforcements from England had arrived with his brother Edmund in September, and the Cypriots were now ready to join in the campaign. Members of the military orders, Templars, Hospitallers, and Teutonic Knights also co-operated, as did the men of Acre itself. The force marched on Qaqun, forty miles south-east of Acre, where they surprised a large force of Turcomans. One estimate was that 1,500 were killed, and 5,000 animals taken as booty. The Moslem report was that one emir had been killed, another wounded, and the governor of the castle forced to abandon his command. But the crusaders failed to take the castle itself, and when a Moslem force approached they retreated rapidly to Acre, losing some men and horses on the way. The raid had hardly been a glorious success: the Turcomans who had been routed were no more than itinerant herdsmen. It was with some justification that Baibars is said to have remarked that if so many men could not take a single house, then it was hardly likely that they could conquer a land such as the kingdom of Jerusalem.[37] Baibars did nevertheless attempt to retaliate, advancing from Damascus upon Acre in December. Heavy rain made it impossible to carry through the attack, and the sultan withdrew to Egypt.

It must have been obvious to the crusaders that continued hostilities held out little chance of success, and Baibars and his men were probably war weary. In May 1272 a truce was agreed at Caesarea, to last for ten years, ten months, ten days and ten hours. It has been suggested that it was Edward who persuaded King Hugh that to accept a truce was the best course of action, but the only support for this view is a letter of 1275, the wording of which is scarcely conclusive.[38] Both western and eastern narrative sources state that Edward was extremely angry at the decision, and such an attitude certainly fits with his earlier

---

[36] Guisborough, 208; G. Hill, *A History of Cyprus* (1948), ii, 168–70; W. Stubbs, *Seventeen Lectures on the Study of Medieval and Modern History* (Oxford, 1887), 205–6; *Receuil des Historiens des Croisades, Lois*, ii, 427–34.

[37] 'Eracles', 461; *Ibn al-Furat*, 155–6; *Makrizi*, 101–2.

[38] *A History of the Crusades*, ed. K.M. Setton, R.L. Wolff, H.W. Hazard, ii (Philadelphia, 1962), 582–3; *Cartulaire Générale de l'ordre des Hospitaliers de St Jean de Jerusalem en Terre Sainte*, ed. J. Delaville le Roulx (Paris, 1894–1906), iii, 170; C. Kohler and C.V. Langlois, 'Lettres inédits concernant les croisades (1275–1307)', *Bibl. de l'école des Chartes*, lii (1891), 53.

determination to proceed with the crusade at all costs.[39] He may have hoped that help would be provided by the Mongols, but Baibars soon entered into negotiations with them, and it became clear that they had no intention of launching a major campaign in the Holy Land.[40]

It was perhaps in the hope of a renewal of hostilities in spite of the truce that Edward remained in the east until 24 September 1272. His brother Edmund, whose heart never seems to have been in the crusade, departed in May, and William de Valence left in August.[41] Edward's own departure was presumably delayed by the need for him to convalesce, after the most celebrated incident of his crusade, the attempt by an assassin on his life in June. There are many accounts of this, not entirely consistent. It is clear that one evening a Moslem came to see Edward, when he was alone in his chamber, and attacked him with a poisoned dagger. Edward, a man of swift reflexes, kicked out at the assassin, and in a brief scuffle managed to kill him. Some have it that the assassin was sent by the Old Man of the Mountains, leader of a heretical Moslem sect, but it is far more likely that responsibility lay with the emir of Ramlah, perhaps acting at Baibars' instigation. Most probably the attack was the result of Edward's opposition to the truce. It seems likely that the assassin was no stranger to Edward, but had been a trusted member of his entourage for some time.[42]

The major disagreement between the sources is not over the attack itself, though there are minor contradictions over the date and the number of wounds inflicted, but over the means used to cure Edward. The most famous story is of how Eleanor of Castile devotedly sucked poison from the wound inflicted by the assassin's dagger, but that version only appeared in the work of Ptolemy of Lucca, a good century later.[43] An Ypres chronicler, again not contemporary, has a circumstantial story of Otto de Grandson sucking the wound, after he alone had suggested that the weapon might have been poisoned.[44] Another version is that Edward was given a special jewel or stone by the Master of the Temple: it may be that this was ground up and given to him to drink, as was done to Baibars on his death-bed.[45]

[39] *Ibn al-Furat*, 159; *Menkonis Chronicon* (Monumenta Germaniae Historica, SS 23, Hannover, 1873), 558.

[40] *Makrizi*, 103ff.

[41] 'Annales de Terre Sainte', 455–6.

[42] Wykes, 249; Guisborough, 208; Rishanger, 69–70; *Ibn al-Furat*, 159, and see 244 for a full list of sources for this incident.

[43] Ptolemy of Lucca, in Muratori, *Rerum Italicarum Scriptores*, xi (Milan, 1727), 1168.

[44] *Johannis Longi Chronica S. Bertini* (Monumenta Germaniae Historica, SS 25, 1880), 856. This author died in 1383.

[45] *Chronicon Hanoniense* (Monumenta Germaniae Historica, SS 25), 464; *Ibn al-Furat*, 168.

Guisborough provides the fullest account. The wound began to putrefy after the remedy provided by the Master of the Temple failed, and Edward began to despair of his life. An English doctor said that he could cure him, though it would be painful, and Edward agreed to the treatment, which involved cutting the decayed flesh away from the wound. His brother Edmund and John de Vescy were asked to take the weeping Eleanor from the room, telling her that it was better that she, rather than the whole of England, should weep. The story may ring true, but it has its flaws. The attack on Edward is placed before Edmund's departure and the agreement to the ten-year truce, and the reported dialogue smacks of literary artifice. In general Guisborough's account of the crusade leaves much to be desired, and there is no reason to give his version of Edward's cure more credence than any other.[46] The various accounts are not in fact mutually exclusive: it is very likely that attempts were made to suck the poison from the wound, that magical potions were tried, and that some surgery was needed.

There was widespread horror at the attempt on Edward's life, but no retaliation took place. Edward, by one account, forbad acts of revenge, lest the lives of pilgrims on their way to the holy places should be put in jeopardy.[47] But although there was no military activity, Edward did not hasten to leave Acre. His own recovery was slow, and Eleanor of Castile had borne him a child, Joan, in the spring: it did not make sense to risk a sea voyage while the baby was in the first months of life. Edward was also engaged in strengthening the defences of the city, building a tower which was to be entrusted in 1278 to the custody of the Order of St Edward of Acre, an entirely obscure English order of knights.[48] It may well have been formed from the few men left by Edward in the east to continue the struggle against the infidels. Finally, towards the end of September 1272, Edward took ship for Italy, no doubt disappointed that he had been able to do so little to help secure the position of the Latin Kingdom, let alone achieve the crusader's goal, the recovery of Jerusalem.[49]

Edward's crusade may have achieved little, and been much smaller than most expeditions to the east, but it was still extremely costly in financial terms. Unfortunately full accounts do not survive, though there is a summary of expenses on the return journey, but enough evidence remains to suggest that the total cost may well have approached £100,000. The contracts made with his followers totalled

[46] Guisborough, 209–10.
[47] Rishanger, 70–1.
[48] *CPR 1272–81*, 296.
[49] According to 'Annales de Terre Sainte', 455–6, Edward left Acre on 24 September; 'Eracles', 462, puts his departure two days earlier.

22,500 marks, but ran only for a year: they were presumably renewed, and further payments made as the expedition was prolonged.[50] The one text dealing with shipping arrangements does not, unfortunately, detail the payments due. It cost St Louis sums varying from 850 to 3,750 *livres* to charter ships for the voyage to Tunis: Edward's expenses in going both to Tunis and to Acre must have been much higher.[51] In addition to the sums due by contract and to transport costs, there must have been heavy expenditure on victualling, equipment, purchase of horses, and the whole range of incidentals involved in medieval warfare.

A more accurate impression of the costs of the crusade is provided by details of the money received by Edward. The French king provided a loan of 70,000 *livres*, and the grant of the twentieth in England eventually provided him with a total of some £31,000.[52] Henry III granted his son 6,000 marks from the English Jewry, of which 4,000 was paid over, with the remainder advanced by Richard of Cornwall.[53] In addition, Edward had his own revenues, many of which must have been diverted to pay for the expedition. Funds appear to have been sufficient until Edward reached Acre, where he had to start borrowing money on a large scale.

On 6 April 1272 he sent a letter to his representatives in England, asking them to send 3,000 marks to Acre, which he was pledged to pay to the Hospitallers by October, and also to send 2,000 marks to pay to the same order in Paris. Edward had borrowed 5,000 marks from various merchants, upon security provided by the Hospitallers. The master of the order also stood surety for a loan of 1,967 *livres* from some merchants from Narbonne. A letter of 12 July set out debts to Pisan merchants of 1,943 *livres*, and on 9 September orders were issued for repayment of 1,526 *livres* borrowed from a Venetian merchant.[54] These surviving letters are probably only a small proportion of the original number: the total borrowed by Edward at Acre cannot be calculated. Some funds were certainly sent to him there: the Italian firm of the Riccardi shipped 2,000 marks out, but such sums were hardly adequate.[55] Nor did Edward's difficulties end when he returned to Europe. The Riccardi were acting as his main financiers, and an

---

[50] Lloyd, 'The Lord Edward's Crusade', 126. This sum includes 1,000 marks due to the earl of Gloucester, who did not of course go on the crusade.

[51] Strayer, *Medieval Statecraft*, 185.

[52] Above, 72.

[53] *CPR 1266–72*, 545–6.

[54] *Cartulaire Générale de l'ordre des Hospitalliers*, iii, 266; *Royal Letters, Henry III*, ii, 347–51; SC 1/12/2.

[55] R.W. Kaeuper, *Bankers to the Crown: the Riccardi of Lucca and Edward I* (Princeton, 1973), 81.

account made by them in 1276, for the period from his landing in Trapani in Sicily in 1274 until his return to England, showed loans totalling £22,364. In addition, the firm paid out £7,687 to Robert Burnell in England on Edward's behalf, the sum including £2,880 repayment to other Italian merchants.[56]

There are references to further loans: the company of the Scoti lent Edward 3,000 marks at Rome, and a Genoese merchant 1,000 marks; 3,000 *livres* was lent to Edward at Paris. Heavy taxation was to be needed to assist the king in paying off the debts incurred on the crusade, and simply by totalling the main taxes allocated for this purpose, and adding the French loan which was secured upon the Bordeaux customs, it seems likely that the overall cost of the expedition was of the order of £100,000.[57] Such a sum represents only the cost to the crown, and takes no account of the considerable efforts men made to raise funds themselves, by selling or leasing their estates.

Edward's crusade may have achieved little for the kingdom of Jerusalem, but it undoubtedly redounded to his credit. The future king of England had proved himself as a champion of a cause to which almost all Christian contemporaries paid at least lip-service, and the dramatic story of the attempt on his life helped to make him famous throughout Europe. The crusade was also of great importance in extending Edward's experience in many ways. His friendship with those who accompanied him must have been deepened by the close companionship of the expedition: particularly noticeable is the emergence of Otto de Grandson as one of Edward's most trusted henchmen at this time. It was on the crusade, too, that Joseph de Chauncy, prior of the English Hospitallers, was recruited into Edward's service to be his treasurer.[58] It is possible that it was at Acre that Edward took into his service the noted Italian lawyer Francesco Accursi, if he can be identified with the man called Accursi d'Arezzo known to have been there at the same time as Edward. Also at Acre Edward made the acquaintance of Tedaldo Visconti, soon to be elected pope as Gregory X. It is even possible that Edward met Marco Polo, who was in Acre with his father and uncle.[59]

[56] *CPR 1272–81*, 132. Curiously, the royal wardrobe account which covers a slightly longer period shows only £9,736 from the Italians, but there is no reason to doubt their account. See Kaeuper, *Bankers to the Crown*, 82 n.

[57] A much fuller attempt to calculate costs is made by B. Beebe, 'Edward I and the Crusades' (University of St Andrews, Ph.D., 1971), 326–90.

[58] T.F. Tout, *Chapters in the Administrative History of Medieval England*, ii (Manchester, 1937), 12–13. Tout's suggestion that Chauncy left office in 1280 through ill-health is not borne out by the fact that he was in Acre in 1282: Kohler and Langlois, 'Lettres inédits', 51n.

[59] Stubbs, *Seventeen Lectures*, 206; Lunt, *Financial Relations of the Papacy with England*, 158; Kohler, 'Deux projets', 417.

John of Acre, employed by Edward as a master of works at the Tower of London, was surely recruited in the course of the crusade.[60] The future builder of castles in North Wales must have been impressed by what he saw of fortifications in the east.

Yet for all that the crusade was important for Edward, it did not show him in an entirely favourable light. He showed little real statesmanship. In the preliminaries to the expedition he displayed a degree of subservience to Louis of France that was surprising in a future king, agreeing to go not as an independent commander, but as if he were a baron of France. After the Tunis debacle, Edward showed remarkable obstinacy in persisting in going on to the east with a totally inadequate force, rather than co-operating properly with plans to launch a really effective large expedition within a few years. In Palestine, Edward's diplomatic efforts to obtain the co-operation of the Mongols achieved little, and in military terms his troops were too few to achieve much. Edward certainly showed full awareness of his limitations, confining his military actions to small-scale raids on vulnerable targets, but his obstinacy remained when it came to the question of negotiating a truce with Baibars. The whole expedition showed a lack of sagacity in financial matters: Edward seems to have had no qualms about mortgaging future revenues, such as the Bordeaux customs, and incurring huge debts with Italian merchants. There was in Edward a curious mix of foolhardiness, in determinedly carrying through his crusade plans against all the odds, with an ultimate sense of caution. Parallels can easily be drawn with his actions in 1297, when he persisted in mounting a campaign against the French with inadequate forces, while virtually bankrupt, and yet was wise enough in the end not to risk battle with his enemy.

Soon after landing at Trapani in Sicily on his return journey, Edward received sad news, firstly of the death of his son John, and then of that of his father Henry III, who had died on 16 November. Charles of Anjou was entertaining him at his court, and was surprised to find him unconcerned about his son, but extremely upset about his father. Edward explained that it was easy to beget sons, but that the loss of a father was irredeemable.[61] Now that Edward was king, it might have been expected that he would hurry back to England, but in fact his journey was to be a leisurely one. A letter from the pope to Eleanor of Castile suggests that Edward was still recovering from the effects of the assassination attempt.[62] On 19 January 1273 Edward was still in

---

[60] *CCR 1272–9*, 444.

[61] Rishanger, 78. The chronicle names Henry, but John must be meant.

[62] *Les registres de Grégoire X et Jean XXI*, ed. J. Guiraud and L. Cadier (Paris, 1892–1906), no. 817.

southern Italy, from where he wrote a distinctly unhelpful letter to the citizens of London, giving no clue as to when they might expect his return. By 5 February he had reached Rome, and a little over a week later arrived at Orvieto, where he was greeted by all the cardinals and led before the pope in grand ceremonial style.[63]

The pope was now Gregory X, whom Edward already knew personally. One matter particularly concerned the two men in their discussions: the murder of his cousin Henry of Almain at Viterbo. A formal complaint was put before the pope, who duly issued a citation ordering Guy de Montfort to appear before the papal curia, but this had no effect. Excommunication followed, but Edward was unable to obtain support for any more effective action. Later in the year Guy was to appear in penitential garb before Gregory, seeking absolution, and by the early 1280s he was restored to the favour of both the papacy and of Charles of Anjou.[64]

From Orvieto Edward and his company rode north through Italy. His passage through Lombardy was thought worthy of note by local chroniclers. He travelled along the Via Emilia, and was entertained in the episcopal palace at Reggio on 20 May. Then he went on through Parma and Milan, aiming next at the relatively easy Alpine pass of the Mont-Cenis.[65] This pass was controlled by the house of Savoy, and Edward's stay in Savoy, particularly the days he spent at the castle of St Georges d'Esperanche (dép. Isère), not far from Lyon, was of considerable significance for the future.

The ruling dynasty of Savoy was much more important in the thirteenth century than its wealth, or the extent of its lands, might suggest. Beatrice, daughter of Thomas of Savoy, had married the count of Provence, and all her four daughters married kings: Louis IX of France, Henry III of England, Richard of Cornwall (who was elected King of the Romans) and Charles of Anjou, king of Sicily. The marriage of Eleanor to Henry III had provided a means for many Savoyards to come to England to seek wealth and power, and, as already shown, they had played a major role in Edward's early years. Otto de Grandson and Jean de Grailly were two important Savoyards present on the crusade. In addition to this, there was a curious territorial connection. As long ago as 1173 four castles in Savoy had been handed over, at least in name, to Henry II, as part of a projected

---

[63] *Liber de Antiquis Legibus*, 158; Rishanger, 78.

[64] *Registres de Gregoire X et Jean XXI*, nos 209, 326, 814. The whole question of Guy de Montfort is fully discussed by Powicke, *Henry III and the Lord Edward*, ii, 608–12. See also above, 27, 74.

[65] 'Memoriale Potestatum Regiensium', Muratori, *Rerum Italicarum Scriptores*, viii, 1135; 'Chronicon Parmense', ibid., ix, 786; 'Annales Mediolanenses', ibid., xvi, 672.

marriage alliance, and a treaty of 1246 provided for the count of Savoy
to do homage to Henry III for four castles in return for 1,000 marks
and an annual pension.[66]

Edward's visit to Savoy in 1273 provided an opportunity to renew
these links. The ruler there was now Philip, youngest son of Thomas,
who had succeeded to the countship in 1268, after a remarkable career
in which he had accumulated a great many ecclesiastical offices, including the archbishopric of Lyon, without ever actually being
ordained. The accounts of his officials show that much was made of
Edward's arrival in Savoy. The castellan of Rivoli sent two messengers
to meet him, and another to inform the count of his arrival. Edward was
then presented with gifts of wine, beef and other foodstuffs. The bailiff
of Montmelian bought ten oxen and fifty-nine lambs ready for a feast
for Edward, and provided him with an escort.[67] The main festivities
took place at St Georges d'Esperanche, the count's new castle which
was still uncompleted. It was there on 25 June 1273 that Count Philip
did homage for the four castles of Avigliana, Bard, Susa and St Maurice
d'Agaune. Edward also, on the previous day, obtained the homage of
William lord of Tournon, as part of the settlement for an attack that
William had made on the crusaders as they marched in the optimistic
days of 1270 towards Aigues-Mortes.

The witness list to this deed reveals that Edward's most important
companions at this stage of his journey were John de Vescy, Roger
Clifford and Otto de Grandson. The last named possibly stayed in
Savoy to see to his own affairs, though he was soon to serve Edward
again. The company was increased in number, however, as various
English magnates had come to Savoy in order to meet their new
sovereign.[68] It must have been on this visit to St Georges that Edward
first met the man who was to be master architect for all his great castles
in Wales, Master James of St George, a man whose imaginative solutions to the problems of castle-building must place him among the
ranks of the greatest of all military architects. James did not return to
England with Edward, but was to be sent for in the late 1270s.[69]

The final adventure of Edward's expedition took place shortly after

---

[66] The complex history of the House of Savoy in the thirteenth century is well
covered by E.L. Cox, *The Eagles of Savoy* (Princeton, 1974). There is a convenient
genealogy on pp. 462–3.

[67] Archivio di Stato di Torino, Inventario Savoia 51, f.257, mazzo 1, no. 8; Inven-
tario Generale, art. 65, f.1, mazzo 1 (I owe these references to the kindness of Dr. A.J.
Taylor, who most generously gave me transcripts of these documents). See also Cox,
Eagles of Savoy, 411.

[68] A.J. Taylor, 'The Castle of St Georges-d'Esperanche', *Antiquaries Journal*, xxxiii
(1953), 33–47; *Foedera*, I. ii, 504.

[69] A.J. Taylor, 'Master James of St George', *EHR*, lxv (1950), 433–57.

he left Savoy. The count of Chalons, Peter, known as the Oxherd, invited the English king to join him in a tournament, which took the form of Edward's men against all-comers. The chronicles suggest that the English were at a two-to-one disadvantage. The tournament was ill-managed, and from the outset was barely distinguishable from a full-scale battle. Infantry attacks upon the English were routed, but the count then charged. He attacked Edward in most unorthodox fashion. Realizing that he was achieving nothing by sword-play, he threw down his weapon and grabbed Edward by the neck, trying to drag him from his horse. Edward was too tall and strong for such treatment: he spurred his horse, and the count was dragged from his saddle, falling to the ground. The conflict became still more unpleasant as the Burgundians saw their lord dismounted, and Edward urged his men to retaliate in kind. The count attacked again, but was forced to surrender. Edward ordered him to give himself up to an ordinary knight: he had disgraced himself too much to be the king's prisoner. The 'Little war of Chalons' did not, fortunately, develop further, and the English eventually reached Paris in safety.[70]

Edward spent from 26 July to 6 August in Paris, where he did homage to the French king Philip III for the lands he held in France. Three letters from an English clerk who had gone to Paris to meet Edward reported briefly that the king had expressed his very great pleasure at the news of the state of affairs in England, that he was in good health, that homage had been done to King Philip, and that there were still matters to be discussed with him. The clerk also told his correspondent that Edward was certainly going to go to Gascony before returning to England.[71] There was serious news from Gascony of the rebellion of Gaston de Béarn, the great noble who, like the earl of Gloucester, should have gone on crusade, but who had considered that his interests were better served by remaining at home. It was not to be until 2 August 1274 that Edward eventually set foot on English soil once more. He was not to go on crusade again, even though he did take the cross a second time in 1287, but it is hard to doubt that the enthusiasm which he had displayed in the course of his expedition was one which would last the rest of his life. It was only right that in the early fourteenth century Pierre Dubois should dedicate his book on the recovery of the Holy Land to Edward, for he despaired of the king of France, but saw in the English monarch the man who might yet provide salvation for the kingdom of Jerusalem.[72]

[70] The fullest account of the 'Little war' is in Guisborough, 210–12. There may be a measure of exaggeration involved.
[71] SC 1/18/88, 89, 90, largely printed by Trabut-Cussac, *L'administration anglaise en Gascogne*, 41, n.3.
[72] See below, 326–33, for discussion of Edward's later policy towards the crusades.

PART II

The King in his Prime

Chapter 4

CORONATION AND CONSOLIDATION

On Thursday 2 August 1274 Edward I at long last returned to England, landing at Dover. His journey back from the crusade had been a leisurely one, and matters in Gascony had taken longer than anticipated; moreover the news he had received from England had not suggested that there was any urgent need for his presence. The arrival of the king was not treated at any length by the chroniclers, and the clerks of the chancery merely noted it in a terse memorandum. Edward was greeted with great state, however, by the earls of Gloucester and Warenne, who entertained him at their respective castles of Tonbridge and Reigate, as he proceeded towards London for his coronation.[1]

Detailed questions of government policy were doubtless set aside in the days following Edward's return: the organization of the coronation ceremony must have been the prime concern. Preparations had been long under way. As early as February 1274 orders had gone out to a dozen countries for the collection of the massive quantities of food needed for the feasting that would follow the actual act of coronation. From Gloucestershire alone 60 oxen and cows, 60 swine, 2 fat boars, 40 bacon pigs and 3,000 capons and hens were requested. Two Londoners were appointed to make purchases of food. Bishops, abbots and priors were asked to prepare as many swans, peacocks, cranes, rabbits and kids as they could, and efforts were made to prevent fishmongers profiting unduly from the demand for pikes, eels, salmon and lampreys.[2] Much work was needed to prepare Westminster, where over £1,100 was spent on works. New lodges, kitchens and stables were built, and by the time that all was ready, every piece of open ground had been used for temporary buildings. There was much redecoration, and new stone thrones were set up in the great hall. Covered ways were erected between the palace and the abbey church.[3]

Many decisions had to be made about the actual ceremony. There had been no coronation in England since that of Edward's mother, Eleanor of Provence, in 1236. On that occasion, a special court had sat

---

[1] CCR 1272–9, 97; CPR 1272–81, 55–6; Flores, iii, 43.
[2] CCR 1272–9, 68–71.
[3] Liber de Antiquis Legibus, 172–3; KW, i, 504.

to hear the various claims and counterclaims regarding the hereditary functions performed by magnates. At issue were such questions as who should carry the three ceremonial swords and two sceptres, and who should bear the canopies over the king and queen. There is no direct evidence as to what took place in these hearings in 1274, but the role to be played by the king's brother, Edmund of Lancaster, was clearly a matter of major controversy. He claimed the right to carry the great sword *Curtana*, but it seems that this was rejected. He probably based his claim on his tenure of the stewardship, and on the day after the ceremony took place he renounced the hereditary grant of the stewardship made to him by Henry III and instead accepted the position for life. A list of magnates present at the coronation omits his name, suggesting that he boycotted the ceremony. The sword was perhaps borne by the earl of Gloucester.[4] Another dispute was over the participation of the archbishop of York, which was bound to reopen the perennial question of the rivalry between Canterbury and York. Walter Giffard of York had carried his cross while he was in the province of Canterbury, a very provocative act. As a result he was excluded from the coronation ceremony, though one chronicler suggests that he was in fact present, but that he took no active part in the proceedings.[5]

Such arguments prior to the coronation were inevitable, as they still are, and it is unlikely that they detracted much from the joyful occasion. On the day before he was crowned, Edward made a triumphal entry into London, which was decorated in his honour. Coronation day, 19 August, saw the conduit at Cheapside running with red and white wine for all to drink.[6] The service itself is not described in any detail by the choniclers. It clearly took a largely traditional form, but there was an innovation in the oath sworn by the newly crowned king. This normally had a tripartite form. According to the legal textbook 'Bracton', the king should promise to work for the peace of church and people, to prevent rapacity and oppression, and to do justice impartially and mercifully. Edward may have agreed to maintain the laws of his predecessors, notably Edward the Confessor: this was certainly a feature of the oath to be used in 1308. Furthermore, Edward also swore an

[4] H.G. Richardson, 'Early Coronation Records', *BIHR*, xiii (1935–6), 130–1. 134–5; *Foedera*, I.ii, 515; H.G. Richardson, 'The Coronation of Edward I', *BIHR*, xv (1937–8), 94–9. The tentative hypothesis made by Richardson, ibid., 98, that the sword might have been carried by Alexander III of Scotland is not very plausible, as if he had performed this duty, it is likely that this would have been used as evidence by Edward I later, in support of his claim of feudal suzerainty over Scotland. I am grateful to Professor E.L.G. Stones for this suggestion.

[5] Richardson 'Coronation of Edward I', 99; *Ann. Dunstable*, 263; Wykes, 260.

[6] *The French Chronicle of London*, ed. G.J. Aungier (Camden Soc., 1844), 13.

oath to preserve the rights of the crown. He referred to this in a letter to the pope in 1275, and on some subsequent occasions. There is also a chronicle story that once Archbishop Kilwardby placed the crown on Edward's head, the king promptly removed it, saying that he would not wear it again until he had recovered the lands belonging to the crown which had been granted away by his father.[7]

After the ceremony in which Edward and Eleanor were crowned, the feasting began. A later story has it that as the king was seated at the banquet, the king of Scots and the earls of Lancaster, Cornwall, Gloucester, Pembroke and Warenne all came before him, each with a retinue of a hundred knights. All dismounted, and the horses were then set free, for anyone to keep those that he managed to catch.[8] The tale is an attractive one, and true or not, catches something of the spirit of the young men who surrounded the king, and of the carefree optimism which accompanied his formal assumption of the crown. The celebration must have been extraordinary, conducted on a scale far beyond anything in the memories of those present.

The business of government did not come to a complete halt during the festivities, but it was not until late September that the reshaping of the administration began. England had been governed with remarkable success during the period between Henry III's death and Edward's return to England, though there was undoubted nervousness that the issues of the civil war might be revived. In 1273 orders had been issued that no one should enter London armed, and Thomas de Clare was appointed to advise the city authority about defences. An order to the sheriffs for the keeping of the peace, which it was said was inadequate, betrays a sense of alarm, as do rumours current in 1274 of a renewed attempt to occupy the Isle of Ely.[9] There had been some trouble when Edmund of Lancaster, after his return from the crusade, tried to pursue his territorial ambitions against Robert de Ferrers to the bitter end. He besieged the Staffordshire manor of Chartley which Ferrers had been allowed to retain, but the earl of Gloucester protested firmly to Robert Burnell, pointing out that 'it does not seem that there can be tranquillity in the land, nor is the king's lordship worth anything if the people of the land can assemble forces like this in time of peace'. The protest was in vain: to judge by a later pardon, Edmund carried the siege through to its conclusion. Gloucester's pressure did result in the issue coming before the council, and it was decided to take Chartley

---

[7] H.G. Richardson, 'The English Coronation Oath', *Speculum*, xxiv (1949), 44–50; BL Cotton Vesp. B. xi (the Hagnaby chronicle), f.27. Bodleian Library MS Rawlinson B. 414 is a shortened version of this chronicle.

[8] Richardson, 'Coronation of Edward I', 98.

[9] *CCR 1272–9*, 10, 25; *CPR 1272–81*, 52.

into royal hands.[10] Other problems the government faced were those of the ambitions of Llywelyn of Wales, and a serious commercial dispute with Flanders: both matters would need Edward's intervention.

Before questions of policy could be resolved by Edward after his coronation, there were matters of personnel to be decided. The most urgent was that of the appointment of Robert Burnell as chancellor, replacing the veteran Walter de Merton. The king's concern for Burnell was shown on 25 August when he appointed him to a church living at Ringwood. Then, on 21 September, Burnell took charge of the great seal and with it the chancery. On the same day the important post of keeper of the wardrobe was entrusted to Anthony Bek, but he held it for less than a month, with his brother Thomas taking over on 18 October. On that day William Louth began his term of office as cofferer of the wardrobe.[11] At the exchequer there was no change: Joseph de Chauncy, who had become treasurer only a year previously, remained in office. These changes did not amount to a political revolution, but were simply the result of Edward's natural desire to see men well-known to him in the highest offices of state. Surprisingly, there were no immediate plans to hold a parliament in which the king could discuss affairs of state with his magnates: there had to be a major inquiry into the state of the realm before appropriate measures could be taken to reform abuses.

Edward's reign was notable for the scale and frequency of the investigations into the way in which the country was governed. The greatest inquest was that of 1274–5 which produced the Hundred Rolls: in many ways this can be seen as the starting point for the major work of reform which was to characterize the first half of the reign. There survives only a fraction of the total returns, but even that fraction is monumental in bulk. The inquiry had its immediate origins in the appointment of two men in January 1274 to investigate the loss of royal rights in eleven counties.[12] It seems that they never carried out their task in full, perhaps because their brief was inadequate, and the government then decided to adopt a much fuller procedure, and began investigations in the autumn. Inquiries into the feudal structure of Gascony during Edward's stay in the duchy may have provided a recent precedent, although the parallel was not very close.[13] In broader terms, the Hundred Rolls inquiry was firmly in the traditions of the middle years of the thirteenth century. In 1255 investigations had taken place into the rights of the crown and the question of whether they had

[10]   *CCR 1272–9*, 17–18; *CPR 1281–92*, 53; SC 1/22, 26. *Flores*, iii, 31–2, refers to a rising in the north: this probably relates to the Chartley incident.

[11]   *CCR 1272–9*, 99; *CPR 1272–81*, 54; Tout, *Chapters*, vi, 6, 26, 30.

[12]   *CPR 1272–82*, 65. Returns for Somerset to this inquiry are printed in *RH*, ii, 118–24.

[13]   Below, 301–3.

been alienated or usurped, as well as into the conduct of royal officials.[14] In 1258 knights were appointed to examine all manner of 'excesses, trespasses and acts of injustice', particularly by royal officials, and the special eyre set up in 1259 provided for the investigation of officials and of the alienation of royal rights.[15]

There was nothing radically new in what Edward I was attempting in 1274. The speed and scale of the inquiry was of a different order to the earlier inquiries, but the nature of the questions being asked was familiar. It is striking that Edward was using methods which had been employed, above all, by the opposition to the crown in his father's reign: even the 1255 inquest had taken place when Henry III was abroad, and did not represent considered royal policy. Edward's own association with the opposition may have been short-lived, but he had picked up ideas about how the country should be governed which he was able to pursue when he came to the throne. The question of how far he himself should be seen as the motivating force behind the Hundred Rolls inquiry is one incapable of resolution, but at the least he must have given new urgency and importance to an existing concept.

It would not have been easy to investigate local government without changing those in charge, and it was surely as a necessary preliminary to the inquiry that in September 1274 the two escheators and the majority of the sheriffs were replaced. A new form of oath to be sworn by the sheriffs and their bailiffs made the government's priorities clear. It stressed first of all that they were to serve the king, and were to maintain his rights. Any usurpations of royal rights were to be ended, and if the sheriffs could not do this themselves, the king or his council were to be informed. Payment of debts due to the crown was to be enforced promptly where possible. Only later in the oath were the sheriffs told to treat people loyally, and in accord with right, rich and poor alike. An oath by itself, however, could achieve little; a cynical clerk termed it, in the margin of the official exchequer roll, 'the sheriffs' perjury'.[16]

On 11 October pairs of commissioners were appointed to put forty or more articles to local juries, each pair dealing with a group of counties. The operation of taking the inquests was remarkably quick. It took only six days to hear the verdicts of the various local juries in Shropshire. Over the whole country, the process lasted between November 1274

[14] Cam, *Hundred and the Hundred Rolls*, 36–7; *Documents of the Baronial Movement*, ed. Sanders, 112–13, 162.

[15] *CPR 1272–81*, 57; *CFR 1272–1307*, 30–33.

[16] E 159/49, m.1d; T. Madox, *History and Antiquities of the Exchequer* (1769), ii, 149n., gives a version of the oath from 1298 which, though rather shorter, does not differ fundamentally from that of 1274; R.J. Maddicott, 'Edward I and the Lessons of Baronial Reform: Local government, 1258–80', *Thirteenth Century England*, I, 20.

and March 1275. Each hundred had its own jury, as did boroughs, large vills and some manors. There might also be juries of knights of the shire, and some individual complaints were noted. The bulk of the material collected was immense, for each session with a jury was recorded in a separate roll, sealed with the seals of the individual jurors. These became known as the Ragman Rolls. In time, extract rolls were compiled, bringing the evidence of the inquisitions into slightly more manageable form, though certainly not one so convenient as the eleventh-century Domesday Book.[17]

The purpose of the inquest was explained succinctly in the heading given to the extract rolls. It was to investigate rights and liberties taken from the king, the excesses of sheriffs and other royal officials, and the misdeeds of private bailiffs. There were some differences in the questions asked by the various commissioners: in the east Midlands six extra articles were added, and only in Gloucestershire and Warwickshire were forgers and clippers of coin the subject of inquiry. The total list of questions provides impressive evidence of the very considerable range of opportunities available to medieval officials to profit by abuse of their position, though the prime purpose of the inquest was to discover what rights and lands had been lost by the crown.

Some of the returns were not particularly satisfactory. In Calne and Ramsbury, in Wiltshire, the jurors produced a string of no less than twenty-five negative answers to the questions put to them. The jurors of Worcester reported that none of the hundreds in the county was in the king's hands: they named those who held the hundreds, but stated that they did not know how long they had had them, nor by what right, nor how much they were worth. Thirty-two 'don't know' answers were provided by the jurors of the manor of Condover in Shropshire.[18] The bulk of the returns, however, were impressively full. The jurors had considerable problems with the questions relating to the alienation of royal rights, for it was very rare for them to know what justification there was for a magnate's claim to hold lands or powers of jurisdiction. It was no part of the inquiry to ask for charters to be produced to justify claims, and the jurors were not in a position to know the details of such evidence. In some cases they were able to provide a long history. For Grantham, in Lincolnshire, the story went back to the days of Queen Matilda, and concluded with Edward's own grant of the place to Earl Warenne, who held it, along with Stamford, for the service of four knights, according to the jurors. It had, they said, an annual value of

---

[17] *RH*, i, 1; the articles of the inquiry are given by Cam. *Hundred and the Hundred Rolls*, 248–56. Ibid., 45, explains that the name Ragman derived from the many seals dangling from the rolls, which gave the appearance of a ragged fringe.

[18] *RH*, ii, 93, 247, 266.

£110, but, for all their detailed knowledge, they had to say that they did not know by what warrant it was held.[19] Some returns must have confirmed the government's fears, even if most were insufficiently specific. In Northamptonshire, for example, the jurors of Huxloe, Polebrook and Wymersley hundreds all reported that the earl of Gloucester had removed his tenants from the hundredal jurisdiction, and had been exercising judicial rights for the past fifteen or sixteen years, though it was not known what right he had to do so.[20] In Shropshire there was alarming evidence of Welsh aggression: Peter Corbet was unable to perform his feudal service, as so much of his land had been lost to the Welsh. Men who used to live under English law were now being forced to accept Welsh law.[21]

The jurors had few inhibitions in providing detailed information about official wrongdoings. Cases where they were intimidated were rare, though Gilbert de Clifton, the earl of Lincoln's bailiff at Staincliffe in Yorkshire, threatened one of the commissioners with the loss of his lands should he proceed with the hearings. This was reported, but it may be that there were other instances where the inquiries were obstructed and which were not recorded. There were considerable regional variations: in Gloucestershire thirty officials were charged with various offences, but in Essex the figure stood much higher, at 188. This probably reflects the much greater authority of private lords in Gloucestershire.[22] The Lincolnshire returns are particularly full. In the wapentake (the local equivalent of the hundred) of Aswardhurn the jurors listed eleven recent sheriffs and eighteen lesser royal officials, along with five seigneurial officials, and accused them of a range of offences. Part of the trouble was that the farm of the wapentake had been increased from its true value of about ten marks to over twenty marks. Corruption and extortion had increased, as efforts were made to raise more revenue. Problems seem to have been particularly acute at this time: when a major judicial inquiry was held later in the reign, in 1298, only five local officials in Aswardhurn were to be accused.[23]

The great majority of accusations made in the Hundred Rolls are monotonous. Few officials had the imagination of the sheriff of Essex who, in 1267, seized cocks which he claimed would be sent flying into London carrying incendiary material tied to their feet.[24] There were

---

[19] *RH*, i, 288.

[20] *RH*, ii, 7–8.

[21] *RH*, i, 362–3.

[22] Cam, *Studies in the Hundred Rolls*, 188–90.

[23] *RH*, i, 241–9; *A Lincolnshire Assize Roll for 1298*, ed. W.S. Thomson (Lincolnshire Record Soc., xxxvi, 1944), 285.

[24] Above, 58–9; *RH*, i, 148–9. It is odd that it was only in one hundred that these charges were made against the sheriff.

some other odd stories. The constable of Shrewsbury allegedly paid a
boy 4d to run through a nearby village shouting 'Wekare! Wekare!' to
insult the inhabitants. A scuffle broke out, the boy was shot and killed
with an arrow, and the village fined a substantial sum by the sheriff.[25]
Some officials emerge very clearly as rogues. Hugh de Dignineton,
constable of Orford castle, was accused of imprisoning a royal official
for three days, and forcing him to swear to leave the place. He took
unauthorized tolls and prises, and extended the bounds of the castle
liberty. One man was thrown into prison in Orford castle, where he was
so badly treated that he died of his wounds, and the coroner was then
prevented from viewing the body, as he should have done.[26] In general
terms, a reading of the surviving Hundred Rolls suggests that there was
a need both for new legislation and for judicial proceedings against
many local officials.

By November 1274 it was planned that parliament would shortly be
held in London. The initial summons was for mid-February 1275, but
just after Christmas the meeting was postponed until 25 April.[27] In this
parliament many matters were considered, and in the first statute
of Westminster various clauses dealt with matters covered in the
Hundred Rolls. Clause 15, for example, dealt with the problems of
bailing prisoners. The Hundred Rolls provided many specific examples.
In Elloe hundred, in Lincolnshire, the jurors detailed nine cases of
criminals wrongly allowed to leave prison after making payments to an
official, and one where the prior of Spalding had unjustifiably detained
a man in such conditions that his feet had completely rotted away.[28]
The statute dealt with problems arising out of wardships, where those in
wardship married without their lord's consent, or where the lords
refused to allow their wards to marry. The Hundred Rolls gave various
examples of the abuse of wardship.[29] Yet the evidence is far from clear
that the statute was affected in its drafting by the returns coming in
from the inquiry. The crown had shown, in the questions put to the
jurors, that it was well aware of the problems that existed, and it is
inconceivable that the legislation could have been based on the huge
mass of returns that came in. In the case of wardship in particular, the
statute did not deal with the main points which emerged from the
inquiry, which related largely to the unlawful concealment of royal
rights.

The Hundred Rolls provided the crown with lengthy lists of official

[25] *RH*, ii, 92. The meaning of 'Wekare' is not clear.
[26] *RH*, ii, 188–9, 191, 199.
[27] *CCR 1272–9*, 137, 229; *Parl. Writs*, i, 1.
[28] *RH*, i, 275; *Statutes of the Realm*, I, 30.
[29] Cam. *Hundred and the Hundred Rolls*, 254; *Statutes of the Realm*, I, 32–3.

wrongdoings, but the inquiry had done nothing to resolve the cases it had exposed, for the commissioners had no powers to give judgement. It was certainly intended to set up a special judicial commission to hear and determine cases against royal and private officials. A document known as the Statute of Ragman provided for this, referring specifically to matters raised in the Hundred Roll inquiry. The date of this is unfortunately not known, but it was probably drawn up not long after Michaelmas 1276.[30] Yet there is no evidence that any commissions were in fact set up, and it is most likely that, as a result of the king's preoccupation with the Welsh war, the matter was put off.

In London a judicial eyre did follow fairly swiftly upon the Hundred Rolls, in 1276, and a comparison between the two records is interesting. The articles of the eyre were not identical to those of the Hundred Roll inquiry, but many cases do appear on both records. In the majority, the eyre roll provides more detail, but that is not so, for example, in the interesting case of Laurence Duket. He killed a doctor, William le Fremound, and in the eyre roll it is simply recorded that he produced a royal charter of pardon. No one came forward to implead him for the offence, and he went free. The Hundred Rolls record that this charter was obtained for Duket by the chief clerk of the city, Ralph Crepyn, who took all Duket's lands and houses in payment, as a result of which the crown, so the jurors alleged, lost what would have been a valuable forfeiture. The story is one of the many examples showing that officials charged in the Hundred Rolls were rarely, in the end, prosecuted. Duket was himself to be the victim of a criminal assault in 1284.[31]

It does not seem that much use was made of the Hundred Rolls in the course of the London eyre, but from 1287 it was laid down that the returns were to be used judicially. Instead of appointing special commissioners, as originally intended, the government determined in the Statute of Gloucester that the whole matter should be dealt with in the general eyres. This proved to be a very slow and laborious process: it was not until 1287 that hearings took place in Gloucestershire. In many cases those accused in the 1274 inquiries died before the cases came to court.[32] The justices had the returns to the Hundred Roll inquiries with them, and annotations prove that they were used. Relatively few cases

---

[30] Cam, *Studies in the Hundred Rolls*, 54, suggests that it may date only from the late summer of 1278, as it resembles the arrangements made in the Statue of Gloucester of that year, but an earlier date seems more likely. See D.W. Sutherland, *Quo Warranto Proceedings in the Reign of Edward I, 1278–1294* (Oxford, 1963), 24–5.

[31] *RH*, i, 415; *The London Eyre of 1276*, ed. M. Weinbaum (1976), no. 207. See below, 265.

[32] *Statutes of the Realm*, i, 46; Sutherland, *Quo Warranto*, 193; Cam, *Studies in the Hundred Rolls*, 191; *RH*, i, 166–74 shows that in Gloucestershire the accused men had died in twenty cases before the matter came to court.

were in fact determined, and in many of those the accused men were found innocent. As for the specific case of Hugh de Dignineton, he did lose office in 1275, but not because of the charges against him, rather because the castle was granted for five years to Robert Ufford. He was appointed as a keeper of the customs in 1277, and also received custody of the bailiwick of Southwark: he was clearly in no way disgraced.[33]

Historians have made much of the Hundred Rolls; contemporary chroniclers, on the other hand, laid no stress on the great inquiry, the Dunstable annalist remarking that no good came of it.[34] Certainly there was no immediate and successful drive against corruption, and there is little evidence to suggest that the returns inspired new legislation. The evidence provided by the jurors was to be more important with regard to the investigation of lost or alienated royal rights in the *Quo Warranto* inquiries.[35] More generally, the fact that the crown had instigated a major inquiry must have helped demonstrate that there was a new determination, a fresh approach, in the new king's government.

Trade and finance were matters of much concern at the outset of Edward's reign. In 1270, years of difficulty and disagreement between England and Flanders had reached a climax, with the dramatic arrest of all goods held by English merchants in Flanders. The order for this was inspired in part by the grievance of the countess of Flanders that an annual pension of 500 marks due to her had not been paid, in part by the efforts of the English to compel overseas merchants to keep to the regulations of the Assize of Cloth, and in part because of the imposition of the new customs duties. The situation was exacerbated by the arrest of Flemish goods at St Ives fair in Huntingdonshire in 1270. In order to place pressure on the Flemings, an embargo was placed on the export of wool from England. This proved hard to enforce. Licences were issued to export to places other than Flanders, and smuggling was almost certainly widespread.

When Edward returned from crusade, he was not pleased with what he learned about the situation, and demanded that steps be taken to compel the Flemings to submit. In August and September 1273 new severe measures were ordered. Trading vessels were to be searched for contraband. Wool exports were again forbidden, and all Flemings were to leave England by Christmas. In April 1274 the king's merchant Luke of Lucca, one of the company of the Riccardi, was appointed to investigate violations of the embargo, and in May he was empowered to arrest

---

[33] *CPR 1272–81*, 89, 210, 240.

[34] *Ann. Dunstable*, 263. The inquest is also noted by the Hagnaby chronicle, BL Vesp. B. xi, f.27.

[35] See below, 258–64.

wool ships in the Humber and the northern ports. The government were setting a thief to catch a thief, for the Riccardi had been deeply involved in attempting to evade the regulations. The new severity, clearly inspired by Edward himself, proved effective, and in June and July 1274 a new treaty with Flanders was negotiated. English merchants and Flemish merchants whose goods had been seized would receive compensation. This would be paid out of the proceeds of the goods that had been taken in England and Flanders, but since more English goods than Flemish had been seized, a balance was due to the English of £4,755, or so Edward claimed. Payment was finally completed in 1287.

The crown was able to profit considerably from the violations of the embargo that had taken place. The Riccardi were employed to collect some £13,300 from alien merchants, and money was also raised from English traders. Payments were made at the rate of ten shillings a sack, and the profitability of the operation may well have contributed to the government's plan to introduce a system of permanent customs duties on the export of wool.[36]

The negotiation of customs duties was one of the prime purposes of the parliament which met in April 1275. The financial position cannot be calculated with any precision, but was certainly very serious. The king's crusading debts were massive, with large sums owed to Italian bankers. What was needed was a simple means of repayment. There was a precedent for a system of customs duties in the so-called new aid of 1266, when Edward had imposed a levy on imports and exports by alien merchants in return for his protection, which yielded 6,000 marks a year. By early 1274 this aid was in the hands of the Riccardi of Lucca, but the bankers were undoubtedly anxious to be provided with a more secure and permanent means of repayment.[37]

The composition of the April parliament shows that it was from the first intended to negotiate a tax on the mercantile wealth of the country. The sheriffs were ordered to obtain the attendance of six or four men from every city, borough or merchant town, as well as four knights from each shire. This meant that the assembly had, almost certainly, a much higher attendance of urban representatives than any other medieval parliament. Indeed, it was roughly twice the size of a normal parliament. In part, the scale of this parliament is to be explained in terms of the king's desire to ensure that the reforms of the first statute of

---

[36] R.H. Bowers, 'English Merchants and the Anglo-Flemish Economic War', *Seven Studies in Medieval English History and Other Historical Essays presented to Harold S. Snellgrove* (Jackson, Mississippi, 1983), 21–54; see also Kaeuper, *Bankers to the Crown*, 142–4, and T.H. Lloyd, *The English Wool Trade in the Middle Ages* (Cambridge, 1977), 25–39.
[37] Kaeuper, *Bankers to the Crown*, 136–8, 141.

Westminster became widely known, but the large number of townsmen can only be explained by the plan to impose a new tax.[38] The crown was in a strong bargaining position, for the embargo on wool exports was still in force, at least formally, and it could offer the merchants abandonment of the measure in return for a grant of customs duties.

According to the Dunstable annals, the new scheme was thought to be the responsibility of the treasurer, Joseph de Chauncy, although its real author was an Italian, whose name is rendered as Poncius de Ponto.[39] Export duties were to be paid on wool, woolfells and hides, at the rate of 6s 8d on each sack of wool. Merchants would have little difficulty in passing this on, most probably in the form of higher prices to their overseas customers. The new custom was, according to the official formula, 'granted by all the great men of the realm and at the request of the communities of merchants of all England', but a draft letter makes it clear that in reality it was the merchant community who made the grant, and that the magnates then gave their consent to it.[40] From the outset it was intended that the proceeds of the customs would be collected at the ports by the Italian bankers and used to repay them for their loans, rather than being paid straight into the exchequer. In each customs port – there were thirteen in all – there was to be one representative of the Italians, with custody of one half of the customs seal, the cocket, and two local men in charge of the other half. The system was simple and effective. There was no question of farming out the customs for a fixed sum, as had been done with the earlier levy of the new aid. The Italians had to account properly for all the money they received. The task of collection was made much easier by the fact that duties were only payable on a very limited range of goods, and for the Italians, the customs provided the solid security they needed if they were to continue to lend to the crown. The yield of the new duties was substantial, averaging some £10,000 a year in the period up to 1279.[41] An important step had been taken towards achieving financial stability.

The main achievements of the spring parliament of 1275 were the first statute of Westminster, and the agreement to grant the new customs duties. Some judicial business was also done, but the

[38] M. McKisack, *The Parliamentary Representation of the English Boroughs during the Middle Ages* (Oxford, 1932), 4–6; C.H. Jenkinson, 'The First Parliament of Edward I', *EHR*, xxv (1910); Maddicott, 'Edward I and the Lessons of Baronial Reform', 14–16.

[39] *Ann. Dunstable*, 258. Who Poncius was is not clear: the chronicler may have meant Orlandino da Pogio, one of the heads of the Riccardi, and a man of great importance.

[40] Kaeuper, *Bankers to the Crown*, 144–5; *Parl. Writs*, i, 2; *CPR 1272–81*, 90.

[41] Lloyd, *English Wool Trade*, 60–2; Kaeuper, *Bankers to the Crown*, 144–6.

parliament was cut short when Edward suddenly fell ill. The wounds he had received from the assassin's blade in the east apparently began to fester again, giving him a fever. Discussion of the payment of an annual tribute to the papacy and various other matters were put off until the next parliament, to be held in October 1275.[42]

During the summer of 1275 Edward and his entourage travelled slowly northwards to Chester, intending to hold talks with Llywelyn of Wales. In the event, Llywelyn refused to attend. On the way, Edward approached the town of Oxford at the end of July. He was met with great pomp, and the place was lavishly decorated in his honour, but the townspeople and students were disconcerted when Edward refused to enter the west gate. He was, it seems, terrified of what the chronicler Wykes called the derisory superstition about the curse of St Frideswide. She was an Anglo-Saxon saint, whose excessive measures in defence of her virginity were thought to have included the imposition of a curse on any king who should enter Oxford, where a church stood on the spot to which she had been pursued by a lustful Mercian prince.[43]

Edward returned to Westminster for parliament in October. What did *not* happen was very significant: Llywelyn of Wales refused to appear to perform homage to the English king. There was some legislation regarding the Jews.[44] A serious dispute between the bishop and prior of Norwich, and the local community was resolved by arbitration. The problem dated back to 1270, when a feud had culminated in the sacking and burning of the monastery, and even the taking of the city into royal hands had not quelled the trouble. By 1275 the ecclesiastical authorities were claiming 4,000 marks in damages, with the citizens offering half that sum. Edward's task was not a particularly difficult one: he set the figure at 3,000 marks, ordered the local community to pay for a gold vessel for the church costing £100, and arranged for sentences of excommunication and interdict to be lifted. What is striking is that Edward, unlike his father, was able to bring the matter to a satisfactory conclusion.[45]

Further steps were taken, in this parliament, to solve the government's financial problems. A tax of a fifteenth, assessed on the value of movable goods, in practice largely foodstuffs and animals, was granted

[42] H.G. Richardson and G.O. Sayles, 'The English Parliaments of Edward I', *BIHR*, v (1928), 136; *CCR 1272–9*, 197–8, Wykes, 263.

[43] Wykes, 263–4; Blaauw, *Barons' Wars*, 121. St Frideswide's shrine is now in Oxford cathedral.

[44] Wykes, 266; Richardson and Sayles, 'The English Parliaments of Edward I', 137.

[45] *The Chronicle of Bury St Edmunds, 1212–1301*, ed. A. Gransden (1964), 59; Cotton, 146–9; *CCR 1272–9*, 217–18.

to the king. There were no urban representatives present, in contrast to the last parliament, but there were knights of the shire to give a measure of popular assent to the decision. The demand for the tax was put by the chief justice, who argued that Edward had spent his own and his father's wealth on the crusade, and that he therefore had to ask for assistance from his subjects. There may also have been an argument that a tax had been promised to Henry III, but not collected. One chronicler saw the matter in very cynical terms, describing the tax as a confiscation. He felt particularly strongly over the way in which it was to be levied on the temporal goods of churchmen as well as laymen. The tax was to be highly successful, with an assessment of over £81,000, and a yield not far short of that sum.[46] Edward also approached the prelates directly for an aid to be paid on the value of their spiritualities, but this was felt to be unreasonable, particularly since the clergy were already paying crusading tenths, imposed for six years by the council of Lyons of 1274. The matter was put off, with the prelates promising a reply by the following Easter.[47]

In the autumn of 1275 measures were also taken to improve the financial administration. A document, known as the statutes of the exchequer, set out the proper procedures to be adopted by the exchequer and those with whom it dealt, all in considerable detail.[48] The major change that took place was in the running of the king's demesne lands, and of the estates that came into royal hands under the system of wardship. It is normally considered that there was little that could be done to increase royal income from land, and most recent historians have considered that crown estates were chiefly of value as a source of patronage, particularly as a means of providing for members of the royal family. This was an age when most landlords retained manors in their own hands, rather than leasing them out, but with the existing exchequer machinery this would have been a difficult task for the government to undertake. In November 1275, however, in accordance with the new statutes of the exchequer, three officials were appointed to the custody of the royal demesnes, each with control of a different region. Ralph of Sandwich, a former Montfortian administrator, had the south and west, Richard de Holebrook the midlands and east, and Thomas de Normanville the north. Small manors were to be leased out; large estates managed directly. In addition to running the demesnes, these three stewards took over the functions of the escheators, dealing with the lands of deceased tenants-in-chief, while at a more

[46] Gervase of Canterbury, ii, 281; G.L. Harriss, *King, Parliament and Public Finance in Medieval England to 1369* (Oxford, 1975), 40, where it is wrongly stated that this was Edward's first parliament. Tax assessments are tabulated in the appendix, below, 569.

[47] Wykes, 265–6.

[48] *Statutes of the Realm*, i, 197–8.

local level the sheriffs performed the tasks formerly undertaken by escheators.[49]

The scheme was a radical one, but the accounts submitted to the exchequer do not suggest that it was particularly successful. Over a three-year period Thomas de Normanville was able to show that he had made payments to the treasury of £3,253, as against total receipts of £6,538 with which he was charged. For the most part, manors continued to be farmed out, though there were exceptions, such as the manors of Woodstock and Wootton in Oxfordshire, and St Briavel's in Gloucestershire. There were many expenses to be met, and the fact that the system was not particularly lucrative provides one reason for its abandonment in 1282. A letter from Richard de Holebrook written in that year reveals further problems. His workload was proving to be excessive, his health not up to it, and he was having considerable difficulty in obtaining the co-operation of some sheriffs.[50] The old system of escheators proved, in the end, more effective than the experiment of 1275.

Early in the new year, 1276, Edward was at Winchester, where, according to the local annalist, he held a parliament, though the proceedings were not honoured with that name in any of the official records.[51] It was at Winchester that the king made an agreement with Isabella de Forz, countess of Aumale, which clearly shows his anxiety to increase the landed endowment of the crown. Isabella had been widowed in 1260, and by 1276 all her children had died, the last, Aveline, in 1274. The bargain that was now struck with her was that she should make over all her lands, apart from four manors, to the king, who would re-grant them to her for life, and would pay her 20,000 marks. On her death the lands would come to the crown, with the rightful heir, Hugh de Courtenay, losing his inheritance. The agreement was not in fact carried through. Perhaps the sum offered was not large enough, perhaps protests from Courtenay dissuaded the countess from her course of action, or maybe the state of royal finances, with the costs of the Welsh war of 1277, was such that the king could not afford the substantial investment involved. The matter was not one which was wholly abandoned, however, and the plan was to be revived in 1293.[52]

Although Edward failed to establish himself as Isabella's heir, he had more success in the case of her daughter Aveline. She had married

---

[49] *CPR 1272–81*, 112. These officials were to receive a grant of £50 a year. The new system is briefly discussed by Cam, *Hundred and the Hundred Rolls*, 202. The scheme is discussed by Maddicott, 'Edward I and the lessons of Baronial Reform', 21–3.

[50] E 372/124, mm.23–7; SC 1/10/157.

[51] *Ann. Winton*, 120.

[52] Powicke, *Henry III and the Lord Edward*, ii, 708–9; McFarlane, *Nobility of Later Medieval England*, 257–8; *CCR 1272–9*, 347–9.

the king's brother Edmund, and died childless, a fact which disqual-
ified Edmund from inheriting her estates. Various claims to her substantial lands were put forward, mostly from descendants of William le
Gros, earl of Aumale, who had died in 1179. The successful claimant
was one John de Eshton, who claimed descent from a daughter of
William's called Avice. His arguments were fiercely contested, with
assertions that Avice had never existed, or alternatively, that she had
been illegitimate, and born of a nun. It is most unlikely that there was
real substance to Eshton's claim, yet his was the one which succeeded.
He was paid £100 by the crown to cover his expenses, and in 1278, soon
after the conclusion of the proceedings, he handed over all his rights to
the Aumale inheritance to the king, receiving land worth £100 a year in
exchange. The whole affair reeks with suspicion, and it seems most
likely that there was collusion between the crown and John de Eshton
from a very early stage in the proceedings. £100 a year was a
remarkably small price to pay for a great inheritance, which included
Holderness, Skipton and Cockermouth.[53]

There were other land deals in Edward's early years on the throne
which form part of the same policy of trying to extend the territorial
strength of the crown. Even before he had returned to England, an
agreement was reached with John de Burgh whereby John effectively
made the king his heir, receiving in exchange the custody of the Tower
of London and Colchester castle. There followed complications when
de Burgh sold the manors of Banstead in Surrey and Saham in
Cambridgeshire without royal permission. The purchaser of Banstead,
William de Appletreefield, was bought out of his rights by the king in
1275 for 200 marks, and although de Burgh's son was allowed to inherit
some of his father's estates, the crown clearly benefited from a complex
affair, as also did Robert Burnell.[54] Queen Eleanor, as well as Edward,
was hungry for land. In about 1278 she acquired Leeds castle in Kent
from William Leyburn, whose father had obtained it ten years previously. William was heavily in debt to a Jewish moneylender, and
when the debt was acquired by the queen, she took Leeds in payment,
handing over 500 marks as compensation to its former owner.[55]

The reasons for Edward's desire to acquire more lands for the crown
were not set out in any contemporary texts. It has been suggested that
his acquisitions in the 1270s 'were almost certainly prompted by the

53   McFarlane, op. cit., 256–7; *Early Yorkshire Charters*, vii, ed. C.T. Clay (Yorks
Arch. Soc., 1947), 23–7, 228. The Lucy family maintained their claim to Skipton: see
Rot. Parl., i, 170, 191; *Select Cases in the Court of King's Bench, Edward I*, ed. G.O. Sayles, iii
(Selden Soc., 1939), 191–2.
54   *Liber de Antiquis Legibus*, 163; *CFR 1272–1307*, 7, 18, 36, 41, 46; *CPR 1272–81*, 41.
55   *KW*. ii. 695; *CCR 1272–9*, 221, 499; *CPR 1272–81*, 335.

prospective needs of his then rapidly growing family'.[56] He had in fact only one son living at this time, Alphonso, born in 1273, and there was certainly no immediate pressure on Edward to build up his territorial position for family reasons. Greed, rather than statesmanship, appears to be the most plausible explanation. Edward was reluctant to grant out his new acquisitions of land, so it was not in order to increase royal patronage that he took the steps he did. It is possible that he quite simply wanted to increase the wealth and power of the crown, and there was no realization on his part as to how limited a contribution the royal estates actually made to government finances. The methods he used did him little credit: he was devious and grasping.

In the early months of 1276 Edward must have felt that matters were going his way. Another of his concerns at Winchester at that time was the case of the rebellious Gascon, Gaston de Béarn, who was brought before the king by Roger Clifford, and placed in comfortable captivity prior to his appearance in parliament at Westminster. Eleanor de Montfort, the intended bride of Prince Llywelyn of Wales, was captured at sea along with her brother Amaury.[57] Little is known of the events of the parliament held at Westminster in May. A chronicle tradition erroneously had it that a tax of a fifteenth was granted, but this perhaps derived from a confused report of the discussions about the assessment and collection of the tax conceded in the previous year. Gaston de Béarn's case was considered, and there was doubtless much legal business to be attended to. The king extended his peace to all those who had fought against him in the civil wars of his father's reign, and ordered the maintenance of Magna Carta and the Charter of the Forest. Once again, Llywelyn refused to attend.[58]

In mid-June Edward attended a grand ceremony at Chichester, where the remains of St Richard, who had died in 1253, were translated to a new shrine. The king's travels that summer extended from Canterbury in the east to Bristol and Worcester in the west. By October he was back at Westminster for yet another parliament. There were continuing problems over the fifteenth granted in the previous year, and in November Ralph de Sandwich and Thomas de Normanville were appointed to hear complaints about the assessment and collection of it. A statute known as *De Bigamis* was drawn up. It took its title from a clause which put into effect a decision of the Council of Lyon concerning men who married twice. The statute also dealt with more important

[56] McFarlane, *Nobility of later Medieval England*, 264.
[57] *Ann. Winton*, 120–1. For Gaston de Béarn, see below, 300–301, and for Eleanor de Montfort, see below, 175.
[58] Cotton, 154; *Flores*, iii, 47; *Ann. Worcester*, 469.

questions regarding the land law.[59] Again there was the problem of Llywelyn of Wales' continued refusal to attend. On 17 November it was announced, in most formal fashion, that the king's tenants-in-chief were to appear, with all the military service that they owed, at Worcester, mustering at Midsummer 1277. From this time on, it was to be the coming war with the Welsh that was to dominate the government's activities, and, no doubt, the king's thoughts.

The initial years of Edward's rule in England had gone smoothly. The fact that he had been absent from the realm since 1270 may have been an advantage for him, making the transition from heir to the throne into king relatively easy. His subjects had perhaps forgotten his faults when he returned a hero from the crusade, and Edward was in a splendid position to make a fresh start. Such problems as his dispute with the earl of Gloucester, which had been so threatening in the late 1260s, could be easily forgotten. A great deal was achieved by Edward in a short time. This was partly thanks to the very competent way in which the country had been run during his absence, but the new vigour with which the problems of government were approached from 1274 to 1276 demonstrates the galvanizing effect of his return. Long-running disputes, notably that with Flanders, were swiftly resolved. Much was done to place the country's finances on a sound footing, with the grant of customs duties and negotiation of a tax of a fifteenth. The Italian company of the Riccardi provided royal finance with a flexibility that was badly needed. The massive inquiry that produced the Hundred Rolls may not have yielded the definitive information about the alienation of royal rights that the king wanted, but it did provide a great deal of valuable evidence, as well as demonstrating the fact that Edward had not discarded the reforming principles which had inspired him for a time as a young man. The promulgation of the first statute of Westminster showed that the new government was committed to a continuing process of reform.

Of course, not all the initiatives taken in this period had quite the results intended. Many new ideas were considered and tried, and some were discarded. Edward's territorial acquisitiveness was prompted to a considerable extent, it seems likely, by a desire to provide the crown with a sounder financial basis: the reorganization of the management of the royal demesnes under the three stewards is strongly suggestive. Yet if an increase in revenue was hoped for, the king must have been sadly disappointed, and the policy was fairly quickly abandoned. These were successful years, however. There must have been fears that the old rivalries of the civil war period would recur, particularly since Simon de

---

[59] *Chron. Bury St Edmunds*, 62; *Ann. Worcester*, 471; *Statutes of the Realm*, i, 42–3; *CPR 1272–81*, 183.

Montfort's sons were actively intriguing with the Welsh prince Llywelyn, but they found no support in England.[60] With his frequent parliaments, Edward had succeeded in winning the co-operation of his subjects in a most impressive fashion.

[60] Fears of a recurrence of the troubles of the 1260s lingered surprisingly long: *CWR*, 218, shows that as late as 1282 there were fears that the king's enemies might once again seize the Isle of Ely, taking advantage of his absence on campaign in Wales.

Chapter 5

THE KING AND HIS FAMILY

In his old age Jean de Joinville wrote a memoir of his master, Louis IX of France, which in its anecdotal style gives a splendid picture of a king much admired by Edward I. It is very unfortunate that Jean's brother Geoffrey, who served Edward long and loyally, did not feel inspired to follow his brother's example. There is no really personal account of Edward I. A stern, perhaps a rather distant figure, he commanded much admiration, but not the affection or concern which might have led someone to write about him in intimate terms. The descriptions provided by the Dominican friar, Thomas Trivet, and by John of London, are too conventional in their eulogistic phraseology to be very helpful: the latter's work is little more than a modification of Peter of Blois's account of Henry II. Royal household accounts, however, do provide evidence of the king's tastes and habits, and a few letters help to illuminate his personality.

Edward was an impressive man in physical terms. He stood head and shoulders above ordinary men. Long arms gave him an advantage as a swordsman, long thighs one as a horseman. In youth his curly hair was blond; in maturity it darkened, and in old age it turned white. The regularity of his features was marred by a drooping left eyelid, an inheritance from his father. His speech, despite a lisp, was said to be persuasive, though few remarks by him were recorded. Even in old age Edward retained his physical presence: he did not develop a stoop, and his eyesight remained keen. He could still readily mount a horse. Such a man did not need to emphasize his royal status by means of ostentatious dress: he apparently eschewed luxurious purple, or lavishly dyed cloth, in favour of ordinary clothes. Entries in the household accounts such as that recording the manufacture of saddles decorated with gold, silver and pearls are rare, and there was certainly none of the extravagant display which Edward III was greatly to enjoy.[1]

Edward I has to be set in the context of the chivalric society of his

---

[1] *Nicholai Triveti Annales*, 281–3; Rishanger, 76–7; 'Commendatio Lamentabilis in Transitu Magni Regis Edwardi', in *Chronicles of the Reigns of Edward I and Edward II*, ed. W. Stubbs (Rolls ser., 1882–3), ii, 4–6; *Records of the Wardrobe and Household 1285–1286*, 44.

day. The ideals of that society were those of honour, *largesse*, loyalty and courage. A late-thirteenth-century romance explained that 'a knight must be hardy, courageous, generous, loyal, and of fair speech; ferocious to his foe, frank and debonair to his friend'.[2] Chivalric culture was a complex blend of different traditions, Christian, Germanic and Celtic, incapable of simple analysis, and often representing an ideal towards which men might strive, rather than reflecting the reality of their conduct. As a young man Edward threw himself into the chivalric world with enthusiasm, taking part in many tournaments, and with his crusade participating in the greatest chivalric adventure of all. Honour was certainly important to him. In the most critical year of the reign, 1297, he stressed that in undertaking an expedition to Flanders he was acting 'for the honour and common profit of his realm'. He feared dishonour if he failed to keep the terms of the treaty he had made with the German king: 'in this affair our honour or our dishonour is at stake, as is that of all who love us.'[3] Of course, Edward's enemies and opponents did not consider him to be an honourable man. There were his changes of side in the 1260s, and in the last years of his reign there were well-justified suspicions that he had little intention of keeping the promises he made in the resolution of the crisis of 1297. Historians have, equally understandably, criticized some of his actions during the Scottish wars. The imprisonment of the countess of Buchan and Mary Bruce in apparently inhuman conditions, caged at Berwick and Roxburgh, may not appear the action of an honourable man, but Edward's own subjects apparently did not condemn him for it, and it would be quite wrong to assume that honour was not a virtue which Edward valued.[4]

Courage was most certainly displayed by Edward on many occasions, though sometimes it might be interpreted as foolhardiness. He showed his bravery in the tournament at Châlons on his way home from crusade. In Flanders in 1297, although there was no fighting with the French, Edward courageously rode full tilt at a chain which his ostensible allies, the Flemings, had stretched across a street in Ghent. At the siege of Stirling, in 1304, he rode close in to the walls of the castle, inspiring his troops, but also exposing himself to enemy fire. He was neither hurt nor panicked when a crossbow bolt lodged in his saddle, or when his horse was felled when a stone from a siege engine landed just by it.[5] In most of his campaigning Edward was not involved in direct

[2] Cited by M.H. Keen, *Chivalry* (New Haven and London, 1984), 80.
[3] *Documents illustrating the Crisis of 1297–8 in England* ed. M.C. Prestwich (Camden Soc., 4th ser., xxiv, 1980), 125, 163.
[4] Above, 27–37, below, 508–9, 517–18.
[5] *Chron. Bury St Edmunds*, 146–7; *Flores*, iii, 317–18.

combat with his enemies, but that was more through their choice than his. The strange story of his cowardice at Kenilworth in 1265 is one which can safely be discarded: Edward was certainly a man of courage.[6]

Largesse, or generosity, was a dangerous virtue for a king to possess in too great a measure. Household accounts provide attractive examples of Edward's generosity in small matters. There was the poor English scholar in Gascony, singing in a church, and given a pound, the little Welsh boy given 21d to buy himself a coat, or the poverty-stricken Welshman who showed the king the way back to his lodging, and earned a shilling.[7] On a larger scale, Edward's patronage was limited. The chronicler Langtoft was in no doubt that the king's *largesse* was inadequate. The problems he had in putting down rebellion in Wales, the absence of earls on the campaign in Flanders in 1297, the difficulties faced in Scotland: these were all attributed by Langtoft to Edward's lack of generosity towards the earls and other great men.[8] Of course, Edward did not attempt to try to rule England without exercising patronage, and the historian can point to such acts as the effective reconstruction of the Welsh Marches by means of major grants to magnates at the time of the second Welsh war.[9] Yet it may be that Edward had a certain distaste for the business of patronage. In the case of one chancery clerk in search of a benefice, instructions went out that he was to be given what he wanted, but that the king was not to be approached any more on the matter.[10]

Loyalty is not an easy quality to assess in the case of a king: Edward expected his subjects to be loyal to him, rather than the other way round. Yet he was consistently loyal to his close circle of friends, with few exceptions. He backed his chancellor, Robert Burnell, and was not moved by arguments that his personal acquisitiveness and dubious morals made him unsuitable for high church office. In the later years of the reign he lent equally full support to Walter Langton, the treasurer, in face of extremely unsavoury rumours. It is no surprise that Edward gave, and received, full loyalty from the Savoyard knight Otto de Grandson, a man of impeccable character. Another Savoyard, Jean de Grailly, did earn the king's displeasure, but there were good reasons, it seems, for this. The same was true of Anthony Bek, bishop of Durham,

---

[6] Above, 50.

[7] *Records of the Wardrobe and Household 1286–1289*, ed. B.F. and C.R. Byerley (1986), 90; A.J. Taylor, 'Royal Alms and Oblations in the Later Thirteenth Century', *Tribute to an Antiquary: essays presented to Marc Fitch*, ed. F.G. Emmison and R. Stephens (1976), 124.

[8] Langtoft, ii, 216, 296, 326, 328.

[9] Below, 204–5.

[10] *CCR 1302–7*, 352.

a friend and companion of long standing, but whose direct challenge to royal authority, in the course of his dispute with Durham Cathedral Priory in the last years of the reign, was more than loyalty could take.[11]

Edward had a violent temper, just as many of his Angevin ancestors had. Trivet told a story of his anger when one of his hunting companions failed to control a falcon properly: the king forced his horse rashly across the river, and chased the man with drawn sword, but checked himself when he humbly submitted. On the occasion of his daughter Margaret's wedding he assaulted a squire with a stick, for no known reason, and later paid him the considerable sum of £13 6s 8d in compensation. A well-known entry in an account book records the cost of repairing his daughter Elizabeth's coronet in 1297, after Edward had hurled it into the fire. Trivet has a story of how in the same year the king was almost thrown from his horse at Winchelsea, when the noise of a windmill made the animal bolt. This almost certainly explains why he sold a horse to Robert de Bures for 50 marks, buying one in exchange valued at 100 marks: surely a transaction decided in a fit of temper.[12]

The accounts provide some glimpses of a pleasanter side to Edward's character. The instance of the king being caught in bed on Easter Monday by the queen's ladies-in-waiting, and of his paying a ransom to them, testifies to a jocularity in court life. This is also reflected by the bet which Edward had with his laundress, Matilda de Waltham, in which she won a warhorse, subsequently bought back by the king.[13] There are indications of his personal tastes. A letter reported his enjoyment of some whalemeat sent to him, and there are several references to the goats and cows kept specifically to provide him with dairy products in the later years of the reign. An inventory of spices includes a mention of a large box of Indian preserved ginger kept for the king's own use. References to fruit – apples, pears, pomegranates, figs, raisins and such like – bought by the royal fruiterer, Nicholas of Gotham, probably reflect Edward's personal likes.[14]

Trivet's description of Edward suggests that he was a man of unsophisticated piety.[15] A lucky escape when a stone fell from the vaulted

---

[11] Below, 234, 305, 541–6, 549–50.

[12] *Nicholai Triveti Annales*, 281–3, 359; C 47/4/5, f.47v.; BL Add. MS 7965, ff.15v, 18. It has been suggested by Adelaide Bennet, 'The Windmill Psalter: the historiated letter E of Psalm One', *Journal of the Warburg and Courtauld Institutes*, xliii (1980), 65, that this illustration may refer to this incident, but this is unlikely.

[13] C 47/4/1, f.27v; *Records of Wardrobe and Household 1286–9*, 108; C 47/4/5, f.47v.

[14] *Documents 1297–8*, 64; BL Add. MS 7965, f.16v, *Liber Quotidianus*, 57, 81; BL Add. MS 8835, ff.7, 8, 18v; E 101/356/21; *Records of Wardrobe and Household 1285–6*, xxxiv.

[15] The question of Edward's piety is discussed more fully in my 'The Piety of Edward I', *England in the Thirteenth Century*, ed. W.M. Ormrod (Harlaxton, 1985), 120–8. For what follows see also Taylor, 'Royal Alms and Oblations', and the almonry account in *Liber Quotidianus*, 16–47.

ceiling on to the seat from which he had just moved, when playing
chess, was attributed by the king to the intervention of the Virgin Mary
and her shrine at Walsingham. The account of his refusal to enter the
gates of Oxford, for fear of incurring the wrath of St Frideswide, implies
a degree of credulity, and the only occasion when he displayed scepticism was when a man appeared claiming to have been cured of blindness
by Henry III. Archbishop Pecham on one occasion suggested that
Edward's declarations of allegiance to God and the church were not
adequately matched by his actions, but there is no suggestion that he
was anything other than conventionally religious in his attitudes.

The accounts of the king's almoners cast some light on Edward's
religious practices, although they cannot reveal his inner thoughts. The
first part of such accounts deals with the regular payments made for the
feeding of paupers. This was a well-established custom of the English
monarchy, but it is striking that the numbers rose from just over 200
paupers a week early in the reign to 666 a week by 1299. Henry III
had, it is true, claimed that it was his custom to feed 500 daily, but this
cannot be tested by documentary evidence. The figures for Edward I's
reign suggest a marked increase in royal generosity. In addition to these
regular allocations, there were special provisions made in honour of
individual saints days and festivals. Again, the numbers rose markedly,
from some 11,090 men receiving alms on church festivals in 1283–4 to
75,000 in 1296–7. In the week which began on Christmas Day 1299, no
less than 4,000 paupers were provided for. There were surprising
changes in the popularity of individual saints, which may well reflect
Edward's own changing views. In 1283–4 Christmas Day and St
Edward's day were the most favoured festivals, but by 1300 as much
was made of the various feasts of the Virgin as of Christmas. In
addition, a very large distribution of alms took place on the birthday of
the king's eldest son. An interesting indication of Edward's own
religious practices is provided by the grants of alms made when he
failed to attend chapel in the morning. This was so unusual in 1289 that
it prompted the largest single distribution of alms in the account, but as
the king aged, so he found attendance more difficult, and in 1305–6 he
did not go to chapel on at least twenty-two days.

The almonry accounts reveal much more than the payments to
paupers. Oblations made by the king and his family reveal a special
concern for the cult of Thomas Becket: in 1285 Edward made not only
the customary offerings at Canterbury, but also presented four elaborate statuettes in gold set with jewels, at a cost of £347. Substantial
offerings were made at Becket's shrine in 1297 and 1300. On the latter
occasion gold florins were placed on the altar, in the name of 'the foetus
then existing in the queen's belly'. Payments to friars occur with great
regularity, though Edward showed no particular preference for any one

order, unlike Queen Eleanor, a noted patron of the Dominicans. The accounts suggest that Edward was not nationalistic in his devotional habits. He had a chapel built in honour of St Louis in 1301, and in 1305–6 he sent clerks to make offerings at the shrines of St Denis in Paris, the Three Kings at Cologne, and the pilgrimage shrine at Santiago de Compostella. The accounts also record minor acts of kindness, such as the grant of 12s to a man whose horse was blown off the bridge over the Medway at Rochester, payments to Englishmen imprisoned in France, and contributions towards the medical expenses of members of the royal household wounded in the wars.

There is much evidence of Edward's practice of touching for the king's evil. This reputed power to heal victims of scrofula was enjoyed only by the kings of England and France, and there is no solid documentary evidence of it until the reigns of Edward I and Philip IV: it has been plausibly argued that it was only established on a regular basis in France after St Louis's return from crusade in 1254, and that Henry III then copied him. The practice was well-established by the start of Edward I's reign, for the earliest details, dating from 1276–7, show that at least 627 invalids were touched, or blessed, by the king. The numbers rose to 1,736 in 1289–90 – inflated because Edward had been out of the realm since 1286 – stood at almost 1,000 in 1299–1300, and went as high as 2,000 in 1305–6. The figures for later reigns are unfortunately not as good, but Edward I probably touched the sick on a greater scale than any other English monarch, showing a remarkable devotion to what cannot have been a particularly pleasant task.[16]

It was characteristic of Edward that the abbey he founded at Vale Royal in Cheshire should have had the largest church of any Cistercian house in England. It is also characteristic of the ambiguities in his career that he should have suddenly and inexplicably dissociated himself from the project, leaving the abbey in a sadly incomplete state. Edward showed no great haste to fulfil the vow to found a monastery, which he made in 1262 or 1263. The first foundation charter was issued in 1270, significantly when Edward was preparing for his crusade. Four years later monks from Dore were recruited for the new house, which was initially planned to be at Darnhall. Dore was selected as some of the brethren had shown kindness to Edward during his captivity after the battle of Lewes. It was in August 1277 that the grand foundation ceremony took place at Vale Royal, attended by four earls and other magnates. This was in part a propaganda move, intended to boost

[16] For this question of the king's curative powers, see M. Bloch, *Les Rois Thaumaturges* (Paris, 1924), and the recent discussion by F. Barlow, 'The King's Evil', *EHR*, xcv (1980), 3–27. I have given fuller figures than those provided by Bloch in my 'The Piety of Edward I', 125.

morale for the coming fighting against the Welsh. It was initially
intended to pay for the building works out of the revenues of Cheshire,
but this proved impracticable. In 1283 the substantial sum of £1,000 a
year was allocated to the abbey, but inevitably payment was not made
in full, and although later tradition had it that Edward paid no less than
£32,000 towards the building costs, he in fact paid out less than a third
of that sum.[17]

In 1290 it was announced that 'the king has ceased to concern
himself with the works of that church, and henceforth will have nothing
more to do with them'. One possibility is that financial peculation had
been discovered; another that the death of Queen Eleanor caused the
king's change of heart. By the late 1290s there were signs of a very
limited return to favour for the abbey: a grant of one tun of wine a year
had not been implemented between 1291 and 1297, but in 1298 orders
went out for the arrears to be made up. Unfortunately for the monks,
Edward had not endowed the house generously with lands, and its
revenues were never adequate for its needs. The building works were
never finished, and in 1360 much of the church was blown down in a
gale.[18]

Edward's piety was not such as to make him subservient to the
church and the clergy. The reverse was the case: his faith gave him a
conviction that he was right, and provided him with the confidence to
challenge prelates such as Archbishop Winchelsey. There are no indications that he took any interest in doctrinal matters, or that he was
much concerned with the spiritual qualities of the clergy. Edward was
not pious in the way that his father Henry III had been, and there was
not the solid religious conviction behind his kingship that can be sensed
in the case of Henry V. Yet he wore a piece of the Holy Cross round his
neck when going into battle, and although he had no reforming zeal,
there was never any question of his being thought to be irreligious, as
William Rufus had been considered to be.[19]

The chronicle descriptions of Edward suggest chess-playing and
hunting as his leisure pursuits. Household accounts confirm that he
played chess, for there are records of his financial losses at the game in
1278, and of the gift of a board to him. The losses do not occur in later
accounts – perhaps his game improved, or possibly no one dared to beat
him – but his continued interest is shown by an inventory of his
possessions from 1300, which includes one ebony chess set, and one of

[17] *The Ledger Book of Vale Royal Abbey*, ed. J. Brownbill (Lancashire and Cheshire
Record Soc., lxviii, 1914), vii–viii, 2–5; *KW*, i, 248–53; *Victoria County History, A History
of the County of Cheshire*, ed. B.E. Harris, iii (1980), 156–9.
[18] *KW*, i, 252, 256; *CCR 1296–1302*, 180.
[19] The relic of the Holy Cross was acquired in the Holy Land by Edward, who later
presented it to Vale Royal Abbey: *Ledger Book of Vale Royal Abbey*, 161–2.

crystal and jasper. His second queen, Margaret of France, had two splendid sets worth £40 each. Edward does not, however, have a major place in the history of chess, unlike his brother-in-law Alphonso of Castile, who commissioned an important manual about the game. Edward also played at 'tables', some kind of board game, and at dice, but there is no evidence that he gambled on any scale.[20]

Trivet claimed that stag-hunting was Edward's favourite sport, and that he preferred to go for the kill with his sword rather than relying on a hunting spear.[21] The documents, however, suggest that the king's real love was falconry. He once explained in a letter to Charles of Salerno that he had no expertise as far as greyhounds were concerned, but there is a considerable amount of surviving correspondence dealing with falcons and hawks.[22] There was a large establishment to look after the royal birds, of which the most prized were the gerfalcons. A splendid mews was built at Charing Cross, featuring a garden with a lead bath for the birds, supplied with running water from a grand fountain with four outlet spouts shaped like leopard's heads, and a statuette of a falcon in the middle.[23] Other birds were kept in a mews at Bicknor in Kent, the home of the chief falconer John de Bicknor, while yet more were placed in the charge of men who held their land by the service of looking after royal falcons. The birds were clearly pampered: as a rule, one falconer or 'ostringer' (the latter for the hawks) was in charge of a single bird. There are, however, no orders from Edward I similar to that from King John, who commanded that his favourite gerfalcon, Gibbon, should have plump goats and good hens to eat, with hare once a week.[24]

Some of Edward's falcons and hawks were given to him as presents. Valuable gerfalcons were sent by the king of Norway in the earlier part of the reign, while the last account book, for 1305–6, shows that Aymer de Valence, William de Braose, Hugh de St Philibert, John of Berwick, and the prince of Wales all gave birds to the king. The names of certain birds suggest that they were presents: Clynton, Strathbogie, Droxford and d'Engayne. Others had names such as Skardebek, Parson, Durham and Blanchepoune. Some birds were bought: accounts for

---

[20] C 47/4/1, ff.7, 8, 9, 16; *Liber Quotidianus*, 323, 350–1; BL Add. MS 7966a, attached schedule; D. Hooper and K. Whyld, *The Oxford Companion to Chess* (Oxford, 1984), 9.

[21] *Nicholai Triveti Annales*, 282. Powicke, *Henry III and the Lord Edward*, ii, 689, has it that Edward 'made no use of the trap of buckstall as a hunter', but this is based on a mistranslation of the Latin *venabulum*, a hunting spear. I am grateful to Professor E.L.G. Stones for pointing this out to me.

[22] *Foedera*, I. ii, 568.

[23] *KW*. i, 559–61.

[24] *Documents 1297–8*, 52, 55; A.L. Poole, *Obligations of Society in the XII and XIII Centuries* (Oxford, 1946), 68; *Records of Wardrobe and Household*, ed. Byerley, xxxix.

1303–4 show that a goshawk and two gerfalcons were purchased, the latter from two Baltic traders.[25] A letter from the king to his falconer Robert Bavent, written near the end of the reign, is illuminating:

> You ask our wishes about the gerfalcon which Sir Philip Kyme wants to give us. We are sending you the letter which we have written to Philip, thanking him for the gerfalcon, and asking if he would present it to us. So, we order you to exercise it with a lure when you receive it on our behalf, and train it for taking herons and cranes, as we have ordered you to do with the other gerfalcons in your keeping. We are sending our huntsman Perkin to help you. And as for buying goshawks or gerfalcons for our use at Boston, which you ask about, you must know that we do not want you to take any of them, unless they are well tried, and the best and most beautiful of any. And if by chance you do find one or two such gerfalcons, tried and better and more beautiful than any others, take them for our use, and let us know quickly what they are, and how expensive, so that we can let you know about it.[26]

In another letter, Edward told Bavent that he had sufficient gerfalcons and falcons, but that he could purchase a goshawk, even if it had broken feathers, provided that it was extremely large and powerful.[27] As in most things, Edward wanted the biggest and best for himself, but his criteria was not, it seems, the sophisticated ones advocated by the emperor Frederick II, who in his book on falconry set out in great detail the precise colouration and build to look for in a bird. Another of Edward's letters to Bavent asked him to train a 'lanner' falcon (a Mediterranean species) to fly after heron with two other birds, as the king had been advised that this was a good method. This was a technique that Frederick II had emphatically not approved in the case of heron, though he considered it satisfactory for cranes. The use of the noise of drums to put up waterfowl was advocated by Frederick, and was certainly employed by Edward and his falconers.[28] Where Edward differed most from the emperor, who had always advocated scientific techniques, was in the means employed to cure his birds when they were ill. On one occasion he had a wax image made of an ailing falcon, which was then presented before the altar of Thomas Becket at

[25] BL. Add. MS 8835, f.69; E 101/369/11. f.157 ff. This account book contains falconry and hunting accounts from 1298 to 1306.

[26] 'Lettres du roi Edouard I à Robert de Bavent, King's Yeoman, sur des questions de venerie', ed. F.J. Tanquerey, *Bull. John Rylands Library*, xxiii (1939), 491–2.

[27] Ibid., 499.

[28] Ibid., 493, 497; BL Add. MS 8835, f.69; *The Art of Falconry, being the De Arte Venandi cum Avibus of Frederick II of Hohenstaufen*, ed. C.A. Wood and F.M. Fyfe (Stanford, 1943), 298, 342. Arabic manuals provide even more detailed accounts of how to judge birds: see *Moamin et Ghatif, traites de fauconnerie et de chiens de chasse*, ed. H. Tjerneld (Stockholm, 1945), 103–4, 106–8.

Canterbury, in the hope of obtaining a cure. Another curious custom was that of bending pennies over the head of the sick bird; these were then sent as offerings to various shrines.[29] There is little justification for arguing that Edward I should have a place alongside Frederick II in the history of falconry. In comparison to the emperor, Edward was little more than an enthusiastic amateur.[30]

The wardrobe accounts do not reveal much about the king's personal hunting exploits, for by their very nature they provide details about the activities of the royal huntsmen when they were away from court, not when they were present. This is just as true of stag and fox hunting as it is of falconry. Only a mention of the purchase of bows and arrows for the king's use suggests that he did not always choose to bring down game at close quarters, as Trivet suggested.[31] Hunting with hounds was more utilitarian than falconry, for the king's huntsmen made an appreciable contribution towards providing the household with food. In 1304, for example, one huntsman, John of Fulham, took eighty deer in Burstwick, which were then salted down to await the king's return from Scotland, and the sheriff of Lincolnshire had to arrange for twenty-four stags, or more probably the venison from them, to be taken to Boston and then shipped to Berwick for the king's table.[32] There are no letters to the keepers of the king's hounds which can be compared with those to Thomas Bavent, and it is reasonable to conclude that while Edward must have enjoyed the exhilaration of the chase, he obtained the most pleasure from falconry.

Edward was, inevitably for a man in his position, a patron of minstrels and heralds, the main publicists of chivalric culture. In the mid 1280s he employed one King Herald, four minstrels and two trumpeters, and by the end of the decade there were ten such men in his household. At Christmas 1288 no fewer than 125 minstrels performed for Edward.[33] Accounts show that minstrels attached to various noble households sometimes played before the king, and that there were also entertainments presented by tumblers and acrobats, such as the aptly named Matilda Makejoy. The greatest occasion was when the king's eldest son was knighted, and hundreds of minstrels attended, in 1306. Yet the scale of Edward's employment of these professional entertainers should not be exaggerated. The account book for 1299–1300 has scant reference to minstrels, merely mentioning payment to one retained by the queen, and to two who performed before Prince

---

[29] A.J. Taylor, 'Edward I and the Shrine of St Thomas of Canterbury', *Journal of the British Archaeological Association*, cxxxii (1979), 26; BL Add. MS 7965, f.115v.
[30] The comparison is suggested by Powicke, *Henry III and the Lord Edward*, ii, 687n.
[31] E 101/351/30. 30 April; above, 115.
[32] BL Add. MS 8835, ff.69v, 70.
[33] *Records of Wardrobe and Household 1285–6*, 167; ibid. 1286–9, 85; E 101/352/24.

Edward.[34] Edward obviously found some solace in music, for when he underwent a blood-letting operation in 1297, a harpist was employed to take his mind off the pain.[35] There is no evidence, however, to suggest that there was anything out of the ordinary in his tastes in entertainment.

To judge by the scanty surviving evidence, Edward did not have a great enthusiasm for literature. When he was in Sicily, Rustichello of Pisa borrowed a book or books of Arthurian romance from him, and this served as the basis for Rustichello's *Meliadus*. The epilogue suggests that the work was written at Edward's express command, but there is no other evidence of his exercise of literary patronage. By 1300, the only work of romance listed by the clerks of the wardrobe as belonging to the king was one with the opening line *Cristiens se voet entremettre*.[36] In one letter Edward employed a literary quotation: it occurs when a coarse proverb about canine excrement was changed to 'Quant la guerre fu finee, si trest Audegier sespee' (Once the war was over, Audegier drew his sword), a reference to the archetypal cowardly knight of thirteenth-century French literature.[37] It could even be that this was the work of a clerk, bowdlerizing the king's initial words. Edward was no great patron of intellectual learning. In 1277 he did pay £1 to a poor scholar, who was off to study in Paris, and he paid for the nephews of one of his Gascon officials, Stephen Lafitte, to study at Oxford, along with one of their compatriots, Jean de Bernadon. Such instances are rare, however, and certainly should not be read as implying any notable enthusiasm on the king's part for the promotion of scholarly education.[38]

Edward's architectural and artistic patronage was more noteworthy than his literary, though unfortunately there is none of the detailed evidence of the king's own instructions to his builders and painters that survives for Henry III's reign. The most notable buildings for which Edward was responsible were, of course, his magnificent castles in Wales, which were in practice the achievement of the Savoyard master mason, James of St George.[39] The Eleanor Crosses, constructed in

[34] Bullock-Davies, *Menestrallorum Multitudo*, provides a full discussion of the minstrels at Edward's court. For 1299–1300, see *Liber Quotidianus*, 162–3.

[35] BL Add. MS 7965, f.54v.

[36] M. Vale, *Edward III and Chivalry* (1982), 19–20. *Liber Quotidianus*, 349. This is identified by M.A.E. Green, *Lives of the Princesses of England* (1850), ii, 284, as a work dealing with the life of William the Conqueror.

[37] P. Chaplais, 'Some Private Letters of Edward I', *EHR*, lxxvii (1962), 79–80.

[38] E 101/350/24; E 101/352/21 (30 Nov.). I am grateful to Dr A.J. Taylor for drawing my attention to these references. For Stephen Lafitte's nephews, see also C 47/4/4, ff.38, 41, 43.

[39] Below, 208–9.

memory of Edward's first queen by masons such as Richard of Crun-
dale and John of Battle, are important in architectural history, as is St
Stephen's Chapel, Westminster, on which work began in 1292. Edward
continued his father's patronage of the painter Walter of Durham, and
on the king's return from Gascony in 1289 a new chamber at Westminster, painted green, was decorated with a Christ in Majesty and figures
of the four evangelists by Walter. It is highly probable that between
1292 and 1297 very extensive additions were made to the pictoral
scheme in the Painted Chamber in the royal palace at Westminster.
These consisted of a series of paintings of Old Testament scenes, the
most important showing the career of Judas Maccabeus. The cycle was
a unique one, and had the chamber not been destroyed by fire in 1834,
these pictures would probably rank as one of the most important of
English artistic achievements in the middle ages. The choice of Judas
Maccabeus as a subject is very interesting, for by the late thirteenth
century he was regarded as one of the great chivalric heroes, along with
such figures as King Arthur and Charlemagne. This was a natural
choice for a warlike king to make, though it has to be admitted that
there is little other evidence to demonstrate Edward's interest in the
book of Maccabees.[40]

It is sometimes suggested that there was a clearly identifiable 'court
style' in Edward I's day, for which the king himself was ultimately
responsible, and which had very considerable influence. The question
is a difficult one, but the products of Edward's patronage were not so
distinct from other works, or so obviously in advance of developments
elsewhere, as to support such a hypothesis. Nor is there such uniformity
of style between, for example, the Alphonso psalter, made for Edward's
eldest son, the fine effigies on the tombs of Henry III and Eleanor of
Castile, the work of the goldsmith William Torel, and the pictures in
the Painted Chamber, as would justify the concept of a single court
school. Edward was eclectic in his artistic tastes, but what can be said is
that in patronizing men such as Walter of Durham and William Torel,
he was employing artists of the very highest calibre.[41]

[40] KW, i, 207, 226–7, 483–5, 498–9, 505; P. Binski, *The Painted Chamber at Westminster*
(1986), is responsible for the suggestion that much of the work in the Painted Chamber
dates from the 1290s. Although the style of dress and armour shown in the pictures (of
which copies were made in the early nineteenth century) is outmoded for such a date,
the architectural detailing in particular fits the 1290s much better than the 1260s, the
period to which they were previously assigned by historians. The subject matter, too,
fits Edward I's reign much better than Henry III's. It should be noted that some
funeral orations for Edward I made use of texts from the book of Maccabees: see below,
558. M.H. Keen, *Chivalry* (1984), 119–21, discusses Judas Maccabeus.
[41] P. Brieger, *English Art 1216–1307* (Oxford, 1957), 200–26, discusses 'the court
school under Edward I', but see the wise comments of Binski, *Painted Chamber*, 108–11,

Edward has been seen by some historians as a great enthusiast for the Arthurian past.[42] His connection with Rustichello of Pisa suggests this, and stronger evidence is provided by the events recorded when the king and queen visited Glastonbury, in the aftermath of the first Welsh war, in 1278. The tomb of Arthur and Guinevere, or what was thought to be their tomb, was opened, and two coffins found, with images of the legendary king and queen on them. The remains were formally re-buried in front of the great altar, in a ceremony like that of the translation of a saint's body. The tomb had first been 'discovered' in 1190, in what was probably an ingenious and successful attempt to develop the lucrative pilgrim traffic to the abbey, but Edward was the first king to take an interest in it, though it is not clear what his purpose was.[43] There was no overt connexion made between the exhumation of the most famous British king, and the recent campaign in Wales, nor was the ceremony accompanied by a tournament or other chivalric activity. Edward does not seem to have tried to develop an Arthurian cult of kingship in the way that his father had developed a cult of Edward the Confessor.

Edward's foundation of Caernarfon castle in 1283 certainly referred back to the mythical past, though not to a specifically Arthurian one. There was a Welsh legend in the tales known as the *Mabinogion* of Maxen Wledig or Magnus Maximus, allegedly the father of Constantine, who had a dream of a beautiful maiden dwelling in a great castle, with multi-coloured towers, at the mouth of a river. His envoys found the castle, and he married the maiden. Edward's castle made a reality of the legend, with its dark coloured bands in the masonry, and its polygonal towers echoing the walls of Constantine's city of Constantinople. Edward was clearly fascinated by the legendary British past, and the great castle of Caernarfon betrays an unexpected romantic aspect of his character. The presentation to him by the Welsh of what was known as Arthur's crown, was well calculated to appeal to him.[44]

In 1284 Edward celebrated his conquest of Wales by holding a Round Table at Nefyn, in the Lleyn peninsula, an act which has been seized on as further evidence of his Arthurian interests. He also held a Round Table at Falkirk in Scotland in 1302. It is far from clear what took place at such gatherings: there is no English evidence that scenes from Arthurian romances were acted out, as was done at Acre in 1285

---

who points out, *inter alia*, that 'we are hardly confronted by the development of a single coherent court idiom, let alone evidence for a single workshop, in this period'.

[42] Notably R.S. Loomis, 'Edward I, Arthurian Enthusiast', *Speculum*, xxviii (1953), 114–27.

[43] *Historia de Rebus Gestis Glastoniensibus*, ed. T. Hearne (1727), quoted by E.K. Chambers, *Arthur of Britain* (1927), 280–1.

[44] *KW*, i, 370; *Ann. Waverley*, 401.

under the patronage of Henry II of Cyprus. Edward's Round Tables
may have involved no more than jousting with blunted weapons, and
some feasting. That in 1284 certainly had something of the character of
a tournament, with one side captained by Edward's friend the earl of
Lincoln, and the other by the earl of Ulster.[45] The great chivalric
occasion of the knighting of the king's eldest son in 1306 does not
appear to have had Arthurian overtones. The high point of the ceremony was the swearing of oaths at a splendid banquet. This was done
at the point when a magnificent device, featuring two gilded swans, was
brought in by a host of minstrels: whether the swans were real, or were
artificial confections, is not clear. Equally unclear is the symbolism
involved. There may have been a link with northern French practices:
poems record vows made there to a peacock and to a sparrow-hawk,
but the choice of swans remains a mystery. The chronicler Pierre
Langtoft commented that no such festivities had been seen since
Arthur's feast at Caerleon, but that does not prove any conscious
imitation on Edward's part of the legendary British ruler.[46] The one
description of an Edwardian feast in Arthurian terms is that given by a
Brabançon chronicler of a royal wedding, complete with Round Table
and acted interludes, which included the appearance of a squire
dressed as the Loathly Damzel. The chronicle is, unfortunately, unreliable in the extreme: the description of Edward's conquest of
Wales is almost wholly fictional, culminating as it does with the king's
descent into a cave containing King Arthur's bones. It cannot be taken
seriously – although some historians have done so – and is best treated
as evidence not of Edward's attitudes, but of the way in which
foreigners viewed him.[47]

The Arthurian myth was undoubtedly of interest to Edward, but it
was certainly not a dominating influence. It could be of use on occasion,
as when he sent a letter to the pope in 1301 justifying English actions in
Scotland. In the historical argument Arthur featured: he had conquered Scotland and installed a subject king there, who did service at a
court held at Caerleon. But this was merely one of a massive list of
precedents cited by the clerks who drafted this letter, and it would be
wrong to make too much of it.[48] Stories of King Arthur, along with tales

---

[45] *Ann. Waverley*, 402; *Ann. Dunstable*, 313; *Flores*, iii, 62; *Annales Cestriensis*, ed. R.C.
Christie (Lancs. and Cheshire Record Soc., xiv, 1886), 114; N. Denholm-Young, 'The
Tournament in the Thirteenth Century', *Studies in Medieval History presented to F.M.
Powicke*, 353–5; Hill, *History of Cyprus*, ii, 181.

[46] Bullock-Davies, *Menestrallorum Multitudo*, xxvii–xxxviii; *Langtoft*, ii, 368.

[47] Lodwijk van Velthem, *Voortzetting van den Spiegel Historiael* (1248–1311), ed. H.
Van der Linden and W. de Vreese (Brussels, 1906), i, 295–321. See also Vale, *Edward
III and Chivalry*, 14–15, 18, where this evidence is taken seriously.

[48] *Anglo-Scottish Relations 1174–1328*, ed. E.L.G. Stones (1965), 98.

of other chivalric heroes such as Judas Maccabeus (whose exploits were featured in the Painted Chamber at Westminster), were part of the common currency of the knightly culture of the day, in which Edward participated eagerly. Pierre Langtoft certainly described Edward in strongly Arthurian terms, at one moment claiming that the king had united Britain more effectively than Arthur, at another comparing him very unfavourably with the legendary figure.[49] What is much less clear is the extent to which Edward saw himself in Arthurian terms: it was probably no more than a conceit he toyed with occasionally.

Medieval chroniclers did not have the inquisitive concern for the family affairs of the monarchy that is a feature of the popular press of the present day. His family, however, was of immense importance to Edward I. His devotion to his first queen, Eleanor of Castile, has become something of a legend, and the evidence suggests that his mother, Eleanor of Provence, exercised an influence over him which should not be ignored. The need to provide for his many children meant that for a king such as Edward, family affairs became a matter of national politics and international diplomacy.

Edward's mother, Eleanor of Provence, was a strong-minded woman, who did not believe that she should retire gracefully from public affairs on the death of her husband.[50] She was a member of a remarkable family, with widespread connexions throughout Europe: the important link with Savoy came through her, and she and her sister Margaret, widow of Louis IX of France, consistently supported Savoyard interests. Her correspondence with her son shows that she felt it was her task to advise Edward on matters of foreign policy, as when in the late 1270s she told him that it would damage English interests should a planned marriage between Charles Martel, son of Charles of Salerno, and Clementia of Habsburg take place.[51]

Edward, understandably, seems not to have consulted his mother as much as she wished. Her letters to him were usually prefaced with a request that she should at least hear from him: 'Know, dear son, that we are in good health, after our fashion, but we will be much better when we hear good news from you', was how one such demand ran. When she wrote to Edward on behalf of Margaret Nevill, who had not seen her son for a long time, Eleanor pointedly laid great stress on the strong desire of any mother to see her son, and have the solace of his company. She could be humorous: a thank-you letter for two cranes

[49] Langtoft, ii, 266, 326.
[50] For an account of her career, see M. Biles, 'The Indomitable Belle: Eleanor of Provence', *Seven Studies in Medieval English History*, ed. Bowers, 113–31.
[51] SC 1/16, no. 180.

Edward sent her made much, in a rather laboured way, of the fact that she liked the bodies, but not the heads. She was concerned not merely for her son, the king, but also for her grandson, suggesting on one occasion that Edward of Caernarfon should not be taken north, as the climate would make him ill.[52] The queen mother was not, of course, present in Edward's household. She had her own entourage, and her own dower estates, and from 1276 resided at Amesbury, in the nunnery there. She took the veil herself in 1286, dying in 1291. Her influence over Edward is hard to assess, but he himself once wrote to Charles of Salerno that since the death of his father, he was more closely bound to Eleanor than to any other living person. She was an indomitable figure, from whom Edward probably inherited much of his own strength of character.

Edward was undoubtedly devoted to his first queen, Eleanor of Castile, yet hers is not a personality that stands out from the pages of the records or the chronicles. Eleanor was the daughter of Ferdinand III of Castile and Jeanne of Dammartin, and it seems that she valued her connections with France more than those with Castile. She did not bring a large number of kinsmen and compatriots to England in the way that her mother-in-law had done, but some of her French relations were given places in her household. She was probably only twelve at the time of her marriage, and her death in 1290 came when she was only forty-nine. Her main activity was the production of children, probably fifteen in all, but she did manage to share Edward's career to a remarkable extent, accompanying him on crusade, and going to Wales and Gascony with him.[53]

Eleanor was a cultured woman. She possessed a library of romances, presumably many of them of the Arthurian type. One at least was copied in France for her, and Girard of Amiens dedicated one of his Arthurian works to her. She employed a couple of scribes to write books, and a painter to illuminate them. In the last year of her life, she sent a messenger to Oxford with letters for a master there about one of her books. It is entirely in character that she should, as it seems likely, have commissioned a translation of Vegetius' work on the art of war for Edward while on crusade. She is also known to have persuaded no less a figure than Archbishop Pecham to write a brief scholarly work for her in French, described by his biographer as 'unfortunately rather a dull and uninspired little treatise'. Eleanor was fond of tapestries, and even engaged in weaving them herself. She was probably not as fond of chess and similar games as her husband, though there is a reference to her

---

[52] SC 1/16, nos 151, 152, 170, 172.
[53] Eleanor's career is discussed by J.C. Parsons, *The Court and Household of Eleanor of Castile in 1290* (Toronto, 1977).

playing the game of Four Kings, probably a four-handed variant of chess. A touching note in the accounts records that her clerks were sent to buy fruit from a Spanish ship which came to Portsmouth – even late in life she missed the figs, pomegranates, oranges and lemons of her childhood.[54]

There is a discordant element in Eleanor's career, concerning the running of her estates. Investigations after her death into the activities of her estate managers produced an unattractive picture of high-handed and extortionate behaviour. One charge, which was upheld, was that one of Eleanor's reeves had seized a house from its owners, falsely procuring their imprisonment, and dumping their baby in its cradle in the middle of the road. Very many years later, the men of Havering recalled the way in which the queen had arbitrarily limited local hunting rights by extending her warren. A jury of twelve leading tenants resisted her claims, only to suffer imprisonment for three days, after which they conceded defeat.

One of the queen's stewards was Hugh Cressingham, fat and unpopular, a man with no reputation for probity. Geoffrey of Aspale, keeper of her wardrobe for a period, was a notorious pluralist, whose nephew married Cressingham's daughter. Geoffrey, though his official career suggests that he was simply another of the efficient yet grasping clerks who flourished in the royal households of the later thirteenth century, was also a scholar of some reputation, an authority on Aristotle's scientific works.[55] In employing harsh officials and building up her estates Eleanor was arguably doing no more than other land-lords. Unlike the king, she was reliant upon her landed income, and although the accounts which survive from the end of her life seem to show that she was well off, it is very possible that it was the inadequate scale of her assignment of lands, to a value of £4,500 a year, which necessitated her adoption of unpopular policies. For unpopular they certainly were. A brief rhyme given in some versions of Guisborough's chronicle includes the couplet:

> The king he wants to get our gold
> The queen would like our lands to hold.[56]

---

[54] Ibid., 12–3; D. Douie, *Archbishop Pecham* (Oxford, 1952), 52; E 101/352/27 provides the name of a further illuminator, Richard du Marche, and another scribe, Hugh of Ireland, to be added to those given by Parsons. For the translation of Vegetius, see L. Thorpe, 'Mastre Richard, a thirteenth-century translator of the "De Re Militari" of Vegetius', *Scriptorium*, vi (1952), 39–50.

[55] Tout, *Chapters in Medieval Administrative History*, v, 236–7, 271n.; Parson, *Court and Household of Eleanor of Castile*, 75n, 93n; M.K. McIntosh, *Autonomy and Community: The Royal Manor of Havering 1200–1500* (Cambridge, 1986), 57–8.

[56] Guisborough, 216n. The translation is that given by Cam, *The Hundred and the Hundred Rolls*, 237.

The allusion to the Queen's land-grabbing policies is very clear. Pecham wrote in very direct terms to Eleanor, telling her that the king's harshness was attributed to her influence, and that her use of Jewish debts to acquire lands amounted to usury and mortal sin.[57]

There is no doubt that the character of Edward's reign changed markedly after Eleanor's death in 1290, but how far the change can be attributed to the loss of her influence on Edward is debatable, for there were many other factors at work. What is very evident is the extent of Edward's grief for his queen, attested by his building the most elaborate series of monuments ever constructed for an English king or queen. Eleanor died at Harby, in Nottinghamshire, and not only did she have three separate tombs, one at Lincoln for the entrails, one at Blackfriars in London for the heart, and the main one in Westminster Abbey, but also the celebrated series of Eleanor crosses were built, twelve in all; one at each stopping point of the funeral cortege. The practice of dividing corpses was quite usual at this time, though it was to be condemned by the pope in 1299, while the commemorative crosses had a recent precedent in those set up to mark the journey of St Louis's bones from Paris to St Denis. The speed and cost of the works on Eleanor's memorials were very remarkable: all was largely complete by 1294, and the tombs and crosses cost almost £2,200. The superb gilt bronze effigy of Eleanor in Westminster Abbey alone cost about £100. The achievement was of great importance in artistic terms, and it provided a visible expression of the monarchy's prestige, but above all it shows how important Eleanor was to Edward.[58]

The problems involved in working out how many children Eleanor had are considerable, even when the fifteenth-century invention of a daughter called Alice is ignored. Children who died in infancy have left little record: all that is known of one is that she died on 29 May and was buried in Bordeaux, but it is not known on which of the royal couple's visits to Gascony this took place. It has generally been assumed that the eldest daughter to survive, Eleanor, was born in 1264, for there was an order issued by Henry III asking Eleanor of Castile to leave Windsor castle with her daughter in June of that year. In fact, this is almost certainly a reference to Katherine who died as a baby, and a writ of June 1269 giving a reward to the messenger who brought Henry III the news of Eleanor's birth is good evidence that she was in fact born in 1269. The following table lists those children for whom there is a reasonable evidence.[59]

---

[57] Douie, *Pecham*, 52.

[58] *KW*, i, 479–85. The question of separate heart and entrail burials is considered by E.A.R. Brown, 'Death and the Human Body in the Later Middle Ages: the legislation of Boniface VIII on the division of the corpse', *Viator*, xii (1981), 221–70.

[59] The problems of listing Eleanor of Castile's children are ably set out by J.C.

		Born	*Died*
1.	Katherine	1261–3	Sept. 1264
2.	Joan	Jan. 1265	Sept. 1265
3.	John	July 1266	Aug. 1271
4.	Henry	May 1268	Oct. 1274
5.	Eleanor	June 1269	Aug. 1298
6.	Unnamed daughter	*c.* 1271	*c.* 1271–2
7.	Joan	1272	April 1307
8.	Alphonso	Nov. 1273	Aug. 1284
9.	Margaret	March 1275	*c.* 1333
10.	Berengaria	May 1276	1277–8
11.	Unnamed child	Jan. 1278	1278
12.	Mary	March 1279	1332
13.	Elizabeth	Aug. 1282	1316
14.	Edward	April 1284	1327

Edward does not seem to have been much concerned with his children when they were young, partly because from a very early age they were placed in their own household, and taken from parental care. Joan of Acre, born on crusade, was for much of her childhood looked after by her maternal grandmother, Jeanne of Dammartin, in Ponthieu.[60] The elder children were entrusted to Richard of Cornwall while Edward and Eleanor were in the east. The practice of sending children to be brought up in other households was a normal one among the aristocracy of the period, and does not imply any lack of parental feeling. Yet it is remarkable that the king, and even more so the queen, should have left their son Henry to be ill and die at Guildford without making the short journey from London to visit him.[61] The almonry accounts show that little attention was paid by the king to the anniversaries of the deaths of his children, and indeed, in 1284, there is no mention of masses for the soul of Alphonso, who died that year, in contrast to the lavish oblations made for Henry of Brittany, son of the duke of Brittany, whose death took place about a month after Alphonso's.[62]

Edward's first three sons all died young. There was widespread popular grief at John's death, for he was apparently a handsome child. Henry died in 1274, aged six. There must have been more hope for Alphonso, who survived until he was ten. Archbishop Pecham wrote to

---

Parsons, 'The Year of Eleanor of Castile's Birth and her Children by Edward I', *Medieval Studies*, xlvi (1984), 249–65, whose conclusions I have accepted. Parsons notes the probable existence of at least two more children, in addition to those in the table.

[60] Parsons, *Court and Household of Eleanor of Castile*, 39n.

[61] H. Johnstone, 'Wardrobe and Household of Henry, son of Edward I', *Bulletin of the John Rylands Library*, vii (1922–3), 397.

[62] Taylor, 'Royal Alms and Oblations', 122.

the king expressing obviously sincere condolences on the news of the death of 'the child who was the hope of us all', but the king's own reaction is not recorded.[63] All these three died before it was felt necessary to provide them with an independent landed endowment. They had their own households, Henry and Alphonso's probably being separate establishments. After Henry's death there was simply one for all the children. Accounts survive for Henry's household, but they are not particularly revealing. He lived together with his sister Eleanor and his cousin John of Brittany, and the expenses show that he was clearly a sickly child, and suggest that he had a sweet tooth, to judge by the consumption of sugary confections. The household was not particularly lavish, with annual expenses of only some £350 a year, a considerable contrast with the elaborate later establishment of Edward of Caernarfon, with its costs of about £4,000 a year.[64]

For obvious reasons, much more is known about Edward of Caernarfon than any of Edward's other sons, and there is little need to summarize his whole career before he came to the throne. With his substantial household, already costing over £2,000 a year by 1288–9, his upbringing largely took place away from the immediate supervision of his father. The most important influence on him was probably that of his 'master', the Gascon knight Guy Ferre, who had been steward to Eleanor of Provence. His cannot have been an easy or a rewarding task: all that Edward excelled in was horsemanship, and perhaps also those mechanical arts, such as hedging, ditching and rowing, which he was to be so criticized for practising when he came to the throne. Edward I was to quarrel bitterly with his son at the end of his reign, even on one occasion physically assaulting him and tearing out his hair, but there are no signs that the father took against his son in childhood.[65] It may well be, however, that much of Edward II's personal inadequacy was the result of his relationship with his formidable father, who must have been a hard man to live up to. Personal details about the king's relationship with his sons are very scant, but it is tempting to see his hand in the choice of toy castles for Alphonso and Edward to play with, the former having a miniature siege engine as well. Henry, more prosaically, had a small cart which cost 7d.[66]

Edward appears to have been fonder of his daughters than of his sons. Five girls survived the perils of infancy and childhood: Eleanor, Joan, Margaret, Mary and Elizabeth. The story of their marriages is

[63] *Reg. Pecham*, iii, 819.

[64] Tout, *Chapters in Medieval Administrative History*, ii, 43, 366; Johnstone, 'Wardrobe and Household of Henry, son of Edward I', 1–37.

[65] Edward of Caernarfon's career prior to his accession is fully discussed by H. Johnstone, *Edward of Caernarvon*; Guisborough, 382–3.

[66] *KW*, i, 202n.; Tout, *Chapters in Medieval Administrative History*, ii, 43n.

part of the diplomatic and of the domestic history of the reign, but it is striking that none was wed at a very young age. There was resistance on the part of the queen and the queen mother to Eleanor being sent off to Spain after she was married by proxy to Alphonso of Aragon in 1282, and in the event she did not marry until 1293, when she was twenty-four. A marriage was planned for Joan at a young age, but nothing came of it, and she was eighteen when she was wed to the earl of Gloucester. Elizabeth was fifteen when she married the count of Holland, but the king was reluctant even after the ceremony to see her leave the court. Some nine months later her husband wrote to the king in anxious tones:

> We have previously asked you if it would please you to send our dear companion to her own land. Dear sire, we beg you humbly again, for her own well-being and for ours, and of our land and people, who are desperate to see their lady, our dear companion, that it may please you to tell us a specific date and place where we can meet, and that it would please you to bring our dear companion into her own land in as honourable a way as she merits.[67]

Elizabeth was a frequent visitor at court, even after her second marriage to the earl of Hereford. So also was the daughter who left the court at the youngest age. This was Mary, who was sent to Amesbury, at her grandmother's insistence, at the age of five, and who became a nun in 1285. Her religious profession did not prevent her from frequently returning to court, with the largest cortege of any of the princesses. Her extravagance, and her gambling debts, suggest that she did not take her vocation very seriously, and this is supported by the later claim of Earl Warenne to have had an affair with her, presumably in the course of one of her visits to court.[68] The most independent of the daughters was Joan of Acre. She displeased her father by leaving court very soon after her marriage to the earl of Gloucester in 1290, and angered him much more in 1297 by her clandestine second marriage to a squire in her household, Ralph de Monthermer.[69] Yet Edward's anger did not last long: his relationship with his daughters, if occasionally stormy, appears to have been a happy one.

Edward's affection for his daughters is evident from his extravagance towards them. He bore with Margaret's tantrums when early in 1297 she rejected some jewellery made for her in London, buying other fine

[67] *Documents 1297–8*, ed. Prestwich, 152.

[68] Green, *Lives of the Princesses of England*, ii, 405–29; F.R. Fairbank, 'The Last Earl of Warenne and Surrey, and the distribution of his possessions', *Yorkshire Archaeological Journal*, xix (1907), 244–5.

[69] Green, *Lives of the Princesses of England*, ii, 331, 343–8.

pieces for her, and paying for a splendid carriage. When Elizabeth returned from Holland after the death of her husband late in 1299, Edward met the costs of her dresses, amounting to some £100 a year. He also bought her a fine carriage when she went to France, which cost £50.[70] The most notable signs of Edward's strong family feelings were perhaps the lavish payments he made to messengers who brought him news of the birth of his grandchildren. He gave no less than £126 13s 4d to the man who brought him news of the birth of a son to Margaret, though news of a daughter to Joan of Acre was not met with similar enthusiasm. The messenger who brought news of a son for Elizabeth, after her marriage to the earl of Hereford, received £26 13s 4d in 1304: news of a second son two years later was better rewarded with £40.[71]

In 1299, as part of the peace process between England and France, Edward married for a second time. His bride was Margaret of France, half-sister of Philip IV. She has left only a slight imprint on history: it was hardly to be expected that the king would be much influenced by a queen some forty years his junior. Edward is said to have been delighted with his new wife, succumbing to a 'fervour of love' once the wedding took place, so that Margaret at once conceived a child. Margaret made a good impression when she visited St Albans in 1299, with generous gifts of alms, and a decision to join the fraternity of the monastery. The chronicler, however, clearly felt that her stay of some three weeks was too long, and her entourage too big.[72] She was extravagant: by 1302 it was necessary for the king to promise her £4,000 out of wardships and marriages, so that she might repay her debts. These included a sum of £1,000 to the Italian firm of the Ballardi of Lucca, probably incurred through purchases of fine cloths and other luxuries. In 1305 her landed endowment was increased by £500, presumably because she was still in financial difficulties.[73]

Despite her youth, Margaret had some influence. A traditional role for the queen was to intercede with the king on behalf of the people seeking pardons. Sometimes she did this by herself, and on other occasions she acted together with other members of the royal family, such as her step-daughter Elizabeth. It was through Margaret's intervention that a certain widow was able to obtain royal permission to remarry, and some grants of a minor character were made at her request. She must have needed more than normal powers of persuasion to obtain a pardon for the man who hid the crown used by Robert Bruce

[70] Ibid., iii, 14; E 101/369/11, ff.104v–105v.
[71] *Liber Quotidianus*, 156, 170; BL Add. MS 8835, f.43; E 101/369/11, f.95v.
[72] Rishanger, 194, 397.
[73] *CPR 1301–7*, 60, 368–9, 372.

at his enthronement in 1306. In 1301 Edward was faced with a problem, when he was not sure whether the earl of Lincoln or the treasurer,
Walter Langton, had proper authorization to agree to a truce with the
Scots. They were therefore asked to approach the queen, as Edward
himself was in Scotland, and show her the letters of authority they had
been given, so that the proper amendments could be made if necessary.
The most important problem that Margaret was able to help resolve
was the bitter dispute between the king and his son Edward in 1305. It
was she who persuaded the king to release a ban he had imposed on the
Londoners to prevent them lending money to the prince, and it was
through her intervention that he was allowed to keep most of his
chamber staff.[74]

A curious story told many years later by Sir Thomas Grey in his
Scalacronica had it that on one occasion Edward had a letter forged, in
which it stated that he had bribed a number of men in the French army
to seize Philip IV. The letter was addressed to the civic authorities of
Ghent, and the king deliberately left it on the queen's bed when he
arose from it. She read it, and promptly told Philip about it, and as a
result he promptly abandoned the siege of Lille.[75] It is highly implausible that this actually happened, but the story may be right in pointing
to the difficulties Margaret faced as a result of the continued suspicion
that existed between France and England.

Some privy seal letters from the king indicate something of his
concern for his young queen in the final stages of his reign. When
Margaret's physician wrote to him for his permission to bleed his
charge, Edward wrote back firmly stating that he should do it as soon as
possible, and a letter to Margaret herself made the same point. The
unfortunate queen then went down with measles, and Edward told her
physician in no uncertain terms that on no account was she to travel
until she was fully recovered, otherwise, 'By god's thigh', he would pay
for it. Edward's concern was shown by orders that he be informed
quickly and frequently how Margaret was progressing. A letter to
Margaret's confessor asked him to break the news of the death of her
sister, Blanche, as gently as possible to her, by comforting and consol-
ing her. If she grieved excessively, Edward suggested that it might be
pointed out to her that Blanche had been as good as dead ever since she
had married the duke of Austria.[76] This may sound ill-considered and
callous, but the king's concern was clearly genuine.

---

[74] *CPR 1301–7*, 503; *CCR 1302–7*, 342; *Calendar of Chancery Warrants, 1244–1326*,
146–7; Johnstone, *Edward of Caernarvon*, 101.
[75] *Scalacronica by Sir Thomas Grey of Heton, Knight*, ed. J. Stevenson (Maitland Club,
1836), 128.
[76] Chaplais, 'Some Private Letters of Edward I', 82–5.

Margaret bore Edward three children: Thomas of Brotherton in 1300, Edmund of Woodstock in 1301, and Eleanor in 1306. An indenture survives giving some of the details of the preparations made for Thomas's birth. Vast quantities of cloth were needed: Thomas's first cradle and bed used thirteen ells of fine Lincoln scarlet, his second the same quantity of dark blue cloth. Fur coverlets were also provided, with sheets made from fifty-five ells of Rheims linen. There were hangings with heraldic arms, and at Edward's orders the young prince's chamber was draped with striped cloth. The birth itself clearly occurred rather earlier than was expected: plans had been made for the confinement to take place at the archbishop of York's manor of Cawood, but Margaret went into labour before reaching it, and gave birth at Brotherton. According to Rishanger, Thomas was a patriotic baby, who rejected the milk of his French wet-nurse, and began to thrive only when he received good English milk. There is documentary evidence which suggests that there is a grain of truth behind the story: one of Thomas's wet-nurses died, and the queen certainly employed a doctor on one occasion to examine and approve the milk of another.[77]

Margaret's three children were of course much too young to play any significant part in the events of Edward's final years. They, like Eleanor's children, had their own household: little more is known of their early years than the fact that their toy drum had to be repaired, and that they were given an iron bird-cage by their mother.[78] The one respect in which they were important was that the king fully appreciated that in time it would be necessary for them to be provided with a proper landed endowment, a fact which undoubtedly influenced his patronage policies.

Edward appears to have been remarkably faithful to his queens. The only breath of scandal contained in contemporary narrative is the suggestion that he became too friendly with the countess of Gloucester in the late 1260s, but there is no evidence to support the charge.[79] The later tale given by the Italian chronicler Villani, that Edward fell in love with a lady sent by his mother to help him escape from Dover castle during the Barons' War, has little plausibility. Then there is the curious inclusion of John Botetourt in a genealogical table in a Hailes Abbey chronicle. His name appears to be written over an erasure, and there is nothing in Botetourt's career to suggest that he was an illegitimate son of the king. He first appeared in royal service as a falconer, but rose to

---

[77] K. Staniland, 'Welcome, Royal Babe! The Birth of Thomas of Brotherton in 1300', *Costume*, 1985, 1–13.

[78] E 101/368/12, 4.

[79] Above, 60–61.

high rank, becoming a banneret in 1298. He was of East Anglian gentry origin, and became lord of Mendlesham through marriage. It is possible that the scribe intended to put the name of Edward's daughter Elizabeth's husband where Botetourt's now features.[80] This evidence places no more than a question mark against Edward's fidelity. Edward's grandfather John and his great-grandfather Henry I I had not been faithful husbands, but attitudes and expectations changed in the thirteenth century. Henry I I I's reputation had been impeccable, as of course had that of Louis I X. It would have been surprising had Edward not followed the precedent set by two kings whom he greatly admired.

In many ways Edward was fortunate with his immediate family. Neither of his queens imported a host of greedy relations and hangers-on, as Eleanor of Provence had done, and neither attempted to play an active political role in the way that Eleanor of Aquitaine had done in Henry I I's reign. Although Edward had an impressive number of children, the fact that only one son grew to adulthood during his lifetime meant that he did not have to make elaborate arrangements to provide for his sons, as Edward I I I was to have to do. Nor was he faced by the political problems presented by a brood of unruly sons, as Henry I I had been. It was no disadvantage to have many daughters, for they were a positive asset in international diplomacy, enabling Edward to create a network of marriage alliances. At home, by marrying them into the English aristocracy the king could hope to increase the loyalty of his nobles. Where Edward was unfortunate was that his son Edward of Caernarfon proved so lacking in ability. It was not possible to rely on him as a military commander, and he could not be sent to rule Gascony. It was the king's nephew, John of Brittany – whom in many ways Edward treated as if he were his son – who was appointed as royal lieutenant both in Gascony and in Scotland, rather than Edward of Caernarfon.[81] It was unfortunate too for Edward that in the decade that proved most difficult for him, both in military and in political terms, the 1290s, he did not have the support of a loyal queen. He had been fortunate to have Eleanor by his side during the really constructive years of the reign. The history of the royal family in this period is not a

[80] N. Denholm-Young, *History and Heraldry* (Oxford, 1965), 38–9; BL Cottonian MS Cleop. D.III, f.51; Prestwich, *War, Politics and Finance under Edward I*, 57–8; C47/4/1, f.15v; *Handbook of British Chronology*, ed. Fryde, Greenway, Porter and Roy, 39. In general terms, the Hailes chronicle is a reliable source, but in the absence of any corroborative evidence, it is difficult to credit the evidence of this genealogical table. It is worth noting that Edward I I's bastard son was duly acknowledged as such in a royal record, there is no such evidence in the case of John Botetourt.

[81] For John's career, see I. Lubimenko, *Jean de Bretagne, comte de Richmond. Sa vie et son activité en Angleterre, en Ecosse et en France (1266–1334)* (Lille, 1908).

dramatic one, filled with scandals such as that in France in 1314 when the king's daughters-in-law were found to have committed adultery. Not all the details of personal relationships emerge clearly from the sources, but there can be little doubt that Edward's family was a source of stability and strength.

Chapter 6

THE ROYAL HOUSEHOLD

The structure of government in medieval England is frequently described as complex and sophisticated. In the exchequer, the king had a long-established office which oversaw the finances of the realm and which followed well-worn bureaucratic procedures. The chancery issued charters and letters under the great seal, transmitting royal instructions to the king's subjects. At the heart of the governmental system, however, lay the king's household, a much more flexible and personal instrument. The household, on one level, was quite simply the king's domestic entourage. Departments such as the kitchen, the pantry and the scullery saw to Edward's day-to-day needs. However, one department, the wardrobe, developed in the thirteenth century a central role in government, taking the place which had earlier been occupied by another household department, the chamber. The wardrobe had, in practice, very considerable financial autonomy, and was capable of expanding to meet the demands created by war in a way that the exchequer could not match. It became the chief spending department of the central government. In addition, the privy seal was kept by one of the wardrobe officials: it was by means of letters authenticated with this seal that instructions were sent to the exchequer and the chancery, and indeed to royal officials and others throughout the realm. The officials of the household, and above all those of the wardrobe, performed vital functions both in peace and war. Without them, Edward would not have been able to organize the affairs of his realm, conduct negotiations with other rulers, or lead campaigns. The household also provided the core of the royal army, in the form of the corps of royal household knights, paid through the wardrobe.

This picture of government through the royal household is made abundantly clear in the account books of the wardrobe from the later years of Edward's reign. They show that the bulk of royal expenditure was channelled through the wardrobe. A large corps of cavalry, along with all the infantry troops and the entire navy, were paid by wardrobe clerks, and supplied by them with foodstuffs. Surviving writs of privy seal show the way in which the king's instructions were transmitted. As one historian, Tout, put it, 'The whole state and realm of England were the appurtenances of the king's household.'[1] Tout considered that there had been a very extensive development of the household, and in particular the wardrobe, in Edward I's reign, for an ordinance of 1279, which set out the organization of the household, did not suggest that at that early stage of his rule, it had much more than a purely domestic function. The ordinance stressed the role of such household departments as the kitchen, the buttery and the pantry, and it did not imply that the officials had duties which extended much beyond the provision of food, drink, clothing and transport. There was no suggestion in the document that the household played a major role in military affairs: it implied that only twenty men-at-arms were retained. The total number of officials was no more, apparently, than about fifty. The contrast with the later establishment of at least 500, and often more, is striking.

The ordinance of 1279, however, is a misleading document, for it was very limited in scope, and did not purport to provide a full description of the whole *familia*. It was simply concerned with the *domus*, the domestic establishment, and in particular with those officials who had accounting responsibilities. The officers of the various departments were named, and details provided of their wages and allowances. Thus Ralph de Waterville, clerk of the kitchen, was paid 7½d a day and received £3 a year for robes. The nightly examination of the officials before the stewards, the treasurer and one of the marshals was outlined. The records of the kitchen, pantry and buttery were to be checked against the number of dishes actually known to have been served, and the amount of wine drunk. It was not any part of the purpose of the document to list the military establishment of the household, the knights and squires, nor did it provide details of the royal huntsmen and messengers. It was probably intended to reduce the scale of the royal establishment: it lists nine men who were entitled to sleep in the wardrobe, and the implication is that many others had been in the habit of taking up residence there. 'Ribalds', or scoundrels, were to be cleared from the household every month.[2]

There are parallels to this text. The *Constitutio Domus Regis* of the 1130s likewise suggests that the household was a housekeeping organization on a fairly modest scale, yet there is ample evidence to show that the royal household under the Norman kings was a vital institution, whose members played a central role in the organization of the state, and which could be expanded rapidly in time of war to form the central core of the king's army.[3] The household ordinance of 1318 was

---

[1] Tout, *Chapters in Medieval Administrative History*, ii, 59.

[2] The ordinance is printed by Tout, *op. cit.*, ii, 158–63.

[3] J.O. Prestwich, 'The Military Household of the Norman Kings', *EHR*, xcvi (1981), 1–35.

in the same tradition: although it gives a better impression of the scale of the household, it was not concerned with the knights and squires.[4] For these, it is necessary to turn to the wardrobe account books. As Edward I's reign proceeded, these became better organized and more complex, but they show that from the 1270s the royal household was a large body, containing a very substantial military element, which was concerned with far more than domestic affairs. In the mid-1280s, lists of those entitled to receive household robes run to some 570 names, ranging from high-ranking bannerets to mere kitchen boys.[5]

Throughout Edward's reign, the household had two aspects. There was the purely domestic establishment with its departments such as the saucery, scullery and kitchen, and there was the larger organization, dominated by the department of the wardrobe, which was of central importance to the state in financial, administrative and military terms. The household certainly changed and developed in the course of Edward's reign, but its transformation was not as dramatic as a comparison of the 1279 Ordinance with the later account books might suggest.

The administrative significance of the wardrobe resulted in large part from the fact that one of its officials, the controller, had charge of the privy seal. Wardrobe clerks wrote the letters and writs that were sent out under this seal. Although enrolled or registered copies of this privy seal correspondence were made, none of these records survives, so only a limited impression is today yielded by the sources of the overall range of privy seal activity. It is clear that this seal was used for the king's own most personal and immediate correspondence. If Edward wanted letters made out by the chancery under the great seal, written in Latin, then he would normally send relatively informal instructions in French to the chancellor, using the privy seal. In the years after the death of the great chancellor Robert Burnell, in 1292, there was a considerable increase in the number of such privy seal warrants to the chancery. During Burnell's period of office they had been common only when king and chancellor were separated, as during campaigns in Wales. In the later years of the reign the post of chancellor was not held by men who enjoyed the king's trust in the way that Burnell had done, and there was a much greater separation of the chancery from the king and his household. As a result, it was necessary to make much more use of the privy seal, and the controller of the wardrobe became a much more influential figure, acting as Edward's private secretary and almost certainly exercising a considerable influence on policy.[6] The privy seal was also used to transmit royal orders to the exchequer, and

---

[4] T.F. Tout, *The Place of Edward II in English History* (Manchester, 1914). 270–314.
[5] *Records of Wardrobe and Household*. ed. Byerley, 164–7.
[6] Tout, *Chapters in Medieval Administrative History*, ii, 60–84, discusses this more fully.

again it is from the later years of the reign that the records show extensive use being made of this technique, notably with a series of angry letters from the king in Scotland to the exchequer officials at York, who were struggling with Edward's incessant demands for funds for his campaigns.[7]

Many orders were issued directly to the king's other officials, and to his subjects, but here the evidence is sadly deficient. A number of draft letters survive, but there is no means of knowing what proportion of the total output they form.[8] It again appears probable that there was a considerable increase in this use of the privy seal in the later years of the reign: it even became worthwhile for criminals to forge the privy seal.[9] The great seal was not superseded, nor was the chancery replaced by a privy seal office developing within the wardrobe, but for many purposes, when great formality was not required, the use of privy seal letters offered a quick and convenient means of communicating royal orders. There was certainly no conflict between privy seal and chancery, for the two formed interlocking parts of the same administrative machine.

The financial functions of the wardrobe are much better recorded than the secretarial. It was the main spending department of the government, used above all for financing war. In the case of the second Welsh war, in 1282–4, a separate account of military expenditure was kept, but in other cases, the general wardrobe accounts include major items of expenditure, such as soldiers' wages and payments to overseas allies, in the same account book as details of the expenditure on the king's hunting establishment. The main reason for the wardrobe's dominance over crown expenditure was quite simply the fact that it was present with the king, whereas even moving the exchequer from Westminster to be near campaigning areas, for example at Shrewsbury or York, did not achieve this. Further, as Tout argued, the wardrobe was far more flexible than the exchequer, less bound by rules and conventions. It had a freedom in times of financial difficulty to issue debentures and bills (promises of future payment) to Crown creditors in a way which the exchequer could not do. In the first half of the reign much wardrobe receipt came in quite independently of the exchequer, notably in the form of loans from Italian bankers, but from the 1290s wardrobe receipts were accounted as coming through the exchequer. In practical terms this was little more than a technicality,

---

[7] Below, 514.

[8] Chaplais, 'Some Private Letters of Edward I', *EHR*, lxxvii (1962), 79–86, prints some privy seal drafts: others are to be found in the class of Ancient Correspondence (SCI).

[9] Tout, *Chapters in Medieval Administrative History*, ii, 79.

and the increasing deficits of the wardrobe in the later years of the reign testify to the inadequacy of exchequer control of the household.[10]

The careers of many household officials have been worked out in some detail, but in all too many cases all that the historian can provide is a dull catalogue of official appointments, records of grants and lists of land-holdings, with no real personal detail. The clerical officials, particularly those who served as keepers and controllers of the wardrobe, were of the very greatest importance in Edward's system of government. It was in the household that most of the men on whom the king really relied received their training, and there that they first gained Edward's confidence. Robert Burnell, by far the most influential and important minister in the first half of the reign, was not of course an official of the royal household, but before his promotion to the chancery he had been in the household of Edward as prince. Walter Langton, who although he was treasurer not chancellor, held a position analogous to Burnell's in the later years of the reign, rose in royal service within the household before he took over at the exchequer.

The first keeper of Edward's wardrobe as king was Philip Willoughby, who held office until October 1274. His functions as keeper during the crusade expedition must have been very different from those of later holders of the office. He moved from the wardrobe to a more settled existence as a baron, and then eventually chancellor, of the exchequer. He never rose to the highest office in either church or state: he became dean, not bishop, of Lincoln, and acted as deputy treasurer, never becoming treasurer in his own right. It is hard to imagine him as other than a colourless civil servant, although in truth the sources do not permit such a character judgement to be made.[11]

Willoughby was succeeded, very briefly, as keeper by Anthony Bek, one of the grand personalities of the reign. He held office for only a month, and was followed by his brother Thomas. The Bek brothers were of a knightly family, a fact which led Tout to suppose that they were 'perhaps too "baronial" in their outlook to be altogether men after Edward's heart'.[12] Such a verdict smacks too much of the traditional view of king and barons in inevitable opposition, and there is nothing to suggest any difference in opinion between Edward and Thomas Bek, who gave up office in 1280 when he became bishop of St David's. Tenure of that position would obviously have been hard to combine with the constant attendance in the household required of the keeper.

[10] Tout, *op. cit.*, ii, 85–130; M.C. Prestwich, 'Exchequer and Wardrobe in the Later Years of Edward I', *BIHR*, xlvi (1973), 1–10.
[11] There is much biographical detail on all these clerical officials in Tout, *Chapters in Medieval Administrative History*, ii. For Willoughby in particular, see ii, 5–7, 108.
[12] Ibid., ii, 14.

After Thomas Bek, the keepership of the wardrobe was held by men who, in the best civil service tradition, had risen through the ranks of the department. William of Louth had been cofferer, in charge of the wardrobe's cash, standing third in the hierarchy of the department under Bek, and took over from him as keeper. The controller, Thomas Gunneys, nominally at least the second most important wardrobe official, was on this occasion passed over. Louth was in charge of the wardrobe for a decade. He held a university degree, and appears to have been of great ability and even integrity. He was warmly praised by one chronicler for his honest and praiseworthy tenure of office. His most difficult tasks were the organization of the finances of the second Welsh war, and his role in Gascony in 1287–8, when he acted as constable of Bordeaux in addition to his household duties, and did much to put the finances of the duchy in order. He was also employed, in 1286, as an ambassador to the French court. Among his rewards was the deanery of St Martin-le-Grand in London, a church closely associated with the wardrobe.[13] Louth left office in 1290, not in disgrace like many who departed from royal service at that time, but because he was elected to the see of Ely. It is rather surprising that he was not promoted to become treasurer, for his predecessor at Ely was John Kirkby, who had held that office. Instead, the king turned to William March.

William March was another major wardrobe official. He had been cofferer from 1280 until 1283, when he rose to the controllership. It has been suggested that he may have played a major part in the development of the wardrobe accounting system, on the basis of his responsibility for the surviving account book of 1285–6, but as this does not show any major advances on the account book of 1276–7, the argument is not a strong one.[14] He was, however, probably responsible for important changes at the exchequer in 1290, after his promotion to the treasurership, and it may well be that by the late 1280s, he was in practice a more important figure in the wardrobe than his master William of Louth. In 1293 he succeeded Burnell as bishop of Bath and Wells, but his official career came to an abrupt end when he was dismissed as treasurer in 1295. He was then able to devote himself to his diocese, gaining a certain reputation for sanctity which was not shared by many of the king's servants.[15]

To succeed William of Louth as keeper of the wardrobe in 1290, the king turned to another wardrobe clerk, Walter Langton. Langton was the most colourful of all Edward's officials. He was a man of great

[13] Ibid., ii, 14–15; *Records of Wardrobe and Household*, ed. Byerley, xvi–xvii; Trabut-Cussac, *L'administration anglaise en Gascogne*, 90, 202; *Ann. Osney*, 325.
[14] *Records of Wardrobe and Household*, ed. Byerley, ix.
[15] Tout, *Chapters in Medieval Administrative History*, ii, 13, 16–17, 21.

ability and little principle. His greed for lands and livings exceeded Burnell's, and while he was to be described later in life as 'conspicuous for the maturity of his counsel and full of discretion', he was also accused of strangling his mistress's husband with her assistance, and of doing homage to the devil. His early career in the wardrobe suggested nothing out of the ordinary. He first appeared as a clerk in 1282, but his abilities were soon noticed, for when the king was in Gascony, Langton took over the post of cofferer from the sick Henry of Wheatley. In 1290 he first became controller, and then keeper. He stayed in that office until March's dismissal from the treasurership in 1295, when he was the obvious candidate to take over from him. It seems very likely that it was he who was responsible for the development of the wardrobe account books into the complex and well-organized form that they had by the later years of the reign, but it was to be as treasurer of the exchequer, not as keeper of the wardrobe, that he was really to leave his mark.[16]

Langton's successor as keeper of the wardrobe in 1295 was, predictably, the man who had earlier succeeded him both as cofferer and controller, John Droxford. Droxford was to remain keeper for the rest of the reign. For a man who occupied a very central place in the royal administration, he remains a curiously obscure figure. Unlike Louth, he attracted no praise from chroniclers. His actions were not disavowed by the king as March's were, nor did he gain any reputation for sanctity, like March. Equally, he did not attract the hostility that was directed at Langton. He came from Droxford, in Hampshire, and was, along with John Benstead, controller from 1295 until 1305, rather an exception among the wardrobe officials in being a southerner: a large number of his colleagues derived from south Yorkshire and north Lincolnshire.[17] Droxford had some affection for his birthplace, for he built a tomb for his mother in the church, and undertook some work of restoration there.[18]

As keeper of the wardrobe, Droxford does not seem to have initiated any major changes in the running of the department. He was the least competent of all Edward's keepers, to judge by his failure to produce his accounts for audit at the exchequer, but this is explained by the

---

[16] Langton's career is fully discussed by A. Beardwood, 'The Trial of Walter Langton, bishop of Lichfield, 1307–1312', *Transactions of the American Philosophical Society*, n.s. liv (1964).

[17] Among the northerners can be counted Philip Willoughby, John Sandale, John Swanland, Robert Cottingham and William Thorntoft: see J.L. Grassi, 'The Clerical Dynasties from Howdenshire, Nottinghamshire and Lindsey in the Royal administration' (Oxford D.Phil. thesis 1959).

[18] N.G. Brett-James, 'John de Drokensford, Bishop of Bath and Wells', *Transactions of the London and Middlesex Archaeological Soc.*, n.s. x (1951), 283.

immense pressure put on the wardrobe as a result of the Scottish wars, rather than by personal inefficiency. As keeper, Droxford, like his predecessors in office, received robes to a value of 16 marks a year, the same as the bannerets of the household. The keepers did not receive a fee, for they could expect rewards in the form of ecclesiastical livings. Droxford was in 1293 granted the church of Childwall in Lancashire, in 1296 that of Kingsclere in Hampshire, in 1297 a prebend in Salisbury cathedral, and in 1304 one in St Mary's, Southwell. He was also able to secure livings for members of his family, such as his brother Roger, who received Childwall in 1299. His efforts, however, on Roger's behalf at the end of the reign, when he tried to obtain a position at York for him over the head of his wardrobe subordinate Walter Bedwin, came to nothing.[19] Droxford did not enter the land market with the guile and enthusiasm of the treasurer, Walter Langton, nor did he lend money on the scale of the chancery official William Hamilton.[20] Yet his wealth and status were such that he was able to campaign with a very substantial retinue. In 1300 he had six knights and twenty-two squires in his company, a larger following than that of his secular counterpart in the household, the steward Walter de Beauchamp.[21]

The records suggest that Droxford was a man of enormous energy. Not only did he have the wardrobe to organize, but he also frequently had to leave court to try to raise money, and to collect supplies needed for Scotland. He deputized for the treasurer, Langton, when he was abroad. One example of his travels is typical. On 10 October 1300, he left the court at Holmcoltram to go to Newcastle, to arrange for victuals to be sent north. He returned to the court at Dumfries, and promptly went to Skinburness, near Carlisle, again to see to victualling. Then he returned to Newcastle, went back to court, by now at Carlisle, and then set out with Walter Langton to see to the provisioning of the castles at Lochmaben, Dumfries and Caerlaverock. He then hurried south, to try to put off the king's Gascon creditors, who had appeared at York demanding payment. On 24 November he came back to court.[22] It was hard work to serve a master such as Edward I.

There were many other important clerks serving Edward in the wardrobe administration, such as the cofferer, Ralph Manton, who held office from 1297 until 1303, when he was killed at Roslin in Scotland. He was harshly rebuked just before he died by Simon Fraser, who, before he joined the Scottish cause, had been a household knight,

[19] *CPR 1292–1301*, 7–8, 200, 228, 254, 429; *CPR 1301–7*, 263; below, 546–7.
[20] Beardwood, 'The Trial of Walter Langton'; R.H. Bowers, 'From Rolls to Riches: King's Clerks and Moneylending in Thirteenth Century England', *Speculum*, lviii (1983), 60–71.
[21] *Liber Quotidianus*, 195–6, 202–3.
[22] Ibid., 82.

for wearing an iron hauberk rather than priestly robes, and for defrauding the king by failing to pay out wages.[23] The first charge was deserved, the second not. Manton rarely had sufficient funds to meet the
demands made on him for cash, and had to resort to the use of bills and
tallies. He was succeeded by Walter Bedwin, another highly competent
official.

John Benstead was one of the most active of all Edward's clerks. He
began his career in the wardrobe in 1292, in the lowly position of usher,
became controller in 1295, and performed the vital task of keeping the
privy seal, being thus in charge of the secretarial aspect of the household. He was described as the king's *secretarius*, and probably did
perform many of the functions of a modern secretary. On one occasion
Edward termed him 'our clerk who stays continually by our side', and
he was one of the king's closest advisers. In 1305 he left the wardrobe to
become chancellor of the exchequer, and early in Edward II's reign he
abandoned his clerical orders, becoming a knight and a royal justice.
He had earlier accepted the full war wages of a banneret, unlike the
other clerks who took pay for their retinues, but not themselves, on
campaign.[24] Another who should be mentioned is John Sandale, whose
career shows the flexibility of which Edward's clerks were capable. He
acted as paymaster in Wales in 1294–5, then performed a similar task in
Gascony, and after a period in charge of the royal mints, became
chamberlain of Scotland at the end of the reign, a position which was
effectively within the wardrobe administration.[25]

Edward was well served by his wardrobe clerks. All of them remained totally loyal to the king, even at times when church and state
were in conflict, notably during the crisis of 1297. They were, of course,
all ecclesiastics themselves. Although March was dismissed from his
post of treasurer in 1295, there were no instances of major household
officials being dismissed from positions within the household for
reasons of incompetence or corruption. The wardrobe's closeness to the
king perhaps made it less vulnerable to purges of administrative personnel, such as that which took place on a wide scale after the king's
return from Gascony in 1289, but the evidence is that the wardrobe
clerks were remarkably efficient in performing a wide range of tasks,
often under severe pressure. They served as paymasters to the king's
armies, and were frequently employed to bring cash from the exchequer to headquarters. They were inevitably also much concerned

[23] Langtoft, ii, 344.

[24] C.L. Kingsford, 'John de Benstede and his Missions for Edward I', *Essays in
History presented to R.L. Poole*, ed. H.W.C. Davis (Oxford, 1927), 332–44; Tout, *Chapters
in Medieval Administrative History*, ii, 19, 69, 141, 225–6.

[25] *The Registers of John de Sandale and Rigaud de Asserio, bishops of Winchester, 1316–23*, ed.
F.J. Baigent (Hants Record Soc., 1897), xvii–xlvii.

with the business of providing sufficient victuals for the armies. Some had more specialized activities than others: the controller had the privy seal, and other clerical responsibilities, which in 1300 included making copies of papal bulls for the king. Some clerks had diplomatic duties: Bonet de St Quentin was a wardrobe clerk, but spent most of his time dealing with the French over problems concerning Gascony, while Stephen of St George acted as Edward's proctor in Rome. The notary John of Caen was retained by the king as wardrobe clerk.[26]

The wardrobe clerks were responsible for drawing up the accounts of the household, and the surviving records show both how much was done in the course of Edward's reign to improve the system, and also how the increasing pressures of the later years proved to be too great for the handful of royal administrators to cope with. Although the surviving evidence for accounting is all in the form of rolls and books, the actual process of calculation was not done with pen and parchment. Accounting tables were an important part of the equipment of the wardrobe: one, bound with iron, was specially made for the Flanders expedition of 1297, and another was made in 1301 and taken on a special cart to Scotland. Counters were used for the actual process of calculation, in the form of copper tokens, or jettons. Money was often weighed out rather than counted: the burden of counting out vast numbers of small silver pennies would have been intolerable, and in 1297 a balance was bought for weighing them.[27] Then the transactions would be noted down in writing, and according to the household ordinance of 1279, accounts were drawn up every night. These would have been simply the accounts of the various domestic departments, the kitchen, buttery, pantry and so forth.[28] In fact, the great expansion of wardrobe business in Edward's reign necessitated a much more complex accounting procedure than the Ordinance envisaged.

Each household department would keep its own records, of receipts and expenditure. Until 1290, account rolls were presented to the exchequer for audit, probably one for receipts, one for household domestic expenses and one for the wide-ranging costs of the wardrobe.

[26] Prestwich, *War, Politics and Finance*, 151–67; *Records of Wardrobe and Household*, ed. Byerley, xxi, 165; *Liber Quotidianus*, 327. John of Caen's career is summarized in *Great Cause* i, 79–80.

[27] BL Add. MS 7965, ff.19v, 20v; Add. MS 7966a, f.39. There have been suggestions that the jettons, coin-like objects, were used as small change, but the evidence of the wardrobe accounts is quite unambiguous, that they were counters: *Edwardian Monetary Affairs (1279–1344)*, ed. N.J. Mayhew (British Archaeological Reports, 1977), 88–9.

[28] Tout, *Chapters in Medieval Administrative History*, ii, 160–1. For an example of a household roll, which gives details of day-by-day expenditure by the domestic departments, see *Records of Wardrobe and Household*, ed. Byerley, 117–63. This is perhaps the dullest of the various types of household record.

At the same time, a different sort of record was kept by the wardrobe;
account books in journal form, listing, on a chronological basis, receipts
and expenses in no very systematic way. The earliest wardrobe account
book dates from 1277–8. By 1286 there were two types of account book
kept. The controller's book still took the form of a journal, by now with
a degree of subdivision, and there was also, probably, a book of prests,
detailing cash advances made by the wardrobe. These books were
probably still internal records, but by the early 1290s account books
were being presented to the exchequer at audit. Under Walter
Langton's guidance, separate books of receipts and expenditure
were kept, and by the end of the century, if not earlier, a single
account book, with details both of expenditure and receipts, was
submitted for audit. Both the keeper and the controller kept copies.
These were systematically organized into sections, dealing with such
matters as the almonry, necessary expenditure of a miscellaneous
type, gifts and restoration of the cost of horses lost in war, fees and
wages of bannerets and knights, wages of squires and sergeants, wages
of infantry, wages of sailors, and the costs of the royal messenger
service, and of the hunting establishment. Lying behind this final
account book was a range of other books, of receipts and prests,
and smaller account rolls for the various different main heads of
expenditure. Journals of daily income and expenditure were kept, in
book form, and books of debts owed by the wardrobe.[29]

The impression given by the vast range of surviving record material,
particularly from the later years of Edward's reign, is of immense
efficiency. Yet, in fact, the logical and clear system which was
developed in the 1290s was too elaborate, and above all could not cope
when national military expenditure was included along with the various domestic elements of household costs. The business of converting
the raw material of the initial accounts into the form of the elegant final
account books took an increasingly long time. The account books for
1296–8 were drawn up reasonably promptly, for a payment was made
for their binding in 1298–9, but the later books took much longer. That
for 1300–1 shows that Adam de Bray, an official in charge of the royal
stable, did not make his account with his superiors until 1314–15, and
the final account book was not therefore written until that date, at the
earliest. The book for 1305–6 cannot, to judge by internal evidence,
have been written before 1315–16. The last accounts of the wardrobe to
be audited in Edward I's reign were those for 1295–8. An entry in the

---

[29] These conclusions are based on a study of the surviving records, which are too
numerous to be listed here. See also *Book of Prests, 1294–5*, ed. E.B. Fryde (Oxford,
1962), ix–xxvi; *Records of Wardrobe and Household*, ed. Byerley, ix–xv, though my views
are not identical with those set out there.

1. Head of Edward as a young man; from the north transept of Westminster Abbey.

2. Figure of a king, very probably either representing, or modelled on, Edward I, painted in the early fourteenth century; from the Sedilia, Westminster Abbey.

3. Miniature contained in the initial S of the Douce Apocalypse, showing Edward and Eleanor of Castile, each holding a shield. (Bodleian Library, MS Douce 180, f. 1)

4. Effigy of Queen Eleanor, by William Torel, on her tomb in Westminster Abbey.

5. Lower border of a page from a psalter made for Edward I's son Alphonso, showing a hawking scene. (British Library, Additional MS 24686, f. 14v.)

6. The Dolgellau Chalice and Paten. This silverware was almost certainly part of Edward I's collection of plate, and may even have been made from silver seized from the Welsh. (Private collection, HM the Queen)

in conſilio impiorum: & in via pec
catorum non ſtetit: & in cathedra pe
ſtilentie non ſedit. Sed in lege domini voluntas eius:
& in lege eius meditabit dic ac nocte.
Et erit tanquam lignum qd plan
tatum eſt ſecus decurſus aquarū.

7. Judgement of Solomon, from the Windmill Psalter. The fact that the scene is, unusually, contained within a letter E, suggests that the figure of the king is modelled on Edward I. (Pierpont Morgan Library, New York, MS M. 102, f. 2)

1305–6 account suggests that it was examined at the exchequer, and some corrections made in it, but only at some date after 1334.[30]

Yet although the impression of order and efficiency given by such account books as the *Liber Quotidianus* of 1300 is a rather spurious one, reflecting the hard work of clerks of Edward II's reign rather than the energies of John Droxford and his clerks, it would be wrong to conclude that the wardrobe altogether failed Edward I. The complexity of the accounting methods that had evolved in the course of the reign was certainly too much for the limited number of clerks who had many more pressing concerns than the writing up of their records. The work of paying the troops, organizing provisioning, assisting in recruiting, raising money as well as running the household on a day-to-day basis was all done, and what is remarkable is not that the accounts were left in some confusion, but that a small staff of a dozen or so men should have achieved so much.

There was no need for the household to be provided with a hierarchy of secular officials to match that of the clerks. The chief lay position was that of steward, or seneschal, of the household, and there were also two marshals. Then there was a varying number of bannerets, knights, squires and sergeants, who were not allocated specific offices, but who might be called upon to undertake a wide variety of tasks.

The steward's only duty, according to the Ordinance of 1279, was to be present along with the other household officials when the accounts were checked every evening.[31] He also presided over the household court, and almost certainly played a leading part in whatever ceremonies took place. Above all, he was in charge of the household's military forces, and when it was necessary to make arrangements for the garrisoning and victualling of castles, it was the steward who sat together with the keeper, and perhaps one or two other officials, to decide what should be done. Until the early 1290s there were, in fact, two stewards holding office at the same time. Hugh FitzOtho had been Edward's steward before his accession, and went with him on crusade: he remained in office until his death in 1283. In 1278, however, Robert FitzJohn was appointed to serve alongside FitzOtho, serving until he died in 1286. John de Montalt was a steward for a decade, from 1284 to 1294, and the Savoyard Peter de Chauvent held office from the late 1280s until 1292. Then Walter de Beauchamp, who had been appointed in 1289, became sole steward, serving until early in 1303. His successor was Robert de la Warde,

---

[30] C. Johnson, 'The System of Account in the Wardrobe of Edward I', *TRHS*, 4th ser. vi (1923), 53; BL Add. MS 7966a, f.46v; E 101/369/11, f.50.
[31] Tout, *Chapters in Medieval Administrative History*, ii, 160.

and for the last six weeks of the reign the office was held by John Thorpe.[32]

These stewards were not men of the highest baronial rank. It would indeed have been surprising had a major territorial magnate been prepared to devote the amount of time to affairs at court that the steward had to do. Equally, these stewards should not be thought of as the royal equivalents of the stewards of great baronial estates. The latter were professional managers, experts in the complex business of auditing accounts, farming out manors and so forth, whereas the household stewards were men whose prime responsibilities were judicial and above all military. They all held the rank of banneret, a position above that of the ordinary knights in the military hierarchy, and were senior and respected men, though their position evidently laid them open to criticism. The author of the *Song of Caerlaverock* described Walter de Beauchamp as 'a knight who would have been one of the best of all, according to my opinion, if he had not been too proud and rashly insolent, but you won't hear anyone talk of the steward without a "but" '.[33]

The office did not bring much more by way of rewards than went to the other bannerets. FitzOtho, according to the Ordinance of 1279, was to receive nothing by way of fees or wages, as the king had given him wardships worth £50 a year. His colleague FitzJohn was to have an annual fee of 10 marks a year, with 8 marks for robes, and land in wardship worth £25 a year. Near the end of the reign, Walter de Beauchamp received the same amount in fees and robes as the other bannerets of the household, £24 a year. He also received £200 in lieu of food, for himself and his retinue in the royal hall, following a reforming ordinance of 1300 known as the Statute of St Albans.[34]

The ordinance of 1279 listed two marshals of the household, Richard du Bois and Elias de Hauville. Their prime responsibility was the maintenance of discipline in the household, while the 1318 household ordinance suggests that they took turns to arrange the seating at dinners in the king's hall.[35] They assisted the steward in giving judgements in the household court, and must also have helped him in the task of organizing the household for war. Unfortunately,

---

[32] The exact chronology of these stewards remains uncertain: see Tout, op. cit., vi, 42, and *Handbook of British Chronology*, 73, 76. The latter includes as a steward in 1306, Thomas Hide, on the basis of a reference in *CCR 1302–7*, 372, but this man does not appear in the list of household knights in E 101/369/11, ff. 106v–107, and was surely an estate steward, not steward of the household.

[33] *The Siege of Carlaverock*, ed. N.H. Nicolas (1828), 30.

[34] Tout, *Chapters in Medieval Administrative History*, ii, 49–50, 158; *Liber Quotidianus*, 92, 188, 311.

[35] Ibid., 158; Tout, *Place of Edward II*, 283.

the lists of knights and bannerets in the household accounts do not
distinguish the marshals in any way, and it is not possible to provide
lists of the holders of this office. There was a connection between the
office of marshal in the household and the position of marshal of
England held by the earl of Norfolk, though it does not seem that the
earl actually appointed any of the household marshals in Edward's
reign. A later treatise on the duties of the marshal of England had a
curious item, in which it was stated that the marshal should have
twelve ladies at court, who were to swear to his representatives that
they knew of no other whores at court apart from themselves. This fits
with some evidence of the service by which the manor of Sherfield in
Cambridgeshire was held, described in about 1280 as 'by finding a
sergeant to keep the whores in the king's army', and under Edward II
as 'by being marshal of the whores in the king's household, and
dismembering condemned malefactors and measuring gallons and
bushels there'. Another sergeanty was described in terms of acting as
'marshal of the twelve girls who follow the king's court'.[36] This was
surely antiquarian material already in Edward I's day, reflecting a
somewhat mythical past. The evidence of the household accounts
provides no support for these statements of the marshal's duties, and
the twelve whores have to be consigned to the realms of fantasy.

The bannerets and knights of the royal household varied considerably in number, in accordance with the scale of the king's military
needs, and the state of his financial position. The evidence becomes
fuller as the reign proceeds, but an account from 1277, the year of the
first Welsh war, suggests that there were then almost fifty household
knights, and an account book of the following year also gives about
fifty names, noting that six men were serving with companions. About
thirty names are in common between the two lists.[37] There is no
accurate list of those retained as bannerets and knights at the time of
the second Welsh war of 1282–4, but there seem again to have been at
least fifty.[38]

From 1285 there survives a roll of payments for robes for the
knights, squires and sergeants of the household, which provides much
better evidence than the earlier lists. There were fourteen bannerets

---

[36] J.H. Round, *The King's Serjeants and Officers of State* (1911), 97–8; BL Cottonian
MS, Vesp. B. VII, f.107.

[37] E 101/3/21; C 47/4/1, f.52.

[38] C 47/2/6. Some of the major household names, such as those of Otto de Grandson
and Robert Tibetot, do not feature on the accounts, although they are listed as
household members on a pay account, E 101/3/6. It may be that it was thought that
they were in receipt of sufficient patronage not to need fees and robes: C 47/4/5. f.33,
shows that Alexander de la Pebrée was deprived of fees and robes when he was granted
lands in Gascony.

listed singly, and then eight noted as having *commilitones*, or companions. The list continues with forty-seven ordinary knights. Denholm-Young suggested that the *commilitones* were some kind of corps d'élite, but this is most unlikely. It was quite common for men to enter into partnerships to share in the profits and bear the losses of war, but it is only at this period that the accounts show this arrangement existing within the household. The total strength in 1285 was seventy-seven.[39] When Edward went to Gascony, numbers fell: in 1288–9 there were sixteen bannerets and only twenty-seven knights in the household, rising in the next year with the king's return to England to twenty-three bannerets and thirty-five knights.[40] The numbers did not rise in the 1290s, as might have been expected from the military situation: although twenty-two men were recruited in 1297, the year of the Flanders expedition, they were an addition to a household that contained only ten bannerets and twenty-six knights. In 1300 there were twenty-eight bannerets and forty-nine knights, but in 1301 the equivalent figures were eighteen and thirty-six. At the end of the reign the figures were much the same: seventeen bannerets and twenty-eight knights.[41]

The figures for squires and sergeants followed a similar pattern. In the mid-1280s there were about a hundred squires and seventy sergeants, falling to eighty and fifty respectively in the later part of the decade. In 1300 there were about sixty squires and forty-five sergeants, with numbers falling in the last years of the reign to fifty squires and some thirty sergeants.[42] Not all of these sergeants were described as sergeants-at-arms: about half their number were allocated to the various household departments, and had largely domestic duties.[43]

In this period, it was becoming increasingly common for nobles to retain knights in their service by means of written indentures, which promised fees, robes, food when they were present in the household, recompense for horses lost on service and other benefits. Edward himself had retained men by means of fees long before he came to the throne: in the autumn of 1259, for example, Drogo de Barentin was promised, in writing, £20 a year for his service with two other

[39] E 101/351/17; Denholm-Young, *History and Heraldry*, 31–2.
[40] E101/352/24; E 101/352/31.
[41] Prestwich, *War. Politics and Finance*, 46–7, with some adjustments to the figures given there.
[42] *Records of Wardrobe and Household*, ed. Byerley, 164–72; E 101/352/24; E 101/352/31; *Liber Quotidianus*; E 101/369/11.
[43] The Latin term *serviens* did not have the almost exclusively military implications of the modern 'sergeant'.

knights.[44] The precise terms of the indentures recording the agreements he made with those who accompanied him on crusade are recorded.[45] In the case of the royal household knights and squires, however, there do not appear to have been such written agreements. There was nothing novel in retaining substantial numbers of men in the king's household, and it seems likely that Edward I simply followed past custom.[46] A well-established system did not need reinforcement with written documents. The accounts show that the knights and bannerets received fees and robes – the latter in the form of a cash payment for the most part – to a value of £24 for a banneret and £12 for a knight. Sergeants-at-arms and squires received much less, with £2 6s 8d or £2 a year. In addition they were entitled to eat in the king's hall (at least until economy measures taken in 1300) received wages while on active duty, and were awarded compensation for horses lost while campaigning in the royal armies.[47]

There was no single avenue for recruitment to the royal household under Edward I. Obviously, those who had served him as prince tended to continue in his household after his accession, but the evidence does not permit any detailed analysis of this type of continuity. There were some who had been Edward's enemies in the Barons' Wars who became loyal household knights. John d'Eyville headed the list of bannerets in a document in 1284–5, and served the king loyally until his death in 1291. John de Vescy was another such, and Nicholas de Segrave was also a Montfortian who became a household knight.[48] There were some men whose careers in the household extended virtually throughout the reign. The Yorkshire knight William Latimer is a splendid example of a long-serving and talented household knight. He went on crusade with Edward, served him in Wales, and accompanied him to Gascony in 1286–9. He assisted in the defence of Gascony against the French in the 1290s, and last saw active service in Scotland in 1300, when he was described in the *Song of Caerlaverock*:

---

[44] C61/4, m.4. Roger de Stokes, Thomas de Ippegrave, Henry de Burn', and the distinguished judge, Henry de Bath, are all also recorded as receiving fees of £20, while Ralph de Aubigny had one of £10. On the dorse of this roll, Hugh Despenser, Roger Clifford, Fulk and Thomas de Orreby, John le Breton and unspecified others are described as being knights of Edward's *familia*.

[45] Above, 68–9.

[46] Prestwich, 'The Military Household of the Norman Kings', *EHR*, xcvi (1981), 1–35.

[47] These terms can be deduced from the wardrobe books, such as the *Liber Quotidianus*.

[48] E 101/351/17; E 101/352/24; *Complete Peerage*, iv, 50–1, ix, 603–4; xii (ii), 278–80.

> Valour and Sir William Latimer
> Fast and firm friends were they;
> His banner red bore a simple charge
> A cross of red patee.

It was with justice that Walter of Guisborough described Latimer as *miles strenuissimus*, but he performed diplomatic and legal duties as well as military ones. His son William followed him into household service, his career beginning in 1294. William junior was knighted on the Welsh campaign that year, and then went to fight in Gascony.[49] William Leyburn was another household knight whose service lasted much of the reign: he was the son of Roger Leyburn, who played so important a part in Edward's early career.[50] Eustace Hatch was a man who rose from being a squire in the household in 1276 to the status of a banneret in the later years of the reign. He served Queen Eleanor as well as the king, and was in charge of the king's daughters during the period when Edward was in Gascony in the late 1280s: like so many household knights, he had abilities which extended well beyond the military sphere.[51]

Such long service as these men gave was rather exceptional: there was a marked change in the composition of the household knights in the 1290s, as age took its toll. Only fourteen of those retained in the 1280s appear in later lists, and conversely, of those in receipt of fees and robes in 1297, only four had featured in the accounts of the previous decade.[52] There was some continuity in family terms: the Latimers and Leyburns were far from unique in providing fathers and sons as household knights. Walter Beauchamp's son followed in his father's footsteps; less auspiciously, the traitor Thomas Turberville was son of a household knight, Hugh Turberville.[53] The tradition of service might go back into Henry III's reign, or even earlier, with such names as Rivers, Tregoz, Grey, Oddingseles and Gorges recurring frequently. The names of Turberville, Lestrange, Mortimer, de la Pole and Mold among the bannerets of the 1280s reflect the importance of the Welsh March in the period of the Welsh wars, but there is no similar bias to the north to be

---

[49] *Complete Peerage*, vii, 461–5; Guisborough, 244; *Records of Wardrobe and Household*, xlii; *Book of Prests, 1294–5*, ed. E.B. Fryde (1962), 150; *The Siege of Carlaverock*, ed. Nicolas, 44.

[50] *Complete Peerage*, vii, 634–7; above, 27–47.

[51] Ibid., vi, 387–9; *Records of Wardrobe and Household*, ed. Byerley, xxxvii, where the evidence of *Liber Quotidianus*, 188, is ignored; *Court and Household of Eleanor of Castile*, ed. Parsons, 63.

[52] Prestwich, *War, Politics and Finance*, 48; BL Add. MS 7965, ff.60–1; *Records of Wardrobe and Household*, ed. Byerley, 164–5.

[53] See below, 383.

detected in the lists for the later years of the reign, when the king's attentions were directed towards Scotland.[54]

There was a significant foreign element among the household knights. It was only to be expected that Edward would employ some Gascons, given the affection which he clearly developed for Gascony from the time of his first visit there in 1254. Two of the Gascons who came to fight for Edward in Wales, during the second Welsh war, Arnold Guillaume and Arnold de Monteny, were recruited into the household, and when the king went to Gascony in 1286, he naturally took on a number of Gascons, including Arnold de Gavaston, father of the notorious Piers, Elie de Caupenne and Alexander de la Pebrée.[55] Few of these men came back to England with Edward, and by 1297 there were only four Gascons among the household knights, one of them a new recruit. In the last years of the reign there was a handful of Gascon household knights, including Arnold Gavaston, Arnold de Caupenne, Guy Ferre and Arnold Guillaume du Puy. They doubtless found the Scottish climate far from congenial when they campaigned in the north.[56]

The other important group of foreigners in Edward's service were the Savoyards. Otto de Grandson was the most important of the Savoyards, and his name does not, rather surprisingly, feature in the lists of household knights. It was probably considered that he was in receipt of sufficient other remuneration, and did not need fees and robes from the king. His importance in the household is attested by much evidence: at Easter 1287, for example, Oger Mote junior, a Gascon, was knighted and admitted to the household by Otto de Grandson acting on the king's behalf.[57] Peter de Chauvant was steward of the household and then chamberlain, and was clearly a figure of great significance.[58] John de Bonvillars, killed at Dryslwyn in 1287, was a distinguished Savoyard knight in the household, and William Cicon and Eble des Montz were among the other members of what seems to have been a close-knit group.[59]

Edward I's very considerable reputation brought other foreigners

[54] See Prestwich, op. cit., 44–5.

[55] *Records of Wardrobe and Household*, ed. Byerley, 164–5; for the names of further Gascon household knights, see Trabut-Cussac, *L'administration anglaise en Gascogne*, 79n. Piers Gaveston was Edward II's favourite.

[56] BL Add. MS 7965, ff.60–61; BL Add. MS 7966a, ff.78v–79.

[57] E 36/201, f.79. Otto's career is fully discussed by Clifford, *A Knight of Great Renown*, and more briefly by C.L. Kingsford, 'Sir Otho de Grandison, 1238?–1328', *TRHS*, 3rd ser., iii (1909), 125–95.

[58] He was still listed as a banneret of the household in 1301: BL Add. MS 7966a, f.135. For his career, see *Complete Peerage*, iii, 154–5.

[59] A.J. Taylor, 'Who was "John Penardd, leader of the men of Gwynedd"?', *EHR*, xci (1976), 79–97.

into his service. In the mid–1280s two Germans, Eustace de Jardin and Rainald Macere, were among the household knights, along with an Italian, Bonvassal of Genoa. In the later years of the reign, the cosmopolitan tradition was continued, with the Spanish knights Jaime, señor de Gerica, and Pascual of Valencia, known as the *adalid*. Within the British Isles Wales was not a fruitful recruiting ground: the social structure meant that there were relatively few men of knightly status, and Owen de la Pole, banneret of the household in the 1280s, was an exceptional figure. Scotland was a different matter. In the first half of the reign the Scot Andrew le Rat was a household knight, and then the king's involvement in Scottish affairs in the last decade of his life brought such men as Simon Lindsay, Simon Fraser, and Thomas and Herbert de Morham into the household. The fact that these men accepted the king's fees and robes did not, however, ensure their loyalty, as the cases of Fraser and Herbert de Morham were to show only too clearly.[60]

The squires formed the rank below the knights in the king's service. They were a very heterogenous group: in 1285–6 the list included the future knight, Grimbald Pauncefoot, and the royal tailor, Adam Bydik. Again, in 1300 the royal goldsmith, harpist, surgeon and tailor were included alongside such aristocratic names as Alan Plugenet, William Montague and Peter Maulay. Those of high birth could expect in due course to be knighted and to rise, if they stayed in household service, to the rank of banneret, while others were never to rise higher in status. The sergeants, a number of whom were Gascons, comprised professional soldiers, sergeants-at-arms and men with particular expertise, such as the king's armourer and his saddler.[61]

The military function of the knights, squires and sergeants of the household was obviously of prime importance. They provided the king with a force which could be readily and swiftly deployed in war, long before the elaborate process of recruiting the host as a whole had been completed. The number of men that could be raised by deploying the knights and others was very considerable, for each banneret and knight would bring his own retinue with him on campaign. In the Welsh wars, some squadrons solely made up of household men can be identified, though some household knights served alongside men who were only temporarily in royal pay. In the second Welsh war, of 1282–3, it seems likely that the household provided as much as a third of the total cavalry strength of the English army. In Flanders in 1297 there were few cavalry who were not of the royal household, and in 1298 the

---

[60] *Records of Wardrobe and Household*, ed. Byerley, xl, 165; Prestwich, *War, Politics and Finance*, 46; E 101/3/13; C 47/4/5, f.32; *Liber Quotidianus*, 188–95.

[61] *Records of Wardrobe and Household*, ed. Byerley, 166–7; *Liber Quotidianus*, 321–3.

household provided 800 cavalry for the Falkirk campaign, out of a total strength of perhaps 3,000. The heraldic poem which describes the siege of Caerlaverock in 1300 shows that the household men formed one out of the four battalions in the army.[62] Nor was the household confined to fighting on land. William Leyburn was named as captain of the king's sailors in 1294, and in the following year he was entitled admiral, the first English bearer of the title, along with his household colleague, John Botetourt. These men were not appointed because they had particular experience of naval matters, as was Gervase Alard of Winchelsea, admiral in 1300, but Leyburn in particular was a seasoned commander who had the king's trust, while Botetourt was rising rapidly to prominence, having begun his household career as a falconer in the 1270s.[63]

The household knights were much more than soldiers. They might be used on diplomatic missions: in the 1280s John de Vescy accompanied Anthony Bek to Bayonne, to the Low Countries and to Paris. In 1301 Robert de la Warde was sent to France to negotiate an extension of the truce between Philip IV and the count of Bar, Edward's son-in-law. Amanieu d'Albret, and other members of the household, were with the earl of Lincoln on an embassy to Rome in the same year, and Arnold de Caupenne was sent to treat with members of the French king's council.[64] At home, household knights might be given administrative duties: in the later years of the reign Robert Clifford was keeper of the temporalities of the bishopric of Durham. They were much used in the preservation of law and order. In 1286 household knights and squires were engaged in the pursuit of criminals. William Latimer served on two commissions to inquire into official malpractices, including the major judicial investigation that took place on Edward's return from Gascony in 1289, in which John de St John, another household banneret, also took part. John Botetourt served on four commissions of oyer and terminer in as many months late in 1298 and early in 1299, and was a man of considerable judicial experience.[65] The political importance of these men is hard to quantify, but a good proportion of the bannerets – two-thirds in 1300 – received summonses to attend parliament as barons, and their support of the king must have been valuable in discussions and debates.

Edward did not, of course, rely exclusively on the household to

---

[62] Prestwich, *War, Politics and Finance*, 50–8, provides a fuller account of the household at war.

[63] *Handbook of British Chronology*, 135; C 47/4/1, ff.15v, 36v.

[64] *Records of Wardrobe and Household*, ed. Byerley, xli; BL Add. MS 7966a, ff.29v, 34, 42v.

[65] Prestwich, 'The Military Household of the Norman Kings', *EHR*, xcvi (1981), 3; *CPR 1292–1301*, 458, 460–1.

provide knights who could perform political, judicial and diplomatic tasks. In some cases, household knights were not used as much as might have been expected. Only three household bannerets were appointed to the many commissions set up in 1297 to receive fines from the clergy in return for the king's protection.[66] Important local men were frequently given commissions to act as justices of oyer and terminer, and some of the appointments of this nature given to household men were probably due very largely to their position in county, rather than court, society. John Botetourt almost certainly received some of his commissions of oyer and terminer because he was an East Anglian landowner of some importance.[67] In 1301 it was two minor knights with no known house-hold connections, Thomas Wale and Thomas Delisle, who were sent to the papal curia with the important mission of putting Edward's case with regard to Scotland to the pope.[68] It is certainly not the case that all the household knights were kept busily employed on royal affairs in times of peace: the reason why Edward retained so many was because of their military function, and in peacetime it was more for reasons of status and prestige that a large establishment was maintained, rather than because the needs of state required a lavish household.

Edward I was never a notably generous master, and the rewards for serving him do not compare with those given out by his grandson Edward III. The clerks probably did best out of all Edward's house-hold servants, with the benefices that came their way. The list of the wardrobe clerks who eventually became bishops – though not all in Edward I's lifetime – is indeed an impressive one, consisting of Louth, Langton, Droxford, Sandale, Melton, Bek, Bicknor, March and Reynolds. There was a considerable increase in royal ecclesiastical patronage in Edward's reign, an increase probably inspired to a great measure by his clerks, who were the chief beneficiaries of it.[69]

The lay members did not benefit from royal patronage to the same extent, even though there were some men who rose strikingly in social status in the household. The king was most reluctant to make any permanent grants of land to his knights: to have done so would have run counter to the policy enunciated in his coronation oath, to maintain royal rights and recover past losses. Wardships and marriages were a different matter, and the household knights were in an excellent position to lay claim to these as they became available. Thus in 1292, John

[66] *CPR 1292–1301*, 239–40. The number could perhaps be raised to four, for William de Leyburn was one of the commissioners, but curiously, he was not included in the wardrobe book, BL Add. MS 7965, ff.60v–62, as receiving fees and robes this year.

[67] As for example *CPR 1292–1301*, 458, 460–1.

[68] E.L.G. Stones, 'The Mission of Thomas Wale and Thomas Delisle from Edward I to Boniface VIII in 1301', *Nottingham Medieval Studies*, xxvi (1982), 8–28.

[69] Below, 546–7.

de St John gained control of the Somery lands, John Botetourt the Drayton estate, and John de Felton, though only a squire, acquired the Middleton wardship. In the same year William FitzWarin's daughter married John de Dagworth, as a form of reward for her father's services.[70] It was through marriage that John Botetourt became an East Anglian landowner, not through any grant of lands from the king. Eustace Hatch, who rose from the rank of squire in 1276 to banneret status, came to hold land in nine counties, but was never a tenant-in-chief of the king. The limited scale of Edward's generosity is shown by the fact that Eustace's executors had to petition in parliament for payment of the debts owed him by the king, so that his legacies to the Holy Land might be paid.[71] William Leyburn even lost Leeds Castle in Kent, acquired by his father in 1268, to the king and queen in 1278, as part of a complex deal which saw his debts to a Jewish moneylender paid off.[72]

Minor gifts might come the way of household knights, as when in 1280 Clifford and Leyburn each received ten bucks and ten does to stock their parks, but it would be wrong to suppose that men served Edward for the sake of material rewards.[73] A king such as Edward did not need to buy loyalty on a lavish scale: there must have been many who felt it a privilege to serve a king of such prestige. There were some signs of discontent at the scant returns for loyalty: in 1305 the senor de Gerica and Pascual de Valencia were given £200 and £100 respectively, on condition that they cease making any further demands for money owed to them. Jean de Lamouilly, whose expertise enabled Edward to use gunpowder at the siege of Stirling in 1304, was so discontented with his treatment at the hands of the English crown that he was later to kidnap and hold to ransom the earl of Pembroke. Such examples were rare, however, and Edward appears to have had no difficulty in recruiting men to serve him. A letter from Katherine Paynel to the chancellor John Langton shows that positions at court were not easy to obtain. She asked for Langton's assistance in placing her son in the king's household, 'where he could learn good sense and manners', and from the fact that she offered to cover his expenses as far as she could, it seems that she was not expecting material rewards to come easily.[74]

If Edward was to exercise good lordship, then he had to provide for his servants in their old age. There was no problem as far as those of knightly status were concerned, for they had sufficient wealth to

[70] CPR 1281–92, 465, 472, 487, 498.
[71] Rotuli Parliamentorum, i, 199; M.C. Prestwich, 'Royal Patronage under Edward I', Thirteenth Century England I, ed. P.R. Coss and S.D. Lloyd (Woodbridge, 1986), 43.
[72] KW. ii, 695; CCR 1279–88, 80.
[73] Ibid., 33–4.
[74] Prestwich, 'Royal Patronage under Edward I'.

maintain themselves, but it was not so easy for the sergeants. Under
Henry III, exchequer pensions had been provided, but this practice
was not followed by Edward. Those pensions in existence at the time
of his return to England in 1274 were rapidly commuted for lump
sums. There were obvious disadvantages in giving men a direct call
on the limited cash resources of the crown, and Edward preferred
a method of rewarding men which cost him nothing. There was a
traditional royal right to demand corrodies, allowances of food and
clothing, from monasteries, particularly royal foundations.[75] Thus
in the hectic month of August 1297, when Edward was both preparing
to sail to Flanders and dealing with intense political arguments, he
found time to demand a corrody in Bury St Edmunds for his sergeant
William de Ponte, and one in Malmesbury for Robert le Despenser.
There was some difficulty at Abbotsbury, where the monks had to
be requested to restore the corrody earlier provided for Henry
Lombard. Many other examples could be given: in March 1293 the
king demanded no less than seven corrodies in seven different religious
houses.[76]

One further element was necessary for the household, and in particular the wardrobe, to serve effectively as a central part of the machinery
of government. It had to possess an effective means of communication,
and the household messengers were far more important than their
relatively humble status suggests. The history of the king's messengers
has been very fully investigated, and many detailed accounts of their
activities survive.[77] There was a small core of men who were retained
on a permanent basis as messengers. They were formally admitted to
the household, just as knights were: one record notes that on 15 March
Geoffrey of Bardney, who had been a member of the English garrison of
Edinburgh, was so admitted, and given a box with the royal arms on it
in which he could carry writs and letters. The total number of such
messengers varied, in the course of the reign, from ten to seventeen.
These regular messengers went about their duties on horseback, but
there were rarely enough of them for the amount of work that needed to
be done, so *cokini* (unmounted couriers) were hired in addition. As
many as forty might be used in any one year, and although not retained
on a permanent basis, many served the king very frequently. The
messengers were busy men: in 1300 the picturesquely named Little
Robin went on at least eleven separate missions, including one to
Gascony. It was not only the privy seal letters, written in the wardrobe,

[75] M.C. Hill, *The King's Messengers, 1199–1377* (1961), 61–85, *CCR 1296–1302*, 122–3,
127; *CCR 1288–96*, 279.

[76] *CCR 1296–1302*, 122–3, 127; *CCR 1288–96*, 279.

[77] Hill, *King's Messengers*.

that they delivered: many chancery writs, such as the summonses to parliament of 1300, were also carried by household messengers.[78]

Messengers had to be reliable, and in the two known cases where they failed Edward, those concerned were almost certainly not members of the household staff. In 1299 when the English garrison at Stirling were in dire straits, they deluded the Scots into thinking that they had ample supplies, by throwing out a quarter carcase of beef and a measure of wheat. However, a messenger they sent to the king, requesting victuals and aid, went to the Scots and revealed their true plight. The castle was therefore blockaded and fell in three days. Later, the treacherous messenger got his due deserts. The other example is of a Welsh messenger, who drunkenly offered to reveal all he knew of the king's secrets to the constable of a besieged Scottish castle. So appalled was the constable by such conduct that he refused to open the letters offered to him, and sent the Welshman back to the English to be hanged.[79]

The importance of the household, and the wardrobe in particular, as the nerve-centre of Edward's government cannot be over-emphasized. Yet at the same time as providing a personal secretariat with the privy seal, serving as the main spending department of state, financing armies, and providing a good many of the troops deployed in those armies, the household still performed its domestic functions. It was a major undertaking to provide for a body comprising up to some 600 people, excluding the inevitable mass of hangers-on, particularly as the household was, for much of the time, itinerant. Food, horses, carts, accommodation, royal almsgiving, even the maintenance of order within the household, all had to be carefully organized.

The demands made by the household in terms of food and drink were very impressive. A contemporary estimate made near the end of the reign, for a six-month period from April to September, put the daily requirement of grain at ten quarters of wheat and ten of malt – the latter for brewing purposes. Over the whole six months, 1,500 cattle, 3,000 sheep, 1,200 pigs and 400 bacon carcases would be required, and the horses would need 3,000 quarters of oats.[80] In addition, of course, great quantities of fish, poultry and wine would be consumed. Some impression of the needs of the household is given by the preparations made for the royal visit to Lenton, near Nottingham, at Easter 1303. As early as February the sheriff was ordered to purvey 100 quarters of wheat and

[78] *Liber Quotidianus*, 280–303.
[79] Hill, *King's Messengers*, 119–20; *Flores*, iii, 310, 320; *Chronicon de Lanercost*, ed. Stevenson, 177–9.
[80] E 101/13/36, no. 220.

600 of oats. Early in March a royal clerk, William Barton, was sent on ahead of the household to collect the grain together. Later that month orders were issued for ten live oxen, thirty beef carcases, twenty live sheep and eighty mutton carcases, along with pots and baskets, to be provided. Peter of Chichester, another household clerk, was sent to obtain forty tuns of ale.[81] The task of the royal officials was simplified by the fact that they could make use of the royal right of prise, which enabled them to compel men to sell their produce to the crown, at arbitrarily fixed prices. For the most part they were not even paid in cash, but received wardrobe bills, or tallies, which promised future payment, a promise which was all too often not fulfilled.

Once the foodstuffs had been collected together, the business of preparation was divided between various departments. The meat was stored in the larder, then cooked in the kitchen. Bread was the province of the pantry, and there was also the poultry and the saucery. Utensils and equipment were looked after by the scullery, and table-linen by the napery. Wine was the concern of the buttery. A full kitchen account survives for 1291–2, which gives some impression of the household diet. The staple items were beef, pork and mutton, with herring and cod on fast days. Most of these would have been preserved by salting, though some was eaten fresh. Chicken and duck were the main items of poultry, and eggs were consumed by the thousand. On special feast days, more luxurious items feature: at Christmas there was veal, and alongside the 1,742 chickens were twenty-two pheasants, seventeen dozen partridges, sixteen dozen mallard duck and six dozen plover. Rabbit might feature occasionally, but it was an expensive item, at no less than 8s 9d for half a dozen on one occasion. Fish days might be enlivened with lampreys, sturgeon, salmon and eels. Vinegar, verjuice and mustard were provided by the gallon to add flavour to what must have been a monotonous diet. Beside all this, of course, there would have been a great deal of bread eaten.

There were two kitchens in the household, according to the Ordinance of 1279: one for the king, and one for his following. The accounts show that Edward ate only rarely in the hall with all his household, going there on such special occasions as the feast of the Nativity of the Virgin.[82] For most of the time he must have eaten in his chamber, and presumably, as a result, usually did better than the general throng. On one occasion, however, in September 1300, the bread was found to be unsatisfactory in both chamber and hall, and the officials concerned were duly fined.[83] There were expensive items in the store of spices kept

[81] E 101/12/4.
[82] E 101/353/2; *Records of Wardrobe and Household*, ed. Byerley, xxx–iv.
[83] E 101/357/16.

by the great wardrobe, and these were obviously destined for the royal table: one inventory lists almonds, rice, ginger, galingale (an East Indian spice), pepper, saffron, caraway, cumin, sugar and other luxuries.[84]

Ale was easily supplied by local brewers, or was produced by the household staff, but wine presented greater problems. Feast days might see a great deal consumed: on Christmas Day 1286 thirteen tuns were needed, though normally the level was much lower, varying considerably in accordance with the number of people present. It could be a costly business to provide sufficient wine: in 1289–90 Matthew de Columbers, the royal butler, bought 1,858 tuns for £3,827. No doubt he was restocking, after the royal expedition to Gascony. The crown did have a right to take one tun of wine from before the mast, and one from abaft, from every ship that came to England, and this was an important source of supply. The procedure was of course unpopular, and one royal chamberlain complained that he had been threatened with the amputation of both arms when one merchant forcibly repossessed the two tuns taken from him. On occasion the crown accumulated enough wine to be able to sell some off: in 1285–6 Columbers obtained almost £300 in this way, and in 1299–1300 his successor as butler, Adam de Rokesle, accounted for almost £500 received from the sale of 172 tuns of wine.[85]

The scale of the provisioning operations for the royal household was vast, and in 1300 an attempt was made to reduce the burden on the clerks, cooks and others with the ordinance known as the Statute of St Albans. This aimed to cut down the numbers of those entitled to meals in the king's hall. The text does not survive, but the accounts provide some hints of its nature. The steward of the household, the keeper, and certain bannerets and knights were allocated cash allowances in lieu of taking meals.[86] If the purpose of the measure was economy, then it achieved little. In 1297–8 expenses of the domestic establishment stood at £12,608. In 1299–1300, the year of the Statute of St Albans, they fell to £10,926, and in the following year to £9,570, but they then rose to £12,021 in 1301–2.[87] However, the ordinance must have simplified the task of the household administrators, and it may well have meant that the demands for foodstuffs, made as the household moved about the country, were not so excessive. The measure could indeed have had some political purpose, to ease criticism of the crown's use of the right of prise.

[84] E 101/356/21.
[85] Records of Wardrobe and Household, ed. Byerley, xxxi–ii, 121; Liber Quotidianus, 15; E 101/352/10; E 101/352/22.
[86] Tout, Chapters in Medieval Administrative History, ii, 49–51.
[87] E 372/144; Liber Quotidianus, 360; BL Add. MS 7966a; E 101/360/25.

The arrangements for feeding the household appear to have been very efficient, to judge by the scarcity of indications of complaint and trouble. There were considerable problems at Conwy early in 1295, when the king was virtually besieged by the Welsh after suffering the loss of his baggage train, but those were exceptional circumstances.[88] There was trouble when Edward was in Flanders. At Ghent early in 1298 the pantry failed to provide enough bread, forcing the knights of the household to go out into the town to buy their supplies. It was held to be an action in contempt of the king when they marched into the hall, each followed by a servant carrying his food. Master Robert, the official in charge of the pantry, said that he could not supply bread, as the wardrobe had not given him sufficient funds: after an angry scene, he was deprived of his wages for a month. There were some difficulties in Scotland in the last years of the reign, as when the poulterer bought poultry, and shipped it north from Berwick in 1304, only for the ship to be driven off course to Norway. The birds died from the effect of the long voyage.[89] In general, however, it is remarkable how well the household administration coped with a difficult task.

The provision of more specialized commodities for the household was the concern of the rather confusingly named great wardrobe. Above all, the keeper of this office bought supplies of cloth, some of it of very high quality, furs and spices. The costs incurred by the king's tailor were mostly included in the great wardrobe accounts. The household ordinance of 1279 laid down that the keeper of the great wardrobe should buy goods at three fairs a year, and that he should have the assistance of the wardrobe usher, to act as his controller. The department was to be firmly under the ultimate control of the keeper of the wardrobe. These provisions were obviously intended to bring the great wardrobe under closer supervision: it had been developing into an office virtually independent of the household. It could never be fully integrated, however, for the nature of the great wardrobe's business was such that it needed to have a permanent base, where the cloth and other goods could be stored, and where work could be done on manufacturing robes. The keeper could not remain permanently in the household, and he had to travel in order to buy goods. The Tower of London provided what amounted to a permanent headquarters, and early in the reign a house in London was hired by Adam Bydik, the king's tailor, as a storehouse.[90]

Close relations were established between the great wardrobe and the

[88] Below, 221.

[89] Tout, *Chapters in Medieval Administrative History*, ii, 32n; Green, *Lives of the Princesses of England*, ii, 313; BL Add. MS 8835, f.29v.

[90] Tout, *Chapters in Medieval Administrative History*, ii, 161–2; iv, 370–1, 394, 398.

merchant community. The bulk of furs were supplied by Londoners, while a wide range of commodities in the later years of the reign were provided by the Italian firm of the Ballardi.[91] It is a measure of the continuing relative independence of the great wardrobe that it preferred to deal with this firm, rather than with the king's main bankers, the Riccardi in the first half of the reign and then the Frescobaldi. The accounts of the great wardrobe give some impression of the luxury and ostentation of the court. While there was much ordinary cloth bought, striped Stamford woollens, worsted and serge, along with plain blue cloth, there were also the cloths of gold, samite, purple, cindon and other high quality items, and a wide variety of furs. The lists of spices, many of them from the east, have an exotic character of their own.[92]

The hunting establishment, like the great wardrobe, had its permanent base, as well as forming a part of the itinerant household. The mews at Charing provided a centre for operations, while hawks and falcons were also sent to many different places, often to be looked after by men who held their lands by performing this particular service.[93] The scale of the royal hunting operations increased considerably in the course of the reign: in 1275–6 the cost was only £378, and in 1279–80 £482. In the next decade it rose as high as £1,002 in 1285–6, with as little as £77 being entered in 1299–1300. This reflects the fact that this was the most inefficient of all sections of the household when it came to accounting, not an actual decline in hunting activity. Many items in the last decade of the reign were not entered in the annual account books, until they came to be included in that for 1305–6, so causing an otherwise inexplicable jump in the total for that year to £1,155.[94] In the mid-1280s there were twenty falconers in the household, and ten 'ostringers' (who saw to the hawks), with ten 'braconers' in charge of the hounds, three huntsmen, six berners or kennel-men, two keepers of harriers, and one each of foxhounds and bercelets (another type of hound). Later numbers stayed at roughly this level.[95] The falconers and huntsmen were not employed merely because the king enjoyed his sport: theirs was also a very practical function, for they were able to supply the royal kitchens with a good deal of game, particularly venison.

The almonry was a small and specialized department, whose functions have already been discussed.[96] Its accounts fall into two sections, the provision made for paupers, some on a regular basis, and some on

---

[91] Williams, *Medieval London*, 159; E 101/127/7.
[92] See for example the fullest printed great wardrobe account, in *Records of Wardrobe and Household*, ed. Byerley, 246–8.
[93] Above, 115.
[94] E 372/123, 124, 130, 136, 144; E 101/369/11.
[95] *Records of Wardrobe and Household*, ed. Byerley, 168.
[96] Above, 112–13.

special saints days and festivals, and the more personal oblations made
by the king. These could include some very miscellaneous items alongside the offerings at various altars and gifts to friars: in December 1299
the almonry paid £45 2s to the bailiff of Darlington for repairs to the
bridge there, so that the royal carts could cross safely, and a month later
£1 4s was paid in alms to a Durham woman who had followed the king
to Berwick, so as to bring an appeal against certain criminals arrested
at the royal court. It was from the royal almonry that a stable boy,
kicked and injured by one of the royal war horses, received 5s by way of
compensation.[97]

The king and his household were frequently on the move. Lengthy
sessions of parliament, the need to take up winter quarters, illness near
the end of his life: such circumstances meant that the king would have
to take up residence in one place for some time, but for the most part it
was rare for him to be more than a few days in any one place. Transport
of the household was therefore a major undertaking. The household
ordinance of 1279 laid down that the wardrobe should have three long
carts, the pantry, buttery and kitchen one long and one short each. An
account of 1285–6 shows that some other departments, such as the
scullery and the larder, also had carts, and that the total then stood at
seven long and five short carts. At the end of the reign there were six
long and seven short carts, each looked after by one carter and one
fore-rider. There were also forty-one packhorses: the king's personal
plate, his robes and bed were all transported in this manner, as was the
furniture of the royal chapel.[98]

The provision of sufficient horses for drawing the carts, carrying
equipment and riding was a complex matter, even though many
members of the household would have had their own mounts. The
marshalsea was the department in charge of the royal horses, and it
organized not only those actually with the household, but also the
various studs and farms where they were bred and kept. Woodstock
and Hertford were two favourite stables, and Odiham was much used.
In the north, royal horses were kept at Macclesfield and the Peak. Other
places included Chertsey, St Albans and Breamore, and there was even
a royal stud at Ardudwy in Wales. A stable for 200 horses was built at
Clipstone in Nottinghamshire in 1282–3. That was an exceptional
number to envisage accommodating: more typical were the figures for
1296–7, when there were some thirty horses at Chertsey, under the
charge of Richard Fohun, a similar number in various places entrusted
to John Gylemyn, and about fifty with Adam de Bray at Hertford.

---

[97] *Liber Quotidianus*, 26–7, 43.

[98] Tout, *Chapters in Medieval Administrative History*, ii, 163; *Records of Wardrobe and Household*, ed. Byerley, 168; E 101/369/11, f.158.

Earlier, an account by William de Perton of the royal horses at Chester in 1284, at the close of the second Welsh war, shows the largest number to have been seventy-three.

A stable account for 1292–3, when the king was in Scotland, gives a better idea of the number of horses required by the itinerant household. In November 1292 there were eighteen royal horses at Berwick, and 164 at Norham. By May of the following year the total number had risen to 269. Of these, thirty-four were specified as being for the king, with others allocated to John of Brabant and the royal children. Fifty were for pulling carts, and forty-five were packhorses.[99] On occasion it proved necessary to buy additional horses. There were some imported from France at the time of the first Welsh war, and in 1297 almost a hundred were purchased for the household, presumably because of the needs of the campaign in Flanders that year.[100] If the horses privately owned by members of the household are included, the total number in the royal entourage becomes very impressive: in 1286 it was estimated that sufficient shipping would be needed to take 1,000 horses across the Channel.[101]

There was a considerable difference between the 'great' chargers used in war, and the carthorses and pack animals. The former could cost up to 100 marks, like the one bought by Edward at Winchelsea in 1297, while an ordinary rouncy, or a sumpter horse, might be worth no more than £2. The warhorses had splendid names, such as Bayard de la Tuche, Bayard de Champagne, Greyley or, slightly more prosaically, Lyndhurst.[102] The citizens of London considered in 1304 that a good way to curry favour with the king would be to present him with a fine horse, and a Spanish charger was duly bought for the purpose. Edward was a little suspicious, and sent Peter de Colingbourn to inspect the animal, but his opinion of it is unfortunately not recorded.[103]

The care of the household horses was a specialized business, and those involved in it, men such as John Gylemyn and Adam de Bray, did not move on to higher positions in other departments. Looking after sick horses, to mention simply one aspect of their overall responsibility, demanded particular expertise. Ailing horses were allocated 3d a day for their expenses, while their grooms received only 2d. Medicines used on them included vinegar, honey, pork grease, olive oil, sulphur and iron sulphate.[104]

[99] E 101/97/3; E 101/13/97; BL Add. MS 7965, ff. 26–7; *KW*, ii, 919.

[100] J.E. Morris, *The Welsh Wars of Edward I* (Oxford, 1901), 115; BL Add. MS 7965, ff. 21v–22v.

[101] *Records of Wardrobe and Household*, ed. Byerley, 46.

[102] E 101/97/12.

[103] BL Add MS. 8835, f.7v.

[104] *Records of Wardrobe and Household*, ed. Byerley, 31; E 101/97/3.

When the household was travelling, it was a major undertaking to
arrange billetting, particularly since there must have been many people
who were not actually retained by the king – merchants, petitioners,
paupers – accompanying the royal entourage. Harbingers and ushers
would be sent on ahead of the main party to make what arrangements
they could. Edward did, of course, possess a substantial number of
castles and manors where he might stay. Castles were not in fact much
favoured: he seems to have preferred to stay at the manor in Windsor
park, rather than in the castle there. The residences on which he was
most prepared to spend money were hunting lodges, such as Clipstone
in Nottinghamshire or Woolmer in Hampshire. At Banstead in Surrey,
acquired from John de Burgh, Edward spent about £200 on repairs,
new buildings and decoration, though in contrast the established royal
lodge at Freemantle in Hampshire was abandoned by the king, and its
buildings demolished.[105] Repairs were frequently needed in advance of
the arrival of the king and his household. In 1300 a writ was sent to the
bailiff of Geddington in Northamptonshire warning him that the king
was coming, and carpenters were duly employed to repair the hunting
lodge there, at a cost of £1 12s 3d. In the next year repairs at Brigstock
in Rockingham Forest cost £3 1s 11½d. At Northampton castle that
year, much work was done because the king was due to visit: a new
chamber was built, along with a wardrobe and a chimney, and a
partition was set up for the queen in the chapel, all at a cost of £22 13s
1d.[106] When the king and queen stayed at Wolvesey castle at Winchester,
in 1302, there was a serious fire, the result of a blocked chimney, from
which they were lucky to escape alive. As a result, when they next
visited the castle, in 1306, a new chamber was built for the queen, and
various repairs done. New glass was fitted to the windows, and the
paintwork renewed. An elaborate painted and upholstered chair was
made for the queen, and a garden with a stream running through
created for her to take her ease in.[107]

Many as the royal castles and houses were, the king and his household frequently had to find hospitality in monasteries, and even houses
belonging to his subjects. Sometimes, indeed, this was preferable to
using a royal castle: in 1306, at York, the archiepiscopal palace was
used as a temporary royal residence rather than Clifford's Tower.[108]
Edward's second queen, Margaret of France, had a strong preference
for staying in monasteries: late in 1299 she spent three weeks at St

[105] *KW*, ii, 919, 1007, 1017.
[106] *Liber Quotidianus*, 62; BL Add. MS 7966a, f.30v.
[107] E 101/369/11, f.46v.
[108] Ibid., f.49. Repairs to the palace came to over £63; BL Add. MS 8835, f.20v,
shows that a chamber for the king was built there in 1304 for just over £47.

Albans, and resisted the king's demands that they should spend Christmas at Clipstone, though in the end she had to compromise on Windsor.[109] A royal visit to a monastic establishment must in many ways have been unwelcome to the monks, but in April and early May 1291 the king came to Bury St Edmunds, dividing his time between the abbey itself and the abbot's nearby manor of Culford, and the house received a useful reward, in the form of a promise that royal justices would not in future sit within the liberty of Bury, which was some compensation for the inconvenience caused. On a later visit to Bury, in 1296, Edward chose not to stay in the monastery, but in the house of one Henry de Lynn: the monks considered that this was something of an affront, and that the accommodation was not really worthy of a king.[110] There certainly might be difficulties in staying in ordinary manor-houses. Early in 1297 the king was at Ipswich, and stayed in William Frank's manor, but there was not room for the wardrobe staff there, and they were put in another house, where they did damage assessed at 6s 8d.[111] Such entries, detailing compensation in the wake of a visit from the royal household, are a common feature of the accounts.

On campaign there was frequently nowhere comfortable to stay, and the royal household was well equipped in time of war with tents and pavilions, but for normal travel around the country little seems to have been done to provide canvas to sleep under, should insufficient accommodation be available. Even when Edward was travelling through France, on his way to Gascony in 1286, curiously the only tents that appear to have been provided were some for the use of a few Welshmen in the royal entourage. Many of the menial servants must often have had to sleep where they could, in the open, or perhaps sheltered under the long carts that carried the equipment. It would certainly be wrong to assume that life in the king's household was luxurious for any but a very few.

With the king's large entourage, there were bound to be problems in keeping order. There were also inevitably arguments with those who lived on the route taken by the household, about demands for provisions. There had to be special jurisdiction, for the crown could hardly be expected to rely on local courts. Edward's reign was very important for the development of the jurisdiction of the household, but the process is not an easy one to trace. The legal treatise known as *Fleta*, written in the 1290s, provides some help, for it states, after mentioning the court in parliament, that 'the king also has his court in his hall before his

[109] Rishanger, 401.
[110] *Chron. Bury St Edmunds*, 134.
[111] BL Add. MS 7965, f. 14r&v.

steward, who now occupies the place of the king's chief justiciar'. The jurisdiction of this court was confined to the verge, an area twelve miles around the king's person. The court was obviously concerned with breaches of the peace in this area, and *Fleta* states that the steward also had the power to receive and determine plaints, without any writ initiating the action, and irrespective of any privileges or franchisal rights that might be claimed. An example is provided of a writ in which the steward of the household commands the sheriff of a county about to be visited by the king, to bring all assizes and pleas, all prisoners in custody and all men on bail, to appear before the household court. The only limitation suggested for this remarkably wide jurisdiction was that the steward should not meddle in cases concerning freeholds, without a writ. It is even suggested that the jurisdiction of the court was still valid when the king was in a foreign country, and a case is cited to prove the point. When Edward was in Paris in 1286, some of the royal plate was stolen. After long discussions in the French king's council, it was decided that the case against the thief should be heard before Edward's steward. The author of *Fleta* was obviously well-informed on these matters, and clearly had access to the court records: he may even have sat as a member of the household court.[112]

Financial records provide valuable information about the workings of household jurisdiction. They make it clear that there were effectively two courts, that of the hall, supervised by the steward and marshal, and that of the market, where the clerk of the market imposed fines for transgressions against trading regulations within the verge. In most years the latter provided more revenue that the former: often local communities would simply pay a lump sum, as in the case of Northampton which was charged £10 in 1301, so that there was no need to hear a large number of petty cases.[113] In 1285–6 the accounts show that it was only the pleas of the market that raised any revenue at all, and that was no more than just over £50.[114] Unfortunately, in the earlier years of the reign the summary accounts of wardrobe receipts do not distinguish between the income from the two aspects of household jurisdiction, so it is not clear how it was that the high figure of £343 was achieved in 1275–6: in the next year income fell to £106. There were startling variations in the 1290s. In 1296–7 market fines were at a normal level, but receipts from the court of the steward and marshal were staggeringly high at £232. This perhaps reflects in some way the fact that this was a year of political crisis. A roll of fines levied in the

---

[112] *Fleta*, ed. H.G. Richardson and G.O. Sayles, ii (Selden Soc., 1955), 109–113. For a discussion of the dating and authorship of this work, see *Fleta*, iii (Selden Soc., 1984), xii–xxv.

[113] BL Add. MS 7966a, f.12.

[114] *Records of Wardrobe and Household*, ed. Byerley, 192–3.

court shows that a great many men simply failed to attend, incurring penalties of between one and two shillings. In the next year, 1297–8, when the Scottish campaign which culminated in the triumph at Falkirk took place, market fines rose to £111, but only just over £5 was raised in the court of the hall.[115] There were no such remarkable fluctuations in the final years of the reign, but the record of the profits made by the court of the steward and marshal in 1299–1300 shows how much might depend on a very few cases. Out of a total of just over £70, £21 came from the silver and plate found in the possession of one Robert Sallowe, arrested for felony within the verge by the bailiffs of Morpeth, and £38 from the forfeiture of the goods of three criminal brothers at Newcastle upon Tyne.[116]

An eminent legal historian, G.O. Sayles, has suggested that 'the evidence at our disposal scarcely justifies a belief in the existence of a steward's court before 1290', and that it was perhaps the experience gained when the king was in France, between 1286 and 1289, that led to the effective creation of the court of the steward and marshal.[117] The financial evidence is to the contrary, and although the accounts for the early part of the reign do not distinguish between the profits of the hall and those of the market, it seems most unlikely that the jurisdiction of the steward and marshal evolved only in the middle years of the reign. One extension of the court's function that undoubtedly did take place was its development as a place where recognisances, or acknowledgements, of debts might be enrolled. In cases where the debtors defaulted, it may have been easier to get speedy action in the household court than elsewhere. The system was not entirely satisfactory, however, for in 1302 merchants asked that they should be allowed to use the machinery of the exchequer to recover debts that had been enrolled before the steward and marshal.[118]

Surprisingly, not all cases that arose within the household were determined in the court over which the steward and marshal presided. In 1291 Nicholas de Lovetot struck another man in the king's hall at Westminster, but it was before the king's bench, not the household court, that he was to be convicted. Two years later, Eustace de Parles and his brother insulted the king's justice, William Bereford, accusing him of corruption and other offences, doing so in the king's hall. This matter was regarded very seriously, and so the case was heard in

[115] See the enrolled wardrobe accounts in E 372/124, 130, 136, 144; E 101/356/3.
[116] *Liber Quotidianus*, 4–5.
[117] *Select Cases in the Court of King's Bench*, ed. Sayles, iii, lxxxiii–lxxxviii. Writing later, however, Sayles pointed to evidence for the jurisdiction of the steward and marshal dating from 1272, and he also suggested that the plea rolls of the household court began much earlier than 1286: *Select Cases in the Court of King's Bench*, ed. Sayles, vii, xliv–xlv.
[118] *Select Cases in the Court of King's Bench*, ed. Sayles, iii, lxxxvii, cxxii–cxiii.

parliament.[119] Nor did the authority of the court extend over the royal army in time of war, as might have been expected, given the fact that the troops were paid through the wardrobe, and that much of the army must have been within the verge. In fact, military discipline was the responsibility of a quite separate court, under the authority of the marshal of England. Only one court roll of this military tribunal survives, for the Scottish campaign of 1296, but it is quite clear from it that the 'pleas of the king's army' were quite distinct from the cases that came before the household court of the steward and marshal.[120]

It was obviously essential, with an itinerant household, that there should be some convenient means of hearing and determining cases as it moved about the country. At the same time, the operations of a prerogative court, which acted upon plaint rather than upon writ, and whose activities were closely connected with the demands made upon the local inhabitants by the household, were bound to create some resentment. In 1300 it was agreed, in the *Articuli super Cartas*, that the jurisdiction of the court should be confined to cases of trespass which occurred within the verge, and in which action could be started before the king had moved on elsewhere, and also to cases regarding debt and other agreements between members of the king's household. The coroner of the household was not to act alone, but in co-operation with local coroners, to obtain indictments of felons within the verge.[121] Complaints along similar lines were to continue in Edward II's reign, and it seems unlikely that the *Articuli* changed much. Edward was not attempting to develop a wide-ranging novel type of jurisdiction for the steward and marshal, and the issue of the limits of the courts functions was not one of major constitutional concern.

In many respects Edward I's government of England saw the adoption of new or revitalized approaches. The techniques which led to the great inquiries, and the production of the statutes, or to the development of consultation through parliament, could hardly be applied to the royal household. Yet, in some respects, fresh attitudes did serve to change this most central of the institutions of government. The very existence of the household ordinance of 1279, unsatisfactory as it is, shows that it was felt that there was a need for some reorganization to take place. It is in the make-up of the records that a transformation is most evident, with a change from the ill-ordered journals of the early years to the well-organized and beautifully written volumes of the final decade of the reign.

---

[119] E 159/65. m. 11; *Rotuli Parliamentorum*, i, 95.

[120] E 39/93/15; partially calendared in *CDS*, ii, no. 822.

[121] *Statutes of the Realm*, i, 138. See also W.R. Jones, 'The Court of the Verge: the Jurisdiction of the Steward and Marshal of the Household in Later Medieval England', *Journal of British Studies*, x (1970–1), 27.

The financial position of the household, and in particular of the wardrobe, changed markedly in the course of the reign. In the early years much of the wardrobe's revenue was received quite independently of the exchequer, whereas in the closing years the bulk of it was allocated by means of block grants through the exchequer. But these administrative changes did not of themselves mean that the fundamental role and character of the household underwent a thoroughgoing transformation. The fine account books of the later years are somewhat deceptive, for they conceal a state of considerable confusion, with accounts submitted years in arrears, and debts mounting up as expenditure far exceeded income. The block allocations of income, through the exchequer, did not mean that in practice the exchequer exercised any effective control over the wardrobe, which was quite as independent as it had been in the early part of the reign. The pressures of war in the years after 1294, rather than a deliberate policy adopted by the crown, do much to explain this. There was certainly no question of Edward attempting to develop the household as a basis for autocratic government, and no way in which it was, or indeed was seen to be, a threat to the established constitutional structure of the realm. There were naturally major changes in the personnel of the household in the course of the reign, with a marked shift taking place in the 1290s, but the new men of the later years of the reign, John Droxford, John Benstead and Walter de Beauchamp among others, were well schooled in the established traditions of the household. This was an institution which evolved gradually, rather than undergoing any sudden, cataclysmic changes.

Chapter 7

THE CONQUEST OF WALES

On 12 November 1276 Edward I formally decided to wage war on Llywelyn ap Gruffydd, prince of Wales. The decision was taken in a council of prelates and magnates, and followed Llywelyn's repeated refusal to come to perform homage to the English king. The conquest of Wales, which was not completed until 1295, was one of Edward's most notable achievements. The princely dynasty of Gwynedd was destroyed, and the most remarkable chain of castles ever constructed stands as a permanent reminder of the power which Edward brought to bear on the Welsh.

It is tempting to assume, with the aid of hindsight, that Edward aimed from the outset at the total subjection of the Welsh principality. He had had little success with regard to Wales prior to his accession: the policies of his ministers had led to revolt in the 1250s, and the Treaty of Montgomery of 1267 had shown that Simon de Montfort's Welsh ally, Llywelyn ap Gruffydd, was still very much a force to be reckoned with. As king, however, Edward was in a much stronger position, and it might be supposed that he embarked on his series of Welsh wars in order to avenge his earlier lack of success. This may have been an element in the English king's policy, but it was Llywelyn's attitude, not Edward's, that explains why war broke out in 1276. The survival of Llywelyn's rule depended on his achieving notable success against the English: Edward, in contrast, did not need to bolster his prestige by means of a struggle with the Welsh.

Llywelyn's career before the 1270s had been astonishingly successful. He had played his hand with great skill in the course of the Barons' Wars, and in the Treaty of Montgomery of 1267 the strength of his position was evident. He was formally acknowledged by Henry III as prince of Wales. The Welsh barons were to hold their lands as fiefs from him, and many of the territorial gains he had made were accepted by the English. He did, it is true, accept that he owed fealty and homage to Henry III, but the nature of the service that he owed as a result was not set out. The treaty was not, perhaps, as clear-cut in all particulars as might have been hoped, especially in some of its territorial terms, but it showed that his authority in Wales was fully recognized by the

English.[1] Significantly the treaty shows the way in which Llywelyn's power was seen by the English. Those responsible for drafting it could not appreciate that the character of Llywelyn's rule was in fact very different from that of an English king, or even an English territorial magnate, and that to describe it in essentially feudal terms was to give a very false impression.

Although Wales had long been exposed to English influence, with English lordship being exercised in the Marches, it was a very different country from England in countless ways. The basic unit of English agrarian life, the manor, had made little progress into Wales, save within the Marcher lordships. After the Edwardian conquest, the earl of Lincoln was to create a brand-new manor at Kilford in his honour of Denbigh, for there had been none there before.[2] Towns had barely begun to appear in the areas not under English influence: it has been estimated that less than two per cent of the population of Merioneth lived in towns. Much of north Wales was remarkably remote, reliant on self-sufficiency rather than on the workings of a market economy. An ordinance of Edward I's, which required one person from every household to come to market once a week, would cause considerable problems, and men had to be allowed to deal in such foodstuffs as cheese, butter and milk as they wished. The constable of Harlech castle was to complain that he had to go as far as Montgomery, or Oswestry, to buy the victuals he needed.[3] The use of money was much less common than in England: in 1318 the men of west Wales were to argue that 'they were never accustomed to have money in the Welshry'.[4]

Lordship was of great importance in Welsh society, but it was not feudal lordship in the English sense. Only to a limited extent were the Welsh adjusting themselves in the thirteenth century to system of grants of land made in return for service. The rules of succession were quite different to those that operated in England, for lands might be divided between sons, rather than descending by a system of primogeniture. The old bonds of kindred were still present, and the legal system took account of the possibility of paying sums of money as recompense for murder, *galanas*, a practice which the lawyers of Edward I's England

---

[1] *Littere Wallie*, 1–4. For the most recent account of Edward's conquest of Wales, which appeared too late to be fully taken into account when this chapter, and Chapter 8 were written, see R.R. Davies, *Conquest, Coexistence and Change: Wales 1063–1415* (Oxford, 1987), 333–88.

[2] R.R. Davies, *Lordship and Society in the March of Wales, 1282–1400* (Oxford, 1978), 109.

[3] *Registrum vulgariter nuncupatum 'The Record of Caernarvon'*, ed. H. Ellis (1838), 212, 224.

[4] *The Merioneth Lay Subsidy Roll, 1292–3*, ed. K. Williams-Jones (Cardiff, 1976), xxiii.

were bound to find illogical and repellent.[5] There was a growing tendency to determine legal cases by an anglicized procedure of inquisitions, but the ancient hereditary position of judge, or *eneyt*, still survived in the north, and there is mention of one *eneyt* in Cyfeiliog, in Powys, so termed because he went to north Wales to learn Welsh law, though he did not, in fact, practice.[6]

Llywelyn ap Gruffydd was the most powerful member of the most important of the Welsh ruling dynasties. He did not, however, face an easy task in establishing his power in face of rivalries, both within his own family and with other Welsh lords. His task resembled that of some Merovingian ruler more than it did that facing a king of the late thirteenth century, such as Edward I. Two of Llywelyn's brothers presented no major threats: the eldest, Owain, had been taken prisoner by him as long ago as 1255, and he remained in custody until 1277. Rhodri was persuaded, in 1272, to hand over his rights to lands in Wales in return for a promise of 1,000 marks. Dafydd, the youngest brother, provided the gravest problem. He opposed Llywelyn in 1255, and in the mid-1260s backed Henry III against his brother. Reconciliation followed, until in 1274 Dafydd became involved in a plot with Gruffydd ap Gwenwynwyn of Powys, directed against Llywelyn.[7]

No doubt Llywelyn wished to extend his power over other Welsh rulers by means of feudal techniques, but the terms of the agreements which he made suggest that this was possible to only a very limited extent. When Gruffydd ap Gwenwynwyn did homage for lands to Llywelyn in 1263, the agreement reads in many ways like a treaty between two rulers of equal authority. It does specify that, provided his own lands were not threatened with invasion, he was bound to join Llywelyn's army, but there was no definition of the nature of this service in normal feudal terms.[8] One means frequently employed by Llywelyn to retain the allegiance of Welsh rulers is evidence of their reluctance to accept his lordship. In 1261 he demanded that Maredudd ap Rhys should hand over twenty-four hostages, and in 1274 Gruffydd ap Gwenwynwyn gave his son Owain to him as hostage. The same technique was used on a wide scale in 1271, when Llywelyn was reinforcing his authority in mid-Wales.[9] The use of such methods is testimony to the fragility of the political edifice that Llywelyn was

[5] R.R. Davies, 'The Survival of the Bloodfeud in Medieval Wales', *History*, liv (1969), 338–57.

[6] *CWR*, 208.

[7] *Littere Wallie*, xxxviii-xl, liii; D. Stephenson, *The Governance of Gwynedd* (Cardiff, 1984), 138–65, provides a fuller analysis of the problems caused by the uncertainty of succession in Wales.

[8] *Littere Wallie*, 77–80, 111–13.

[9] Ibid., xliv-xlv.

trying to construct, and it is small wonder that Edward I was to have little difficulty in gaining support from some of those who had been subjected to Llywelyn's arbitrary techniques of rule.

Llywelyn did not have the same kind of administrative resources as did the English king. His central government was scarcely departmentalized, and the custom of rewarding ministers and officials with hereditary grants of land was a drain on already inadequate princely estates. There were various traditional renders which could be commuted into cash, and although there was an occasional levy, taken on the basis of the number of cattle owned, there was not the tradition of taxation which existed in England. Llywelyn's expenses were very considerable. Military service beyond forty days appears to have been at his expense.[10] Castles had to be strengthened: Llywelyn appears to have engaged in extensive building works at Ewloe, Dolwyddelan, Criccieth and Castell y Bere, and in 1273 a new castle was started at Dolforwyn.[11] In addition, the financial cost of the Treaty of Montgomery of 1267 was heavy. The Welsh prince agreed to pay the English 25,000 marks, in instalments, and to that was added a further 5,000 marks in 1270, when Henry III conceded feudal lordship over Maredudd ap Rhys, of Ystrad Tywi in south Wales, to Llywelyn.[12] Remarkably, in the years up to 1272 Llywelyn kept up with his payments, which were set at 3,000 marks a year. Given that the income available to Edward prince of Wales in 1304–5 from north Wales was just over £3,000, it is evident that Llywelyn must have placed his subjects under enormous pressure.[13]

A list of complaints against his rule, drawn up after his death and presented to Edward I, makes it plain that his regime was aggressive and unpopular. He overrode traditional customs, and imposed considerable increases in traditional obligations. The *census annuus* in the Lleyn peninsula was doubled, and units of measure were manipulated to his advantage.[14] It was only by engaging in a policy of further expansion of his dominions that Llywelyn could hope to retain the loyalty of his officials and his subjects: only by winning lands and booty could he provide them with sufficient rewards.

Conflict began in the early 1270s between Llywelyn and the Marcher lords. In 1270 the Welsh seized the earl of Gloucester's new fortress at

[10] Stephenson, *Governance of Gwynedd*, provides a full discussion of Llywelyn's government.

[11] R. Avent, *Cestell Tywysogion Gwynedd* (Cardiff, 1983), 21–2.

[12] *Littere Wallie*, xliii, li, 1–4; *Calendar of Ancient Correspondence concerning Wales*, ed. J.G. Edwards (Cardiff, 1935), 207–8; *CPR 1266–72*. 457.

[13] *Merioneth Lay Subsidy Roll*, xviii-xx.

[14] L. Beverley Smith, 'The Gravamina of the Community of Gwynedd against Llywelyn ap Gruffydd', *Bull. Board of Celtic Studies*, xxxi (1984), 158–76.

Caerffili in Glamorgan, though by 1274 it appeared that the earl had regained the upper hand. There was also fighting between Llywelyn's men and the earl of Hereford, whose lordship of Brecon was under attack.[15] There was trouble between the Welsh prince and Roger Mortimer. Llywelyn claimed that Mortimer's castle-building activities in Maelienydd went beyond what was permitted by the Treaty of Montgomery, and that his own claims to the land, acknowledged in the treaty, had not been heard. In these circumstances, Llywelyn was not prepared to continue payment of the money under the terms of the treaty. He asked Edward in 1273 or 1274 (the letter is undated) to 'compel the earl of Gloucester, Humphrey de Bohun and the rest of the Marchers to restore to Llywelyn the lands by them unjustly occupied and more unjustly detained'. If this was done, then payment would be resumed.[16] The building of Dolforwyn castle in Montgomeryshire was also at issue in this period. In June 1273 the English government forbad the construction of the castle, and the creation of an associated borough and market. Llywelyn responded firmly, arguing that he had full power to build castles and set up markets on his own land, and that although he held his principality from the king, the rights of that principality were quite distinct from the laws of the English realm. He suggested that the prohibition had been issued without Edward's knowledge (the king was in Gascony at the time), and implied that he would not have taken such action himself. Building continued: in the year up to April 1274, £174 6s 8d was paid to the constable of the new castle to pay for the works.[17]

The question of Llywelyn promising fealty to Edward I was raised soon after Henry III's death, but the Welsh prince did not answer a summons to come to Montgomery at the end of January 1273. Nor did he appear at Edward's coronation in 1274, but arrangements were made for him to come to Shrewsbury in November of that year, so that he could perform homage. Edward, unfortunately, was struck by illness and could not attend: it is conceivable that had the meeting taken place, the course of events might have taken a very different turn. In June 1275 Llywelyn was asked to come before Edward at Chester in late August. This time Edward attended – a few days late – but the Welsh prince did not. However, he claimed in proclamations to his own people that peace had been made, and raised a tax, on the pretext that he needed the money to pay Edward what was due to him. This alarmed some of the Welsh, and it must be suspected that Llywelyn was

[15] Altschul, *A Baronial Family*, 129–33.
[16] *Cal. Anc. Corr. Wales*, 92–4.
[17] Ibid., 86; *Littere Wallie*, 23–4; *CCR 1272–9*, 51; M.W. Beresford, *New Towns of the Middle Ages* (1967), 44, 239–40.

in fact collecting funds with a view to war. Further summonses were issued by Edward, requesting Llywelyn's presence at Westminster in October 1275, at Winchester in January 1276 and finally again at Westminster in April 1276. Llywelyn steadfastly refused to attend, and the sums due under the terms of the Treaty of Montgomery remained unpaid.[18]

Llywelyn had strong reasons for acting as he did. He considered that the English had not kept to the treaty of 1267, and worries about the efficacy of Edward's offers of safe-conducts made him very reluctant to undertake a journey into England. More serious was the plot hatched early in 1274 between Gruffydd ap Gwenwynwyn of Powys and Llywelyn's brother Dafydd, which aimed at the assassination of the Welsh prince. The conspiracy was discovered, but both Gruffydd and Dafydd managed to escape to England, where they were well received by Edward.[19] Further provocation came over Llywelyn's marriage plans. He had long been betrothed to Simon de Montfort's daughter Eleanor, and it seems that he thought, quite misguidedly, that it would be possible to reawaken the rivalries of the 1260s in England. He was in league with Earl Simon's surviving sons, Guy and Amaury, and one of the executors of their mother's will, Nicholas de Waltham, was acting as his secret agent at the English court.[20] These links were strengthened by the proxy marriage ceremony between Llywelyn and Eleanor which took place in 1275. Disaster struck when Eleanor and her brother Amaury tried to come to Wales by sea, for they were captured in the Bristol Channel, probably by a Cornish knight, Thomas Larchdeacon. Some chroniclers considered that this incident was what drove Llywelyn to make war upon the English, but it seems unlikely that the Welsh prince would have persisted in his marriage plans had he not in fact already been determined on settling his disputes with Edward by force. It is certainly the case, however, that Edward's refusal to release Eleanor aggravated an already tense and difficult situation.[21]

In 1276 matters continued to deteriorate. In May Llywelyn complained about Roger Mortimer's activities in the March, and about raids by Gruffydd ap Gwenwynwyn's men. Payn de Chaworth was also attacking Welsh territory. In the autumn, Bogo de Knoville told the king that the area around Oswestry and Montgomery was being constantly harried by the Welsh, and that he was powerless to resist. An

[18] *Littere Wallie*, lvi; *Cal. Anc. Corr. Wales*, 64, 105; *CPR 1272–81*, 72.
[19] *Littere Wallie*, liii-lv.
[20] D. Stephenson, 'Llywelyn ap Gruffydd and the Struggle for the Principality of Wales, 1258–1282', *Trans. of the Honourable Society of Cymmrodorion*, (1983), 44; F. Pollock and F.W. Maitland, *The History of English Law* (2nd edn, Cambridge, 1898), ii, 507.
[21] *Chron. Bury St Edmunds*, 60; *CCR 1272–9*, 292.

offer by Llywelyn to come to do homage to Edward at either of these two places was not acceptable to the English king. The conditions placed on the offer included the receipt of elaborate safe-conducts, the confirmation of the treaty of 1267 and the release of Eleanor de Montfort.[22] Edward no doubt considered that the question of fealty and homage was not negotiable: it was Llywelyn's duty to fulfil his obligation to appear before him, and if he would not do so, he would be treated as a rebel. Edward was determined on war. He must have considered that he had been patient long enough, although in practice, the length of time needed to make military preparations would allow the Welsh one last opportunity to try to achieve a peaceful settlement.

The main muster of the English feudal host was ordered to take place at Worcester on 1 July 1277. It was essential to make arrangements for the defence of English-held lands much more immediately than that, in view of the prospect of further Welsh raids. Accordingly, in the council at Westminster where the decision to make war on Llywelyn was taken, appointments were made to provide for the protection of the Marches. The earl of Warwick was to be captain at Chester, Roger Mortimer at Montgomery, and Payn de Chaworth in west Wales.[23] Royal household knights were moved swiftly westwards: in November and December they received pay successively at London, Windsor and Cirencester. In January 1277 John de Beauchamp was appointed to the custody of the castles of Cardigan and Carmarthen, and by the end of the month he had a force of over a hundred cavalry. In the next month the earl of Lincoln had a similar sized troop at Oswestry. Warwick's force at Chester was clearly substantial, costing £1,094 in wages between January and May. Unpaid service was provided by the men of Shropshire and Herefordshire.[24]

These forces did much more than hold their own against the Welsh. Lincoln retook Bauseley in Montgomeryshire, and the men of Gorddwr surrendered to the Marcher lord Peter Corbet. Gruffydd ap Gwenwynwyn, loyal to Edward, won over many Welshmen to his side. Bogo de Knoville also reported to the king that the three most powerful men in the cantred of Arwystli had come to terms, provided that Edward would agree to maintain their rights. Further south, Payn de Chaworth succeeded in negotiating the surrender of two important lords, Rhys ap Maredudd and Gruffydd ap Maredudd ap Owain, in March, and although they failed to appear later that month to perform

[22] *Cal. Anc. Corr. Wales*, 27–8, 86–7; *CCR 1272–9*, 360.
[23] *Parl. Writs*, i, 193; *CCR 1272–9*, 358.
[24] E 101/3/12, 13, 21; Morris, *Welsh Wars of Edward I*, 118–22.

fealty to Edward as they had promised, peace with Rhys was concluded on 11 April, while Gruffydd finally made his full surrender on 2 May. Llywelyn's power received a direct blow when, at the end of March, the garrison of Dolforwyn promised that they would surrender on 8 April if they had not been relieved by then. The castle was duly handed over to Roger Mortimer, who appointed Gruffydd ap Gwenwynwyn to be in charge of it. The full extent of the success achieved by the English forces must have been very clear to Edward when, on 1 July, five important Welsh rulers, Rhys ap Maredudd, Rhys Wyndod, Gruffydd and Cynan ap Maredudd ap Owain, and Rhys Fychan, all appeared before him and performed homage.[25]

The extent of English success in the Marches, and in the south, before the main expedition had even mustered, must have made Llywelyn think hard about the wisdom of offering armed resistance to Edward I. Early in the year attempts had been made to negotiate an agreement: the bishop of Bangor, with a clerk, had been sent to Edward, and some mediation was attempted by the archbishop of Canterbury. Llywelyn argued that the English had more to gain from him than from 'those who now by the king's war seek their own profit and convenience rather than the king's honour'.[26] This met with no response from Edward. In what was in many ways a civil war in Wales, it must have been obvious to the English king that it was to his advantage to give full encouragement to Prince Dafydd, Gruffydd ap Gwenwynwyn and those Welsh rulers who were ready to throw off their allegiance to Llywelyn.

Many preparations had to be made for Edward's expedition into Wales. The formal feudal summonses were issued on 12 December 1276, asking all those who owed service to muster at Worcester on 1 July.[27] There was a shortage of suitable cavalry horses in England: the bailiffs of the French port of Wissant were asked, also on 12 December, to allow the passage of seventy-five horses. In February 1277 Matthew de Columbers, a royal sergeant, was sent to France to buy twenty mounts for the king, and in June he returned there for another forty.[28] Abbeys and priories were asked to provide carts to transport the king's tents and pavilions from London to Wales: at least nineteen such carts were used.[29] Arrangements were made for the recruitment of infantry, and some steps were taken to ensure that there would be sufficient

[25] *Cal. Anc. Corr. Wales*, 30–2, 55–6, 71–2, 81; *Littere Wallie*, 36–7, 41; *Brenhinedd y Saesson*, ed. T. Jones (Cardiff, 1971), 255; R.A. Griffiths, *The Principality of Wales in the Later Middle Ages*, i (Cardiff, 1972), 3; Morris, *Welsh Wars of Edward I*, 120–1, 124–5.
[26] *Cal. Anc. Corr. Wales*, 87, 91.
[27] *Parl. Writs*, i, 193, 195–6.
[28] *CPR 1272–81*, 184, 193, 212.
[29] E 101/3/15.

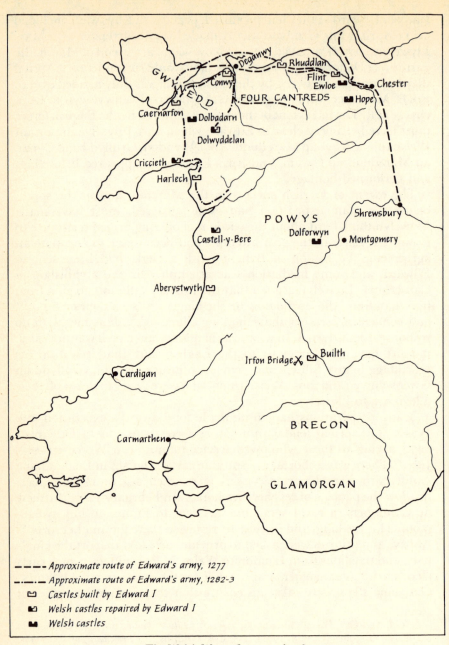

1. The Welsh Wars of 1277 and 1282–3

THE CONQUEST OF WALES

supplies of food and weapons. In February, the justiciar of Ireland was asked to send 600 quarters of wheat and 1,000 of oats to Chester by Midsummer. In the next month there must have been frenzied activity at St Briavel's castle, in Gloucestershire, where Edward requested the manufacture of 200,000 crossbow bolts.[30] Money was needed as well as men, equipment and victuals. In February, arrangements were made to borrow just over £3,700 from Italian merchant companies operating in England, and in May, the steward of Ulster was asked to take all the issues of his county to Chester at Midsummer, 'the king being in great need of money for the furtherance of arduous affairs in Wales'.[31] In comparison to the massive efforts made for Edward's later wars in Wales and in Scotland, all this activity was on a small scale, but the vital precedents for the future were now being set.

The records of the feudal muster show that a total service of 228 knights and 294 sergeants was provided by the king's tenants-in-chief.[32] This was not, of course, the total cavalry force at Edward's disposal: many men served for pay, and some Marchers at their own expense. From Worcester, some men were sent to join an army under the command of the king's brother, Edmund of Lancaster, operating from Carmarthen. By 25 July they had reached Llanbadarn, the future Aberystwyth. The activities of this force thoroughly alarmed Rhys Fychan, who had earlier surrendered to Edward. He now fled to join Llewelyn, and his lands were seized by the English.[33]

The majority of those who mustered at Worcester in July moved swiftly northwards, to Chester, which was to be the base for the king's own advance against Llywelyn. The fleet of the Cinque Ports, which also owed feudal service and consisted of twenty-six ships, came to Chester as well. The campaign was a surprisingly uneventful one. The army, consisting of perhaps 800 cavalry and some 2,500 infantry, advanced swiftly from Chester to Flint by 25 July, cutting a wide road through the forest. Edward himself then returned to Cheshire, to supervise the collection of supplies and equipment needed to set up a strong base. Great quantities of timber were brought from the Wirral and elsewhere; picks, axes and other equipment were bought in Chester. By mid-August, Edward was back at Flint, where a great ditch had been dug to provide defence against the Welsh: the ditchers were given a reward of 8s 9d for their good work. Carts brought crossbow bolts along the newly made road and, no doubt most welcome to the troops, five barrels full of silver pennies for their pay. The main army moved on

[30] E 101/3/15; *CCR 1272-9*, 373.
[31] *CPR 1272-81*, 209.
[32] Morris, *Welsh Wars*, 45.
[33] Ibid., 136-8; *Brenhenidd y Saesson*, 255; Griffiths, *Principality of Wales*, i, 4.

to Rhuddlan by late August, its numbers building up rapidly. At the end of the month there were some 15,000 infantry in pay, of whom about 9,000 were Welshmen drawn from the Marches and the south. By that time they had reached Deganwy, and a substantial force under the command of John de Vescy and Otto de Grandson was sent off by sea to occupy Anglesey. A total of 360 harvesters were taken across, to collect the harvest in the island: at one and the same time victuals would be provided for the English troops, and pressure put on the Welsh by threatening them with starvation.[34]

Medieval warfare was rarely an affair of gaily caparisoned knights riding out to defeat a chivalrous foe in battle, winning fame and glory. Llywelyn did not have the forces to oppose the English in open battle. Although there are reports from the early 1260s that he could muster up to 300 cavalry, these were almost certainly not fully equipped as knights, and there are no similar references from the 1270s or 1280s.[35] The Welsh infantry, mostly spearmen in the north, were adept at guerilla warfare, and Edward was too cautious a commander to risk an advance into the heartland of Llywelyn's dominions, Snowdonia. The chronicler Bartholomew Cotton described the operations of this first Welsh war as a siege of Snowdonia, and they certainly had something of that character, with the Welsh being steadily encircled and their food supplies cut off.[36]

On 12 September Edward withdrew from Deganwy back to Rhuddlan, to await events.[37] There was no immediate settlement, but on 2 November Otto de Grandson, Anthony Bek, Robert Tibetot and others of the king's council were authorized to negotiate on Edward's behalf.[38] They went to Conwy, and on 9 November terms were agreed with Llywelyn. The Welsh prince came, according to one account, to seek the king's mercy, rather than judgement. The terms imposed on him were far from merciful. He was to pay an indemnity of £50,000, abandon his claims to the Four Cantreds and all other lands seized by Edward, with the exception of Anglesey, which he was permitted to retain in return for 1,000 marks a year. His brother Owain was to be released

---

[34] Morris, *Welsh Wars*, 126–35, provides a detailed account. See also E 101/3/11, 15 for further details.

[35] *Merioneth Lay Subsidy Roll*, cxxiv.

[36] Cotton, 155.

[37] Morris, *Welsh Wars*, 136, suggests that Edward left Rhuddlan in mid-October, going as far as Shrewsbury. This he appears to have deduced from the chancery rolls, but the evidence of the enrolments is not reliable as far as the king's own whereabouts are concerned, and the dating of writs from Shrewsbury probably indicates no more than the transfer, for a time, of the chancery from Rhuddlan to Shrewsbury. *Cal. Chancery Warrants*, 4, shows that the king was at Rhuddlan for at least some of the time that writs were being dated at Shrewsbury.

[38] E 101/3/15.

from captivity, and the hostages he had taken from various Welsh lords returned. He was to retain the homage of only five Welsh magnates. Surprisingly, he was allowed to keep his brother Dafydd's hereditary lands: Edward promised to compensate Dafydd with lands elsewhere. Llywelyn was to swear fealty to Edward at Rhuddlan, and then come to London to do homage. Ten hostages were to be handed over, to ensure that the terms of the treaty would be maintained.[39]

One clause of the treaty was impossible for Llywelyn. There was no way in which he could have paid out £50,000, even though he did hand over 2,000 marks at the time of the negotiations, and later made the payments for Anglesey. It was not uncommon for heavy fines to be imposed in legal cases, with no real expectation that payment would ever be made in full, and it was perhaps sufficient for Edward that Llywelyn should concede that he was guilty of offences which merited so huge a fine. Accordingly, on 11 November the fine was pardoned. Eleven months later Edward went further and freed the ten hostages he had taken, in recognition of Llywelyn's good faith since the treaty had been agreed.[40]

The war of 1277 has, very reasonably, been described as a disaster for Llywelyn, and the treaty as a humiliation.[41] Yet was this all that Edward had hoped for from the war? On 23 August 1277 he had promised Dafydd that, in the event of his defeating Llywelyn, he would restore half of Snowdonia, Anglesey and Penllyn, with the Lleyn peninsula, to Dafydd and his brother Owain. Alternatively, should Edward decide to keep the whole of Anglesey, all the rest of Llywelyn's territory would be divided between the brothers. The continuing grants of protections to men in the king's service, made in September and October, and in some cases lasting until Easter 1278, suggest that Edward was still envisaging a lengthy campaign.[42]

It is likely that Edward faced difficulties, not on the scale of Llywelyn's, but sufficient to persuade him that it was better to make terms than to continue with the war until the Welsh prince was totally annihilated. Victuals were probably running short in the autumn of 1277: though royal clerks and knights had been sent to six counties to buy up supplies, the operation had cost only £416, and cannot have produced much. A messenger was sent on 19 September to hasten the process of collecting supplies, an indication of difficulties.[43] The grain

---

[39] *Littere Wallie*, 118–22. The terms are conveniently summarized by Powicke, *Henry III and the Lord Edward*, ii, 649–51.

[40] *CWR*, 157, 159, 169. For further evidence of payment of the money for Anglesey, see William de Perton's account for 7–8 Edward I, in E 372/124.

[41] Stephenson, 'Llywelyn ap Gruffydd', 44.

[42] *CPR 1272–82*, 222, 225.

[43] E 101/3/15, 16.

harvested in Anglesey must have eased the position in the English
army, but it is unlikely that Edward could have kept a large force
together for much longer. Finance, too, was a problem. The war was
not particularly expensive, with the accounts showing a total cost of
only just over £23,000, but the prospect of continued campaigning
cannot have been an attractive one to the king's financial advisers.[44]
There was no prospect of obtaining further unpaid feudal service, and
large numbers of troops would have been required, at great cost, if
Llywelyn was to be directly challenged in Snowdonia.

If Edward's fullest hopes for the war were not fulfilled, he must
nevertheless have been well satisfied with his achievement. Llywelyn
had fully acknowledged his authority, and had seen his own power
radically reduced. New castles were built to hem the Welsh in:
Aberystwyth and Builth from the south, Flint and Rhuddlan from
the north-east, threatened the lands of the principality.[45] Yet Wales
was not conquered, and Edward's problems there had hardly begun.
His campaign of 1277 had been little more than a brief military
promenade, followed by successful negotiations. The second Welsh
war, which began in 1282, was to be a very different matter.

The second war began, for the English, quite unexpectedly. Prince
Dafydd, expected as a guest at Roger Clifford's castle of Hawarden for
Easter, appeared instead on the night before Palm Sunday with an
armed band, and stormed the castle. Clifford was dragged from his bed,
and many of his companions were slain.[46] The attack was not an
isolated incident. Oswestry was attacked on the same day, 22 March,
and two days later the constable of Aberystwyth was taken by a ruse.
He was invited to dine with Gruffydd ap Maredudd, who took him
prisoner. On 26 March the castles of Carreg Cennen and Llandovery
were taken. Llywelyn ap Gruffydd himself was not slow to join in what
was rapidly becoming a nationwide rebellion, and took part in attacks
on Flint and Rhuddlan.[47]

To explain the rising, it is first necessary to examine Dafydd's
grievances: he had, after all, supported Edward in 1277, and it was his
action at Hawarden which marked the start of hostilities in 1282.
Dafydd had not been the easiest of allies in 1277. There had been

[44] Morris, *Welsh Wars*, 140–1.

[45] See below, 207–15, for a discussion of Edward's castle-building in Wales.

[46] *CWR*, 212, gives an official account of events at Hawarden, which are also dealt
with by most of the chroniclers. An account printed in *Historical MSS Commission, Various
Collections*, i (1901), has it that shortly before the attack Dafydd sent Clifford two salmon
as a sign of friendship.

[47] *The Welsh Assize Roll, 1277–1284*, ed. J. Conway Davies (Cardiff, 1940), 352; *Cal.
Anc. Corr. Wales*, 44–5.

problems when he refused to hand over the due share of booty taken to the king or his officials, and he had been disappointed in the territorial settlement. He had, certainly, been granted the land of Hope, and two of the Four Cantreds, Dyffryn Clwyd and Rhufuniog, but he had not recovered his share of his family lands.[48] An ambitious man, Dafydd attempted to increase his power by building a new castle at Hope, the last purely Welsh castle to be constructed. He found, however, that he was thwarted in many ways by the justiciar of Chester, Reginald de Grey, and claimed that he had been told of a plot to capture him, or take his sons hostage, destroy his castle, and cut down his forests. He resented the way in which he had been forced to appear at the shire court of Chester to answer a plea brought by William de Venables, regarding his tenure of Hope and Estyn: Dafydd's claim was that this was Welsh land, not subject to English law.[49]

Dafydd was not the only Welsh noble to feel that Edward had not displayed sufficient gratitude to him in the aftermath of the war of 1277. Gruffydd ap Maredudd had presented a petition in parliament in 1278 complaining that he had lost half of his lands, despite his labours on the king's behalf, fighting at his own expense in Cardigan.[50] The lack of a satisfactory response does much to explain the events at Aberystwyth at Easter 1282. Many of those lords of south Wales who had surrendered early to the English in 1277 clearly found Edward's lordship no more to their liking than Llywelyn's, and certainly gained nothing from their abandonment of the Welsh cause. Gruffydd ap Gwenwynwyn of Powys, and Rhys ap Maredudd of Ystrad Tywi, were exceptional among Welsh magnates in not joining in the great rising of 1282.[51]

A central problem in determining the origins of the rising is that presented by Prince Llywelyn himself. He argued that he knew nothing of the attack on Hawarden until it had taken place, and one argument has it that his decision to join in the rebellion 'was not made until the twelfth hour had already struck'.[52] Yet Llywelyn more than anyone had his grievances against Edward, and although he was punctilious in performing his obligations to the English king after 1277, it appears that he was, at the same time, working to restore his power and authority in Wales. He, more than anyone else, was capable of organizing nationwide resistance to the English, and it is hard to imagine that he was merely drawn into the rebellion at the last minute.

[48] *CPR 1272–82*, 227, 231. The grant of Dyffryn Clwyd and Rhufuniog was in fact a renewal of one made by Edward prior to his accession.
[49] *Cal. Anc. Corr. Wales*, 72–3; *Reg. Peckham*, ii, 445–7.
[50] *Rot. Parl.*, i, 5.
[51] The allegiance of the Welsh magnates at this time is discussed by D. Stephenson, *The Last Prince of Wales* (Buckingham, 1983), 26–30.
[52] J.G. Edwards, in *Littere Wallie*, lxiv.

Initially, Edward I's behaviour towards Llywelyn, after the agreement of the treaty of Conwy in 1277, was reasonable. When he came to Rhuddlan in September 1278, there was considerable argument when the Welsh prince's brother Rhodri appeared, demanding his share of the family inheritance, on the grounds that he had not been paid the 1,000 marks promised him by Llywelyn. Edward could have used the case to deprive Llywelyn of some of his lands, but instead it was agreed that he should simply make full payment to his brother.[53] It was not long, however, before problems became evident. Some relatively minor matters were a source of obvious irritation. Before the war of 1277, Llywelyn had exercised right of wreck when an English merchant, Robert of Leicester, lost his ship in a storm. Robert later obtained royal writs ordering the justiciar of Chester to obtain restitution for his losses, and when Llywelyn sent men to Chester to buy honey, this, with their horses, was seized. Edward wrote to Llywelyn in July 1280 promising that he would order release of the goods seized, but later orders to the justiciar confirmed that they were to be confiscated. Llywelyn's surprise at this contradiction of what he had been told is very understandable.[54] Other issues included the hanging of two men, who Llywelyn claimed were members of his household, under a royal safe-conduct. His huntsmen were maltreated, and their prey taken from them when they trespassed on royal land, 'a thing almost unheard of'.[55]

The major issue which saw Llywelyn increasingly frustrated by the English and Edward in particular was the case of Arwystli. In 1274 he had seized this land, lying to the south of Gwynedd, from his enemy Gruffydd ap Gwenwynwyn of Powys. Now, in the aftermath of the war of 1277, the question of right to this land was to be determined in the courts. One immediate problem was, which courts? Llywelyn held that the matter should be determined under Welsh law; Gruffydd that, as he was a Marcher baron, the law of the March should apply. The roll of pleas held before royal justices began with a case brought by Adam de Montgomery against Gruffydd. Adam was a former constable of Oswestry castle, and his case was almost certainly not a genuine one, but brought collusively, simply with the intention of proving that Edward's justices had rights of jurisdiction over Arwystli.[56] Llywelyn was not going to be convinced by such machinations, and when the matter was put before Edward at Rhuddlan in September 1278, it was adjourned.

The treaty of 1277 had provided simply that 'controversies and

[53] *CCR 1272–9*, 506.
[54] *Cal. Anc. Corr. Wales*, 60, 62, 78, 89.
[55] *CWR*, 165; *Cal. Anc. Corr. Wales*, 88–9.
[56] *Welsh Assize Roll*, 125–9.

disputes moved or to be moved between the prince and anyone whatsoever, shall be determined and decided by March law when they arise
in the Marches, and according to Welsh law when they arise in
Wales'.[57] Llywelyn demanded from Edward a declaration that in this
case, Welsh law should apply, and by 1280 was writing with understandable impatience that 'it seems that three years should suffice for
the settling of one article'.[58] Edward's position was that he was bound
by his coronation oath to root out bad laws and customs: he could not
allow any Welsh laws to be observed, other than those which were just
and reasonable. It was therefore necessary to set up a commission, to
find out just what the laws and customs of Wales were. It seems that a
decision to do this was taken in May 1280, although it was not until 4
December that the appointments to the commission were in fact made.
The commission did not proceed with any sense of urgency. It was not
until June 1281 that Edward finally informed Llywelyn that his case
against Gruffydd ap Gwenwynwyn could go ahead before royal
justices. The writ, couched in Delphic terms, failed even now to make it
clear which law should apply, though a letter from Llywelyn to the king
suggests that he understood it to be in fact Welsh law. Further delays
followed. Gruffydd argued that, as a baron, he should not have to
answer without a royal writ being brought against him. Llywelyn's
attorney stated that there had been such a writ issued, but, either
through incompetence or deliberate prevarication, it proved impossible for Edward and his officials to locate it. The case never reached a
final conclusion, for the rebellion of 1282 brought the proceedings to an
end.[59]

Historians have laid great stress on the Arwystli case, for it provides
perhaps the best test of Edward's intentions and good faith with regard
to Wales. His view that the only laws and customs which he could
accept in Wales were those which he and his predecessors had been
accustomed to exercise there has been condemned as 'an outrageous
example of special pleading, which could only issue from a distorted
legalistic mind'.[60] Yet Edward's case was not quite so unreasonable.
He could not be expected to concede points as a result of the treaty
of 1277 which he would not have been prepared to countenance previously. While an inquisition held by Reginald de Grey and William
Hamilton, in 1278, had found that in cases between Welsh lords, the
Welsh laws of Hywel Dda should apply, this did not cover the point in
the Arwystli case, where one of the litigants, for all his Welsh ancestry,

[57] Ibid., 8; *Littere Wallie*, 120.
[58] *Cal. Anc. Corr. Wales*, 89.
[59] *Cal. Anc. Corr. Wales*, 61–2; *CWR*, 188, 210–11.
[60] *Welsh Assize Roll*, 142.

claimed to hold as a Marcher lord. Nor did it meet the arguments being put forcibly by Archbishop Pecham that Welsh laws were in many cases unreasonable and contrary to the teachings of the Bible.[61]

Much obviously depended on the findings of the commission set up in December 1280. Edward has been accused of giving it a biased composition, but its effective head, Walter de Hopton, was not obviously any worse than most of the English justices of his day. The evidence is certainly not adequate to characterize him as a man 'both greedy and avaricious: he was false and ambitious. He could be relied upon to work the king's will irrespective of justice or equity.'[62] It is not surprising that two of the Welshmen associated with Hopton were men who had taken the English side in the war of 1277, but Goronwy ap Heilyn had been one of Llywelyn's negotiators in that year and, for all that he may have had English connections, took the Welsh side in 1282.[63]

The commission's task was not an easy one, but there is nothing to suggest that its findings were dishonest. The findings revealed a complex situation. No adequate answer was forthcoming from Arwystli itself, where only four men gave evidence. Elsewhere it appears that the disputes were settled either by Welsh legal procedures, or by inquest. One Welsh witness indicated that the preference of the country was for the latter method: significantly, a marginal note in the roll drew attention to this. It was of course the case that Llywelyn and his predecessors had themselves been turning away from traditional Welsh law and had begun to imitate their English neighbours to an increasing extent. It is hard not to sympathize with the Welsh lord whose unhelpful reported evidence on these thorny legal matters concluded: 'Of the other articles he knows nothing, because he gives more attention to hunting than to the discussion of law.'[64]

While Edward was not being deliberately dishonest in denying Llywelyn an immediate recourse to Welsh law in the Arwystli case, he can be considered guilty of excessive delay in reaching a resolution in what was certainly a difficult matter. This was surely not the result of any distorted legalism on his part, but because the case presented an insoluble political difficulty. Gruffydd ap Gwenwynwyn was his ally of 1277, a man who expected a just reward for his service, and a man content, unlike Prince Dafydd, with a new status as a Marcher lord. To deny him Arwystli, which he and his ancestors had held for forty-two years, would very probably drive him into rebellion. Yet equally, a

---

[61] *Welsh Assize Roll*, 143; *Reg. Peckham*, i, 135–6.
[62] *Welsh Assize Roll*, 142. See ibid., 97ff., for a detailed examination of the composition of the commission.
[63] Stephenson, *Governance of Gwynedd*, 104.
[64] The report of the Hopton commission is printed in *CWR*, 190–210.

decision in Gruffydd's favour might well have disastrous consequences. There was a very obvious temptation to rely on the inertia of the law, and leave the matter unresolved for as long as possible. In the event, Edward's calculations failed, but it is hard to see that he had any better option than prevarication.

It is hardly surprising to find signs, as early as 1278, that Llywelyn was attempting to revive his political authority in Wales. In May of that year, he received the homage and fealty of a southern lord, Trahaearn ap Madog of Brecon, with sureties provided by a number of influential south Welsh magnates, including Rhys Fychan, and Gruffydd and Cynan ap Maredudd ap Owain. In August of the same year, he reached an agreement with Gruffydd ap Gwen, steward of no less a man than Gruffydd ap Gwenwynwyn of Powys.[65] In 1281 he made a treaty with the English Marcher lord Roger Mortimer, in which the two men made promises of mutual support, saving their fealty to Edward I. This was taken by J.G. Edwards as evidence that Llywelyn was not planning a war against the English, but equally it does strongly suggest that he had finally lost patience with the legal proceedings in the Arwystli case, and that he was intending to take military action against Gruffydd ap Gwenwynwyn, whose lands lay between his own and Mortimer's. He must have been aware that such action might very well develop into a conflict on a much larger scale, into which Edward I would inevitably be drawn.[66]

The grievances of the two princes, Dafydd and Llywelyn, are of central importance in examining the causes of the rebellion of 1282, but it is also clear that the English had been provocative in a great many other cases. One chronicle singled out, with some cause, the activities of Reginald de Grey as causing the war.[67] He had been appointed justiciar of Chester in November 1281, and had made every effort to introduce English methods of law and administration into north Wales. He was accused of bringing cases involving offences committed as long ago as the reign of Henry III, of threatening to decapitate Goronwy ap Heilyn over a dispute he had with Robert de Creuker, and of making similar threats to some Welsh messengers. The men of Ystrad Alun in Flintshire complained of the way in which Roger Clifford had forced them to purchase their rights and privileges for twenty marks, and had imposed on them the English custom of using juries of twelve men. Complaints were not confined to the north: the constable of Oswestry came in for criticism, as did his colleague at Whitchurch.[68]

---

[65] Stephenson, 'Llywelyn ap Gruffydd', 45–6.
[66] Edwards, in *Littere Wallie*, lxii, 99–100; Stephenson, op. cit., 45.
[67] The Hagnaby chronicle, BL Vesp. B. xi, f.27v.
[68] *Reg. Peckham*, ii, 455–8, 459, 463.

The evidence for the grievances of the Welsh comes primarily from bills presented to Archbishop Pecham, when he attempted mediation in 1282. There is a consistent thread running through them, of a deep hostility to the introduction of English laws and customs into a Welsh environment. The similarity of the arguments put forward by the Welsh shows that there was a deliberate policy of making use of the law as a symbol of national identity, and it is very likely that it was Llywelyn himself who determined what this policy should be.[69] In one significant statement, he argued that every province of Edward's *imperium* had its own laws and customs: Gascon in Gascony, Scottish in Scotland, Irish in Ireland, English in England, and that accordingly the Welsh prince should have the right to use Welsh law.[70] The sons of Maredudd ap Owain put it more dramatically: 'All Christians have laws and customs in their own lands; even the Jews in England have laws among the English; we had our immutable laws and customs in our lands until the English took them away after the last war.'[71] Prince Dafydd used the argument: 'Since the king is, by grace of God, lord of divers countries and of divers tongues, and divers laws are administered in them and are not changed, let the laws of Wales, if it please the king's reverence, be unchanged like the laws of the other peoples.'[72]

The claim that the English were threatening the national identity of the Welsh provided a unifying theme to the various grievances, and elevated the argument to a high plane. There were difficulties with the argument, for not all the evidence goes to show the unpopularity of English law in Wales. At Carmarthen, in 1280, the county court was ordered to sit twice a week, not once as in the past, 'by reason of the multitude of suitors, both Englishmen and Welshmen'.[73] But the emotional appeal of Llywelyn's case overrode such problems, with powerful propaganda suggesting that the Welsh were being treated by the king's bailiffs worse than if they had been Saracens or Jews.[74] Yet for all the importance of the legal issue, the fact remains that the main question was one of power, and of who was to exercise it in Wales.

The war which began in 1282 was a far greater undertaking for the English than that of 1277 had been. This was not a campaign intended simply to deal with a recalcitrant vassal: it was a war of conquest. There

---

[69] R.R. Davies, 'Law and National Identity in Thirteenth Century Wales', *Welsh Society and Nationhood*, ed. R.R. Davies, R.A. Griffiths, I.G. Jones and K.O. Morgan (Cardiff, 1984), 57.

[70] *Welsh Assize Roll*, 266.

[71] *Reg. Peckham*, ii, 454.

[72] *Cal. Anc. Corr. Wales*, 73.

[73] *CWR*, 184.

[74] *Reg. Peckham*, ii, 439.

was no time for a steady build-up towards the campaign, as there had been in 1276–7: Edward had to respond quickly to the news of the Easter uprising in Wales. On 25 March, three days after Hawarden was attacked, he appointed Reginald de Grey to command at Chester, Roger Mortimer in the central Marches, and Robert de Tibetot in west Wales. A council was rapidly summoned to meet at Devizes on 5 April. On the next day, writs were issued asking the magnates to muster at Worcester on 17 May. Household knights were rapidly deployed: the pay roll for the war starts as early as 7 April, with Amadeus of Savoy leading a force off to reinforce Grey's men at Chester, and then to relieve Rhuddlan. By late May there were probably over 200 cavalry in royal pay, divided between the various commands.[75]

When the troops mustered at Worcester, as ordered, plans were rapidly changed. Edward had demanded paid service, but now issued new commands on 20 May, which required feudal, unpaid service, with a muster at Rhuddlan on 2 August.[76] The change to Rhuddlan was obviously dictated by military considerations, Edward deciding to repeat his strategy of 1277. It is less clear why he adopted a feudal summons at such short notice. J.E. Morris suggested that the magnates may have brought pressure on him. The evidence of the pay roll does not suggest that recruiting was going badly in May, but many magnates may have resented the subordination involved in accepting pay, and may have insisted on performing their traditional feudal duties. This could have been important in a war of conquest, where those doing feudal service might have expected a better share of the spoils than those in receipt of pay. Yet they could have simply served voluntarily at their own expense, without insisting on a feudal summons, as many magnates were to do, later in the reign, in Scotland. Possibly the earl of Hereford, as Constable of England, demanded a feudal summons: he was certainly insistent upon receiving the rights due to his office.[77] The evidence is simply not adequate to explain the change in the method of recruitment, and it may be that Edward had all along intended to issue a feudal summons: he did request, as early as 10 April, the men of the Cinque Ports to provide their service.[78]

Edward's advance to Chester, and then on to Flint and Rhuddlan, went smoothly. Reginald de Grey conducted operations against Prince Dafydd, to ensure that no attack should be made from the flank on Edward's army. He and his men took Hope castle, which the Welsh had themselves slighted, and Richard de Grey captured Ewloe.

[75] Morris, *Welsh Wars*, 154–6.
[76] *Parl. Writs*, i, 224–5.
[77] Morris, *Welsh Wars*, 155, 157–8; Prestwich, *War, Politics and Finance*, 71–2.
[78] *CWR*, 247.

Edward's army at Rhuddlan was rapidly built up in strength: by the end of August he had at least some 750 cavalry in his command, and about 8,000 foot.[79] The next objective, as in 1277, was Anglesey. A naval force was sent there, and on 18 August Luke de Tany was appointed to command the troops on the island. The most ambitious part of the plan was to link Anglesey to the mainland by means of a bridge of boats, so establishing a new invasion route into Snowdonia and outflanking Llywelyn's defences.[80] The operation was not easy: the pontoon boats, forty in number, that had originally been proposed were too large and heavy for the ships of the Cinque Ports to transport, and ships had to be purchased specially at Chester. Teams of carpenters were set to work, and by November the bridge was complete.[81] In the second half of October, Luke de Tany, Roger Clifford, William Audley and others sailed for Anglesey to prepare for their attack on the Welsh.[82] Meanwhile, the forces under Edward's command were steadily consolidating their position. Ruthin was taken in early September, and in October Denbigh and Dinas Bran fell. The Welsh were steadily pushed back into their fastness of Snowdonia.[83]

In the south, the English were less successful. In June, the earl of Gloucester had been roundly defeated, probably in an ambush; William de Valence the younger was killed. His father replaced Gloucester in command on 6 July, and in August and September he conducted a lengthy raid, reaching Aberystwyth, but failing to engage the Welsh on any scale. The kind of warfare that the English were able to engage in is illustrated by a letter from one of their ablest commanders, Robert Tibetot, announcing that the garrison of Cardigan had recently been able to take 'a great booty', though they had lost eighteen men captured in the process. Then spies had reported the whereabouts of Gruffydd ap Maredudd ap Owain and his brother; a dramatic night march by Tibetot, and his Welsh ally Rhys ap Maredudd, almost succeeded in taking them, and did result in the release of the eighteen men captured earlier. Some horses were lost, but they took a great many cattle, put by Tibetot at 3,000, a clear exaggeration.[84]

With the onset of autumn, the position of the English in the Marches worsened. In October Roger Mortimer, lord of Wigmore, died of natural causes, and the loss of so great a lord had its inevitable effect on morale. In November the sheriff of Shropshire reported that he found the inhabitants of Mortimer's lordship 'very fickle and haughty, as they

---

[79] Morris, *Welsh Wars*, 160–1, 174.
[80] *CWR*, 235.
[81] *KW*, i, 354–7.
[82] E 101/4/1.
[83] Morris, *Welsh Wars*, 177–8.
[84] Morris, *Welsh Wars*, 165–6; *Cal. Anc. Corr. Wales*, 131–2.

were on the point of leaving the king's peace, because they have no definite lord', and he begged that the business of handing over the lands to Roger's heir Edmund be hastened. In the same month, Roger Lestrange reported that he could not attack the enemy in his district, as they had retreated into the 'difficult and repellent' mountains. He was doing his best to prevent any supplies from reaching the Welsh, but it was clear to him that a good deal was getting through.[85]

The war was evidently not reaching a point of resolution, and in what may have seemed a situation of stalemate, Archbishop Pecham decided to try to mediate. His task was a hopeless one. Edward was determined that the status of the Four Cantreds in the north should not be altered: he made lavish grants of conquered lands in the north to Reginald de Grey, earl Warenne, and the earl of Lincoln in October 1282, and would not go back on his action. Nor was he prepared to bring Anglesey into discussion.[86] Edward was ready to countenance an extraordinary offer to Llywelyn, of an English earldom with lands worth £1,000 a year, provided that he hand over Snowdonia to Edward. Should Dafydd go to the Holy Land, Edward would provide for him.

Such offers were hardly attractive to the Welsh, and their distrust of Edward is very clear from the reply made on Dafydd's behalf, referring to fear of death, imprisonment or perpetual disinheritance. The war, it was argued, was a just one, and it ill behoved Pecham to issue excommunications against the Welsh when the English were engaged in the destruction of churches and the slaughter of babies at the breast.[87] The Welsh took the opportunity of Pecham's peace mission to put their case as strongly as they could, for it was the only chance they had to obtain any kind of hearing, but little can have been expected of a prelate whose view of the Welsh was apparently quite as hostile as was Edward's own. Edward himself had expected that the assistance of the church, with its spiritual weapons of excommunication, would help to bring about a rapid end to the rising, but he sought victory, not mediation, and Pecham's peace mission did not meet with his approval. By 14 November the archbishop had returned to Rhuddlan, despairing that any solution could be found.[88]

The hope of reaching a settlement had indeed been completely dashed on 6 November, with the dramatic defeat of an English force under Luke de Tany, which gave the Welsh new heart, and made Edward's men determined on revenge. There are various accounts of the defeat, which are unfortunately not entirely consistent. One is that

[85] Ibid., 84, 131.
[86] *Reg. Peckham*, 436. For grants, see below, 204.
[87] *Reg. Peckham*, ii, 467, 471-3.
[88] Pecham's mission is discussed more fully by Douie, *Pecham*, 235-53.

de Tany and his men crossed the bridge from Anglesey and advanced
inland. When they returned, their route to the bridge was cut off by the
rising tide. The Welsh swooped, and drove them into the sea, where
many drowned.[89] An alternative tradition is that the English force was
retreating back to the bridge, having been surprised by the Welsh, and
that in their haste to get to safety, the structure was overloaded,
perhaps breaking with the force of the tide. As the barges sank, so the
men drowned.[90] This seems the more plausible story, but whatever the
truth of the matter, the disaster was a major one. Knightly casualties
were, as a rule, low in medieval warfare, and now, at one blow, at least
sixteen were lost, along with many lesser men. William Latimer was
fortunate indeed in that his charger had the strength to swim to safety
through the waves. Otto de Grandson was another who apparently had
a narrow escape from death.[91]

Various explanations were given for the disaster. One chronicler,
Walter of Guisborough, thought that Luke de Tany acted incautiously,
in the hope of winning glory; the Hagnaby writer blamed the younger
Roger Clifford, for a move primarily intended to rescue his father from
captivity. Wykes thought that the English were deliberately attacking
during Pecham's peace negotiations, in an attempt to catch the Welsh
off guard.[92] There is no evidence that there was any 'cease-fire' in
operation during Pecham's mission, but it is easy to see that the men
in Anglesey could have felt very frustrated at the thought that a
negotiated peace was possible early in November. They had not
received any grants of lands in Wales, and must have seen their hopes
of gain, as well as glory, receding rapidly. The raid across the bridge
was premature, and may well have been meant either to thwart
Pecham's mission, or to achieve major gains before the negotiations
were concluded. Whatever the truth of the matter, one chronicler,
Pierre Langtoft, was surely correct when he blamed the English
commanders for not employing spies, or scouts, to warn them of the
movements of the Welsh.[93]

Edward was determined to continue the fight. On 12 November he
ordered thirty-nine magnates to go to join Valence's force at Carmarthen,
along with a levy of knights from the south-western counties. On 24
November, and again on 6 December, orders to recruit fresh infantry
were issued. Powerful reinforcements appeared in November, to give
fresh heart to the English: Gascon troops began to reach Edward's

---

[89] Guisborough, 219–20. For problems in this account, see Morris, *Welsh Wars*, 180.
[90] Rishanger, 101–2; Langtoft, ii, 179; *Ann. Dunstable*, 292; *Flores*, iii, 57.
[91] Guisborough, 219–20; *Annales Cestrienses*, 110–12. This latter source provides the
fullest casualty list.
[92] Guisborough, 291; BL Cotton. Vesp. B. xi, f.28; Wykes, 290.
[93] Langtoft, ii, 178.

headquarters, and by December there were in the army 21 knights, 52 mounted crossbowmen and 533 ordinary footsoldiers from Gascony.[94] But Edward was wary of making any fresh moves. He was a cautious commander, and he must have known that time was on his side. He had the resources for a long war, which the Welsh did not.

It was Llywelyn who made the unexpected move in November, marching out of Snowdonia towards the central Marches and then to Builth. He clearly hoped to profit from the confusion resulting from Mortimer's death, and appreciated that in the end, if he stayed in Snowdonia, he would be starved out. But, just as in the game of chess a king which is forced out of its own territory in the middle game is liable to be hunted down, so Llywelyn met with disaster, and was killed on 11 December. The unreliability of medieval news reporting is made very clear by a comparison of the chronicle accounts of the events which led to Llywelyn's death, and it is unfortunately not possible to provide a reliable reconstruction of what took place. Possibly the Welsh army were taken by surprise when the English army attacked them, having avoided the bridge over the river Irfon, which was well guarded, but making their crossing over a ford. By this account, Llywelyn was not with his men at the time, but hurried back on hearing noise of battle. One Stephen de Frankton saw him, but did not recognize him. Had he done so, he would surely have taken him prisoner: as it was, he ran him through with his lance. This is Guisborough's account.

A Peterborough chronicle has it that Llywelyn and the Welsh were surprised by forces under Roger Lestrange (not commanded by John Giffard and Roger Mortimer the younger, as Guisborough has it). A fierce battle took place late in the day, during which Llywelyn was killed. A related source names the man who decapitated Llywelyn as Robert Body. This is not necessarily in conflict with the evidence that the slayer was Frankton, for in Guisborough's account, it was only when the body was found and recognized that the head was cut off. Both Frankton and Body are known to have had connections with Lestrange. The Hagnaby chronicle however, describes a long battle, with casualties on both sides, which saw the English victorious. Llywelyn fled into the woods with his squire, but was discovered. He fought bravely, but fell, shouting his name, thereupon to be promptly decapitated.[95] Documentary sources are not of very much assistance in

[94] Morris, *Welsh Wars*, 188–9; E 101/3/27.

[95] Guisborough, 220–1; *Chronicon Petroburgense*, ed. T. Stapleton (Camden Soc., 1849), 57–8; BL Cotton. MS Vesp. B.xi, f.28. For a full discussion of the sources, see the important article by L. Beverley Smith, 'The death of Llywelyn ap Gruffydd: the narrative reconsidered', *Welsh History Review*, xi (1982), 200–13. Although this article is surely correct in casting doubt on the accuracy of Guisborough's version of events, it is a little far-fetched to suggest that the chronicler somehow conflated the battles of Irfon

resolving the conflict between the chronicles, though a letter from Lestrange makes it quite clear that it was he who was in command of the force, and reported the really significant facts: 'Llywelyn ap Gruffydd is dead, his army defeated, and all the flower of his army dead.'[96]

Conspiracy theories have always had their attractions, and it is not surprising to find that Llywelyn's death was attributed by some contemporaries to a plot. The Hagnaby chronicle is the most circumstantial, alleging that Roger Mortimer the younger sent word to Llywelyn, asking him to come to receive his homage and that of his men. Mortimer and other magnates then arranged to ambush the Welsh prince, and it was this that resulted in his death. The Dunstable chronicle and various others refer to the same tale, which finds some corroboration in two letters from Archbishop Pecham. It seems that a letter was found on Llywelyn's body, 'expressed in obscure words and with fictitious names', implying treasonable intentions towards Edward on the part of some of the Marcher lords.[97] The link with Mortimer is given added force by the fact that the prince had of course made an agreement with the elder Roger in 1281, and it is conceivable that he could have been persuaded that this was to be renewed late in 1282.[98]

Llywelyn's death was a disaster for the Welsh. He was the one man who could perhaps have succeeded in uniting Wales against the English invader, a man who, for all his mistakes, had the prestige and experience to provide Edward I with worthy opposition. Yet the events near Builth did not end the war. Prince Dafydd sent Roger Clifford and his wife to Edward to plead for peace, but this proposal was abruptly refused, and Clifford returned into captivity.[99] Dafydd held a meeting of his followers, and decided on resistance.[100]

The English did not choose to wait for a Welsh surrender: instead, once Edward had built up his forces, he took the war to the enemy. The men recruited by means of orders issued in November and December were ready by mid-January, and in a bold move Edward marched inland from his base at Rhuddlan. By 18 January he was at Bettws-y-Coed on the upper Conwy, and on the same day his troops entered

---

Bridge and Stirling Bridge. See also the discussion in Stephenson, *The Last Prince of Wales*, 75–8.

[96] *Cal. Anc. Corr. Wales*, 83–4.

[97] BL Cotton. MS Vesp. B.xi, f.28; *Ann. Dunstable*, 292–3; *Reg. Peckham*, ii, 489–90; *Cal. Anc. Corr. Wales*, 129; *Receuil des lettres Anglo-Françaises, 1265–1399* ed. F. Tanquerey (Paris, 1916), 32–3.

[98] Above, 187.

[99] BL Cotton. MS Vesp. B.xi, f.29v.

[100] Langtoft, ii, 181. Morris, *Welsh Wars*, 185, plausibly suggests that if this meeting did take place after Llywelyn's death, it must have been at Dolwyddelan rather than Denbigh, as the chronicle has it.

Dolwyddelan castle, a key strategic point.[101] It does not seem that there was any resistance, and it is very likely that Edward had in advance secretly negotiated the surrender of the castle. It is unlikely that he would have risked so hazardous an adventure as a push into Snowdonia in January without prior assurance of success. Further, an entry in the royal accounts shows that the constable of Dolwyddelan stayed at the court for twelve days, receiving double the wages his rank entitled him to, at about this time.[102] This is very suggestive of some deal between the English and the defenders of the castle. Once it had surrendered, Dolwyddelan was given an English garrison, which was hastily equipped with camouflage clothing of white tunics and stockings, suitable for winter warfare in the mountains. A new siege engine was made at Bettws, and carried to Dolwyddelan, to reinforce the defences.[103]

Following this success, a garrison was soon established on the coast, at Bangor, and the forces from Anglesey were sent along the coast of the mainland, towards Harlech. In March the royal headquarters were moved from Rhuddlan to Conwy. By April the main activity recorded in the royal pay rolls was the sending out of parties to seek Prince Dafydd. A small group of a dozen men was sent to Meirionydd and Ardudwy, and a larger troop of fifty to Ardudwy and Penllyn. Others were engaged in a hunt for booty.[104] Yet even with Snowdonia secure, Edward did not consider that his task was done. He was contemplating a major campaign in mid-Wales, and in March writs to nine earls and seventy-seven other magnates ordered them to muster at Montgomery, in May. Infantry was to be recruited as well, and arrangements were made for victualling the troops.[105]

In the event, these elaborate preparations proved not to be needed. The forces of Roger Lestrange, based on Montgomery, and those of William de Valence, moving up from Aberystwyth, converged on the last remaining substantial Welsh castle, Castell-y-Bere, and forced its surrender on 25 April, after a ten-day siege.[106] Dafydd still evaded capture, but the chase finally ended on 21 June. The Welsh prince had only a few men with him, and his seizure was not a major military undertaking. He was taken by Welshmen, probably through treachery:

[101] E 101/3/30 testifies to the king's presence at Bettws-y-Coed; for the entry to Dolwyddelan, *KW*, i, 336, no. 1.

[102] E 101/4/1, in an entry which starts on 5 December, but clearly covers a fairly long period, refers to the presence at court of Tudor ap Gruffydd, constable of Dolwyddelan. The scribe has possibly given the name wrongly, and intended Gruffydd ap Tudor, later given command of Dolwyddelan by the English: see D. Stephenson, *Governance of Gwynedd*, 111–12, 132; *CWR*, 288.

[103] *KW*, i, 336, no. 1; E 101/359/9.

[104] E 101/4/1, 30; Morris, *Welsh Wars*, 190–2.

[105] *Parl. Writs*, i, 245–7.

[106] Morris, *Welsh Wars*, 192–5; C 47/2/4.

there was a struggle in which he was wounded, and he was then taken off to captivity.[107] Resistance was now at an end. Peace was ensured by taking large numbers of Welsh hostages, who were marched off, under escort, to England.

The war of 1282–3 had involved an immense effort on the part of the English. The surviving records do not, unfortunately, allow a complete reconstruction of the numbers of English troops involved in the war, one difficulty being that the forces were split up to such an extent, and another being that many magnates served at their own expense, so that the crown had no need to record the size of their contingents. The feudal summons yielded a force of at least 123 knights and 190 sergeants, who served at their own expense for a forty-day period: not a very substantial contribution, in view of the total scale of manpower, and long duration of the campaign.[108] The crown appears to have been satisfied with the response to the summons: only Nicholas de Stuteville was later charged with neglecting it. He submitted to the king's will, and was fined 100 marks for each knight's fee he held: a substantial sum, as he was in possession of twenty.[109] Most of the feudal quotas were very small, because of a major reduction in the levels of service which had taken place in the first half of the thirteenth century. The number of men actually owed bore little relationship to the number of knight's fees held, and even so great a magnate as the earl of Gloucester only owed ten knights for the host. In practice no man of standing would come on campaign without bringing an adequate retinue with him, and there is no doubt that the earls and barons appeared with far more men than they were technically obliged to bring, and that they served for much longer than the required forty days. None of the English earls on the campaign was paid wages – Robert Bruce, earl of Carrick, father of the future king of Scots, did accept pay – and the sums paid as prests, or cash advances, to the earls of Warwick (£65), Lincoln (£1,655) and Norfolk (£410) were most probably for the wages of the infantry under their command, and not for themselves or their knights.[110]

J.E. Morris, in his classic study of the Welsh wars of Edward I, made various calculations of the strength of the paid forces employed by the king. At Chester there were some 276 heavy cavalry, according to the main pay roll, but this figure excludes Reginald de Grey's men. In the

[107] BL Cotton. MS Vesp. B.xi, f.29v; *Ann Dunstable*, 293. Guisborough, 221, puts Dafydd's capture in the autumn, another example of this chronicler's unreliability.

[108] Morris, *Welsh Wars*, 45. This is the number of those at headquarters only: others may have performed feudal service elsewhere.

[109] E 159/57, m.70.

[110] E 101/4/1.

south, there was a paid force of almost exactly 100 cavalry available to reinforce the unpaid levies of the Marcher lords. Later in the war, there are no detailed accounts for the detachment sent to Anglesey, but wages amounted to £3,761 for cavalry, and £3,540 for infantry, suggesting a substantial force.[111] A full pay roll survives for the Gascon contingent: at its peak, early in 1283, this numbered some 40 knights, 120 other horsemen, mostly mounted crossbowmen, and up to 1,300 infantry.[112] The central element of the paid cavalry was, of course, provided by the royal household. One list details 36 bannerets and knights, who, with their retinues, provided a force of 173 horse. There were also 72 squires, making the total strength 245.[113] It would probably be reasonable to estimate the total strength of the paid cavalry employed by Edward in this war at 700 or 800, if not more.

The feudal summons no doubt served as a general invitation to men to come and serve the king in his Welsh war. One problem, as in 1277, was that there was apparently a considerable shortage of suitable war-horses in the realm. On 26 May 1282 writs ordered everyone in possession of £30 worth of land or more a year, to provide themselves with a suitable horse and military equipment. In June a concession had to be made, and anyone owing service who did not have an adequate horse was permitted to pay a fine in lieu of attending the muster at Rhuddlan. The May order is particularly significant, in that it shows that Edward was beginning to think in terms of a system of military obligation dependent simply upon wealth, and not on position in the feudal hierarchy. Summonses issued on 20 November took the principle further: all those who had at least £20 worth of land, and were fit to bear arms, but were not fighting in Wales, were summoned to meet in regional assemblies at Northampton and York. There was clearly some idea of encouraging them – or forcing them – to go and fight, while county representatives were also summoned to these assemblies, so that a grant of taxation might be made. At Northampton it looks as if a straightforward grant of a tax was made, but the form of the grant at York appears, in the first instance, to have been of military service, with payment of fines as an alternative available to those who did not wish to fight. This was then abandoned in favour of the same type of tax that had been conceded in the south.[114] In general, the recruitment of cavalry forces for the war caused no great problems: there was sufficient

---

[111] Morris, *Welsh Wars*, 159, 163, 176.

[112] There were some notable men among the Gascon leaders, such as Elie de Caupenne and Arnold de Gavaston, who both served Edward later. Guitard de Bourg had been mayor of Bordeaux, and Auger de Mauleon headed a large contingent: E 101/3/27; Trabut-Cussac, *L'administration Anglaise en Gascogne*, 69–70.

[113] Prestwich, *War, Politics and Finance under Edward I*, 51, citing C 47/2/6.

[114] *Parl. Writs*, i, 10–11, 14.

enthusiasm for the king's policies, or for the chance of fighting, on the part of the magnates to ensure that he had sufficient men at his disposal.

Infantry were required for the war in large numbers, as well as cavalry. There is much less information available on the process of recruitment than there is for the later wars of Edward's reign, but the pay rolls suggest that at any one time up to 8,000 foot were employed. As in 1277, it proved possible to recruit substantial numbers of Welshmen from the Marches. Shropshire and Cheshire were obvious areas to draw from, because they were so close to the campaigning areas: Lancashire also provided a good many men. One select troop of 100 archers from Macclesfield were paid 3d a day, rather than the normal 2d, perhaps because they were better equipped or trained than the majority of the troops.[115] As well as foot soldiers, workmen were needed in large quantities, partly so that roads might be cut through the Welsh forests, and partly for the work of fortification that was a necessary and vital element in the king's policy in Wales. It was as early as 15 April that writs were issued, calling for 1,010 diggers and 345 carpenters from 28 counties: no other evidence demonstrates so well the systematic planning that went into the war.[116]

Considerable thought went into the complex business of victualling for the army. Much was done to encourage merchants to come to Wales, or to such English centres as Oswestry and Chester, and there were stern prohibitions on trading with the enemy. Markets were prohibited in the Marches, so as to compel merchants to take their goods to the armies. Safe-conducts and protections were of course provided for them. Private enterprise could not be wholly relied upon, and the crown sent its officials to buy up food supplies. On 14 April 1282 the sheriffs of Essex, Surrey, Sussex, Kent and Hampshire were each ordered to assist John de Maidstone in collecting 1,500 quarters of wheat and 2,000 quarters of oats from each county for shipment to Wales.[117] The bishopric of Winchester, in the king's hands through episcopal vacancy, provided 1,000 quarters of wheat, 300 quarters of barley and 600 quarters of oats, all of which was sent to Chester.[118] In July 1282 royal clerks were sent to buy up victuals in Staffordshire, Derbyshire, Nottinghamshire and Lancashire.[119] Edward also called upon his overseas dominions. Ireland was to provide 2,000 quarters of

[115] E 101/3/11; Morris, *Welsh Wars*, 174.
[116] *KW*, i, 182–3, 331; A.J. Taylor, 'Castle-Building in Wales in the later thirteenth century: the prelude to construction', *Studies in Building History*, ed. E.M. Jope (1961), 105–6, 111.
[117] *CWR*, 217, 235, 248, 257–8.
[118] M. Howell, *Regalian Right in Medieval England* (1962), 151.
[119] E 101/351/9.

wheat, 4,000 quarters of oats, 400 quarters of beans and peas, 500 quarters of barley, 600 tuns of wine and 1,000 salt salmon. Ponthieu was assessed at 2,000 quarters of wheat, the same quantity of oats, and 300 quarters of beans and peas. From Gascony the king requested 2,000 quarters of wheat, 1,000 quarters of oats, 300 quarters of beans and peas, 500 tuns of wine, 1,000 bacon pigs and other commodities.[120]

The accounts of the wardrobe, the household department which took on the immense task of organizing the war effort, show that a great central victualling depot was set up at Chester, under the charge of William de Perton, Ralph the clerk of the market, and various other officials. At Rhuddlan a new royal mill was constructed, and much flour was laboriously ground using the many hand-mills supplied to the army. A special war account shows that 5,741 quarters of wheat and flour were sold to the army, along with a smaller quantity of oats and other foodstuffs. The ordinary wardrobe account for 1282–4 includes mention of large quantities of victuals, totalling some 23,000 quarters of grain. Not all of this was for household consumption: some supplies were handed out gratis to the soldiers, and the king's favoured commanders received substantial gifts of wine: twenty casks to Otto de Grandson, and twenty-six to John de Vescy.[121]

In addition to the great efforts made by the crown to provide foodstuffs for the campaign, the magnates also made their own arrangements. There is little documentation on this, but in the case of Roger Bigod, earl of Norfolk, there is a list of the victuals supplied to him from two of his Irish manors. It details about 100 quarters of wheat, 200 quarters of oats, 77 beef cattle, 120 sheep, 57 pigs and 28 tuns of wine. This proved more than could be sent across the Irish Sea, and some of the meat and wine was kept back, but the grain, and much of the rest, was transported to Rhuddlan early in 1283. The whole operation cost the earl the substantial figure of £176, one indication of the fact that the figures of crown expenditure on the war should not be taken as an indication of the total cost to the country.[122]

It was not only victuals that were supplied to the army. The various accounts dealing with the war give a vivid impression of the multiplicity of supplies that were needed. There were carts, collected by Matthew Cheker from various abbeys and priories at the start of the campaign; constant expenditure on the tents and pavilions used by the king and his entourage; cloth bought to provide armbands with the Cross of St George on them to serve as a kind of uniform for the infantry

[120] *CWR*, 214–16.
[121] *Chronica Johannis de Oxenedes*, ed. H. Ellis (Rolls ser., 1859), 332; E 101/3/29; E 101/4/6.
[122] E 101/4/3.

(and as an indication, perhaps, of the holy character which Archbishop Pecham's excommunications of the Welsh gave the war); lances to carry the royal banners; even bran used to polish the king's armour. Ready-made hurdles, or *bretasches*, to form palisades were shipped from Chester; iron and lead were provided for the smiths in the army. Sheaves of arrows and crossbow bolts were bought in London, and sent to Wales.[123]

The costs of the war of 1282–3 were indeed heavy. J.E. Morris made careful calculations from the accounts, and reached a total of just over £60,000, which excluded the expenditure on castle-building. If this was added, a grand total was reached of £98,421.[124] However, Morris did not use the enrolled account of the wardrobe, which provides some additional figures, notably for the purchase of victuals, compensation paid for horses lost in the war, and some wage payments. Various other accounts also include expenditure on the war, such as that for the vacant bishopric of Hereford, which includes £80 given to Grimbald Pauncefoot for purchase of victuals, in the March, and £240 paid to the troops based at Oswestry. An entirely accurate total of royal expenditure on the war cannot be worked out, but a figure of about £120,000, including costs of castle-building incurred up to 1284, is indicated by the evidence.[125]

Such a total is impressive enough, but does not give much impression of the practical difficulties involved in financing a war in which the military impetus had to be maintained over a long period in hostile terrain. There was constant activity, as knights, and above all clerks, were sent to various parts of England to raise money, and bring it to Wales. On one occasion even the king's tailor, Adam Bydik, was employed on this task. The largest single payment into the royal wardrobe was one of £4,000, delivered at Devizes when the campaign was being planned: thereafter cash deliveries varied from between 1,000 marks to £3,000. Records show that by the time of Dafydd's death in 1283 at least £38,000 in cash had been carried to Chester for the use of the king's forces in the north, while further sums were taken to the troops operating further south.[126] Details of the transport of one

---

[123] E 101/351/9.

[124] Morris, *Welsh Wars*, 196–7, provides a very convenient tabulation.

[125] Oxenedes, 326–36; E 372/128, m.34d; E 372/130, 136 (wardrobe accounts). In my *War, Politics and Finance under Edward I*, 170, I gave a higher total, of £150,000. It is hard to distinguish military from ordinary expenditure, but the main reason why that estimate was higher was that I included in it, as part of military expenditure, £20,000 that the wardrobe account included as repayment of loans. These had been received in 1282–3, and were repaid in the next year, and should not be counted as true military expenditure.

[126] E 101/351/9.

sum of 1,000 marks taken from Boston in Lincolnshire to Carmarthen reveal something of the problems that might be encountered. It took six days for the money to reach Chepstow, from where a dozen footsoldiers escorted it to Neath. From Neath a substantial force of four cavalrymen and 400 foot brought it to Swansea: the Welsh were thought to be in force in the Tawe valley. A smaller troop of sixty infantry then took the money on to Kidwelly, and then it was not far to the final destination. It is noticeable that not very much use was made of the Italian bankers in these operations, though they were no doubt busily engaged in raising funds for the king in London and elsewhere. Only one substantial payment at Chester was made by the Italians, while in the south two members of the Riccardi firm came with a royal clerk, Vincent de Hulton, when he took £833 6s 8d, which they had lent the crown, to Carmarthen.[127]

By the summer of 1283 Edward had destroyed the power of the princes of Gwynedd. His victory was considerable, yet hardly surprising in view of the scale of the resources he could pour into the war. The Welsh achievement, in resisting for as long as they did, was also notable. The war had been of their making, but Llywelyn and Dafydd did not rule a united principality. In view of the rivalries and divisions within Wales, and the massive scale of English influence in the country, it was astonishing to have achieved as much as they did. Their eventual failure presented Edward I with a new set of problems, in a way more difficult than that of organizing the war: a proper settlement of Wales now had to be devised, a real test of the English king's statesmanship.

[127] Kaeuper, *Bankers to the Crown*, 184–5; C 47/2/4.

Chapter 8

WALES: SETTLEMENT AND REBELLION

The settlement of Wales following the English triumph in the war of 1282–3 presented Edward I with many problems. The defeated Welsh leaders had to be dealt with. The English magnates who had served in the war needed to be rewarded. A new administrative and legal system had to be created in the conquered territory, and English military dominance had to be assured by means of castle-building. The programme was a considerable one.

Clemency towards his enemies was not in Edward's character. After Llywelyn's death the prince's head had been sent to the king at Rhuddlan, and far from showing respect for a gallant opponent, Edward had it sent to London, where it adorned the Tower of London for many years on the end of a pike. Almost as soon as the king knew of Dafydd's capture, he had writs issued for a parliament to be held at Shrewsbury, at Michaelmas 1283, to discuss what should be done with him. Both magnates and representatives of shires and boroughs were asked to attend, the latter presumably to be there as witnesses.[1] Significantly, no clergy were asked, as from the outset it was envisaged that a judgement of blood would be given, in which they could not participate. The parliament was not intended to be the occasion for any general settlement of Wales: it was, rather, a celebration of victory.

The judgement on the unfortunate Dafydd was a fourfold one, though the sources vary as to the precise details. The Dunstable annals, in what seems the most plausible version, have it that he was sentenced to be dragged by horses to the scaffold, because he was a traitor. He was to be hanged alive for homicide, to have his bowels burned because he had committed his crimes at Easter, a holy period, and because he had plotted the king's death his body was to be quartered.[2] The sentence was comprehensive and savage, if not unprecedented in its viciousness: a man who tried to kill the king had been drawn, hanged, beheaded and quartered in 1238.[3] Dafydd's executioner, one Geoffrey of Shrewsbury,

---

[1] *Parl. Writs*, i.

[2] *Ann. Dunstable*, 294.

[3] Pollock and Maitland, *History of English Law*, ii, 501, n.1, where the theory of these multiple punishments is briefly discussed.

was paid a pound for his labours. There then followed some un-
seemly squabbling over the distribution of the pieces of the body: the
Londoners carried off the head in triumph, but the citizens of York and
Winchester disputed possession of the right shoulder. The men of
Lincoln refused to accept any part, and as a result incurred royal
displeasure, only remitted once a substantial fine had been paid.[4]

No general bloodbath took place after the English victory. One
Welsh knight was drawn and hanged at Shrewsbury, but imprisonment, rather than death, was the general rule.[5] Despite the obvious
danger involved in leaving any members of the Welsh princely family
alive, Dafydd's sons were sent into captivity at Bristol. The elder,
Llywelyn, died in 1287, but the younger, Owain, lived until at least
1325. Though he received a financial allowance, and had servants to
provide for his needs, he was kept in what seem unduly harsh conditions. Around 1305 he was put into a wooden cage at night, for reasons
of security, and rather later asked pathetically 'that he may go and play
within the wall of the castle'. Llywelyn's baby daughter Gwenllian, and
Dafydd's daughters, were banished to various nunneries in England.
Gwenllian, by her own account, was promised £100 a year in land or
rent by Edward, but in practice only received £20 from the exchequer.[6]
The lesser Welsh leaders mostly languished long in prison. A few were
released to serve Edward in Flanders in 1297, but at least one of them,
Rhys Fychan, returned to captivity at Windsor, where he died in 1302.
Edward at least directed the constable to have the body properly and
courteously buried, and agreed to meet the costs himself.[7]

From Shrewsbury Edward went on a leisurely progress through
England, going to York in January 1284 for the consecration of his
friend and servant Anthony Bek as bishop of Durham. He returned to
Wales via Chester in March, and embarked on a tour of Wales, plainly
as a means of consolidating his conquest of the previous year. He
concentrated his time in the north, only moving into south Wales in
November. He stayed for quite lengthy periods at Caernarfon, spent
about three weeks at a manor near Lake Bala, and went into the Lleyn
peninsula as well as to Criccieth and Harlech.[8] When he was at Conwy,
a presentation symbolic of conquest took place, when a group of
Welshmen presented him with 'that part of the most holy wood of the

---

[4] *Ann. London.*, 92; BL Vesp. B. xi (the Hagnaby chronicle), f.29v; E 101/359/9.
[5] BL Vesp. B. xi, f.29v.
[6] *Accounts of the Constables of Bristol Castle in the thirteenth and early fourteenth centuries*, ed.
M. Sharp (Bristol Record Soc., 1982), xxx; *Calendar of Ancient Petitions relating to Wales*,
ed. W. Rees (Cardiff, 1975), 458, 521; Powicke, *Henry III and the Lord Edward*, ii, 684–5.
[7] Stephenson, *The Last Prince of Wales*, 17–18; *Cal. Anc. Corr. Wales*, 261–2.
[8] Edward's itinerary is given in *Itinerary of Edward I, part 1: 1272–1290* (List and Index
Soc., 103, 1974).

cross which is called by the Welsh "Croysseneyht", which Llywelyn son of Griffin, late Prince of Wales, and his ancestors, princes of Wales, owned'. It was a former clerk of Llywelyn's, Hugo ap Ythel, who was responsible for this action: he was rewarded with a robe worth 20 shillings, and sufficient funds to enable him to study at Oxford. The Cross Neith was later taken regularly by Edward on his travels: his esteem for it is demonstrated by the considerable sum of £104 spent in 1293–4 on adorning its pedestal with gems set in gold.[9] Not only did Edward worship at Llywelyn's cross, he also dined off plate made from Llywelyn's treasure. A London goldsmith, William de Farndon, was entrusted with £57 worth of silver for this purpose. From the seal matrices of Llywelyn, his wife and Dafydd, Edward had a chalice made, which he ordered to be given to Vale Royal Abbey. It has been temptingly suggested that the Dolgellau chalice, found in 1890, is that very piece. Edward is also said to have been presented with what was claimed to be Arthur's crown, a further symbol of his success.[10] With clear deliberation, Edward had removed from Wales the regalia of Llywelyn's dynasty.

The business of territorial settlement was a very important one. The major grants to the king's followers had all been made in the initial phase of the war. In October 1282 Earl Warenne was granted Dinas Bran, with the lands of Bromfield and Yale. Dyffryn Clwyd, with Ruthin castle, went to Reginald de Grey. The cantreds of Rhos and Rhufoniog, with the commote of Dinmael, went to the earl of Lincoln, forming the great lordship of Denbigh. The Mortimers were well rewarded for their part in the war. In June 1282 the younger Roger was granted Llywelyn Fychan's lands, and he also received the land of Chirk. The sheriff of Shropshire, Roger Springhose, received lands in Mechain Iscoed, though he never developed his power there to any real extent. John Giffard of Brimpsfield was given the commote of Iscennen in November 1283, but in the south there was not the territorial revolution in the March that took place in the north. It is very striking that the earls of Gloucester and Hereford received no major territorial rewards for their war service. William de Valence was another who may well have felt that he deserved more from Edward, who seems to have resented his territorial ambitions.[11]

---

[9] *CWR*, 274; Taylor, 'Royal Alms and Oblations', 119–20; E 101/352/21.

[10] E 372/138, wardrobe account; A.J. Taylor, 'A Fragment of a Dona account of 1284', *Bull. of the Board of Celtic Studies*, xxvii (1976–8), 256–8; Rishanger, 107.

[11] *CWR*, 223, 240–1, 243, 265, 283; *Cal. Charter Rolls, 1257–1300*, 262; R. Morgan, 'The Barony of Powys, 1275–1360', *Welsh History Review*, x (1980–1), 41; Davies, *Lordship and Society in the March of Wales*, 26–9.

Grants to those Welshmen who supported the English were not many, but in July 1282 the king granted Rhys ap Maredudd the cantreds of Mawbynion and Gwynionydd, and some other lands in the hands of rebels.[12] Gruffydd ap Gwenwynwyn was no doubt content to see his claims in Powys upheld by Edward against Llywelyn's ambitions. He had served Edward well in the war, even though his physical powers were probably failing. A story has it that his son Owain surrendered his lands to Edward in 1283, receiving them back as an English barony; this may not be true, as it lacks documentary corroboration, but it expresses neatly the process that saw Powys transformed at this time from a Welsh to a Marcher lordship. Owain became Owen de la Pole of Welshpool.[13]

The precise status of the lands granted out by Edward was not made very clear at the outset, with the charters merely indicating that they were to be held in traditional manner, 'as freely and wholly as other neighbouring cantreds are held'.[14] In practice, however, they became Marcher lordships, even though they lacked the traditions of the old-established lordships on the border, and even though they were held in chief of the principality of Wales after 1301, rather than being held directly from the crown.[15] It is surprising that at a time when Edward's lawyers were very much concerned with the precise status of baronial rights, investigated in the *Quo Warranto* inquiries, there should not have been absolute clarity about the status and rights of these newly created lordships.

There remained the question of the lands that Edward himself retained in Wales. No grants of Llywelyn's territories of Snowdonia or Anglesey were made, as they were retained for the crown, like Flintshire, and also Carmarthen and Cardigan in the south. The Statute of Wales, issued at Rhuddlan on 19 March 1284, set out the provisions for the king's lands in north Wales, including Flintshire. It began with a splendidly grandiloquent preamble, explaining how Wales, feudally dependent on England, was now 'wholly and entirely transferred under our proper dominion', united and annexed to England. Welsh laws and customs had been duly considered and some were to continue, while others were corrected or added to. The king appealed to divine providence as justifying his actions, and good government was promised to the Welsh who, by implication, had not enjoyed this in the past.[16]

The body of the Statute of Wales had a precision and a matter-of-fact

---

[12] *CWR*, 233–4, 236–7.
[13] Davies, *Lordship and Society in the March of Wales*, 31, n.56.
[14] *CWR*, 243.
[15] Davies, *Lordship and Society in the March of Wales*, 27–8.
[16] *Statutes of the Realm*, i, 55–68.

quality somewhat at odds with the style of the preamble. It was more an administrative provision than a new legal code. It set out the new structure of local government, with the creation of the new shires of Flint, Anglesey, Caernarfon and Merioneth. Within these, the old organization of cantreds and commotes was maintained: there was no intention of complete anglicization. There was to be a justiciar of north Wales, with sheriffs, coroners and bailiffs under him in the shires. County courts were to be held monthly, and the sheriff was to conduct his tourn twice a year, holding sessions in the commote courts. A long list of offences to be tried in these courts ranged from treason, rape and homicide to breach of the assize of bread and ale. Welsh law still might apply in matters regarding debts, sureties, contracts and so forth, but in criminal questions, English law should be used. The statute provided examples of the writs to be used in Wales in the future. Although they were based on English practice, the number of writs was very small, for an attempt was made to simplify the incredible complexity of the English writ system. A single writ of right was devised to cover what in England needed perhaps some fifteen different formulae, and it can be argued that Edward, or rather his legal advisers, succeeded in creating legal processes which were a distinct improvement on English practice.[17]

While much was done to bring the administration of Wales into line with that of England (a continuation of a policy which Edward's officials had been engaged in as early as the 1250s), the statute did not seek to create unity between English and Welsh law. Nor did it suggest any particularly novel solution to the question of the status of Wales under the English crown. Neither in the preamble, nor in the main body of the text, is there, for example, any echo of imperial concepts of rule, or of justification for Edward's policy expressed in terms of Roman law. Yet for all that the statute was limited in geographical scope, and inadequate in that it did not anticipate all the legal complexities that might arise in the future, it does represent a most statesmanlike attempt to resolve many of the problems posed as a result of the Edwardian conquest of north Wales. It did not, however, bring together all the aspects of Edward's policies in Wales, and it is not sufficient evidence on which to judge the king.

The appointments which Edward made to positions of power in his newly conquered Welsh lands show that he intended the Welsh themselves to play only a minor part. He appointed Otto de Grandson as justiciar of north Wales. Otto, however, was to spend little time in the country after 1284, being more concerned with affairs in France and the

[17] L. Beverley Smith, 'The Statute of Wales, 1284', *Welsh History Review*, x (1980–1), 127–54, provides a detailed and important analysis of the statute.

Holy Land.[18] His personal deputy was a Savoyard compatriot, John de Bonvillars, appointed as constable of the new castle of Harlech in 1285.[19] On John's death in 1287 William de Grandson took over, but it is striking that the Savoyards did not attempt to establish themselves as a new aristocracy in Wales, being content with official positions rather than with grants of lands. As deputy justiciar in north Wales, Edward appointed John de Havering, who held office until 1287, when he became seneschal of Gascony. He returned to Wales as royal lieutenant, following the revolt of 1294–5. Englishmen were appointed as sheriffs in the newly formed counties, and the finances were in the hands of English clerks holding the offices of chamberlain and controller. The English and Savoyard constables of the castles also played an important part in the administration of north Wales. Below these exalted ranks, local office was largely the preserve of the Welsh. The introduction of anglicized methods of rule seems to have resulted in a considerable increase in the number of such positions as those of *rhaglaw* and *rhingyll*, roughly equivalent to English bailiffs. The old Welsh aristocracy was in rapid decline, but through office-holding a way was open for the advancement of the gentry. Yet only one Welshman, Gruffydd ap Tudor, was constable of a castle, and only one, Gruffydd ap Dafydd, rose to be a sheriff.[20]

In physical terms, the English consolidated their hold on north Wales by means of the construction of a magnificent series of castles, with their associated towns. Wales was not a country without castles prior to Edward's wars: both Llywelyn the Great and Llywelyn ap Gruffydd had seen a programme of castle-building as one means of increasing their power and prestige. The Welsh castles, such as Ewloe or Dolwyddelan, were not, however, well suited to English strategy. They were built primarily for defensive purposes, perched on relatively inaccessible sites to serve as places of refuge. They were not designed to be easily supplied, to serve as bases for the operation of large armies, to act as administrative headquarters, or to protect mercantile settlements, and this was what the English needed. They did make use of Criccieth, Castell-y-Bere and Dolwyddelan, but after the rising of 1294–5 it was only the first named of these that continued to be of any importance.[21]

The English programme of castle-building began with the war of

[18] W.H. Waters, *The Edwardian Settlement of North Wales* (1935), 9–11.

[19] A.J. Taylor, 'Who was "John Penardd", leader of the men of Gwynedd', *EHR*, xci (1976), 79–97.

[20] For the appointment of officials, see *CWR*, 283–4; Morris, *Welsh Wars*, 199; Waters, *Edwardian Settlement of North Wales*, 5–30.

[21] The Welsh castles are discussed by Avent, *Cestell Tywysogion Gwynedd* (conveniently, the text is in English as well as Welsh).

1277, when Builth, Aberystwyth, Flint and Rhuddlan were founded. Much the most important were Flint and Rhuddlan, which served as bases for the royal advance into north Wales. The second Welsh war saw the start of work at the major sites of Conwy, Caernarfon and Harlech, while the rebellion of 1294–5 prompted the king to order the building of Beaumaris, in Anglesey. The strategy of castle–building altered and developed with the changing circumstances of the wars. When Rhuddlan was begun in 1277, it was clearly intended to become the major royal centre in north Wales, the administrative capital of a shire and the seat of the bishopric, which Edward hoped to transfer from St Asaph. The creation of the new Marcher lordships with the grants to the magnates of 1282 changed the position, and the shire administration went to Flint, the bishopric stayed at St Asaph, while the function of a forward military base was taken over by Caernarfon and the other new castles to the west.[22]

Yet there was a consistency in what Edward was doing. In contrast to the seigneurial castles built in Wales, such as the earl of Lincoln's Denbigh, the royal castles in the north were all designed to be victualled and reinforced by sea. So much stress was laid on this that at Rhuddlan the river Clwyd was diverted so that it would be navigable right up to the castle walls. Conventional wisdom would have had the castle built on some rocky eminence, as Henry III's nearby fortification of Dyserth had been, but such sites could be blockaded, and the garrison forced to surrender. There was consistency, too, in the way in which the castles were linked to new urban foundations. It was not always possible to provide these with town walls, but at Conwy Edward built one of the finest of all medieval walled towns in conjunction with the castle.

The part played by the king himself in the planning of the new castles is unfortunately far from clear. A letter from Bogo de Knoville about the poor state of affairs at Aberystwyth in 1280 makes it clear that the problems were to be explained to the king himself, but the surviving records do not reveal in Edward's case the kind of detailed orders about architectural matters that survive from Henry III's reign. It is only in the case of Linlithgow, in Scotland, that there is a surviving agreement between the king and his chief mason.[23] Edward's orders would normally have been given either by word of mouth, or by means of writs under the privy seal, and these have unfortunately not survived. It is, however, inconceivable that so great a building programme could have been undertaken had the king himself not taken a deep interest in it.

The man who is known to have dominated the whole enterprise was

[22] *KW*, i, 323; A.J. Taylor, *Rhuddlan Castle* (Official Guide, 1956).
[23] *KW*, i, 302–3, 413.

Edward's great master mason, James of St George. He was a Savoyard, who must have met Edward when he stayed at St Georges d'Esperanche on his return from the crusade. By early 1278 he had been recruited by Edward, for he was then in Wales, 'to ordain the works of the castles there'. He was employed throughout the second Welsh war, and stayed in Wales as master of the king's works until he was summoned to Gascony in 1287. In the 1290s he was responsible for Beaumaris castle, and he played an important part in Scotland during Edward's last years.[24] Other Savoyards assisted Master James. John de Bonvillars, a knight, was paid late in 1283 to go to Wales 'to supervise the king's works there', and the accounts of building work at Conwy show that he was involved in the details of allocating work to teams of masons. William Cicon, a Savoyard household knight, constable at Rhuddlan and then at Conwy, was probably influential, and Otto de Grandson doubtless had a part to play. There were other masons from Savoy serving under Master James, along with other craftsmen. One Guy de Vergers, for example, appears alongside Master James in accounts both in Savoy and in Wales. Master Giles of St George was employed at Aberystwyth, and another Savoyard mason, John Francis, worked at Conwy. It may even be that the painter simply called Stephen who decorated the royal chamber at Rhuddlan had earlier performed the same task for the count and countess of Savoy at St Laurent-du-Pont.[25] There were, of course, some important English masons, such as Walter of Hereford who worked at Caernarfon from 1295 until 1309, but it was the Savoyards who were the elite of the men employed in castle-building.

By the late thirteenth century castle design had progressed far beyond the deceptively simple motte-and-bailey forms of the Norman period. Keeps were not universally employed, many castles relying on the strength of curtain walls and flanking towers. White Castle in Monmouthshire is a good example of such a castle, built by Edmund of Lancaster, and consisting of a polygonal enclosure with a high curtain wall flanked by circular towers. Two such towers were brought together to form a gatehouse in characteristic English style, copied by the Welsh at Criccieth castle.[26] Square towers were hardly ever used;

[24] A.J. Taylor, 'Master James of St George', *EHR*, lxv (1950), 433–57; *KW*, i, 203–5. My debt to Dr Taylor's work is immense: his studies have transformed knowledge of Edward's castles. Many of his articles have been collected together in his *Studies in Castles and Castle-Building* (1985).

[25] A.J. Taylor, 'Some notes on the Savoyards in North Wales, 1277–1300, with special reference to the Savoyard element in the construction of Harlech castle', *Genava*, ns, xi (1963), 289–315.

[26] There is some argument over the Criccieth gatehouse. The Official Guide by C.N. Johns (1970) claims that it is Edwardian work, but the level of expenditure at Criccieth

perhaps because they were vulnerable at the corners to mining and battering, or perhaps simply because fashions had changed since the twelfth century. The Welsh preference was for a D-shaped plan for the towers, the English for a round one. In Edward's new castles, the existing elements of keeps, towers, gatehouses and curtain walls were all employed, being developed in more complex ways without the adoption of any totally radical innovations.

The castles built by Edward I in north Wales fall, in terms of their ground plans, into clear groups. Flint, like Builth in mid-Wales, has a true keep. In the later castles only Caernarfon possesses, in the Eagle Tower, anything like a keep. Rhuddlan, Harlech and Beaumaris were all built on fairly level ground, which did not dictate any obvious plan. These castles show the development of the concept of a concentric castle, with an outer ring of relatively slender defences, constructed so as to provide massive fire-power from arrow-loops and crenellations. At Rhuddlan the inner ward was trapezoidal in plan, with twin towers at two corners forming gatehouses. At Harlech a square inner ward featured round corner towers, and a massive twin-towered gatehouse in the centre of one wall. This was developed on the courtyard side into what looks more like a mansion than a fortification. At Beaumaris, last of the castles, additional flanking towers were added to the plan, and two great gatehouses built rather than one, making for complete symmetry. The outer defences, too, were far more elaborate than those at Rhuddlan or Harlech. At Conwy and Caernarfon the sites compelled Master James to adopt an elongated rather than a concentric plan. Both castles have two wards, intended to be separated by a cross wall, though this no longer stands at Caernarfon. At Conwy, the entrances are protected by barbicans, with no true gatehouse, but Caernarfon features two massive gatehouses. Unlike the other castles, it has multi-angular towers. The south curtain is most ingenious, for it is tunnelled through, in order to provide a gallery for archers, while the design of the wall-head is such that any attacker was faced with triple banks of arrow-loops.

It is not so much in the overall conception of the castles, as in the details of the architecture, that the Savoyard connection is shown most clearly, though the castle of St Georges d'Esperanche itself, with a symmetrically planned inner ward and octagonal towers, has some obvious general resemblance to the Edwardian castles. St Georges has one very precise link with Harlech, for the form and measurement of a latrine chute, at the abutment of curtain wall and corner tower, are just the same in both castles. The design of the windows, with shallow

---

by Edward was not such as to suggest he built so massive a structure, and Avent's view, *Cestyll Tywysogion Gwynedd*, 31, that it is Welsh work seems preferable.

curved heads, is also very similar, though here the exact parallel in terms of measurement is with the Savoyard castle of Chillon. Full-centred round arches elsewhere at Harlech are also of Savoyard design. The building technique of using inclined or sloping scaffolds was one common to the Welsh and Savoyard castles, and was not normally employed by English masons.[27]

Medieval master masons were not afraid to copy other men's work, and many influences lay behind the north Welsh castles. The king's own travels, particularly to the east, may well have provided some of the inspiration for the building programme. The crusader port of Aigues Mortes, built by St Louis, provides some possible precedents. A formally planned town with its own port, Aigues Mortes may well have been in Edward's mind when such stress was laid on the ease of access from the sea to his new castles and their associated boroughs. The great circular tower, the Tour de Constance, at Aigues Mortes has been suggested as one possible inspiration for one of the most puzzling features of any of the Welsh castles, the keep at Flint. This consists, in effect, of two concentric drum towers, one inside the other, and the circular galleries of the Tour de Constance have something of the same effect. Another possibility is that Flint parallels Castel del Monte in Apulia, which Edward could have visited on his return from the east. The difference in scale between the celebrated Apulian castle and Flint makes this connection rather unlikely.[28] A closer connection with an Apulian castle is Lucera, which, although not circular, did have what amounted to one tower built within another. The purpose of the design at Flint was probably to provide comfortable, well-lit accommodation in the upper levels of the keep, the inner drum being open to the sky, forming a kind of small open courtyard. It would be a gross error to assume that all the architectural features of the castles are to be explained in terms of purely military need. That comfort was a consideration is shown by the provision at Rhuddlan, of a garden for the queen, which featured a pleasant fishpond surrounded by seats.[29]

The most intriguing origin of any of the architectural features adopted by Edward's masons is that of the remarkable multi-angular towers and dark stripes in the stonework at Caernarfon. This has been

[27] Taylor, 'Some notes on the Savoyards in North Wales', 309–12; 'The castle of St Georges d'Esperanche', 42–6.

[28] R.A. Brown, *English Castles* (3rd edn, 1976), 110; *Flint Castle* (Official Guide, reprinted 1971), 2.

[29] *KW*, i, 324. For an absurd 'military' explanation of the design of Flint, see W.D. Simpson, *Castles in England and Wales* (1969), 283, where it is suggested that attackers would be forced down into the basement of the inner drum, and then picked off at leisure by the defenders, from the circular gallery.

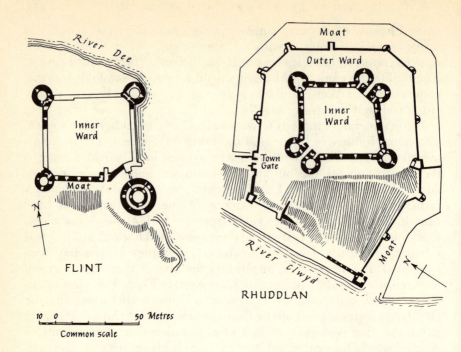

River Dee

Inner
Ward

Moat

N

FLINT

Moat

Outer Ward

Inner
Ward

Town
Gate

River Clwyd

Moat

N

RHUDDLAN

10 0   50 Metres

Common scale

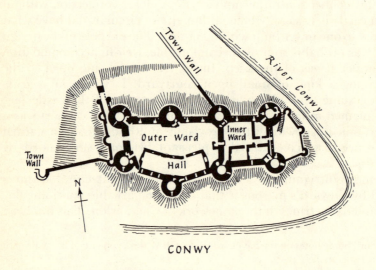

Town Wall

River Conwy

Outer Ward

Inner
Ward

Hall

Town
Wall

N

CONWY

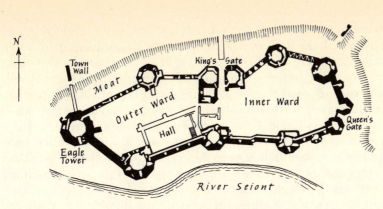

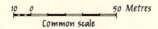

CAERNARFON

10 0   50 Metres

Common scale

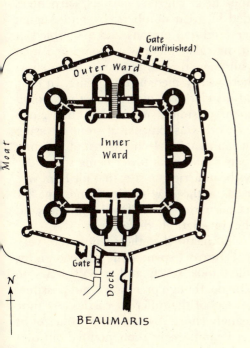

BEAUMARIS

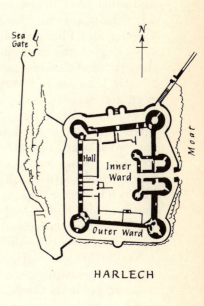

HARLECH

2. Edward I's Castles in Wales: ground plans

convincingly demonstrated by A.J. Taylor.[30] Strong traditions linked Caernarfon with the Roman past, and in 1283 Edward was involved in re-burying the body of what was thought to be Magnus Maximus, 'father of the noble emperor Constantine'. The style of the castle is very clearly derived from the walls of the imperial city of Constantinople. Imperial links were further emphasized by placing eagles on the tops of the triple turreted Eagle Tower: conveniently, these also provided a link with Savoy, for the eagle was the count's symbol. There was perhaps less Savoyard influence in the architecture of Caernarfon than in the other castles. The man initially in charge of the whole building operation was the English knight Eustace Hatch, and later the main responsibility for the building works lay on the shoulders of Walter of Hereford. Yet there is little doubt that Master James of St George was the man primarily responsible for the design of the castle, and in 1288 the Savoyard knight William de Grandson was sent to supervise the works at Caernarfon.[31]

The organization of a building programme on the scale of that undertaken in Wales was a tremendous task. Diggers, masons, carpenters and other workmen were needed in great numbers: by mid-August 1277, 1,845 diggers, 790 sawyers and 320 masons had assembled at Chester and Flint. At Harlech, in 1286, there were some 950 men labouring on the castle in the summer, though in winter when short days reduced working hours, there were a mere 60 on the site. In 1295 Master James of St George and his clerk calculated that they would need 400 masons, 200 quarrymen, 30 smiths and no less than 2,000 labourers at Beaumaris. Skilled work was expensive: stone dressing might cost 1¼d or 1½d per stone, and at Harlech the cost of building the two seaward towers was 45s per foot, each tower being some fifty feet high. Stone could not always be quarried on site: that for Flint was taken from Shotwick and ferried to the new castle. Limestone for Harlech had to be shipped from Caernarfon or Anglesey. Timber, sand and coal also had to be brought considerable distances.[32]

All this manpower and material meant that the castles were very costly. Between 1277 and 1304, Edward I spent some £80,000 on his works in Wales. Harlech, which took seven and a half years to complete, probably cost about £9,500, though precision is not possible, as some accounts combine the costs of the different castles. As time wore on, money became increasingly short. A letter from James of St George and his clerk, working at Beaumaris in 1296, pointed out that 'the work we are doing is very costly and we need a great deal of money',

[30] *KW*, i, 369–71; above, 120.
[31] *CPR 1281–92*, 302.
[32] *KW*, i, 313, 359–61, 399.

and concluded with a desperate postscript: 'And, sirs, for God's sake be quick with the money for the works, as much as ever our lord the king wills; otherwise everything done up till now will have been of no avail.'[33] In the last years of the reign matters became more difficult still, and it is the lack of funds which explains the incomplete character of the works, particularly at Caernarfon and Beaumaris. At the latter, the towers never rose up above the level of the curtain walls.

Yet incomplete as they were, the castles ringing north Wales must have been astonishingly impressive in about 1300. They gleamed with white plaster or wash, their crenellations were capped with pinnacles, their towers with watch turrets, and they were a most formidable symbol of the English conquest. Yet to understand their importance, it is not enough to study merely the physical appearance and military strength of the castles. Their institutional place in society was, in many ways, quite as important.

Many of the men appointed as constables of the castles were, like their builders, Savoyards. William Cicon at Flint and then Conwy, John de Bonvillars at Harlech, James of St George himself at the same castle, and Otto de Grandson at Caernarfon: the list is an impressive one. The Englishmen who served in the Welsh castles were not men of such note, with the exception of William Leyburn at Criccieth from 1284. It is striking that few of the constables had much territorial interest in Wales: Hugh Turberville who commanded Castell-y-Bere for a time, was the only real Marcher lord among them. Nor did becoming a constable give a man direct control over Welsh estates, for Edward's technique was to allocate fees at the exchequer, rather than linking lands with the office. Cicon received £190 for Conwy, Leyburn £100 for Criccieth, Turberville 200 marks for Castell-y-Bere.[34] Such an arrangement was obviously not wholly satisfactory to the constables, and in 1305 the commanders at Harlech and Criccieth both petitioned for the grant of local offices, only to have their demands refused.[35] These castles were not the centres of castleries in the traditional English manner, and only Caernarfon, as the main seat of the justiciar of north Wales, and Flint as the centre of its county, had a full administrative role to play. Nor, for all their splendour, were the castles heavily garrisoned. In 1284 thirty or forty men to each was regarded as appropriate. In the rebellion of 1294–5 Harlech had twenty men, of whom two died during the siege, until reinforcements came from Ireland. With some townsmen who had taken refuge in the castle, the

[33] *KW*, i, 399.
[34] *CWR*, 291–2, 296, 302, 325–6.
[35] *Record of Carnarvon*, 224.

total strength came to thirty-eight men, and in addition there were
seven women and five children of the castle, and twelve women, with
twenty-one children, of the town.[36]

The castles were a part of an English colonizing process, for they
were linked with the establishment of new towns in Wales. Archbishop
Pecham advised Edward that the Welsh should be encouraged to live in
towns, as a means of civilizing them.[37] He had perhaps picked up, and
misunderstood, discussions at court, for the purpose of the new towns
was not to convert the Welsh to an English way of life, but to create
English enclaves, protected by the castles, and provide them with some
economic viability. Urban settlements were associated with the castles
of the first Welsh war, as well as with those of the second, but it was not
until September and November 1284, that the important step was
taken of granting charters to Flint, Rhuddlan, Conwy, Caernarfon,
Bere, Criccieth and Harlech.[38] The most striking of the new towns were
Conwy and Caernarfon, both carefully planned, and provided with
superb town walls. In contrast, Harlech and Criccieth were little more
than huddles of houses sheltering under the castle walls. There was
little enthusiasm to settle in remote Bere, or Harlech, but by the early
1290s there were 74 taxpayers at Flint, and 75 at Harlech. A rental of
1298 recorded the names of 110 burgesses at Conwy, and there were 62
at Caernarfon.[39] The success of the towns is shown by the fact that they
were soon imitated: three more towns were founded in Flintshire in the
early 1290s, at Caerwys, Overton and New Mostyn, though none of
these was linked with castles. The magnates created towns as well: the
earl of Lincoln at Denbigh, earl Warenne at Holt, and Reginald de
Grey at Ruthin.[40]

Edward's policy was an imaginative one, which in time was to do
much to transform the economic and social structure of north Wales. In
the king's own day, however, the new English boroughs were isolated
outposts, separated by language, as well as by fortifications, from the
surrounding Welsh. The English settlers were none too comfortable in
an alien land. Prior to receiving their charter in 1284, the men of
Rhuddlan had complained bitterly that they had to use Welsh law, and
they threatened to move out if the king did not keep his promise to allow

[36] *CWR*, 291–2, 296; J. Griffiths, 'Documents relating to the Rebellion of Madoc,
1294–5', *Bull. of the Board of Celtic Studies*, viii (1935–7), 149–50.

[37] *Receuil des lettres Anglo-Françaises*, ed. Tanquerey, 47.

[38] The charters are conveniently printed together by E.A. Lewis, *The Medieval
Boroughs of Snowdonia* (1912), 279–83.

[39] A.J. Taylor, 'The earliest burgesses of Flint and Rhuddlan', *Flintshire Historical
Society Publications*, xxvii (1975–6), 152–60; *Merioneth Lay Subsidy Roll*, lxiv.

[40] Beresford, *New Towns of the Middle Ages*, 547–51. Caerwys was exceptional in that
most of its inhabitants were Welsh.

them to use the customs of Hereford. They objected on another occasion to the fact that 'so many Welsh are lodged near to the town on the outside that they disturb the profit and the market of the English, and give voice to much treason among them'.[41]

It was hardly to be expected that the Welsh would be well treated by their new masters after the conquest. Strenuous efforts were made by Edward's officials to increase the paltry revenues that came their way. A concern with the valuation of newly conquered lands came very early, for in August 1283 Guncelin de Badlesmere and Peter de Lek, along with a Welsh friar, were engaged on this task.[42] Officials such as Roger de Pulesdon, sheriff of Anglesey, found themselves in a difficult position. His accounts for 1291–2 show outgoings of almost £400, mounting to nearly £600 if arrears from previous years are included. His income came to only £341, and it is hardly surprising that he was destined to be accused of unjust practices in his attempts to make ends meet.[43] The queen had been granted the lands of Hope and Maelor Saesneg after Prince Dafydd's execution, and her officials, notably Roger de Bures, behaved in a very high-handed manner. It is very clear that every opportunity had been taken to raise rents, and many customary rights were overridden. When the king had ordered the widening of the roads, Bures had gone to excessive lengths, clearing large tracts of land, turning it into arable, even where the queen had no rights in the area.[44] In the lordship of Denbigh there was wholesale expropriation of Welshmen, and the lands granted to them in compensation were infertile and inadequate. The Welsh of Dyffryn Clwyd complained, many years later, about Reginald de Grey's actions, driving men 'from their wood, pasture, mountains and mills; and this of his own will'.[45]

A document drawn up after Edward's reign made note of various ordinances issued by the king, described in it as the conqueror. These possibly date from the mid-1290s, and provide a telling contrast to the statesmanship indicated by the Statute of Wales. Welshmen were prohibited from holding gatherings without royal permission, and in the absence of royal officials. Welshmen might not hold lands in the newly founded towns. They were not to bear arms in the towns, and could not give hospitality to strangers for more than one night. They

[41] *Cal. Anc. Pet. Wales*, 461, 491.
[42] E 101/359/9.
[43] Waters, *Edwardian Settlement of North Wales*, 16–17; *Record of Carnarvon*, 216.
[44] N.M. Fryde, 'A royal enquiry into abuses by Queen Eleanor's ministers in north-east Wales, 1291–2', *Welsh History Review*, v (1970–1), 366–76.
[45] R.R. Davies, 'Colonial Wales', *Past and Present*, 65 (1974), 11; *Cal. Anc. Pet. Wales*, 168.

could only sell their goods in market towns. The traditional custodians
of the peace, known as *keys*, were to be removed from office.[46]

It is hardly surprising that there were two rebellions against English
rule in the years following the conquest. Both took place when the king
was distracted with overseas affairs. The first, in 1287, was the product
of Edward's lack of generosity towards those Welsh who had served
him in the wars, while the second, in 1294, was a much more serious
general rising against the English, which had extensive popular
support.

Rhys ap Maredudd, lord of Dryslwyn, had been conspicuously loyal
to the English, both in 1277 and in 1282–3. Yet he had not been able to
extend his lordship in south Wales by acquiring Dinefwr castle as he
wished, and at the conclusion of the second Welsh war he suffered the
humiliation of trial in parliament at Acton Burnell, for entering lands
he had been granted prior to their being formally handed over by the
justiciar. He became entangled in legal disputes with the justiciar of
west Wales, Robert Tibetot, and had considerable difficulties with
some of his own tenants. The crisis came in 1287, following repeated
refusals by Rhys to attend the justiciar's court at Carmarthen. He had
done all he could to obtain Edward's support, and in the previous year
had even been to France in person, to put his case.[47] In a letter to
Edmund of Cornwall, his lieutenant in England, the king stated that
he did not wish Rhys to be molested, and asked that his grievances
be seen to. However, there was no sympathy in England for Rhys: a
clerk noted at the foot of Edward's letter that 'the whole world knows
Rhys stands against the English allegiance'.[48] Although in April 1287
the king forbad any action for two months after the end of the legal
proceedings, should they go against Rhys, there was little hope of
avoiding conflict.

The rising began when Rhys seized Llandovery castle on 8 June
1287. Dinefwr and Carreg Cennen soon fell to the Welsh. Edmund of
Cornwall made elaborate plans for four armies to converge on the
rebels, and by 13 August he had reached the Welsh stronghold of
Dryslwyn. Disaster struck the English when a mine dug by them
collapsed prematurely while it was being inspected by a group of
knights, including the important Savoyard John de Bonvillars. Yet the

---

[46] *Record of Carnarvon*, 131–2. There is no contemporary version of such an ordinance
issued by Edward, and so there are doubts about this document. Yet it does fit in well
with much of what is known of Edward's policy in Wales.

[47] This visit is noted by the Hagnaby chronicler, BL Vesp. B. xi., f.32. Rhys may
have brought back with him the letters of protection given in *Littere Wallie*, 169–70.

[48] J. Beverley Smith, 'The Origins of the Revolt of Rhys ap Maredudd', *Bull. Board of
Celtic Studies*, xxi (1964–6), 163.

siege continued, with the attackers using a great stone-throwing trebuchet, rather than continuing with undermining the walls. In September the castle fell, but Rhys, his wife and most of the garrison escaped. In November he took Newcastle Emlyn by surprise, and it was not until the following January that it was recaptured. Again Rhys escaped, and the rest of his life was spent as a fugitive in the hills and woods of Wales. He was eventually betrayed by his own men in 1292, and suffered a similar fate to that of Prince Dafydd.[49] The revolt was costly to suppress, perhaps because the government over-reacted in the early stages, and ordered up far more troops than were really needed. The Italian bankers provided at least £8,288 out of the total of over £10,000.[50] Edmund of Cornwall had to make extensive use of them, as the normal administrative machinery of the wardrobe was not available for the organization of the war, since it was in Gascony with the king. Improvisation was highly successful, however, and the revolt never threatened the central features of the Edwardian settlement of Wales. One striking aspect of it, indeed, was the degree of support that Edmund of Cornwall was able to obtain in Wales itself, even from Rhys's own men. The next rising was to be very different.

There is no statement of the specific grievances of the Welsh in 1294, but it is not hard to see why rebellion took place in that year. In addition to the generally harsh character of English administration, there was the matter of the tax which was imposed on the country in 1292. A massive tax of a fifteenth was granted in England in 1290, but as Wales was not part of the parliamentary machinery whereby county representatives gave their consent to taxation, it was necessary for the various Marcher lords to be approached separately for their agreement. This all took time. The tax in Wales was a fifteenth, just as in England, but in practice the assessment was much heavier than it was there. Merioneth, for example, was to pay £566, as compared with, for example, £1,604 for the much wealthier English county of Essex. The average Merioneth taxpayer was asked for 4s 3d, whereas his Colchester counterpart owed only 1s 9d. The total assessment for the whole of Wales was probably in the region of £10,000, and although only just over £3,000 is recorded as being paid into the English exchequer, there can be little doubt that the tax was generally regarded as insupportable by the Welsh. Much was probably paid to local officials, and never reached the exchequer. The final instalment of the tax was due to be paid in the autumn of 1294. A further demand on Wales was for soldiers to go and fight in Gascony, and it was surely no coincidence

[49] The fullest account of the rising is given by R.A. Griffiths, 'The Revolt of Rhys ap Maredudd', *Welsh History Review*, iii (1966–7), 121–43.
[50] Kaeuper, *Bankers to the Crown*, 195–9.

that the outbreak of rebellion at the end of September coincided both with the date for payment of the last instalment of the tax and with the muster of the Welsh troops at Shrewsbury. The military preparations provided an opportunity for rebellion, as well as an inducement, for they meant that many major English magnates were due to leave Wales to sail for Gascony.[51]

The leadership of the revolt was not taken by men who had played a leading role in earlier resistance to Edward. Madog ap Llywelyn in the north was the son of a lord of Meirionydd who had been dispossessed by Llywelyn ap Gruffydd. He had probably spent some time in England, and received payment from Edward in 1277. He must have been resentful that in the aftermath of the conquest of 1282–3 he was not restored to Meirionydd, but had to be satisfied with a small estate in Anglesey.[52] Cynan ap Maredudd's identity is not wholly clear, but he may have been of noble origins. It is not even certain where he was operating. Maelgwyn ap Rhys in Cardiganshire and Morgan ap Maredudd in Glamorgan were not men of great distinction.[53] Edward had destroyed the power of the house of Gwynedd so effectively that leadership had to be found elsewhere.

The rising was almost certainly premeditated, with attacks on English castles throughout Wales. At Caernarfon the half-built castle was overrun, and Roger de Pulesdon was put to death in a manner which recalled the savagery of Dafydd's execution. The new royal castles which were reasonably complete, Flint, Rhuddlan, Conwy and Harlech, all held out, though at Flint the English deliberately set fire to the town. At Builth an English official was killed. Baronial castles fared less well. A number of those belonging to the earl of Gloucester in the south fell, as did Denbigh, Ruthin, Mold and Hawarden.[54]

The fact that preparations were far advanced for a Gascon campaign meant that it was a relatively easy, if bitter, task for Edward to divert troops, money and material to Wales. On 15 October writs were issued to the leading magnates to meet the king at Worcester on 21 November. Musters were planned at Brecon, Cardiff and Chester, the king's own forces assembling at the latter venue. Some of the provisions collected for Gascony were transferred to Wales, and further supplies were

[51] *Merioneth Lay Subsidy Roll*, xxiv–xxxv and *passim*.

[52] J.G. Edwards, 'Madog ap Llywelyn, the Welsh Leader in 1294–5', *Bull. Board of Celtic Studies*, xiii (1950), 207–10; Stephenson, *Governance of Gwynedd*, 143–4.

[53] *Brenhinedd y Saesson*, 261; *Book of Prests*, xxviii.

[54] Morris, *Welsh Wars*, 241–2; Altschul, *A Baronial Family*, 154; M.C. Prestwich, 'A New Account of the Welsh Campaign of 1294–5', *Welsh History Review*, vi (1973–4), 89–94. For a fuller commentary, with corrections, on the chronicle account printed there, see R.F. Walker, 'The Hagnaby Chronicle and the Battle of Maes Moydog', *Welsh History Review*, viii (1976–7), 125–38.

collected.[55] While these measures were being taken, matters were deteriorating in Wales. On 11 November, the earl of Lincoln was attacked by his own tenants as he advanced towards Denbigh, and was forced to flee.[56] An expedition, which seems to have failed, was mounted to relieve Castell-y-Bere. Archaeological evidence of destruction by fire at about this period is highly suggestive of disaster there. The one success was that John Giffard did manage to relieve the beleaguered garrison at Builth.[57]

When the English armies mustered in December, the original plan was modified. The king's forces assembled at Chester as planned, but Warwick's troops mustered at Montgomery, and a third army, under William de Valence and the earl of Norfolk, gathered at Carmarthen. In all, the English forces were larger than ever before. Some 21,000 infantry were engaged in operations in north Wales, 10,700 were serving under Warwick in late December, and there were at least 4,000 in the south. The size of the cavalry forces cannot, unfortunately, be calculated, but it must have been considerable.[58]

Edward himself marched from Chester to Wrexham, then on through Denbigh, to reach Conwy by Christmas. Other troops, under Reginald de Grey, took the more usual coastal route. At some point a large number of Welshmen came to the king, who pardoned them their rebellion, on condition that they agreed to serve him in France. They promised to capture Madog, but when they went to the Welsh leader, he made a powerful speech, which made them change their minds.[59] The English suffered a major setback when the baggage train was attacked and destroyed by the Welsh, and Edward found himself effectively besieged in Conwy castle. Walter of Guisborough has a touching story of how the king refused the small quantity of wine that had been kept back for him, and insisted that it be shared out between his troops. There certainly was for a time an acute shortage of victuals.[60] In January the king undertook an astonishing march, leaving Conwy on the 7th, advancing through Bangor, and riding right on to Nefyn in the Lleyn peninsula, where he stayed on the 12th and 13th. By 20 January he was back at Conwy, apparently with little to show for this raid. The long stay at Conwy which followed was a tedious one,

[55] *CWR*, 359–61.
[56] Guisborough, 251.
[57] Morris, *Welsh Wars*, 252, argues *ex silentio* that the relief of Castell-y-Bere must have been successful, but the evidence cited in *KW*, i, 368–9 points to a different conclusion.
[58] *Book of Prests*, xxix–xxxi.
[59] Prestwich, 'A New Account of the Welsh Campaign', 89–94; Walker, 'The Hagnaby Chronicle and the Battle of Maes Moydog', 126–7.
[60] Guisborough, 251–2; *Book of Prests*, xxxii–iii.

ANGLESEY

Beaumaris
(April–May '95)

FLINT

Conwy
(Dec '94–
April '95)
(June '95)

Rhuddlan

Flint

Chester
(Dec. '94)

Caernarfon

Denbigh

Ruthin

CAERNARFON

MERIONETH

Chirk

(Jan '95)

Criccieth
Harlech

Oswestry
(June '95)

Maes Moydog ✕
(5 March '95)

(May '95)

Montgomery

Aberystwyth

CARDIGAN

Builth

Cardigan

(June '95)

CARMARTHEN

Brecon

Carmarthen

- - - -   *Approximate route of Edward and his army, 1294-5*
   ⌐⌐ *Castles built by Edward I*
   ⌐⌐ *'Lordship' castles*
FLINT *Counties created by Edward I (Flint is in three parts)*

3. The Welsh Rebellion of 1294–5

and in March the infantry begged the king for action. They made a sortie, accompanied by some cavalry, surprised their enemies, killing some 500, and recovered some of the baggage lost earlier. In April the king mounted an attack on Anglesey, recrossing the Menai straits to Bangor on 6 May. He then advanced southwards towards Aberystwyth and Cardigan.[61]

Events elsewhere in Wales were more dramatic. In the south the earl of Gloucester's forces had little success against Morgan ap Maredudd, but on 5 March Warwick's troops achieved a notable triumph against Madog. The Welsh leader had evidently copied Prince Llywelyn's strategy of 1283, and broken out of Snowdonia. A newsletter in the Hagnaby chronicle gives the following account of events:

> Know that the Montgomery army went to Oswestry to take some plunder. Then the prince came into Powys with the elite of his Welshmen, and our spies came by night to Oswestry, and told us that the prince had gone as far as Cydewain. They [the English] went as quickly as they could to Montgomery, on the Friday and Saturday, 5 March. The prince's host awaited our men on open ground and they fought together, our men killing a good six hundred. Then our men from Llystynwynnan joined battle with those who were transporting the prince's victuals, and killed a good hundred, and took from them, over six score beasts laden with foodstuffs. And we lost only one esquire, the tailor of Robert FitzWalter, and six infantrymen, but a good ten horses were killed. For the Welshmen held their ground well, and they were the best and bravest Welsh that anyone has seen.[62]

The force involved at this battle of Maes Moydog was small, consisting of only about 119 horse and 2,500 infantry. Another account of the engagement suggests that the earl of Warwick employed novel tactics, interspersing crossbowmen with the cavalry, but the fact that there were a mere thirteen crossbowmen and archers listed in the pay roll for the army casts considerable doubt on this version of events.[63] At all events, an important victory was achieved, even though Madog himself was neither killed nor captured.

In the south, Hereford's men defeated a Welsh force which had been lured into a trap. Reginald de Grey, marching south-west from Rhuddlan, had considerable success in routing out Madog's men from the

---

[61] *Book of Prests*, xxxii–iv, xxxix–xli, and see 222–5 for the royal itinerary; Prestwich, 'A new account of the Welsh Campaign', 89–94.

[62] Prestwich, 'A New Account of the Welsh Campaign', 91; Walker, 'The Hagnaby Chronicle and the battle of Maes Moydog', 128–30.

[63] Prestwich, *War, Politics and Finance under Edward I*, 107–8. For this campaign and battle, see also J.G. Edwards, 'The Battle of Maes Moydog and the Welsh Campaign of 1294–5', *EHR*, xxxix (1924), 1–12; J.G. Edwards, 'The Site of the Battle of "Meismeidoc", 1295 (Note)', *EHR*, xlvi (1931), 262–5.

forests where they had taken shelter.[64] Even without the capture of the leaders of the rebellion, the collapse was rapid. Morgan ap Maredudd made his peace with the king in the south, claiming that he was only fighting against the earl of Gloucester. It was possibly as a result of a dispute over Morgan's surrender that the king took Glamorgan into his custody for a time.[65]

Eventually the leaders were, for the most part, caught. There was some argument as to who was responsible for taking Madog: John de Havering claimed the 500 mark reward offered by the king, but Enyr Fychan of Meirionydd was to claim that he held the rhaglawry of Talybont as a result of capturing the north Welsh leader. He was, surprisingly, not put on trial and executed, but was imprisoned in the Tower of London, where he probably remained for the rest of his life. Cynan ap Maredudd and two of his associates were brutally executed for treason at Hereford, but within a couple of years Morgan ap Maredudd would be serving Edward as a squire of the household on various business, in Flanders and elsewhere. Maelgwyn was killed in the fighting at the close of the rebellion. Large numbers of hostages were taken to England, as a means of ensuring future peace in Wales.[66] Edward's clemency to Madog in particular is surprising: perhaps he considered that he was not of sufficiently exalted social status to be worth a show trial and execution, or perhaps he was simply in merciful mood when Madog's submission took place. He was certainly not benevolent in all cases. When he was on his triumphal journey round Wales in the aftermath of the rebellion, the abbot of Strata Florida unwisely promised that he would bring the leading men of Cardiganshire to Edward to receive his peace. When they failed to appear, the king angrily ordered 'Burn it! Burn it!'. The abbey was duly fired, along with all else in sight.[67]

A study of the campaign of 1294–5 shows a well-oiled war machine in operation. The system of recruiting was well established: men such as Thomas de Berkeley, Osbert de Spaldington and Alan Plugenet had ample experience, and seem to have had little difficulty in bringing together the large numbers of infantry the king required. When Robert de Rye went to Chester to get 300 ditchers, 30 carpenters and 20 masons to come to Conwy, he was on a mission familiar to many of

[64] *Cal. Anc. Corr. Wales*, 108–9.

[65] Altschul, *A Baronial Family*, 155.

[66] J. Griffiths, 'The Revolt of Madog ap Llywelyn, 1294–5', *Trans. Caernarvonshire Historical Society* (1955), 21–3; *Book of Prests*, xliii–iv; *Flores*, iii, 277; J. Beverley Smith, 'Edward II and the Allegiance of Wales', *Welsh History Review*, viii (1976–7), 142. The story in Guisborough, 252, that Madog surrendered and was admitted to the king's peace on condition that he captured Morgan makes no sense.

[67] *Ann. Worcester*, 520

Edward's officials. James of St George prepared bridging equipment in the Wirral: it was probably not used, but the formula adopted in 1282 must have been in his mind. Victuals were brought from the south coast where they had been stockpiled ready to go to Gascony, while clerks collected additional supplies from various English counties. Ireland too was an important source. Richard de Havering went there to organize the revictualling of Harlech and Criccieth castles, an important operation carried out early in April 1295.[68] Finance was no great problem, as large reserves of cash had been accumulated by the crown for the French war, and it proved possible to send consignments of up to £4,000 at the rate of two or three a month to Wales from Westminster. A total of £54,453 was sent in this way between the outbreak of the rebellion and the following October, with a further £1,000 from Ireland. This sum does not, of course, represent the total cost of putting down the rebellion, but it is unfortunately not possible to isolate all the Welsh items in the royal accounts from the broader entries, and an accurate total cannot be calculated.[69]

The chronicler Pierre Langtoft provides an interesting explanation for the length of time that it took to put down the rebellion in Wales. He argued that had Edward been prepared to reward his followers with the lands that they took, to hold of him in feudal service, the war would have been won virtually at a stroke.[70] There is no other evidence to suggest any reluctance on the part of the magnates to serve Edward in Wales, but Langtoft's view almost certainly reflects the views of men who found themselves largely unrewarded for their services, save for the payment of wages, which almost certainly did not cover their costs in full. Edward did not choose to use the opportunity presented by the rising to make any radical changes in the landholding structure or government of Wales: his policy was to permit the heirs of Welshmen who had fought against him to retain their lands, under severe threat of what would happen if there was further rebellion.[71] There was a commission appointed to investigate what had taken place in Wales, but it is unlikely that those appointed to it, John de Havering and William Cicon, had any degree of sympathy with the Welsh point of view.[72] Nor did the king draw the obvious lesson from the rebellion, and lighten the financial burden placed on the Welsh. In 1300 he even

[68] *Book of Prests*, 54–6, 61–5, 76; J. Griffiths, 'Documents relating to the rebellion of Madoc, 1294–5', 149–55.
[69] The finances of the war are fully discussed in *Book of Prests*, l–liii, and tabulated 226–7.
[70] Langtoft, ii, 216.
[71] *Ann. Dunstable*, 386–7.
[72] *CPR 1292–1301*, 165.

collected a tax of a fifteenth in Wales, raising £2,776, not including what was raised in the Marches.[73]

The major change in the government of Wales came in 1301, not as a result of Madog's rebellion, but because of the need to provide for the king's son Edward. In the sixteenth century the story was that Edward, after defeating Llywelyn and Dafydd, promised to give the Welsh a prince born in Wales, who could not speak a word of English. Accordingly, he presented to them in 1284 his son Edward, born at Caernarfon on 25 April 1284, a baby then incapable of any speech at all. It is an attractive tale, but there is little plausibility to it. In 1284 Alphonso, not Edward, was the king's heir, the *primogenitus*, and it is most unlikely that Wales would have been promised to a younger son at a time when no landed endowment had been provided for the elder. It is possible that Caernarfon was deliberately selected as the baby's birthplace, because of its legendary imperial past. It would certainly have been more sensible to leave Queen Eleanor in the relative comfort of Rhuddlan, than bring her to give birth in the building-site that was Caernarfon in 1284. Whatever the truth of the matter, there are no indications of any link between the young prince and Wales until 1301.[74]

At the Lincoln parliament of 1301, on 7 February, Edward I granted the royal lands in Wales, together with the earldom of Chester, to his son.[75] This was obviously reminiscent of the grant made to Edward himself forty-seven years before, although it was less generous. The act is surely better explained in terms of past tradition than in terms of any possible promise to the Welsh in 1284. It was consistent with the precedent of 1254, in that it did not give the heir to the throne any specific title: it was not until May 1301 that he began to be termed Prince of Wales. The young man was sent to Wales very promptly: he spent some five weeks there in April and May, receiving the homage of his Welsh tenants. He did not, however, visit his birthplace of Caernarfon, where the building works were virtually in abeyance and the castle in a sadly incomplete condition.[76]

The transfer of control from Edward I to his son in 1301 was not marked by any change of policy. The prince was not a man to challenge his father over important affairs of state, however much the two may have quarrelled over such matters as the prince's questionable relationship with Piers Gaveston. The young Edward never in fact visited Wales after 1301, though evidence suggests that he did intend to do so.

[73] *List of Welsh Entries in the Memoranda Rolls, 1282–1343*, ed. N.M. Fryde (Cardiff, 1974), xviii–xix.

[74] H. Johnstone, *Edward of Carnarvon*, 6–7; *KW*, i, 371.

[75] *CChR 1300–26*, 6.

[76] Johnstone, *Edward of Carnarvon*, 62; *KW*, i, 382.

The grants he made were solidly in line with Edward I's policies, and the responses to a great number of petitions from Wales presented to him at Kennington reveal that nothing new was to be done without consultation with the king.[77] The prince's attitude towards Wales is indicated by a frivolous letter he sent to Louis of Evreux in 1305:

> We send you a big trotting palfrey which can hardly carry its own weight, and some of our bandy-legged terriers from Wales, which can well catch a hare if they find it asleep, and some of our running dogs, which go at a gentle pace; for we well know that you take delight in lazy dogs. And, dear cousin, if you want anything from our land of Wales, we can send you plenty of wild men if you like, who will know well how to teach breeding to the young heirs or heiresses of great lords.[78]

Edward II was, in fact, to receive substantial support from Wales during the political problems of his reign, but this was a reflection not of any skill he exercised during his rule as prince, but of a growing preference by many Welshmen for royal rule, in place of the harsh exercise of authority by the lords of the March.

The conquest and settlement of Wales by Edward I were undoubtedly great achievements. He has received much praise. J.E. Morris considered that his real skill lay in the organization of his wars, the way in which English armies were steadily improved and their equipment brought up to date, with a new emphasis on archery. 'The conquest of Wales was effected by patience and resolution, which are not so interesting to record or read, but which are more serviceable in war than dashing bravery in the open battlefield.'[79] The fact that Edward's methods of warfare were successful means that there is a tendency to assume that they were indeed the most effective that could have been employed, but for H.G. Richardson, 'however good a tactician he may have been, he was a pitiable strategist. His capacity was on a level with that of Sir Redvers Buller.'[80] The policies adopted by Edward in Wales have been described by F.M. Powicke as 'wise and equitable', and 'in closer accord with previous tendencies in Welsh law and government than national feeling in Wales has usually realized'.[81] More recently R.R. Davies has pointed to Edward's failing in Wales: 'he had not the imagination to enter into other men's sensitivities; his pride in his own status and dignity as king of England was such that it blinded him

---

[77] Waters, *Edwardian Settlement of North Wales*, 31–44. The Kennington petitions are printed in *Record of Carnarvon*, 212–25.
[78] Johnstone, *Edward of Carnarvon*, 64.
[79] Morris, *Welsh Wars*, 105.
[80] H.G. Richardson, reviewing *KW*, i and ii, *EHR*, lxxx (1965), 555.
[81] Powicke, *Thirteenth Century*, 437.

entirely to the status and dignity of others.' He has also written of the 'extortionate and unimaginative rule of English officials'.[82] There is no simple answer.

To take first the question of Edward's military skill, it may be frivolous to look back to the Roman general Suetonius Paulinus as an early exponent of the strategy of marching along the coast of north Wales and then crossing to Anglesey, but it is certainly true that Edward's troops were tramping on a very well-worn route.[83] In 1157 Henry II had advanced his army from Chester along the coast, and organized a naval attack on Anglesey. Henry III adopted a similar strategy in 1245 and, as his son was to do, made use of supplies brought by sea from Ireland. Of course, Edward did not rely solely on the advance of royal armies from Chester: there were precedents for attacks on several fronts, such as Henry I's three-pronged assault on Gwynedd in 1114. Even the scale of recruitment of workmen which is such a striking feature of Edward's careful war preparations was not new. In 1212 King John had summoned no less than 8,000 labourers to assist in the task of forest clearance and fortification, which was an important part of his Welsh strategy.[84]

There was nothing wrong, of course, in taking a familiar strategy and adapting it to new circumstances. The use of other routes by the English had not been particularly successful. Henry II's 1165 expedition, which had mustered at Shrewsbury, then advanced to Oswestry and marched on to the upper stretches of the Dee, had been frustrated by geographical obstacles and bad weather. John had more success in 1211, when he drove through from Oswestry to the coast at Bangor, but under Henry III the campaigns of 1228 and 1231 showed that it was hard indeed to launch a major expedition into mid-Wales.[85] Edward's strategy was certainly a cautious one, but the wisdom of caution was shown only too clearly in 1282, when Luke de Tany and his men paid such a heavy price for their rashness. On two occasions Edward did display boldness; in 1283 with the march into Snowdonia, and in 1295 with the remarkable January raid as far as the Lleyn peninsula. On neither occasion was any signal triumph achieved, but this is not to Edward's discredit. He was probably well aware of the sensible teachings of the classical theorist Vegetius, whose advice was that every

---

[82] R.R. Davies, 'Llywelyn ap Gruffydd, Prince of Wales', *Journal of the Merioneth Historical and Record Society*, ix (1983), 270, 275.

[83] M.C. Prestwich, *The Three Edwards: war and state in England 1272–1377* (1980), 17.

[84] W.L. Warren, *Henry II* (1973), 161; Powicke, *Thirteenth Century*, 399; A.L. Poole, *From Domesday Book to Magna Carta 1087–1216* (Oxford, 1955), 287; S. Painter, *The Reign of King John* (Boston, 1949), 266.

[85] Warren, *Henry II*, 163–4; Poole, *From Domesday Book to Magna Carta*, 299; Powicke, *Thirteenth Century*, 395–7.

conceivable resort should be tried before incurring the inevitable risks involved in battle.[86] Further, the Welsh were themselves simply not prepared to challenge the king in open conflict, and this is one reason why it was Edward's commanders in mid-Wales, not he himself, who won victories in battle in 1282 and 1295.

Two of the most common elements of medieval warfare were largely lacking from Edward's campaigns in Wales. In 1173 the count of Flanders is said to have advised the Scots on their war against the English: they should ravage and waste the countryside, and then besiege the castles. Much medieval military strategy can be explained in these terms.[87] Edward's armies do not seem to have engaged in burning and plundering Welsh territory on a large scale. No doubt this was in part because there were not quite the same opportunities for ravaging as there would be in more prosperous and densely populated countries, but such techniques would have created great problems in the aftermath of conquest. It was possible for Edward to bring considerable economic pressure on the Welsh simply by blockading Snowdonia, harvesting rather than burning the grain crop in Anglesey, and capturing the enemy stores of victuals.[88] Some destruction certainly did take place, but it was not as systematic and extensive as might have been expected. As for sieges, Edward was not faced with the problem of strong castles held by the enemy. The war of 1287, with the siege of Dryslwyn, was exceptional, as for the most part the Welsh did not try to hold out within fortifications. In 1282 Prince Dafydd abandoned Hope, slighting the walls before the English arrived at the castle, and in general the Welsh castles were simply not strong enough to resist Edward's forces.

One aspect of Edward's military planning that seems of doubtful wisdom is that of recruitment. There was much attention paid to providing the heavy cavalry that were the backbone of English thirteenth-century armies. Horses of sufficient size, strength and stamina to carry heavily armoured knights were in short supply, and much was done to remedy this deficiency. Yet the type of warfare that was waged by the Welsh meant that it was never possible to make use of the heavy cavalry to their best advantage, in a massed charge such as had dominated the battlefields of Lewes and Evesham. The terrain was not suitable, nor were the Welsh prepared to face the English on such

[86] For Edward's copy of Vegetius, see above, 123.

[87] For a recent valuable discussion, see J.B. Gillingham, 'Richard I and the Science of War in the Middle Ages', *War and Government in the Middle Ages*, ed. J.B. Gillingham and J.C. Holt (Woodbridge, 1984), 78–91.

[88] See *Cal. Anc. Corr. Wales*, 172, for evidence of the capture of Welsh food stores in Edeyrnion in 1282–3.

terms. Equally, the value of the enormous contingents of infantry employed by Edward seems dubious. It was never possible to put them all into battle at one time, and to have over 30,000 men engaged in a campaign made for immense logistical problems. It is certainly true that the rising proportion of archers among the foot was a considerable advance, but the crown could have done much more to ensure that its troops were properly equipped. What was surely needed were relatively small forces of well-equipped men, capable of the same kind of swift movement that characterized their enemies. Lightly armed cavalry were almost completely lacking from the Edwardian armies in Wales, but such troops would surely have been ideal for Welsh conditions. It is striking that both in 1282 and 1295 it was the small armies that achieved the victories over the Welsh, rather than the large and unwieldy hosts that the king himself led into north Wales.

A most impressive aspect of Edward's military enterprises was the organization of supplies. The provision of victuals and transport was very competently organized, especially from 1282 onwards. A memorandum drawn up at Devizes in April 1282 shows how concerned the king's officials were with these matters. At the very start of the process of organizing the campaign, they were working out the numbers of workmen needed, promising to refund merchants for any losses incurred through coming to Chester, noting the quantities of grain needed from particular officials, and even including a note that salt meat should be obtained in Gascony.[89] It was only when the baggage train had been attacked by the Welsh, early in 1295, that major difficulties were faced by the English troops in Wales. How far Edward in person concerned himself with these questions of supplies is not very clear, but his return to Cheshire from Flint in the early stages of the 1277 campaign suggests that he was very well aware of the necessity of ensuring that his forces were properly supplied. The contrast between the efficiency of the logistics of war under Edward I, and the severe problems that had been faced in his father's reign by English armies in Wales strongly points to the importance of the king's own personal leadership.

The strategy of castle-building adopted by Edward has obvious clear logic. The Welsh heartland of Gwynedd was to be surrounded by strong fortresses, easily supplied by sea. In any future conflict, Snowdonia would be much easier to isolate than had been the case in 1277 or 1282. Yet for all the magnificence of Master James of St George's creations, the wisdom of the castle-building can be questioned. The new castles were capable of holding out in the face of the most up-to-date siege equipment, yet there is no evidence that either Llywelyn

---

[89] Taylor, 'Castle Building in Wales in the later thirteenth century', 112–13.

or Dafydd was capable of launching the kind of operation that had eventually compelled the garrison of Kenilworth to surrender at the end of the Barons' Wars, or which was to be successful at Stirling in 1304. There was no immediate need to build on the scale of Caernarfon or Beaumaris, and the English can hardly have expected the Welsh, once conquered, to develop military capabilities they had not had when independent. Master James of St George certainly appreciated the political importance of his work: in 1296 he wrote: 'But as you know, Welshmen are Welshmen, and you need to understand them properly.'[90]

The ever increasing ambitiousness of the castles is best explained not by military or political need, but by the determination of Master James to make each creation more splendid than the last, and to build everlasting symbols of his master's success. In practice, the value of the castles in future warfare proved mixed. In the war of 1294–5, while Flint, Rhuddlan and Conwy all had their value as bases for military operations, Harlech and Criccieth served no such purpose. The need to organize a difficult and costly revictualling programme for them from Ireland was a diversion of valuable resources, and it is doubtful whether the existence of the castles distracted many Welsh troops from more important objectives. Further, the very fact that there was such a major rebellion as that of 1294–5, shows that the castle-building programme had not cowed the Welsh into total submission. It is certainly far from clear that the expenditure of some £80,000 on the castles, in the course of the reign, was the best use that could have been made of such a large sum. In the longer term, Edward's failure to provide the new castles with their own financial resources, such as an allocation of land to the castles could have provided, meant that they were to fall rapidly into a sorry state of disrepair.

The conquest of Wales was a matter of politics as well as of warfare. Neither Edward, nor his greatest Welsh adversary, Llywelyn ap Gruffydd, displayed any sympathy for, or understanding of, each other's position. Llywelyn faced serious internal problems, and he may have felt that if he showed weakness towards the English king, his domestic enemies might find encouragement in his conduct. The essential dynamic of his rule was one of expansion. He clearly failed to appreciate the importance for Edward I of the question of homage: his initial failures to respond to Edward's requests that he appear before him did not result in any dire consequences. Edward, for his part, probably did not think that Llywelyn would resort to arms in the late 1270s, and failed to appreciate the importance for the Welsh prince of his various grievances over the implementation of the Treaty of

[90] *KW*, i, 399.

Montgomery of 1267. Edward must, however, have felt well satisfied
with the way matters went in 1277. It was after the first Welsh war
that he made political errors. To have driven two men who had been
such bitter rivals as Llywelyn and Dafydd into the same camp was
remarkably inept. The king's handling of the legal difficulties in Wales
that resulted from the peace treaty of 1277 was insensitive and unwise,
and it is remarkable that he and his officials failed to be aware of the
degree of resentment that was building up, and which caused rebellion
to break out in 1282. A similar insensitivity led to Rhys ap Maredudd's
rebellion in 1287, though here the king was less blameworthy than his
officials.

The rising of 1294–5 was not the result of the mishandling of individual Welsh magnates, in the same way as those of 1282 and 1287, and
was much less possible to foresee. The fact of that rebellion, however,
does suggest that the settlement of Wales in the aftermath of the war of
1282–3 was not quite so capable as has sometimes been suggested. The
statute of Wales of 1284 was certainly a skilled piece of work, which
testifies to the ability of the lawyers on Edward's council. The system of
government it set up in Gwynedd was in many ways a reasonable one,
for all that the officials that were placed in charge were just as overbear-
ing and intolerant as ever. Yet an opportunity was surely missed after
Llywelyn's death. Much more could have been done to provide redress
for the grievances that abounded against the late prince's rule. The
virtues and advantages of Edward's legal innovations were considerable, but were not stressed.

Although it is possible to criticize much that Edward did in Wales,
the fact remains that he was in the end thoroughly successful. Of course
his resources were immeasurably greater than those of the Welsh, but
the Welsh had succeeded in retaining a considerable degree of independence in the face of powerful English kings ever since the Norman
Conquest. Edward had now taken a major step towards the eventual
political unification of the British Isles, though in his later years he was
to find that he could not repeat in Scotland what he had achieved in
Wales.

Chapter 9

THE GOVERNMENT OF ENGLAND, 1278–86

The process of administrative change which had begun in 1274, when Edward I returned to England, was only briefly halted in 1277 by the first Welsh war. The years from 1278 until 1286, when Edward sailed for Gascony, did not witness dramatic political crises at home, and did not provide much for the chroniclers to write about. This was, however, a period of constructive and important achievement in finance, administration and law. Edward himself was forty in 1279, and these years saw him in his prime. He still had many of the associates of his youth around him, both magnates and officials, and was in a good position to put into effect all he had learned by hard experience.

The dominant figure, after Edward himself, in the government was the chancellor, Robert Burnell. He was almost constantly at the king's side, except when he was sent on an important mission to Gascony in 1278, or on such occasions as that in 1280, when the king went hunting in the New Forest and Burnell went to Westminster to see to the business of chancery.[1] The fact that the two men were so close means that there is little surviving correspondence to show what kind of advice Burnell was giving to Edward, but there is no doubting his influence. What does survive in profusion are letters and petitions addressed to Burnell, and these, though often routine in character, certainly indicate the extent of his power. Many requests concerned patronage of various sorts. Roger Lestrange, seeking a grant of Maelor Saesneg or other lands in Wales, approached Burnell and Anthony Bek, rather than putting his demand directly to the king.[2] The bishop of Exeter sought the chancellor's assistance when he was involved in a dispute with the chief justice of the king's bench, Ralph Hengham. William de Valence wrote in support of one of his retainers who was charged with rape, and whose accuser seemed to be prepared to bring the case in every county in succession. The letters suggest that Burnell was thoroughly approachable. One from the earl of Gloucester explained that when he had returned from London to Glamorgan, he had found that one of his

---

[1] Below, 304; *Ann. Waverley*, 393.
[2] *Cal. Anc. Corr. Wales*, 124.

children was ill, and that, as a result, he would be delayed in coming to the royal court. He did not want the reason for this delay to be made public, and asked the chancellor to make excuses for him. A wide range of administrative questions was put to Burnell. The escheator in Cornwall suggested that a survey of lands held directly from the king should be made in his county. The bishop of Worcester asked that the city of Worcester should be allowed to pay a lump sum as its contribution to a tax. The bishop of Norwich complained that by some error both he and Richard de Holbrook had been given similar commissions to keep the peace.[3]

Other sources give a less favourable picture of Robert Burnell. He was described as being affable, but slippery. His accumulation of many church benefices was a scandal, but not as much as was his sexual life. Although he was a bishop, he had a mistress called Juliana, who claimed that she had borne him five sons. Gossip also had it that he had many daughters, whom he married off into the nobility.[4] Burnell denied the accusations against him, but the rumours meant that advancement to the sees first of Winchester, and later of Canterbury, which Edward wanted to secure for him, was blocked. The king himself was apparently not concerned about questions of personal morality, provided that the business of government was conducted efficiently and energetically, and there could be no faulting of Burnell on that score.[5]

There was not the same stability at the exchequer as there was in the chancery. Joseph de Chauncy had been treasurer since 1273. He was prior of the Hospital of St John in England, and resigned his office in 1280, when he left for the Holy Land.[6] There are no indications that he was anything more than competent in office. His successor was Richard Ware, abbot of Westminster, not a man of any great significance. He was followed in 1284 by John Kirkby, a protégé of Burnell, and an important figure, who was almost certainly the driving force behind major improvements in the financial administration. The chronicler Bartholomew Cotton quoted some Latin lines about him, suggesting that he was greedy, bitter and quarrelsome, but the Dunstable annalist saw some good in him, arguing that, for all his contentiousness, he was invariably truthful and just. Like many of Edward's clerks, he was a pluralist, and it was because of this that Archbishop Pecham quashed his election to the see of Rochester in 1283, although no objections were

---

[3] SC 1/22, 156; SC 1/23, 97, 99; SC 1/24, 14, 64, 163, 199.

[4] *Reg. Peckham*, i, 46–7; *Ann. Dunstable*, 373.

[5] For a fuller discussion of Burnell, see Powicke, *Thirteenth Century*, 335–9, and U.W. Hughes, 'A Biographical Sketch of Robert Burnell, with materials for his life' (Oxford B.Litt thesis, 1936).

[6] Tout, *Chapters in Mediaeval Administrative History*, ii, 13, assumed that Chauncy resigned because of illness, but SC 1/12/118 shows that he went to the Holy Land.

raised to his becoming bishop of Ely three years later.[7] The other office of major importance in the administration was that of keeper of the wardrobe, which has already been discussed in Chapter 6. The post was held by Thomas Bek from 1274 until 1280, when the able and upright William of Louth took over.[8]

The business of government was not the concern simply of the king and his officials. The participation of the magnates, both formally and informally, was vital if an effective consensus was to be achieved. The mechanisms of council and parliament provided for this, and they are discussed later, in Chapter 17. Unfortunately, there is no good evidence from these years to show who was in regular receipt of summonses to parliament. However, the lists of those who witnessed royal charters show that the earls were very regular in their attendance on the king: it was only during Edward's journey round Wales in 1284 that his charters were not witnessed by a good number of earls. The most frequent witness was the earl of Lincoln, a man whose loyalty to Edward was consistent and striking, and after him came the earl of Gloucester. The names to appear rarely were those of Richmond and Oxford. The former was duke of Brittany, and rarely in England, while the latter was a nonentity, whose wealth was not equal to his comital status. The 1290s would not see such a consistent presence of earls round the king, and while this is not necessarily evidence that they were critical of his policies – those fighting in Gascony could hardly witness charters in England – it does suggest that there was not the same unity of purpose that had existed in the first half of the reign.[9]

The inquiry which had yielded the Hundred Rolls had provided a starting point for the reforms of the mid-1270s, and the pattern of detailed investigation at a local level was continued. Late in 1278 most of the sheriffs were replaced, an essential preliminary. In March 1279 a new, wide-ranging inquiry was set up, which produced what must have been the most comprehensive survey of England ever made in the middle ages. It has unfortunately never been given a convenient name for ready reference. Returns survive for only five counties. According to

---

[7] Cotton, 167; *Ann. Dunstable*, 358; *Reg. Peckham*, ii, 575–6.

[8] Above, 138–41. Convenient lists of officials are given by Tout, *Chapters in Mediaeval Administrative History*, vi.

[9] Between January 1278 and Edward's departure for France in May 1286 the earls appeared as witnesses of royal charters with the following frequency: Lincoln, 129; Gloucester, 114; Lancaster, 106; William de Valence, 76; Cornwall 76; Norfolk, 71; Warenne, 67; Hereford, 53; Warwick, 51; Oxford, 8; Richmond, 4. These figures are derived from the Charter Rolls, C 53. I am extremely grateful to Miss Elizabeth Davies for lending me her tabulation of the witness lists on these rolls, and my addition is reliant on the data she collected.

the Russian historian Kosminsky, who studied them in great detail, the inquiry was intended 'to provide the completest possible picture of the division of rent and the tangle of feudal relationships'.[10] That, however, is the purpose for which historians have used these rolls, and it was not necessarily that of Edward and his advisers. In the first place, the inquiry was set up to investigate a recent order that all those with lands worth at least £20 a year should become knights. The commissioners were also asked to investigate encroachments on demesne lands, knights' fees, feudal rights and liberties, which had resulted in losses both to the king and to others.[11] In contrast to the 1274–5 inquiry, there was now no investigation of official malpractices. Rather, the commissioners concentrated on the question of who held which land, and by what services. Remarkably full details were given about such matters as how much land was held in demesne by lords, how much by free tenants, and how much by villeins, as well as about rents and labour services.

It is not easy to discover what use was made of the returns to this inquest.[12] It had been intended that they should be put together in book form, but this was never done, probably because they were far too bulky. The sections dealing with the rights of jurisdiction exercised by magnates may have been of some value in the crown's legal investigations known as *Quo Warranto*, but there is no clear evidence for this. One possibility is that the returns were, in part, intended to provide a basis for future taxation. The evidence they contained would have made the introduction of an effective land tax possible. One chronicle records a demand made by the king in 1280, at a meeting in London, of four pence from every bovate, or oxgang. This the magnates rejected, and they then declined to attend a subsequent assembly at Oxford, so that nothing was achieved. The story is not confirmed by other sources, but such a request for a tax could have been related to the 1279 returns.[13] Some other uses were doubtless found for these massive rolls, but it must be suspected that they were in practice too vast to be of much value.[14]

The next major inquiry was to be of much more long-term use than that of 1279. In 1285 exchequer officials under the leadership of John Kirkby conducted what became known as Kirkby's Quest. There was a long list of questions put to local juries. Debts to the crown were one

---

[10] E.A. Kosminsky, *Studies in the Agrarian History of England in the Thirteenth Century* (Oxford, 1956), 14.

[11] *CPR 1272–83*, 342–3.

[12] Kosminsky, op. cit., 23, commented 'I am not clear what was the practical application of the 1279 survey.'

[13] BL Vesp. B.xi (the Hagnaby chronicle), f.27v.

[14] The surviving rolls are printed in *RH*, ii.

major concern, and there were further inquiries about dues and rents. The status of vills, whether they were in royal or private hands, was investigated, but the major task proved to be that of finding out what knights' fees were held in chief from the crown, and by whom. Jurisdictional liberties were also the subject of inquiry. There are few full returns that survive: the bulk of the evidence for Kirkby's Quest consists of later abridgements, which concentrated upon the question of knights' fees, though in 1285 that was only one element of a wide-ranging investigation. The context of this inquiry was that of recent reforms in exchequer procedure, but the officials chose to broaden its scope considerably.[15] What both Kirkby's Quest and the 1279 inquest show is that Edward's officials had a remarkable desire for information on a wide range of matters. Then, as in more recent times, full knowledge of the country was essential for good government. Not since Domesday Book had royal officials discovered so much about England as they did under Edward I.

Major steps had been taken in 1275 to provide financial stability. The customs duties had been instituted, a tax granted, and a new system of management for royal estates set up.[16] Yet, important as those measures were, there were still financial problems. The accounts for the first Welsh war suggest a total cost of only about £23,000, but the war of 1282–3 involved the crown in expenditure of some £120,000. The ordinary revenues of the crown were quite inadequate for such demands. According to an estimate made in 1284, the traditional sources of royal income, such as the farms of the counties, profits of justice, vacant bishoprics and so forth, brought in under £19,000 a year, with a further £8,000 coming from the customs duties.[17] This was scarcely sufficient for the normal peacetime needs of the crown; the wardrobe accounts show that the domestic household of the king cost some £8,000 a year in the early part of the reign, while in the period between the two Welsh wars, total wardrobe expenditure varied from £19,302 to £30,992 a year.[18] It was evidently necessary to raise fresh taxes, to borrow money, and to improve the administration of the main financial department of state, the exchequer.

War provided the crown with a good reason for asking for the grant of a tax, but the laity were not asked for a tax for the first Welsh war. It

[15] *Feudal Aids, 1284–1431* (1899), i, viii–xxii; *The Survey of the County of York taken by John de Kirkby*, ed. R.H. Skaife (Surtees Soc., xlix 1867), v–xi.

[16] Above, 99–103.

[17] Above, 182, 200; below, 242–3.

[18] The wardrobe accounts are conveniently tabulated by Tout, *Chapters in Mediaeval Administrative History*, vi, 78–9.

may be that it was felt that the fifteenth of 1275 had been conceded so recently that to ask for a new grant would not be politic. One chronicler does state that a twentieth was granted in 1277, but there is no confirmation from any other source for this, and it does not even seem very likely that the report reflects some abortive negotiations for a tax.[19] The clergy, however, had not made a grant in 1275, and in 1279 the Canterbury clergy were persuaded to pay a fifteenth for three years, and their York brethren agreed to a tenth for two years in 1280.[20] These taxes were paid on the assessment made for papal taxation in 1254, which was a low one, putting the total wealth of the church at only about £102,000. The yield of these taxes was therefore limited, but the wardrobe accounts show that between 1280 and 1284 a useful £13,225 was received from clerical taxation. Of this sum, £2,451 came from the northern province and was handed over to the royal paymaster at Chester.[21]

   The onset of war at Easter 1282 was so sudden that there was no time to summon a parliament which could make a conventional grant of taxation. Other means had to be adopted, and in June 1282 the king sent John Kirkby to negotiate financial assistance from local communities, particularly towns. Money was sought in the form of both loans and gifts, and in all £16,535 was raised, £4,000 of it from London. Not surprisingly, places near the Welsh border were more co-operative than those which were in no immediate danger from the enemy.[22] Much more money was needed than this, however, and in November it was decided to negotiate a tax on a more general basis. Two assemblies were summoned to meet in January, one at Northampton and one at York. These appear to have discussed both military service and taxation, and a grant of a thirtieth was made. The tax had, to some extent, the aspect of an alternative to active service in the field. The major magnates fighting in Wales were exempted from payment, and the sums already paid to Kirkby were set against the new tax. The tax was assessed at £42,765, but the sums paid to Kirkby should be added to that figure, since they were, in effect, advance payments of tax. A statement of wardrobe revenue put the income from the tax, together with the money received by Kirkby, at £55,358. Taxes upon moveable goods were obviously one of the most effective means of raising money

    [19] Rishanger, 92.
    [20] Below, 252–3; H.S. Deighton, 'Clerical Taxation by Consent, 1272–1301', *EHR*, lxviii(1953), 163.
    [21] E 372/128, 130; *CPR 1281–92*, 151–2. The figures given by Deighton, op. cit., 165, are not reliable.
    [22] E 372/136, m.31; *Lancashire Lay Subsidies, i, 1216–1307*, ed. J.A.C. Vincent (Record Society for Lancashire and Cheshire, 1893), 169.

available to the crown.[23] The grant from the laity was followed by a demand for further clerical taxation. Edward's demand in 1283 for a triennial twentieth was rejected by the Canterbury clergy, who promised in its place a twentieth for two years, while the northern clergy delayed their grant of a triennial thirtieth until 1286.[24]

There were some miscellaneous sources of revenue which helped to ease Edward's difficulties during this period. The vacancy in the bishopric of Winchester, which lasted from February 1280 until August 1282, provided the appreciable sum of £11,332.[25] The sale of the wardship of Baldwin Wake's heir to the earl of Cornwall in 1282, yielded a useful 7,000 marks, and in the next year John de Bohun paid 2,500 marks for the wardship of John le Marshal's heir.[26] In March 1283, Edward ordered the seizure of the proceeds of a crusading tenth which were stored in churches and monasteries, totalling about £40,000, but protests at this action had some effect, and the bulk of the money was returned in its original sacks, the seals untouched. £4,125 was kept by the crown, to be repaid out of the tax of the thirtieth.[27]

The various sources of income available to the crown were not sufficient to meet the needs created by the wars in Wales. It was necessary to borrow money, and the assistance of the Italian bankers proved to be vital. Edward's involvement with the Italians went back a long way. Their help had been essential during the crusading expedition, and the firm of the Riccardi, in particular, were owed substantial debts at the outset of the reign. If the bankers were to have any hope of obtaining repayment, then they had to retain the king's favour, and the best way to do that was to continue to advance money. In all, the crown's aggregate debt to the Riccardi by 1294 was to amount to some £392,000. Through their involvement in the wool trade, and their role in collecting royal customs duties and papal crusading taxes, they had substantial deposits from which they could make loans. The Riccardi also acted as agents for the king, borrowing money on his behalf from other Italian companies.

At the time of the first Welsh war the Riccardi paid £22,476 into the wardrobe, and in 1277–8 they advanced a further £18,233. Out of the proceeds of the fifteenth granted in 1275, 37,000 marks went to repay

[23] Above, 101–2; E 101/4/2. The tax assessments are tabulated in Prestwich, *War, Politics and Finance*, 179.

[24] *Councils and Synods, II, 1205–1313*, ed. F.M. Powicke and C.R. Cheney (Oxford, 1964), ii, 828–51.

[25] Howell, *Regalian Right in Medieval England*, 241.

[26] *CPR 1281–92*, 40, 65.

[27] Lunt, *Financial Relations of England with the Papacy*, 336–7, and see also the account for the thirtieth in E 359/4A.

the Riccardi, and there was an additional 17,250 marks repaid to other Italian firms, who had lent money to the crown using the Riccardi as intermediaries.[28] The Riccardi did not play quite such a dominant part in the financing of the second Welsh war, perhaps because the firm was rather hard-pressed at the time. The record of receipts in the special war account shows nothing paid over by them, but this gives a rather false impression, for it includes £22,916 from the customs, which were in their hands, and £37,432 from the tax of the thirtieth, almost £16,000 of which passed through their hands. By one estimate, the Riccardi were concerned in nearly two-fifths of the war account, and contributed much to the ordinary wardrobe account as well. Half of the cost of the force of Gascon mercenaries in the war was met by the Riccardi. It was necessary to look to other companies as well, and some £20,000 was raised by means of forced loans from other Italian companies operating in England. Such was the pressure that the king put on the merchant community that by the end of the war period, in 1284, the Riccardi could not raise £1,000 requested by the treasurer immediately, but wrote to him to say that they would have to ask their partners overseas to send them money.[29]

The services of the Riccardi were not confined to the emergencies of wartime. In the period following the first Welsh war, the wardrobe account book shows that most of the department's income came in the form of advances from the merchants. Although this was not the case by the 1280s, the Italians continued to provide valuable services, such as making funds available to English ambassadors to the papal curia, and arranging other transfers of funds. The normal disadvantage of relying on bankers to the extent that Edward I obviously did is that interest payments are needed to service the loans. Yet, although historians have usually assumed that the Riccardi received rewards in the form of interest payments, the evidence for this is very inadequate.

Payment of interest was forbidden under canon law, and this Edward accepted, as his father had done. The terms of the Statute of Jewry of 1275 are testimony to his determination to stamp out usury.[30] There were means of evading the prohibition on usury, however, such as the technique of manipulating exchange rates, lending one currency and paying back in another, but the crown's accounts with Riccardi do not suggest that this was being done. There is only one recorded grant to the company to make up losses incurred as a result of their loans: this was of 5,000 marks, 'for their services in the court of Rome', but there

---

[28] Kaeuper, *Bankers to the Crown*, 178, 202; E 372/123, account of the fifteenth; E 372/124, wardrobe account.

[29] Kaeuper, *Bankers to the Crown*, 182–90; E 159/163, m.14.

[30] *Statutes of the Realm*, i, 220–1.

may well have been other similar payments for which no evidence survives. On two occasions, in 1276 and 1293, Edward made promises of repayment in an impossibly short period of time, and this may have been a device to make the imposition of an additional charge for 'damages' legitimate in the eyes of the church. The evidence as a whole, however, indicates that the Riccardi received little by way of financial reward for their services from the king. Their loans were not expensive for Edward.[31]

Why, if they did not profit from it, did the Italians lend to Edward? In part it must have been to protect their original investment: if they were to receive repayment in time, they needed to keep the king sweet with continuing loans. There were also very significant indirect benefits that came their way. As early as 1274 the exchequer officials were ordered to treat debts owing to Luke of Lucca, head of the Riccardi, just as if they were crown debts, and throughout their association with the crown the merchants were able to use the machinery of the exchequer to collect money due to them from other debtors. They received exemptions from local tolls and duties, and their offences against currency and trading regulations were generally overlooked or pardoned. Orlandino da Pogio, one of the most important members of the Riccardi partnership, was among the few men named in the household ordinance of 1279 as having the right to sleep in the king's wardrobe. He had the ear of government officials, and as an acute businessman must have been able to put his position to financial advantage. Yet the Riccardi did not receive many open favours from Edward. There were no grants of English estates to them, no ecclesiastical livings on a grand scale for their dependants, and it cannot be shown that they exercised any political influence over the king or his ministers.[32] The debt that the king owed them generally stood in the region of £25,000, not an impossibly large sum.[33] Reliance on the bankers in the first half of Edward's reign did not therefore mean that the king was running his finances in an improvident manner, accumulating large debts which could not be repaid.

In the aftermath of the second Welsh war, major efforts were made to overhaul the financial administration, and the exchequer in particular. It is very likely that the appointment of the energetic John Kirkby as treasurer was responsible for the fresh approach that was adopted. The

[31] CPR 1281–92, 394; Riccardi account in E 372/143; Kaeuper, Bankers to the Crown, 120.

[32] E 159/49, m.3v; Kaeuper, Bankers to the Crown, 121–4; Tout, Chapters in Mediaeval Administrative History, ii, 163.

[33] CPR 1272–81, 355, and E 101/126/1 show a debt in December 1279 of £23,000, almost the same sum as was owing in 1290, as shown by the customs account for 17–18 Edward I in E 372/134.

book-keeping methods of the exchequer were reformed, the sources of
royal income were analysed, and a campaign was launched to try to
recover unpaid debts, a campaign which involved yet another nationwide inquiry. The first step was the issue of a statute at Rhuddlan in
March 1284. One aim of this was to clear the large number of old and
largely unrecoverable debts from the main exchequer records, the pipe
rolls. Attempts had been made to deal with this problem in the past,
most recently in 1270. It had then been laid down that such old debts
were to be marked with a 'd', and not copied in the accounts for
subsequent years. They would only be entered later if they were
cleared. In practice, however, many old debts were left on the pipe
rolls, particularly if they concerned large sums or important men.[34]
Now, in 1284, it was decided that unrecoverable debts should be placed
in a separate roll. Further, the first part of the county entries, which
gave the details of the county farm and did not change from year to
year, was also to be removed from the pipe into another roll. This
system was maintained until 1298, when it was decided that the county
farms should once more be entered on the pipe, where they remained
until 1311. The statute of 1284 set out arrangements for men who had
paid off debts, and who had tally receipts as evidence of this, which for
some reason had not been accepted in the past by the exchequer, to
hand the tallies over to the sheriffs so that the debt could be duly
cancelled. This met the complaints that had been made in 1274–5
about the way in which the crown often attempted to collect the same
sum over and over again. In order to speed up the operation of the
exchequer, the hearing of pleas there was limited to matters specifically
concerning the king and his officials. Commissioners were to be sent
round the country to inquire into the whole matter of debts owed to the
crown.[35]

After the statute of Rhuddlan was issued, the exchequer officials
made a calculation of crown revenues. Their estimate made depressing
reading. The county farms, due every Michaelmas from the sheriffs,
were valued at only £10,168 a year, and the only other major source of
income was the customs, assessed at £8,000 a year. Profits from the
central courts, and the justices in eyre, were put at £1,100. Vacant
abbeys and priories were expected to yield £666, and wardships only
£333. The value of the chancery was given as £666 a year. Payment of
debts in instalments was expected to raise an annual £1,414. There
were many other miscellaneous sources of income, but the total
amounted to no more than £26,828 3s 9d. A memorandum for

[34] C.A.F. Meekings, *Studies in Thirteenth-Century Justice and Administration* (1982),
chapter XX.
[35] *Statutes of the Realm*, i, 69–70.

discussion shows that the main priority was to put the provisions of the statute of Rhuddlan into effect. Procedures were outlined to speed the collection of judicial fines: the justices were to list and assess such fines, and send lists of them to the chancellor before Michaelmas. As an inducement, they would not receive their own fees until this was done.[36]

The next step in the process of reform was the inquiry into crown debts at a local level, which formed one element of Kirkby's Quest.[37] It proved to be a difficult matter to collect these debts, and the new drive by the exchequer soon aroused protests. As a result, a royal writ was sent to the exchequer in July 1285, pointing out that many men simply could not afford to pay without severe hardship, and officials were ordered to try to recover debts in future by setting reasonable terms for payment in instalments.[38] There are many examples of this being done. John de Vaux owed the crown £213 8s 8d. He was pardoned £80 of this (due from the time when he had been sheriff of Norfolk and Suffolk), and the remainder was to be paid off at the rate of £20 a year.[39] The abbot of Abingdon had been fined £133 for various offences, and instalments of £20 a year were arranged. Roger Bigod, earl of Norfolk, was much encumbered by debt throughout his career. At this stage, he owed the crown £1,052, and he was allowed to pay in annual instalments of £100.[40]

The number of such instructions issued in 1284 and 1285 shows that the exchequer officials were pursuing the question of crown debts with assiduity, but it is also clear that this campaign barely altered the crown's financial position. Little was done to recover the large sums that were owed by some magnates. When the barons of the exchequer were ordered to raise 400 marks from the earl of Gloucester, he protested that he was due more from the king than he owed him, and the matter was accordingly postponed. Various sums were later set against the earl's debts. The demand for payment of debts made in the case of the earl of Cornwall was put off, for he claimed that he was quit of the bulk of them.[41] In the case of the great men, at least, political considerations proved more important than financial need.

An examination of the receipts at the exchequer does suggest that the overhaul of the administrative machinery did, however, achieve results in terms of revenue. One index of the efficiency and activity of the

[36] M. Mills, 'Exchequer Agenda and Estimate of Revenue, Easter Term 1284', *EHR*, xl (1925), 229–34.
[37] See above, 236–7.
[38] E 159/58, m.11v.
[39] E 159/58, m.58.
[40] *CFR 1272–1307*, 214, 217; E 159/58, m.11.
[41] E 159/57, m.70; E 159/58, m.5v; E 159, m.16v.

financial bureaucracy is that of the sums of money paid by the sheriffs, when they made their annual appearance at the exchequer. The figures for the earliest part of the reign are very low, but they rose in 1275, fell back, and by 1285 had again risen sharply, as the following table shows.

Sheriffs' Payments to the Exchequer[42]

1273	£2,419	1278	£3,449	1283	£4,360
1274	£3,223	1279	£3,463	1284	£4,780
1275	£4,529	1280	£4,717	1285	£7,435
1276	£3,405	1281	£4,643	1286	£6,846
1277	£2,567	1282	£5,016	1287	£8,210

These figures, it must be stressed, in no way represent total royal income. Much money collected by the sheriffs was disbursed locally: much money was brought to the exchequer by other officials. Yet the change that took place in 1285 is striking, and surely shows the effects of the new attitude created by the reforms of that year.

Another way in which the financial system of the 1280s contrasted with that of the 1270s was the degree to which the wardrobe, the main financial department of the household, became dependent for its income on the exchequer. When Bek was keeper of the wardrobe, the most that came in from the exchequer was £6,861 in 1279–80. The bulk of wardrobe income was derived at that time from loans made by Italian bankers. When William of Louth succeeded Bek, the pattern changed, and save for the exceptional period of the second Welsh war, exchequer allocations to the wardrobe usually ran at about £20,000 a year. The independent receipts of the wardrobe were still substantial, representing over half the total income of the department, but there was a greater integration of the household financial system with the household than had been the case earlier.[43]

Another financial necessity was the reform of the currency. There had been no full recoinage since 1247, and inevitably much of the money in circulation had deteriorated through wear and tear, as well as through clipping. Gresham's law operated: the bad coins drove out the good. Thomas Wykes, no doubt exaggerating, claimed that the coinage weighed only half what it should, and that foreign merchants were not coming to England as much as in the past because of the poor state of the currency. Prices had risen, he argued, as a result. There is some evidence to support this: the trend of both livestock and grain prices in the 1270s was steadily upwards, and in certain cases very marked rises

[42] M. Mills, '"Adventus Vicecomitum", 1272–1307', EHR, xxxviii (1923), 340.
[43] Tout, Chapters in Mediaeval Administrative History, ii, 88–9; vi, 76–9.

were taking place at the end of the decade.[44] The escheator in Cornwall complained that the coinage was in such a poor state that collection of taxes 'is not only difficult, but almost impossible'.[45]

The first decision was taken at a council meeting at Windsor in October 1278. All Jews and goldsmiths were to be arrested, for they were the prime suspects as coin-clippers. This was done, in so far as it was possible to carry out such a drastic measure, on two separate days in November. Next, in January 1279, commissions were set up to hear the charges against coin dealers and clippers, and the officials of the exchanges and mints.[46] The chroniclers are agreed that a bloodbath followed, two suggesting that in London alone the death toll among the Jews was 293. Record evidence, however, suggests that only nineteen Jews were executed in south-eastern England. One of the king's moneyers, Philip de Cambio, was found guilty of issuing coin with more copper in the alloy than was permitted, and he, along with one of the assayers of the mint, was hanged. It is not clear whether this drive against coin-clippers was intended as a preparatory step for the introduction of a new coinage, but it is most probable that the evidence produced by the inquiries made the government aware that the only effective remedy for the situation was to order a total recoinage. It was conceivably hoped that the action against the Jews and goldsmiths would bring in enough bullion to provide the mints with sufficient silver to start the work of recoinage, but in fact the operation yielded only £10,815, some of which went on expenses.[47]

By January 1279, the king had decided on a recoinage. It may be that he was influenced by the example of the count of Savoy, for not long before Edward's visit to Savoy, on his return from crusade, Count Philip had reformed his coinage, producing new coins of heavy weight and high quality.[48] Edward appointed Gregory de Rokesle, a Londoner, and Orlandino da Pogio, one of the Riccardi banking house, as wardens of the exchanges at London and Canterbury. In March two moneyers from Marseilles, William de Turnemire and his brother Peter, were recruited.[49] Loans from Italian merchants totalling £20,300

---

[44] Wykes, 278; M. Mate, 'Monetary Policies in England, 1272–1307', *British Numismatic Journal*, xli (1972), 41; D.L. Farmer, 'Some Livestock Price Movements in Thirteenth-Century England', *Economic History Review*, 2nd ser., xxii (1969), 3, 5, 7–8, 13.

[45] SC 1/24, 199.

[46] *CPR 1272–81*, 338.

[47] Mate, 'Monetary Policies in England', 42–3; *The French Chronicle of London*, ed. G.J. Aungier (Camden Soc., 1844), 16; *Ann. London*, 88.

[48] Cox, *Eagles of Savoy*, 398.

[49] Mate, 'Monetary Policies in England', 44; in addition, Hubert Alion of Asti was hired, but he does not seem ever to have taken up office as a royal moneyer.

were the main source of bullion in the initial stages of producing the
new currency: once the mints were well in operation, men would bring
in old coins to be exchanged for new, and there would be a steady
supply of bullion. Large numbers of workmen were recruited from
abroad: some did not find conditions to their liking, and tried to leave,
either back to the continent, or to Scotland. Much work had to be done
to make new dies, refurbish buildings, and buy necessary equipment.
The main mints were those at London and Canterbury, while there
were also the bishop's mint at Durham and the abbot's at Bury St
Edmunds. This was not sufficient, and in 1280 five provincial mints
were opened, at Bristol, Lincoln, York, Newcastle upon Tyne and
Chester. In the same year the recoinage was started in Ireland.[50]

The new coinage was issued at a slightly lower standard than the old
had been originally, although as so much of the coin in circulation was
worn and clipped, the new money was in practice considerably
superior. The number of pennies (the only coins hitherto current) struck
from each pound of silver was 243 rather than the original 240, and for a
period in 1280 this went up to 245. The proportion of copper in the alloy
was slightly raised. The most obvious change was the introduction of
new coins alongside the traditional pennies. There were groats, each
worth 4d, which did not prove to be very successful, and round half-
pennies and farthings, which obviated the need to cut pennies to make
small change. A stylized bust of the king was featured on the obverse,
while on the reverse there was a cross extending to the edge of the
design, as in the previous 'long-cross' coinage. A new method of manufacture was introduced by William Turnemire. The blank coins were
cut from a silver rod, rather than being stamped out from a sheet, and
this method appears to have been highly efficient.[51]

The scale of the recoinage was most impressive. The absence of
accounts for the provincial mints makes it impossible to give any
precise figure for the output of coin, but by 1281, at a conservative
estimate, £500,000 worth had been minted. The bulk of the old 'long-
cross' coins that had been in circulation had by then been reminted, but
the mints continued to be very active for the rest of the decade. A
considerable, though varying, proportion of the silver acquired by the
mints came from abroad, particularly from the Low Countries, and all
the indications are that the country's stock of silver was rising fast in the
1280s. English mints offered a better price for silver than those in
France or in the Low Countries, and it seems likely that, despite a royal
prohibition in 1283, some of the new good-quality sterling coinage was

[50] Mate, 'Monetary Policies in England', 47, 49–51. The enrolled accounts for the
recoinage are to be found in E 372/132.
[51] Mate, 'Monetary Policies in England', 49–51.

exported to the continent. An estimate of the late 1280s put the level of English coin circulating in France at £50,000. This means that it is not possible to calculate the total size of the currency in England simply by adding up the figures for the mint output. What is clear is that Edward's recoinage was a resounding success.[52]

Edward I, there can be little doubt, reformed the coinage because by 1279 it was in a bad state. He may have been influenced by a natural desire to mark his rule of England by producing a new coinage with his head on it, but it is also the case that there were substantial material gains for the crown from a recoinage. The king was entitled to take a deduction from each pound of silver minted, partly to cover the expenses of reminting, but also as seignorage, a traditional due. In 1279 the deductions totalled 19d, of which seignorage came to 9d, but in 1280 this went up to 12d, falling again in 1281. It is not easy to calculate the profits made by the crown from the recoinage, but by the end of 1281 the London mint alone had yielded £18,219. In all, profits in this period probably stood at a substantial £25,000. The accounts of the wardrobe alone show receipts from the mints of £9,424 in 1279–80, and of £10,620 in 1281–3. Mint profits were also paid out for a variety of miscellaneous purposes: a repayment of a loan from Florentine merchants to the king when he was at Amiens, works on the Tower of London, and even a small sum to the friars at Oxford.[53] The mints were, during the period of the recoinage, a valuable addition to the range of royal financial resources, and it would not be safe to dismiss profit as one of the motives for the change in the currency ordered by the king.

In most cases, when medieval rulers instituted a recoinage, men were induced to exchange their old money for the new because, through debasement, the new coins were offered at an apparently attractive price. Edward I, however, did not need to persuade his subjects to bring their old money to his mints. He had, in August 1280, simply demonetized the previous 'long-cross' coinage, forbidding its use. The recoinage does not seem to have been unpopular: the new coins were not very different from the old, and the price that the mint gave for silver was an attractive one. Further, and significantly, there were no adverse economic consequences that resulted from the introduction of the new coinage.

[52] Ibid., 53, 56, and see 75, 78, for tables of mint purchases of silver; M.C. Prestwich, 'Edward I's Monetary Policies and their Consequences', *Economic History Review*, 2nd ser., xxii (1969), 407–8.

[53] Profits are discussed by Mate, 'Monetary Policies in England', 50–1, 54, with tables at 76, 79. The wardrobe accounts are in E 372/124, 128. The figures in my 'Edward I's Monetary Policies and their Consequences', where they are derived from Sir James Ramsay's work, are not reliable.

The effects of the change in the currency are hard to assess. The one indication that can be used is that of price changes: if the coinage was in bad condition, prices would be high, whereas a sound coinage implies low prices. Yet if the reforms were highly successful, and the mints turned out a great deal of new coin, the quantity of it in circulation would tend to drive prices up. The major difficulty in making deductions from price movements is, of course, that the main determinants of prices were those of supply and demand, not the volume of the currency. The quality of harvests was of prime importance. The very considerable fluctuations that took place in the prices of grain and animals in the 1270s and 1280s make it hard to discern the effect of the monetary reforms, to such an extent that one historian has been led 'to conclude that Edward achieved very little with his recoinage because wheat prices rose far more in those years of reform than they should have done'.[54] Yet a comparison of two seven-year periods does suggest that the recoinage had a clear effect. The average price of wheat from 1268–75 was 6.70 shillings per quarter, and the average yield from one bushel sown was 3.6 bushels. The yield was exactly the same in the period 1283–90, yet the average price was markedly lower, at 5.14 shillings.[55] The evidence of livestock prices, not as subject to sudden fluctuations as those of grain, also strongly suggests that the effect of the new coinage was to bring down prices. Oxen fell in price from about 14 shillings each in 1278, to less than 10 shillings by 1282.[56] Edward had intended to provide the country with a sound and stable currency, and in that aim he was, by medieval standards, very successful.

The financial reforms of the late 1270s and the 1280s were not characterized by startling, radical initiatives. Indeed, one of the innovations of 1275, the appointment of the three stewards to supervise royal estates, was abandoned in 1282, in favour of the old methods.[57] The major inquiries of 1279 and 1285 did not yield dramatic results, and led to no fundamental reforms. The changes that took place in exchequer procedures were mostly technical in character, and the innovations in record-keeping did not result in any reduction in the ever-increasing size and complexity of the pipe rolls. Much was done, however, to improve and simplify procedures, and it is striking that efforts were made to provide for every eventuality. One ordinance, early in 1286, laid out in detail the procedure to be followed should someone lose the tallies given to him as receipts, before he came before

[54] A.R. Bridbury, 'Thirteenth Century Prices and the Money Supply', *Agricultural History Review*, xxxiii (1985), 17.

[55] Prestwich, 'Edward I's Monetary Policies and their Consequences', 415.

[56] D.L. Farmer, 'Some Livestock Price Movements in Thirteenth-Century England', 12.

[57] Above, 102–3.

the barons of the exchequer in the final accounting process.[58] The campaign to collect crown debts was not as effective as the officials had doubtless hoped, but the rise in receipts from the sheriffs shows that the general tightening up of procedures was effective. The recoinage was in the tradition of the past: it proved to be the last full reminting of the currency to take place in England.[59] That it was not possible ever again to conduct a total recoinage is testimony to the scale of Edward's achievement. What Edward and his officials could not do was provide complete financial stability. There was no way in which the crown's revenues could be raised sufficiently to meet the needs of such emergencies as the Welsh wars without obtaining grants of taxation, and borrowing from Italian bankers.

The first half of Edward I's reign did not see any major political crisis in which the king's authority was challenged in the way it would be later, notably in 1297. The demands made by the government on the people were not excessive. Measures were taken to curb abuses by officials. The king's ambitions in Wales met with no opposition at home. Yet affairs did not go smoothly throughout, and in particular there was a succession of arguments between church and state. There was little danger of a complete breakdown of relations, but in the archbishop of Canterbury, John Pecham, Edward found a formidable opponent.

In 1278 the see of Canterbury unexpectedly became vacant, when Robert Kilwardby was nominated by the pope to become cardinal bishop of Porto, near Rome. Nominally a promotion, this was in reality nothing of the kind. Nicholas III was probably angry at the way in which Kilwardby had encouraged resistance to the collection of a papal tenth, and at the limited progress that had been made in England towards carrying out the reforms of the Council of Lyons of 1274. Edward naturally wished to see his friend Robert Burnell succeed Kilwardby, but although the Canterbury monks did not object, such an appointment was hardly in line with papal policy. An eloquent plea by Edward's Bolognese lawyer Francesco Accursi to the pope was in vain, and a further embassy achieved nothing. Early in 1279 Nicholas III nominated the distinguished scholar John Pecham as archbishop of Canterbury: conveniently for him, he was present in the Curia at the time that the matter was under discussion.[60]

Pecham's first encounter with Edward was on his journey to England,

---

[58] E 159/59, m.22v.

[59] Even when the currency was decimalized in the 1970s, some old coins, 2s and 6d pieces, remained in circulation, though with a new nominal face value.

[60] Douie, *Archbishop Pecham*, 47–8; Powicke, *Thirteenth Century*, 469–71; G.L. Haskins and E. Kantorowicz, 'A Diplomatic Mission of Francis Accursius and his Oration before Pope Nicholas III', *EHR*, lviii (1943), 424–47.

when the two men met at Amiens. All went well: the new archbishop
gave Edward his full support in the negotiations with Philip III, and in
return he was at once granted the temporalities of his see, and made a
royal councillor.[61] Once arrived in England, Pecham summoned a
church council to meet at Reading on 29 July: he had a sense of urgency
about the need for reform. At the council, past ecclesiastical legislation
was renewed, and new measures, especially concerning pluralism and
non-residence by ecclesiastics, were agreed. Pecham claimed that the
pope had personally commanded him to rid England of the evil of
pluralism, though on non-residence he was prepared to compromise, so
that clerks might be allowed to leave their livings in order to study.
Pecham then turned to Magna Carta. This was read out in the council,
and sentences of excommunication were issued against anyone who
dared to interfere with the liberties of the church, or do anything
against the terms of the great charter.[62]

The interests of the crown were affected in various ways by the
decisions taken at Reading. The campaign against pluralism was
bound to affect the king's clerks, for a standard means of rewarding
them for their services was to grant them church livings. Few were quite
as notorious as Henry de Bray, escheator south of the Trent and justice
of the Jews. He was not even in priestly orders, but between 1275 and
1277 he had been presented to four churches in south Wales. He
attended an ordination service conducted by Pecham, provocatively
dressed in secular clothes.[63] Others were less blatant, but even more
successful, in accumulating livings. A list of pluralists drawn up in 1280
credited Adam Stratton with twenty-three benefices, and Geoffrey of
Aspale with fifteen. It also included Bogo de Clare, brother of the earl of
Gloucester, not himself a royal clerk, but a man of great importance,
and holder of at least thirteen churches.[64] Such men bitterly resented
the plan to curb pluralism. One royal clerk argued that it was beneficed
clerks who effectively ruled the country, and he suggested that they
might respond to extreme measures by seceding from papal authority,
with disastrous results. He pointed to the sufferings of royal clerks
earlier at the hands of the Montfortian rebels, and to the burden of
paying crusading taxes. The measures against pluralism would be like
death following upon wounds.[65]

One of the Reading proposals was directed against the crown's use of
writs of prohibition. These were used to remove cases from ecclesiastical

---

[61] Douie, *Archbishop Pecham*, 51.
[62] *Councils and Synods*, II, ii, 828–51.
[63] Douie, *Archbishop Pecham*, 105; *CPR 1272–81*, 75, 160, 166, 234.
[64] Altschul, *A Baronial Family*, 178.
[65] *Councils and Synods*, II, ii. 853–4.

jurisdiction, and Pecham went much further than his predecessors in attacking their use. Edward was bound to resent such an attack on his jurisdiction, and to judge by a rather garbled account of the proceedings, sent emissaries to the council of Reading to oppose Pecham's plans. As a result, the offending clause was removed. In more general terms, the king was angry at the implications behind Pecham's ostentatious appeal to Magna Carta, which were that royal officials were acting in contravention of its terms. The archbishop's action on 24 October, when in the hall of his palace at Lambeth he solemnly excommunicated the 'Sons of Belial' allegedly plotting against him, with a pointed exclusion of the royal family and the bishops, made matters even worse.[66]

In parliament at Westminster in November 1279 Archbishop Pecham was forced to retreat. He was made to withdraw his sentences of excommunication on those seeking writs of prohibition. He conceded that there were adequate penalties in the royal courts for dealing with those who seized church lands, and he agreed not to excommunicate royal officials who had, for example, released excommunicates from prison. Copies of Magna Carta that had been posted in church entrances were to be removed. The king and his successors were not to be prejudiced in any way by the legislation of the council of Reading. The king even stepped into the long-running dispute between the archbishops of Canterbury and York, and stated that Pecham was not to hinder his fellow metropolitan by forbidding people to sell food to him when he was in the province of Canterbury.[67]

It is usually argued that Pecham's surrender on so many issues resulted from the king's enactment of the statute of Mortmain in this same parliament. This statute forbad the grant of land to the church, and looks very like a measure intended to bring the archbishop to heel. As so often with legislative matters, the situation was not so simple. Demands for measures against such grants were nothing new, and the question had been dealt with in the Provisions of Westminster of 1259. The clause had not been re-enacted in the statute of Marlborough in 1267, but the courts still treated it as valid, as cases in 1277 and 1279 show. In one of these the master of the Templars argued that there was no royal legislation dealing with the question, and he asked for a postponement until the king's will was known. It looks very much as if the statute of 1279 was, at least in part, drafted in response to this request. It seems that Pecham's submission was made before the statute of Mortmain was published, and it is odd that it should have

---

[66] Douie, *Archbishop Pecham*, 113–18; *Wykes*, 285–6; *Councils and Synods*, II, ii, 829–31, 845–8.

[67] *Councils and Synods*, II, ii, 856–7.

been thought necessary to put into effect threats made with the intention of forcing him to come to terms with the king, after he had done so. Even so, while there were good legal reasons for issuing the statute in parliament in the autumn of 1279, it is unlikely that Edward would have done so had his relations with Pecham not been at a low ebb.[68]

If the statute of Mortmain was not the instrument used to compel Pecham to retract, why then did he do so? Pressure from the king's clerks, threats of appeals to Rome against him, and perhaps even requests from the papal curia to take a more moderate line may all have been important. Pecham's own financial position may have played its part as well. He had borrowed 4,000 marks from the Riccardi to cover the costs of his journey to England and of his inauguration. The banking firm had the ears of both pope and king, and soon after his arrival in England Pecham was himself under threat of excommunication if he did not repay the loan. His problems increased with a further loan of 2,000 marks, but he was rescued by the king in December 1279 with an advance of £1,000. A man in such a state of indebtedness was not in a good position to conduct an effective campaign against the power of the crown.[69]

If Pecham was in a weak financial position, so too was the king. The archbishop was soon able to use Edward's need for a grant of taxation to obtain concessions in exchange. The king had been anxious for a grant from the clergy for some time: his request for one in 1275 had been turned down on the grounds that a tenth was being paid to the papacy. Letters to the bishops in November 1279 asked for a subsidy, which was obviously intended to be the clerical counterpart to the lay tax conceded in 1275. The York clergy obliged early in 1280, with a grant of a tenth for two years, but from the fact that it was not until later that the diocese of Carlisle and the archdeaconry of Richmond made their grants it seems likely that there was some argument.[70] Pecham summoned his clergy to a council in January, which proved inconclusive. Further meetings were held at London in May, and Lincoln in October, and consent was finally given to a grant of a fifteenth for three years. At the same time a massive list of clerical grievances was drawn up, which was presented in parliament in November 1280. Although the grant of taxation was not made conditional upon the redress of these

---

[68] *Statutes of the Realm*, i, 51; P.A. Brand, 'The Control of Mortmain Legislation in England, 1200–1300', *Legal Records and the Historian*, ed. J.H. Baker (1980), 29–40.

[69] Douie, *Archbishop Pecham*, 49, 65–7; Kaeuper, *Bankers to the Crown*, 25–6.

[70] *Reg. Peckham*, i, 78–80; *Councils and Synods*, II, ii, 868–70; H.S. Deighton, 'Clerical Taxation by Consent, 1279–1301', *EHR*, lxviii (1953), 163. Douie, *Archbishop Pecham*, 121, and Powicke, *Thirteenth Century*, 478, are wrong in thinking that a lay tax was also granted.

grievances, there was no doubt an expectation that the king would give the clergy a sympathetic hearing.[71]

The list of complaints was long, and for the most part technical. Most of them covered familiar ground, though there was naturally a new demand for the repeal of the recent statute of Mortmain. There was a lengthy discussion, with answers given by the king to the grievances. Edward made it clear that these were only preliminary, and would not put them in writing. Pecham, however, had them recorded, and they were to be important in the future, providing precedents for the division between lay and ecclesiastical jurisdiction. Edward was certainly not wholly unsympathetic towards the clergy. One complaint was that the sheriffs were negligent in arresting excommunicates, and in reply Edward told a story of how he had ordered a sheriff to bring eighteen named individuals before him. The right number of men were produced, but only two of those actually requested were among them. The prelates, suggested the king, should not be surprised at the misdeeds of sheriffs, but he promised to do all he could to punish them. Edward was fully prepared to negotiate, and was willing to make changes, where there were obvious abuses. On the important issue of writs of prohibition, it was suggested that doubtful writs should be examined by a committee of suitable royal clerks. Fines or imprisonment were to be imposed where writs were sought for incorrect purposes, and the prelates could bring wrongful writs before the king and council in parliament for correction. What Edward was not prepared to do, was to enter into any fundamental reassessment of the relationship between church and state, and he would not accept any infringement of what he regarded as his royal rights.[72]

It was clear that Pecham's climb-down in 1279 had not marked the end of the arguments between church and state. He was issuing excommunications at a most remarkable rate, and the sentences he issued against the king's bailiffs of Southwark in May 1280 showed that he had not, in reality, retreated far from the position he had adopted at the council of Reading.[73] In 1281 another council, this time at Lambeth, was held, to continue the work of reform. Royal orders forbad the clergy from doing anything adversely affecting royal rights, but one clause of the canons of the council dealt with the excommunication of those who

---

[71] *Councils and Synods*, II, ii, 865–8, 870–1.
[72] Ibid., II, ii, 872–82; Douie, *Archbishop Pecham*, 121–7.
[73] *CCR 1279–88*, 56. F.D. Logan, *Excommunication and the Secular Arm in Medieval England* (Toronto, 1968), 67–8, shows that at this period Pecham was issuing far more significations of excommunications than was the case at any other period. For 1275–9 the total was 1,443, and for 1280–4, 1,536. In the next five-year period the number fell to 935, and from 1290–4 it stood at 702, dropping to 485 from 1295–9.

violated the liberties of the church, and went right back to the principles
laid down at Reading.

After the council was over, Pecham sent a long and uncompromising
letter to the king, in which he stressed Edward's obligation to bring
English practices into line with those of the rest of Christendom. The
argument was put in historical terms: the present evil practices dated
from the times of Henry I and Henry II. Pecham even appealed to
Edward's sense of family, pointing out that the king's great-uncle
Boniface of Savoy had laboured for the liberties of the church. Pecham,
as he was later to point out in a different context, was not 'a reed shaken
in the wind', and his submission of 1279 had not meant that he had
given up the fight.[74] All seemed set for a renewal of the crisis, particularly since there were further issues dividing the king and his
archbishops in the early 1280s.

The royal free chapels were few in number, but they were important
for Edward as a source of patronage, notably that of St Martin's le
Grand in London. The crown claimed that the chapels were free from
ordinary ecclesiastical jurisdiction, but Pecham set out powerful arguments against the claimed exemptions. When on a visitation of the
diocese of Coventry and Lichfield in 1280 he totally disregarded a royal
order forbidding him to investigate the chapels, and he even went so far
as to excommunicate some of the clerks holding office in them. It was
thought necessary to post armed guards to prevent the archbishop's
entry to St Mary's, Stafford. Pecham wrote in typical outspoken style to
Edward: 'It weighs heavily on me that you, whom God preserve,
should set yourself to defend the iniquity of Hell, for which God give
you pardon. And sire, saving your reverence, it was not right that you
should have ordered the chapels to be held against me by force, by
armed men.' The king was not moved by this, and when the question
was discussed in the Easter parliament of 1281, Pecham had to climb
down, suspending publication of sentences of excommunication. In the
summer a compromise was reached. Royal chapels were to remain
exempt from episcopal visitations, though bishops were to be received
with due ceremony should they pass through, and might preach and
perform other duties in the royal chapels, by grace, not of right. The
issue was a complex one, and would cause trouble later in the reign, but
Pecham, perhaps by pressing his case too hard, had achieved little.[75]

There were three important episcopal vacancies in 1280: at London,

[74] *Councils and Synods*, II, ii, 892–918; H. Johnstone, 'Archbishop Pecham and the
council of Lambeth of 1281', *Essays in Medieval History presented to T.F. Tout*, ed. A.G.
Little and F.M. Powicke (Manchester, 1925), 171–88; *Reg. Peckham*, i, 239–44; iii, 889.
[75] Douie, *Archbishop Pecham*, 145–7; J.H. Denton, *English Royal Free Chapels 1100–1300*
(Manchester, 1970), 103–16; *Reg. Peckham*, i, 112; below, 546.

Lincoln and Winchester. There was little argument over the election of Oliver Sutton at Lincoln, and after due inquiries into possible pluralism, Pecham confirmed the election of Richard of Gravesend at London. At Winchester, on the other hand, royal pressure for the election of Robert Burnell met with immediate rejection of the candidate by the papacy. The next candidate was turned down by Pecham, on grounds of pluralism, and it was only when the issue went to the papal curia, that the matter was eventually resolved by Martin I V's nomination of John of Pontoise, himself a pluralist, but one who had had the sense to seek papal dispensation. Edward was doubtless none too pleased that not one of these sees went to a royal clerk, but there was no open conflict between himself and Pecham over any of the appointments.[76]

The outbreak of the second Welsh war in 1282 provides one reason why no major crisis in the relations between church and state took place at this time, for Pecham's sympathies lay with Edward, not the Welsh, whose customs he found repugnant. In addition, Pecham's own position in the church was not strong enough for him to be able to mount a full-scale challenge to royal authority. There was considerable episcopal resentment at his interference in the affairs of various dioceses, and the campaign against pluralism was hardly a good recipe for popularity.[77]

Once the Welsh war was over, the argument began again. At the same time that he extracted the grant of the thirtieth from the laity, Edward sought financial aid from the church. The northern clergy appear to have refused, while the southern agreed to no more than the collection of the final instalment of the fifteenth conceded in 1280. Demands for a new tax were firmly rejected, as the clergy claimed that they had been burdened enough in the recent past, and papal permission would be needed. To a third request, that the archbishop should provide service for the war in Wales, or pay a sum in commutation, it was replied that clerks were forbidden to take part in the shedding of blood, and so the request had to be denied. Edward was not prepared to leave the matter there, and eventually, in October 1283, a biennial twentieth was granted to pay off the king's war debts.[78]

The problems of taxation were not the only difficulties at this time: there was also debate in 1284 over the question of criminous clerks. This, of course, was the issue that had been so important in the dispute between Henry I I and Thomas Becket. The problem was hardly as important now as it had been then, but two *causes célèbres*, the

---

[76] Douie, *Archbishop Pecham*, 106–8.

[77] Douie, *Archbishop Pecham*, 131–2.

[78] *Councils and Synods*, II, ii, 944–5; Deighton, 'Clerical Taxation by Consent', 165–6; E 159/58, m.5v.

murder in London of Laurence Duket, and in Exeter that of the precentor of the cathedral, both involved clerks. In the latter case, the dean of Exeter was widely thought to have instigated the murder himself.[79]

At parliament in May 1285 the clergy initially put forward seventeen articles of grievance. After the promulgation of the statute of Westminster II, further articles objecting to some of the measures in the statute were presented, and a final set of grievances protested at the treatment of the clergy in royal courts. The initial articles took up once more the issues raised at Reading and Lambeth, and were answered by a group of officials headed by Robert Burnell. As far as writs of prohibition were concerned, it was suggested that ecclesiastics who received such writs might consult four named justices. Later Burnell suggested that they might take the problem to the exchequer, or the King's Bench. To the demand that imprisoned clerics should be handed over to the church when this was requested, a matter relevant to the recent criminal cases, Burnell's retort was simply that this was current practice. It was likewise his contention that Magna Carta was being properly observed. The complaints against Westminster II were nine in number, and ranged from technical problems about executors of wills to the claim of the church to have full jurisdiction over the question of the abduction of nuns. This was particularly relevant to the case of Osbert Giffard, who had taken two nuns from Wilton abbey, and upon whom Pecham was to impose an impressive set of penances. The royal answers to these complaints were hardly satisfactory to the church, and as regards the matter of Mortmain in particular, the reply was uncompromising in the extreme.[80]

The third set of grievances followed the issue of an edict, which unfortunately has not survived, which set out the limits between lay and ecclesiastical jurisdiction. Its terms are clear from a writ to the diocese of Norwich of 1 July 1285, which listed pleas claimed by the crown, and left to the church little save matrimonial and testamentary matters. Protests were prompt, and the last of the sixteen articles on the matter presented in parliament appealed to the celebrated thirty-ninth clause of Magna Carta. It was argued that just as free men should not be disseized of their liberties or free customs without judgement of peers, in accordance with the law of the land, 'much more so should the church not be despoiled of its rights and liberties'.[81]

[79] Douie, *Archbishop Pecham*, 302–4; below, 265.

[80] *Councils and Synods*, II, ii, 956–67; Douie, op. cit., 304–11; H.G. Richardson and G.O. Sayles, *The English Parliament in the Middle Ages* (1981), VIII; *Reg. Peckham*, iii, 916–17.

[81] *Councils and Synods*, II, ii, 967–72; Douie, *Archbishop Pecham*, 312–16.

The debates during the parliament of May 1285 had been vigorous, but the chief protagonists of church and state had not been directly involved. Pecham was occupied with a visitation of the diocese of Salisbury, and the king had left discussion of the clerical grievances to his experts, notably Robert Burnell. This was not the stuff from which major crises were made, and little was decided. It was the activities of Richard of Boyland and the sheriff of Norfolk and Suffolk that led to a resolution of at least some of the problems voiced in parliament. These two men were commissioned, by the writ of 1 July 1285, to inquire into past breaches of royal jurisdictional rights in the bishopric of Norwich. This diocese was probably deliberately chosen as a test case, since the bishop had been particularly active in pressing his claims. Over 150 cases were reported in which the church courts had allegedly over-stepped their proper bounds. The bishop eventually paid a fine of 1,000 marks in return for freedom from further action for his clergy: one Gregory of Pontefract, who had shown contempt for royal writs of prohibition, was excluded from these terms. Not surprisingly, one of the items on the agenda for a church council in October 1286 was 'the new oppression of the church, especially in Norfolk'.

By the time that the council met in October 1286, the crisis had largely been resolved, for when Edward was in Paris in early summer, on his way to Gascony, he had issued a writ which became known as *Circumspecte Agatis*. This was addressed to Boyland in his capacity as justice in eyre, and his companions, and ordered them to act with due circumspection towards the clergy. Instead of providing a list of pleas claimed by the crown, as had been done in the writ of July 1285, this writ listed the cases that the church courts could try. Not only did the list cover matrimonial, testamentary and moral questions, but it also included slanderous and even physical attacks on the clergy, provided that no financial penalties were involved, and that the courts were concerned with the correction of sins. Later copies of *Circumspecte Agatis*, which were included in collections of statutes, added to it a revised version of one of the clauses of the ecclesiastical grievances of 1280, dealing with the same question of the rights of church courts to hear certain types of cases. This may have been issued by the king at Paris as a separate document, or added by a later compiler. *Circumspecte Agatis* had not been intended as a statute, but in time it came to be regarded as such. It certainly had the desired effect of calming the situation.[82]

Edward's readiness to compromise with the church over the issue of

[82] E.B. Graves, 'Circumspecte Agatis', *EHR*, xliii (1928), 1–20, provides a full discussion of the writ and its background, but his account needs to be modified in the light of Richardson and Sayles, *English Parliament in the Middle Ages*, VIII.

jurisdiction was probably the result of a desire to prevent controversy during his absence from the kingdom, while he was in Gascony. Pecham's conduct had been wiser than in the past, and Edward had been careful to ensure that the disputes did not develop too far. He had distanced himself from the debates in parliament in 1285, and had limited the attack on the church courts to a single diocese. He could let his ministers and justices see how far they could go, without attracting too much odium himself. The king could then demonstrate his own statesmanship by intervening with a reasonable compromise. The issue of *Circumspecte Agatis* marked the conclusion of Edward's arguments with Pecham: it did not end his arguments with the church, which, under Archbishop Winchelsey, was to present further challenges to his authority later in the reign.

At the start of his reign Edward had much reason to be concerned by the fact that many royal rights had, or were thought to have, been usurped by magnates and others. Jurors had reported in the Hundred Rolls inquiry that many rights, particularly of jurisdiction, were being exercised by private individuals, and they did not know by what warrant this was done. The investigation, by means of legal proceedings, of private rights of jurisdiction was an important aspect of royal policy from 1278 until the early 1290s. Such investigations were not entirely novel. There were good precedents from Henry III's reign for inquiries, but Henry had done little more than investigate. He had not wished to limit the franchises held by the magnates, preferring to try to retain their friendship. Edward's approach was more aggressive and much more systematic.[83]

The initial plan had been for the crown to challenge franchisal rights in parliament, but by Easter 1278 it had become clear that this method had not worked. Other business had been too pressing, and cases had been postponed again and again. It was then decided to revive the system of general eyres, following a gap of six years. This was a system by which justices were sent on circuit round the country, and from 1278 it was to be before these justices that franchisal rights would be investigated. The procedure was that anyone who possessed rights of jurisdiction should appear to set out their claims. If it was alleged that they had usurped them from the crown, they would have to answer the court, even if no writ had been taken out against them, but if they claimed that their ancestors had held the franchise, then the crown might proceed against them by means of a writ of *Quo Warranto*, inquiring by what

---

[83] M.T. Clanchy, 'The Franchise of Return of Writs', *TRHS*, 5th ser., xvii (1967), 65–7; D.A. Carpenter, 'King, Magnates and Society: the Personal Rule of King Henry III, 1234–1258', *Speculum*, lx (1985), 50–2.

warrant they exercised their rights. This was worked out at a parliament held at Gloucester in August 1278.[84]

What was not done at the Gloucester parliament was to set out the criteria the courts were to use to decide whether claims were justified or not. The theory put forward by many royal attornies was developed from the earlier thirteenth-century legal treatise known as Bracton. This was that all judicial franchises were delegated by the crown, and that they could be revoked at any time. This was even developed, by about 1290 in the treatise called *Fleta*, into the view that liberties of any kind should not be granted out at all, and that the king was obliged to revoke them.[85] Such ideas were not universal. There was no well-articulated theory to set against the arguments of the royal attornies, but there was a strong sense that franchises that had been acquired through conquest in the eleventh century, or by long and uninterrupted tenure by a single family, could not be revoked, and should not be challenged. The celebrated story told by Walter of Guisborough about Earl Warenne makes the point. When challenged by royal justices to prove his rights, the earl produced not a royal charter as his proof, but a rusty sword, declaring: 'Look, my lords, here is my warrant. My ancestors came with William the Bastard, and conquered their lands with the sword, and I will defend them with the sword against anyone wishing to seize them.' There are many problems about the story, which bears the marks of legend, but it did express a strongly held view about the nature of franchises, that they had been acquired by conquest, not by royal grant.[86] Another expression of hostility to the royal viewpoint was put by the elderly abbot of St Mary's, York, in 1290, when he argued that the objections raised to his rights to the proceeds of justice arose from 'the subtlety of the moderns'.[87] It was felt that old and established ways were threatened by new ideas.

In 1279 the earl of Gloucester's attorney tried to argue that there was no need to answer a writ of *Quo Warranto*, as it did not name the king as

---

[84] D.W. Sutherland, *Quo Warranto Proceedings in the Reign of Edward I* (Oxford, 1963), 17–27. The order for the investigation of franchises made at Gloucester is printed ibid., 190–3. My debt to Sutherland's important book cannot be properly expressed in footnote references.

[85] The arguments are well summarized by Sutherland, op. cit., 1–15.

[86] Guisborough, 216. Two versions of this tale specify the earl of Gloucester, not Warenne, and in some respects he is a more obvious candidate. However, Warenne was considerably provoked by the *Quo Warranto* proceedings, notably over Grantham, and the story could well fit him. See M.T. Clanchy, *From Memory to Written Record* (1979), 21–8; Clanchy, 'The Franchise of Return of Writs', 74–5; G.T. Lapsley, 'John de Warenne and the Quo Warranto proceedings in 1279', *Cambridge Historical Journal*, ii (1926–7), 110–32.

[87] M.T. Clanchy, '*Moderni* in Medieval Education and Government in England', *Speculum*, 1 (1975), 671.

plaintiff, nor did it detail the royal case. The council ruled against this argument, and in its decision stated that all liberties were royal, and belonged to the crown, unless the holder could produce a charter, or show that he and his ancestors had held the franchise in question since before the time of legal memory.[88] This question of tenure from time out of mind – in practice since 1189 – was extremely thorny. In some of the early proceedings, claims made on this basis were accepted by the courts. A jury accepted Earl Warenne's argument that he and his ancestors had held rights in Reigate, and elsewhere in Surrey, from time immemorial. There was more argument with a royal attorney, William of Gislingham, over Warenne's franchisal rights in Sussex, but again, he was allowed to retain them.[89] Royal attorneys became increasingly hostile to claims based on prescriptive right, or tenure from time out of mind, but there was little consistency in their attitude until 1285. From that date, they uniformly attacked prescriptive claims, arguing that long and unchallenged tenure did not amount to royal approval for a franchise. In Essex, in the autumn of 1285, a claim to tenure from time out of mind, put forward by Hugh Despenser's attorney, was met by William of Gislingham, acting for the crown, with a firm statement that all liberties of the type in question belonged to the crown, and that no one could exercise them without royal warrant.[90]

These questions as to what kind of claims were acceptable should have been settled at an early stage in the proceedings, but even as late as 1285 the justices were still very uncertain. In that year, John de Vaux, and his colleagues on the northern circuit, addressed a series of questions to Chief Justice Hengham. They wanted guidance on a number of points, one of which was what to do with claims to tenure based on prescriptive right. Hengham's answer was pragmatic. As far as return of writ and view of frankpledge were concerned, tenure from time out of mind should be acceptable, not by virtue of Magna Carta, as one argument had it, but simply because so many franchise holders were exercising their rights with no other title. To disallow such claims would be quite impracticable. On a different issue, that of the use of *Quo Warranto* writs for the recovery of free tenements which the crown claimed as part of its ancient demesne, Hengham interestingly reported the king's own opinion, which was that he was not bound by any prescription, but that in some cases he would, as an act of grace, accept a plea based on the principle of long-user.[91] Hengham's advice may

---

[88] Sutherland, *Quo Warranto Proceedings*, 8–9, 195–7.

[89] *Placita de Quo Warranto* (Record Commission, 1818), 745, 750–1; Sutherland, *Quo Warranto Proceedings*, 73.

[90] Ibid., 72; *Placita de Quo Warranto*, 239.

[91] P.A. Brand, '"Quo Warranto" Law in the reign of Edward I: a hitherto undiscovered opinion of Chief Justice Hengham', *Irish Jurist*, n.s. xiv (1979), 133–8, 167–8.

have helped the northern justices to clarify their minds, but in general there was still considerable uncertainty. The only possible course was to postpone judgement, and by 1290 it has been estimated that there were some 250 unfinished cases waiting to be settled.[92] The situation had undoubtedly been made more difficult by Edward's absence in Gascony since 1286. Only with his return to England would it be possible to settle the difficult issues.

Claims to franchises based on tenure from time out of mind, or on conquest, were among the most difficult. Yet even if the holder of a franchise had a royal charter, there might still be problems. Earl Warenne's claim to the right of return of writ – the right to put royal writs into effect, excluding the sheriff from a liberty – in Grantham, was based on a charter issued by Edward himself before he had become king, and on Henry III's confirmation of that charter. Yet in 1281 Gilbert de Thornton, an aggressive royal attorney, argued that the general words used in the charters were not sufficiently explicit, and did not cover return of writ. He argued too, that Edward as king was 'as if another person' from the Edward who had made the grant. The case was a difficult one, postponed several times, and it was eventually determined by the council in parliament in 1282. Predictably, the verdict went against the earl.[93]

A general political philosophy underlay the *Quo Warranto* investigations, with the view that all judicial authority was derived from the king. There was also a general assumption that many royal rights had been usurped, and that it was an important part of Edward's kingly duty to recover them. Were there, however, more specific political motives involved in the *Quo Warranto* proceedings? The earl of Gloucester was certainly singled out in the early stages. A special roll was drawn up detailing the franchises which he and his father had allegedly usurped, and in the Kent eyre of 1279 five out of eight actions of *Quo Warranto* were brought against him. In other counties particular care was taken to bring actions against him.[94] The earl was, not surprisingly, aggrieved. A petition from him in parliament, in 1278, began with a plea that 'our lord the king should allow him to enjoy the seisin of his franchises, which he has had, and now has, in peace. And he does not wish, if it please the king, that the king's will should be done to him contrary to the law of the land.'[95] Edward had his quarrels with Gloucester, but it would be wrong to assume that political malevolence

---

[92] Sutherland, *Quo Warranto Proceedings*, 85–6. These 250 postponed cases were from the eyres of 1286–9; there were others from the earlier hearings as well.

[93] Clanchy, 'The Franchise of Return of Writs', 70–1; *Placita de Quo Warranto*, 429–30.

[94] Sutherland, *Quo Warranto Proceedings*, 146–7; *Placita de Quo Warranto*, 336–41.

[95] *Rot. Parl.*, i, 8.

inspired the use of *Quo Warranto* against the earl. The proceedings are far more likely to have been based on a genuine belief that Gloucester and his father had indeed usurped royal rights extensively in the 1260s.

The king's main baronial opponents of later years, Roger Bigod and Humphrey de Bohun, earls of Norfolk and Hereford, do not seem to have suffered particularly at the hands of the attornies and justices conducting the *Quo Warranto* campaign. Bigod lost a right to view of frankpledge in Norfolk but most of the cases in which he was involved were postponed and probably never concluded. When Bohun lost his rights in two Huntingdonshire manors in 1286, because his attorney failed to appear in court, they were soon returned to him by grace of the chancellor of the exchequer.[96] Not surprisingly, men close to the king suffered little. A massive list of franchises held by the earl of Lincoln in Lancashire was drawn up, but the earl's claim that he held them by prescriptive right was upheld by a jury, and no further action was taken. Edmund of Lancaster, the king's brother, was challenged in a good many cases, but does not appear to have lost anything as a result of the proceedings. A case against Robert Burnell, concerning liberties he held as bishop of Bath and Wells, did not proceed far.[97]

The proceedings were not universally unpopular. The many presentations made in the course of the Hundred Rolls inquiry in 1274-5 suggest that the exercise of private jurisdiction was not welcomed by all those who lived under the system. In 1278 Robert Aguylon petitioned the king, complaining about Earl Warenne's franchisal rights in the barony of Lewes, and his claims to free warren and hunting rights throughout Sussex, and he asked to be allowed to prosecute the earl himself. Robert Burnell, in his episcopal capacity, asked for the earl of Gloucester to be impleaded over the rights he exercised in various hundreds in Somerset.[98]

The magnates certainly disliked *Quo Warranto*. Some versions of Guisborough's chronicle include a story of how the king questioned the sons of the great men, to find out what they were saying about him in private, and they confessed that a rhyme was current, which went as follows:

> The king he wants to get our gold,
> The queen would like our lands to hold,
> And the writ Quo Warranto
> Will give us all enough to do![99]

---

[96] *Placita de Quo Warranto*, 303, 482-3.
[97] *Placita de Quo Warranto*, 381, 703.
[98] *Rot. Parl.*, i, 6; E 159/55, m.lv.
[99] Guisborough, 216. The translation is that given by Cam, *The Hundred and the Hundred Rolls*, 237.

Yet in the period before the king's return from Gascony in 1289, there were no concerted protests at the proceedings. In part this was because they did not all take place at once, so aggravating the entire body of the baronage simultaneously, and in part it was because the extent of royal success in recovering usurped franchisal rights was very limited indeed. In Kent substantial gains were made at the expense of the earl of Gloucester, but it has been shown that the Yorkshire proceedings of 1279–81 'were an almost ludicrous failure' in terms of the recovery of royal rights.[100] A further important point is that Edward did not challenge some of the most jealously guarded privileges, those of the Welsh Marcher lords. It is tempting to see this in political terms, of the king's need for Marcher support in his Welsh wars.[101] There may be some truth to this argument, but it was also the case that the system of judicial eyres did not extend into the Welsh March, so there was no convenient way of bringing actions under writs of *Quo Warranto* there. Had Edward been deliberately courting the favour of the Marchers, then he would have made sure that they received preferential treatment as far as the franchises they held in England were concerned, and that was not the case.[102]

Quo Warranto was a specifically English campaign. In Ireland it looks as if Edward had similar plans at the outset of his reign, for in October 1274 he wrote to the justiciar, Geoffrey de Geneville, stating that he had heard that many holders of liberties had usurped royal rights. In such cases, the liberties were to be taken into the king's hands, pending Edward's decision on the matter. A memorandum for the administration of Ireland, probably dating from 1278, put the problem in extreme terms: for every six or seven legitimate franchises, there were twenty-four illicit ones. Yet when Agnes de Vesey's liberty of Kildare was taken from her in 1278, royal sympathy for her was such that she recovered it for a fine of only £100, and the king gave instructions that she was not to be distrained when this was not paid.[103] Equally, there was no *Quo Warranto* campaign in Gascony.

The government had certainly not achieved all that might have been expected from the *Quo Warranto* hearings. The failure to provide clear definitions as to what types of claims were acceptable, and what not,

---

[100] Sutherland, *Quo Warranto Proceedings*, 145–61.

[101] Prestwich, *War, Politics and Finance*, 231–4.

[102] J. Beverley Smith, 'The Legal Position of Wales in the Middle Ages', *Law Making and Law-Makers*, ed. A. Harding (1980), 38–9. In a Shropshire case in 1292 Peter Corbet roundly declared that some of his manors were 'in the Welshry and wholly outside the county', and therefore not liable to *Quo Warranto*: *Placita de Quo Warranto*, 686.

[103] *CDI*, ii, no. 1050, 1503, 1974, 1977; *Documents on the Affairs of Ireland before the King's Council*, ed. G.O. Sayles (Dublin, 1979), 18–20.

meant that very many cases were never brought to a proper conclusion. In the absence of defined principles and objectives, the campaign had all too often blundered aimlessly through very difficult terrain. Yet it had served to make it clear that the exercise of local rights of jurisdiction was a delegation of royal authority. Arguments that the proceedings brought incidental advantages to the crown by providing a survey of franchises, or supervision of their operation, are not convincing, but they undoubtedly made franchise holders aware, as never before, of the fact that they owed their position to the crown. They must have deterred men from attempting any fresh usurpations of royal rights. At the same time, the *Quo Warranto* cases had clogged up the eyre proceedings, making hearings that were already very cumbersome and lengthy almost unmanageable. While important questions of law had been raised, they had all too often remained unresolved. At least the ineffectiveness of the *Quo Warranto* hearings meant that a policy which could have provoked a serious confrontation with the magnates did not destroy the essential harmony that existed in the late 1270s and in the 1280s between the king and his greater subjects. When a confrontation did eventually come, at Easter 1290, Edward showed his statesmanship in realizing that this was a question over which he could well afford to compromise.[104]

There was one further sector of society with which Edward came into conflict in the 1280s. Royal policy towards the towns, and in particular towards London, took a very aggressive turn. Urban judicial privileges and rights of self-government did not accord well with the king's concepts of his authority. He had imposed his will and his law on the Welsh, and it would have been surprising had he not done the same with the Londoners.

From 1281 to 1284 the mayor of London, Henry le Waleys, was a loyal supporter of the king. He served Edward in many capacities, and had been mayor of London before, in 1273–4, then moving on to Bordeaux.[105] In 1281 he was told to take exceptional measures to bring order to London. He began the practice of dragging bakers convicted of fraud through the streets of the city. He set up a new prison, the Tun, and he instituted new methods of trial. A new food-market was created, known as the Stocks, and houses were built on vacant plots, and the rents used to maintain London Bridge. These measures aroused the hostility of many of the London oligarchs, and in October 1284 Gregory de Rokesle, who had been mayor from 1274 until 1281, regained office. This came at a difficult moment in the city's relationship with the

<hr />

[104] See below, 346–7.
[105] His biography is summarized by Williams, *Medieval London*, 333–5.

king. In the summer before Rokesle's election, the *cause célèbre* of the murder of Laurence Duket took place. Duket had attacked and wounded a clerk, and then took refuge in the church of St Mary-le-Bow, where he was found hanged five days later. The initial verdict was suicide, but a boy who had been in the church with Duket revealed the truth, and a number of those responsible for the murder were hanged. Duket's mistress, who was said to have been responsible for his death, was burned. The king was outraged at the murder, and the attempt to conceal the truth, and his opinion of the Londoners was confirmed by the riots that took place in the next year, when five prisoners broke out of Newgate gaol and climbed on the roof.[106]

Edward responded to the disorder in London by appointing a special judicial commission, headed by John Kirkby, in June 1285. He also gave permission to the canons of St Paul's to enclose their churchyard and precinct 'for the prevention of homicides, fornications and other evils in the streets and lanes', a move which deprived the city of the ancient site of the Folkmoot. Gregory de Rokesle, with the aldermen, entered the Tower to appear before Kirkby and his colleagues, but before he did so he resigned his office of mayor in protest. His objections at the unconstitutional nature of the proceedings were met by Kirkby's summary seizure of the city into royal hands. The citizens were ordered to appear before the king at Westminster, and when they appeared, eighty were detained. Ralph de Sandwich was appointed to take over custody of the city. The mayoralty was not destined to be restored until 1298. The royal officials were able to continue Henry le Waleys' policies, and indeed to take them much further. Alien merchants were given full rights in the city, so breaking the old monopolies. Much work was done to bring the legal system in London into line with that of the rest of the country, and the city became far more open to intervention by the departments of central government than it had been in the past.[107]

There were no events elsewhere in England as dramatic as those in London, but Edward was certainly not reluctant to intervene in urban affairs. In 1280 both York and Canterbury were taken into the king's hands: in the former case, the mayoralty was not restored until 1282. At Scarborough, trouble arose in 1282 when the young men and the newcomers to the town banded together, to 'subvert the customs and rights of the said town', and royal justices were sent to investigate. The butchers guild at York was fined by the crown, in the same year, for allowing the escape of four prisoners entrusted to their custody. Four

---

[106] *Ann. London*, 92–3; *Ann. Dunstable*, 314; *Cotton*, 166; *CPR 1281–92*, 143; SC 1/24, 195, 195A; Douie, *Archbishop Pecham*, 302–3.
[107] Williams, *Medieval London*, 254–6.

years later, a commission was set up to investigate the activities of
vagabonds in the same city, whose crimes were such that some citizens
did not dare to leave their homes without an armed escort. The city of
Bristol was fined £500 for contempt in 1285. At Canterbury there was a
furious row, which began in December 1285, between the archbishop's
bailiffs and the men of the city's Westgate, which necessitated royal
intervention.[108] A very different type of royal involvement in urban
matters took place at Winchelsea, where the town was suffering badly
from erosion of the site by the sea. The plan to create a new town was
first conceived in 1280, and the setting out of the streets, market place
and harbours was started in 1283. The inhabitants of the old town did
not start moving into the new one until 1287, but the project was one
which proved to be totally successful, and which deserves to be set
alongside Edward's other new town foundations, in Wales and in
Gascony.[109]

The government of England in the years between the first Welsh war
and the king's departure for Gascony in 1286 was not characterized by
dramatic incidents. There were arguments, notably with Archbishop
Pecham, but these, like the debates over *Quo Warranto* and the intervention in the affairs of the city of London, did not threaten to develop into
a major crisis. The king and his officials did not achieve all that they
aimed at. The inquiry of 1279 yielded massive returns, but little use
appears to have been made of them, and it seems likely that some plan,
perhaps for developing a new system of taxation, was abandoned.
Kirkby's Quest was of more value, but did not yield the financial
dividend that was almost certainly hoped for. The *Quo Warranto* campaign shows that energetic intentions could not always be carried
through, and that muddle and confusion might win the day. Yet these
were years of positive achievement. The reform of the coinage was
efficiently done, and worthwhile improvements took pace in exchequer
procedures. The burden of paying for the war in Wales did not seriously
threaten financial stability. The many surviving records testify to the
general efficiency of the day-to-day running of affairs. The greatest
achievements of this period, however, have still to be discussed, for
this was above all the age of the statutes. It was now that the bulk of the
legislation for which Edward is so well known was promulgated, and
that is the subject of the next chapter.

[108] *CPR 1281–92*, 41, 50, 178, 256; *CFR 1272–1307*, 130, 161; E 101/159/60, m.3;
Douie, *Archbishop Pecham*, 75–6.
[109] Beresford, *New Towns of the Middle Ages*, 14–19; *CPR 1281–92*, 81–2.

Chapter 10

THE STATUTES AND THE LAW

The reign of Edward I was one of the most important periods in the development of English law. The majestic series of statutes marked a major advance in legislative practice, and it is not surprising that the king has received the accolade of being termed 'The English Justinian'. Of course, such a title will not bear close scrutiny: Edward did not try to codify law as Justinian had done, nor were his statutes based on Roman law. Yet, as Bishop Stubbs put it in the nineteenth century, it is a term 'which, if it be meant to denote the importance and permanence of his legislation and the dignity of his position in legal history, no Englishman will dispute'.[1] The story of the law under Edward I, however, is not one of consistent triumphs. The king's return from Gascony in 1289 was followed by serious accusations against many of the judges, and their subsequent dismissal. It was suggested by none other than the king himself that at the end of the reign the country was on the verge of civil war, so serious was the breakdown of law and order.

The English legal system of Edward I's day was very complex. Courts ranged in type from the manorial right up to parliament, and different jurisdictions overlapped and competed. There was an important element inherited from the Anglo-Saxon past, with local courts in vill, borough, hundred and shire, and there were feudal courts. The church had its own jurisdiction. Royal justice had the central courts of King's Bench and Common Pleas, and the exchequer also had rights of jurisdiction. Royal justices toured the country in the general eyres, and were also employed on more specialized commissions, such as those of gaol delivery or oyer and terminer. Private jurisdictions might, in rare cases, such as that of the palatinate of Durham, almost rival that of the king himself: royal writs did not run in Durham. At a lower level, much of the exercise of judicial authority lay in private hands. It has been calculated that only 270 of the English hundreds were in royal hands in the 1270s, as against 358 in private possession.[2]

Legal proceedings could take many different forms. Cases might be initiated by means of a writ obtained from the royal chancery: by

[1] W. Stubbs, *The Constitutional History of England* (4th edn, Oxford, 1906), ii, 109.
[2] Cam, *Hundred and the Hundred Rolls*, 137.

Edward's day there were a large number of standardized writs to meet many different circumstances. An important development in the thirteenth century was the increasing use of more informal methods of starting proceedings, by plaint of *querela*, rather than by writ. A plaintiff might simply go straight to the justices with his complaint, which would usually be presented in written form. This was particularly useful procedure when the crown wished to hear grievances against its officials.[3] Criminal cases might be brought forward by juries of presentment, empanelled locally to inform justices about crimes that had been committed since the last judicial visitation. It was possible for the injured parties to bring appeals against criminals, and justices also made use of approvers, men who brought accusations against their former companions in crime.

The main instrument of legal change in Edward's day was the statute, but it was only in retrospect that it became clear that the statutes were a distinct type of legislative instrument. It was the courts and those who practised in them who came to regard certain documents as statutes, rather than those who drafted and promulgated them. The legislators were not consciously producing a new type of law, nor indeed were they doing something very new in issuing written legislation. Magna Carta, with its various reissues, had made alterations to the law, as the statute of Merton of 1236 had done. Much legislation took place during the period of baronial reform, although, because of their opposition origins, texts such as the Provisions of Westminster were not included in later collections of statutes. There was no such problem with the statute of Marlborough of 1267, however, of which thirty copies were made for distribution.

Statutes under Edward I were far from being standardized in form. Some were in Latin, some French. They were not enrolled in a systematic way in the thirteenth century as they would have been if it had been considered that they were a new and distinctive type of document: only from 1299 was the Statute Roll used to record statutes as they were issued.[4] Lawyers, however, had volumes of statutes drawn up for their use from a surprisingly early date. One example, written between 1286 and 1290, was probably written for someone in the service of Isabella de Forz, who was very possibly the infamous Adam Stratton. Interestingly, this uses the term 'statute' only for documents promulgated under Edward I: for its compiler, there obviously was some dividing line

---

[3] For bills and plaints, see *Select Cases of Procedure without Writ*, ed. G.O. Sayles and H.G. Richardson (Selden Soc., lx, 1941); A. Harding, 'Plaints and Bills in the History of English Law, mainly in the period 1250–1350', *Legal History Studies*, ed. D. Jenkins (Cardiff, 1972), 65–86.

[4] *Select Cases in the Court of King's Bench*, ed. Sayles, iii, xv–xvi.

between the Marlborough legislation of 1267, and that of Westminster in 1275.[5] The latter was described as 'certain provisions and statutes', and sealed copies were sent to every county, with instructions that it be read and solemnly proclaimed in every hundred, city, borough, vill and other suitable place.[6] It was, however, repute more than anything else which made a statute, and it was in this way that texts such as the writ *Circumspecte Agatis* acquired statutory status.[7] The inclusion of a privately drawn-up tract on the king's rights, the *Prerogativa Regis*, in collections of statutes, provided this text with something of the force of a royal statute.[8] The authenticity of some of the texts of the major statutes is open to question. A writ issued in 1282 recited the initial clause of the statute of Westminster I, giving it in Latin rather than the original French, but although the gist is the same, the differences are too great for it to be possible to assume that one is a bad translation of the other.[9] Contemporaries were confused on occasion: in 1298 appeal was made to a statute of conspirators which never existed.[10] The problems should not be exaggerated, however, for people generally knew what they meant when they referred to statutes, and judges showed little hesitation in cutting through difficulties caused by bad drafting.

The question of who was responsible for the statutes is not an easy one. The preamble to the relatively unimportant statute of Bigamy of 1276 is more explicit than anything in the other statutes: it explained that the articles were recited and recorded in the presence of Walter de Merton, Robert Burnell, Francesco Accursi, and other clerics and judges of the royal council. They were then heard and published before the king and council, and it was agreed that they should be adhered to in future.[11] The drafting of statutes was a technical business, and the range and complexity of many suggest that it is a mistake to look for a single author. The phrases such as 'The king ordains and establishes', or 'Firstly the king wishes and commands' should certainly not be

---

[5] V.H. Galbraith, 'Statutes of Edward I: Huntingdon Library MS H.M. 25782', *Essays in Medieval History presented to Bertie Wilkinson*, ed. M.R. Powicke and T.A. Sandquist (Toronto, 1969), 181.

[6] *Statutes of the Realm*, i, 39.

[7] Above, 257–8. By Edward III's reign doubts were being expressed about the authenticity of *Circumspecte Agatis*, and one judge declared that it had been made by the prelates themselves: *Select Cases in the Court of King's Bench*, iii, xiv.

[8] F.W. Maitland, 'The "Praerogativa Regis"', *EHR*, vi (1891), 367–72.

[9] *CPR 1281–92*, 28; *Statutes of the Realm*, i, 26–8. The study of Edward's statutes is severely hampered by the lack of a modern edition of them: it would be an extremely difficult task to produce proper texts, as there are so many manuscripts with minor variants.

[10] *Select Cases in the Court of King's Bench*, ed. Sayles, iii, lix, 63.

[11] *Statutes of the Realm*, i, 42.

taken as an indication of Edward's involvement in the detailed work of drafting the various clauses of the statutes.[12] There are no records of the discussion within the council to reveal the attitude that he took, but it seems most likely that his concern was with the overall direction of policy, not the specific details of the measures themselves. Argument in court in 1311 about the interpretation of the first clause of the statute of Westminster II of 1285 led Chief Justice Bereford to set out what he believed 'he that made the statute intended'. Earlier, in discussions about a different clause of the same statute, Chief Justice Hengham had expostulated, 'Do not gloss the statute: we know it better than you, for we made it.' It would be wrong to conclude from this that Hengham was the author of the whole of Westminster II: it may well be that his remark was intended to refer collectively to the judges or the king's council, rather than to himself.[13]

Edward's statutes were not, like the *Liber Augustalis* of Frederick II, or the *Siete Partidas* of Alphonso X of Castile, the work of a single legislator. Many clauses – probably more than can ever be so demonstrated – had their origins in specific problems arising in the courts. Matters which were revealed in the course of inquiries, or which were the subject of petitions to the king, might also lead to legislation. The specific instance of the abduction of two nuns by Osbert Giffard lay behind the drafting of part of a clause of the statute of Westminster II.[14] Pressure from many magnates explains why Edward issued the statute of *Quia Emptores* in 1290. Yet, behind the diversity of the various measures taken in the statutes, certain general principles can be seen. There was a drive to make the law more efficient and effective, to produce measures for the relief of the people and the speedy execution of justice.[15] The king and his advisers were not trying to create a new system of law. The were operating within the common law, which they were constantly amending and improving. There was no narrow sectional interest that predominated: remedies were provided where lords had grievances against their tenants, and equally, tenants were given new protection against oppression by their lords. The problems were met by providing proper, clear-cut procedures to follow in future, and the legislation was carefully thought out in terms of the realities facing the courts.

The range of Edward's legislation was immense, and it is not possible to summarize more than a few of the important measures. The statutes

---

[12] *Statutes of the Realm*, i, 26.

[13] T.F.T. Plucknett, *Legislation of Edward I* (Oxford, 1949), 73, 133, where it is assumed that Hengham *was* the author of Westminster II.

[14] Douie, *Archbishop Pecham*, 311.

[15] See the preamble to the Statute of Westminster II. *Statutes of the Realm*, i, 71.

were not, with few exceptions, limited to a single topic, and equally, a single theme was often pursued in the courts of several statutes. The land law was one subject of importance, and a good illustration of what Edward and his lawyers were doing is provided by the changes that were made to one of the most popular forms of action, that of novel disseisin. This was the most celebrated of the so-called possessory assizes introduced by Henry II, and was intended to provide a swift and efficient means of recovery for someone ejected from lands he occupied.[16] A jury would be asked if the plaintiff had been disseised unjustly, and if they agreed that he had lost his lands without judgement, the sheriff would restore them to him. The action related only to seizin, or occupation, and not to the question of ultimate right. It was originally intended to apply only to recent acts (hence, 'novel' disseisin), but the process of bringing forward the date before which it could not apply had been haphazard. In the statute of Westminster I of 1275 it was set at 1242, and remained there for the rest of the medieval period.

The rule that the action could be brought only by the man who lost his land against the man who had taken it was accordingly more effective than the date of limitation in preventing actions of novel disseisin being taken long after the event to which they referred. In Westminster I this was changed, and it became possible for the heirs of both parties to continue the action. It was also laid down that if the disseisin took place with robbery or violence, then the plaintiff was to recover all he had lost, with damages, and the defendant was threatened with a fine and imprisonment. If it was a royal official who had carried out the disseisin, without a proper warrant, then the plaintiff need not even obtain a writ of novel disseisin, but could simply use the plaint procedure. The guilty official was threatened with double damages. In Westminster I it was also laid down that the action might take place even during Advent, Septuagesima or Lent: the permission of the bishops had been obtained for this.[17]

The question of novel disseisin was taken up again in the Statute of Gloucester of 1278. If the defendant had granted out or leased the land he had seized, then the new tenant would have to pay the damages. Plaintiffs were now entitled to recover their costs, as well as damages. The statute of Westminster II of 1285 extended the scope of the action.

---

[16] The classic explanation of this is provided by Pollock and Maitland, *The History of English Law*, ii, 47–56.
[17] *Statutes of the Realm*, i, 33, 35–6, 38–9. The action is very fully treated in D.W. Sutherland, *The Assize of Novel Disseisin* (Oxford, 1973). The effect of the church's prohibition on the taking of oaths in penitential seasons is explained in *Handbook of Dates*, ed. C.R. Cheney (1970), 65–6.

It was laid down that it could be used in the case of lands being held as a means of recovering a debt: in such cases, a debtor might very well attempt to recover his lands by force. Novel disseisin could also be used where rights to collect fruit and nuts in woodland, annual deliveries of annuities in kind, or profits from tolls and bridges were concerned, but it was not available in cases where common pasture was encroached upon by the building of a windmill, or creation of a sheepfold. The statute emphasized the speed of the action. Neither plaintiffs nor defendants could excuse themselves from presence in court, so delaying matters, and the use of bogus arguments, such as a mendacious claim that the issue had already been the subject of litigation at a higher level, was to be punished with double damages and a year's imprisonment. Later measures included the statute of Joint Tenants of 1306, which provided remedies to prevent delays caused by a defendant's claim that he did not hold the land in question by himself, but was a joint-tenant.[18]

In the various measures refining the action of novel disseisin certain principles can be detected. Edward was determined to enhance the force of the law by introducing stiffer penalties where this was appropriate, and especially harsh treatment was to be given to royal officials who transgressed. There was no sympathy for those who attempted to delay judgement by means of legal quibbles. The legislation was clearly based on practical experience in the courts: indeed, the clause of Westminster II which prevented the use of 'false exceptions' (bogus arguments), was probably based on a specific case, Hengston v. Kyriole.[19] Edward was not overthrowing the established principles of novel disseisin: he was ensuring that it continued to be effective and efficient.[20] This indeed it was. It had been calculated that 84 per cent of some 500 cases that came up before Ralph Hengham between 1271 and 1289 were concluded with a judgement on the first day. In a case in 1281, the abbot of Ramsey was able to recover six square miles of land only twelve days after obtaining his writ of novel disseisin.[21] In the Huntingdon eyre of 1286, when thirty-three cases of novel disseisin were heard, a similar record of efficiency is evident. Only one case was not settled by the justices in eyre. In it, the tenement in question had been taken into the king's hands, and then granted to the Savoyard knight John de Bonvillars. He had then handed it over to the keeper of the wardrobe, William of Louth. Both Bonvillars and Louth were

---

[18] *Statutes of the Realm*, i, 47, 82, 84–5, 89, 145–6.

[19] Sutherland, *Assize of Novel Disseisin*, 133, no. 1.

[20] The argument that Edward I reversed earlier policy on seisin is refuted by N.D. Hurnard, 'Did Edward I reverse Henry II's Policy upon Seisin?', *EHR*, lxix (1954), 529–53.

[21] Sutherland, *Assize of Novel Disseisin*, 127, 129–30.

named as defendants, and with such important men involved, it was inevitable that the justices would decide that the matter should be referred to the court of King's Bench.[22]

In some important aspects of the land law, Edward's statutes did much more than refine existing actions. The initial clause of Westminster II of 1285, known as *de donis conditionalibus*, which governed the making of conditional gifts, had a fundamental effect on the workings of the land market. The concern here was with family settlements. When land was granted to a son or daughter, particularly when they married, the donor would often try to ensure that the land would remain in his family, and revert to him should the line of descent of the donees fail. In practice, however, before 1285 it was impossible to create entails in this way. The statute of Westminster II expressed the king's intention that the conditions attached to a gift of land should be observed, and 'in a new case new remedy must be provided'. Writs, known as Formedon in Descender, were to be available to enable the giver to recover his lands where the conditions were not kept.

There were considerable difficulties with the statute, for it could be read in such a way that the conditional quality of gifts lasted for only one generation. However, in 1311 Chief Justice Bereford was to argue: 'He that made the statute intended to bring within it not only the donees but also the issue in tail until the entail was fully accomplished in the fourth degree; and the fact that he did not do so by express words concerning the issue was only due to his negligence.' It may be that the poor drafting of the clause was the result of last-minute changes, caused by alarm at the prospect of the creation of permanent entails, or simply that it shows the difficulty involved in resolving problems by means of a single legislative act. What the statute proves is the obvious determination of the king and his council to meet an evident grievance. The clause that was produced, and its later interpretation, was to effect very substantial changes in the landholding structure of England, with the creation of secure entails.[23]

A major problem facing landlords in this period was that, with the increasing subdivision of holdings, it became more and more difficult to exact such profitable feudal rights as wardship, marriage and escheat. The difficulty was not a new one in Edward's day: in the 1217 reissue of Magna Carta it had been laid down that a tenant should not alienate so much of his fee, that he could no longer maintain his services to his lord.

---

[22] *Royal Justice and the Medieval English Countryside*, ed. A.R. DeWindt and E.B. DeWindt (Toronto, 1981), i, 255–6.

[23] T.F.T. Plucknett, *Legislation of Edward I* (Oxford, 1949), 131–3; A.B.W. Simpson, *An Introduction to the History of the Land Law* (Oxford, 1961), 75–82; *Statutes of the Realm*, i, 71–2. The term 'formedon' is derived from the Latin *forma doni*.

The problem, as far as grants to the church were concerned, had featured in the Provisions of Westminster of 1259, and had been dealt with by Edward I in 1279 with the statute of Mortmain. Also, the crown had guarded its own position with regard to tenants-in-chief. An ordinance of 1228 forbad them to grant lands to the church, and writs of 1256 had forbidden any alienations by tenants-in-chief without special permission.[24] Tenants-in-chief, however, did not have equivalent rights over their own tenants, who might make ingenious arrangements to grant their lands to another, who would regrant it under different terms, so as to deprive the lord of his rights.[25]

The statute of *Quia Emptores* of 1290 dealt with this problem with a deceptive clarity. At the request of the great men of the realm the king, it states, 'granted, provided and ordained that from henceforth it should be lawful for every free man to sell at his own pleasure his lands or tenements or part of them so that the same feoffee would hold the same lands or tenements of the chief lord of the same fee, by the same service and customs as his feoffor had held before'.[26] This meant that in future lands could be granted out, but not subinfeudated. The new tenant would hold them directly from the original lord, whose rights would be preserved. The statute was not quite so general in its operation as initially appeared. The crown still retained its rights over the tenants-in-chief, and the statute did not cover estates held on conditional terms, either entailed or for a term of years. Unfortunately nothing is known of the arguments that must have taken place prior to the issue of this statute, but it is best seen as a compromise between the magnates' desire to establish freedom of alienation without loss of feudal rights, and the crown's continued desire to maintain full control over its tenants-in-chief.[27]

Much was done in the course of the legislation to deal with the problems inherent in the relationship between lords and tenants. When tenants failed to provide services, lords would first of all try to recover their rights in their own courts, but this might well prove difficult, as the abbot of Ramsey found in 1294, when faced by the recalcitrance of his tenants who were asked to provide military service for the royal expedition to Gascony.[28] Lords could use distraint, that is, seizure of beasts, chattels or even lands, against unwilling tenants: they in turn could use an action known as replevin as a means of recovering what

---

[24] Bean, *Decline of English Feudalism*, 40–79.

[25] Ibid., 86–9.

[26] *Statutes of the Realm*, i, 106.

[27] Bean, *Decline of English Feudalism*, 79–97. The statute is discussed by Plucknett, *Legislation of Edward I*, 102–8.

[28] *Select Pleas in Manorial and other Seignorial Courts*, ed. F.W. Maitland (Selden Soc., i, 1889), 79–80.

had been taken from them. The system was obviously open to abuse. In Westminster I, 1275, it was even provided that, where all else failed, a man trying to recover goods improperly detained could get the sheriff to take the extreme measure of knocking down the castle where they were kept. Westminster II of 1285 gave a tenant entitlement to treble damages in cases of unjust distraint, and also provided checks against legal tricks employed by tenants. An action was provided whereby, if a lord distrained the goods not of his own tenant, but of a sub-tenant, the latter could bring a writ against the tenant who had defaulted in not providing services. The writ of *cessavit* was made available to lords in cases where services had not been performed for two years: if the action was successful, they would recover their lands.[29]

The interests of great landowners were served by clause 11 of the statute of Westminster II, which dealt with the problem of unreliable bailiffs. This was an age when direct management of estates was normal, rather than their being rented out, and it was essential to have proper safeguards against fraudulent officials. The statute provided for a bailiff who owed money to his lord to be imprisoned, and if there were problems with the accounts, then they might be heard before the experts of the royal exchequer. In the last resort, a bailiff guilty of embezzlement or fraud would suffer outlawry.[30] Edward had, of course, had problems himself with his steward Roger Leyburn in the early 1260s, though it is not likely that that case was the precedent for this clause of the statute.[31] The new procedure was certainly used by landlords: the earl of Gloucester employed it to have one of his bailiffs imprisoned in the Fleet for arrears of £200, and another of his officials was held in prison at Clare, owing no less than £614 4s 1½d.[32] The measure was not universally popular: the *Mirror of Justices*, a tract of about 1290, commented, 'It is an abuse that lords should appoint auditors to hear their bailiffs' accounts without consent of the bailiffs. . . . It is an abuse that bailiffs cannot recover damages against tortious auditors.'[33]

Another example of legislation which met the demands of the great landowners comes from 1293, when Edward, at their request, conceded that foresters and other such officials should not be punished if they killed poachers who resisted arrest after the hue and cry had been raised. In future they were to be regarded just like thieves trying to escape. It may be that the duke of Brittany, lord of Richmond, was

---

[29] Plucknett, *Legislation of Edward I*, 59–63, 90–4.
[30] *Statutes of the Realm*, i, 80–1; Plucknett, *Legislation of Edward I*, 153–6.
[31] See above, 37.
[32] Denholm-Young, *Seignorial Administration in England*, 158–9.
[33] *The Mirror of Justices*, ed. W.J. Whittaker and F.W. Maitland (Selden Soc., 1893), 164–5.

particularly concerned about this, for he had protected one of his foresters for a time after he had killed a man in the course of his duties. Once royal policy changed, the forester received a pardon from the king.[34]

Much was done in the course of the legislation to try to make the operation of the law more effective. One problem faced by plaintiffs was that even if they won their case, sheriffs might not implement the judgement properly. In the statute of Westminster I of 1275, it was established that if a defendant defaulted, grand distress, or distraint on all his property, would be ordered. The sheriff would be 'grievously fined' if he did not comply with his instructions. Ten years later, in Westminster II, the problem of false returns by the sheriffs was tackled – they often set a low valuation on the goods distrained, or declared that there were no proceeds to be had from the lands. The plaintiff could now demand that the sheriff's return should be heard, and he could apply for a writ to have an inquest into the value of the goods and lands taken. It was made clear that all movable goods were liable to distraint, save a riding horse, clothes and household utensils. In a case between the abbot of Hyde and Earl Warenne in 1288, the sheriff of Sussex imposed grand distress when the earl defaulted, and returned a value for the goods taken of £135. The plaintiff alleged that they were worth much more, and an inquest jury put a valuation on them of £189 6s 8d. The procedure was not much used, however, and a further revision of it took place in the statute *De Finibus Levatis* of 1299. This laid down that the exchequer was to charge the person distrained with the money due, rather than the sheriff, in an attempt to prevent corruption by the sheriffs. Unfortunately, this meant that the sheriffs had less chance of profiting from imposing distraint, and the procedure lost much of its effectiveness. Well-intentioned legislation foundered on the problems of putting it into practice.[35]

It was not possible for the legislators to envisage every possible eventuality, and clause 24 of Westminster II permitted the clerks of chancery to make new writs when 'a writ is found in one case, but none is found in a similar case'. Alternatively, if there was no obvious parallel for the new writ, the matter could be adjourned to parliament, and a new writ made there 'by those learned in the law'. The statute gave three examples, all relating to the land law, in all of which a swift and convenient remedy, in full accordance with existing principles in closely allied cases, was introduced. It was thought that the origins of the

---

[34] N.D. Hurnard, *The King's Pardon for Homicide* (Oxford, 1969), 237 n.1, 274, 288 n.4.
[35] D.W. Sutherland, 'Mesne Process in the early Common Law', *Law Quarterly Review*, lxxxii (1966), 482–96; *Statutes of the Realm*, i, 37–8, 90–1.

wide array of actions known as 'case' lay in this clause, but this was almost certainly not so: Plucknett argued persuasively that what was really important in it was not the limited element of discretion given to the chancery clerks to produce new writs, but the fact that the statute laid down, in unambiguous terms, the power of parliament to create new remedies.[36] The principle that the chancery could produce writs based upon similar cases had been enunciated earlier than the statute of Westminster II. In a case heard in 1276, the dowager countess of Gloucester's attorney objected to a writ which had been granted to the dowager countess of Devon, on the grounds that it was novel and not based on any similar cases.[37] It may even be that this instance was in the minds of those who drafted the relevant clause of Westminster II.

Legal historians have emphasized Edward I's changes to the land law, for that is the part of the legislation that was perhaps of the greatest long-term significance. The statutes themselves, however, were concerned with a much wider range of issues. One problem was that of how merchants could obtain repayment of debts. England was not an advanced country in commercial terms at this time, and lacked the complex mechanisms that existed elsewhere, notably in Italy, for the registration and enforcement of commercial contracts. In England, if a trader failed to meet his obligations, his creditors would often simply distrain the goods of some other merchants who came from the same town or country. This practice was limited in the statute of Westminster I, which forbad the distraint of Englishmen who had not agreed to act as pledges for a given debt. This, however, merely made it harder to collect debts, and did not deal with the problems facing overseas merchants.[38] A petition to the king, in the summer of 1283, from Raymond Trespas explained that he had sold goods in London, Salisbury and Winchester, and that although he had tallies and written promises of payment, he could not obtain the money due to him.[39] A long-running case which began under Henry III, that between James le Roy of Dixmude and John de Redmere, showed how difficult it was to collect debts even if judgement was obtained. The two men had been partners, and when James le Roy finally obtained judgement that he was owed 200 marks, he could not recover it, for the sheriff of

---

[36] Ibid., 83–4; T.F.T. Plucknett, 'Case and the Statute of Westminster II', *Columbia Law Review*, xxxi (1931), 778–99; S.F.C. Milsom, *Historical Foundations of the Common Law* (2nd edn, 1981), 284. For a broader exposition of case, see A.K. Kiralfy, *The Action on the Case* (1951).

[37] Galbraith, 'Statutes of Edward I', 188–91.

[38] *Statutes of the Realm*, i, 33.

[39] SC 1/24, 3A.

Lincolnshire reported, almost beyond doubt fraudulently, that
Redmere had no lands in his county from which he could raise the
money.[40]

These matters were discussed at the parliament held at Acton
Burnell in the autumn of 1283, and a statute was enacted to meet an
obvious need. There was a real fear, according to the preamble, that if a
swift remedy was not provided for the problems they faced, then foreign
merchants would cease coming to trade in England. The statute
provided for the registration of debts before the mayors of London,
York and Bristol. If repayment was not made as specified, then the
mayor was empowered to sell the debtor's movable goods and burgage
tenements up to the value of the debt. If the debtor had no goods within
the mayor's jurisdiction, then the sheriff in whose county he did have
possessions was to levy the debt. If all else failed, he was to be imprisoned until he made arrangements for repayment.

These measures were not successful. Three places where debts could
be registered were too few, the limitation to movable goods and
burgage tenements was excessive, and the sheriffs were unwilling to
co-operate with the new procedures. The system was therefore considerably modified in the statute of Merchants of 1285. More towns were to
be used as registries, and if a debt was not paid off promptly, then the
debtor was to be imprisoned at once, and given three months to raise
the money. If he failed to do so, then his creditor would receive all his
lands and goods, to hold by a new form of tenure until the debt was fully
paid off from the proceeds. This was a very severe procedure, much
more so than that set out in clause 18 of the statute of Westminster II of
the same year, which made a new writ, *elegit*, available for the recovery
of debts or damages awarded in court. There were some local parallels,
in Yarmouth and the Cinque Ports, to the new procedures, but the use
of imprisonment and the creation of tenure by statute merchant were
innovations.[41]

It is tempting to think that the crown's connection with the Italian
bankers may have lain behind the legislation on debt, but the Riccardi
had little need of the new procedures, for they enjoyed the privilege of
using the machinery of the exchequer to collect debts owed to them.[42]
Among those who did benefit notably from the new measures, however,
were the king's own officials, notably the unscrupulous treasurer Walter
Langton. At the time of his arrest soon after Edward I's death there
were some eighty-five recognisances in force under statute merchant in

---

[40] *Select Cases in the Law Merchant*, ed. H. Hall, ii (Selden Soc., 1929), 18–27.
[41] *Statutes of the Realm*, i, 98–100; *Select Cases in the Law Merchant*, iii (Selden Soc.,
1932), xxii–xxiii; Plucknett, *Legislation of Edward I*, 136–48.
[42] Kaeuper, *Bankers to the Crown*, 121–2.

his favour. He used highly unprincipled methods, as the case of Richard of St Valery shows. He had entered into a recognisance for £200 with Langton in 1299, but failed to pay off the debt. In 1305 he was imprisoned, and when he refused to make over two of his manors in fee to Langton, he was cast into a deep dungeon, in irons. His house was broken into, and his property-deeds seized. His resolution failed him, and he granted one of his manors to Langton in perpetuity. The treasurer also gained £340 more than he was entitled to under the terms of the statute.[43] It is most unlikely that this type of use had been envisaged when the legislation was first enacted, and it is hardly surprising that the Lords Ordainers in 1311 were to limit use of the statute simply to cases between merchants. This was, most probably, what had originally been intended.

The reforms introduced by Edward I into the criminal law have not received as good a press from legal historians as his other measures. In part this is because the king failed to solve the problems presented by the crime wave that took place in his later years, and in part because the criminal law cannot be represented as an intellectual system in the way that property law can be. For S.F.C. Milsom, 'The miserable history of crime in England can be shortly told. Nothing worth-while was created. There are only administrative achievements to trace.'[44] The historian of Edward's reign cannot dismiss the criminal law so lightly, for the maintenance of law and order was a most important aspect of the duties of kingship, and one of which Edward was highly conscious.

Criminal matters received considerable emphasis in the first statute of Westminster in 1275. All men were to be ready to join in the pursuit and arrest of felons. Notorious felons who refused to undergo jury trial were to suffer prison *forte et dure*, which then amounted to only food on one day, and only drink on the next. Extortion and other offences by royal officials were condemned. These measures were probably not innovations, but what was new was the way in which imprisonment was specified as a penalty in certain instances. One was rape, where it was established that if no accusation was brought within forty days of the offence being committed, the king might take over the prosecution. If guilt was established, the punishment was two years in prison. Poachers and trespassers in parks and hunting reserves faced a stiffer penalty of three years incarceration. Royal and other officials who concealed felonies, or who granted bail to prisoners who should not be

---

[43] Beardwood, 'The Trial of Walter Langton', 30, and idem, *Records of the Trial of Walter Langeton, 1307–1312* (Camden Soc., 4th ser., vi, 1969), 262–70.
[44] Milsom, *Historical Foundations of the Common Law*, 403.

released, would also serve a three-year sentence.[45] Edward's approach was clear: more efficient methods of arrest were needed, and stiffer penalties should be imposed.

The statute of Westminster II continued along similar lines. Anyone who made a false accusation of homicide, or other felony, should be imprisoned for a year. Abduction of children, if the lucrative right of controlling their marriage belonged to someone else, carried a two-year sentence. Strict penalties were imposed for poaching salmon. Rape was now dealt with much more seriously still than in Westminster I: it was now treated as a serious felony, punishable with loss of life or limb. The statute made it quite clear that the offence was not confined to the violation of virgins, but covered attacks on all women. Abduction of nuns, even with their consent, meant three years in prison.[46]

The major changes of 1285 in criminal law came not in the statute of Westminster II, but in that of Winchester. This began with the statement that crime was more frequent than in the past, and that it was difficult to get juries to indict felons. It was laid down that a prompt suit should be made after crimes took place, and that in cases of robbery, the hundred in which the offence took place should be responsible for loss and damage. The local community was allowed forty days to produce the criminals before the authorities. The idea of making the local hundred responsible was not a new one, dating back to the Norman period for cases of murder, but when Henry III had tried to introduce such a principle regarding robbery in 1253, the magnates would not accept what they regarded as a Savoyard innovation. The statute of Winchester provided, in addition, for security in towns and cities, with arrangements for watch and ward at night. Roads were to be widened, so that there should be no undergrowth or bushes within two hundred feet on either side in which robbers might lurk. Edward's experience of road cutting and widening in Wales may have influenced this decision. The statute went on to update the twelfth-century regulations regarding the military equipment that all free men were to possess: to ensure that law-worthy men were properly armed might deter criminals. Justices were to be assigned to see that the statute was kept, and were to report to the king in parliament.[47]

The efficacy of these measures is hard to assess. Statistics drawn from

[45] Statutes of the Realm, i, 26–39, especially clauses 9, 12, 13, 20; H.R.T. Summerson, 'The Early Development of Peine Forte et Dure', Law, Litigants and the Legal Profession, ed. E.W. Ives and A.H. Manchester (1983), 117–18. Peine forte et dure became more severe still in the early 1290s: prisoners were laden with as much iron as they could bear, and rarely survived long.

[46] Statutes of the Realm, i, 81, 87–8, 94–5.

[47] Ibid., 96–8; T.F.T. Plucknett, Edward I and the Criminal Law (Cambridge, 1960), 89.

court records reveal how much crime was discovered, not how much there actually was. One concern expressed in the statute of Winchester was that many crimes were not being reported, and the truth of that supposition cannot be tested. What the government at the time was particularly aware of was the number of offences which caused a major scandal. The case of Laurence Duket, murdered in St Mary-le-Bow, was one such. A conspiracy in 1287 on the part of some sailors at Dunwich was a serious matter. They had prevented the local court from sitting, had appropriated fines imposed by royal justices, and prevented the execution of royal writs and judgements. In the following year, the burning of Boston Fair in the aftermath of a tournament, in which one side dressed as monks, the other as canons, achieved much notoriety: there had been fires and serious crimes there earlier in the reign as well.[48] The murder of Edmund of Cornwall's steward, Roger de Drayton, as he was walking to parliament in 1292, caused a furore. It was said that Roger had maliciously contrived to have the mother of one of his murderers put in the stocks at Berkhampstead, and that revenge was the motive for the attack. The guilty men succeeded in finding sanctuary, and went into exile abroad.[49] Relatively minor disputes might take a violent turn. In 1293 Edward FitzJohn, acting rector of the church at Thame in Oxfordshire, found himself besieged for four days by a force acting under the authority of the bishop of Lincoln. Ditches were dug in the roadway outside the church, and it was even said that the attackers had broken down the bridge at Thame, though they alleged that the force of floodwater had done this.[50] A matter of particular concern to the magnates was the number of incidents of parks being broken into, particularly while their owners were away fighting for the king. During the second Welsh war the earls of Cornwall, Gloucester, Norfolk, Oxford and Lincoln all suffered in this way, as did many lesser men. It was noted that criminals became bold once the king was out of the country.[51]

In certain respects it seems that Edward's policy of imposing stiffer penalties, far from deterring crime, simply had the effect of making it harder to obtain accusations and convictions. The changes in the law on rape are a case in point. Prior to the reforms of the statutes of Westminster I and II, cases of rape are far from uncommon. In the Wiltshire eyre of 1249 there were nineteen appeals of rape, the same

---

[48] *CPR 1281–92*, 279, 397, 401–2, 474; *CCR 1279–88*, 92; Guisborough, 224–5; above, 265.
[49] *Ann. London*, 100; *CPR 1292–1301*, 143.
[50] *Select Cases in the Court of King's Bench*, iii, 11–16; *CPR 1292–1301*, 109; *Rot. Parl.*, i, 101–2.
[51] *CPR 1281–92*, 64, 66, 73, 91–2, 94–7, 100, 102.

number as homicides.[52] What frequently happened was the imposition of a light fine if the case came forward by means of a presentment, and if it were brought by appeal, then frequently the parties concerned would come to an agreement to marry. There was even a popular song, retelling the woes of a man who 'chanced to go on the earth with a maid', who then took him to court, and screamed 'By my gabbing it shall not go so, and that be on you all, that you shall wed me and have me to wife'.[53] The changes made in the law by Westminster I, with the imposition of a statutory period of imprisonment, made the courts reluctant to convict rapists. In one apparently clear-cut case in 1282, where the deed took place 'with dreadful violence', the justices over-ruled the refusal of the defendant to plead benefit of clergy, and handed him over to the church authorities. In another instance, the defendant was acquitted because the plaintiff had failed to specify the precise whereabouts of the door through which her attacker entered the grange where the crime took place.

The case which seems to have inspired the king and council to insert, almost certainly at a later stage, the clause about rape in the statute of Westminster I I was that of Rose Savage who accused John de Clifford of rape. He had abducted her and taken her to his hall at Middleton in Oxfordshire (she specified that it lay north and south, with the door to the west), raped her, and then imprisoned her from January 1280 until November 1282. The case was initially dismissed because the precise date of the offence was not specified, but prosecution was taken over by the crown. The case came before the King's Bench, at the start of the parliament in which the statute of Westminster I I was enacted.[54] That statute imposed yet stiffer penalties, and well-intentioned as it undoubtedly was, this made conviction still more difficult to obtain. There is a remarkably detailed accusation, brought by Matilda, daughter of Michael, of Chiswick, in 1293, in which the details of the dress she was wearing at the time of the assault are described – it cost 2s – and the whereabouts of the incident are set out with great care. Her case failed, however, because she failed to state what metal the knife she was wounded with was made of, nor which hand her assailant used to hold her down.[55]

---

[52] *Crown Pleas of the Wiltshire Eyre*, ed. C.A.F. Meekings (Wiltshire Archaeological and Natural History Soc., Records Branch, 1961), 74.

[53] *Political Songs*, ed. Wright, 155–9. This particular case was brought in a church court. J.B. Post, 'Ravishment of Women and the Statute of Westminster', *Legal Records and the Historian*, ed. J.H. Baker (1978), 155, refers to one case, of seduction rather than rape, where the man was given the choice of death, kissing the girl's backside, or marriage. He chose the third option.

[54] *Select Cases in the Court of King's Bench*, i, 101–2; Post, 'Ravishment of Women', 156.

[55] KB 26/146, m.22.

The reforms to the law regarding rape were thoroughly criticized by the author of the *Mirror of Justices*, primarily on the dubious grounds that a number of quite different offences had been conflated into one: rape of virgins had been put together with adultery, fornication and incest. What was true was that the offence of abduction of women (ravishment) became unjustifiably identified with rape, and questions of the property involved became in time more important than those of personal violence. The change in the frequency with which rape cases came before the courts is striking. In the Huntingdon eyre of 1286, only one appeal for rape was brought, and as the defendant was not brought to court, it failed. Only two cases were presented by jurors.[56] It does not seem likely that Edward's legislation had affected the number of sexual assaults as strikingly as this: what it had done was to reduce substantially the number that came to court, as compared with the situation in the mid-thirteenth century.

There are no exact parallels to the story of the changes in the law on rape, but it was certainly difficult to obtain convictions for any crime. The Huntingdon eyre of 1286 shows that of some 190 men accused of homicide, only a third were brought to trial, and less than nine per cent convicted. In the case of theft, the crown was more successful, with ninety-five men found guilty out of a total of 239.[57] There are, unfortunately, few figures of the numbers of men kept in prison in this period, but it does not look to have been very large. Evidence of charitable deliveries of bread to York prison indicates that there were 80 prisoners there in 1289, but there were no less than 310 four years later, shortly before an eyre was due.[58]

The problem of maintaining law and order became increasingly acute in the 1290s, and in the first years of the fourteenth century. A celebrated statement in the Yorkshire eyre roll of 1294 stated that 'justice and truth are completely choked', as a result of the way in which influential men manipulated legal proceedings. A decade later, as the king was returning from the triumphant conclusion of the siege of Stirling, loud complaints were put to him about the activities of gangs who, it was alleged, offered to beat up people, and extort money from them, for a mere three or four shillings. The chronicler Pierre Langtoft thought that if a stop was not put to this, civil war might follow, and the king himself used similar phraseology later, referring to the troubles as being 'like the start of war'.[59]

The situation was indeed serious. The concentration of both king

---

[56] *Royal Justice and the Medieval English Countryside*, ed. deWindt, nos 558, 805.
[57] Ibid., 59–63.
[58] R.B. Pugh, *Imprisonment in Medieval England* (Cambridge, 1968), 366.
[59] Langtoft, ii, 360; *Select Cases in the Court of King's Bench*, ed. Sayles, iv, lvi.

and nobility on the wars had meant that little attention had been paid
to the question of law and order. Their absence on campaign gave
encouragement to criminals, as it had done during the Welsh wars. The
system of general eyres had been virtually abandoned in 1294, and
infrequent as these visitations had been, they had provided a full
investigation into county affairs. The practice of pardoning men in
return for good service in war began in 1294. In that year, Roger
Brabazon and William de Bereford were commissioned to recruit
criminals for the Gascon campaign. It was said that there were many
men, accused of crimes, 'who wander about the countryside, doing,
committing and procuring many evil deeds', and that the king 'was
moved to pity for that so many and divers men of our kingdom so often
incur the penalty of life and limb'. In practice, the ease with which
pardons could be obtained as a result of the new policy – in one case a
soldier in Scotland obtained his within eight weeks of killing a man –
encouraged crime, rather than brought criminals back into law-
abiding society.[60]

One change in the law may have deterred people from bringing
accusations against criminals. An ordinance of 1293 provided a form of
action to be used in cases of conspiracy to hinder justice. The crime was
very widely interpreted, and a defendant, once acquitted, now had a
form of writ available which he could use to bring an action against the
original plaintiff. It had to be shown that the latter had acted maliciously
in an attempt to pervert the course of justice, and in some cases the
procedure was obviously valuable. In 1298, for example, William Bell
brought an action of conspiracy against Hugh le Cornwaleys and
others who had, he claimed, falsely procured his indictment for robbery
and burglary, planting a stolen charter in his bed. In another case, a
vicar was charged with wrongly accusing a woman of adultery with a
monk. There were precedents for such an action before 1293, but it was
now widely available. If an accused man was found not guilty, as was so
often the case, there was a very real danger that he would then accuse
those responsible for his indictment of conspiracy. Not until 1304 was a
rule introduced forbidding use of the action in this way against the
indictors.[61]

The main weapons against the crime wave before 1304 were the
normal judicial proceedings of gaol delivery and commissions of oyer
and terminer. The latter, *ad hoc* appointments to deal with specific
crimes, help to reveal how serious the situation was by 1303–4, not only

[60] Hurnard, *The King's Pardon for Homicide*, 248, 313–17.
[61] *Select Cases in the Court of King's Bench*, ed. Sayles, iii, liv-lxxi, 61–2, 95–6; *Cal.
Chancery Warrants*, i, 241–2; A. Harding, 'The Origins of the Crime of Conspiracy',
TRHS, 5th ser., xxxiii (1983), 93–7.

as regards ordinary criminal activity but also concerning the involvement of gentry and nobility in violent affrays. A feud between the
Berkeley family and the people of Bristol was the occasion for a violent
attack on the manor of Bedminster, and the mayor of Bristol was so
badly beaten up that the marrow oozed from his shin bones. Thomas
earl of Lancaster was engaged in a violent dispute with the prior of
Tutbury, some of whose men were imprisoned for six months in the
earl's castles. Royal officials were maltreated: in Norfolk a coroner was
assaulted and his rolls torn up and trampled. At Shrewsbury, there
were complaints that the town had been besieged, the bailiffs assaulted
and new ones installed, and also that one Isabella Borry and her men
had been raiding and plundering. There was what was described as a
league of vagabonds 'who commit depredations by night, and refuse to
submit to justice' at Newcastle upon Tyne.[62]

A systematic approach to the problem of law and order was clearly
needed, and special 'trailbaston' commissions were duly set up. The
earliest appointment was made in November 1304, when justices were
given a specific brief to inquire into such offences as the hiring of men to
assault others, especially at fairs and markets.[63] This was a commission
to make inquiries and arrests, rather than to determine cases, and by
March 1305 so many criminals had been taken that it was a matter of
some urgency to arrange for them to be tried. In parliament that spring
the Ordinance of Trailbaston was promulgated – the name comes from
the bastons, or staves, carried by criminal bands. Five judicial circuits
were set up, to hear cases that had occurred between the summer of
1297 and Easter 1305.[64] Peter Maulay, who headed the northern
commission, objected to this limitation, and Edward duly suggested
that any crimes committed up to 15 August next should also be heard.
He described the activities of the justices as being like a drink taken
before medicine: the medicine was to be a full visitation by justices in
eyre, but that never materialized. Instead, the trailbaston commissions
were renewed, with some modifications, in the autumn of 1305 and
early in 1307.[65]

The trailbaston inquiries certainly revealed a disturbing situation.
Brutality of all sorts was rife, with a host of apparently unprovoked

---

[62] *CPR 1301–7*, 193–4, 270–1, 285–6, 288, 347–8, 353–4, 356.
[63] *CFR, 1272–1307*, 504. For discussion of the origins of trailbaston, see A. Harding,
'Early Trailbaston proceedings from the Lincoln roll of 1305', *Medieval Legal Records*, ed.
R.F. Hunnisett and J.B. Post (1978), 144–6; R.B. Pugh, *London Trailbaston Trials*
(1975), 2–4.
[64] *CPR 1301–7*, 348, 354; *Rot. Parl.*, i, 178. For another explanation of the word
'trailbaston', see J.H. Denton, *Robert Winchelsey and the Crown 1294–1313* (Cambridge,
1980), 212n.
[65] *Select Cases in the Court of King's Bench*, ed. Sayles, ii, cl–cli; *CPR 1301–7*, 404, 542–3.

assaults and murders. Fairs and markets were the scene of a good many crimes, as when a royal bailiff was assaulted by Thomas de Aston and his two brothers, pursued, and beaten up publicly in the market at Stafford. In some cases the use of standard formulae makes it hard to assess the gravity of the offences, but many accusations were very specific. In Lincolnshire, Ralph Tokel entered Adam Swanson's house, and attacked Adam's son Hugh, breaking his left arm. Later, he met Hugh again, broke both his arms and three ribs, and then cut away the soles of his feet with his sword. Members of the gentry were involved in many cases. John d'Eyville of Egmanton broke up a session of the county court in Lincolnshire, because of a case involving a member of his family. Another Lincolnshire knight, Ranulph de Friskeney, used his position as a royal justice to influence pleas, and retained a couple of thugs, who had appeared before him in court, in his service. John of Brunscote in Staffordshire was accused of various beatings, and in one case he broke his sword on an unfortunate man, and then charged him 2s for the cost of repairing it. Protection rackets of various sorts were rife. At York, justices found an alarming situation, for a group of wealthy citizens held the city in a complete stranglehold, under the colour of a religious guild. The scale of the hearings is indicated by the fact that in Staffordshire about 300 men were outlawed as a result of them.[66]

The records of the London trailbaston proceedings, however, suggest that earlier royal intervention in the affairs of the city had been of some effect. There had been no major disturbances of the peace in the city, with the exception of a riot between the tailors and the tawers. In some cases there seems to have been an excessive enthusiasm to arrest and indict men. One John of London was suspected of evil-doing, because he often left town for two or three weeks, was well-clad and spent lavishly, although he did not practise any trade. Another man, Walter Foyl, was indicted because 'he commonly leaves the city with arms and a greyhound at the time of vespers, and returns in the morning'. Such conduct led to a presumption that he must be a vagrant and an evil-doer, and he duly suffered a long period of imprisonment.[67]

The trailbaston commissions were unpopular. A poem of the period, known as the Song of Trailbaston, told the tale of an ex-soldier who had served loyally in the wars, and who had committed no worse an offence than giving his servant a buffet or two. For this he would have to pay a

---

[66] Harding, 'Early Trailbaston Proceedings', 154–7; 'Plea Rolls of the Reign of Edward I', ed. G. Wrottesley, *Staffordshire Record Society, Collections for a History of Staffordshire*, vii, 153, 156, 166; G.O. Sayles, 'The Dissolution of a Guild at York in 1306', *EHR*, lv (1940), 83–98.

[67] Pugh, *London Trailbaston Trials*, 61, 76.

fine of forty shillings to escape imprisonment, and so he had taken refuge as an outlaw 'in the wood of Belregard, where the jay flies and the nightingale sings every day'. The poet explained that anyone who knew how to use a bow and arrow was liable of being accused of belonging to a criminal band, and that anyone who knew some law might be accused of conspiracy. Justices with local connections – in this case William Martin and Gilbert de Knoville – met with some approval, but others, specifically Henry Spigurnel and Roger de Beaufoy, were described as men of cruelty. A London chronicler considered, cynically, that the inquiries were introduced as a means of restoring the king's financial position, and suggested that he did indeed acquire much treasure as a result of them.[68]

These trailbaston proceedings attracted much more comment from the chroniclers than any other legal measure taken in Edward's reign, for they had a more immediate effect on people's lives than the great statutes. The proceedings were comprehensive, and evidently successful in the short term. But Edward had created an expedient which could be used only on occasion, and had not developed a new system of local peace-keeping. No changes were made to the system that had been set out in the statute of Winchester of 1285, even though in some regions at least that system was either inoperative or inapplicable. At the end of the reign the men of Shropshire set out an elaborate case against the statute. They pointed to the absence of the frankpledge system in their county – this was the practice of placing men in sworn groups of ten, taking mutual responsibility for each other. They claimed exemption from the obligations placed on the hundred by the statute, and even from the system of local constable and watch and ward. There was a strong basis in local custom for these claims. In contrast, the county community of Cumberland, in an undated petition, complained that in their county there was no system of indictment, but that criminals could be arrested by bailiffs only on suspicion, and the full operation of the common law, in accordance with the statute of Winchester, was requested.[69] There was much that remained to be done if the problems of law and order were to be resolved. Edward hoped in his last years, 'that we may promote pleasantness and ease and quiet for our subjects dwelling in our realm, for in their quiet we have rest, and in their tranquillity we are inwardly cherished with the scent of satisfaction amidst the flowers of hoped-for peace'.[70] The words are doubtless those

[68] *Political Songs*, ed. Wright, 231–6.

[69] D.C. Cox, 'Peace-keeping without Frankpledge: Shropshire Claims in 1307', *Transactions of the Shropshire Archaeological Society*, lx (1975–7), 81–95; *Select Cases in the Court of King's Bench*, ed. Sayles, iii, cxvii.

[70] *Statutes of the Realm*, i, 147.

of a clerk, not the king himself, but the laudable wishes they expressed were scarcely fulfilled.

Edward's other dominions, Ireland, Gascony, and through conquest Wales and, as it seemed in 1305, Scotland, had their own legal systems. Examination of Edward's legislative policies in them helps to set the English statutes in perspective. The question of Wales has already been discussed: there, for all the distaste expressed in English propaganda for Welsh law, there was no attempt at a full anglicization. The statute of Wales of 1284 did, however, extend many of the principles of English land law and criminal law into Wales, and the simplification of the forms of writ available shows the way in which Edward's advisers were seeking for clarity and simplicity in legal procedure.[71] In Ireland, Irish law still held good in the unconquered districts, and elsewhere the native Irish had no access to the English law courts, unless they had obtained a charter granting them the right to use English law. The English – or Anglo-Norman – settlers employed English law. Early in Edward's reign there was an attempt to extend the privileges of English law to all the Irish. Edward declared in the course of the negotiations, in 1277, that 'the laws which the Irish use are detestable to God and so contrary to all law that they ought not to be deemed laws'. The phraseology is very similar to that used of the Welsh and Scottish laws. The origins of the proposal to give the Irish English law almost certainly lay in conversations which Edward had with the archbishop of Cashel in 1274, and it seems clear that the initiative was, as far as the Irish were concerned, primarily an ecclesiastical one. The privilege was one considered worth paying for, and the initial offer was 7,000 marks, but this was thought inadequate, and by 1280 the amount had risen to 10,000 marks, a huge sum in terms of the resources of Ireland. The English administrators in Ireland had no enthusiasm for the scheme, and no more was heard of it after 1280: the price was perhaps too high. Edward's enthusiasm for the divinely approved English laws was not such that he was prepared to grant them to the Irish for nothing.[72]

In Scotland, Edward did not have sufficient time to make changes in the law. The intention in 1305 was to go through the existing laws, and make such changes as were needed, so that they should contain nothing 'openly contrary to God and reason'. The 'usage of Scots and Brets' was abolished: this almost certainly refers to the anachronistic survival of wergild payments – compensation payments for death or injury – in

[71] Above, 205–6.
[72] Otway-Ruthven, *History of Medieval Ireland*, 188–9; A. Gwynn, 'Edward I and the proposed purchase of English Law for the Irish, c. 1276–80', *TRHS*, 5th ser., x (1960), 111–27.

remote parts.[73] As for Gascony, the legal system there, which was largely based on Roman law, was not such that any innovations along the lines of English practice were practicable, and the only resemblances between the king's policies in England and Gascony lie in a desire to see greater order and efficiency in legal administration.

Legislation could not be effective without efficient courts and competent judges. The central royal courts of King's Bench and Common Pleas did not undergo any notable changes in the course of Edward's reign, though the volume of business certainly increased markedly. The system of itinerant justices on the general eyre, which had been introduced in the twelfth century and was systematized by Henry II, was, however, virtually abandoned after 1294. The eyre system was not employed immediately upon Edward's return to England in 1274, but was started, after a six-year gap, in 1278. Proceedings under the commissions issued then lasted until 1289, and thirty-two counties in all were visited. A visitation in a single county could take a long time: those in Yorkshire lasted from May 1279 until May 1281. From 1292 to 1294 another series of eyres took place, but this time only eleven counties were involved. In the rest of the reign there were only two visitations by justices in eyre, to Cambridgeshire in 1299 and to Cornwall in 1302.[74] Eyres bore heavily upon the counties: a total of almost 3,000 individuals were named in the records of the Huntingdonshire eyre of 1286–7, and a calculation of the potential financial benefit to the crown of the proceedings puts the total at £554 19s 11½d, though not all of this would in fact have been collected.[75] The effective abandonment of the eyre system in 1294 coincided with the start of Edward's war with France, and while administrative reasons provide one explanation, it may also be that, just as the *Quo Warranto* proceedings were stopped 'as a favour to the people', so also were the general eyres.[76]

The cessation of the general eyres did not mean that royal justices no longer toured the countryside. There were other types of more limited judicial commissions which in many ways served the crown's interests better than the cumbersome eyres. Commissions of gaol delivery had been used since the 1220s. A good many special commissions of this type were set up in the first years of Edward's reign, to hear cases concerning those who had not come to the king's peace in 1267. In 1275–6 an experiment took place, in which the normal four-man commissions were replaced by pairs of professional justices and local

[73] Below, 504.
[74] Sutherland, *Quo Warranto Proceedings*, 28–30, 216–20.
[75] *Royal Justice and the Medieval English Countryside*, ed. deWindt, 73, 103.
[76] Sutherland, op. cit., 213.

knights, but this did not last long. In the early 1290s the use of four-man commissions was in turn abandoned, amidst allegations of incompetence and corruption, and in 1294 new types were set up, composed partly of justices and partly of permanent commissioners, properly sworn into office. It was clearly necessary to take greater care over these proceedings, following the virtual abandonment of the eyres. It made sense to combine the business of gaol delivery with that of hearing assizes. A system of circuits for assize hearings had begun to emerge in 1272, and twenty years later four circuits were properly established. In the statute *De Finibus Levatis* of 1299 the logical step was taken of giving assize justices the task of delivering gaols, though this was not to become a standard system until Edward III's reign.[77]

It was very often necessary to supplement the regular judicial sessions with special oyer and terminer commissions, set up to hear and determine particular cases or types of case. Edward I's reign saw an explosion in the use of these commissions, starting in 1275. They were much used for cases of trespass brought by means of plaints, and there was obviously a very considerable demand for them. By 1285 the government was concerned at the number being set up, and in the statute of Westminster II it was stated that such a commission should only be issued in cases of 'heinous trespass where it is necessary to provide speedy remedy, and the lord king has seen fit to issue it of his special grace'.[78] The numbers issued fell for a time, but soon rose again. Appointment of commissions, such as those of 1298 into the activities of royal officials during the years of the French war, or the trailbaston inquiries of the last years of the reign, meant a cut in the number of special oyer and terminer appointments made. These commissions were an important adjunct to the regular courts of law, though the need for them points to the inadequacy of the latter.

One problem with special oyer and terminer was that influential men could use their position to have sympathetic justices appointed to hear their case. In one instance Edmund of Lancaster asked that Ralph Hengham and Robert Waleys be named to hear a case concerning forest offences, and this was duly agreed to. When the earl of Cornwall suffered a raid on one of his parks, allegedly by 200 men, he successfully asked that William de Bereford and John Neyrmouth should hear the case.[79] John Langton wrote to the king on one occasion, on behalf of his cousin, Margaret de Hardsull, about a dispute she was engaged in with

[77] Pugh, *Imprisonment in Medieval England*, 265–6, 272–3, 280.

[78] *Statutes of the Realm*, i, 85. Maddicott, 'Edward I and the Lessons of Baronial Reform', 24–5, discusses plaints and the use of oyer and terminer.

[79] R.W. Kaeuper, 'Law and Order in Fourteenth-Century England: the evidence of special commissions of oyer and terminer', *Speculum*, liv (1979), 734–84.

Philip Marmion, to ask for the appointment of justices likely to be sympathetic. He suggested Henry de Bray and Henry de Michelsone, and argued that on no account should Ralph Hengham hear the case, as he was in receipt of a fee from Marmion.[80] The use of special oyer and terminer commissions was obviously convenient, and met a widespread demand, but it was clearly very open to abuse.

Edward's reign saw an extension of royal justice at the expense of other courts. It has been suggested that a conscious decision was made to draw cases from the county courts, because the Hundred Rolls inquiry had shown the extent of popular dissatisfaction with the sheriffs, but it may simply be that the initiative came from the king's subjects, rather than the king or his officials. From 1274 until 1281, widespread use was made of the writ *pone*, which transferred a case from the county court to the king's court, but there is no indication that measures were taken to make this writ more widely available. There was, however, a change in 1275 in the use of the writ *recordari*, which made it possible for the first time to remove from lower to higher courts cases begun by plaint. So popular did trespass litigation before the royal courts become that it was necessary, in the 1278 statute of Gloucester, to declare that 'sheriffs shall hold pleas of trespass in county courts as they used to and that no one from now on shall have a writ of trespass before justices unless he declared on oath that the goods taken away are worth at least forty shillings'. It became impossible to use *recordari* to transfer cases of trespass, but the introduction of a new viscontiel, or sheriff's writ of trespass for use in the county court, did meet some at least of plaintiffs' demands, and relieved the everincreasing burden imposed on the central courts.[81]

It was often less easy to transfer cases from private courts to royal ones, than it was from the county courts. In 1290, the parson of Attleborough complained that false judgement had been given in a case brought against him in the court of the abbot of Bury St Edmunds, but no proper record of the case could be provided for consideration by the King's Bench, as no suitors of the abbot's court would swear to the record, or put their seals to it. In the same year a similar problem occurred in the court of John Fitz Reginald at Talgarth in the Welsh Marches, for when the writ of *recordari* was brought, 'immediately the steward of the court and the suitors withdrew from the said court that they made no record and took no pains to make one'.[82] Such obstructive tactics could not succeed in the long term, however, and it was not

---

[80] SC 1/26, 38; SC 1/30, 24.

[81] R.C. Palmer, *The County Courts of Medieval England 1150–1350* (Princeton, 1982), 228–62.

[82] *Select Cases in the Court of King's Bench*, ed. Sayles, ii, 3–6.

possible to stem the tide of litigation away from local tribunals into the king's courts, a tide which resulted as least as much from popular demand as from any conscious royal policy.

Much of the credit for the work of legal reform in Edward's reign must go to the judges, and yet the great purge of the judicial establishment that Edward conducted when he returned from Gascony in 1289 suggests that there must also have been much to their discredit.[83] There was great variety among the judges: some were clerics, some laymen, and to produce a collective biography of them would take too much space. One judge's career in particular, however, obviously deserves consideration. Ralph Hengham was the dominant figure on the King's Bench during the great period of reform. He first appeared as a judge in 1269, but his importance dates from 1274, when he was promoted to be chief justice of King's Bench on the death of Martin of Littlebury. He probably owed this rise to his connections with Robert Burnell.[84] The justices of Edward's day did not produce any great treatises on the law such as that which goes under the name of Henry of Bracton, written earlier in the thirteenth century. Hengham's fame, however, rests in part on the attribution to him of two widely circulated tracts, the *Summa Magna* and the *Summa Parva*. The former, however, was almost certainly not his work, but was a production of a slightly earlier generation. In style it is very different from the *Summa Parva*, which is characterized by short, sharp sentences, rather than by a rhetorical style. The *Summa Parva* was Hengham's work, and has a close relationship with the statute of Westminster II, explaining how much of it was to work in practice. It is the work, above all, of a practical lawyer.[85]

Hengham was not an out-and-out supporter of the king in all legal matters. The answers he made to the judges on the northern circuit in 1285, when they put various questions concerning *Quo Warranto* before him show this: he was ready to allow men to retain franchises if they and their ancestors had held them from time immemorial. On another occasion, he opposed the validity of a writ summoning the countess of Aumale, as it did not specify the case that she was to answer. His forthright tones are preserved in the retort he made to one of the judges who had supported the writ: 'Would you make such a judgement here

---

[83] See below, 339–42.

[84] *Radulphi de Hengham Summae*, ed. W.H. Dunham (Cambridge, 1932), lxviii, notes the marriage of Andrew Hengham, possibly Ralph's brother or nephew, with Burnell's daughter Amabilla.

[85] P. Brand, 'Hengham Magna: a thirteenth-century English common law treatise and its composition', *The Irish Jurist*, xi (1976), 147–69.

as you made at the gaol delivery at C. when a receiver was hanged and the principal criminal was afterwards acquitted before yourself?' It has been very plausibly suggested that his dismissal from office in 1290 was a result of his independent attitude.[86]

Hengham's fall was a part of the great purge of the judicial and official establishment that took place after Edward's return from Gascony in 1289.[87] Later legend had it that he incurred the massive fine of 8,000 marks merely for remitting half a mark of a fine, and altering the court records accordingly. Legal mythology has no more truth in it than any other, but the charges against Hengham were few, and his offences not serious. The charges he faced provided no more than an excuse for dismissing him. The real reason must have been a more fundamental dissatisfaction on the king's part with his role. Perhaps, as Langtoft had it, it was because he had argued too much.[88] Hengham paid off the bulk of his fine without evident difficulty. His fee as chief justice was sixty marks a year, and certainly does not explain his wealth. There were, of course, many other fees paid to him: in one of the cases against him in 1290 it was said that he took a fee from the abbot of Bury St Edmunds.[89] On one occasion his advice was sought in a case about ownership of a manor, and he asked bluntly what his reward would be. When offered a ploughland, his response was that he would not as much as walk from his house to Westminster for so little. The offer of half the proceeds of the suit was more satisfactory, but the other party in the litigation offered him 200 marks, and he won the case. Much to Hengham's credit, he gave the unsuccessful claimant fifty marks to placate him for his loss.[90]

It is likely that the dismissal of Hengham – and many of his fellow justices – contributed to the change in the pattern of legislation after 1290. That year marked the conclusion of the great series of statutes, and the legislation of the later years was much less comprehensive and systematic in character. Robert Burnell's death in 1292, and the concentration of the king and his officials on war after 1294, are also factors of significance. Gilbert de Thornton, for all that he too wrote a legal

---

[86] P. Brand, ' "Quo Warranto" law in the reign of Edward I: a hitherto undiscovered opinion of Chief Justice Hengham', ibid., xiv (1979), 124–72; *Select Cases in the Court of King's Bench*, ed. Sayles, i, lxx.

[87] See below, 339–42.

[88] Langtoft, ii, 186; Brand, ' "Quo Warranto" Law in the reign of Edward I', 167.

[89] *State Trials of the Reign of Edward I*, 49; J.R. Maddicott, *Law and Lordship: Royal Justices as retainers in thirteenth- and fourteenth-century England* (*Past and Present* supplement 4, 1978), 14, notes receipt of a pension of £5 p.a. from Christ Church Canterbury by Hengham.

[90] G.O. Sayles, 'Medieval Judges as Legal Consultants', *Law Quarterly Review*, lvi (1940), 247–54.

treatise, was not a man of the same stamp as Hengham.[91] There was a change coming over the character of the judicial benches. Hengham, like many of his contemporaries, was a cleric. He had begun his career in the 1250s as clerk to one of the judges of the day, but the newer generation were coming to be drawn from the ranks of the 'narratores', the pleaders in court. There was an increasing secularization of the judicial profession evident by the end of Edward's reign.[92] Hengham himself, however, was not forgotten, and his disgrace did not last. He was appointed to the politically sensitive task of investigating the boundaries of the royal forests in 1299, was summoned to parliament in 1300, and in September of the following year became Chief Justice of Common Pleas. He was now once again a member of the king's council, but without the support of such allies as Robert Burnell, his position and influence were not as strong as they had been in the heady days of the 1280s.[93]

Edward I's own attitude to the law is hard to determine. It is necessary to distinguish between the views expressed on his behalf in the courts, and his own personal opinions. In 1292 it was said on his behalf that his prerogative placed him above the laws and customs of the land, but this should not be taken as an arrogant and arbitrary assumption of royal supremacy. Rather, it was a legal doctrine intended to protect the public interest when it conflicted with established usage.[94] Edward's own attitudes do emerge, however, from a few recorded interventions by him in legal proceedings, which suggest a very real concern on his part that justice should be done, along with a certain impatience with the technicalities of the law.

The case involving the countess of Aumale, in which Hengham denounced the writ employed against her, was finally concluded by Edward himself, who was present in court, and rose, declaring 'I have nothing to do with your disputations, but, by God's blood, you shall give me a good writ before you arise hence.' The king was not prepared to let the case go on when it was based on a dubious writ.[95] The story is one of the rare pieces of evidence for Edward's presence in court. Another example of his intervention in a lawsuit dates from 1280, and

---

[91] For Thornton, see A.L. Spitzer, 'The Legal Careers of Thomas of Weyland and Gilbert of Thornton', *Journal of Legal History*, vi (1985), 67–77.

[92] Maddicott, *Law and Lordship*, 19.

[93] For the later stages of Hengham's career, see *Radulphi de Hengham Summae*, ed. Dunham, lvii-lviii; P. Vinogradoff, 'Ralph of Hengham as Chief Justice of the Common Pleas', *Essays in Medieval History presented to T.F. Tout*, ed. A.G. Little and F.M. Powicke (Manchester, 1925), 189–96.

[94] *Rot. Parl.*, i, 71; below, 352.

[95] *Select Cases in the Court of King's Bench*, ed. Sayles, i, lxx.

also concerns Hengham. Agnes of Sparkford brought a case against William of Patney, claiming that he had promised to marry her, once she had enfeoffed him with all her land. She kept her part of the bargain, only for him to claim that he was already married. William claimed that he had simply acquired the land for 200 marks, with no question of marriage. Hengham stated that Agnes had gone to the queen to complain about her treatment, and 'on this there came the lord king himself who clearly understood that deed, and at once ordered speedy justice to be done to the aforesaid Agnes'. Edward himself firmly rebutted William's claim that he should not have to answer in the absence of a royal writ. The matter was not finally resolved in 1280, however, despite the royal intervention, and came up in court again in 1290, by which time the lands in question had been acquired by the queen, who had presumably exacted a heavy price from Agnes in return for helping her.[96]

A Peterborough chronicler told a vivid story of the king's part in a case brought against his monastery by the earl of Gloucester. One of the monks representing the house asked in court to see the writ that the earl had obtained. Pointing out with delight that it omitted the word 'sheriff' in the address, he successfully argued that the case should be dismissed. The abbot, aware of what would happen next, sent three monks to the royal court. When they arrived, they were too frightened to approach Edward, for he was deep in conversation with their opponent, the earl. Only when he had left did they dare go up to the king, and explain that as their house was a royal foundation they claimed the privilege of not answering any case brought against them without royal consent. Edward was sympathetic, but the earl had already received a new writ, which could not be cancelled. The chancery clerks were consulted, and the question was resolved by the issue of a new writ granting protection to the monastery, dated prior to that given to the earl. When the case next came up before the eyre justices at Northampton, the monks triumphantly produced their writ, and the earl's plea was promptly dismissed.[97] The story is an attractive one, even if it does suggest that the king was prepared on occasion to cut through the knots of legal procedure in a distinctly questionable manner.

Some instances show that where his own interests were concerned,

[96] Ibid., i, 65–6; ii, 20–3.

[97] *Historiae Anglicanae Scriptores Varii*, ed. J. Sparke (1724), 148–9. The story names William de Woodford as the monk with legal expertise, and *CPR 1281–92*, 257–8, confirms the likelihood of this. However, the story has it that the time on the writ was altered, rather than the date, but writs did not, of course, specify the time of issue. The record of the case is in Just. 1/620, mm. 18d, 38d. The abbot in fact claimed that he need not answer the earl without consulting the king, as the matter – a claim to the manor of Bigging – involved the interpretation of a royal charter, issued by King Edgar.

the king was certainly prepared to manipulate or ignore the law. The matter of the inheritance of Aveline de Forz is one, and at the very end of the reign, the way in which Edward blocked a case brought against Walter Langton by John de Ferrers, eventually giving the treasurer a pardon which effectively admitted that Ferrers' case was well-founded, is another.[98] Yet Edward did not ride rough-shod over law and custom in many cases, and his political opponents in 1297 and later did not accuse him of doing so. A eulogy written on his death praised him for his qualities as a judge and legislator, and in particular for his care towards the poor and unfortunate, and there must have been a good many of his subjects who did regard him in such a light.[99] In 1297 a case came up in London of debt between two men, Roger of York and Richard of Montpellier. The sum involved was only 36s, and the sheriffs failed to implement the judgement in Roger's favour. The court roll records the king's anger and astonishment at this, a reaction entirely typical of the man.[100]

The legislative achievement was without doubt one of the elements which went to make Edward's reign a great one. It would be dangerous to impute too high a purpose to the king: although the statute of *Quia Emptores* was to help transform the feudal landholding structure of the realm, all that was intended in 1290 was the correction of an obvious wrong. The stress laid by legal historians, interested in the development of 'case', on clause 24 of the statute of Westminster II would surely have astonished those who drafted it. The provision of that same great statute dealing with conditional gifts had an effect on the aristocratic land market in the long term which could hardly have been anticipated in 1285. It would not be right, on the other hand, to adopt a cynical approach, and to assume that the legal reforms of Edward's reign were merely a device to draw cases, and with them profits, into the king's court.[101] The purpose was to make the law more efficient, to make justice speedier by introducing improved procedures, and to correct errors and abuses. A wide range of grievances were met in the statutes, some of them revealed by inquiries, others by complaints, and

---

[98] McFarlane, *Nobility of Later Medieval England*, 255–7.

[99] John of London, in *Chronicles of the Reigns of Edward I and II*, ed. Stubbs, 6.

[100] *The Pleas of the Court of King's Bench, Trinity Term, 25 Edward I*, ed. W.P.W. Phillimore (British Record Society, 1898), 229.

[101] This is not to deny that justice could be profitable. It is striking, however, that the exchequer estimate of revenue made in 1284 put income from the courts at no more than £1,000 a year: see above, 237. Much of Edward's legislation was concerned with civil law, and in the 1286 Huntingdon eyre, civil pleas raised little more than £100 at most: *Royal Justice and the English Countryside*, ed. deWindt, i, 101. Edward I never attempted to use the courts as a means of raising money in as blatant a fashion as Edward III was to do: Harriss, *King, Parliament and Public Finance*, 405–6.

some as a result of cases in the courts. The process of legislation was a pragmatic one. Edward had no grandiose notion of romanizing English law, of codifying it in accordance with abstract principles. The common law was too complex for such treatment to be possible in the late thirteenth century, and what Edward and his advisers did was far more effective than any codification could possibly have been. Justinian's legislation had preserved the past: Edward I's created openings for the future.

Chapter 11

THE DUKE OF AQUITAINE, 1273–94

For all that he bore an English name, Edward I was much more than an English king. His royal ancestors were by tradition buried in the Angevin abbey of Fontevrault. His mother was of Savoyard descent, and his queen was of the Castilian royal house. There was a strongly cosmopolitan character to his entourage, typified by such men as Otto de Grandson, Geoffrey de Geneville, Count Amadeus of Savoy and John of Brittany. Edward was, as his title proclaimed, duke of Aquitaine and lord of Ireland, as well as king of England. Ireland was never particularly important to Edward, who, like so many kings, never went there. Gascony, the land that was his by right of his title of duke of Aquitaine, was a very different matter.[1] The duchy had been very important to him in his early career. Not only had he been there in 1254–5, but he returned in the winter of 1260–1, and was there again in the following autumn. He may well have visited it again in 1262.[2] It was in Gascony that Edward had his first taste of political power, and it was to Gascony that Edward first directed his attention on his return from crusade in 1273, coming back to England only in 1274. He went there again from 1286 to 1289. Edward's rule in Gascony provides interesting parallels and contrasts to his policies in England, and helps to show what general principles of government may have been behind his style of rule.

Gascony was an immense contrast to England. For all that the duchy had been in English hands since the marriage of Eleanor of Aquitaine and Henry II, it had never experienced the same sort of centralized government that existed in England. Noble society was highly individualistic and competitive, as a result partly of a tradition of partible inheritance and of the fact that much land was not held under terms of feudal tenure. There were a few great lords, such as Gaston de Béarn or

[1] In the thirteenth century the terms Aquitaine, Guyenne and Gascony were effectively synonymous. The English had, by 1224, lost most of the northern part of the old duchy of Aquitaine, but the title of duke of Aquitaine was not given up. The term Gascony (*Vasconia*) was usually used to designate the territory held by the English in south-western France. See Trabut-Cussac, *L'administration anglaise en Gascogne*, xi.

[2] See the itinerary in J.R. Studd's thesis, 'A Catalogue of the Acts of the Lord Edward, 1254–1272'.

Amanieu d'Albret, and major ecclesiastical estates, such as that of the archbishopric of Bordeaux, but in general this was a land of fragmented lordship, with a large but often impoverished aristocracy. The great towns of Bordeaux and Bayonne were wealthy and independent-minded, and in the former, the constant feuding of the Colomb and Soler factions created an instability akin to that of many Italian cities. The wealth of Gascony was largely provided by the wine trade, with the bulk of exports going through Bordeaux, whose excellent communications inland by river provided access to a wide hinterland.

The duchy was not easy to rule, as Edward appreciated. In 1278 he fell into the temptation of thinking in terms of national characteristics, when he described his Gascon subjects as notorious for their changeableness, never adhering to promises that they made.[3] There was little sense of unity between Gascony and England. Gascony was not a colony which accepted English laws and administrative methods, and Gascons were clearly regarded as aliens in England. On one occasion the exchequer had to be sharply reminded to treat Gascon merchants politely, since they were Edward's subjects just as much as Englishmen were.[4]

An essential difference between Gascony and Edward's other dominions was that it was held as a fief from the French throne, as had been agreed in the Treaty of Paris of 1259. This meant that there was always the possibility of French interference in Gascon affairs, particularly in legal matters. Discontented Gascons who felt that they had not obtained justice could, and often did, appeal to the *parlement* of Paris. Edward's authority was thus much less complete than it was in England, and his policies had to be tempered accordingly.

Save for the relatively brief periods when Edward was himself in Gascony, the duchy was ruled by men acting on his behalf. Normally the chief official was the seneschal, who had judicial authority and political power, while the finances were in the charge of the constable of Bordeaux. At some periods a royal lieutenant was appointed, to act as the king's deputy. At the same time, much attention was given to Gascon affairs by the government in England. Whereas, in the case of Ireland, there was a separate Irish chancery which issued letters in the king's name, as there was for Wales after 1284, and for Scotland when it was under English control, many documents dealing with Gascon matters were issued by the English chancery, and enrolled on special Gascon rolls. Gascons petitioned parliament in considerable numbers, and from at least 1290 there were separate auditors of petitions for England, Ireland and Gascony. The duchy may have been distant from

---

[3] *Foedera*, I, ii, 554.
[4] *Documents 1297-8*, 150.

England, but the constant comings and goings of Gascons at Westminster meant that the king was never out of touch with affairs there.
Of course, as well as the Gascon writs and letters issued by the English
chancery under the great seal, there were many documents issued
locally by the lieutenants and seneschals, but these were in their own
names, not that of the king. This was very possibly, it has been argued,
a result of French feudal suzerainty. If appeals were to go to the
parlement of Paris, then it was better that they should be against
decisions of the seneschal, rather than involving Edward directly, as
this might lead to the embarrassing possibility of his being summoned
to appear in the French court.[5]

When Edward left Paris in the course of his return journey from the
crusade in 1273, he turned south to Gascony, rather than going to
England to be crowned king. It was the activities of the greatest Gascon
noble, Gaston de Béarn, that led to this decision. It had been intended
that Gaston should go on the crusade with Edward, but the plan had
fallen through. The marriage of Gaston's daughter Constance to
Edward's cousin Henry of Almain in 1270 had been designed to cement
the links between the English crown and the Gascon noble, but Henry's
murder at Viterbo, in the same year, put paid to that. In 1273 Gaston
refused a summons to appear in the seneschal of Gascony's court to
answer charges against him. It may be that he was offended by the
aggressive policies of the newly appointed seneschal, Luke de Tany, or
that he deliberately chose to reassert his independence at the start of a
new reign. When Edward arrived in Gascony, Gaston did not come to
perform homage to him at St Sever along with other magnates. Instead,
he threw a royal envoy into prison. Edward did not hesitate, and in a
swift military action captured Gaston, who promised to accept the
judgement issued against him at St Sever, handed over his lands and
castles, and promised not to leave the royal court. He promptly did
exactly that, and returned to Orthez in defiance of the king.

Edward was careful to act in accordance with the law. A court was
held, and it was decided that if Gaston de Béarn disobeyed one final
summons, then the king could march against him. The summons was
duly rejected, and an army assembled at the start of November 1273.
Gaston's daughter Constance surrendered at the end of the month.
Gaston's own surrender was soon negotiated, but no sooner was it
agreed than he appealed to Philip III of France, the feudal overlord of
Gascony. Legal resistance served him better than military. He
appeared as plaintiff before the French king, charging Edward and his
officials with damages committed in Béarn. The matter was far from

---

[5] P. Chaplais, 'The Chancery of Guyenne', *Essays in Medieval Diplomacy and Administration* (1981), VIII, 61–7.

settled by the time that Edward left Gascony for England in the late April of 1274. There were dramatic scenes in the *parlement* of Paris when the Gascon lord accused Edward of treason and false judgement, and demanded that the matter be settled by single combat. A letter from Giles de Noaillan survives, asking that he should be allowed to champion the king, but in the event no judicial duel took place. After a lengthy series of adjournments, the influence of Edward's aunt, Queen Margaret of France, and careful negotiation by Otto de Grandson and Robert Burnell, led to agreement with Gaston de Béarn in 1278.[6]

From the late 1270s until his death in 1290, Gaston de Béarn caused Edward no more trouble. The English king was more successful in dealing with him than with others whom he regarded as rebellious vassals, notably Llywelyn of Wales and John Balliol, king of Scots. The position of a great lord on the frontiers of Gascony, with an ultimate overlord in the form of the king of France, was very different, however, from that of subordinate rulers within the British Isles. Edward had to be particularly careful in this case to tread within the bounds imposed by law and custom, while Gaston had to compare the merits of subordination to Edward and to Philip. The affair is one, however, in which Edward displayed considerable skill.

On his first visit to Gascony as king Edward was concerned with much more than the affair of Gaston de Béarn. He was naturally anxious to reassert and define his powers of lordship. At St Sever, in September 1273, he asked the ninety lords present to set out the feudal duties which they owed him. This they could not do, probably not as a result of recalcitrance, but out of ignorance. A survey of the feudal obligations of the duchy had been planned in 1259, but had never taken place. Edward now began a general inquiry, but the task proved difficult. In late February 1274, in a proclamation at Lectoure, south of Agen, he asked all his tenants in the region to come before him to make their claims, but none appeared, for this was a frontier district, where allegiance was uncertain. There was much trouble at Bazas, where two of Luke de Tany's squires were killed in a scuffle, and the town gates were locked to keep Luke out. Nevertheless, massive returns known as the *Recognitiones Feudorum* were eventually drawn up, though the process was not complete by the time of Edward's departure for England in 1274.

There is an obvious temptation to compare this Gascon inquiry with that in England which yielded the Hundred Rolls, but it was in fact

---

[6] The affair is summarized by Powicke, *Thirteenth Century*, 284–6, largely relying on Trabut-Cussac's work. See Trabut-Cussac, *L'administration anglaise en Gascogne*, 42–4, 49–51; *Foedera*, I, ii, 505–7, 511–12, 533, 563, 569; *Gascon Register A*, ed. Cuttino, i, no. 21, ii, nos 83, 86, 299.

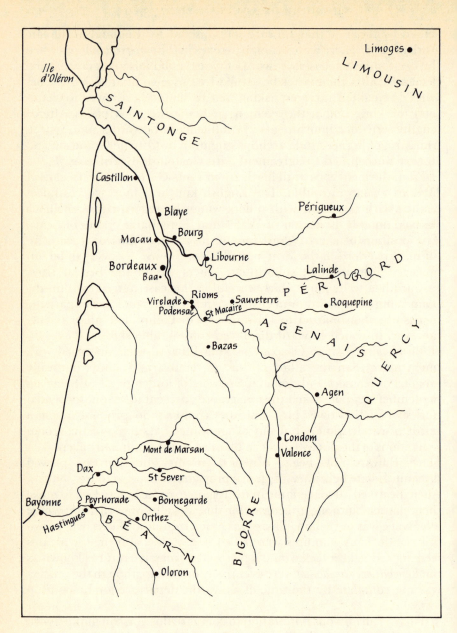

4. Gascony

very dissimilar. It may have been based on an inquiry conducted by Alphonse of Poitiers in 1259 into his fiefs. It was not concerned with taxation, or official wrongdoings, but was simply a survey of feudal lordship. As such, it turned up some very strange services. One family were bound to prepare a meal for the king and ten knights, which if not otherwise specified was to consist of beef, pork, chicken, onion and cauliflower. If one of the family was a knight, then he was to serve the dinner wearing red shoes with silver spurs. More inexplicably still, one tenant had to go with the king to a particular oak tree, with a cartload of firewood drawn by two tail-less oxen. He was then to set fire to the tree, and let it be completely burned unless the two oxen could make their escape. In general, military service was light and ill-defined, particularly in the case of the great nobles. The great inquiry probably yielded few tangible benefits for the crown, but it did have the important effect of bringing home to the Gascon nobles and townspeople the fact that Edward was their feudal lord.[7]

Shortly after setting out on his return journey to England, Edward became involved in the complex question of Limoges. The place had been disputed between the English and French, but Henry III had abandoned his claims there in 1272. Now, the townspeople looked to Edward for support against the French vicomtesse. When he lodged in the abbey there, the keys of the city were brought to him, and he was begged to defend the place. He was moved to tears, but said that he had to obey the king of France, though he would not desert those who swore fealty to him. Some English troops were left in Limoges, and a month after Edward had moved on, William de Valence, with a Gascon force, came there, and mounted a siege of the vicomtesse's stronghold of Aixe. The siege was lifted when a French herald ordered a cease-fire, and summoned the parties to appear before the *parlement* of Paris. In 1275 the vicomtesse won her case: the oaths to Edward were annulled, and he was ordered to pay damages. Final settlement was reached through arbitration in the following year.[8] Edward had undoubtedly exceeded his rights, as a result of the flattery of the citizens of Limoges, but it is striking that in the end he was prepared to accept Philip III's lordship and jurisdiction.

Edward I did not return to Gascony until 1286, though he certainly did not neglect the affairs of the duchy. He left Luke de Tany in charge, as seneschal, but his rule was not a success. There was a succession of difficult legal matters, with appeals to the *parlement* of Paris when de

---

[7] Trabut-Cussac, *L'administration anglaise en Gascogne*, 45–6; E.C. Lodge, *Gascony under English Rule* (1926), 200; *Receuils d'actes relatifs à l'administration des rois d'Angleterre en Guienne*, ed. Bémont (Paris, 1914), 73.
[8] Trabut-Cussac, *L'administration anglaise en Gascogne*, 46–8.

Tany failed to resolve them. A major dispute took place in Dax, where the bishopric had been taken into Edward's hands in 1272 because of a vacancy, and the townspeople resisted de Tany with force. There was also trouble at Bazas. It was clear that action had to be taken, and in 1278 Otto de Grandson and Robert Burnell went to Gascony to investigate the situation, with firm royal instructions to obtain written agreements, reinforced by oaths and penalties, to prevent further trouble.[9]

The royal envoys were in Gascony from May until September 1278. Luke de Tany was removed from office, but he was not disgraced or brought to trial. His failure had been the result of trying to rule with too strong a hand, not of omissions or corruption. Agreement was reached with the men of Dax, and at Bordeaux the right of electing the mayor was restored to the citizens. Peace between the rival city factions was assured by means of marriage alliances. A parliament was held at Bordeaux, at which the men of St Sever and Bazas received guarantees that the construction of new towns, or *bastides*, would not be to their disadvantage. A hearth-tax was granted, the first since 1261, though its collection was to be postponed for a time, in part because of a poor harvest, and in part to prevent the French laying claim to some of the proceeds.[10] The mission of Otto de Grandson and Robert Burnell appears to have been thoroughly successful, and good relations between Edward and his Gascon subjects were fully restored: the incident is one which testifies to the immense political skill of the king's most important advisers.

The new seneschal to replace Luke de Tany was a Savoyard, Jean de Grailly. His links with Edward and with Gascony went back to the early 1260s, and he had, indeed, briefly held the position of seneschal at the end of that decade, before going on crusade. By the late 1270s he was in a strong position, holding important estates in Gascony. His task as seneschal was not to be an easy one. The addition of the Agenais to the Gascon lands in 1279, as a result of the treaty of Amiens, increased the burden of his office. He was inevitably much involved in litigation at the *parlement* of Paris. The complex matter of the succession to the county of Bigorre proved very troublesome. The count died in 1283, leaving a host of claimants, including Constance de Béarn. Edward was determined to take the inheritance for himself, and even resorted to the expedient of giving de Grailly superior authority to that he possessed as seneschal, by naming him royal lieutenant, and nominating John de Vaux as seneschal. Rebellion threatened over the question of Bigorre, but was averted when Constance was persuaded to go to England and make her peace with Edward. In the end, rather ironically, it was the

[9] Ibid., 52–6; *Foedera*, II, ii, 554.
[10] Trabut-Cussac, *L'administration anglaise en Gascogne*, 57–8, 325–6.

8. The north-east tower at Flint castle.

9. Rhuddlan castle, viewed from across the river Clywd,
showing one of the two twin-towered gatehouses.

10. Conwy castle, seen from the town, showing the main entrance.

11. Caernarfon castle, showing the southern facade,
with the Eagle Tower on the left.

12. Harlech castle, showing the eastern front with the great twin-towered gatehouse.

13. Beaumaris castle in Anglesey, showing the moat, outer walls and inner ward behind.

longtain vonatge. qui souffrra de porter seulemet ong
sae de soye a vng ymatge de saint george pendat a icellui.
Aussi se ledit colier doz auoit besoing de reparacion il porra
estre mis en la main de louurier iusques a ce quil soit
repare. Lequel colier aussi ne pourra estre enrichy de
pierres ou daultres choses reserue ses ymatge qui pourra
estre garny au plaisir du cheualier. Et aussi ne pourra
estre ledit colier vendu engaitge donne ne aliene pour
necessite ou cause quelconque que ce soit

Alexander Rex Scocie   Lewellin princeps wallie

14. A sixteenth-century imaginary reconstruction of parliament under Edward I, showing the king flanked by Alexander III of Scotland and Llywelyn ap Gruffydd of Wales, a situation which never in fact occurred. (Royal Library, Windsor Castle, Wriothesley MS, quire B)

claim of Philip IV's queen, Jeanne de Navarre, which was to be successful in the early 1290s.[11]

At a more local level, Jean de Grailly was involved in settling a remarkable dispute between the bishop of Bayonne and the civic authorities. In 1279 an adulterous couple were being paraded naked, bound together with a rope, as was apparently customary in such cases, when a clerk, Menald d'Ax, who it was claimed had also slept with the woman concerned, attacked the man, and cut the rope with his sword. Menald was promptly imprisoned in the castle of Bayonne, his right hand was cut off and then publicly displayed on a gibbet near the cathedral. The bishop objected vigorously to what he considered to be an invasion of his rights of jurisdiction, and his palace was attacked and entered by adherents of the mayor. The bishop wished to take the whole matter to the papal curia, while de Grailly was anxious to preserve Edward's rights of jurisdiction. He wrote a lengthy report to the king, and eventually the matter was resolved by royal arbitration.[12]

In 1285 Bonet de St Quentin, an experienced legal expert who had acted as Edward's proctor in the *parlement* of Paris, was sent to Gascony to investigate abuses, though with what results is not known.[13] There were obviously considerable problems arising from Jean de Grailly's rule, and his last mention as seneschal of Gascony in the English records was in March 1286. The arrival of the king himself in the duchy in the summer of that year meant that, for the time being, there was no need for a seneschal. De Grailly was not at first in disgrace, but was employed on a diplomatic mission to Aragon. It was only after his return from Spain, in 1287, that he was put on trial before a powerful commission, presided over by the bishop of Norwich, and including Robert Burnell, the earl of Lincoln, John de Vescy and Otto de Grandson. He was found guilty of misappropriating royal rights of justice in St Emilion and elsewhere, and his Gascon career came to an end. Edward does not seem to have punished him severely, however, and he fought at Acre in 1290, alongside Otto de Grandson, his compatriot, and reappeared in Edward's service in the Scottish campaign of 1296.[14]

On his second visit to Gascony since his accession, which lasted from the autumn of 1286 until the summer of 1289, Edward was much preoccupied with questions of international politics, especially the release of Charles of Salerno from captivity in Aragon.[15] The opportunity was also taken for a major reorganization of the government of the

[11] Ibid., 72-7.

[12] *Gascon Register A*, ed. Cuttino, ii, 475-9; *Rôles Gascons*, ii, 127; iii, xxxvi, n.

[13] Trabut-Cussac, *L'administration anglaise en Gascogne*, 77, 232.

[14] Jean de Grailly's career is discussed by Bémont in *Rôles Gascons*, iii, xxxiii-xlvii. His presence in Scotland in 1296 was reported by Cotton, 312.

[15] Below, 323-6. For Edward's itinerary during his stay in Gascony, see J.P.

duchy. An investigation of feudal obligations in the Agenais, along the lines of that of 1273–4, was carried out. A succession of urban charters was issued, notably to the king's new foundations. The Jews were expelled from the duchy in the spring of 1287, a move possibly linked with Edward's taking the cross for the second time. Some new lands were purchased for the crown: there was remarkably little ducal demesne in Gascony, and estates were needed, in particular for the new *bastides* that were created at Bonnegarde and elsewhere.[16] The major reforming enterprise came shortly before Edward left Gascony, after the various inquiries had been completed, and the king and his officials had gained some real experience of how the duchy worked. A council was held at Condom in March 1289, where ordinances for the government of the duchy were drawn up. These were then promulgated at a parliament held at Libourne in May and June.

The Ordinances for the rule of Gascony were quite unlike the statutes issued in England.[17] No attempt was made to change substantive law, but much was done to summarize and systematize existing administrative practice. There was to be a sharp division between the role of the seneschal, which was judicial, military and political, and that of the constable of Bordeaux, in charge of the finances. Officials were to be paid at set rates, in an obvious move against corruption: the seneschal was allocated an annual fee of 2,000 *livres* of Bordeaux money. There was to be an appeal justice permanently at Bordeaux, and a proctor to look after the affairs of the duchy in the *parlement* of Paris. The document even specified the appointment of an engineer to supervise the castles of the duchy, with an armourer to supply munitions. Separate ordinances dealt with Saintonge, Périgord, Limousin, Quercy and the Agenais, but in the first four of these, the local sub-seneschals were to be subordinate to the main seneschal of Gascony. The Agenais, however, was not so fully integrated with the rest of Edward's possessions in France. Each of these regions was to have its own proctor in the *parlement* of Paris, although it has been argued that one purpose of the direct subordination of the sub-seneschals to the seneschal of Gascony was to prevent the recent practice of appealing directly from the local level to the *parlement*.[18]

There is little in the Ordinances that obviously reflects English practice, and certainly no attempt to bring Gascon administration into

---

Trabut-Cussac, 'Itinéraire d'Edouard I en France, 1286–89', *BIHR*, xxv (1952), 160–203.

[16] Trabut-Cussac, *L'administration anglaise en Gascogne*, 81–101.

[17] The Ordinances are printed in *Gascon Register A*, ed. Cuttino; see also Powicke, *Thirteenth Century*, 300–5.

[18] P. Chaplais. 'The Chancery of Guyenne', *Essays in Medieval Diplomacy and Administration*, VIII, 66–7.

line with that of Wales or Ireland. The problems that Edward faced in Gascony were very different: above all, what was needed was to regularize and make more efficient the administrative and judicial system, so as to prevent, or at least limit, the practice of discontented litigants appealing to the *parlement* of Paris against judgements in the Gascon courts. The use of *defensores* to look after royal interests was hardly needed elsewhere in Edward's dominions. The most that there was in common between these Gascon Ordinances and Edward's reforms in England and Wales was a sense of providing order and system where there had previously been confusion.

Edward's stay in Gascony did not see all the problems of the duchy resolved, and in some ways it created fresh difficulties. The financial situation had never been as satisfactory as that in England. The currency did not have the stability of English sterling, and it was not possible to institute any system of regular taxation. Proceeds from the sale of local offices, from tolls and from rights of jurisdiction brought in some profits, but the main resource was the customs on wine exports. The structure of duties was complex, and became more so after negotiations conducted by Jean de Grailly in 1284, which allowed many merchants from the French lands surrounding Gascony to export their wine from Bordeaux at preferential rates.[19] The Gascon revenues were quite inadequate for the support of the king during his stay in the duchy. An account of the constable of Bordeaux, Itier d'Angoulême, from June 1289 until November 1290, indicates annual receipts of under £12,000 a year.[20] Between May 1286 and August 1289, Edward incurred a debt approaching £110,000 (380,609 *livres tournois* and £12,632) to his Italian bankers, the Riccardi of Lucca.[21] The only solution was to hand the revenues of the duchy over to them until they were repaid. As a consequence of this, officials were not paid their salaries, and other debts mounted up.

When Edward left Gascony in June 1289, he decided that the form of government set out in the Ordinances was not sufficiently powerful, and that in addition to a seneschal, a royal lieutenant was needed. He appointed Maurice de Craon to this position. He was the son of a half-sister of Henry III, and was hereditary seneschal of Anjou, Maine and Poitou. He had been employed previously as a diplomat in the English cause, and such a man, linked by blood with Edward, and at the same time an important landholder in France, was well placed to

---

[19] Gascon finances are fully discussed by Trabut-Cussac, *L'administration anglaise en Gascogne*, 287–331.

[20] E 159/66, m. 41. The precise breakdown of Itier's receipts was as follows: 20,036*li.* 0s 7½d black *tournois*; 22,161*li.* 4s 5d old Bordeaux money (*chipotenses*); 6,559*li.* 14s 3d new Bordeaux money.

[21] Trabut-Cussac, op. cit., 104; *CPR 1281–92*, 318.

defuse any possible problems that might arise between the English and
Philip IV of France. It was unfortunate that he died in 1293, shortly
before the Anglo-French crisis broke.[22]

John de Havering, the seneschal appointed in 1289, was not a man of
great standing. An Essex knight with judicial and administrative experience in England, he did not prove to be a good choice.[23] At the very
start of his period of office, his intervention in the affairs of Bordeaux,
before he had sworn to observe the customs of the city, caused a major
crisis, in the course of which a group of citizens appealed to the French
parlement. This in turn provoked the authorities in England to confiscate
the wine that they had exported but not yet sold. Only a year after the
Ordinances had been promulgated at Libourne, Edward was so
alarmed at reports that officials in Gascony were not obeying orders
that an inquiry was ordered. He complained that sub-seneschals were
using the revenues from their offices for their own private ends. It is
clear that there was a lack of proper control over the lower officials, and
that the practice of sale of office encouraged corruption and other
abuses. A decision in 1291, that posts would not necessarily go to the
highest bidder, but that a good man might be retained in office, did not
make a marked difference to the situation. In the early 1290s, many of
the inhabitants of the Ile d'Oléron fled to escape the exactions of the
local prévot, Richard of Winchester.[24] When the crisis came in 1294, and
the French attempted to confiscate the duchy of Gascony, the English
administration, and Gascons themselves, were not in good heart.

One element of Edward's policy in Gascony which was strikingly
successful, was the creation of the bastides. The founding of new towns
was a feature of his activities in Wales, while New Winchelsea and
Kingston upon Hull were two important English foundations. The
scale of this policy was very much greater in Gascony, however, with
over fifty bastides created in the course of the reign.

The bastides were new towns, characterized for the most part by a
quadrilateral plan, with a central market place, often with attractive
arcades or cornières round it. The crown was involved in the foundation
of about three-quarters of these towns, but of these, only a half were
solely royal foundations. In the case of the now-vanished bastide of Baa,
the site was purchased from the lord of Blaye for 3,000 livres of local
currency (£547) in the winter of 1286–7, and Gerard de Turri was sent
to plan the new town. Later, Richard of Eastham was paid £7 12s for

[22] Rôles Gascons, ed. Bémont, iii, l–liii.
[23] Ibid., iii, liii–lxi. Trabut-Cussac, op. cit., 143n., explains that Bémont was wrong
to suspect the existence of two men of the same name.
[24] Trabut-Cussac, L'administration anglaise en Gascogne, 179, 189, 203–4; Rôles Gascons,
ii, no. 1791; iii, no. 1966.

expenses on the works there, and the king himself paid for drinks for the men when he visited the site.[25] In many cases, *bastides* were founded by means of partnership agreements with local lords. They would provide the site, and the king would give the new town his protection and grant it liberties. Profits would then be shared. This was not a novel system, but one which had been employed extensively by Alphonse of Poitiers in nearby French territory: it was well-suited to a place where there was little royal demesne land.[26]

It is tempting to assume that the creation of the *bastides* was intended to provide for the defence of the duchy of Gascony against the French. Yet two-thirds of them had no defences, and where defences did exist, they were normally added under Edward I I or Edward I I I. The great majority were founded during the period of relatively good relations between England and France, and many were sited on good land, low-lying and near rivers, well-suited to commerce but of little military value.[27] There were exceptions: at Bonnegarde the *bastide* was dominated by the royal castle, but because of its site never became viable in commercial terms. One motive for creating *bastides* was to provide administrative centres: in 1290 Edward ordered the construction of one to serve in this way for Quercy, and a high proportion of the *baillages* of the duchy were centred upon *bastides*.[28] Lords regarded the creation of *bastides* as a weapon against lawlessness: in 1305 Arnaud-Loup of Estibeaux petitioned Edward, asking for his agreement to a joint foundation for 2,000 inhabitants, as a means of pacifying the local populace.[29] The main purpose of the *bastides*, however, was undoubtedly economic. The new towns would yield valuable rents, and other dues, and the foundations in Gascony were part of a wider movement of creating new urban settlements throughout south-west France.

The new *bastides* were not always welcome. At Sauveterre de Guyenne, work had to be halted and a lengthy inquiry held, with the new settlers stressing the economic potential of the place, as did the local abbot, while neighbouring lords and towns feared loss of business to the new community. Eventually work was allowed to continue. Elsewhere orders had to be issued to prevent villeins being taken into *bastides*, so as to protect the interests of local nobles. In 1282, the abbey of Condom received a promise that no new towns would be founded in

---

[25] E 36/201, ff.15, 33, 34. The question of Baa is fully discussed by J.P. Trabut-Cussac, 'Date, fondation et identification de la bastide de Baa', *Revue Historique de Bordeaux*, n.s. x (1961), 133–44.

[26] Beresford, *New Towns of the Middle Ages*, 99–100.

[27] Ibid., 184–6, 361; C. Higounet, 'Bastides et Frontières', *Le Moyen Age*, liv (1948), 113–21; J.P. Trabut-Cussac, 'Bastides ou Forteresses?', *Le Moyen Age*, lx (1954), 81–135.

[28] Beresford, *New Towns of the Middle Ages*, 362.

[29] Ibid., 84.

the Condomais without their agreement. Edward himself was prepared to object to seigneurial foundations when these threatened his own interests.[30]

Edward's direct role in the foundation of the *bastides* should not be exaggerated. For the most part, they were the work of his officials, as a petition from Bertrand de Panisseau shows. He claimed that he had built the *bastide* of Roquepine in 1283, that he was responsible for Molières in the same period, and had founded Montpazier in 1285. In addition, he had done much to improve Lalinde.[31] Yet for all that the Gascon *bastides* were largely the work of Gascons, and the product of a wider movement of urban creation in south-western France, rather than of English policies, there were interesting connections between the new towns in the duchy and those in Britain. Henry le Waleys served as mayor both of London and of Bordeaux, worked on the planning of the new town at Winchelsea, and advised the king on the rebuilding of Berwick upon Tweed. In 1284 he was appointed to farm the revenues of six of the new Gascon *bastides*, and his career thus links Edward's urban policies in an intriguing way.[32] The names of some of the new *bastides*, too, are a roll-call of great men of Edward's reign, and emphasize the English role in Gascony: Libourne (Leyburn): Baa (Bath, for Robert Burnell, bishop of Bath and Wells); Hastingues (Hastings); Nichole (the earl of Lincoln): Valence (William de Valence).

Although the *bastides* were not founded, in the majority of cases, for military purposes, it would be wrong to assume that Edward neglected the question of the defence of the duchy. There were relatively few castles in Gascony under his control, and it is clear that this was a situation he was determined to remedy. In 1274 Luke de Tany was ordered to build a new stone castle near Bordeaux. Jean de Grailly was given permission in 1279 to fortify and build castles. In 1281 the constable of Bordeaux was told to repair the castle at Saintes, and all other royal castles in the duchy. After the Agenais was taken over in 1279, a new castle was founded at Sauveterre-la-Lemance, and work on defences undertaken elsewhere. Attempts were made to acquire existing fortresses: in 1283 Edward bought Talmont for 1,322 *livres tournois*, and in 1290 the motte of Tontoulon, near Bazas, was acquired for 3,500 *livres* of Bordeaux. Edward had hoped for more acquisitions, but his designs on Lourdes and Gramont in 1274 came to nothing, and he failed later to gain Montferrand, near Bordeaux. His financial resources in Gascony were inadequate for a programme of castle-building such as that undertaken in Wales, and it was symptomatic of

    [30] Ibid., 235–6, 243.
    [31] Ibid., 96–7; Trabut-Cussac, *L'administration anglaise en Gascogne*, 203, shows that Panisseau was *bailli* at Montpazier, Lalinde and Molières.
    [32] Beresford, *New Towns of the Middle Ages*, 7–9, 29; Williams, *Medieval London*, 333–4.

this that the castle planned near Bordeaux in 1274 was never built, and that fortifications ordered at Miramont in Tursan in the same year were only carried out in earth and timber. He was, however, able to increase his military authority by means of partnership agreements akin to those involving *bastides*, and could exercise some control over the defensive resources of the duchy by means of his power to license men to build or refortify castles. By the early 1290s, he controlled about twenty major castles in Gascony, and many minor defensive sites and walled towns.[33]

It would be a mistake to try to draw close parallels between Edward's government in Gascony and his practices in England. The very different local customs, the very structure of society, made it impossible to pursue the same policies in duchy and kingdom. The drive of Edward's legal reforms, and the investigation of franchises by means of *Quo Warranto*, have no real counterpart in Gascony. The Gascon feudal inquiry of 1273–4 has greater similarities to French precedents than to the inquests conducted by Edward's officials in England. Even when documents such as licences to construct castles were issued, they were very different in England and Gascony, for in the latter case Edward was able to insist on the French custom of 'rendability', requiring that the castle should be handed over to him on request.[34]

It is true that some of Edward's English ministers, notably Robert Burnell, played a leading role in the reorganization of Gascony in the later 1280s, but their work shows that they were fully capable of appreciating the differences between Gascony and England, and there was no attempt to impose standardized and inappropriate solutions. The Angevin empire, so called, had never possessed administrative unity, and Edward did not seek a revolutionary change in the interrelationship of his various lands. What he and his officials did was sufficient to ensure that English rule over the duchy of Gascony was far more effective in the first part of his reign than it had ever been before, and indeed than it ever was to be again. He had not, however, resolved all the problems. The nobility still had great independence of spirit, and many of the citizens of Bordeaux resented English rule. In military terms the duchy lacked adequate defences against possible French attack. The events of 1294 and the succeeding years were to show how fragile the English hold on Gascony still was.

[33] J. Gardelles, *Les Châteaux du Moyen Age dans la France du sud-ouest: la Gascogne Anglaise de 1216 à 1327* (Geneva, 1972), 28–33.

[34] *Gascon Register A*, ed. Cuttino, ii, 546. For 'rendability' in general, see C.L.H. Coulson, 'Rendability and Castellation in Medieval France', *Château Gaillard*, vi (1972), 59–67.

Chapter 12

DIPLOMACY, 1274–94

Edward I was king of England, but in some senses he was not an English king. In terms of descent he was largely French, with an important Savoyard element on his mother's side. He retained strong family connections with France, notably through his aunt Margaret, widow of Louis IX. His marriage to Eleanor of Castile gave him an involvement in the affairs of the Iberian peninsula. The cultural world in which he was brought up was the international one of chivalric society, and such was his reputation that rulers in the Low Countries requested him to knight their sons. Even Italians asked Edward to do them this honour.[1] Edward's crusade had done much to foster his reputation, and he was widely looked to as the man most likely to redeem the situation in the East, by leading a successful expedition against the infidel. In the 1280s, in particular, Edward saw himself as playing a central part in the ordering of European affairs, a necessary task if a further crusade was to be mounted.

International diplomacy in this period was a skilled and difficult art. There were complex cross-currents of dynastic and commercial rivalries, feudal relationships and marriage ties. The concerns of the papacy had to be considered, as well as those of secular powers. Allies might be bought by subsidies, or obtained by means of marriage alliances, the mortar with which the building blocks of foreign policy were cemented together. There were many problems. Children might die, or might prove to be too closely related for a marriage alliance to meet with the approval of the church. It might prove impossible to fulfil the promises to pay subsidies, or rival powers might step in with a higher bid. The physical problems facing medieval diplomats, in terms of travel and communications, were also themselves considerable.

There were no resident ambassadors in this period, so each fresh initiative required a new embassy, which had to be provided with the proper letters of accreditation and protection. In 1278, documents given to envoys going to negotiate the marriage of Edward's daughter Joan to Hartmann of Habsburg were unsatisfactory. The word 'marks' had been omitted, where it should have been stated that the dowry

---

[1] *Foedera*, I, ii, 529; *Documents 1297–8*, 166–7.

should be of 10,000 marks. The letters of credence were sealed close, and it was considered by Otto de Grandson's brother, the bishop of Verdun, that they should have been made out in patent form, so that all could read them. The embassy did not have letters authorizing it to give and accept sureties, and this defect had to be made good.[2]

Once the documentation was complete, ambassadors faced the problems of travel. Roads were bad, robbery frequent, maps inadequate or non-existent. An account submitted by Otto de Grandson for a mission to the Roman curia, which lasted from May 1289 until March 1290, reveals, in its cold financial details, something of the hardships and difficulties Edward's diplomats faced. Otto was accompanied by William de Hotham, and a substantial entourage, with at times as many as sixty horses. The men needed food and other necessities bought, and shoes, harness, saddle-cloths, fodder and medicaments were needed for the horses. Disease struck the party as they crossed the Alps, and Edmund de Bonvillars and three servants died. Funerals had to be organized and paid for. In the Alps the horses had to be led, and local mounts, perhaps mules, hired to carry the party and their baggage up the steep paths. When they reached Rome, one of the party, Ralph le Alemaunt suffered from what was probably an attack of gastro-enteritis, and had the further misfortune of breaking his arm. The financing of the expedition was not easy, for at least twelve different local currencies had to be used, as well as gold florins and silver *tournois*.[3]

The problems facing Otto de Grandson and his entourage were slight when compared to those that Geoffrey de Langley and his companions had to overcome when they travelled with a message from Edward I to the Il-Khan of Persia in 1292. The accounts submitted to the exchequer are tantalizingly mundane, but the purchase at Trebizond, on the Black Sea, of cotton for tents, and of parasols, indicates something of the problems presented by the middle-eastern climate. Language was not a problem for envoys in Europe, where Latin and French could be used, but Langley and his companions had to hire interpreters. They took with them, as a gift for the Il-Khan, some highly prized gerfalcons, which were a good deal easier to transport than the leopard which they brought back as a present for Edward. The diet recorded in the remarkably complete accounts of this embassy was, at least to modern eyes, much better than Langley would have enjoyed in England, with ample fruit, dairy produce, preserved ox-tongue, fresh beans, and a range of spices and sauces.[4]

[2] P. Chaplais, *English Medieval Diplomatic Practice* (1982) II, ii, 719–20.
[3] *Documents illustrative of the History of Scotland*, ed. J. Stevenson (1870), i, 134–8.
[4] C. Desimoni, 'I Conti dell' Ambasciate al Chan di Persia nell mccxcii', *Atti delle Società Ligure de Storia Patria*, xiii (1879), 540–698.

Once envoys reached their destination, they might find their task very daunting. Raymond des Pins had a very difficult time in a hostile papal curia in 1300. He was ill for a time, and could not obtain an answer to his requests from the papal authorities. He could find only one friend prepared to assist him, and to make matters worse, he ran out of money, and found it impossible to borrow any, which, as he pointed out, was to Edward's shame.[5] As for Geoffrey de Langley and his mission to the East, he found when he arrived that the Il-Khan Arghun whom he had gone to see had died: as one Arab writer put it, 'The parakeet of the soul of the Il-Khan left the cage of his body to go and dwell among the peacocks of the palace of the sublime garden.'[6] Arghun's successor Gaikhatu was extremely difficult to locate, and it appears that the embassy came back to England virtually empty-handed.

Relations with France form one dominant theme in English diplomacy under Edward I. Under the terms of the Treaty of Paris of 1259, Henry III had abandoned his claims to Normandy, Anjou, Maine, Touraine and Poitou, all part of the old Angevin empire and lost under King John. Certain territorial concessions to the English were made in the south-west, and Henry had agreed that he would perform homage for Gascony to the French king. Previously, Gascony had been held free of feudal obligation towards the French crown; it now became a fief, and Louis IX had extended the bounds of his lordship from the Garonne to the Pyrenees.[7] Homage had to be performed only on the accession of a new king in either England or France. On Louis IX's death in 1271, Henry III was not fit to journey to perform the ceremony to Philip III. Edward I, on his return from crusade, made no difficulties about doing homage to Philip when he was in Paris in 1273. Some people considered that the phraseology Edward used, 'Lord king, I do homage to you for all the lands I ought to hold from you', implied a revival of English claims to Normandy, but it is likely that this was simply the form of homage employed by Henry III, and that the implication that there were lands which the English should, but did not, hold was no more than a reference to the territorial concessions promised in the Treaty of Paris. There were certainly no signs of conflict in 1274: the two kings met as friends and cousins.[8] The fact that Gascony was held

[5] Chaplais, *English Medieval Diplomatic Practice*, II, i, 266–8.

[6] H.H. Howarth, *History of the Mongols* (1888), iii, 343.

[7] P. Chaplais, 'Le traité de Paris de 1259 et l'infeudation de la Gascogne allodiale', *Essays in Medieval Diplomacy and Administration* (1981), II, 121–37.

[8] *Flores*, iii, 31; Chaplais, 'Le duché-pairie de Guyenne', *Essays in Medieval Diplomacy and Administration*, III, 18.

as a fief from the king of France meant that the French could claim rights of jurisdiction in Edward's duchy, and appeals to the *parlement* were certainly encouraged by the French. But such affairs as that of Gaston de Béarn did not cause a breach in Anglo-French relations,[9] and it would be wrong to interpret the situation in the 1270s and 1280s as one where conflict between Edward and the Capetian kings constantly threatened.

During his stay in Gascony in 1273–4, Edward was involved in two sets of marriage negotiations. One plan was to marry his eldest daughter Eleanor to the eldest son of Peter, infante of Aragon. Peter was certainly looking for allies against the French, for his own marriage to Constanza, daughter of Manfred of Sicily, gave him a claim to intervene against Charles of Anjou, conqueror of southern Italy and Sicily. The recent loss of the county of Foix to the French gave him a further motive to look for allies. It is very doubtful if Edward saw the marriage in such anti-French terms, however, and the plan proceeded no further for the time being.[10] The other projected marriage was to be between Edward's son Henry, and Jeanne, daughter and sole heiress of Henry I of Navarre, whose baby son had died tragically when carelessly dropped over the battlements of a castle by his nurse. Henry died in 1274, and Jeanne's mother Blanche took her to the French court for safety, where arrangements were made for her to marry Philip III's son, and eventual successor, Philip. However, this did not end the English interest in the house of Navarre, for the widowed Blanche married Edward I's brother, Edmund of Lancaster. She held the county of Champagne during the minority of her daughter, and this marriage placed one of the great French fiefs under a degree of English control. This match was not a triumph for Edward I's diplomacy, however, but was the work of Louis IX's widow Margaret. Edmund was not much of a politician, nor indeed a military leader, and probably with good reason, he never made much of his position in Champagne. In 1284, he and his wife gave in to French arguments that Jeanne, now all of twelve years old, had come of age, and accepted, in compensation for Champagne, payment of 60,000 *livres* and a dower of five castellanies. Edward clearly regarded the whole business as Edmund's affair, and it never became a source of friction between himself and Philip III of France.[11]

Edward's reluctance to become involved in the affairs of Navarre was

[9] Above, 300–1.
[10] F.D. Swift, 'Marriage Alliance of the Infanta Pedro of Aragon and Edward I of England', *EHR*, v (1890), 326–8; Chaplais, *English Medieval Diplomatic Practice*, II, ii, 469–70.
[11] W.E. Rhodes, 'Edmund earl of Lancaster', *EHR*, x (1895), 213–25; R. Fawtier, *L'Europe occidentale de 1270 à 1380* (Paris, 1940), 266–9; *Foedera*, I, ii, 508.

made clear in 1275, when his father-in-law, Alphonso of Castile, who had his own interests in Navarre, asked to know what his position would be, in case of conflict with the French. Edward duly expressed his readiness to assist Alphonso, but qualified this by stating that he was not prepared to involve himself against the king of France. In 1277 in a further letter to Alphonso, Edward indicated his lack of enthusiasm for war. He was engaged against the Welsh, and expressed his desire to see peace between France and Castile. In view of the close family ties between the English and Castilian royal houses, Edward saw no need for any formal alliance.[12] When a French embassy demanded his personal service against Castile, Edward found himself in an embarrassing position. He had no wish to offend either Philip III or Alphonso X, and replied that he did not want to serve, but that he would do all in his power to settle their quarrel. He was not prepared to go so far as to deny the French king's right to summon him to join his host, and as the war did not materialize, Philip chose to press him no further.[13]

In 1279, outstanding differences between the English and French were the subject of negotiations at Amiens. The Agenais, to the north of Gascony, was one of the districts which should have been ceded to the English under the terms of the Treaty of Paris, once Alphonse of Poitiers' widow died. Quercy and Saintonge were claimed on the same basis. However, Philip III had taken possession of these lands in 1271. Now, at Amiens, he conceded the English right to the Agenais and the southern part of Saintonge, though the issue of Quercy, which was also claimed by Charles of Anjou, was not settled until 1286, when Edward abandoned his claims in return for 3,000 *livres* a year. A further issue was the provision of the Treaty of Paris of 1259 that the English king's vassals in Saintonge, Limousin, Périgord and Quercy should swear to support the French king should the English fail to observe the terms of the agreement. Edward's efforts to implement this clause had been in vain, and Philip now abandoned this demand. In exchange, Edward gave up his claims in the bishoprics of Limoges, Périgord and Quercy.[14]

At the same time the county of Ponthieu, in northern France, came under English rule. Queen Eleanor's mother Jeanne was the daughter of Marie, countess of Ponthieu, and on her death in 1279 the county came by descent to Eleanor, who received it upon payment of a relief of 6,000

---

[12] *Foedera*, I, ii, 540–1.

[13] *Flores*, iii, 48. This passage is dated 1276, but it seems likely that it actually refers to the events of 1277, when there is documentary evidence both for the French summons, and the English response: *Foedera*, I, ii, 607; *Treaty Rolls 1234–1325*, ed. P. Chaplais (1955) no. 177. However Chaplais, 'Le duché-pairie de Guyenne', 19–20, assumes summonses both in 1276 and 1277.

[14] *English Medieval Diplomatic Practice*, ed. Chaplais, II, ii, 621–3; Powicke, *Thirteenth Century*, 289; Trabut-Cussac, *L'administration anglaise en Gascogne*, 61–2.

livres parisis. It was Eleanor, not Edward, who did homage for Ponthieu, but the acquisition did bring the English king, in effect, into an even closer feudal relationship with Philip III.[15]

Further marriage plans were afoot in the late 1270s. In 1277 the German king, Rudolph of Habsburg, authorized envoys to negotiate the marriage of his son Hartmann to Edward's daughter Joan. The scheme was the work of Edward's aunt Margaret, dowager queen of France. Her hope was that Rudolph would endow his son with a revived kingdom of Arles, which lay within the empire, and included Provence. Margaret bitterly resented the fact that she had been ex-cluded from what she regarded as her rightful inheritance in Provence, which had gone to her sister Beatrice, who had married Charles of Anjou. A possible obstacle to Margaret's design was the quarrel be-tween the count of Savoy and Rudolph of Habsburg over lands in what is now western Switzerland: in May 1278 Edward was authorized by Rudolph to make peace between himself and the count. Little came of these elaborate notions. The papacy was negotiating for a marriage alliance between the Habsburgs and the Angevins, and there was more powerful backing for this than there was for Margaret's plan. Her hopes were dashed on a rock in the fog-shrouded Rhine in 1281, on which a boat carrying the young Hartmann was wrecked. He drowned in the accident.[16] On Edward's side, much of the negotiation was the work of the Grandson family. Otto met the German ambassadors in England, James went to Germany to discuss the question of Joan's dower lands, and Gerard, the bishop of Verdun, was deeply involved in the whole affair. Queen Margaret of France was herself of Savoyard descent, of course, and this whole project is in some ways better viewed as an aspect of the foreign policy of Savoy rather than of England.[17]

In 1278 negotiations took place with the duke of Brabant for the marriage of the duke's heir John to Edward's daughter Margaret. Although she was only three at the time, the arrangements were very detailed, providing for a subsidy to be paid by the English, and the allocation of dower by the Brabantines.[18] The marriage was not in fact to take place until 1290. It could be argued that in trying to establish links by marriage with Aragon, with the Habsburgs in Germany, and with Brabant, Edward was attempting an encirclement of France. This is not the way in which contemporaries would have thought about these matters. Edward was doubtless much concerned to provide fitting

[15] H. Johnstone, 'The County of Ponthieu, 1279–1307', *EHR*, xxix (1914), 435–52; Powicke, *Thirteenth Century*, 235.

[16] Ibid., 246–7; *Foedera*, I, ii, 545, 555–7; Cox, *The Eagles of Savoy*, 417–18.

[17] E.R. Clifford, *A Knight of Great Renown* (Chicago, 1961), 59–60.

[18] *Foedera*, I, ii, 549–50.

husbands for his daughters, but there is no indication that he was attempting to put any strategic concept into operation, or that he regarded France and its king as a potential foe. When in 1281 Philip III took exception to the fact that charters issued in Gascony were dated by reference to Edward's regnal years in England, it was decided by the Gascon authorities, after consultation with Edward, that both Philip and Edward should feature in the dating clauses.[19] The issue might have been explosive in other circumstances, but this was not a period when the English considered that French ambitions posed any major threat to their interests. Nor did Edward have ambitions to recover the possessions in France which had been lost under King John.

The decade of the 1280s was dominated to a considerable extent, as far as English diplomatic activity was concerned, by the problems presented by the house of Anjou. Charles of Anjou, the ambitious and unscrupulous younger brother of Louis IX, had established himself in southern Italy and Sicily in the 1260s, when he took advantage of the collapse of the house of Hohenstaufen. In 1282, in the celebrated rising known as the Sicilian Vespers, the people of Palermo turned against their French masters. The rebellion spread, and the Sicilians turned for support to Peter of Aragon, whose queen was a descendant of the Hohenstaufen, and so had a legitimate claim to Sicily and southern Italy. In the subsequent war, Charles of Salerno, Charles of Anjou's son, was captured by the Aragonese in a naval engagement in 1284. Charles of Anjou himself died in the next year. The situation remained critical, as the French planned a major offensive in the form of a crusade against Aragon. The peace of all Europe was threatened, but Edward did all he could to prevent war.

Edward's first involvement with Charles of Salerno came in 1280. There was a difficult situation in Castile, where Alphonso X's second son, Sancho, opposed the claim to be heir to the throne put forward on behalf of the sons of Ferdinand, Alphonso's elder son who had died in 1275. They had the support of the French, but Alphonso reluctantly accepted the decision of his nobility to back Sancho. The English acted as intermediaries: in 1279 William de Valence and Jean de Grailly, acting on Edward's behalf, negotiated a truce, and in the following year this was extended for a year, after Alphonso asked Edward to act again.

---

[19] Ibid., I, ii, 602–3; P. Chaplais, 'La souveraineté du roi de France et le pouvoir législatif en Guyenne au début du xive siecle', *Essays in Medieval Diplomacy and Administration*, V, 453. In practice, the new formula was only regularly used in the Agenais, for in Gascony Edward's subjects continued to date charters simply by reference to his reign.

It was agreed that the kings of Castile and France should meet in Gascony. Then, in July 1280, Alphonso suddenly announced that he had empowered Charles of Salerno to mediate on his behalf with the French. One theory was that this was done out of pique, because Edward had reached agreement with Philip III at Amiens in 1279 without taking account of the Castilian affair. Arrangements went on for the meeting of the kings in Gascony, but Edward presented his apologies to both of them for not being able to proceed at once to the duchy. He was distinctly hostile to Charles of Salerno, for he had lent his support to Simon de Montfort's son Guy, a man Edward could never forgive, above all because of his involvement in the murder of his cousin Henry of Almain. In the event, the negotiations held under the guidance of Charles of Salerno were abortive, and Edward's own hopes of going to Gascony to take charge of the matter again were dashed when the rival kings turned instead to the papacy for mediation. Edward's own concerns were soon shifted to the problem of Wales.[20]

Edward persisted in his policy of neutrality in 1281, when his aunt Margaret, the French dowager queen, planned to create a great alliance directed against the Angevins. She was still pursuing her ambitions in Provence. At a meeting at Mâcon in the autumn, Jean de Grailly was present, along with Edmund of Cornwall. Charles of Salerno wrote indignantly to complain that he gathered that Edward was going to assist Margaret, even to the length of handing over Gascony to her, but this the English king denied. He explained that he was in a difficult position, because his mother, to whom he was devoted, was involved (she backed her sister Margaret), but that his heart was not in the affair. He hoped that papal arbitration might settle the issue. Edward was certainly under considerable pressure from his mother: she wrote to Philip III to seek his assistance in establishing her own rights in Provence, and sought to have the letter sent in Edward's name.[21] It was hard to see how Edward could have remained neutral without giving offence, but he was fortunate. The Welsh war made it impossible for him to consider taking any part in plans for the conquest of Provence, and the news of the Sicilian Vespers at Easter 1282 transformed the whole European situation.

Edward's involvement as a peace-maker in the struggle between the Angevins, based on Naples, and the Aragonese monarchy was only to be expected, but the way in which he was brought in was surprising. Neither Charles of Anjou nor Peter of Aragon had the resources for a

---

[20] These negotiations are conveniently summarized by Trabut-Cussac, *L'administration anglaise en Gascogne*, 67–8, and Powicke, *Thirteenth Century*, 242–5. See also *Foedera*, II, ii, 580–6, 594; *Treaty Rolls*, i, 63–4; *English Medieval Diplomatic Practice*, II, i, 264–6.

[21] *Foedera*, I, ii, 600, 611; Powicke, *Thirteenth Century*, 248.

long-drawn-out war, and in negotiations between the two, the proposal was put forward that the issue should be determined by single combat between the two men. Such proposals were to be common in the fourteenth century, but were often no more than a negotiating ploy, a part of the complex ritual game of diplomacy. In this case, however, both parties appear to have been serious. It was obviously unsuitable, however, that the two men should fight it out singly: Charles was certainly well past his prime as a warrior. So it was decided that each king should appear with a hundred knights, who would fight on their behalf. The venue was fixed, apparently without consulting Edward, at Bordeaux, and the date of 1 June 1283 agreed.

Pope Martin IV was appalled at the prospect of the duel, and did all he could to prevent it, asking Edward to prevent the two kings entering Gascon territory. Although Edward refused to go to supervise the proceedings in person, he was not prepared to go so far as the pope wished. Although he wrote to Charles that 'we could not find it in our heart that we should permit such cruelty to take place before us, nor within our lands', he did allow Jean de Grailly to make the requisite arrangements in Gascony. When the appointed day came, what should have been a climax turned into farce. Peter of Aragon came in disguise with only a few knights, rode early in the morning on the field, had his challenge to the Angevin ruler formally proclaimed and recorded, and claimed victory by default, in the absence of any opponent. Some hours later Charles of Anjou arrived, in great pomp and style, rode round the field, and just like Peter, claimed that the victory was his. No time for the engagement had been fixed, merely date and place, but it has to be suspected that even if an hour had been fixed, some other trick might well have been devised to preserve both the honour and lives of all parties in this quite extraordinary affair.[22]

Was it because of Edward's reputation both for chivalry and as a peacemaker that the participants in this farce had selected Bordeaux for their meeting? It seems rather that there was no realistic alternative. Charles's relationship to Philip III, his nephew, ruled out French territory, and the imperial dominions were too remote. Obviously the duel should take place before a man of high status, and the obvious answer was that it should take place in Gascony, which could be reached quite easily by both men, and which could fairly be seen as neutral ground.

At this time, the question of the marriage of Edward's daughter Eleanor to Peter of Aragon's heir Alphonso was still very much under consideration. The Aragonese had hoped that it might take place when

---

[22] For this affair, see S. Runciman, *The Sicilian Vespers* (Harmondsworth, 1960), 251–64; Powicke, *Thirteenth Century*, 254.

Edward came to Gascony to mediate between the French and Castilians, but as Edward's services had been rejected by Alphonso of Castile in favour of those of Charles of Salerno, his planned expedition did not materialize. Negotiations continued with Aragon, however, and early in 1282 Anthony Bek and John de Vescy were sent there to conclude the marriage by proxy. There were considerable problems in getting the documentation correct for the envoys, but after discussion of the financial provisions, agreement was reached in August, and the ceremony of marriage performed. All that remained was for Edward to send his daughter to Aragon, which he was remarkably reluctant to do. He used the Welsh rebellion as an excuse, while the girl's mother and grandmother raised objections on the grounds of her age: she was only thirteen at the time of the proxy marriage. The war with Charles of Anjou provided a good reason for not despatching Eleanor to Aragon. Then came papal intervention against Aragon, and with it objections from Martin IV to the marriage. The couple were related in the fourth degree, and no papal dispensation had been obtained, nor was Martin prepared to provide one. It seemed increasingly unlikely that the marriage would ever be consummated.[23]

The French hostility towards Aragon, which followed from the Sicilian Vespers, placed Edward in a difficult position. The French demanded that he do his duty as a loyal vassal, and provide troops for their planned campaign against Aragon. He, however, had no desire to join in the war: to have done so would have run counter to his policies of promoting peace in Europe. The first summons from the French king was issued in 1282, and in 1283 the English officials in Ponthieu responded to it by raising troops. They were marched to Bordeaux to join other contingents, but no campaign took place that year. The king of Aragon also asked Edward for aid: the English king's reply was that he could not go against his homage to Philip III of France, and that he could not be seen to be rebelling against his lord. The issue came to a head in 1285, when the French expedition was finally ready. At the start of the year, Edward was preparing to go overseas, and the chronicler Thomas Wykes believed that he was intending to fulfil his military obligations and join the French forces. It was, according to Wykes, news that a truce had been agreed that led him to abandon his plans, and to go to Norfolk. It is more likely that he received a vigorous protest from the Gascons and the men of the Agenais, and that their arguments

<hr/>

[23] Chaplais, *English Medieval Diplomatic Practice*, II, ii, 473–81, provides a full discussion of the marriage. He assumes that Eleanor was born in 1264, but 1269 is much more likely: see above, 125. The marriage negotiations are also discussed by F. Kern, 'Edouard I von England und Peter von Aragon', *Mitteilungen des Instituts für Osterreichische Geschichtsforschung*, xxx (1909), 412–23.

that there was no precedent for them serving against Aragon led Edward to ignore the French summons. He had certainly not planned to involve the English in the war: no military preparations appear to have been made in England, and the letters of protection for those intending to go abroad with him were only valid until Easter, hardly long enough for a campaign in Aragon.[24]

Edward's subjects could hardly fail to be concerned about the situation, and the whole question of the French summons to serve in the Aragon campaign was hammered out in the Easter parliament of 1285. Unfortunately only summary extracts of the ordinance that was issued survive. It is clear that an Anglo-French commission was suggested, to deal with questions relating to the interpretation of treaties and agreements between England and France. Gascon advocates and proctors were not to place such questions before the French *parlement*, nor were they to agree to any French inquiries concerning English-held lands. The matter of military service was presumably to go before the joint commission. It would have been unwise for Edward to have refused outright to serve under the French king, but by placing the matters before arbitrators, he perhaps hoped to delay any action until it was too late.[25]

The English envoys who set out for France in May 1285 were indeed late, for the campaign against Aragon had already begun. It proved to be a costly disaster for the French. The Aragonese were victorious at sea, and refused battle on land. Short of supplies, and decimated by disease, the French were forced to retreat in the autumn. Philip III himself died soon after his army returned to French territory.[26] Events had been kind to Edward. In the circumstances of the accession of a new king, Philip IV, who needed to establish himself firmly on the throne, and to come to terms with Aragon, it was unlikely that any action would be taken against Edward for his failure to fulfil his feudal military obligations as duke of Gascony. A potential crisis had been averted, more through chance than as a result of any diplomatic skill on Edward's part.

Philip IV's accession meant that Edward now had to go abroad, to perform the act of homage. It was a good time to renew the question of the fulfilment of the territorial conditions of the Treaty of Paris, and to discuss the problems caused by Gascon appeals to the French *parlement*.

---

[24] Chaplais, *Essays in Medieval Diplomacy and Administration*, III, 20–2; Wykes, 300–1. Rishanger, 109, has it that Edward turned back on hearing that his mother was ill at Amesbury, but this does not fit the royal itinerary, as Edward did go to East Anglia, as Wykes says.

[25] Chaplais, op. cit., 23–4; *The War of Saint-Sardos (1323–1325)*, ed. P. Chaplais (Camden Soc., 3rd ser., lxxxvii, 1957), 87n.

[26] J.R. Strayer, *Medieval Statecraft and the Perspectives of History*, 107–22.

Further, Edward had hopes of resolving the dispute between France and Aragon, and of securing the release of Charles of Salerno. In addition, it was time that he revisited Gascony, to resolve internal problems there.

Edward crossed the Channel on 13 May 1286. It must have taken several days to transport all of the royal household, for some of the ships made three crossings. No fewer than 1,000 horses were taken across, twenty-four to a ship. Eight vessels carried the kitchen equipment, and other household paraphernalia. The journey to Paris was a leisurely one, taking a route through Ponthieu and then Amiens. At Paris Edward established himself at the abbey of St Germain-des-Prés. From there he could easily go by boat across the Seine to the French court at the Louvre. The king's Italian bankers brought £4,000 from London to cover the heavy expenses incurred in Paris, such as the banquet given to celebrate the Feast of the Trinity at a cost of £151.[27]

Edward's stay in Paris brought considerable success, at least in the short term, for English diplomacy. The question of homage to the French king went smoothly. Robert Burnell made a speech on Edward's behalf, setting out past history since the Treaty of Paris of 1259. He explained that, although the king has been advised to challenge the French claims to homage, and despite the fact that, in some cases, his rights had been threatened by the French, he nevertheless wished to do homage for the sake of peace. The formula Edward used was: 'I become your man for the lands which I hold overseas, according to the terms of the peace made between our ancestors.' Philip made some concessions on the tricky question of appeals to the *parlement* from Edward's Gascon subjects, in which, for example, he made provision for Edward and his officials to have three months to deal with matters raised by appellants, before any French intervention took place. The question of Quercy was finally settled by compromise. Everything augured well for future relations between Edward and Philip.[28]

Edward was also successful in his role as mediator between France and Aragon. Both sides agreed that he should negotiate a truce, and on 26 July a formula was agreed. Hostilities were to cease until March 1287. Edward wrote to the pope, Honorius IV, asking him to agree to the truce. This he duly did, as did Peter of Aragon's rebellious brother James, king of Majorca.[29] There remained one outstanding difficulty. Charles of Salerno was still captive in Aragon, and king Alphonso II,

[27] *Records of Wardrobe and Household 1285–6*, 46, 51–5, 58, 60, 65, 137, 140.
[28] Chaplais, *Essays in Medieval Diplomacy and Administration*, III, 24–5; Trabut-Cussac, *L'administration anglaise en Gascogne*, 79–80; *Foedera*, I, ii, 665, 672–3.
[29] *Foedera*, I, ii, 668–74.

who had succeeded his father Peter in 1286, was determined not to give
up this trump card lightly.

Edward left Paris at the end of July 1286, on an unhurried journey to
Gascony. The route he followed swept east, to Pontigny, where offerings were made at the shrine of St Edmund, and then to Auxerre. He
met the count of Bar at St Fargeau, and went on to Orléans. The royal
party visited Fontevrault, burial place of many of Edward's ancestors,
and it was not until the end of September that the isle of Oléron was
reached. The journey had not been easy, for many of the royal entourage had been struck with illness, and had to be left behind to recover.[30]

There was intense diplomatic activity in the winter of 1286–7 in
Gascony, with embassies coming and going. Then, in May 1287, John
de Vescy was sent to see Alphonso of Aragon, and a meeting between
him and Edward was arranged for July, at Oloron-Sainte-Marie in
Béarn. Both men duly arrived, and despite moments of alarm when the
lion which Edward had brought with him escaped and killed a horse,
and when two of Alphonso's Saracen followers ran away, negotiations
were successfully concluded.[31]

The king of Aragon had already shown that he intended to take every
possible advantage from the fact that he had Charles safely in his
charge. He had tried to impose harsh terms in the treaty of Cefalu of
1286, under the terms of which Sicily and some Calabrian lands were to
be handed over to James of Majorca, while Alphonso was to receive full
recognition as king of Aragon. A marriage alliance accompanied these
proposals, which were anathema to the papacy, and were not carried
out. Alphonso's demands at Oloron-Sainte-Marie continued to be
outrageous. Charles of Salerno was to be freed upon payment of 50,000
marks, 30,000 of which was to be in cash. His three eldest sons were to
be handed over as hostages, along with no fewer than sixty Provençal
magnates. Charles was to make a final peace within three years, and
return to captivity should he fail to satisfy the king of Aragon. All this
was conceded by Edward. This time there could be no papal objections,
for Honorius had died in April 1287, and there had been no new
election, though when Nicholas IV became pope in February 1288, he
promptly annulled the treaty. Philip IV put every obstacle he could in
the way, being particularly alarmed at the clause of the treaty which
provided for the Aragonese to gain Provence should peace not be finally
agreed within the three-year period.[32]

[30] *Records of Wardrobe and Household 1285–6*, 66–8, 70–4, 147–56, 200–1.

[31] Trabut-Cussac, *L'administration anglaise en Gascogne*, 87; *Records of Wardrobe and
Household 1286–9*, 108.

[32] E.G. Léonard, *Les Angevins de Naples* (Paris, 1954), 167–9; Powicke, *Thirteenth
Century*, 259; *Foedera*, I, ii, 677–8.

It is remarkable that Edward should have agreed on such disadvan-
tageous terms with Alphonso. His own desire to see the marriage of
Eleanor to Alphonso take place weakened his bargaining position, and
he was clearly determined to see Charles of Salerno released at whatever cost: he seems to have had a real personal concern for an attractive
and chivalrous figure. The treaty of Oloron-Sainte-Marie, however,
can only be seen as a triumph for Aragonese diplomacy. But if that
treaty was surprising from the English point of view, the sequel to it was
extraordinary. Following Nicholas IV's condemnation of the treaty,
fresh negotiations took place, and in October 1288, at Canfranc in
Aragon, Edward effectively agreed that he would personally provide
the cash and the hostages to ensure Charles's release; 30,000 marks
were to be paid over, and seventy-six English and Gascon hostages
handed to the Aragonese until such time as they might be replaced by
Provençals, an improbable eventuality. Among the hostages were such
great men as Gaston de Béarn, Otto de Grandson and John de Vescy,
along with important household knights such as William Latimer,
Hugh Audley and John de St John. The terms of captivity for these men
in Aragon were not harsh: each was allowed to go where he wanted by
day, provided that he returned to his lodgings every night. Each had
two guards to prevent escape. John de Vescy and Arnaud de Gironde
were given total freedom to go where they wished for three months.

The financial terms proved hard to carry out, given the state of
Edward's finances in Gascony, but 23,000 marks was paid over by
William of Louth, keeper of the wardrobe, and 7,000 marks was prom-
ised from Gascon sources. The hostages were released quite quickly, by
March 1289, as Charles fulfilled some of his undertakings to Alphonso,
who was probably anxious to improve his international standing by an
act of goodwill. The intention was, of course, that Charles should repay
Edward the money handed over to Aragon, but although the count of
Bar was empowered in 1298 to collect 10,000 marks from Charles, it
does not appear that the English ever received repayment.[33]

An acute English observer of these events, William de Hotham, later
archbishop of Dublin, found little to encourage him. Things had gone
badly during Edward's stay in Gascony: the release of Charles of
Salerno had been an occasion for grief, not joy, because the hostages
had to be handed over. Their release, at least, gave pleasure, because it
presaged the end of a stay which all felt had been too long. When he left
Gascony, Hotham went on an embassy with Otto de Grandson to the
papal curia. What he learned there of Charles of Salerno's government

---

[33] *Foedera*, I, ii, 687–704, 893; Léonard, *Les Angevins de Naples*, 170–1; Trabut-
Cussac, *L'administration anglaise en Gascogne*, 90–3; Powicke, *Thirteenth Century*, 260–1,
283–4.

of his kingdom of Naples was thoroughly discouraging. 'I fear that we have worked so much for him all in vain', he wrote dispiritedly.[34] The English ambassadors must have been angry to find that the pope had granted Charles absolution from the terms of the treaty of Canfranc, which became a dead letter. Charles was crowned king of Sicily, and was given the use of a crusading tenth in his realms, to pay for renewed war against Aragon. A Sicilian chronicler reported Otto de Grandson's speech of protest to the pope. He expressed the English king's astonishment that the pope should be permitting the conflict between the Angevins and the Aragonese to continue, and criticized both opposing kings, but to no effect.[35] Otto worked hard to secure a further truce, but by the time that Alphonso was forced to come to terms with his enemies, in negotiations at Tarascon in 1291, the English were no longer exercising any real influence. Alphonso died soon afterwards, leaving his brother James to become king of both Sicily and Aragon. With Alphonso's death, even the long-planned marriage alliance between England and Aragon came to nothing.[36]

The policies that Edward adopted in Europe in the 1270s and especially in the 1280s stand in striking contrast to his aggressive approach towards the Welsh. In his attitude towards the French, and the problems that arose from his feudal relationship with the king of France, Edward was conciliatory. There was little that presaged the Anglo-French conflict of the 1290s, although the French themselves may well have resented the increasingly prominent role Edward took in diplomatic affairs. The marriage alliances that Edward sought were not intended as a means of providing him with allies in some future war. As Powicke stressed, Edward's policies have to be seen in family terms: his concern for Charles of Salerno had much to do with the fact that the two men were cousins. His involvement, such as it was, with Queen Margaret of France's plans for Provence was not a part of a grandiose plan to encircle France with English allies, but stemmed from the complex family policies of the house of Savoy.[37] Edward's diplomatic initiatives in Europe were not simply intended to promote peace, however. Peace was no more than the first necessary stage, which had to be achieved if a new and successful crusade was to be mounted, and it is in many ways the crusade which provides the real key to Edward's policies.

It does not seem that Edward contemplated a further crusade with

[34] *Report on Manuscripts in Various Collections*, Historical Manuscripts Commission, i (1901), 253, 256.

[35] Clifford, *A Knight of Great Renown*, 100–1.

[36] Powicke, *Thirteenth Century*, 262–4.

[37] Ibid., 246–8.

real seriousness until the 1280s. Gregory X had hoped to revitalize the crusading movement at the Council of Lyons in 1274, where a tax of a tenth payable for six years was agreed. The only opposition came from the English: the dean of Lincoln handed the pope a memorandum, pointing out the way in which the English church had suffered as a result of previous papal taxation, and the civil war. He was deprived of his post for three days for his pains.[38] Gregory promised that any king who took the cross could receive the proceeds of the tax. This was very tempting, and in 1276 Edward wrote to the pope, promising that he would either go on the next crusade, or send Edmund of Lancaster on his behalf. In 1278 he sent John of Darlington to the pope – by now Nicholas III – to ask for the proceeds of the tenth, but the response was a meagre one. He was offered 25,000 marks once he actually took the cross, and provided he promised to pay it back should he not go. Negotiations continued, with Edward seeking in 1280 and 1281 to have the grant paid to his brother Edmund. Edward's policy seems to have been a cynical one, aimed at the acquisition of the tax. In 1282 he gave orders that none of the money was to be allowed to leave the country, and in the next year, when he had to pay for the Welsh war, he ordered his officials to seize the deposits from churches and monasteries.[39]

Edward's conduct was not as outrageous as might seem. There was every reason to suspect that the papacy would itself misuse crusading funds in 1282, in an attempt to reinstate Charles of Anjou in Sicily: the French pope Martin IV certainly lent Charles large sums out of the tenth. Further, Edward returned most of the confiscated money in its original sacks, untouched: only about £4,000 had been used, and that was rapidly repaid.[40] Martin IV's fury at what had happened soon abated, and discussions began about the projected crusade.

The negotiations were lengthy and complex. The long journey between England and Rome was an obstacle in itself, and matters were complicated by the successive deaths of Martin IV in 1285, and Honorius IV in 1287. Edward wanted adequate financial provision from the papacy. His suspicions about the corrupt practices of papal tax collectors were not well received at Rome, nor was his suggestion that he should appoint a nominee of his own to act jointly with the papal nuncio. English envoys failed to provide the papacy with clear answers to the question of how many men he intended to take to the East, or of how long he intended to stay there. Edward was anxious to

---

[38] Guisborough, 214–15.
[39] Lunt, *Financial Relations of England with the Papacy to 1327*, 334–6; above, 239; *Foedera*, I, ii, 357.
[40] Strayer, *Medieval Statecraft and the Perspectives of History*, 150–1; above, 239.

ensure that all those who took the cross actually went on crusade: the papacy had been permitting the widespread commutation of crusading vows. The situation in the East was relevant: the papal view was that there was little point in Edward organizing a general crusade, if there was a truce between the rulers of the kingdom of Jerusalem and the Mamluks.[41] Both sides were responsible for delays in the negotiations, but the indications are that, in spite of the various conditions he tried to impose, Edward was in earnest about going on a new crusade. There is no justification for any accusations that he was merely attempting to acquire the proceeds of crusade taxation for his own ends.

Edward's determination to go to the East once again is best attested, of course, by his taking the cross in 1287. Yet the way in which he did this was curious. He did not take the crusading vow in a major public ceremony, as he had done at Northampton in his youth, and it is not even quite certain exactly when the promise was made, or where. It seems that the king was ill when staying at Blanquefort, and that he took the crusading oath when he recovered, either there, or at Bordeaux. It may be that his illness was connected with an unfortunate accident, which took place when the floor of the room that he was in collapsed, and Edward fell, breaking his collar-bone. It was almost certainly in the spring of 1287 that he made the crusading promise, for in July he made gifts to some of his household, who had agreed to go with him to the East.[42] It is also unlikely that he would have taken the cross after hearing news of the death of Honorius IV, which took place just before Easter, for to do so during a papal vacancy would create complex problems. As it was, the archbishop of Ravenna, who conducted the ceremony, and the archbishop of Canterbury, and others who granted crusading privileges in England were not properly authorized to do so, and their actions had to receive retrospective approval from the papacy.[43]

The election of a new pope, Nicholas IV, and the consequent need for new negotiations about the crusade, certainly delayed matters. The expedition was high on the agenda of the embassy, led by William de Hotham and Otto de Grandson, to the papal curia in 1289 and 1290. Nicholas IV proved co-operative, renewing the grant of papal taxation to Edward, and making over financial provisions. The

[41] *Calendar of Papal Registers, Papal Letters, i, 1198–1304,* 473–4, 479–80; *Foedera,* I, ii, 642, 652–3, 663, 674–5.

[42] Trabut-Cussac, *L'administration anglaise en Gascogne,* 85; Lunt, *Financial Relations of the Papacy with England to 1327,* 338n; Oxenedes, 269–70. It may be that Edward took the cross in a private ceremony at Blanquefort, and this was followed by a more public one at Bordeaux.

[43] *Calendar of Papal Registers,* i, 552.

pope set the date for departure to the East at June 1292, but Edward changed this to June 1293, demanding that half of the new crusading tax should be paid to him before he set out. In 1291 the king at last obtained the financial concessions he had long sought, when the pope agreed to his terms. A series of bulls expressed Nicholas's pleasure at Edward's decision to go to the East.[44]

By that time, the situation in the East was changing radically, and the complacency that had existed in the West in the 1280s was proving to have been entirely unjustified. In 1289 the port of Tripoli had been lost to the Egyptian Mamluks, and in the next year a small force of galleys was sent to Acre, with a small, badly disciplined force of crusaders. They all promptly disregarded the truce that had been agreed with Egypt, and massacred all the Arab traders they could find, along with a good many local Christians. This gave the Mamluks the excuse to renew their attacks. The death of their sultan, Kalavun, provided a brief respite, but in March 1291 the Moslem army set out. There was a small English force under the valiant Otto de Grandson present in Acre: his arrival had given the defenders a false sense of optimism, for it was thought that Edward would soon follow with a full expedition. The siege did not last long. A fierce bombardment from mangonels and catapults took place, and on 18 May the final assault was launched. Otto de Grandson and Jean de Grailly distinguished themselves in the fighting, the latter being badly wounded before the two men reached a Venetian ship, and sailed off to safety in Cyprus. The unkind pun on Otto's name, that he should change his name as he had made little noise ('Grandson' meaning 'large noise'), was certainly not justified.[45]

The news of the fall of Acre reached the pope in late August 1291, and spread rapidly through the Christian world. The shock was immense. The need for a major initiative to recover the lost lands of the Crusader states in the East was now obvious, but at the same time, the fact that the last remaining outpost, Acre, had fallen meant that there was no longer any immediate urgency to organize a new crusade. The main evidence of debate in England about the new situation comes from the reports of a church council, held in February 1292, under Archbishop Pecham's leadership. The king was not involved in these discussions, and would not have been flattered by the view put forward that there should be an immediate imperial election, so that an emperor could impose peace in Europe and, very

[44] Lunt, *Financial Relations of the Papacy with England to 1327*, 339-40; *Les Registres de Nicholas IV*, ed. E. Langlois (Paris, 1886-1905), 889-92.

[45] Guisborough, 228-9; *The Later Crusades 1189-1311*, ed. R.L. Wolff and H.W. Hazard (Philadelphia, 1962), 592-8.

probably, provide leadership for the crusade. The French clergy, in their parallel debates, emphasized the need for a powerful leader, and may have been thinking in terms of Edward, but the English church appears to have laid no stress on the part their king might play in the forthcoming expedition.[46]

Edward was certainly still determined to go on crusade. He made this clear in a letter to the king of Hungary written in June 1292, and one sent to Norway bears the same implication.[47] The embassy that he sent under Geoffrey de Langley to the Persian Il-Khan, in the same year, was an important part of the diplomatic preparations for the crusade. Edward had first opened relations with the Mongol rulers at the time of his expedition to the East, when he had sent an embassy to the Il-Khan Abagha, and it is clear that he regarded an alliance with the Mongols as the best hope for the salvation of the Holy Land.[48] This was not as far-fetched an idea as it sounds. At this stage the Mongol rulers had not been converted to Islam, and there was a substantial Nestorian Christian element in their courts. They were themselves anxious to find allies against Mamluk Egypt. Contacts between the Mongols and the West continued in the 1270s and 1280s. When Edward was in Gascony in 1287, he received an embassy sent by the Mongols. An account of this mission survives, written by one of its leaders, a Nestorian monk of Chinese origin, called Rabban Sauma. Unfortunately he was so impressed with the wealth of relics, particularly in Constantinople, Rome and Paris, that he recorded little else. He did, however, record Edward's speech to the embassy: 'We, the king of these cities, have taken the sign of the cross upon our body, and have no other thought than this affair. My heart swells when I learn that what I am thinking is also being thought by King Arghun.'[49]

In 1289 a further Mongol embassy arrived, this time headed by an adventurous Genoese traveller and trader, Buscarello de Gisolfo, who had taken service with the Il-Khans. He brought letters from the Il-Khan Arghun for Philip IV and Edward I: unfortunately only the former survives, but the two were probably identical in their terms. He declared his intention of being outside Damascus in the spring of 1291, and even offered to supply the crusaders with horses, to ease their transport problems. Edward in his reply thanked Arghun for this

---

[46] *Councils and Synods*, II, ii, 1104–1113; Douie, *Archbishop Pecham*, 333–6.
[47] *Foedera*, I, ii, 760, 788.
[48] Above, 75, 78.
[49] N. McLean, 'An Eastern Embassy to Europe in the years 1287–8', *EHR*, xiv (1899), 299–318; J.B. Chabot, 'Histoire du Patriarche Mar Jabalaha III', *Revue de l'orient Latin*, xi (1894), 110.

offer, congratulated him on his intention of attacking the Egyptian sultan, and informed him that he intended to set out, as soon as he obtained papal permission.[50] Yet another Mongol embassy arrived in 1290, led by a Christian noble called Zagan, and including Buscarello. The pope was somewhat sceptical of Mongol claims to support the Christian cause, and was dubious of the orthodoxy of the Nestorians, but he wrote to Edward, asking that he should see this new mission.[51]

It was the Mongols who took most of the initiatives in this long-range diplomacy, but Edward's decision to send Geoffrey de Langley to the East, at a cost of perhaps £6,000 shows that he took them very seriously. Unfortunately, the Il-Khan Arghun died in 1291, and his successor Gaikhatu was a man of weak character, who had great difficulty in maintaining his position. Marco Polo, who was returning westwards from Gaikhatu's court at about this period, wrote that 'Gaikhatu was not the legitimate lord, and therefore the people had less scruple to do mischief than if they had a lawful prince'.[52] Geoffrey de Langley must have returned from his long journey with pessimistic reports for Edward. The prospects for the crusade were undoubtedly diminished in the absence of the hoped-for Mongol alliance.

Edward's belief in an alliance with the Mongols, so different in culture and customs from the rulers of the West, may suggest a remarkable gullibility on his part. Yet the Il-Khan's armies would not have had to travel as far as the crusader host; there was a Christian element in the Mongol courts; and there was a genuine desire to join in a common enterprise. The proof, at least as far as contemporaries were concerned, that the concept of a joint operation was not wholly fantastic came in 1300. In that year the West rejoiced at news that a Mongol army under a new Il-Khan, Ghazan, had retaken Jerusalem, which was now thought to be safe for Christianity. The news was, of course, a considerable exaggeration of the facts, for Ghazan's control of the Holy Land only lasted a few months, and he was the first of the Il-Khans to accept the Moslem faith, a piece of information his envoys withheld from the West.[53] Had there been a

[50] J.B. Chabot, 'Notes sur les relations du roi Argoun avec l'occident', *Revue de l'orient Latin*, xi (1894), 592–3, 610–13; T.H. Turner, 'Unpublished Notices of the Times of Edward I', *Archaeological Journal*, viii (1851), 48–9; B. Spuler, *History of the Mongols* (Berkeley and Los Angeles, 1972), 141–2.

[51] Chabot, op. cit., 616–23; J.D. Ryan, 'Nicholas IV and the Evolution of the Eastern Missionary Effort', *Archivum Historiae Pontificum*, xix (1981), 79–95.

[52] Howarth, *History of the Mongols*, iii, 367.

[53] S. Schein, 'Gesta Dei per Mongolos 1300. The genesis of a non-event', *EHR*, xciv (1979), 805–19.

crusader army in the East at the time of Ghazan's invasion, it might have been able to re-establish a Christian outpost in Palestine, and Edward's policy would have been vindicated.

The failure of the Mongol alliance was but one of the many obstacles in the way of Edward's crusade in the early 1290s. Finance was an important problem. It had been agreed with the papacy that the proceeds of the crusading tenth, which had been imposed as long ago as 1276, should be paid to Edward in two instalments in 1290 and 1291. He seems to have received very little of the money, for the Italian bankers, with whom the money had been deposited, found great difficulty in suddenly paying it over. They had, quite naturally, used these funds to finance their trading activities, and, under-capitalized as they were, could not meet the unexpected demand made of them.[54] A new tenth was also imposed on the church in 1291 by Nicholas IV, but collection took time. In 1293 Edward borrowed £10,000 from the collectors for expenses in Gascony, but he certainly did not receive sufficient funds from this tax to finance a crusade.[55]

The political problems which faced Edward in the early 1290s also made a crusade virtually inconceivable. In 1291 and 1292 the affair of the Scottish succession dominated his thoughts, and by 1294, a year after he had promised to set out, his war with France meant that any plans to go to the East had to be postponed. A further factor was the death of Pope Nicholas IV in 1292. There followed a long vacancy, and when agreement was eventually reached in 1294, the man selected was the elderly, and entirely unsuitable, Celestine V. He was removed from office in the year of his election. Boniface VIII then accepted the papal tiara. He was a wholly different figure, who might in other circumstances have been capable of organizing a crusade, but as war broke out between England and France in 1294, he never had the opportunity.

Edward did not altogether abandon his dream of leading a successful crusade. In June 1294 he wrote to Florence, prince of Achaea in Greece, expressing his firm hope that he would be able to go on crusade, and to visit Greece. He explained, however, that the course of events at home, which greatly displeased him, meant that he

[54] Lunt, *Financial Relations of the Papacy with England to 1327*, 339–41. Lunt argued that Edward did receive money from the Italian merchants from the crusading tenth, but Kaeuper, *Bankers to the Crown*, 211–12, 219–20, suggests otherwise. The fact that a receipt for 100,000 marks was issued by the chancery on 13 June 1292 does not mean that the money was paid over: the document was prepared in the expectation that the funds would be forthcoming, but the lack of any indication of such a massive influx of funds in the financial records suggests that the Italians failed to produce the cash. See *CPR 1281–92*, 494–5.

[55] Lunt, op. cit., 361.

did not know when he would be able to set out.[56] There is no reason to disbelieve the chronicler Langtoft's summary of Edward's plans, once affairs in Scotland appeared to be settled in 1296: 'Now all he has to do is arrange his expeditions against the king of France, to conquer his inheritances, and then bear the cross to where Jesus Christ was born.'[57] In practice, the circumstances of Edward's last years, with political troubles at home, and war with the Scots, meant that there was no real hope of the king's embarking on a crusade. Yet the French crusade propagandist thought that Edward was the right person to whom to address his tract on the recovery of the Holy Land, rather than Philip IV. According to one account, Edward expressed the desire on his deathbed that his heart should be sent to the East, and that eighty knights should be sent with it.[58]

Edward's diplomacy had failed by the early 1290s to achieve the king's main aims. He had hoped to bring peace to Europe and then to proceed with a major, successful crusade. Edward planned various marriage alliances, but those with Navarre, Aragon and the Habsburgs all failed for various reasons, and it was only the marriage of his daughter Margaret to the heir of the duke of Brabant that was actually carried through. Edward had secured the release of Charles of Salerno from captivity, but only at great cost to himself, and without securing the lasting peace between Aragon and the Angevins that he sought. This period saw the final collapse of the crusader states in the East, and all Edward's efforts to organize a fresh crusade came to nothing. It had been argued that 'his long deferment of his second vow of crusade ... had a disastrous effect on the possibility of a vigorous crusade in the final years of the Crusader states'.[59] This is an extreme point of view: Edward's delays were not of his making, and there is no justification for taking a cynical view of his intentions. It could be argued, however, that he should have realized that his hopes of a major expedition mounted from a peaceful Europe, in which the crusaders would co-operate with the Mongols, were over-ambitious. The men of Acre and Tripoli would have been better served, perhaps, by smaller and more manageable expeditions. Edward's concern to promote peace in Europe meant that, in his relations with the kings of France, he did less than he might have done to limit French claims to jurisdiction over the English possessions in Gascony, so arguably

---

[56] SC 1/13/66, 67.

[57] Langtoft, ii, 266.

[58] Pierre Dubois, *De Recuperatione Terrae Sanctae*, ed. C.V. Langlois (Paris, 1891), 1; Wright, *Political Songs*, 247.

[59] M. Purcell, *Papal Crusading Policy 1244–1291* (Leyden, 1975), 113.

creating problems for his later years. Yet his conciliatory approach to the French did mean that the difficult question of the Agenais was settled in his favour in 1279, and that no problems were raised as a result of the English acquisition of Ponthieu. It is very doubtful whether a more aggressive attitude towards Philip III and Philip IV would have achieved more.

The fact that few of Edward's schemes in these years achieved the results he wished was because the task he set himself was too great. Edward should not be condemned because his aspirations extended so far: peace in Europe followed by a crusade was an ideal which was widely shared, and it is only with hindsight that it appears as an impossible dream. Edward was an international figure, and it was right that his policies should have been aimed at much more than the immediate protection of English interests. This was, however, an age when national concerns were becoming more and more important, and in his later years Edward was to be forced to play a very different role in European affairs.

Edward may not have achieved all he hoped for in international affairs in the first half of his reign, but nevertheless he had been astonishingly successful in the 1270s and 1280s. There had been few problems resulting from any continuing bitterness caused by the civil conflicts of the 1260s: as king, Edward showed a statesmanship towards his former opponents that had not always been evident in his conduct as prince. He was never prepared, however, to extend forgiveness to the Ferrers family. Part of the reason for Edward's success in these years of his prime must be the fact that he was prepared to adopt some elements of the baronial reform movement of the 1250s and 1260s. Many features of the legislative programme of Edward's statutes can be traced back to such documents as the Provisions of Westminster of 1259. The technique of holding thoroughgoing inquiries into local affairs was one which Edward took over and developed, to considerable effect. Edward was also, of course, very conscious of his position as king, and as custodian of royal rights. This might on occasion cause him to go too far, most notably perhaps in his policy of land acquisition, but it also provided a driving force for a thorough reassessment or revision of much of the machinery of government. His defence of his rights as he saw them, combined with an insensitivity towards the rights of others, led him into war against the Welsh. Of course, Edward's resources were vastly greater than those of his opponent, Llywelyn ap Gruffydd, but nevertheless, the English king's achievement in mobilizing and in making use of those resources was very considerable.

There was no single motive behind Edward's many achievements in these years, no one ideal. There must, undoubtedly, have been a measure of genuine idealism. The cultural world of chivalry was important to Edward, and his construction of Caernarfon Castle along the lines suggested by the Welsh legend in the *Mabinogion* suggests what would now be interpreted as romanticism. Edward was also surely motivated by a desire to do justice as a king should. At the same time, he was a hard-headed ruler, determined to uphold his rights as he saw them, and ruthless in the methods he adopted to achieve his ends. There was for him no inconsistency between his pursuit of such ideals as the crusade, and the determined practicality of the way in which he ruled in England. Circumstances undoubtedly favoured him in the 1270s and 1280s, thought it also has to be said that he used those circumstances well. The remaining years of Edward's reign, however, were to see him put to a sterner test. The pressures of war were to become far greater, and the king would be less in control of events. The demands he would make of his subjects were to lead to political crisis of a sort that he had not had to face since succeeding to the throne. Edward had showed that he could rule well in good times: it was now to be seen how he would respond under much greater pressure.

PART III

The Later Years

Chapter 13

BEFORE THE STORM, 1289–94

On 12 August 1289 Edward returned to England after his lengthy stay in Gascony. Although the country had been ruled with reasonable efficiency during his absence, there was much for the king to do. He was convinced that major abuses had been prevalent, and that a purge of the justices, and other officials, was required. The financial situation, due largely to the debts Edward had incurred in Gascony, was precarious. Although the Welsh rebellion of 1287 had been successfully put down, trouble was threatening in the Marches, as a result of the rivalry between the earls of Gloucester and Hereford. The king would also have to deal with the problems caused by the *Quo Warranto* campaign, with its massive arrears of cases.

Edward showed no great urgency on his return to go to Westminster and see to affairs of state there. He spent some time in Kent, notably at Leeds castle, and crossed the Thames into Essex, where he hunted at Rayleigh. He visited Bury St Edmunds, and the shrine at Walsingham in Norfolk, before arriving at Westminster for the Feast of St Edward on 13 October.[1] Even then, no parliament was held until after Christmas. The first scandal, however, had broken in September. The chief justice of Common Pleas, Thomas de Weyland, had protected two of his men from justice after they had committed a murder. It is not clear exactly when the case against him was heard, but by 19 September officials were appointed to take charge of his confiscated estates. Weyland escaped from custody, and took refuge in a friary at Bury St Edmunds. This was blockaded on royal orders, and after two months, during which the friars were allowed to leave, Weyland was starved out and taken to the Tower. When parliament met, he was given the choice of standing trial, permanent imprisonment, or exile, and not surprisingly chose the last of these.[2]

Whether the Weyland case alerted the king to the possibility of more widespread corruption, or whether many complaints began to reach him, is not clear. On 13 October, however, the sheriffs were informed

[1] *Itinerary of Edward I*, i, 274–7.
[2] Cotton, 171, 173; *Chron. Bury St Edmunds*, 92–3.

that a commission, consisting of the bishop of Winchester, Robert Burnell, the earl of Lincoln, John de St John, William Latimer, William Louth and William March, had been appointed to hear complaints against royal officials, and to report on them in parliament. Anyone who wished to make a complaint was to come to Westminster on 12 November.[3] In practice, complainants probably came forward over a long period of time, and the task of hearing and then determining the cases lasted until 1293. In all, about 1,000 defendants were named, in some 670 actions. The most important were tried before a commission headed by the bishop of Winchester, who was succeeded by Peter of Leicester, an exchequer official, in 1291. Minor offenders went before the archdeacon of Norwich.[4]

The view of the chroniclers, that the justices had been responsible for widespread corruption and subversion of the law, is hardly borne out by the records. The greatest of those brought down in the proceedings was Ralph Hengham, chief justice of the King's Bench. He faced nine charges, and escaped unscathed on five. The one which led to his being fined 8,000 marks involved the issue of a writ ordering an arrest, prior to an inquisition which had been ordered. The crucial question was the dating of the writ, and part of the defence was that 'in the chancery on one and the same day one clerk would put one date, and another a different one'.[5] This was not convincing, but the offence was hardly commensurate with the fine, and it must be suspected that the king had other reasons for wanting to be rid of Hengham. One possibility is that Edward found him too independent, particularly where *Quo Warranto* cases were concerned.[6]

William de Saham, Hengham's colleague on the Bench, was found guilty in the same case, and was fined 2,500 marks. William de Brompton, a justice of Common Pleas, was probably one of the most culpable of those against whom prosecutions were brought. He was accused of taking bribes, forcing a jury to change its mind, adjourning cases incorrectly, and a range of other offences, in twenty-eight actions. He was fined 6,000 marks. John de Lovetot, also a justice of Common Pleas, was fined 2,000 marks: his worst offence was concealment of murder. Some of the justices were convicted on what now appears to have been slender evidence, or merely technicalities. Walter of Hopton and Thomas of Siddington were both found guilty only in one case.

---

[3] *CCR 1288–96*, 55.

[4] The cases are analysed in *State Trials of the Reign of Edward I*, ed. Tout and Johnstone, 100–253. Their conclusions, however, have been substantially modified in an important article by P.A. Brand, 'Edward I and the Judges: the "State Trials" of 1289–93', *Thirteenth Century England I*, ed. Cross and Lloyd, 31–40.

[5] *State Trials of Edward I*, ed. Tout and Johnstone, 35.

[6] Above, 293.

Hopton later argued convincingly that he was in fact innocent, while Siddington's responsibility was little more than formal.[7]

The purge extended far beyond the judicial benches. The infamous Adam Stratton, chamberlain of the exchequer, was a notable victim. He had already experienced similar judicial proceedings, when in 1279 the king had sought *querelae*, plaints, against him. He had then been pardoned, on the intercession of Isabella de Forz, on payment of a substantial fine. It is possible that the case against Stratton now preceded the main hearings: one account has it that he was tried by some of the justices against whom action was taken. He was convicted of forging a deed relating to Bermondsey Priory, a house from which he had acquired five manors, and which, he claimed, owed him £6,000. On his arrest, a vast fortune was found in his house in London, consisting of £11,333 in new money, and £1,317 in old coins. In addition, according to Bartholomew Cotton, a silk-lined chest was discovered, which contained fingernail and toenail clippings, women's pubic hair, the feet of toads and moles, and other items used in witchcraft. This was sealed up by royal officials, but Stratton broke the seals, and threw it down a latrine. Even Stratton was not found guilty of all charges: an apparently circumstantial story, of how he had torn the seal from an acquittance for a debt and then thrown the document into the Thames, was not found to be true.[8] Henry de Bray, escheator south of the Trent, was another important official to be arrested. He tried to drown himself when being taken by boat to the Tower, and then attempted suicide again, by dashing his head against a brick wall. The trial records show that he was charged with misappropriating estates, rather than the rape of virgins, as the chronicler Cotton would have it.[9]

The proceedings provided excuses for many men who had been disappointed in legal proceedings to reopen cases, and in a good many it is far from clear that the king's justices and officials had behaved as improperly as was alleged. Robert, son of Simon of Staunton, complained that although his father was a lunatic, in the habit of visiting ladies when he was wearing only a sword, he had been allowed to sell one of his manors. The matter was investigated, and the unfortunate Simon was found imprisoned, in irons, in his chapel, but there was no evidence of his insanity. No guilt in this case was attached to the justice involved, William de Saham. In other cases, justices had behaved in a biassed and unreasonable manner. Thomas de Goldington and his wife

---

[7] Brand, 'Edward I and the Judges', 36–8; *State Trials of Edward I*, ed. Tout and Johnstone, xxxi–xxxii; *Select Cases in the Court of King's Bench*, ed. Sayles, i., li, lvi.

[8] *Ann. London*, 98; Cotton, 171–2; R.H. Bowers, 'From Rolls to Riches: King's Clerks and Moneylending in Thirteenth-Century England', *Speculum*, lviii (1983), 69.

[9] Cotton, 176; *State Trials of Edward I*, ed. Tout and Johnstone, 17–18, 208.

had failed to obtain justice in a murder case, as after bribery, the judge, Nicholas de Stapleton, had held the inquiry secretly, in Newcastle-upon-Tyne, even though the offence had been committed in Westmorland. Richard de Boyland, another judge, had compelled William de Derneford to pay 200 marks to the earl of Gloucester, by detaining him and threatening him.[10]

The downfall of so many judges met with general approval, to go by the reaction of the chroniclers, but this was followed by dismay at the punishments imposed. For the most part, Edward was content to take fines from the guilty men, and, as Cotton put it, 'the iniquity of Mammon intervened, and peace was made between them [the judges] and the king, though he did remove them from his service'.[11] The author of the *Mirror of Justices* provided a long list of judges allegedly executed by King Alfred, to contrast with Edward's leniency.[12] Some of the fines were certainly very heavy, but it does not seem that Hengham, for example, paid his in full. Nicholas de Stapleton was fined 2,000 marks, but in October 1290 he received a pardon in return for only 300 marks. Adam Stratton's friends successfully offered the king 500 marks to obtain his release in 1291.[13] Even so, the king made substantial financial gains from these proceedings. Exchequer receipt rolls show receipts by 1293 of over £15,500 from ten of the chief offenders. If allowance is made for the money found in Adam Stratton's house, and the fines on lesser offenders, then the overall total may well have reached £30,000.[14] It would be quite wrong to think that the king had started these proceedings with the aim of making money out of them, but once they had begun, it made sense to profit from them. The trials must have had a salutary effect on the new judges appointed in 1290, but it was also thought necessary to introduce a new oath for them to swear, forbidding bribery, and preventing the taking of fees without royal consent. All that they might lawfully accept was food and drink on a daily basis.[15]

By the spring of 1290 there was an urgent need to replenish the royal coffers. An attempt to negotiate a tax while Edward was in Gascony had failed, as Gloucester and the other magnates had refused to make a grant in the king's absence.[16] No steps were taken to obtain a grant in the parliament held early in 1290, but in that which began in April,

---

[10] *State Trials of Edward I*, ed. Tout and Johnstone, 5–11, 71–7, 81–4.
[11] Cotton, 173.
[12] *Mirror of Justices*, ed. Whitaker and Maitland, 166–9.
[13] *CFR 1272–1307*, 284, 292.
[14] *State Trials of Edward I*, ed. Tout and Johnstone, xxxviii.
[15] E 159/64, m.10; Oxenedes, 276.
[16] Wykes, 316. There is no evidence to support the chronicler's view that an attempt was made to collect a tallage, once the tax grant had been refused.

Edward obtained agreement for the levy of a feudal aid. He was quite entitled to take this tax, as his daughter Joan was marrying the earl of Gloucester, and feudal custom entitled him to an aid on such an occasion, but he obviously considered it more politic to have the agreement of the magnates. However, a feudal aid was unlikely to raise much money, and the plan was shelved, not to be revived for ten years. Instead, knights of the shire were summoned to Westminster, to appear on 15 July. Whether parliament was still in session is not clear, but the knights gave their consent to the collection of a tax of a fifteenth, to which the magnates had already agreed.[17]

This grant of a fifteenth was not prompted by the usual arguments of national emergency or military need. No canon or Roman lawyer would have recognized the reason for the tax as legitimate in terms of the theories of the day, though churchmen no doubt approved wholeheartedly of what was done. The chroniclers were quite clear that the grant of the tax was made in exchange for the expulsion of the Jews from England: the edict for this was issued on 18 July, immediately after the tax was conceded. Some other reasons for the tax were put forward: the debts incurred in releasing Charles of Salerno, and the defence of the Holy Land were two, but it was probably the expulsion which persuaded Edward's subjects to be so generous. The tax was astonishingly successful, with an assessment of £116,346, and a yield not far short of that sum. It is not surprising that the Oseney annalist considered that it was much heavier than any in the past, and that 'the people groaned inconsolably'.[18] The clergy were also asked for a tax, and in the autumn and winter of 1290, tenths for one year were granted by those of both Canterbury and York.[19]

The treasurer for the past six years, John Kirkby, died early in 1290, following an unsuccessful operation to bleed him,[20] and his successor William March made important changes in the administration of the new taxes. For the first time, tax income was recorded on special exchequer receipt rolls, and the exchequer officials took a much more active part in the business of assessment and collection. March also cut back, at least in formal terms, the financial independence of the wardrobe, and the bulk of this department's income was now channelled through the exchequer. During Walter Langton's keepership of the wardrobe, from 1290 to 1295, the exchequer contributed over eighty-

---

[17] *Parl. Writs*, i, 21; *Select Charters*, ed. W. Stubbs (9th edn, Oxford, 1921), 472–3; Richardson and Sayles, *The English Parliament in the Middle Ages*, V, 144.
[18] Guisborough, 227; *Ann. Dunstable*, 362; *Ann. London*, 99; *CCR 1288–96*, 95–6; Wykes, 326.
[19] Deighton, 'Clerical Taxation by Consent', 169–71.
[20] Cotton, 174.

four per cent of the total wardrobe receipt. In practice, tax-collectors and others still paid money into the wardrobe, but the sums involved were now entered on exchequer rolls, and the whole process was subject to greater supervision.[21]

No novel sources of revenue were found in 1290, and it proved necessary to take substantial loans from Italian merchants, totalling £18,900, as it was not for some time that the tax receipts began to come in. However, the grants of taxation, combined with the changes in exchequer practices, meant that in the early 1290s royal finances were in a healthier state than they had been for many years.

Part of the price for financial stability was the expulsion of the Jews from England. This action met with almost universal approval from contemporaries, although to modern eyes it does not appear creditable. The Jews in England were not many: by this time there were probably no more than about fifteen communities, with a total population estimated at some 3,000. They were moneylenders and traders, with a unique role in the economy that was made possible by the fact that their law permitted them to lend money to Gentiles at interest. Canon law forbad Christians to take interest. In legal theory, they were the property of the king, and they were always subject to his will. In particular, they could be taxed arbitrarily. They had been tallaged heavily in the 1270s, and had suffered during the campaign against coin-clipping that was associated with the recoinage.[22] The scale of royal profits in this period from the Jewry is indicated by the fact that the account of the king's Italian bankers, the Riccardi, for 1272–9 includes receipts of £2,758 from the Jews, while the wardrobe account for 1279–80 includes £1,356 from the sale of confiscated Jewish goods. In 1282–4, however, wardrobe income from the Jews stood at only £222.[23] For much of the 1280s the Jews were spared arbitrary tallages, but that policy was dramatically reversed in 1287. The chronicle tradition is that on 2 May 1287 all the Jews in England were imprisoned, and released only after agreeing to pay £12,000. This sum was an exaggeration: the receipt rolls show that £4,023 was actually paid.[24]

The extent of royal demands on the Jews had been such that their

[21] J.F. Willard, 'An Exchequer Reform under Edward I', *The Crusades and other Historical Essays presented to Dana C. Munro*, ed. L.J. Paetow (New York, 1928), 326–40.

[22] H.G. Richardson *The English Jewry under Angevin Kings* (1960), 19, 214–20.

[23] Riccardi account, E 101/126/1; wardrobe accounts in E 372/124, E 372/130.

[24] *Ann. London*, 96; Oxenedes, 268; Richardson, *English Jewry under Angevin Kings*, 227. Richardson finds the story of universal imprisonment implausible, but there was a precedent in 1273, when all Jews had been ordered to go to Canterbury from December until the following Easter. It may be that expulsion was being considered even then: E 159/48, m.4.

financial resources had been severely depleted, and in expelling them from the country Edward was hardly depriving himself of a substantial source of future revenue. He was, indeed, providing himself with funds, for he took over the debts that had been due to the Jews, and collected as much as he could from them, though interest payments were remitted. He also gained the property left behind by the Jews, raising about £2,000 from the sale of their houses. There was a precedent for all this, for it was only three years before that he had expelled the Jews from Gascony, and had confiscated their debts and goods.[25] An argument has been put forward suggesting that Edward was able to expel the Jews because the part that they had played in royal finance could be filled by the Italian merchants, but this is valid to only a limited extent. The role of the Italians, as bankers providing loans, was very different from that of the Jews, from whom money was taken by means of taxation.[26]

One reason that was given at the time for the expulsion of the Jews was that they had not fulfilled the terms of the statute of Jewry of 1275. This was a remarkable enactment which provided for the complete abolition of usury, and permitted Jews to become merchants and artisans, and even to lease land so that they could farm it. The Jews were set a fifteen-year period in which to adjust to their new role in life, and this they had clearly not done by 1290. In fact, papal intervention would have made it difficult to integrate the Jews even in the limited manner suggested in the statute.[27] In about 1285 a proposal was made that, since the Jews had not abandoned their practice of usury, but had merely disguised interest payments, the crown should legitimize such payments, and regularize them at about forty-three per cent a year.[28] This was not done, and expulsion must have appeared to be a much more satisfactory means of dealing with the question of usury.

The expulsion of the Jews should not be analysed solely in financial or economic terms. There was undoubtedly very considerable prejudice against the Jews in England. There were stories of ritual child-murder and torture, which, although they now appear groundless on the basis of the recorded evidence, were generally believed. The most famous was that of the death of Little St Hugh of Lincoln in 1255, but there were others. The chronicle of Bury St Edmunds recorded the

---

[25] E 159/64, m.4; Richardson, *English Jewry under Angevin Kings*, 225-6; 230.

[26] P. Elman, 'The Economic Causes of the Expulsion of the Jews in 1290', *Economic History Review*, vii (1936), 145-54.

[27] *Statutes of the Realm*, i, 221; B.L. Abrahams, *The Expulsion of the Jews from England in 1290* (1895), 75, provides full discussion.

[28] *Select Pleas, Starrs, and other Records from the Exchequer of the Jews, 1220-1284*, ed. J.M. Rigg (Selden Soc., xv, 1901), liv-lx.

crucifixion of a boy by the Jews at Northampton.[29] Edward's mother, Eleanor of Provence, was anti-Semitic, and obtained Edward's permission in 1275 to lay down that in future no Jews should live on her estates.[30] Queen Eleanor of Castile, in contrast, had many dealings with Jews, from which she profited considerably, though this does not reveal what her personal attitude to them was.[31] As for the king himself, he appears to have been very interested in Jewish matters, giving verbal instructions to his officials and justices about their dealings with the Jewry. While he does not seem to have been virulently hostile to the Jews, Edward showed them little sympathy. In 1276 he had intervened in a case dating from Henry III's reign, in which an apparently unjustified case of child murder was levied against some London Jews, but he was eventually persuaded of the truth of the charges. When a Jew petitioned the king in parliament in 1290, complaining that a Jewish boy had been forcibly baptized, his reply was uncompromising: 'The king does not want to revoke the baptism. No inquiries are to be made of anyone, and nothing is to be done.'[32] Edward cannot have had many doubts about the wisdom of the decision to expel the Jews.

The expulsion itself went surprisingly smoothly, and was not the occasion for massacres, as it might well have been. Royal safe-conducts were given to the Jews making their way to the Cinque Ports, and the sailors were ordered to charge moderate rates for the Channel crossing. The chroniclers reported one horror story. A shipmaster anchored in the Thames as the tide was going out, and when the ship grounded, he persuaded the Jews on board to go for a walk on the sands. He led them far from the vessel, and managed to get back on board himself in time as the tide rose, leaving his passengers to drown.[33] In another incident, a ship containing Jewish refugees drifted ashore near Burnham-on-Crouch, and all were robbed and killed. The sheriff put the remaining cargo on sale, but three cartloads were removed by his brother, who was tried for this offence at the exchequer.[34] Such occurrences fortunately seem to have been rare, and the exodus proceeded quietly. Only a few converted Jews remained in England, and it was not until 1656 that Edward I's action was reversed.

The year 1290 was important for the king's relationship with the magnates. The question of the *Quo Warranto* inquiries into the rights

[29] C. Roth, *History of the Jews in England* (Oxford, 1941), 56–7; *Chron. Bury St Edmunds*, 69.

[30] *CPR 1272–81*, 76.

[31] *The Court and Household of Eleanor of Castile*, ed. Parsons, 18.

[32] *CCR 1272–9*, 271–4; *Rot. Parl.*, i, 46.

[33] Guisborough, 226–7; Cotton, 178, reports what is probably the same story.

[34] E 13/16, m.5d.

that men had to exercise franchisal jurisdiction reached a point of crisis. With the dismissal of Ralph Hengham, Gilbert de Thornton became chief justice of the King's Bench. He had been one of the most aggressive of the royal attorneys in the *Quo Warranto* proceedings, and it seems that the judgements he now delivered in cases that had been adjourned from previous hearings were firm. Tenure from time out of mind was not now adequate warrant for the exercise of rights of jurisdiction which properly belonged to the king. The Dunstable chronicle reports two cases, those of Robert FitzWalter of Daventry and Henry de Grey of Newbottle, which caused widespread concern among the magnates. In parliament at Easter 1290 pressure was clearly put on the king, and on 21 May the statute of *Quo Warranto* was issued. The terms of the statute allowed anyone who could show continuous use of a franchise by himself and his ancestors since 1189 to have his position confirmed by means of royal letters patent. In cases which had gone against defendants since Easter 1290 – presumably those of FitzWalter and Grey came into this category – those concerned could go to the king and have their franchises restored. *Quo Warranto* actions were removed from Westminster, where Thornton and his colleagues had been hearing them, and sent back into the eyres.[35]

The statute of *Quo Warranto* was an ingenious compromise, which both preserved the theory that all liberties were delegations of royal authority, and also permitted tenure since 1189 as a sufficient warrant for the exercise of rights of jurisdiction. It would, however, have been an extraordinarily time-consuming task to issue letters patent to all those who claimed tenure from time out of mind, and what was put into effect was not the statute itself, but a summary of it. This simply stated that anyone who could show that a given liberty had been held since 1189 could continue to hold it. Should he be challenged in his right, then the king would confirm it. This was a simpler, more convenient procedure. The issue was not finally settled in 1290, however, for when eyres started once again in 1292, some royal attorneys continued to challenge claims just as they had done in the past. Once again, many cases were postponed, and the whole campaign at long last came to a halt. When war broke out with France in 1294 the king abandoned it, 'as a favour to his people'.[36] The *Quo Warranto* proceedings had shown the king to be something of a paper tiger as far as baronial liberties in England were concerned. Yet, in the early 1290s, Edward showed that he was a tiger with sharp claws and teeth, when it came to the great liberties of the Welsh March, which *Quo Warranto* had not touched.

---

[35] *Ann. Dunstable*, 360; Sutherland, *Quo Warranto Proceedings*, 94–6, 203–4; *Statutes of the Realm*, i, 107.

[36] Sutherland, *Quo Warranto Proceedings*, 93–4, 99–110, 213.

It was a feud between the earls of Gloucester and Hereford which prompted royal interference in the March. The trouble had broken out while Edward was in Gascony, but the roots of it went back to 1265, when Gloucester had been granted rights of wardship over Hereford. When Hereford came of age in 1270, he purchased his right of marriage from his fellow earl for £1,000, and Gloucester claimed in 1290 that he had received only 390 marks. There was a territorial dispute between the two men: in the aftermath of the 1287 campaign against Rhys ap Maredudd, Gloucester began to build a castle at Morlais, which Hereford claimed lay within his territory. An order in 1286 from Edmund of Cornwall, as regent, ordering construction to cease had no effect, and the efforts of the archbishop of Canterbury to settle the dispute were of no avail.[37]

The traditional method of resolving disputes in the March was, firstly, by negotiation which took place on the boundaries between lordships, and secondly, if that failed, by means of private war. That sounds drastic, but there were well-recognized conventions for the conduct of such war, which should be seen as an extension of legal procedure, not a substitute for it. The earl of Hereford, however, was not very powerful in the Marches, and lacked allies: he was already in dispute with another neighbour, John Giffard, over territorial claims. He refused to play the game according to the Marcher rule-book, and presented his complaints to the crown. He received a sympathetic hearing, and Edward promptly ordered hostilities to cease. Gloucester ignored this. In February 1290 his bailiffs raided Hereford's land of Brecon, and the fact that the earl received the customary third part of the booty indicated his complicity.[38]

At this juncture, Gloucester was in a strong position, for his long-planned marriage to the king's daughter Joan of Acre was about to take place. This match had been agreed in 1283, about eighteen months after the death of Hartmann of Habsburg, whom Joan had originally been intended to marry. There were delays, as Gloucester's first marriage had to be annulled by the pope, and a dispensation obtained for his second, but these obstacles had been overcome late in 1289. Both Edward I and the earl had, potentially, much to gain from the marriage. Gloucester agreed to surrender all his lands to the king, to receive them back, jointly with his bride, with the provision that they should pass to his heirs by Joan, or in the absence of such heirs, to her children by a later marriage. The earl ensured that any children of his marriage

---

[37] Altschul, *A Baronial Family*, 146–7; KB 27/130, m.10v.

[38] For the details of the dispute between the earls, see Morris, *Welsh Wars of Edward I*, 225–38; Altschul, *A Baronial Family*, 147–52. In addition to the sources cited there, a version of the trial is enrolled in KB 27/130, mm.17–20.

to Joan would be close to inheriting the throne, while the king made an excellent provision for his daughter in territorial terms, and ensured that future earls of Gloucester would be closely tied by blood to the throne.[39] The regranting of the lands to Gloucester did not affect the earl's enjoyment of his liberties, or his status as a Marcher lord. The marriage took place early in May, at the time that parliament was in session, and in June Gloucester showed that his new relationship to the king had not curbed his independence, and he mounted a further raid on Hereford's lands.

In October 1290 Gloucester suffered a defeat in a dispute with the crown, over his claim to the custody of the bishopric of Llandaff during vacancies. He was forced to surrender his rights to Edward, and received them back for life only.[40] His response to this was to send his men once more into Hereford's estates. Hereford's case against Gloucester, meanwhile, appeared to be getting nowhere, for Gloucester simply failed to appear in court, causing a series of adjournments. In January 1291, however, the king appointed a powerful judicial commission to investigate, and it was made clear that even if the earls failed to take the case forward (a hint that Marcher pressure may have been making Hereford think of withdrawing his plaint), it should be continued by the king, as it concerned matters prejudicial to the crown. Gloucester continued his tactics of failing to appear and his fellow Marchers made it plain that they would co-operate with the king only if Marcher customs were respected. Eventually a jury of twenty-four was assembled, and the story of the raids rehearsed. Before the king could hold further hearings at Abergavenny, in September 1291, news reached him of yet more disturbances in the March, in which Hereford's men had retaliated and raided Gloucester's estates. Now, both Hereford and Gloucester were tried at Abergavenny before king and council.

Hereford's case was a simple one: he had, he claimed, done his best to obey the king's orders. However, according to the jury, he retained the cattle taken by his men from Gloucester's estates, and had appropriated the disputed land even though the issue was not yet determined in court. It was therefore decided that he, and his constable of Brecon, should be imprisoned. Gloucester's arguments were more complex, and rested on a number of legal technicalities. He argued, for example, that the royal prohibition on further hostilities had been rendered

[39] McFarlane, *Nobility of Later Medieval England*, 259–60. In the event, the earl's son by Joan, Gilbert de Clare, died in a suicidal charge at Bannockburn in 1314, and after a protracted feigned pregnancy by his widow, the estates were partitioned between his three sisters.

[40] For this matter, see Altschul, *A Baronial Family*, 274–5; *Rot. Parl.*, i, 42–3.

invalid by his surrender of his lands to the king, and their subsequent
regrant to himself and Joan of Acre. This was all to no avail: Gloucester,
like Hereford, was sentenced to imprisonment, 'because all these things
were done by the earl and his men of Glamorgan most boldly and
presumptuously, believing that they would escape by their liberty of
the March from the penalty and peril that they would deservedly have
incurred if they had committed such an excess elsewhere in England
outside the March'.[41]

The proceedings at Abergavenny did not conclude the case. The two
earls were promptly bailed, and their liberties restored to them until
they should appear before king and council at Westminster. The next
stage took place in Otto de Grandson's house in Westminster, where
the case was adjourned, as the king had not had time to take proper
advice about it. Finally, the earls appeared in parliament in January
1292, and submitted themselves to the king's will. Gloucester's liberty
of Glamorgan was declared forfeit, but as the earl was married to the
king's daughter, this forfeiture was to last only for his lifetime.
Hereford's liberty of Brecon was to be treated in the same way, for he
was married to a relative of the queen. Both earls were imprisoned, but
they were promptly released, with a fine on Gloucester of 10,000 marks
and one on Hereford of 1,000 marks.[42]

The eventual outcome of the case against the two earls was an
anti-climax. In May 1292, a mere four months after sentence was
passed, Gloucester received Glamorgan back from the king, and in July
Hereford regained Brecon. The fines were not paid. It could be 'that the
king knew when to stop', or that he gave in to pressure from other
magnates, who were sympathetic to the two earls. The support they
received is shown by the lists of those who guaranteed that they would
appear in court. For Gloucester, there were the earl of Lancaster,
William de Valence, the earl of Lincoln and John de Hastings, and for
Hereford, Reginald de Grey, Robert Tibetot, Robert FitzWalter and
Walter de Beauchamp.[43] Both men, therefore, had substantial backing
from men close to the king. Edward had gone as far as he could in
attacking the position of two of his greatest magnates, and he had
emphasized his authority in very definite terms. Yet in the end the
Marcher liberties were returned intact, though clearly no one would
dare to try to settle his disputes by means of private war in the future.

The humbling of the two earls has received much attention from
modern historians, and deservedly so, for it provides a splendid

[41] *CWR*, 346.
[42] The case is summarized ibid., 334-9, and conveniently printed in *Rot. Parl.*, i,
70-7.
[43] *Rot. Parl.*, i, 77.

example of Edward's masterful policies in operation. Yet contemporary chroniclers did not give it much attention: Bartholomew Cotton noted the birth of a son to the earl of Gloucester and Joan of Acre, but made no mention of the dispute between the earls, and the royal intervention.[44] The disaster of the loss of Acre, and then the disputed Scottish succession, dominated the attention of the chroniclers to the exclusion, to a great extent, of domestic affairs.

The case of the two earls was not the only Marcher affair in which Edward intervened in the early 1290s. In 1290 Bogo de Knoville, royal bailiff of Montgomery, complained that Edmund Mortimer had imprisoned, tried and executed a criminal in spite of Bogo's requests that he be handed over. In parliament, in the autumn of 1290, Edmund placed himself at the king's will, and was sentenced to lose the liberty of Wigmore. However, just as in the case of Gloucester and Hereford, the sentence was then substantially reduced. Edmund was to pay a fine of only 100 marks, and a remarkable instruction given that he should hand over an effigy to Bogo, to be hanged by him in lieu of the already executed felon. In fact, Edmund failed to do this, and the liberty was confiscated for a second time, but it was eventually given back to him, and his powers of jurisdiction were left unaltered.[45]

Another Marcher magnate who was tried before Edward was Theobald de Verdun, who had been involved in disputes with the prior of Llantony. His stewards had used a substantial armed force, allegedly 600 strong, to prevent the sheriff from taking an inquisition at Ewyas Lacy.[46] Theobald appeared before the king and council at Abergavenny, in the same session as Gloucester and Hereford, and was duly sentenced to imprisonment and loss of his liberty of Ewyas Lacy. Following the pattern of the other cases, he in fact paid a fine, of £500, and his liberty was restored, possibly in return for services he performed in Gascony. A catalogue of further cases includes royal intervention in a private war in 1293 between the earl of Arundel and Fulk FitzWarin, the royal seizure of the lordship of Elfael from Ralph de Tony, and of the hundred of Purslow from Arundel. Ystlwyf was recovered from William de Valence, and incorporated into the county of Carmarthen. The grant of a fifteenth, to which the Marchers gave grudging consent during 1292 and 1293, led to a further extension of royal authority into the Welsh border lands.[47]

Edward's dealings with the Marchers were very different from the

[44] Cotton, 199.

[45] *Rot. Parl.*, i, 45.

[46] KB 27/129, m.54.

[47] Davies, *Lordship and Society in the March of Wales*, 260–1; *Rot. Parl.*, i, 81–2; Morris, *Welsh Wars*, 238–9.

Quo Warranto inquiries. There was no concern with the specific terms of charters, or arguments over tenure from time out of mind. The king was not concerned to recover allegedly lost royal rights, and was not determined to reduce what he recognized as the legitimate jurisdictional rights of the Marchers. He was quite firm, however, that his prerogative should not be limited: it was argued, in the course of the case between Gloucester and Hereford, that the prerogative might override any local privileges and customs. Where possible, Edward based his actions on direct refusals by Marcher lords to obey royal instructions, for these provided him with clear-cut, and indeed unanswerable, cases. Once the king had proved his point, he was quite prepared to allow the Marchers to continue to exercise their rights, so long as they did not engage in private war, disobey further royal orders, or infringe royal rights. The Marchers were not challenged as a group, and as Edward's actions did not threaten their collective position, he did not face united opposition from them in these years.[48] His actions were to be remembered, however, in 1297 when he faced his greatest political crisis.

In 1291 and 1292, the affair of the Scottish succession meant that Edward had little time for political matters at home. The only English parliament held in 1291 took place in January at Ashridge in Hertfordshire, and in 1292 the only one was in London, again at the start of the year. In 1293 a lengthy parliamentary session began in the spring at London, moved to Canterbury, and ended in July.[49] There was much legal business to be done. One important case was brought against the archbishop of York. He had excommunicated Anthony Bek, bishop of Durham, because he had permitted the arrest and imprisonment of two clerks in Durham. Bek was under royal protection at the time, as he was in royal service in Scotland. It was argued on behalf of the king that Bek had acted in his capacity as an earl palatine, not as a bishop, and that the archbishop of York had, by his action, attempted 'to occupy and usurp upon the royal crown and dignity'. As in the case of the earls of Gloucester and Hereford, great emphasis was placed on the royal prerogative. It was decided that the archbishop should be imprisoned, but before sentence was pronounced, he submitted to Edward, and a fine of 4,000 marks was agreed.[50]

Later in 1293, in November, Edward was presented with a rare opportunity to acquire substantial estates. He had long had designs upon the lands of Isabel de Redvers, the mother of Aveline de Forz, but his attempts to purchase the reversion of her inheritance in 1276 had

---

[48] Davies, *Lordship and Society in the March of Wales*, 262–9, provides a full discussion.
[49] For the sessions of parliament at this time, see *Handbook of British Chronology*, 549.
[50] *CCR 1288–96*, 330–4; *Rot. Parl.* i, 102–5.

been unsuccessful. There were further discussions, but the matter suddenly became urgent when it became clear that Isabel was dying. Anthony Bek, accompanied by Walter Langton, hastened to her deathbed, and a charter was rapidly drawn up in which the Isle of Wight and three manors were promised to Edward in return for 6,000 marks. Bek was only just in time: the charter was dated 9 November, and Isabel died in the early hours of the next morning. The money was duly paid on the next day to her executors, and the king acquired the lands.

The affair was undoubtedly suspicious: for seventeen years Isabel had not acceded to royal requests, and for her to agree during her last hours, when she can hardly have expected to be able to make use of the 6,000 marks, was surprising. It is true that her rightful heir, Hugh de Courtenay, was under age, and not particularly closely related to her, but it was expected that he would inherit her lands. Indeed, a contemporary letter reported that the lands had merely been taken into royal hands until he should come of age. The truth of what had taken place was not widely known for some time. When Hugh achieved his majority in 1297, he began a long and fruitless struggle to gain what he felt was his rightful inheritance. He was at least to receive from Edward III, in 1335, the title of earl of Devon which should have been his under Edward I.[51] The story is a shabby one, but the king's own part in it is far from clear. The initiative for drawing up the charter so soon before Isabel's death is more likely to have come from Bek or Langton than from the king himself, and when Courtenay came to press his claim, Edward could hardly have disavowed their actions. The acquisition of the Isle of Wight and the three manors was, it has to be said, of a piece with other questionable deals by means of which Edward increased his landed endowment.

Edward was never very much concerned with affairs in Ireland, but events there developed in these years in a way which was potentially embarrassing for the king. In 1290 William de Vescy was appointed justiciar of Ireland, and in the same year he inherited, through his mother, the lordship of Kildare. He had not previously spent much time in Ireland, and he appears to have behaved in a high-handed and autocratic manner when he took up his post there. In particular, he aroused the hostility of John FitzThomas, baron of Offaly and head of the powerful family grouping of the Geraldines. In 1293 a feudal summons to muster at Kildare was issued, and it is very likely that de

[51] N. Denholm-Young, 'Edward I and the Sale of the Isle of Wight', *EHR*, xliv (1929), 433–8; Powicke, *Henry III and the Lord Edward*, ii, 710–11; McFarlane, *Nobility of Later Medieval England*, 257–9. I have largely followed McFarlane's interpretation. The letter concerning this matter is in SC 1/48, 165. It also reveals that Warin de Lisle claimed the inheritance, and that the council would not hear him until Hugh de Courtenay came of age.

Vescy was planning a campaign against FitzThomas, but when complaints about the justiciar's conduct reached the king, Edward acted quickly, and the summons was cancelled.[52] John FitzThomas' revenge took a remarkable form. According to William de Vescy, he first complained to the king and council in England that de Vescy had tried to persuade him to enter into a sworn alliance against the king. John denied this, and when pressed produced a written statement of what he alleged de Vescy had said to him about the king. The statement was explosive: de Vescy had argued that the Irish were the most miserable people he knew, for if they had anything about them, they would be well able to do without the king. If they knew what de Vescy knew, they would realize that Edward was the most cowardly and idle knight in the realm. The statement went on to detail Edward's alleged cowardice at Kenilworth, shortly before the battle of Evesham.

William de Vescy's response to this was to offer to prove himself in battle, and FitzThomas also agreed to a trial by combat. The case was adjourned several times, and an inquest into the matter was ordered by Edward. All parties were ordered to Westminster to receive judgement, and on the appointed day in August 1294 William de Vescy appeared there in full armour, claiming judgement in his favour by default in his opponent's absence. The affair was, however, adjourned again. Delays continued, for Edward claimed that other business was too pressing. He could not let the trial by battle go ahead, lest the result be seen as justifying the slander against him. Conveniently, it was finally settled in parliament in 1295, when it was decided that the whole case had been contrary to the law and custom of the land from the very outset, and both parties were dismissed. It had taken a long time to reach this conclusion: the case must have caused heart-searching among Edward's legal advisers, as to how best to deal with such a troublesome matter which brought the king's own reputation into question.[53] It had, hardly surprisingly, brought de Vescy's dismissal from the justiciarship of Ireland in June 1294. As for FitzThomas, he was involved in another feud, this time with the earl of Ulster whom he imprisoned for a time, finally surrendering himself to the king's will in August 1295. Edward did not break his power, however, but in time he managed to curb the aggressive instincts of this powerful Anglo-Norman magnate.[54] It is to Edward's credit that he did not automatically take the side of his nominee, William de Vescy, and that he understood the important role that men such as FitzThomas had to play in Ireland.

*   *   *

[52] *CDI 1293–1301*, nos 62–4; Otway-Ruthven, *History of Medieval Ireland*, 205, 209–11.

[53] *Rot. Parl.*, i, 127–8, 132–4; *CDI 1293–1301*, no. 147. See also above, 50.

[54] Otway-Ruthven, *History of Medieval Ireland*, 211.

Important changes in the personnel surrounding the king took place in the early 1290s. Eleanor of Castile died in 1290, and the king's mother, Eleanor of Provence, ended her days in the next year. Both women had a strong influence on Edward, though that of his mother had declined in her last years. There was a marked change in the corps of household knights, as a new generation began to take the place of those who had served Edward through the Welsh wars of the 1270s and 1280s.[55] The appointment of Walter Langton as keeper of the wardrobe in 1290, and of John Droxford as his controller, marked the advent to high office of two of the dominant administrators of Edward's later years. Outside the household, there were major changes. Kirkby's death in 1290, and his replacement by William March, has already been discussed. The death of Robert Burnell, in October 1292, removed from the scene the most important of all Edward's advisers in the first half of the reign. John Langton, who replaced him in the chancery, was not a man who began to approach Burnell in power and influence. Further, the dismissal of so many of the justices transformed the senior personnel of the courts, and of the king's council. Gilbert de Thornton and the man who succeeded him as chief justice of the King's Bench, Roger Brabazon, arguably lacked the commitment to reform that Ralph Hengham had possessed. This pattern of change in personnel was not universal. The only change among the earls was the addition to their number of Richard FitzAlan, whose claim to the earldom of Arundel was recognized by Edward early in 1291. He did not, however, witness any royal charters until 1296, and was never a man on whom Edward relied to any great extent.[56] The continued presence of such men as Henry de Lacy, earl of Lincoln, in Edward's circle was not sufficient to maintain continuity of policy with that of the 1270s and 1280s, given the changes in the ranks of the king's officials.

Changed international circumstances, in addition, meant that Edward's government of his country was to be very different in the 1290s. There was some concern in 1293 at the deteriorating relationship with France, and that concern was soon to turn to alarm. Instead of Edward being able to play the role of the peace-maker in Europe, and the leader of a future crusade, the English king found himself facing the prospect of fighting Philip IV of France in defence of Gascony. Welsh rebellion in 1294, and Scottish hostility to Edward in 1296, meant that the government had to direct most of its energies towards war and its organization. The king's achievement in giving his realm stability and unity was perhaps not to be a lasting one.

---

[55] Above, 150.
[56] *Complete Peerage*, i; C53/82.

Chapter 14

THE GREAT CAUSE, 1291–2

According to the annals of Waverley Abbey, Edward I gathered his magnates and councillors together in 1291, and announced that he intended to bring Scotland under his control, just as he had subjugated Wales.[1] With hindsight, this sounds very plausible. It suggests that from the outset of his involvement in Scottish affairs, the king had a consistent policy aimed at extending his rule over all of Britain. By 1296, the chronicler Langtoft was able to compare Edward favourably with King Arthur for his achievement in creating one realm out of two kingdoms. Yet in discussing the events of 1291 and 1292, Langtoft had suggested that at that stage all Edward had wished to do was to establish who had the proper right to rule as king in Scotland, and that he had simply exercised his rights as feudal lord of Scotland so that a tricky succession dispute might be resolved.[2] More recent commentators have also produced very varied verdicts on Edward's actions. For Sir Maurice Powicke, Edward was a man who 'respected without question the customs and institutions of Scotland', while at the same time being determined 'to maintain order and justice'. In contrast, G.W.S. Barrow has suggested that Edward took undue advantage of the Scots when they had no leader, extracting such recognition of his authority as he could, and imposing 'his own prejudiced and highly questionable view of the relationship between the English and Scottish crowns'.[3]

There was nothing in the relations between Scotland and England in the first half of Edward's reign that presaged the conflicts that were to dominate the second half. Alexander III, king of Scots, had married Edward's sister Margaret in 1251, and although she died in 1275, letters from both Alexander and his elder son and daughter testify to a

---

[1] *Ann. Waverley*, 409. As the chronicle breaks off, with the final pages being lost, it is not clear how much hindsight the author had. Powicke, *Thirteenth Century*, 603, no. 1, discounts this passage as being 'casual and isolated'.
[2] *Langtoft*, ii, 192, 264–6.
[3] Powicke, *Thirteenth Century*, 610; G.W.S. Barrow, *Robert Bruce and the Community of the Realm of Scotland* (1965), 44, 70. There has, of course, always been a difference between English and Scottish writers.

continued family affection towards the English king.[4] The issue of homage, which proved so divisive in the case of Wales, does not appear to have been raised by Edward when Alexander came south in 1274 for the English coronation. The matter was brought up in 1278, and Alexander clearly had considerable reservations: his demand for a most impressive escort, to consist of the archbishops of Canterbury and York, and the earls of Gloucester, Warenne and Lincoln, shows that he did not expect to be treated by his brother-in-law as an ordinary feudal tenant-in-chief. The problems were smoothed over, however, and in the autumn parliament of 1278 Alexander did homage to Edward. It is clear, even though the English and Scottish texts are not in full agreement, that this was for the lands that Alexander held in England. The Scottish king was not prepared to concede that his realm was held as a fief from Edward, and although the English reserved their position, the matter was not pressed.[5] Edward did not adopt an aggressive attitude towards Alexander. When, for example, Alexander's liberties in Cumberland were taken into the king's hands in the course of *Quo Warranto* inquiries in the late 1270s, Edward firmly ordered them to be restored. Alexander's attitude towards Edward was a friendly one, as is shown by a letter he sent, along with a present of four gerfalcons, inquiring after the English king's health.[6]

In addition to the links between the English and Scottish royal families, there were also important connections between England and Scotland among magnates. Many families of Norman and French origins had major landed interests on both sides of the Anglo-Scottish border. Roger de Quincy, earl of Winchester, had remarkably widespread estates in the mid-thirteenth century in both England and Scotland. The Umfraville family was another whose concerns were shared between both countries. Of great significance for the events which were to unfold in the 1290s was the case of the Balliols, who had a strong power-base at Barnard castle in County Durham, as well as other English estates, and who also acquired much land in Galloway.[7] The Bruce family, too, possessed lands in England. Robert Bruce, earl of Carrick, father of the future king, was lent money by Edward I, served him in Wales, and was appointed constable of Carlisle castle,

---

[4] *Anglo-Scottish Relations*, ed. Stones, xxiv, 42–3; *CDS*, ii, nos 185, 204, 253. There was also a great deal of correspondence of a more official character: see, for example, the letters in SC 1/20, nos 142–68.

[5] *Anglo-Scottish Relations*, ed. Stones, 38–41; *CDS*, ii, no. 120.

[6] *CDS*, ii, nos 146, 253.

[7] G.G. Simpson, 'The *Familia* of Roger de Quincy, earl of Winchester and Constable of Scotland', *Essays on the Nobility of Medieval Scotland*, ed. K.J. Stringer (Edinburgh, 1985), 103; G. Stell, 'The Balliol Family and the Great Cause of 1291–2', ibid., 151–7.

and sheriff of Cumberland.[8] Many other Scottish nobles had interests in England, and these cross-border links, it appears, tended to promote harmony between the realms.

The situation that had existed for much of the thirteenth century was transformed by the extraordinary succession of tragedies which over-took the Scottish royal house. Alexander III had two sons. The younger, David, died in 1281, and the elder, Alexander, in 1284. A letter from the king of Scots to Edward thanked him for his sympathy over the death of his heir: he could not have known that Edward's almonry account reveals that only 1s 5d was spent by the king on offerings for the young Alexander's soul, and that the queen and her ladies gave only 2s.[9] King Alexander's daughter, Margaret, died in 1283, but she had married Eric, king of Norway, and left a daughter, also called Margaret. She thus became the sole heiress to the Scottish kingdom. It was obviously prudent in these circumstances for Alexander to remarry, and this he did in October 1285. Hopes that the new queen, Yolande of Dreux, a French noblewoman, would produce a new male heir were in vain. In March 1286 Alexander rode out from Edinburgh in ferocious weather, to rejoin his queen whom he had left at Kinghorn in Fife. He crossed the Forth successfully, and then insisted on riding on through the night. He was found dead on the seashore the next morning, killed in a fall from his horse.[10]

Alexander's death left Margaret of Norway as the heir to the king-dom, once it became clear that Queen Yolande was not pregnant. Margaret was only seven when she left Norway for Scotland in 1290: she fell ill on the voyage, and died in Orkney.[11] The dynastic situation that resulted from her death was complex. There was no obvious heir, and no less than thirteen claimants to the throne were to appear. Some, such as Nicholas de Soules, William de Ros and William de Vescy, claimed through illegitimate lines of descent from Alexander II, who had died in 1249. Much more powerful were the claims through descent from Henry, earl of Northumberland, who had died in 1152. He was the son of David I of Scots, and father of both Malcolm IV and William the Lion, but it was through his youngest son, David, earl of Huntingdon, that the claims of John Balliol, Robert Bruce and John Hastings were derived, all through daughters of the earl. As the principle of primogen-iture did not apply in feudal law to daughters, all three had justifiable claims. In addition, there were claims put forward by Florence, count of Holland, and Robert de Pinkeney, based on their descent from

---

[8] Barrow, *Robert Bruce*, 32–3; *CDS*, ii, nos 200, 236–7; above, 196.
[9] *CDS*, ii, no. 250; Taylor, 'Royal Alms and Oblations', 114.
[10] Barrow, *Robert Bruce*, 3–4, 19–20; *Chron. Lanercost*, 116–17.
[11] See below, 362.

daughters of Henry, earl of Northumberland. One claim, that of John Comyn, went back even further, to the younger son of King Duncan, Donald Ban, who had died in 1099. The king of Norway also put in a claim, as Margaret's father. Despite the number of claimants, however, it was clear that the central issue was in practice between John Balliol and Robert Bruce.[12]

Edward I showed no immediate desire to become involved in Scottish affairs when he heard the news of Alexander III's death in 1286. Two Scottish friars were sent to him on behalf of those present at the late king's funeral, but no English embassy was sent to Scotland. There was no English participation in the process by which six Guardians were chosen – two bishops, two earls, and two barons – to govern the kingdom.[13] Edward was not to be diverted from his expedition to Gascony, and it was on his journey through France that two Scottish embassies found him in the spring and summer of 1286. The bishop of St Andrews was the first to reach him; the bishop of Brechin with other envoys caught up with him in Gascony. Later tradition has it that the Scots were seeking Edward's advice and protection, and it has even been suggested that he may have replied that he would only provide assistance if his rights of lordship over Scotland were recognized.[14] Such an attitude would certainly have been consistent with his later policy, but the only clue to the nature of the negotiations in the English records is an order issued in mid-September delaying legal proceedings in the March between England and Scotland.[15]

There was no haste shown by Edward's subjects to take advantage of the problems facing the Scots. The earl of Ulster and Thomas de Clare did make an agreement with an important group of Scottish nobles, including James, steward of Scotland, the earls of Menteith and Dunbar, Robert Bruce of Annandale and his son, the earl of Carrick, in September 1286. The document is a puzzling one. Some historians have seen it as evidence of some Irish project by the Scots, but it could also represent an unsuccessful attempt by the Bruces and their supporters to gain allies in case civil war broke out.[16] There was a brief Bruce

---

[12] The various claims to the Scottish throne are very conveniently summarized in *Edward I and the Throne of Scotland 1290-1296. An Edition of the Record Sources for the Great Cause*, ed. E.L.G. Stones and G.G. Simpson(Oxford, 1978), i, 13-21. My debt to this important work, elsewhere in this book referred to as *Great Cause*, is very considerable indeed.

[13] *Documents illustrative of the History of Scotland*. ed. J. Stevenson (1870), i, 4-5.

[14] A.A.M. Duncan, 'The Community of the Realm of Scotland and Robert Bruce', *SHR*, xlv (1966), 189.

[15] *Documents*, ed. Stevenson, i, 21-2.

[16] Ibid., i, 22-3. For comment on this text, Powicke, *Thirteenth Century*, 597-8; Barrow, *Robert Bruce*, 25-6; Duncan, 'Community of the Realm of Scotland', 188.

rising in south-western Scotland, probably in the winter of 1286–7, but
it achieved little.[17] By then, it was clear that Yolande was not pregnant.
There was no doubt that the heiress was Margaret of Norway, and this
presented a new avenue by which Edward could gain effective control
of Scotland, if that was his intention.

Margaret, born in 1283, had been accepted as the rightful heir to the
throne in 1284, so there was no problem about her right, even though a
woman had never ruled as queen of Scots. In view of her age, however,
her father, Eric of Norway, was reluctant to see her leave Norway for an
uncertain future in Scotland. The obvious solution was to arrange for
her marriage, and a plan duly emerged for Margaret to be wed to
Edward of Caernarfon, Edward I's heir. It is, unfortunately, far from
clear who conceived this scheme.[18] Edward was certainly active in
promoting it, for he sent an emissary to Norway in April 1290, and one
of the aims of Otto de Grandson's embassy to Rome which set out in the
next month was to obtain papal dispensation for the marriage.[19] The
original initiative, however, could well have come from the Guardians
of Scotland, or even from the Norwegian king. From the Guardians'
point of view, the marriage would give Edward I a direct interest in
preserving the peace in Scotland, and it would remove one reason for
King Eric's reluctance to send Margaret to Scotland. From the latter's
standpoint, a marriage alliance with the English was plainly desirable.

Negotiations between the English, Scots and Norwegians took place
at Salisbury early in 1289. It was agreed that Margaret should come to
Scotland, or England, by 1 November 1290. Assurances were given
that she would not be married without Edward's consent, and that of
the king of Norway. The Scots agreed that she was the true heiress, and
conceded that unsuitable Guardians or officials might be removed from
office, with the consent of English and Norwegian envoys. Should the
Scots and the Norwegians differ, the English might settle matters. The
agreement was ratified by the Scots, at Birgham, on 14 March 1290.[20]
It is possible that Edward was not being entirely open in his dealings,
for a curious entry on the Close Rolls noted that certain documents
concerning Norway were sealed in secret, in February 1290, at Robert

---

[17] Barrow, *Robert Bruce*, 25; *Formulary E, Scottish Letters and Brieves 1286–1424*, ed.
A.A.M. Duncan (University of Glasgow, Scottish History Department, Occasional
Papers, 1976), 41, provides evidence that a feudal summons may have been issued to
recruit troops to deal with this rising.

[18] G.W.S. Barrow, *Kingship and Unity: Scotland 1000–1306* (1981), 159, implies that
Edward I was responsible, but the same historian in his *Robert Bruce*, 38–9, suggests
that it was the Guardians who took the initiative.

[19] *CDS*, ii, no. 368; *Documents*, ed. Stevenson, i, 134.

[20] Ibid., i, 105–11, 129–31. The modern 'Birgham' is often given as 'Brigham' in the
records.

Burnell's house in London, and were then enrolled in the wardrobe, rather than the chancery.[21] In May an English embassy set out to fetch Margaret, the Maid of Norway. Elaborate preparations were made, with the ship made ready at Yarmouth, lavishly provisioned with wine, beer, salt meat and fish, and a stock of luxuries to tempt the young heiress, such as sugar, spices, almonds, figs and raisins. There was even an organ for her amusement, and banners and pennons so that the vessel could be decked out in splendour.[22] Unfortunately, not all the diplomatic problems had been overcome, and the envoys returned in June empty-handed.

Further negotiations were needed, and on 18 July the Treaty of Birgham was agreed between the English and the Scots. It was confirmed by Edward at Northampton at the end of the following month. This dealt with the arrangements to be made once the young Edward had married Margaret. Scotland would remain 'separate, free in itself without any subjection to England, and divided by its proper frontiers and marches as in the past'. The Scottish administration was to be kept quite separate from the English, and the relics and muniments of the Scottish kingdom were to be kept under seal in Scotland until Margaret had come there, and had given birth to an heir.[23] These guarantees on Scottish independence show that the Guardians were extremely cautious in their dealings with Edward I. The English king, however, was not pressing hard any claims to his feudal rights over Scotland at this stage. A letter prepared for use by Anthony Bek in the negotiations, which was not apparently needed, omitted a phrase demanded by the Scots, which stressed that Scotland should not be subject to England. The phrase, however, was duly included in the final treaty. Edward, hardly surprisingly, resisted a Scottish request that no work of fortification should take place in the March on the English side, and he ensured that his rights in the March were not prejudiced.[24] At this stage the issue of any possible claims to overlordship of Scotland by Edward was not, perhaps, very significant, for if the crown were to be linked by marriage, then the English would not need any other justification for intervention in Scottish affairs.

Although Edward did not press any theoretical claims to his overlordship of Scotland in the summer of 1290, his actions showed no respect for Scottish traditions of independence. On 4 June he appointed

---

[21] *CCR 1288–96*, 149.
[22] *Documents*, ed. Stevenson, i, 149, 186–92; *CDS*, ii, no. 464; C 47/4/5, ff.9v–10. As the ship made two voyages to Norway, it is not clear what supplies were provided on each occasion.
[23] *Documents*, ed. Stevenson, i, 162–73.
[24] *Documents*, ed. Stevenson, i, 160, 167.

Walter de Huntercombe to the custody of the Isle of Man, claiming that the earl of Ulster had surrendered it to him, and ignoring the strong Scottish claim to the island. He then gave authority, on 20 June, to Anthony Bek, bishop of Durham, to admit the warring inhabitants of the Western Isles to his peace. However justified this was by conditions there, it was a surprising intervention in the affairs of another realm. Then, on 28 July, the very day that he confirmed the treaty of Birgham, Edward nominated Bek to act on behalf of Edward of Caernarfon and the young queen Margaret in Scotland, 'to administer justice and set that realm in order'. Bek was to act in conjunction with the Scottish Guardians, and Edward asked them to be obedient to him.[25] The evidence does not suggest that Scotland was in so serious a state as Edward implied, and Bek's appointment was a remarkable step to take before Margaret had even come to Scotland. Whatever his motives were, it is plain that Edward had decided that he should exercise power in Scotland.

The situation was transformed in the autumn of 1290, with Margaret's death in Orkney, where her ship put in on its way from Norway.[26] The thread on which the future security of Scotland depended had snapped. Bishop Fraser of St Andrews wrote to Edward I on 7 October, reporting the rumour of Margaret's death, which he still hoped might prove to be false. He feared that civil war might break out, for Robert Bruce the elder had come to Perth, where the magnates had assembled to wait for Margaret, with a considerable following and uncertain intentions. The bishop asked Edward to come north to the Scottish border, so that, if Margaret had died, he might prevent trouble, and place the rightful claimant on the throne. He added, tactfully, 'as long as he is ready to accept your counsel'. Bishop Fraser did not explicitly state who the heir should be, but he implied that his candidate was John Balliol. If Balliol came to see Edward, then he should be treated, said the bishop, in such a way that the English king's own honour and position should not be prejudiced.[27]

It is likely that Edward also received approaches from a different faction in Scotland. An undated document, known as the Appeals of the Seven Earls, asked for his help against Bishop Fraser and John Comyn, both of whom were Guardians. It claimed that the Seven Earls of Scotland had the right to make the king, and to place him on the throne,

---

[25] Ibid., i, 156–7, 161–2; *CPR 1281–92*, 386; Barrow, *Robert Bruce*, 41–2.

[26] Barrow, *Robert Bruce*, 42; *Foedera*, I, ii, 741.

[27] *Great Cause*, i, 5–6; ii, 3–4. There are considerable problems in translating the terms used by Bishop Fraser. The phrase regarding Edward's position should Balliol come to him is that *honor vester et commodum* should be preserved. The rightful claimant should be enthroned *dum tamen ille vestro consilio voluerit adherere*.

and complaints were made against subordinates of the Guardians who had been ravaging Moray.[28] John Balliol, meanwhile, was describing himself as heir to the Scottish kingdom. His promise to Anthony Bek of land worth 500 marks a year in Scotland shows a ready awareness of the importance that the English were bound to have in the settlement of the succession.[29] Edward probably intended to go north in the autumn of 1290, but the death of his queen, Eleanor, on 28 November put an end to any such plans. He spent Christmas at the religious house at Ashridge, founded by his cousin Edmund of Cornwall, and it was perhaps at the parliament held there in January that he began to consider the Scottish question again. Anthony Bek, possibly with others, was sent to Scotland, and attempts were almost certainly made to persuade the Scots to submit the question of the succession to Edward.[30]

Edward and his advisers decided that the dispute over the Scottish throne should be resolved by the English king acting as feudal overlord of Scotland. Invitations from the Scots to Edward to arbitrate as an influential outsider, if such were received, which is uncertain, were not acceptable to him. On 8 March 1291 the abbot of Evesham, and probably some thirty other heads of monastic houses, were asked to provide information from chronicles 'touching in any way our realm and the rule of Scotland'. Presumably some research had been undertaken in the royal archives, with insufficient results. In most cases, the replies from the monasteries were also unhelpful, but in a few instances, such as that of Tewkesbury, useful material was found. Some monks were asked to bring their chronicles to Norham, where Edward was to meet the Scots.[31] This was a remarkable procedure. Although appeals to past history were common in the middle ages, this was the first time that the king had tried to use the accumulated knowledge of the monasteries. There is a striking contrast with the methods used by Edward in his dealings with the French monarchy. In that case, argument could largely proceed from the Treaty of Paris of 1259, so there was not the same degree of uncertainty about the central facts of the relationship between the two countries that existed with regard to Anglo-Scottish affairs. Further, Edward used trained lawyers, men such as Bonet de St Quentin, in his dealings with the French, and the arguments accordingly reached a high level of legal sophistication. As far as the Scots were concerned, Anthony Bek was particularly

---

[28] *Anglo-Scottish Relations*, ed. Stones, 44–50. For other possibly related documents, see *Great Cause*, ii, 185–7.

[29] *Documents*, ed. Stevenson, i, 203–4.

[30] *Great Cause*, i, 7.

[31] Ibid., i, 137–48, for a full discussion.

influential in advising Edward: one usually well-informed chronicler said that the appeal to the monastic chronicles was his idea.[32]

The hearings which were to determine the issue of the Scottish succession began at Norham, where English and Scottish magnates had gathered, on 10 May 1291. A remarkably full record of the proceedings was drawn up on behalf of Edward I by a notary, John of Caen, and another version made, in Edward II's reign, by Andrew Tange.[33] It was not usual for court or parliamentary proceedings to be recorded by public notaries, but it must have been felt that on so sensitive a question as the succession to the Scottish throne, it was essential that the author of the record should have a standing and a reliability that ordinary royal clerks did not possess. A notary's reputation depended on his accuracy. Yet there are problems. The record was not produced absolutely contemporaneously: the earliest reference to it dates from 31 May 1297. John was an employee of the English king, and in 1303 he was prepared to make a very significant emendation to his roll, 'in the most significant part of the whole process'.[34] Careful selection by John of Caen of what to include could bias the record in Edward's interest, and unfortunately there is no equivalent Scottish source which can be set against his roll. Nor could such an official record be expected to reveal the complex undercurrents of political dealing that undoubtedly existed, but are often no more than hinted at by scraps of evidence.

The first stage of the hearings was dominated by arguments over Edward's rights of jurisdiction. At Norham, on 10 May 1291, the chief justice of the King's Bench, Roger Brabazon, asked the Scots to recognize Edward's overlordship, so that he might do justice, and bring peace. It is likely, though the English sources do not reveal this, that Robert Wishart, bishop of Glasgow, protested firmly that Scotland was not under feudal subjection to England.[35] An adjournment was required so that the Scots could consider the English demands, and the proceedings reopened on 2 June. It was probably then that the Scots presented a careful written statement, pointing out that in the absence of a king of Scots, they were not empowered to give an answer to Edward's claim. Only a king could deal with such a matter.[36] One view is that Edward rejected this argument 'out of hand', but the procedure that he adopted suggests that he and his advisers took the logical view,

---

[32] Langtoft, ii, 190; above, 314–15; below, 376.

[33] John of Caen's roll, and Andrew Tange's, are discussed in *Great Cause*, i, 40–52.

[34] Ibid., i, 50.

[35] Barrow, *Robert Bruce*, 48; P.A. Linehan, 'A Fourteenth Century History of Anglo-Scottish Relations in a Spanish Manuscript, *BIHR*, xlviii (1975), 120.

[36] *Great Cause*, ii, 30–1; *Anglo-Scottish Relations*, ed. Stones, 53–4.

hinted at in the Scots' reply, that if there was no king, then the best step would be to obtain the necessary recognition of his overlordship and jurisdiction from the candidates for kingship.[37]

John of Caen's record set out in considerable detail, with much repetition, two speeches made by the chancellor, Robert Burnell, and one by Edward himself, made on 2 and 3 June. Edward's speech was originally given in French, though for the record it was translated into Latin. It is by far the longest he is known to have made, but as given by John of Caen, it has an implausibly literary flavour and too close a resemblance to Burnell's speeches to be regarded as authentic.[38] The solution to the impasse that the Scots had placed Edward in was for the various competitors to acknowledge the English king's right to lordship and jurisdiction. They conceded that he might take the realm of Scotland into his hands, with the proviso that he agreed to grant it to the successful claimant. An ingenious fiction got round the problem that the competitors themselves did not have seisin of Scotland, and the initial refusal of the keepers of the royal castles in Scotland to hand them over to the English. The castles were handed over to Edward in his capacity as a competitor (he had reserved his own right to claim the throne), and to the other candidates for the throne. The latter then entrusted the castles to Edward in his role as feudal overlord of Scotland, a position which they, though not the Scots as a whole, were prepared to concede he held.[39]

There have, inevitably, been doubts cast upon the propriety of Edward's actions in obtaining recognition of his overlordship, and seisin of Scotland, from the competitors, when this had been refused by the Guardians and the assembled Scottish magnates. Pope Boniface VIII in 1299, echoing arguments put to him by the Scots, implied that Edward had used improper force, and the charge was made explicit by 1321.[40] Certainly, on 16 April, Edward had asked sixty-seven northern magnates to attend at Norham, with their feudal quotas of armed men. There was also a small force of crossbowmen and archers present from 2 June until 6 August, and an English fleet lurking off Holy Island. Yet such a force was hardly sufficient for purposes of conquest, and was perhaps recruited to provide the king with a substantial formal retinue,

---

[37] Barrow, *Robert Bruce*, 47; Duncan, 'The Community of the Realm of Scotland', 191. I follow Duncan's interpretation here. It should be noted that the reply by the Scots to Edward was not included in the English record of the proceedings, though it was, it seems, inserted by Edward's clerks into the Exchequer register called *Liber A*: *Great Cause*, i, 116.

[38] *Great Cause*, ii, 32–41, 46–65.

[39] Ibid., ii, 68, 100, 112–13; Barrow, *Robert Bruce*, 50–1; Duncan, 'The Community of the Realm of Scotland', 192.

[40] Barrow, *Robert Bruce*, 70, 85–6.

or simply to assist in the preservation of public order.[41] Edward's rejection of the Scots' refusal to acknowledge his overlordship has been described as 'the first thoroughly discreditable action in his dealings with the Scottish nation'.[42] Yet, from the English point of view, if the succession to the Scottish throne was to be resolved without bloodshed, it was essential that Edward should hear the case, and it was impossible for him to act unless those concerned recognized his right of jurisdiction. Simply to have acted as an arbitrator would have meant Edward neglecting what he regarded as his right of feudal overlordship. It is plain that he was determined to use the opportunity presented by the disputed succession to establish that overlordship, as the elaborate arrangements that were made for him to receive fealty from as many Scots as possible in July and August 1291 show. Overlordship for Edward was not a mere legal fiction that would allow him to hear the case, but a right that he was anxious to establish and exercise, by obtaining seisin of Scotland.

Once the competitors had agreed to accept Edward's jurisdiction, a court was set up, composed of 104 auditors. Forty were nominated by Bruce, forty by Balliol and twenty-four by Edward. The division between Bruce and Balliol does not necessarily reflect the fact that they had the strongest claims, but may have been a recognition of the factional split in Scottish politics at this time. The attractive idea that the court was based on the classical Roman tribunal of the *centumviri* is implausible. Edward's court did not adopt procedures based on Roman law, and the main function of the auditors appears to have been to investigate the various claims put forward, and to answer questions on specific legal points.[43] Final judgement was to be the work, it appears, of Edward and his council.

It was decided to hold the hearings at Berwick, starting early in August 1291. They proved to be extraordinarily protracted. The first stage took little more than a week, and was largely devoted to the submission by the various competitors of their petitions. An adjournment until 2 June 1292 followed, when the problem of deciding what

---

[41] *Anglo-Scottish Relations*, ed. Stones, 84; *Parl. Writs*, i, 256; *Documents*, ed. Stevenson, 204–5. The document printed by Stevenson states that the fleet was stationed so as 'to prevent victuals coming to Scotland', which suggests an economic blockade, but it goes on to list the substantial quantities of foodstuffs sent to the king on the border, and it seems likely that the entry was garbled by the clerk. The question of this military force is discussed further in *Great Cause*, i, 175–6.

[42] Barrow, *Robert Bruce*, 47.

[43] *Great Cause*, i, 33, 221; ii, 371–2. The suggestion that the court was based on the *centumviri* was made by G. Neilson, 'Bruce *versus* Balliol', *SHR*, xvi (1919), 1–14. *Rishanger*, 238, states that the auditors were selected 'ad jus dictorum petentium diffiniendum'.

law should apply to the case dominated matters, though it was also decided that the vital issue to be determined was that between Bruce and Balliol. Another adjournment followed, and the case was finally concluded in a session which began in mid-October 1292, and ended when final judgement was given on 17 November.[44] There can be no doubt that the decision in favour of John Balliol was a fair one: he had the best claim by the principles of primogeniture. He was the closest hereditary heir to the late queen, Margaret, and to her grandfather, Alexander III. What has to be decided, however, is whether Edward reached the decision in favour of Balliol in the right way, or whether he was throughout attempting to manipulate the legal process in his own interests, delaying matters so that Scotland would remain for as long as possible in his hands, and ensuring that the new king would start his reign at a considerable disadvantage.

The long adjournment between August 1291 and June 1292 was intended, according to the record, to give time for one of the claimants, Florence, count of Holland, to find a document vital to his case. This allegedly showed that David, earl of Huntingdon, had surrendered his rights, and those of his descendants, to the Scottish throne. If this was so, then the claims of John Balliol, Robert Bruce and John Hastings would all fail. It was obviously right that this question should be resolved at an early stage of the hearings, but it is odd that so long was allowed for the adjournment. The count was not able, even so, to produce the document in court, and claimed that it had been removed from the Scottish treasury by the prior of Pluscardine, who still retained it. Yet the Dutch national archives contain two copies of the deed in question, both dated in November 1291, one of them authenticated by the prior himself. The count's attorney appears to have had a good knowledge of the text. It is certainly a forgery, but it is not clear who was responsible for it, or why Florence was unable to produce it in court.[45]

Florence's claim may seem rather frivolous, but it did have important implications. These were, G.W.S. Barrow has persuasively argued, well appreciated by Robert Bruce, who saw in it the best means of defeating the Balliol claim. Count Florence and Robert Bruce made a remarkable agreement, on 14 June 1292, which provided for each to help the other. If either were successful, then he would compensate the other. Of course if Florence's argument was successful against Balliol, it would also invalidate Bruce's hereditary claim, but Bruce might still succeed, on the grounds that he had been designated as future king by

[44] The chronology of the hearings is conveniently set out in *Great Cause*, i, 236-85.
[45] G.G. Simpson, 'The Claim of Florence Count of Holland to the Scottish Throne, 1291-2', *SHR*, xxxvi (1957), 111-23; *Great Cause*, i, 122-5; ii, 150-1, 325.

Alexander II, or so he alleged, and that he was the choice of the Seven Earls. Interestingly, Gilbert de Clare, earl of Gloucester, was among the witnesses to the agreement. He had a family connection by marriage with Bruce, but his appearance in this witness list suggests that Bruce was looking for influential English allies, much as Balliol had looked to Anthony Bek for support.[46] There was, no doubt, much political manoeuvring, and many deals struck, during the long adjournment.

When the sessions resumed in the summer of 1292, a vital question to be decided was that of what system of law should be employed. In his arguments, Robert Bruce suggested that his claim was the strongest 'by the natural law, by which kings reign', and he flattered Edward by appealing to him 'as his sovereign lord and emperor'. John Balliol argued that for the case to be heard under imperial law would be prejudicial to the rights of the English crown, and he demanded the application of the customs of England and Scotland.[47] Roman law favoured a claim by proximity (Bruce); the feudal custom of primogeniture favoured a claim by primogeniture (Balliol). A further question was whether the kindom was partible, as an earldom was, in which case Scotland could be divided between the claimants descended from the earl of Huntingdon's daughters.

Edward acted meticulously in reaching a decision on these points. Representatives had been summoned from Oxford and Cambridge to Norham, evidently to provide legal expertise.[48] In the summer of 1292 the king went further, and made extensive inquiries from legal experts overseas. The question put to them assumed that Scotland was held by homage from the king of England, and that it was impartible. The issue was whether proximity or primogeniture should be preferred. In general, the surviving replies, from lawyers in Paris, suggested that local custom should be followed. An examination of the problem, however, in the light of the Lombard *Libri Feudorum* suggested the elimination of all the candidates, which would have meant the kingdom escheating to Edward I. Remarkably, Thomas Weyland, the recently disgraced chief justice, proffered his advice. Ignoring the instruction that the kingdom should be regarded as impartible, he suggested its division between Balliol, Bruce and Hastings, as this would be to Edward's greatest advantage.[49] Escheat or partition must have been tempting to Edward, and it is to his credit that there are no indications that he considered

[46] Ibid., ii, 162–4; Barrow, *Robert Bruce*, 63–7.

[47] *Great Cause*, ii, 167, 170, 179, 183.

[48] Ibid., i, 8; ii, 5.

[49] Ibid., ii, 358–65; G.J. Hand, 'The Opinions of the Paris Lawyers upon the Scottish Succession c. 1292', *The Irish Jurist*, n.s. v (1970), 141–55.

such solutions seriously.[50] He may well have considered, of course, that partition would be a dangerous precedent, as it might be applied to England should he die without leaving a male heir.

The final stages of the case went quickly in the autumn of 1292, with only brief adjournments. Edward's councillors unanimously agreed, on 3 November, that a candidate descended from a younger sister, even if closer in degree to the throne (Bruce), should not be preferred to one descended from the elder sister (Balliol). On 6 November the Scots auditors concurred with this view, and judgement was given against Bruce. Then the demands made by Bruce and Hastings that the kingdom should be divided were considered, and after the Scottish auditors were consulted, the decision was that they had no case. By then, the rest of the competitors had either withdrawn, or been told that their claims were invalid as they had not been properly pursued. The final judgement, on 17 November, accordingly went to John Balliol.[51] There can be little doubt that this was an entirely proper outcome to the proceedings.

Once judgement was pronounced in favour of John Balliol, Edward did not hesitate to hand the kingdom over to its new ruler. Instructions for Balliol to be given seisin of Scotland were issued on 19 November.[52] Early in the proceedings, on 12 June 1291, Edward had formally promised to maintain the laws and customs of Scotland, and to restore the realm to the rightful claimant, within two months of judgement being given. If he failed to do so, he would be liable to a penalty of £100,000 in aid of the Holy Land. A saving clause preserved Edward's rights in the Marches, and he made it clear that he had the right to receive homage from the new king, and the rights that went with it, and that 'sovereign lordship' was his. He renounced, however, any claims to exercise rights of wardship or marriage over the rulers of Scotland.[53] Now that Scotland had a new king, in the form of John Balliol, Edward had the opportunity to establish in practice what was entailed in his sovereign lordship, and what obligations towards him would ensue from the act of homage.

The judgement in Balliol's favour was immediately followed, according to the insertion made in the roll in 1303 by John of Caen, by a warning that if he did not govern justly, Edward would have to intervene.[54] On the same day that seisin of Scotland was granted to Balliol, the seal that had been used by the Guardians in the

---

[50] Pollock and Maitland, *History of English Law*, ii, 265.
[51] *Great Cause*, i, 127-35; ii, 198-247.
[52] Ibid., ii, 250-1.
[53] Ibid., ii, 98-9.
[54] Ibid., ii, 248-9; above, 364.

interregnum was broken, and the pieces sent to England, as evidence of
Edward's rights over Scotland.[55] When Balliol was enthroned at Scone,
the ceremony was performed by Anthony Bek and John de St John. The
latter was deputizing for the infant earl of Fife, whose hereditary task
this was, but the fact that two English magnates played such a role
emphasized the new subjection of the Scottish crown to England.[56] If
there were any doubts about Balliol's position, they must have been
largely resolved on 26 December, when the new king did homage to
Edward I in unambiguous terms, which recognized the English king's
sovereign lordship, and acknowledged that homage was owed in
respect of the whole realm of Scotland.[57]

Edward did not live in an age when a man could be content with a
mere recognition of his authority: he had to exercise his rights in order
to establish them. The first issue arose so quickly that some have
suspected that it may have been engineered by the English. On 7
December 1292 a Berwick burgess, Roger Bartholomew, appealed to
Edward against three judgements delivered in the court of the
Guardians. It was decided, very properly, that Scottish law should be
followed, but the appeals were heard by Edward and his council, sitting
at Newcastle-upon-Tyne. In one of the three cases, the previous judgement against Roger was overthrown, in a ruling made on 22
December.[58] Five days later the Scots protested that Edward had not
kept his promise, made in the Treaty of Northampton, that Scottish
cases would not be heard outside Scotland. In reply, Roger Brabazon
argued that Edward was keeping his promise not to delay in doing
justice in Scottish cases, that he had a right to hear matters concerning
officials who had acted under his authority as overlord during the
interregnum, and lastly, and this was the sinister note, that Edward
was not obliged to keep promises made when the throne of Scotland
was vacant, now that there was a king.

Four days later the matter was discussed in a well-attended meeting
in the king's chamber. Edward himself explained in unambiguous
terms that he intended to hear any cases brought to him as superior lord
of Scotland, when and where he chose, and that if need be, he would
even summon the king of Scots to appear before him in England.[59] This
was going well beyond the issues raised by Roger Bartholomew's case,
which had not been concerned with the relationship of Balliol with

[55] *Great Cause*, ii, 252–3.
[56] Ibid., 259; Guisborough, 239.
[57] *Great Cause*, ii, 260–3.
[58] Stevenson, *Documents*, i, 377–89. Barrow, *Robert Bruce*, 71–2, argues that this was a
deliberately organized test case.
[59] *Great Cause*, ii, 264–8.

Edward I, and must cast some doubt on the view that this was an arranged test case. It could be that Roger's complaints were seen by the English as providing a welcome opportunity for clarifying the legal position. John Balliol was clearly put under considerable pressure by Edward at Newcastle, and on 2 January 1293 he acquitted the English king of all the promises he had made, and annulled the terms of the Treaty of Northampton, which had provided for the independence and freedom of Scotland. The only promise Edward was prepared to renew was his agreement that he would not demand wardship or marriage from any future heir to the Scottish realm.[60] Edward had now got what he wanted: it remained to be seen how he would treat John Balliol.

It was rarely easy in the middle ages for a magnate to undergo the metamorphosis into kingship successfully, as the career of King Stephen in the twelfth century showed. John Balliol was certainly not the man to be able to make the change effectively, although, of course, Robert Bruce was to show that it was certainly not impossible. Balliol was the fourth son of a wealthy Anglo-Scottish magnate, who had held various official positions in England. John had probably been intended for the church, and does not appear to have had the training in war and politics that would have been needed for him to become an effective king. His connections were largely with England: his wife was a daughter of Earl Warenne, and he was a landowner on a substantial scale in the north of England.[61] Like so many magnates, he was in debt to the crown, owing £1,223, which he was told, in May 1293, that he could pay off in instalments of £40 a year.[62]

It was the question of appeals to the English king's court that was the first test of Edward's strength, and of John Balliol's weakness. Records exist of nine appellants in all, of whom two, the abbot of Reading and the bishop of Durham, were English, one a Gascon, and the rest Scots. The most important case was that of Macduff, younger son of Malcolm, earl of Fife. He claimed that he had been unjustly deprived of his inheritance and then imprisoned by John Balliol. The Scottish king was summoned to appear in the English parliament to answer the charge, and the procedure to be used in such cases was set out in an ordinance. It was made clear that Balliol had to attend in person, and this he did at Michaelmas 1293. Initial defiance did not last long when he was threatened with forfeiture of his three most important castles and towns. He acknowledged Edward's lordship, and obtained an

[60] Ibid., ii, 270–4.

[61] G. Stell, 'The Balliol Family and the Great Cause of 1291–2', *Essays on the Nobility of Medieval Scotland*, 150–65. In addition to the evidence cited there, the song quoted by Langtoft, ii, 258, suggests that Balliol had a scholarly education.

[62] *CDS*, ii, no. 671.

adjournment in the case, which was never concluded.[63] Balliol did at
least succeed in establishing his rights to the lands that Alexander III
had held in Scotland, in face of a renewed claim from John Hastings,
but Edward missed few opportunities of demonstrating what were the
practical implications of the superior lordship he claimed. Edward
asked, for example, that Balliol should pay £20 to the chamberlain, for
the fee due to him on the occasion of the performance of homage.[64]
There are hints, too, that Edward was intervening actively in Scottish
affairs. He paid the travel and other expenses of the sheriff of Fife, and
ordered him to hand over some lands in Fife to the bishop of Glasgow.
In 1294 Edward granted a weekly market at Crail in Fife to Isabella de
Vescy.[65]

All this might have been tolerated by the Scots. In the summer of
1294, however, Edward took a new step. He summoned John Balliol
and eighteen Scottish magnates to perform feudal service against the
French. Edward had demanded – and received – service from Scots
before, during his Welsh wars, but this had been for the lands they held
in England. Now, he was using his claim to superior lordship over
Scotland to ask for military aid. John Balliol had been in parliament at
Westminster shortly before this summons was issued, and according to
Guisborough's chronicle, he and the Scots with him had promised aid,
saying that they would be ready to muster when given sufficient warning, but it seems most unlikely that even Balliol would have been
prepared to concede that this warning should take the form of a feudal
summons.[66] The Welsh rebellion in the autumn of 1294 meant that this
feudal muster never in fact took place, and a major crisis in relations
between England and Scotland was temporarily averted.

Edward's war with France, which began in 1294, injected a new and
dangerous element into Anglo-Scottish relations. Not only did it pro-
voke Edward into making unprecedented demands on the Scots, but
also it gave the Scots a potential ally against the English. Before this
time, it would have been foolhardy to try to resist Edward. Now, they
could seek the assistance of Philip IV. One interpretation of the
immediate origins of the war against the Scots, which broke out in 1296,
has as a central element the political revolution in Scotland of 1295,
when power was taken from Balliol by a council of twelve, and a treaty
of alliance made with the French. The ratification of this treaty in
February 1296 was tantamount to a declaration of war against Edward

[63] Barrow, *Robert Bruce*, 78–83; *Rot. Parl.*, i, 112–13; *Anglo-Scottish Relations*, ed.
Stones, 65–7.
[64] *Rot. Parl*, i, 114–16; *CCR 1288–96*, 317.
[65] *CDS*, ii, nos 701, 704, 708.
[66] *Foedera*, I, ii, 804; Guisborough, 243.

I, and the Scottish host was accordingly called out. The English army had already been summoned to muster at Newcastle upon Tyne. This is the version of events ably set out by G.W.S. Barrow. An alternative view, however, sees the English invasion of Scotland in 1296 as the culmination of legal process. Balliol had refused to come to court to conclude the Macduff case, and had refused to hand over the three castles and towns as security. Edward therefore prepared his army to take them by force, and the war was, therefore, the final stage of the arguments over appeals from Scottish courts to Edward I.[67]

The official version of events, prepared by English notaries and appended, twenty years later, to the record of the Great Cause, was that the Macduff case was continually postponed, because of Edward's other preoccupations, until a parliament held at Bury St Edmunds after Martinmas 1295. Macduff appeared at this parliament, and pressed his case. Balliol did not attend, but sent the abbot of Arbroath and others, who excused their king, and complained about the injuries done by the English to the Scots. Edward promised remedy according to the law, and announced a further delay in the Macduff case until 1 March 1296, when the parties were asked to come to Newcastle-upon-Tyne. News then reached Edward of the alliance made by the Scots with the French. Edward demanded the surrender of certain border castles, and reminded Balliol that he was to appear at Newcastle. Instead, the Scots invaded England, committing 'notorious atrocities': infanticide, cutting off women's breasts, and burning two hundred schoolchildren alive at Corbridge. Edward's invasion of Scotland was therefore fully justified. It was only a later version of the text that laid any stress on the alliance with the French: the first account made only one brief allusion to it. This evidence has been, at least in part, discredited, because of its reference to a Martinmas parliament at Bury St Edmunds, but it is likely that there was only a small measure of confusion, and that a meeting at Bury in January 1296 was intended.[68] Certainly, the war can be seen as the final outcome of the legal disputes in which Edward and Balliol were involved.

It would not be right, however, to ignore the Scottish treaty with the French. Edward was certainly well aware of the possibility of such an alliance, for the French spy, Thomas Turberville, advised his masters to send an influential embassy to Scotland, 'for if they get there, you will benefit forever'.[69] Edward issued orders on 16 October 1295 for the

---

[67] Barrow, *Robert Bruce*, 87-96; W.C. Dickinson, *Scotland from the Earliest Times to 1603*, 3rd edn, revised by A.A.M. Duncan (Oxford, 1977), 151-2.

[68] *Great Cause*, ii, 284-91. The safe-conduct issued on 23 January 1296 to the abbot and prior of Arbroath, for their return to Scotland, lends some credence to the official record: *CPR 1292-1301*, 183.

[69] Cotton, 305.

seizure of all the lands and goods held by Scotsmen in England, and for Roxburgh, Jedburgh and Berwick to be handed over to him. This was clearly related to the French situation, for it was expressly stated that the three castles were not to be returned until the war with France was over.[70] The Macduff case meant that Edward was able to argue that John Balliol was a contumacious litigant, wilfully refusing to accept the jurisdiction of his superior lord, but to see the origins of the war purely in legal terms would not be correct. It was also a part of the wider manoeuvrings of the conflict between Edward I and Philip IV of France.

If Edward I had done no more with regard to Scotland than hear and determine the succession dispute, his reputation would have been high indeed. The Scots faced an extraordinary situation after the death of Margaret, the Maid of Norway, and the best means of resolving it was undoubtedly the proper hearing of the various claims in a court of law. Edward's conduct of the case itself is hard to fault. The claimants were given ample opportunity to present their arguments, the question of what law should apply was carefully considered, and the final outcome, in legal terms, was eminently satisfactory. The Great Cause, however, was only a part of a wider story of a deepening involvement in Scottish affairs by Edward, and he has been charged with taking 'advantage of the leaderless state of Scotland to extract something like the admissions he required', and then humiliating the new king, John Balliol, in a thoroughly merciless fashion.[71]

The question of how far Edward's claims to lordship over Scotland were justified can probably never be properly answered. There were certainly precedents to be found in the twelfth century: an effective English overlordship had existed from 1174 until 1189, and there were five examples of Scottish kings serving in English armies, on one occasion in France. There is, however, no clear evidence as to the precise nature of the feudal relationship in that period between the English and Scottish kings.[72] Edward I did, therefore, have a case, though not an unanswerable one. During Alexander III's reign, there was little purpose in pursuing the matter, and Edward had other preoccupations, notably in Wales. With Alexander's death, Edward had the opportunity of extending his influence in Scotland by means of the proposed marriage of his son to Margaret of Norway. In order to ensure the success of that plan, Edward was quite prepared to make extensive promises of independence to the Scots in the treaty of

---

[70] *Rotuli Scotiae* (Record Commission, 1814–19), i, 22.
[71] Barrow, *Robert Bruce*, 44.
[72] Warren, *Henry II*, 177–9.

Birgham, which he confirmed at Northampton. Margaret's death changed the situation completely. It became necessary for Edward to press his claims to overlordship, firstly so that he could hear the succession dispute, and then so that he could exercise some control over the new king. It is hardly reasonable to expect a ruler, because there was little opposition to him, to abstain from pressing home his case. Edward was presented with a splendid opportunity to establish what he saw as his rights, and many of his own subjects might well have felt that he was in dereliction of his duties had he not done so.

There is no doubt that, on Balliol's accession, Edward went back on promises that he had made previously. The English records of the hearings of the Great Cause carefully omitted the concessions, and did not include the rejection by the Scots of Edward's demand that they acknowledge his overlordship. But that rejection had made it clear that an answer could be given once there was a new king of Scots, and Edward certainly felt justified in regarding the situation once Balliol had been enthroned as entirely new. There was a case for regarding promises made when circumstances had been very different as no longer binding.

A parallel is often drawn between Philip IV of France's treatment of Edward as duke of Aquitaine, and Edward's own treatment of John Balliol. In both cases, the issues of legal appeals and of military service were very important.[73] There is no means of knowing whether Edward himself was influenced by the example of Philip IV's policies in determining his attitude towards the Scots, and John Balliol in particular.[74] Questions of jurisdiction and service were part of the essence of the feudal relationship, and the precise circumstances of Gascony and Scotland were very different. What Edward should have appreciated from his knowledge of Gascon affairs was the sensitivity of a feudal vassal to oppressive claims by an overlord. His own resentment at being summoned to appear in the *parlement* of Paris should have made him appreciate the problems that faced John Balliol. Edward, however, was not a man to draw such lessons. He was very well aware of his own honour and his own rights, but invariably lacked awareness of the susceptibilities of others. In Wales his policies drove the Welsh to rebellion, and in Scotland the story was a similar one. There is much that can be criticized in Edward's policies towards the Scots, but perhaps the most serious failing was that his unsympathetic treatment of John Balliol drove the Scots into alliance with the French, so diverting the king's attention and resources away from the conflict with Philip IV.

[73] For Edward's relations with Philip IV, see above, 323-4 and below, 376-81.
[74] Barrow, *Robert Bruce*, 74-5.

Chapter 15

THE WAR WITH FRANCE, 1294–8

The outbreak of war with France in 1294 must have been a bitter blow for Edward I. In personal terms, it dashed his hopes of a second marriage, but far more seriously, it meant that there was now no longer a realistic possibility that he might mount a crusading expedition. The conflict with Philip IV of France gave hope to the Scots, and in 1296 Edward found himself at the head of an invasion of Scotland. The wars meant that burdens of a new order of magnitude were placed on the English people, with demands for money, men and food supplies. Edward found himself faced by political opposition at home of a kind he had not had to deal with since his accession. Many of the achievements of the first half of the reign were seriously threatened.

The central problem in Anglo-French relations was the fact that, by reason of the Treaty of Paris of 1259, the king of England now held Gascony as a vassal of the king of France. The French considered that they were now entitled to hear, in the *parlement* of Paris, appeals against Edward's jurisdiction in Gascony, and even claimed the right to military service. From the point of view of the French rulers, Gascony was a great fief, in just the same way as was Flanders. There was a clear royal policy, especially under Philip IV, of asserting sovereignty over such fiefs beyond any possible doubt, and of making that sovereignty effective. Yet in the first half of Edward's reign, relations between England and France had not approached a point of crisis. Several difficulties were resolved, and none apparently created, when Edward performed homage to Philip IV in 1286.[1]

The immediate issue which led to the breakdown of relations between Edward I and Philip IV in the early 1290s was unexpected. For reasons which are unclear, rivalries between the sailors of England and Gascony, and those of other nations, reached new heights. Initially, in 1292, the problem was one of hostility directed against the Flemings by the men of the Cinque Ports in south-eastern England and Bayonne. Agreement was reached with Count Guy of Flanders, however, without much difficulty. In the next year there were problems over

[1] Above, 323.

the maltreatment of sailors from Bayonne in the port of Lisbon, and there was also trouble involving Castilian ships.[2] The major conflict, however, was that between Edward's subjects and Norman sailors, subjects of Philip IV. The feud seems to have begun in 1292, when there was a scuffle in Normandy when some men from the Cinque Ports and the crew of a ship from Bayonne went ashore. In response, there was a Norman raid up the Gironde estuary, and attacks upon English and Irish ships at sea. In 1293 matters became worse. According to one account, Philip IV sent a knight to Bordeaux to proclaim peace, and to announce that he had forbidden any attacks on English shipping. Trade, which had slackened to a negligible level, duly picked up, but the Normans promptly attacked the English fleets. When a large English convoy sailed from Portsmouth, it was attacked by a Norman fleet, with banners of war flying, off Cap Saint-Mathieu on 15 May.[3] This was followed by another battle, and it was perhaps on this occasion that the encounter was carefully planned in advance, by joint agreement, with an empty ship moored to mark the location of the fight. Despite heavy losses, the English eventually won the day. Edward was careful not to implicate himself in what was a private war conducted by some of his subjects, and although much booty was taken, he refused to accept any of it for himself.[4]

There is nothing to suggest that Edward was in any way responsible for the war at sea, despite the assertions of some modern French historians to the contrary.[5] He had shown an anxiety to settle the matter from an early stage, agreeing, in August 1292, that an investigation be made, in co-operation with the French authorities. In one case that came before the royal courts at this period, merchants from La Rochelle seem to have received reasonable treatment when they protested at the demands of an English shipmaster that they pay full freightage charges, when owing to a shipwreck and subsequent robbery he had not fulfilled his promises to them. In another case, in which some Dutch merchants accused English sailors of robbery, it was noted by the crown that if redress was not given in the courts, because of the delaying tactics of the defendants, the realm might be placed in real danger of war. That Edward did not want. After the naval battles of 1293, Edward ordered his subjects to cease hostilities. Admittedly, the first writ which he issued afterwards noted, somewhat provocatively, of the English that 'God has given them victory over the malice of their

---

[2] *Foedera*, I, ii, 759, 760, 789–90.
[3] *Lettres des rois, reines et autres personnages*, ed. M. Champollion-Figeac, i (Paris, 1839), 392–8; Guisborough, 240–1.
[4] *Chron. Bury St Edmunds*, 117; *Flores*, iii, 84–5.
[5] As, for example, J. Favier, *Philippe le Bel* (Paris, 1978), 210.

enemies', but when the order was repeated, no such phrase was included.[6]

In May 1293, a high-ranking embassy was sent to Paris, to consult Philip IV and to try to arrange a truce. It was headed by Edmund, earl of Lancaster, Edward I's brother, and Henry de Lacy, earl of Lincoln. In July a further embassy, with greater legal expertise, was sent, made up of the bishop of London, Roger Brabazon and William Greenfield, later to be archbishop of York. They suggested three solutions. One was that Edward would do justice to any Frenchmen who had suffered loss at the hands of the English. If that would not do, then a commission of two Englishmen and two Frenchmen might be set up, and the third option was to place the dispute in the hands of the papacy. Philip IV laid particular stress on the involvement of the men of Bayonne, and treated the affair largely as a Franco-Gascon one. Although the English envoys conceded that Philip had rights of sovereignty in Gascony, they also pointed to his failure to observe the agreement that he had reached with Edmund of Lancaster, and concluded that Edward was no longer bound by feudal ties to Philip.[7]

The French were intransigent. Philip IV ordered the English lieutenant in Gascony to surrender the civic officials, and a hundred leading citizens of Bayonne, into custody at Périgueux, a command which, not surprisingly, was disobeyed. It was seen as a flagrant violation of the customary methods of resolving disputes. Edward was duly summoned to appear before the *parlement* of Paris soon after Christmas.[8] It seems doubtful whether even a prompt offer by Edward to pay full restitution for all French losses in the naval conflict would have prevented Philip from taking such a step: it looks as if the French king was determined to use the issue of the war at sea as a pretext for a demonstration that his lordship over Gascony was effective, rather than nominal. It could be that Philip was influenced by knowledge of the way in which Edward had been summoning John Balliol to appear in his parliament, and his attitude was probably hardened by his brother, Charles of Valois, who was regarded as being partly responsible for the naval war.[9]

Early in 1294, Edmund of Lancaster, assisted by the experienced

---

[6] *Rot. Parl.*, i, 125–6; *Placita Parlamentaria*, ed. G. Ryley (1661), 184–6, 188, 207–9; *CPR 1292–1301*, 16, 30–1.

[7] *CPR 1292–1301*, 15; *Lettres des rois*, ed. Champollion-Figeac, i, 404, 426–9; Chaplais, *English Medieval Diplomatic Practice*, I, i, 394–6. A convenient summary of the negotiations is provided by M.C.L. Salt, 'List of English Embassies to France, 1272–1307', *EHR*, xliv (1929), 263–78.

[8] Chaplais, *Essays in Medieval Diplomacy*, IX, 271–9; *Foedera*, I, ii, 793.

[9] Guisborough, 241. Charles of Valois may well have been strongly anti-English because Edward's policies helped to prevent him from acquiring the Aragonese throne in the aftermath of the Sicilian Vespers.

clerk John de Lacy, made a final attempt to negotiate a settlement. When progress seemed impossible, the French queen Jeanne, and Marie, the widow of the late King Philip III, intervened with Philip IV on Edmund's behalf. An agreement was reached by which various fortresses and towns would be handed over to the French, and twenty Gascon notables given as hostages. Philip would revoke the summons to Edward to appear in the *parlement* of Paris, which had been issued in the previous October, and he agreed to meet the English king at Amiens. Further, Edward was to marry Philip IV's sister Margaret. Edward was told of the plan, and gave his agreement: he would have considered that it would promote peace, and bring nearer the day when he could set off on crusade. The agreement was a secret one. To satisfy opinion in France, it was to be announced in public that Edward would surrender all of Gascony, and letters patent to this effect were issued by the English king. The private understanding was that these letters would not be put into effect, and it was also agreed that the Gascon towns and fortresses that were handed over to Philip would be rapidly restored to Edward. Edmund was satisfied by Philip IV's statements of intent, which were made before witnesses, and John de Lacy was sent to arrange the surrender to the French. This duly took place in March, and effectively the whole duchy, including Bordeaux, was handed over to the French. When Edmund asked Philip to provide Edward with a safe-conduct to go to Amiens, he was told not to be alarmed if the French appeared to be taking a hard line in public. Then, before his councillors, Philip announced that Gascony was not to be restored to the English, and the summons to Edward to appear before the *parlement*, instead of being withdrawn, was renewed.[10]

Edward's reaction was inevitable. He rejected the summons to the *parlement*, and was duly condemned by the French to lose his fief of Gascony. Edward appointed four friars to go to Philip to renounce his homage formally, and to protest at the way in which the terms of the secret treaty had been ignored. Now, with the feudal tie dissolved, Edward could challenge Philip on equal terms, one crowned and anointed king against another, rather than appearing as a rebellious vassal turning on his lord. The letters of credence given to the friars were dated 20 June, the same day that letters were issued to envoys sent to arrange an alliance with the German king Adolf. In fact, the friars probably did not set out until early August, and it may be that their letters were deliberately backdated, so as to prevent any accusations that Edward had conspired against the French king while he was still his vassal. The choice of friars for this mission is interesting:

---

[10] *Foedera*, I, ii, 793-6. Chaplais, *English Medieval Diplomatic Practice*, I, ii, 428n. provides an excellent summary of these events.

presumably the English feared that lay envoys might be captured and imprisoned in what had now become hostile territory. As it was, the friars suffered a few days incarceration before their status as diplomatic envoys was accepted by the French.[11]

These events were quite extraordinary. The diplomatic failure of the English in 1293 and 1294 must rank with the appeasement policies before the Second World War as among the most dismal episodes of English foreign policy. One contemporary explanation was that Edward was so overcome by his lust for the king of France's sister that he acted without counsel. The chancellor, John Langton, in particular, opposed the plan. The stumbling block to the agreement with the French was, according to this explanation, the French princess's reluctance to marry someone as old as Edward.[12] There are many implausibilities in all this. The chroniclers all name the object of Edward's desires as Blanche, though the actual scheme was for him to marry her sister Margaret. Lust seems unlikely, as Edward could not have seen the French princess since 1286. He had, it is true, been sent a portrait of her, according to one chronicler, yet even if he obtained from his envoys in addition such remarkable details as those requested by Henry VII about his intended bride, which extended to the size of her nipples,[13] it is not conceivable that his acceptance of what was essentially his brother Edmund's scheme was dictated by sexual rather than political considerations.

What is much more likely is that, as the chronicler Walter of Guisborough suggests, Edmund of Lancaster was simply duped by the French. Someone with such strong connections with the French court as he had through his wife, the queen of Navarre, could well have been too trusting in what was said to him.[14] As far as Edward was concerned, the secret treaty offered major attractions. Points at issue with the French would be settled, and a marriage alliance such as this was likely to reduce the possibility of future disagreements. It is likely, however, that it was the prospect of advancing the cause of the crusade that weighed most heavily with him. Where Edward's envoys, and indeed the king as well, failed, was in their assessment of Philip IV's intentions. This was not surprising, as the French king was one of the most taciturn and impenetrable of men, an enigma to both contemporaries

[11] Ibid., I, ii, 417–19; *Foedera*, I, ii, 807; *Treaty Rolls*, i, 92; Guisborough, 243; Langtoft, ii, 204–10.

[12] *Chron. Bury St Edmunds*, 118–20; Langtoft, ii, 196–8; Cotton, 232; *Ann. Worcester*, 515.

[13] Chaplais, *English Medieval Diplomatic Practice*, I, i, 92–3; Langtoft, ii, 196–8. It is not quite clear whether the envoys brought back an actual picture, or merely provided the king with a description.

[14] Guisborough, 242; above, 315.

and historians. It could be that his abandonment of the plan in the secret treaty was the result of factional infighting in the French court, or it could be that Philip harboured some long-standing resentment against the successful Edward I. Whatever the truth of the matter, the war, when it came, was of Philip's choice, not Edward's.

The war with the French which began in 1294 was the last of the series of thirteenth-century military failures on the continent. It was a complicated and ultimately futile conflict. Edward's strategy was to conduct a holding operation in Gascony, while creating a massive alliance of continental princes that could be directed against Philip IV. The king aimed to campaign in person in the north, fighting side by side with the Flemings and others against the French. This all took time to organize, and the Welsh rebellion of 1294–5, followed by the need to act against the Scots in 1296, delayed the full operation of the plan until 1297. Therefore, contrary to what was probably intended, it was in fact in Gascony that most of the military activity took place: the campaign that Edward himself led in Flanders in 1297 proved to be sadly anti-climactic.

It took some time before Edward was in a position to send military aid to his Gascon subjects. A muster was ordered to take place at Portsmouth on 1 September 1294, but it had to be postponed until the end of the month. Even then, it seems that few responded to the king's request, very probably because there was considerable reluctance to perform feudal service overseas.[15] It was not until about 9 October that the first contingents finally set sail, under the command of the king's inexperienced nephew, John of Brittany, and of John de St John. These were paid troops, for the attempt to obtain unpaid feudal service had been quietly abandoned.

On 10 October payment of almost £2,000 was authorized to the next planned force, which was to have been headed by Edmund of Lancaster. Large numbers were clearly assembled at Portsmouth: one account shows that there were no less than 1,537 horses waiting there for shipment to Gascony, and letters of protection show that Lancaster had at least 278 men in his own retinue.[16] The number of infantrymen is not known, but one striking feature about their recruitment was that this was the first time that Edward employed the technique of pardoning criminals in return for service. At least three hundred men were taken on in this way.[17] In the event, however, the news of the Welsh rebellion

---

[15] *Parl. Writs*, i, 259–63; below, 406.
[16] Prestwich, *War, Politics and Finance*, 75–6; C 62/71; E 101/4/30; *Rôles Gascons*, iii, cxxxiv, cxlvi–cxlvii.
[17] Ibid., cxxxviii; Hurnard, *The King's Pardon for Homicide*, 311–12.

meant that Lancaster's force had to be diverted, and it was not until
early 1296 that he was able to go to Gascony. The full responsibility
for defending what was left of the English possessions in south-
western France fell upon what had been intended as no more than an
advance-guard, the force under John of Brittany and John de St
John.

The small expedition which sailed in October 1294 achieved more
than could have been anticipated. On the way south, Cap St Mathieu
and the Ile de Ré were raided. The fleet then sailed up the Gironde,
taking Castillon and Macau, then Bourg-sur-Mer and Blaye. An
attack on Bordeaux failed: one ship was holed by a stone hurled from a
siege engine. The fleet moved on up river, receiving the surrender of
Podensac and Virelade, and then of Rioms. Only then were the horses
disembarked from the ships where they had been for seventeen weeks.
John of Brittany and William Latimer remained with part of the force
at Rioms, while John de St John with the remainder marched to
Bayonne, where the citizens gladly handed the town over to them. The
French were compelled to surrender the castle, and two fine galleys
were captured.[18] The mobility which the fleet provided had enabled the
English to move against French garrisons with speed and surprise. It
remained to be seen what would happen once a major French army was
put into the field. The fact that Bordeaux was still in enemy hands
posed a major problem.

The French counter-attack came at Easter 1295, when Charles of
Valois invaded Gascony with a large army. Rioms was besieged, and
when a sortie was attempted, the English were driven back 'like sheep
into the fold'.[19] Disaster came as a result of the news of the surrender of
Podensac by the elderly John Giffard. He agreed terms which allowed
the English to go free, and left the Gascon inhabitants to the far from
tender mercies of the French. Some fifty were duly hanged. The marshal of the English army, Ralph Gorges, tried to pacify Gascon anger by
putting Giffard and others on trial, but this merely provoked a riot
among the English troops. John of Brittany and many other knights
fled by ship, and the French were able to enter the town without much
difficulty. They captured a dozen English knights, including Thomas
Turberville, who was soon to turn traitor. Further south, the English
did not fare quite so badly. Although Hugh de Vere was forced to
surrender St Sever after a gallant defence, once the French army left
the English were able to recapture the place without much difficulty.
By the summer of 1295, though, the English were hard-pressed in
Gascony. They held Bourg and Blaye, beleaguered and isolated in the

---

[18] *Ann. Worcester*, 519–20; Guisborough, 244–5; *Rôles Gascons*, iii, cxlvii.
[19] Guisborough, 246.

north of the duchy, and Bayonne with its outposts in the south. The rest was largely in French hands.

The news from Gascony was doubtless depressing, but yet more alarming for the English was the fact that in the summer of 1295, the French began to raid English seaports. Philip IV had brought shipbuilders from Genoa to build galleys in Marseilles and in Normandy, and in 1295 a squadron sailed from the Mediterranean to fight the English. In August, a raid was mounted on Dover. Part of the town was set on fire, the priory was attacked, and two monks killed. An assault on Winchelsea was foiled by a fleet from Yarmouth and a French galley which attempted to attack Hythe was captured.[20] There was widespread public alarm. Edward made much of the threat of invasion in a summons asking the clergy to come to parliament. He even suggested that the French aimed to destroy the English nation itself.[21] The atmosphere of hysteria was heightened by the discovery of Thomas Turberville's treason. He had appeared in England, claiming to have escaped from prison in France. He had in fact been released on condition that he spied for the French. A letter he wrote to the provost of Paris was discovered by the English. In it, he reported, among other things, on the defenceless state of the Isle of Wight, on the troops to be despatched to Gascony, and on the king's diplomatic efforts. On 22 September, men were sent to seek Turberville out, and he was soon taken, tried and executed for treason. The affair must have shaken the king, for Turberville had been a household knight, and therefore in a trusted position.[22]

Edward had anticipated the danger of attack by French naval forces, and late in 1294 had ordered the building of thirty galleys, each with

---

[20] *Flores*, iii, 94-5; Cotton, 295-6; A.Z. Freeman, 'A Moat Defensive: the coast defense scheme of 1295', *Speculum*, xlii (1967), 446.

[21] Stubbs, *Select Charters*, 480. The Latin word used for nation in this writ is *lingua*, which can, of course, mean 'tongue' or 'language', and it may be that it should be read here with the implication that language was a element in the English national identity. In a lawsuit of 1297, it was alleged that in 1295, shortly before the issue of this writ, the prior of St Neots had expelled all who used the English tongue (*linguam anglicanam*) from his service: *Select Cases in the Court of King's Bench*, iii, 50-1. Earlier, however, in 1283, *lingua* was used by the English chancery in referring to the Welsh nation: Stubbs, *Select Charters*, 460-1. The term could also be used in a geographical sense. A document of slightly later date refers to Languedoc as *Linguam Occitanam* in such a way: *Chronicles of the Reigns of Edward I and Edward II*, ed. Stubbs, ii, cv. It should, of course, be observed that the English upper classes spoke French, or rather the Anglo-Norman dialect of that language, rather than English. I am grateful for suggestions on this point received from Professor E.L.G. Stones and Professor J.S. Roskell.

[22] J.G. Edwards, 'The Treason of Thomas Turberville, 1295', *Studies in Medieval History presented to F.M. Powicke*, ed. R.W. Hunt, W.A. Pantin, R.W. Southern (Oxford, 1948), 296-309. E 404/1/5 provides the additional information that William Wither was paid £1 to spy on Turberville in Gloucestershire, on 23 September.

120 oars. The plan was a very ambitious one, and Grimsby and Hull, at least, were told that vessels of 100 oars would suffice. How many galleys were in fact built is not known, but the orders were certainly obeyed at London, Newcastle-upon-Tyne, Southampton, Lyme Regis, Grimsby, King's Lynn and York.[23] In addition, merchant ships were taken into royal service, and by 1295 a system whereby separate naval squadrons each guarded a section of coast was instituted. Arrangements were also made for the recruitment and organization of defence forces on land. In 1296, perhaps in part because of the revelations of the Turberville affair, these became more complex. The Isle of Wight was now defended by seventy-six cavalrymen, and large naval forces prevented any repetition of the raids of the previous year.[24]

Not many troops were sent to Gascony in 1295. Some forces were sent there in July under John Botetourt, but in August a group of magnates, headed by the earl of Arundel, resisted the king's demands that they go to Gascony. They eventually agreed to go only after they had been put under severe financial pressure, by means of threats to collect all the debts they owed to the crown. It was not until October that orders were issued for the recruitment of 25,000 infantry. Ships were gathered at Winchelsea and Plymouth, but departure was delayed until late January 1296 by the illness of the commander of the force, Edmund of Lancaster. He was accompanied by Henry de Lacy, earl of Lincoln, and both men served under contract, being paid at the rate of 4,000 marks and 2,000 marks a year respectively.[25]

The 1296 expedition followed the example of that of 1294, and sailed up the Gironde to Bourg and Blaye. They were not as successful as their predecessors: the French had now had time to prepare. Bordeaux proved impregnable: after making a feigned retreat, a few of the English forced an entry to the city, but the gates were closed behind them, and they were captured. An attempt to bribe some citizens into handing the city over to the English was discovered. At St Macaire a gallant defence of the castle by a French garrison culminated in the relief of the siege by Robert of Artois.[26] According to one account, the English army was saved from complete disaster as a result of a premonition of danger which the earl of Lincoln had. A search took place, and three French spies were discovered. After two were executed, the third revealed that a French attack was imminent.[27] Money ran short, and the army was

[23] Prestwich, *War, Politics and Finance*, 138; E 159/68, m.77; E 159/69, m.4d; E 368/69, m.4d.

[24] Prestwich, *War, Politics and Finance*, 139–40; Freeman, 'A Moat Defensive', 446–58.

[25] *Rôles Gascons*, iii, clii; Prestwich, *War, Politics and Finance*, 76.

[26] Guisborough, 261.

[27] The Hagnaby chronicle, BL Cotton Vesp. B. xi, f.40.

demoralized by the illness of its commander, Edmund of Lancaster. Before he died, on 5 June 1296, he asked that his bones should not be buried until his debts were paid. Henry de Lacy replaced Lancaster in command. A lengthy siege of Dax failed, and little was achieved in the rest of the year.[28]

A fresh disaster struck in January 1297. Henry de Lacy organized an expedition to revictual the *bastide* at Bellegarde. The army was divided into three battalions, following normal practice, under John de St John, John of Brittany and Henry himself. As they came out of a wood, the vanguard, under St John, was ambushed by a large army under Robert of Artois. Henry de Lacy tried to rally his forces, but many fled in the confusion. The fight took place at dusk, and it proved to be impossible to bring order to the English troops, as the columns fell back one on another. Henry de Lacy and John of Brittany made their escape, but John de St John was captured, along with a number of other knights. Infantry casualties were very heavy. Decisive battles, however, were rare in the middle ages, and this engagement was no exception to the rule. In the summer of 1297, Henry de Lacy was able to take advantage of the withdrawal of the French army, and conducted a successful raid into French territory, towards Toulouse, burning and plundering as he went.[29] That was the last active operation of the war in Gascony, for events to the north, in Flanders, led to a truce being negotiated between Edward I and Philip IV in the autumn of 1297.

It would be wrong to give the impression that the war in Gascony was largely fought by English expeditionary forces. The accounts of the costs of the war show that the wages of English cavalry came to £37,051, while English, Spanish and other footsoldiers were paid £17,928. In comparison, Gascon troops wages amounted to £137,595, and their rates of pay were lower than those of the English.[30] These figures alone show the extent to which the English commanders relied upon local recruitment. Records show that Gascon nobles had begun to receive pay in return for their service as early as 1293.[31] The chronicler Walter of Guisborough explained that John de St John's beneficent rule of the duchy was remembered,[32] so that many were anxious to serve under his banner. The English were not reliant on the loyalty of the ducal

---

[28] Guisborough, 262.

[29] The precise course of the battle is very hard to reconstruct from the surviving sources: see Guisborough, 262–3; Rishanger, 168–9; Langtoft, ii, 282; *Rôles Gascons*, iii, clxiv–clxv; Lubimenko, *Jean de Bretagne*, 21–5.

[30] E 372/160, m.41. This account is summarized in *Rôles Gascons*, iii, clxvii–clxix.

[31] M.G.A. Vale, 'The Gascon Nobility and the Anglo-French War, 1294–8', *War and Government in the Middle Ages*, ed. J. Gillingham and J.C. Holt (Cambridge, 1984), 134–46, provides the fullest discussion of this question.

[32] Guisborough, 245.

officials, for the disastrous diplomacy of 1294, and the subsequent surrender of Gascony to the French, meant that there were not many such men available. It was rather the small, independently minded nobles, and some of the townspeople, who rallied to the English cause. Wages were probably not particularly important as a lure, for pay was received at best irregularly. Petitions heard by Edward at Plympton, in Devon, in 1297 testify to the discontent many Gascons indeed felt at their inadequate financial rewards. Barrau de Sescas, for example, admiral at Bayonne, had spent in four months 100 marks more than he was entitled to receive in wages.[33] Loyalty to Edward was probably due to far more intangible factors: a devotion to the lord of Gascony, as opposed to a northern French king, and a desire to maintain the traditional customs of Gascony, combined, no doubt, with the hope of winning both glory and booty in war.

The English received substantial backing from many Gascon towns, such as Bayonne, Bourg, Blaye and St Sever. Townspeople were prepared to invest in hopes of English success: loans from Bayonne alone totalled £45,763. Money was also raised in such places as Peyrehorade, Sorde and Bonnegarde.[34] Commercial connections with England through the wine trade may have had some influence on the townspeople. Yet affection for the English was not universal, and it is noteworthy that the city of Bordeaux, on which the hand of English government had fallen most heavily in the past, sided firmly with the French. In taking 153 hostages from the city in 1294, the French may have been able to remove the most anglophile of the inhabitants, but what the men of Bordeaux wanted above all was independence, as they were to show in 1303 when they rose against Philip IV's officials.[35] If, however, the loyalty of many Gascon nobles and townspeople is taken as evidence of the effectiveness of English government in the duchy, and of the solidity of Edward's achievement during his visit there from 1286 to 1289, the case of Bordeaux presents a major exception.

The fighting in Gascony was only one part of the English war effort. Edward can never have had hopes that the French would be defeated there, and he realized that the struggle had to be widened. The chronicler Peter Langtoft described the council meeting, in 1294, at which the action to be taken against Philip IV was discussed. When Edward

---

[33] *Rôles Gascons*, iii, clxxxix.

[34] Ibid., iii, clxiii.

[35] R.P. Lawton, 'Henry de Lacy, Earl of Lincoln (1272–1311) as *locum tenens et capitaneus* in the duchy of Aquitaine' (London Ph.D., 1974), 203, gives the figure of 153 hostages as a correction to that of 182 provided by *Rôles Gascons*, iii, cxxviii. This thesis provides a valuable account of Gascon support for the English cause.

asked for advice, Anthony Bek, bishop of Durham, advocated war in unambiguous terms: 'Mount the warhorses, take your lance in your grip.' He encouraged the king to buy allies abroad, specifying the king of Germany, the archbishop of Cologne, the count of Savoy, the count of Burgundy and the king of Aragon. The barons present concurred, arguing that the French king, with his great resources, could only be defeated by means of a sworn alliance.[36] There are dangers in taking such an account at face value, but Bek's importance is underlined by the fact that it was he, along with the archbishop of Dublin, Hugh Despenser and Nicholas Segrave, who was sent to negotiate with the German king and the archbishop of Cologne.[37] The next few years were to see intricate and costly diplomatic manoeuvring by both English and French, as each side tried to construct alliances, and to neutralize the efforts of their opponents.

To start with, the English schemes prospered. Agreement was reached with the German king, Adolf of Nassau, in August: he was promised a subsidy of £40,000 by Christmas 1294, with a further £20,000 once Edward began his campaign in the Low Countries. The archbishop of Cologne promised to serve with 1,000 cavalry, in return for 10,000 marks by Christmas 1294, and the promise of an additional £2,000. Other, less important, Germans, such as the count of Katzenellenbogen, were brought into the alliance at the same time.[38] There were no great difficulties in reaching agreement with the duke of Brabant, who had married Edward's daughter Margaret in 1290. He was present in Anglesey with Edward in the spring of 1295, and agreed to serve for six months with 2,000 cavalry in return for a grant of 160,000 *livres tournois*, or about £40,000.[39] He was also promised a further fee of 40,000 *livres*, and payment of £4,000 out of the customs revenue was ordered. An alliance was made at the same time with the count of Guelders, who was promised 100,000 *livres tournois* in

---

[36] Langtoft, ii, 200–4.

[37] *Treaty Rolls*, i, 89–90.

[38] Details of the alliances of this period are to be found in *Treaty Rolls*, i, 89–90, 98–112, 124, 129–33; E.B. Fryde, *Studies in Medieval Trade and Finance* (1983), II, 1168–87; M.C. Prestwich, 'Edward I's Wars and their Financing' (Oxford D.Phil thesis, 1968), 445–54; Prestwich, *War, Politics and Finance*, 172–3, and the further references given there.

[39] In 1294 the exchange rate was roughly one pound sterling to four *livres tournois*, but French debasement brought the rate down to one to six in the course of 1297. By 1305 it had reached one to eight. See B.D. Lyon, 'Un compte de l'échiquier relatif aux relations d'Edouard I d'Angleterre avec le duc Jean II de Brabant', *Bulletin de la Commission Royal d'Histoire*, cxx (1955), 86–7. For fluctuations in the rates in Edward I's last years, see M.C. Prestwich, 'Early Fourteenth-Century Exchange Rates', *Economic History Review*, 2nd ser., xxxii (1979), 471–5. See also P. Spufford, *Handbook of Medieval Exchange* (1986), 209.

return for six months service. An embassy to Holland was successful in buying the support of the count, Florence V, with a promised 80,000 *livres*.

If a campaign was to be launched against the northern borders of France, one further ally was vital for geographical reasons. Flanders was the obvious place for an English army to land, and from which to attack the French. A marriage between Edward's heir, Edward of Caernarfon, and Count Guy of Flanders' daughter had been under discussion since 1292, but early in 1294 Edward I had indicated his strong preference for a French marriage for his son, as part of the abortive peace negotiations. Now the old plan was revived, and Guy was promised in addition a subsidy of 200,000 *livres tournois*. Philip IV acted swiftly to counter this danger. He summoned the count to Paris, and ordered him to hand his daughter over into royal custody. She was kept, in comfortable conditions, in the Louvre, and her father was allowed to return to Flanders. There was no possibility of the English marriage taking place, and Philip wisely lifted much of the pressure which his officials had been placing on the count and his subjects. There was no future, at least for the time being, for Guy's alliance with Edward I.[40] This success for the French, which was achieved in 1295, was followed by another. In a treaty of 6 January 1296 the count of Holland was detached from the English alliance. In part this was because he resented the favour Edward showed to the duke of Brabant, and in part it was because of the promise of a fee of 4,000 *livres* for life, and a lump sum of 25,000 *livres*.[41]

With both Flanders and Holland siding with Philip IV, the prospects for Edward's planned campaign were bleak by 1296. The French alliance with the Scots was another major problem, necessitating an expedition northwards to dethrone John Balliol. The measures that were taken to reverse the situation in Holland reveal the darker side of the diplomacy of the period. The immediate English reaction to the news of the count's switch of allegiance was to impose a trade embargo upon Holland. Then a plot was organized to kidnap the count. John, lord of Cuyck, a subject of the duke of Brabant, who was in receipt of a grant from Edward of 200 *livres tournois* a year, was deeply involved. The kidnap was followed by the murder of the count. It is not clear how far Edward I himself was involved in all this, but he was to show favour to one of the murderers, John de Renesse, and at the least he condoned what had happened. The murdered Count Florence was succeeded by his anglophile son John, whose marriage to Edward's daughter Elizabeth had been agreed as long ago as 1281, and finally took place in

[40] *Treaty Rolls*, i, 108, 111–12; Strayer, *Philip the Fair*, 328–9.
[41] *Acta Imperii Angliae et Franciae*, ed. F. Kern (Tübingen, 1911), 279–80.

January 1297. This, along with a fresh subsidy, cemented the new Anglo-Dutch alliance.[42]

More important than the re-establishment of the alliance with Holland at the start of 1297 was Edward's success in winning the count of Flanders to his side once again. Count Guy had been placed in a difficult position in the previous year, when the towns of Lille, Bruges, Douai and Ypres appealed to the *parlement* of Paris against him, and were placed under the French king's protection. The pressure of the English embargo on wool exports to Flanders was beginning to take effect, and in renewing his alliance with Edward, Count Guy was hoping to win the support of the artisans in the cities, as opposed to the oligarchic civic authorities who were looking to the French for assistance. A further element in a complex situation was Guy's resentment at the favours accorded by Philip IV to the count of Hainault. In addition, of course, the alliance with the English promised to be profitable, with 100,000 *livres tournois* promised for the first year, and 200,000 *livres* later.[43]

By January 1297 Edward had succeeded in buying the support of an impressive coalition which extended from the Rhine to the Channel coast. This was not all he sought, however. Allies were needed on the eastern frontiers of France. Two Edward had there already. In September 1293 his daughter Eleanor had married Henry, count of Bar, and so it was hardly surprising that in November 1294 a treaty was drawn up, in which the count promised to serve Edward with 1,000 horse for six months, in return for at least 30,000 marks.[44] The English could also count on the support of Amadeus, count of Savoy. It was not until May 1297, however, that other allies were found who could attack Philip IV from the east. A group of Burgundian noblemen from the Franche-Comté, headed by Jean de Chalon-Arlay, reached agreement with English envoys at Brussels. They were to receive 60,000 *livres* for the first year of the alliance, and 30,000 in each subsequent year. They were also promised a gift of £2,000. In return they promised to provide a force of 500 cavalry.[45] There had been hopes in 1294 that aid might also be found in Spain, from James of Aragon, but these were groundless. In 1295 he came to terms with the papacy, and married Charles of

---

[42] Cotton, 303; *Acta Imperii*, ed. Kern, 76–7; F. Trautz, *Die Könige von England und das Reich, 1272–1377* (Heidelberg, 1961), 135; *Documents 1297–8*, 34, 164.

[43] Chaplais, *English Medieval Diplomatic Practice*, I, ii, 491–3; *Foedera*, I, ii, 850–1.

[44] C 62/71

[45] *Treaty Rolls*, i, 132–3; J. de Sturler, 'Le paiement à Bruxelles des allies franc-comtois d'Edouard Ier, roi d'Angleterre (Mai 1297)', *Cahiers Bruxellois*, v (1960), 18–37.

Salerno's daughter: there was no means by which Edward could win his assistance.[46]

A French memorandum about the war, probably written some forty years later, suggests that Philip IV achieved one final triumph in the diplomatic game before Edward at long last set out on his expedition to Flanders. It claims that secret negotiations took place with Adolf of Nassau, the German king, in which Italian bankers acted for Philip IV. There has been much controversy among historians over this. The document is inaccurate in many particulars. It makes no mention of Albrecht of Habsburg, an ally of the French, and it is very tempting to assume that the author confused Albrecht with Adolf, whom he succeeded on the throne in 1298. It was in fact Albrecht's activities that were to prevent Adolf from campaigning in Flanders alongside Edward I. The English certainly had no inkling that Adolf might have deserted them, and it seems most unlikely that he had in fact accepted subsidies from the French in secret.[47]

The English diplomats who had tried to secure an agreement with the French in 1293 and 1294, headed by Edmund of Lancaster, had failed disastrously. It is not surprising that Edward turned to different men in his efforts to build up the great coalition of allies. As already shown, Anthony Bek played a leading part in the summer of 1294, conducting negotiations in the Low Countries and in Germany. Alongside him, and the other magnates with him, was a clerk, Robert de Segre. He played a major role, for he was put in charge of making the payments to the various allies. He was not an important royal clerk: he had been with Edward in Gascony in the late 1280s, but there is no clue in the records to explain why he was given such a major function in 1294. It is perhaps a measure of how the onset of war had stretched the administrative resources of the government that he was employed. Between July and October 1294 he was based at Dordrecht, with charge of £22,000, most of which was issued to the German allies on the instructions of Anthony Bek and John Sandford, archbishop of Dublin. His next mission lasted from mid-November 1294 until November 1296. He took just over £25,000 with him, and obtained further funds in Dordrecht from English merchants there. His account reveals some of the activities of Edward's diplomats, with payments to Itier de Angoulême and Raymond Arnaud de Rama, both Gascons, sent to see

---

[46] J.N. Hillgarth, *The Spanish Kingdoms* (1976), 264.

[47] F. Funck-Brentano, 'Document pour servir à l'histoire des relations de la France avec l'Angleterre et l'Allemagne sous le règne de Philippe le Bel', *Revue Historique*, xxxix (1889), 326–48. The arguments of G. Barraclough, 'Edward I and Adolf of Nassau', *Cambridge Historical Journal*, vi (1940), 225–62 are not convincing: see Trautz, *Die Könige von England und das Reich*, 149–72; *Documents 1297–8*, 33–4.

Adolf of Nassau. The employment of Christian de Raphorst, sent on the instructions of the council in England to Holland and Zeeland, demonstrates the way in which Edward made use of foreigners to further his diplomacy.[48] Two German brothers, Eustace and Gerlach, were valuable to him in his dealings with Adolf of Nassau: the former was a knight of the English household, the latter simultaneously a canon of Aachen and a royal clerk in England.[49] Such men obviously had a vested interest in establishing a firm Anglo-German alliance.

The main envoys in the second diplomatic initiative, that of 1296–7, were the treasurer Walter Langton, Otto de Grandson, Hugh Despenser, the clerk John of Berwick and the count of Savoy. Langton's account book, fortunately, has survived to show how he spent a total of almost £35,000. Until the autumn of 1296 the main energies of the English envoys were directed at furthering the peace initiative which had been launched by the papacy: Boniface VIII had appointed two cardinals to try to end the war. The ambassadors did not remain together as a group. Langton's own movements extended from Brabant in the north to Paris, but Otto de Grandson went into the Auvergne, to Burgundy and to Savoy. Two envoys journeyed to the papal curia, and the account is full of the many comings and goings as contact was maintained between the allies.[50]

The ambassadors were allowed considerable freedom of action, but Walter Langton returned to England in the autumn of 1296 for the parliament at Bury St Edmunds, where there must have been lengthy discussions with the king, as the next stage of the diplomatic moves was planned. Elaborate letters authorizing the negotiations of an armistice and a peace were issued, but by early 1297, they were given powers to make alliances with various named rulers in the Low Countries and Burgundy, and even 'the nobility and other persons of whatever kingdom, status or condition'.[51] The initiative was not, of course, invariably taken by the English. Instructions to John of Cuyck, Henry de Blâmont and the receiver of Flanders, sent by the count of Flanders to England to negotiate Edward I's final agreement to the Anglo-Flemish alliance, suggest that the first moves were made by the count. The terminology

[48] J. de Sturler, 'Deux comptes "enrolés" de Robert de Segre, receveur et agent payeur d'Edouard Ier, roi d'Angleterre, aux Pays-Bas (1294–1296), *Bulletin de la Commission Royale d'Histoire*, cxxv (1960), 561–612. For Edward's relations with Brabant, and the importance of the wool trade in this respect, see J. de Sturler, *Les relations politiques et les échanges commerciaux entre le duché de Brabant et l'Angleterre au moyen âge* (Paris, 1936).

[49] Chaplais, *English Medieval Diplomatic Practice*, I, i, 352.

[50] G.P. Cuttino, *English Diplomatic Administration 1259–1339* (2nd ed., Oxford, 1971), 177–83, 224–50. Cuttino prints Langton's account book; the original is E101/308/19.

[51] *Treaty Rolls*, i, 122–4, 129–31.

of the final treaty was Flemish, rather than English.[52] Many hands were involved in building the alliance, and their achievement by the summer of 1297 had done much to make up for the damage caused by the mistakes made in 1293 and 1294, when Edmund of Lancaster had been duped by Philip IV. It remained to be seen whether Edward, with his military expedition to Flanders, could capitalize on the work that had been done.

Edward I faced very great difficulties in recruiting an army to go to Flanders, for reasons to be explained in the next chapter. The force which finally sailed on 24 August was far too small, consisting of only 895 cavalry and less than 8,000 infantry.[53] Admittedly, Henry V was to win the battle of Agincourt with a smaller force, but his troops, particularly his archers, were far better equipped than Edward's. The English army in 1297 should, rather, be compared with that which was to win the battle of Falkirk in 1298, which was almost 30,000 strong. Not only was Edward's army too small, it was also too late. The French had invaded Flanders in mid-June, and proceeded to invest the town of Lille. The allies were understandably reluctant to act in Edward's absence, but when the margrave of Jülich, with some of Edward's German and Brabancon allies, did muster a force, it was routed by Robert of Artois on 20 August. Five days later Lille surrendered.[54] Edward, therefore, arrived to find the war already half-lost.

The English were involved in some fighting as soon as the fleet arrived in the Zwyn estuary, but it was of a kind that Edward must have deplored. There were 273 ships in all in the English fleet, 73 of them from the Cinque Ports, and 59 from Yarmouth. There was intense rivalry between these two major contingents, and the men of the Ports seized the opportunity to attack the Yarmouth vessels. At least seventeen, and perhaps as many as thirty-seven, ships were lost. Most of the equipment belonging to the royal wardrobe was all on one ship, the *Bayard* of Yarmouth, and it was only saved when a man called Philip of Hales quick-wittedly cut the mooring rope, so that the vessel drifted free of danger. Edward took hostages from both sides, but the affair was hardly a good omen for the expedition.[55]

Once the army had disembarked, they faced the danger of a French

[52] K. de Lettenhove, 'De controvertia Bonifacium inter et Philippum Pulchrum agitata', Migne, *Patrologia Latina*, clxxxv (Paris, 1860), 1853–4; Chaplais, *English Medieval Diplomatic Practice*, I, ii, 491–3.

[53] N.B. Lewis, 'The English Forces in Flanders, August–November 1297', *Studies in Medieval History presented to F.M. Powicke*, 310–18.

[54] Favier, *Philippe le Bel*, 223–4.

[55] Prestwich, *War, Politics and Finance*, 142–3; F.W. Brooks, 'The Cinque Ports Feud with Yarmouth', *Mariners' Mirror*, xix (1933), 26–51.

attack. According to one account, Edward managed to deceive his enemies into thinking that his force was much larger than it was, for he sent his Welsh infantry forward with lances erect, so that from a distance they looked like a large cavalry force. No engagement took place, and the English were able to advance to the town of Bruges. Edward met his ally, the count of Flanders, there. The place was not strongly fortified, but the citizens rejected an English offer of paying half the cost of new defences – in view of the state of Edward's finances, this was probably wise. There were rumours that the citizens were about to rise in support of the French, so Edward and Count Guy moved further inland, to Ghent, early in September. There Edward was faced by the threat of a French blockade, and there were also troubles with the local citizenry. On one occasion he left the city on a brief sortie. The gates were then barred in his absence, and the Flemings began to attack those English who were left behind. It was only with difficulty that they held out until the king's return. Further problems were caused by the undisciplined looting engaged in by Edward's Welsh infantry.[56]

In September hopes were high in the English army that Adolf of Nassau would soon come to their assistance. By the middle of the next month, however, John of Cuyck reported on a visit he made to the German king. Adolf was still expressing hopes that he would set out, but John noted that he did not have sufficient troops with him.[57] It was clear that Edward's chances of victory were extremely slight, and that negotiation, not battle, offered the best chance of escape from a difficult situation. The man primarily responsible for arranging a truce was the archbishop-elect of Dublin, William de Hotham. He had studied in Paris, and was well acquainted with Philip IV and some of the French nobility. He obtained permission from the French king to travel through France, so that he could deal with some problems arising from his nomination by the papal curia to the see of Dublin. He used this opportunity to see Philip, and persuaded him to start negotiations for a truce. On the fifth day of talks, the cease-fire was agreed, and it was promulgated at Vive-Saint-Bavon on 9 October.[58]

It is easy to see why Edward should have agreed to the truce, particularly since the terms permitted the German king to reopen hostilities should he decide to enter the war. Not only was Edward in a difficult position in Flanders, but he also would now have had news of the events in Scotland, where Earl Warenne had been defeated in the

---

[56] Documents 1297–8, 32–3; Chron. Bury St. Edmunds, 143–4; Rishanger, 177.

[57] Documents 1297–8, 148–9, 161–2.

[58] Guisborough, 316–17; see also Chaplais, English Medieval Diplomatic Practice, I, i, 353.

battle of Stirling Bridge. More difficult to understand are Philip IV's motives, for in October 1297 Edward I was apparently at his mercy. Financial considerations may have been important,[59] and Philip may have decided that Flanders was more important to him than Gascony. If he could break Edward's alliance with Count Guy, then he could proceed to deal with his Flemish enemies. It is also probable that Philip failed to appreciate the true weakness of Edward's position. Initially, the truce was to last only until 7 December 1297 in the Low Countries, and Edward explained, in a letter to the government in England in late November, that he needed reinforcements, so as to impress the French with his power, and thus obtain better terms.[60] There seems, in fact, to have been little difficulty in renewing the truce.

Edward could not extricate himself from Flanders immediately that the truce was agreed. He still had obligations to his allies, who were owed large sums of money, though strikingly, no mention was made in the letters sent to England requesting funds of his debts to the count of Flanders.[61] Problems continued with the Flemings, who perhaps realized that Edward was deserting them. Early in February 1298 a plot was hatched in Ghent, with the object of capturing Edward, and handing him over to the French. At dawn on the appointed day the city gates were closed, so that the infantry billeted in the suburbs could not come to assist the king. The rising began within the walls, and there were many English casualties. Those troops outside the fortifications, however, managed to force an entry by setting fire to the gates, and the English were duly victorious. Flemish pleas for mercy were heard sympathetically by Edward, but this did not prevent the English infantry from engaging in an orgy of plunder. Many were subsequently convicted and hanged: if it had not been for the mercy shown by the bishop of Durham, nearly all would have been condemned to death.[62]

The king's patience was clearly wearing thin. On 5 February he sent William of Gainsborough and John Lovel back to England with a firm request for funds, so that his Burgundian allies might be paid. Only then could 'the king and his men be delivered from this land'. A hundred ships were to come to Sluys to take the force home.[63] Early in March payment was duly made to the Burgundians, though they were

[59] Papal pressure, preventing both Edward and Philip imposing taxes on the clergy, had not proved effective, for Philip retaliated by preventing the transfer of funds from France to the papal curia. For a recent revision of views of this, see C. Zuckerman, 'The ending of French interference in the papal financial system in 1297: a neglected episode', *Viator*, xi (1980), 259–88.

[60] *Documents 1297–8*, 174–5.

[61] Ibid., 148–9, 162–4, 184.

[62] *Chron. Bury St Edmunds*, 146–7; Guisborough, 332.

[63] *Documents 1297–8*, 174–5.

not fully satisfied until 1306.[64] In the middle of the month the king at long last returned to Sandwich. Early in the morning of 15 March a ceremony took place, in which the seal that had been used in England during the king's absence was handed over, and the great seal itself, which had been with Edward in Flanders, was entrusted to the chancellor.[65]

It was one thing to negotiate a truce with the French, but quite another to agree on final peace terms. It is not possible in a short space to do full justice to the arguments employed. Many issues were at stake. There was the central question of Edward's position as duke of Gascony, and vassal of Philip IV. There were territorial and jurisdictional matters regarding Gascony to be settled. There was the question of compensation for losses by merchants, and others, on both sides, during the war and the truce. Nor was the war simply a question of Anglo-French relations: it was complicated by the position of Edward's allies, the Flemings, and Philip's allies, the Scots.

Both sides accepted an offer of arbitration from the pope, Boniface VIII, though the French insisted that he act in his private, not his public, capacity. A detailed memorandum of the English case, very probably the work of Raymond de la Ferrière, has survived. He was a Gascon, a trained lawyer, and a royal clerk of considerable seniority, who had acted as Edward's proctor in the *parlement* of Paris. His arguments centred upon the question of the status of Gascony, starting from the proposition that the duchy had been held as an allod, not a fief. Even if it were a fief, the memorandum pointed out that Philip's failure to observe his obligations as a feudal lord meant that he had deprived himself of any rights he might have possessed. Various solutions were proposed: Edward should hold Gascony freely, or the French should renounce the right to hear appeals from Gascony, or the duchy should be held as a fief from the papacy.[66] Such arguments were quite unacceptable to the French, and Boniface's arbitration decree, issued in June 1298, was that in territorial terms the pre-war status quo should be re-established, and that until that was done, the lands should be handed over to the papacy. Peace was to be ensured by the conventional means of a marriage alliance. Edward was to marry Philip IV's sister Margaret, and his son the French king's daughter Isabella.[67]

The arbitration by Boniface made no mention of the question of

---

[64] BL Add. MS 7965, f.156; *CPR 1301-7*, 432.

[65] *CPR 1292-1301*, 335.

[66] H. Rothwell, 'Edward I's case against Philip the Fair over Gascony', *EHR*, xlii, (1927), 572-82; Chaplais, *English Medieval Diplomatic Practice*, I, ii, 422-30; Chaplais, *Essays in Medieval Diplomacy and Administration*, III, 34.

[67] *Foedera*, I, ii, 894-5.

Flanders, nor indeed of that of Scotland. A tacit, and surely cynical, part of the peace process was that Edward I and Philip IV were both left free to pursue their designs upon their northern neighbours. A series of letters from the Flemish negotiators at the papal curia is revealing. They show that the Flemings objected to the fact that Philip was holding some of their compatriots prisoner, contrary to the terms of the truce, and they pointed out to the English envoys that Edward had failed to meet his financial obligations towards their count. The count of Savoy, who was one of those acting for Edward, was distinctly unsympathetic, pointing out that Edward, with his concerns in Scotland, Gascony and England itself, would not be able to assist the Flemings, 'nor will the English ever return willingly to your land'. Protestations about the importance of the Anglo-Flemish alliance were in vain. The English argued that no money was owed to the count, as the treaty had specified that it was only due in time of war, not truce. The Flemish envoys pointed out bitterly that in their view, and that of many others, the French king had done much better for John Balliol than Edward I had done for his ally, the count of Flanders.[68] Balliol, indeed, was handed over by the English into the hands of a papal envoy in June 1299, and there was much justice in the Flemish accusation against Edward, for all that the English king may have resented the treachery of the citizens of Bruges, and the rising in Ghent against him.

Agreement was reached, in June 1299, between the English and French ambassadors at Montreuil, and subsequently confirmed by the two kings.[69] In the following September, Edward duly married Margaret of France. Yet this was not the end of the story. The French failed to hand over to the papacy the Gascon lands they still held, and the only solution was for further negotiations to take place at the papal curia. A detailed report by Pierre Aimery, one of the English negotiators, reveals the blunt way in which Boniface VIII approached the matter. He pointed out that in many respects Edward was at fault. He would have done better to limit himself to the defence of Gascony, rather than becoming involved in Flanders and constructing his grand alliance. He had not observed papal decrees. The pope had no doubts, of course, about the initial stupidity of the English in 1294, when they had handed Gascony over to the French. Boniface explained that 'he who deals with the French deals with the devil'. Given their innate greed, there was no hope that the French would accept his verdict, when he was acting in his private capacity, and Boniface suggested that appeal should be made to him as pope, against a king whom he regarded, along with the

---

[68] De Lettenhove, 'De controvertia Bonifacium . . .', 1857–1890, notably 1869, 1881.
[69] *Foedera*, I, ii, 894–5.

French prelates, as excommunicate.[70] Little came of these negotiations. It must have been clear to Edward that little would be achieved by following the pope's suggestions, especially since Boniface continued to be critical of English activity in Scotland.

In 1302, the situation was transformed. Ironically, this was the work of the Flemings, who, despite being deserted by Edward, defeated the French army in an astonishing battle at Courtrai, in which urban levies defeated the aristocratic cavalry host of Philip IV. There was much delight at this in England, where the battle was the subject of a song written in English.[71] It was evident that Philip had little chance of retaining the territory he still held in Gascony: the citizens of Bordeaux rebelled against him early in 1303. It was vital for him to ensure that the Flemings did not receive English assistance, and so in May 1303 a final peace was negotiated with Edward, who was represented in the negotiations by Amadeus of Savoy, Henry de Lacy and the ever faithful Otto de Grandson. The essence of the treaty was simple: a return to the position that had existed prior to the outbreak of war in 1294.[72] Edward does not, in fact, appear to have been much tempted by the suggestion that he make a fresh alliance with Flanders. When Flemish envoys came before him in March 1303, they were rebuffed with a string of arguments and excuses. The matter could only be decided in a parliament; the regent of Flanders, John of Namur, was of insufficient standing.[73] It was clear that Edward was prepared to leave Philip a free hand in Flanders, provided he had a free hand in Scotland.

The treaty of 1303 did not resolve all the problems between the English and the French, but there was no danger of renewal of war. The transfer of territory in Gascony proceeded slowly, but without major problems. It proved impossible to arrange for either Edward or his son to go to France to perform homage to Philip, but no crisis resulted. The question of the various claims to damages, particularly by merchants who had suffered loss during the period of truce, was highly complex. A joint Anglo-French commission began sitting at Montreuil in the summer of 1306, but little came of it. Both sides overstated their claims, and the proceedings ended in farce, when one of the English commissioners, John Bakewell, went to Paris in October 1306 as it had been agreed he should, but completely failed to locate his French counterparts there.[74]

---

[70] J.G. Black, 'Edward I and Gascony in 1300', *EHR*, xvii (1902), 522-7; Chaplais, *English Medieval Diplomatic Practice*, I, i, 269-75.
[71] Wright, *Political Songs*, 187-95. Courtrai was remarkable, in that like Stirling Bridge, it saw the defeat of well-armed cavalry forces by footsoldiers.
[72] Chaplais, *Essays in Medieval Diplomacy and Administration*, III, 37-8; *Foedera*, I, ii, 952-4.
[73] Chaplais, *English Medieval Diplomatic Practice*, I, i, 116-18.
[74] Chaplais, *Essays in Medieval Diplomacy and Administration*, III, 135-42; Cuttino,

The peace did not bring friendship and co-operation with it, and the planned marriage of Edward of Caernarfon with Philip IV's daughter Isabella had not taken place by the end of Edward I's reign. There were still many tensions in the relationship between England and France, but there was no spark that might have ignited another war.

The war against France was Edward I's most unsuccessful venture. It had not been a war of his choosing: the outbreak of the conflict was not the result of Edward's obduracy in the face of French demands, but rather of the weakness shown by the English diplomats, which led Philip IV into thinking that he could win an easy victory. Appeasement, not aggression, by the English led to war. The strategy that Edward then adopted was a logical one, which had a close resemblance to that used unsuccessfully by King John in his attempts to recover Normandy from Philip II. The troops fighting in Gascony probably did as well as could be expected against more numerous French forces. The English had not yet developed the tactical skills which were to prove so effective in the hands of Edward III and the Black Prince during the Hundred Years War. The great alliance of princes ringing the northern and eastern borders of France was carefully constructed, and it was unfortunate for Edward that the situation in Scotland should have enabled the French to delay his planned expedition to the continent for so long.

In 1297, Edward showed extraordinary stubbornness in persisting with his plan. One reason, clearly, was that he considered that his honour was at stake, though his propaganda also stressed the extreme danger that the realm was in, and that the best defence was to fight at a distance, rather than at home.[75] The king's arguments had some force: had he not gone to Flanders, then Philip IV would not have conceded a truce, and the English would have had to continue to finance the defence of Gascony. Yet Edward's protestations about his obligations to his allies were revealed as distinctly threadbare when the truce was negotiated, and he showed no inclination to continue to defend the interests of the count of Flanders. The outcome of the expedition was hardly an honourable one for Edward.

The war against the French was also remarkably expensive. The cost of fighting in Gascony was considerable, as not only did troops have to be transported on the long sea-voyage to the Gironde, or to Bayonne, but they also had to be kept in the field and on garrison duty for lengthy periods, to meet the French threat. The main war account, submitted

English Diplomatic Administration, 62–87. The negotiations referred to, ibid., 63–4, as taking place in 1297 were, of course, those of 1294.

[75] _Documents 1297–8_, 134.

by John Sandale, details costs from November 1294 until August 1299 totalling £359,288. It includes expenses during the period of truce, which in Gascony began on 24 March 1298, but it does not give the costs incurred by the first English paymaster in Gascony, Peter of Aylesford. Nor does it include the money spent by the wardrobe in England on shipping and victuals for the armies going to Gascony. At a rough estimate, the war in the duchy probably cost in the region of £400,000. That is not to say that such a sum was exported from England in support of the military operations in Gascony during the war years. Between 1294 and Easter 1297, about £148,000 was sent from the exchequer in substantial lump sums to the paymasters in Gascony. Advances on wages, paid in England, to the main commanders, totalled at least £5,000, and this money was presumably taken by them to Gascony. Sale of victuals sent from England brought in £11,149. The one substantial local receipt was £45,763, lent by the merchants of Bayonne.

There was a massive debt accumulated by the crown. The account showed that military captains had been given promises of payment totalling £154,570, of which £75,707 were paid off by the English exchequer during Edward I's reign. The Bayonne loan was eventually repaid out of the English customs revenue, between 1299 and 1304. When John Sandale and his colleague, Thomas of Cambridge, finally made their account with the exchequer in 1314, they claimed a deficit of £59,139, though the exchequer officials were not satisfied with all the evidence that was put forward, and claimed that the total owed by the two men was no less than £97,989.[76] Whatever the rights and wrongs of that argument, it is abundantly clear that the war cost more than Edward I could afford. The calculation that about £265,000 was transferred from England to Gascony during the period of the war, and the truce that followed it (from 1294 to 1301) is probably very close to the mark. The costs to the French, it is worth noting, were of a similar, or slightly greater, order of magnitude.[77]

The great alliance did not cost as much as the defence of Gascony, but the obligations that Edward entered into were heavy enough. His various allies were probably promised a total of about £250,000, and it seems likely that they actually received some £165,000. In 1294 Robert de Segre had charge of about £47,000 exported from England. Walter Langton, when on his diplomatic mission, received one payment of £10,000 from the exchequer in England, which went to the count of

---

[76] E 372/160, m.41. This account is summarized in *Rôles Gascons*, iii, clxvii–clxix.

[77] J.R. Strayer, 'The Costs and Profits of War: the Anglo-French Conflict of 1294–1303', *The Medieval City*, ed. H.A. Miskimin, D. Herlihy, A.L. Udovitch (New Haven, 1977), 272, 290.

Flanders, part of a total of £24,300 paid to him in 1297. Substantial sums were paid over to foreign envoys in England: those sent by the duke of Brabant received £23,000 in 1295. Some of the money paid out in subsidies was raised on the continent. Two of Edward's agents, Gilbert Chesterton of Stamford and Elias Russel of London, collected almost £34,000 from the sale of English wool, and from customs duties paid by English merchants. Funds were also raised in loans from Italians, and other merchants in the Low Countries.[78] When the policy of constructing the grand alliance was initiated in 1294, those responsible could not have anticipated that it would take until 1297 before the English campaign in the Low Countries could be set in motion. That delay proved very expensive, as subsidies had to be renewed and new alliances formed.

The Flanders campaign itself was not so expensive, although as the account book only goes up to 19 November 1297, it is not possible to give a precise figure. The cost of wages and victualling, and other items directly attributable to the war, amounted to about £25,000 up to that date, but it is not easy to separate military expenditure from other items. The total cost of the expedition, from August 1297 until March 1298, is, however, not likely to have much exceeded £50,000.[79]

The war with France was not, of course, Edward's sole military expense during these years. There was also the Welsh rebellion of 1294–5 which had to be put down, and there was the Scottish campaign of 1296. The accounts of the royal wardrobe show that from November 1294 until November 1297 expenditure of £341,423 was incurred. That sum does not include the costs of the Gascon war which were charged to the paymasters there. Precise calculations are not possible, but it is likely that the total cost to Edward of the wars between 1294 and his return from Flanders in 1298 was in the region of £750,000.[80] That was an immense sum of money, and Edward had very little to show for such an investment. It is hardly surprising that his principal subjects were bitterly resentful, and that these were not merely years of extreme difficulty abroad, but also of intense political controversy at home.

---

[78] Above, 390; Cuttino, *English Diplomatic Administration*, 250; E 372/146 (Chesterton and Russel's account); Prestwich, *War, Politics and Finance*, 173; Fryde, *Studies in Medieval Trade and Finance* II, 1168–87, where slightly lower figures than mine are given.

[79] Prestwich, *War, Politics and Finance*, 175.

[80] Ibid., 175; the wardrobe expenses are tabulated in the appendix below, 570.

Chapter 16

THE YEARS OF CRISIS, 1294–8

War imposed a great strain on the English state in Edward I's later years. The cost of paying wages to the soldiers, of collecting sufficient food supplies, of maintaining fleets, and of arranging a system of home defence was very high, and the administrative difficulties considerable. It may seem strange that the burden of putting into the field armies which were never more than about 30,000 strong, and which were, by later standards, appallingly ill-equipped should have been as great as it was. There was, however, little surplus wealth in the economy which could be diverted to pay for the war, and the yields of the harvests were needed to feed the population, much of which existed at subsistence level. The total amount of money in circulation was small, in comparison with more modern periods: it was probably about one million pounds, and set against that, the costs of the wars of the 1290s were large indeed. Edward I had an extremely difficult task facing him between 1294 and 1298. He had to recruit armies, collect taxes, and persuade his subjects that his policies were the right ones. By 1297, his army was too small, his revenues inadequate, and his people close to rebellion.

The crisis caused by the French rejection in 1294 of the secret peace treaty, which Edmund of Lancaster had negotiated, was unexpected.[1] Rather than summon a large parliament, with full representation from shires, boroughs and clergy, Edward instead called together sixty-two barons to discuss the problems he faced. The writs were issued on 8 June, and the meeting was in session within ten days. The first important financial measure was heralded by an order on 12 June, before Edward had even renounced his homage to the king of France. The sheriffs were asked to organize the seizure of all the wool in the country, ostensibly so as to prevent any of it being exported to France. The real purpose soon became clear, when the magnates agreed to a plan whereby the wool would be exported by the crown, at what was hoped would be a very substantial profit. Repayment would eventually be made to the growers.[2]

---

[1] Above, 397.
[2] Lloyd, *English Wool Trade in the Middle Ages*, 75; E 159/68, m.82.

This project met with fierce hostility from the merchants, one of whom wrote a memorandum suggesting alternative methods of financing the war. He put forward various proposals, including one for a sales tax similar to those which operated in France and Castile, but his most important suggestion was that heavy customs duties, at the rate of five marks, or £3 3s 4d, on each sack of wool, should be imposed.[3] Such a tax, unlike the seizure of wool, would not put the merchants out of business, and it would be possible for them to pass the burden of it on, to the growers in the form of lower prices, and to the consumers in higher prices. The suggestion was a tempting one, and was supported by the greatest English wool merchant of the time, Laurence of Ludlow. On 26 July, therefore, the seizure of wool was cancelled. Three days later officials were appointed to collect the new customs duties, which were set at five marks from a sack of the best-quality sorted wool, and three marks from an ordinary sack. This differential rate proved impossible to enforce, and it was not long before three marks, or forty shillings, became the standard rate. Figures for receipts are not quite complete, but over £110,000 was collected between 1294 and late November 1297, when the tax was abolished.[4]

The introduction of the new customs duties saw the king break with the Italian banking house of the Riccardi of Lucca, who had been so closely involved with the creation of the customs system in 1275. The firm was not granted the receipts of the new duties in July 1294, and by October their assets in Ireland, and by implication also in England, were being seized by royal agents. It is not easy to explain why the king moved against a company which had been one of the mainstays of his financial system. It may be that the firm, with its extensive interests in both England and France, suffered so much from the news of the outbreak of war, with a consequent panic by its depositors, that it was simply unable to meet its obligations. It might have been action by the French king that caused the crisis. It has also been suggested that the root of the problem lay in the crusading tenth which had been imposed in 1274, and finally promised to Edward in 1291. The Riccardi were asked to act as agents in collecting the money, which was held by various different companies, and it appears that they failed in this task. The sum involved was 100,000 marks, or £66,666, as the first instalment. Edward's anger when this money was not forthcoming is understandable, and it seems very likely that it was this specific issue which

---

[3] C.V. Langlois, 'Project for Taxation presented to Edward I', *EHR*, iv (1889), 517–21.

[4] Lloyd, *English Wool Trade in the Middle Ages*, 76–80; Prestwich, *War, Politics and Finance*, 196–7.

led him to turn against the company which had served him so well since before his accession.[5]

The failure of the Riccardi meant that Edward no longer had the services of bankers ready and willing to supply him with cash. He was able, in the autumn of 1294, to compel eight companies to lend a total of £12,000, probably under threat of expulsion from the realm, and further loans of this type followed. Between 1294 and 1298 he raised a total of almost £29,000 in forced loans from eleven Italian companies, but this was hardly an adequate substitute for the wide-ranging assistance which the Riccardi had provided earlier in the reign. In 1297 the company of the Frescobaldi did lend voluntarily to Edward, but it was not until the king's return from Flanders in 1298 that they gradually came to occupy a position similar to that held by the Riccardi in the years before 1294.[6]

Edward had to find other means of raising money quickly in 1294. An extraordinary expedient was adopted on 16 June, when commissioners were appointed to scrutinize all deposits of money in churches and religious houses in England. The ostensible reason for this was to search out counterfeit and clipped coins, but in reality the king was looking for funds. It may be that he hoped to locate some of the crusading tenth, and he also intended to take what amounted to a forced loan. A total of £10,795 removed from private deposits was taken to the treasury. A careful record was made of the money's ownership, but only about £2,000 was in fact to be repaid. What caused particular offence about the operation, which took place on 4 July, was the way in which entry was forced to churches, and chests then smashed when keys could not be found.[7] This was followed by seizure of the crusade deposits, which totalled £32,480. This, however, was money to which the king was entitled, in contrast to the private funds which had been appropriated in the course of the scrutiny.[8]

All these actions were still not enough. Edward did not at first approach the laity for the grant of a tax, for the magnates had granted him the wool that had been seized, and they were expected to provide military service. Instead, the king summoned an ecclesiastical council, drawn from the provinces of both York and Canterbury. The writs demanding attendance were very like those used for a normal parliament: Edward now had freedom to act as he wished, as Archbishop Pecham had died in 1292, and his successor, Robert Winchelsey, did

[5] These problems are fully discussed by Kaeuper, *Bankers to the Crown*, 209–20.

[6] Prestwich, *War, Politics and Finance*, 208–10.

[7] *Rôles Gascons*, iii, 143–4; Cotton, 238; Guisborough, 248; J.H. Denton, *Robert Winchelsey and the Crown 1294–1313* (Cambridge, 1980), 67–8.

[8] Ibid., 64–5; *Book of Prests*, ed. Fryde, li.

not return from his consecration in Italy until January 1295. The archbishop of York was in a weak position, being in debt to the crown, and the powerful bishop of Durham, Anthony Bek, was abroad on an embassy for the king. According to Walter of Guisborough, Edward addressed the clergy in person when the council met in September. He stressed his desire for peace, but explained that he would fight to the death for his rights. He tried to justify the seizure of wool, and the scrutiny of church deposits, and promised to make amends for wrongs. Edward pointed out that the earls, barons and knights were risking their lives in war, and suggested that the clergy should assist the military effort by paying a tax. Oliver Sutton, bishop of Lincoln, asked for time to discuss the request, and after three days an offer was made of two tenths in one year, double the usual rate of tax. Edward was furious, and sent John de Havering and others to threaten the clergy. If they did not pay a half of the assessed wealth, they would be excluded from royal protection, in effect suffering outlawry. There was little resistance, but much bitter feeling. The demand was enormous. The tax was to be collected on the basis of the new papal assessment made in 1291, which totalled £200,000. The clergy were therefore asked to provide £100,000, and in fact, by Michaelmas 1294, the yield approached £70,000.[9]

It was probably the news of the rising in Wales in 1294 which convinced the king and his advisers that funds were still insufficient. Early in October knights of the shire were summoned to Westminster, along with earls and barons. Whether or not this assembly was a true parliament is a moot point: it may be that at the Michaelmas parliament the magnates had refused to grant a tax, on the grounds that there were no representatives present, and that therefore a special gathering was summoned.[10] According to one account, Edward demanded a tax of a third and sixth, but the earl of Gloucester and other magnates protested, and the grant was then made on 12 November, at the reduced rate of a tenth and sixth. The higher rate was paid by the towns and the ancient demesnes of the crown. The tax should have been fully collected by May 1295, but only about £45,000 had in fact come in by then. By the following January, however, the total stood at £72,820.[11] Although this tax was granted by a purely secular assembly, the temporalities of the clergy were included in the assessment. It was

---

[9] *Councils and Synods*, II, ii, 1125–34; Guisborough, 249–50; *Book of Prests*, ed. Fryde, li; Denton, *Winchelsey*, 69–77. Lists of protections issued to the clergy are given in *CPR 1292–1301*, 89–95, 117–24.

[10] *Parl. Writs*, i, 26–7; Richardson and Sayles, *English Parliament in the Middle Ages*, V, 149; below, 457.

[11] Prestwich, *War, Politics and Finance*, 181; the Hagnaby chronicle, BL Cotton Vesp. B.xi, f.36.

probably this issue which led the dean of St Paul's to go to the king to protest. Such was the emotion of the moment that he had a stroke and died, just as he approached Edward.[12]

The crown's financial difficulties continued, as expenditure on war remained at a high level. Fiscal policies were unaltered, despite the dismissal of the treasurer, William March, in August 1295. It may be that the king welcomed the chance to use March as a scapegoat for the unpopular scrutiny of church deposits in the previous year, but in addition, serious charges were brought against the treasurer by the Londoners.[13] March was replaced by Walter Langton, and he in turn was succeeded as keeper of the wardrobe by John Droxford. The question of further, badly needed grants of taxation was raised in parliament in late November and early December 1295. There was little difficulty in obtaining a grant of an eleventh and seventh from the laity, which probably yielded about £46,000.[14] The clergy presented a greater problem. Edward had taken the unusual step of summoning to parliament not only the prelates, but also representatives of the lower clergy. The church now had a determined leader in the form of Archbishop Winchelsey. A tenth was offered to the king, and despite pressure put by the chief justice of Common Pleas and the chancellor, Winchelsey would not increase it. He did promise, however, that if the war continued, further assistance would be forthcoming in the following year. The clerical tenth probably yielded only about £11,500.[15]

Instructions from Edward to the exchequer, in January 1296, show that he was worried by the financial situation. Every effort was to be made to collect the taxes, both direct and indirect, and the exchequer officials were told to take no vacations. All possible means were to be employed to collect debts owed to the crown, and all royal building works were to cease, with the exception of the castles in Wales and the decoration of the Painted Chamber at Westminster.[16] It was not possible to negotiate further taxes until November 1296, when a parliament was held at Bury St Edmunds. There, the laity granted a twelfth and eighth, with little argument. The clergy, however, were

---

[12] *Flores*, iii, 275−6. The dean may have made his protest earlier, over the clerical tax of a half, according to ibid., 90. *Chron. Bury St Edmunds*, 124, does not connect his death with the king's request for taxation, but sees him, as does *Ann. Dunstable*, 389, as a supporter of royal policy. See also Denton, *Winchelsey*, 73−4.

[13] *Select Cases before the King's Council, 1243−1482*, ed. I.S. Leadham and J.F. Baldwin (Selden Soc., xxxv, 1918), li-lvi, 8−18.

[14] Cotton, 299; tax yield calculated from E 372/151.

[15] *Flores*, iii, 282−3; Cotton, 299. The tax should have raised some £21,000, as the table given by Denton, *Winchelsey*, 299, shows. However, the evidence of the special receipt rolls is that between January and September 1296 only £11,233 was paid to the exchequer. The tax should have been fully paid by 1 July 1296.

[16] E 159/69, m.11; *KW*, i, 379−80.

much less amenable. The papal bull *Clericis Laicos*, drawn up in February 1296, was in Winchelsey's hands at the time parliament met. It prohibited the payment of taxes by the clergy to the lay power, and provided a good reason for him to postpone giving an answer to Edward until a church council, which was to be held in January 1297. The scene was set for a major confrontation between king and clergy.[17]

Military service was very possibly the subject of considerable argument between the king and his magnates in 1294, though this can only be deduced from the writs issued by the chancery, and not from the chronicle accounts of events. Edward issued a feudal summons for troops to muster at Portsmouth, ready to sail for Gascony. There was no precedent for such service there, and the request was bound to be resented. On 17 August the muster, which had been ordered for 1 September, was postponed until the end of the month, but it does not seem likely that many men appeared. The abbot of Ramsey certainly took the summons seriously, but he had great difficulty in persuading his tenants to provide the service that they owed. The earl of Oxford, in particular, proved unco-operative. It has been suggested that the muster was cancelled because of the news of the revolt in Wales, but the full seriousness of the rising was not evident until after the date set for the troops to assemble.[18] It is striking that neither the army that went to Wales, nor the troops that sailed for Gascony, included any feudal contingents, that is, men performing their obligation to serve the king for forty days at their own cost. It seems likely that resistance, perhaps of a purely passive character, forced Edward to change his recruitment methods.

In 1295 and 1296 there was little argument over military service, but later problems were foreshadowed. An important innovation was made in February 1296, when inquests were ordered to find out who held land worth more than forty librates, that is £40 a year. All such men were ordered to be ready to go on campaign at three weeks' notice, duly armed and mounted, in return for royal wages. In the past, the wealth qualification had been used as a means of compelling men to take up knighthood: now the question of knighthood was ignored, and service demanded from all those rich enough to have the right equipment. The technique was, it seems, successful in raising reinforcements for the Welsh war, and did not apparently arouse any opposition, though similar techniques were to be bitterly resented in 1297.[19]

[17] Denton, *Winchelsey*, 95–6; *Flores*, iii, 288–9; Guisborough, 286; Cotton, 314–15.
[18] *Parl. Writs*, i, 259–63; H.M. Chew, *The English Ecclesiastical Tenants in Chief and Knight Service* (Oxford, 1932), 99; *Select Pleas in Manorial Courts*, ed. Maitland, 76, 80.
[19] *Parl. Writs*, i, 267–8; Morris, *Welsh Wars*, 77, 262–3; M.R. Powicke, *Military Obligation in Medieval England* (Oxford, 1962), 110.

There was clear resentment shown when Edward asked nineteen magnates to go to Gascony in 1295, even though this was to be at wages. Several of them, including the earl of Arundel, were reluctant to comply, and in an angry letter the king ordered the exchequer to distrain them harshly. All the debts that they owed to the crown were to be collected without fear or favour. In some cases the sums involved were impressive: Arundel's debts amounted to £5,232, largely the result of an unpaid relief in John's reign. The threat was effective, and the disgruntled nobles duly sailed for Gascony.[20] In contrast, there were no arguments about the recruitment of the army that Edward led on his successful Scottish expedition in 1296. The magnates were summoned simply in accordance with their fealty to the crown, and asked to bring appropriate contingents. There was no question of feudal quotas, and there could be little objection to such a demand.

Infantry were needed as well as cavalry, and Edward recruited large numbers for the Welsh campaign of 1294–5, and that in Scotland in 1296. There was no argument about his needs on those occasions, but there were difficulties over recruitment for Gascony. In 1295 men were mustered and then not used by the crown, as the expedition was so long delayed. The chronicler Bartholomew Cotton recorded the arrival of Hugh Cressingham and William Mortimer in Norfolk to recruit soldiers. Large numbers were selected, and equipped with white tunics, swords and knives, all at the expense of the local communities. The men were mustered at Newmarket. Some were immediately dismissed as being inadequate, and the rest were sent home after four days, as they were not needed. A record of the cost of this operation in the hundred of Launditch shows that the various villages raised an average of six men each, and that expenses totalled £52 10s 8½d, which compares to a tax assessment for the tenth and sixth of 1294 of £241 10s 6d.[21] Such a costly and fruitless exercise must have been deeply resented. In addition to recruitment for the armies going to Gascony, there were also the forces raised for coastal defence. These were not paid for by the central administration, but must have imposed a considerable burden on the localities. When the Londoners provided twenty men-at-arms to serve in Kent in 1296, for a four-week period, each man received a generous twenty marks.[22]

In addition to the need for money and manpower, Edward had to collect food for his armies. The system of compulsory purchase, or

---

[20] *Parl. Writs*, i, 269; *Book of Prests*, ed. Fryde, xlviii; E 159/68, m.65.

[21] Cotton, 307; E 401/1656; Prestwich, *War, Politics and Finance*, 101. Recruitment was not, of course, confined to East Anglia: E 101/13/34/30 is a record of payments to some 1,400 men recruited from seven Midland counties, almost certainly for service in Gascony at this date.

[22] Prestwich, *War, Politics and Finance*, 140.

prise, was an old one, but in the past it had largely been limited in use to provisioning of the royal household. It had been used, on a small scale, for the first Welsh war, and more systematically in 1282–3, but it was now greatly extended, with demands reaching new heights in 1296. In March and April that year, 13,500 quarters of wheat and almost as much oats were demanded from twelve southern counties. There was a complaint to the king, the text of which has unfortunately not survived, as a result of which instruction went out in May to the effect that people were to be left with enough food to live on. Exactions continued, with fresh commissions issued to purveyors in June. In July news came from Gascony that the English troops there were in severe distress as a result of a lack of victuals, and in September Richard of Louth brought orders to the exchequer from the king, the first of which was that 100,000 quarters of grain should be purveyed, and sent to Gascony. The officials protested that such a quantity was impossible. Edward replied that he had indeed specified such an amount, but that his intention was simply that as much as possible should be collected, without burdening the people excessively. In the event, the exchequer issued orders for the collection of 33,000 quarters of wheat, 20,400 quarters of oats, 5,800 quarters of barley, and 3,200 quarters of beans and peas, largely from the south and the midlands.[23] Efforts were made by the crown to try to ensure that the burden of providing supplies was shared equally within counties, though it was inevitable, given the difficulties of transporting large quantities of goods, that some regions were called upon more often than others. There was a process of local assessment, and in the autumn of 1296, orders were given to use the tax records as a way of checking that the poor were not being burdened, while the rich were spared.[24]

It is not easy to show the degree to which the king's demands affected his subjects. The overall figures are very impressive. One calculation is that in the early stages of the French war, between June 1294 and November 1295, Edward I accumulated, and disposed of, some £250,000, probably about a quarter of the total currency of the realm. At a rough estimate, during the years from 1294 to 1297, Edward raised about £150,000 in direct lay taxes, and £130,000 in taxation of the clergy.[25] There was a startling decline in the assessment figures for the lay taxes, from £81,838 for the tenth and sixth of 1295, to £53,870 for the

[23] Ibid., 120–1; E 159/69, mm.19d; 76d; 80d; 85d.
[24] J.R. Maddicott, *The English Peasantry and the Demands of the Crown 1294–1341* (Past and Present Supplement 1, 1975), 24–5, discusses local assessment of prise. The royal instructions for the great prise of the autumn of 1297 are in E 159/70, m.119.
[25] M.C. Prestwich, 'The Crown and the Currency. The circulation of money in late thirteenth- and early fourteenth-century England' *Numismatic Chronicle*, cxlii (1982), 54, 56.

eleventh and seventh of 1295, down to £38,484 for the twelfth and eighth of 1296. The ninth granted in the autumn of 1297 was assessed at a mere £34,419. This suggests that the country's wealth was dramatically reduced, and it is probably true that the export of coin in support of the war effort did reduce the amount of currency in circulation in England to a marked extent. Grain prices fell, from a high level of an average 8s 2½d a quarter for wheat in 1294, to 4s 10d in 1296, and this might have had the effect of reducing the assessment figures. In addition, and perhaps this was the main reason for the fall, men became more adept at tax evasion, persuading and bribing tax assessors to return low figures.[26]

The customs duties of forty shillings on each sack exported were substantial, and it was argued in 1297 that as the value of English wool amounted to half that of the land, then the duty came to no less than a fifth of that value.[27] That was, of course, a considerable exaggeration, and as an indirect tax, the maltolt, as the new duties were termed, had perhaps less immediate and evident effects than the direct levies. The tax yielded, on average, about £33,000 a year. One chronicle suggested that the tax consisted of 20s paid by the wool grower, and 20s by the buyer, and it is very likely that wool merchants were in fact able to pass on the duty in precisely this way. The evidence of wool prices in the war years does suggest a fall of about 20s a sack, or by another calculation twenty-four per cent. Large-scale wool producers must have seen their income declining as a result.[28]

The overall value of the goods taken by way of prise cannot be calculated with any precision. At the prices set out in the ordinance for the prise of November 1296, the crown was asking for the collection of victuals worth some £30,000, a massive request. But, for some reason, the ordinance gave price levels far in excess of reality, and in practice all the foodstuffs ordered to be taken in 1296 (including those before

---

J.H. Denton, *Winchelsey*, 299, gives higher figures for the tax burden on the clergy, but these are based on assessments, not yields, and include the proportion of the lay taxes that the clergy paid, unlike my figures.

[26] Prestwich, *War, Politics and Finance*, 179, tabulates the overall assessments, but for county-by-county valuations, see J.F. Hadwin, 'The Medieval Lay Subsidies and Economic History', *Economic History Review*, 2nd ser., xxxvi (1983), 215, and note his comments ibid., 207; D.L. Farmer, 'Some Grain Price Movements in Thirteenth Century England', *Economic History Review*, 2nd ser., x (1957), 212; J.F. Willard, *Parliamentary Taxes on Personal Property, 1290 to 1334* (Cambridge, Mass, 1934, 343–7; E. Miller, 'War, taxation and the English Economy in the late thirteenth and early fourteenth centuries', *War and Economic Development*, ed. J.M. Winter (1975), 19.

[27] *Documents 1297–8*, 117.

[28] The Hagnaby chronicle, BL Vesp. B.xi, f.36; Miller, op. cit., 14; Prestwich, *War, Politics and Finance*, 199. Wool prices are fully set out in T.H. Lloyd, *The Movement of Wool Prices in Medieval England* (Economic History Review Supplement no. 6, 1973).

November) probably had a market value of around £17,000.[29] The crown did promise to pay for what it took, but even those who were fortunate had to wait a long time for their money.

What were the implications of these levels of taxation for individuals? In theory, the very poorest were exempt from lay taxation, the principle being that if a tax was set at a tenth, then no one assessed at less than ten shillings would have to pay. In practice, there was little point in tax collectors trying to raise money from those who had scarcely any, but lords would, of course, have passed on some at least of their own burden to their poor tenants. The great magnates did not pay tax in true proportion to their wealth. Some were exempted, because they were serving in Gascony. The earl of Cornwall's property was, for the most part, rented out, and as only movable goods, not rents, were assessed for tax purposes, he paid remarkably little. In 1296 he appears to have been charged only about £10, and he was very probably the richest lay magnate. Roger Bigod's estates were not managed in the same way as the earl of Cornwall's, but it has been calculated that, taking eighteen of his manors, the most that was paid in tax during this wartime period was no more than about four and a half per cent of net annual income. For those in between the extremes of wealth and poverty, the lay taxes were spread surprisingly evenly. It has been shown that in Bedfordshire, the proportion paid by lords as against peasants paralleled very closely the relative amounts of land farmed by each group.[30]

The effect of a tax on an individual's budget is impossible to estimate. Petronilla 'ad Petram', of Heighmongrove, in Huntingdonshire, had to pay 1s 1¾d in tax in 1295. A few years earlier her movable goods had consisted of six quarters of grain, ten sheep, some hay, 500 reeds and 500 turves. For such a person, a request for a sum which could have bought her, say, four bushels of oats, was a considerable one. To put it differently, it would probably have taken two weeks' work for her to earn enough to pay her tax.[31] One small Northamptonshire landlord, Henry de Bray, kept notes of his main items of capital expenditure during this period, which were largely on building. He did not record details of how much he had to pay in taxation, but a table does show that he was spending much less during the years of the war with France than he had before, or was to later, and this may reflect the crown's demands upon his resources.

---

[29] The Ordinance is in E 159/70, m.119: it specified a price for wheat of no less than 12s a quarter. My calculations are based on Farmer's price figures, op. cit., 212. For 1296 he gives an average for wheat of 4s 10d.

[30] Miller, 'War, Taxation and the English Economy', 15.

[31] *Early Huntingdonshire Lay Subsidy Rolls*, ed. J.A. Raftis and M.P. Hogan (Toronto, 1976), 52, 64. For a similar example, see Miller, 'War, taxation and the English economy', 18.

Expenditure of Henry de Bray[32]

1289	£12	(hall and chamber built)
1290	£5 7s 4d	(land purchased; courtyard enclosed)
1291	£5 10s	(chamber built)
1292	£2 7s 8d	(wall built)
1293	£4 17s	(fishpond; watercourse diverted)
1294	£1 3s	(repairs to gateway)
1295	£1 10s 4d	(cottage built; pound and wall repaired)
1296	£2 13s	(sister's marriage; cottage built)
1297	£3 2s 4d	(walled garden constructed)
1298	£2 16s	(pigsty, chicken-house, wall built)
1299	£9 6s 4d	(water-mill built)
1300	£6 14s 4d	(repair of mill, purchase of cottage, tower built)

The church, and those who lived on its lands, bore a much heavier load of taxation than did the laity. Clerical taxes were taken on the basis of an assessment for crusade taxation made in 1291. Instead of valuing the property of individuals, this assessment placed values on entire estates. Major ecclesiastical landowners were thus charged with large sums, notably in the case of the tax of a half of 1294, which they would then pass on, at least in part, to their tenants. At Bolton Priory payment of the half took twenty-two per cent of total expenditure in 1294, and at Christ Church, Canterbury, the figure was even higher, at about thirty per cent. At God's House, Southampton, the hospital could not pay one instalment of the tax, which came to £25, and so eighteen oxen were seized by the crown.[33] At Worcester Cathedral Priory one instalment of the half came to £150 4s 1½d; £134 17s 0¼d was raised by means of a tax on the unfree tenants, while only £34 16s 2½d came from the obedientaries of the house.[34] The great monasteries were, in general, able to afford to pay their taxes. At Canterbury, there was less wine drunk, but this was probably an economy forced on the monks through shortage of supplies. The number of monks fell, and productive investment ceased, but the clear profit shown in the accounts for 1297, of £444, shows that the house had not been forced into poverty by the king.[35] Lesser churchmen, however, probably found the situation more

[32] *The Estate Book of Henry de Bray*, ed. D. Willis (Camden Soc., 3rd ser., xxvii, 1916), 48–50.

[33] M. Mate, 'The Impact of War on the Economy of Canterbury Cathedral Priory, 1294–1340', *Speculum*, lvii (1982), 763; Prestwich, *War, Politics and Finance*, 193.

[34] *Early Compotus Rolls of the Priory of Worcester*, ed. J.M. Wilson and C. Gordon (Worcestershire Historical Society, 1908), 27–8, 31. I am grateful to Professor R.H. Hilton for drawing my attention to this source.

[35] Mate, 'The Impact of War on the Economy of Canterbury Cathedral Priory', 764–5.

difficult, and the peasant tenants on church lands must have found it harder still to make ends meet.

Although the country was hard-pressed by Edward, he was able to carry his subjects with him until late in 1296, when the clergy's refusal to grant a tax at Bury St Edmunds marked a major setback. The king had done as much as he could, in an age of poor communications, to explain the need for the taxes and prises, and to win the support of his people. At the start of the war with France, he asked for prayers to be said for the success of his enterprise, and a similar request was made in January 1296: all congregations were thus made aware of the problems facing the country.[36] Summonses to parliament made much of the dangers threatening the realm. That addressed to the clergy in 1295, suggesting that the French aimed to destroy the English nation, was particularly notable. The same writ, in a celebrated phrase drawn from Roman law, stressed the need for universal approval for the measures needed (*quod omnes tangit ab omnibus approbetur*), so that a common danger might be met by a common remedy.[37] Diplomatic successes, such as the treaty with Adolf of Nassau, made in 1294, were widely publicized, to judge by their treatment in chronicles.[38] The unpopular *Quo Warranto* hearings were halted in 1294, and in the same year the king adopted a much more generous policy towards tenants-in-chief who wanted to grant out lands.[39] Though there may have been debate over the feudal summons to serve in Gascony in 1294, there had been no major objections of a political or constitutional character to the king's actions. Matters were to be very different in 1297, when further demands for men, money and food would be seen as arbitrary, unreasonable and excessive.

Before the complex issues involved in the political disputes – and near civil war – of 1297 are discussed, one further element to the background of the crisis needs to be examined. Some of the leading participants in the events had their own reasons for resenting the king and his policies. One such was the archbishop of Canterbury, Robert Winchelsey. He was a tough and occasionally irascible man, and a worthy opponent of Edward I. The impact he might have on those who crossed him is

[36] *Foedera*, I, ii, 802, 834. For a full discussion, see D.W. Burton, 'Politics, Propaganda and Public Opinion in the Reigns of Henry III and Edward I' (Oxford D.Phil. thesis, 1985), 368–71, 409–10.

[37] Stubbs, *Select Charters*, 480; see also below, 465–6.

[38] The treaty is given in full by Cotton, 240–5, and is widely referred to in other chronicles, such as Rishanger, 142; Guisborough, 248; *Ann. Worcester*, 516. Ironically, Edward's own officials could not locate the original document in 1297: *Documents 1297–8*, 80.

[39] Sutherland, *Quo Warranto*, 213; Bean, *Decline of English Feudalism*, 75.

demonstrated by the instance of the fatal heart-attack suffered by the abbot of Oseney when he was rebuked by Winchelsey in 1297.[40] Relations between king and archbishop started badly, when the archbishop swore his oath of fealty at Conwy in February 1295, and added a statement which made it clear that he was only swearing in respect of the temporalities of his see, not the spiritualities. Disputes over rights of presentation to churches aggravated the situation. Thomas de Capella, a royal chancery clerk, obtained the church of Sevenoaks in 1294. There were grounds for doubting his sanity, and he was a pluralist, so Winchelsey refused to take any steps to admit him to his living. The archbishop was duly taken to court, and damages of £7,000 were claimed from him. He was forced to back down. Edward's request, in 1295, that Winchelsey pay off a debt of £3,568 to the crown in the brief space of three years testifies to the antagonism that existed between king and archbishop.[41]

The leaders of the lay opposition to Edward in 1297 were the earls of Norfolk and Hereford, Roger Bigod and Humphrey de Bohun. The earl of Gloucester, who would have carried some more weight, had died in 1295. The earls of Lincoln and Cornwall were fighting in Gascony, and earl Warenne was in Scotland. The earl of Oxford was an obscure figure, so the only earls left to play a political role in England were Bigod, Bohun, Arundel and Warwick. Humphrey de Bohun's treatment at the king's hands, in the case between himself and the earl of Gloucester, must have rankled, and he probably considered that Edward had not paid due regard in military matters to his hereditary role as constable of England.[42] Roger Bigod had still stronger reasons to be angry with the king. His position as hereditary marshal had been ignored by Edward in 1294, when a household knight, Roger de Molis, had been appointed marshal of the army in Wales, an action which could have been the consequence of arguments over the feudal summons to serve in Gascony that year. There was also a long history of arguments over debts that Bigod owed to the crown. As early as 1277, the earl had promised to hand his manor of Bosham, with other lands in Sussex and elsewhere, to the king within two years, as surety for a loan of 1,000 marks. In the mid 1280s the exchequer calculated that Bigod owed just over £1,000 and he was allowed to pay this off in instalments of £100 a year, but by the early 1290s the debt had risen to at least £1,400. That figure the earl conceded, but the exchequer argued that the real total was in fact no less than £3,326. Bigod appeared in parliament, and petitioned to be excused payment. Once again he

[40] Denton, *Winchelsey*, 126.
[41] Ibid., 5–6, 81, 126, 274–5; Prestwich, *War, Politics and Finance*, 237.
[42] Above, 348–50.

received permission to pay off his debts at the rate of £100 a year, but the humiliation of having to beg for this favour in parliament must have rankled.[43] John de Ferrers was another man with a personal grievance, for as a result of the treatment accorded to his father, Robert, in the aftermath of the Barons' Wars, he had lost most of his inheritance, as well as his title of earl of Derby.[44] Many of the lords of the Welsh March considered that they were threatened by Edward's treatment of their franchisal rights. The feelings that could be aroused are illustrated by the incident in 1294, when a royal writ, which interfered with the liberty of Leominster, in Herefordshire, was seized, and those responsible 'trampled it in the mud so that it could not be found, and the king's command contained therein could not be executed'.[45]

The grievances of the Londoners contributed a further element to the coming political crisis. Unfortunately, the section covering the years from 1293 to 1300 is missing from the London Annals, but there was undoubtedly much bitterness against the king in the city, as a result of the system of direct rule which had begun in 1285.[46] After 1293 none of the old city dynasties had provided officials, and resentment against the crown grew. The charges the Londoners brought against William March provide one indication of their anger. Restoration of the mayoralty and of the franchises of the city was demanded, but Edward was unbending. Many of the key events in 1297 were to take place in London, and it is hardly surprising that the citizens gave their backing to Edward's opponents.[47]

The first issue to be raised in 1297 was that of clerical taxation. Archbishop Winchelsey summoned a council to meet in London, at St Paul's, so that the request for a grant made by the king at Bury St Edmunds in the previous November might be answered. The main obstacle to a grant was the papal bull *Clericis Laicos*. The archbishop had ordered this to be made public, in December and January, and it was read out to the assembled council. The proctors of the lower clergy argued strongly against the grant of a tax. They noted the king's failure to restore the liberties of the church in return for the last tax, and pointed out that grants made over the past two decades had not resulted in any worthwhile royal concessions. They argued that the king should approach the pope, for if they made a grant without papal consent then they would be excommunicated. Winchelsey himself did

[43] Above, 243; E 159/58, m.11; E 159/66, mm.25, 33; Prestwich, *War, Politics and Finance*, 237.

[44] Above, 61.

[45] *CPR 1292–1301*, 113.

[46] Above, 265.

[47] Williams, *Medieval London*, 258–60.

not put the case in such an extreme way, but stated the problem to Edward in terms of the need to find a middle way between the obligation to assist the realm in time of necessity, and the prohibition, in the papal bull, against the payment of taxes to the lay power. Only if the danger was very great, could the church consider making a grant in face of the papal instruction. The letter ended with a complaint against the seizure of grain from clerics, which threatened to reduce them to beggary.[48]

This argument was firmly couched in terms of the Roman law doctrine of necessity, which permitted a ruler to request and obtain aid from his subjects if the state was in danger. If it was accepted that a state of necessity existed, then the subjects were bound to grant such aid. The Third Lateran Council of 1179 had laid down that the clergy might, in a case of urgent necessity, pay taxes to a lay power, and Winchelsey clearly saw a conflict between this principle, and the firm prohibition of such payments made in *Clericis Laicos*.[49] The implication of the argument was that Winchelsey did not consider that the French war created a sufficient necessity for him to suggest that the papal bull be overridden.

Edward I did not appreciate the difficulty of the clergy's position, or the subtlety of Winchelsey's arguments. According to Bartholomew Cotton, when a clerical deputation put their case to him, the king replied bluntly: 'Since you are not keeping the terms of the homage and the oath by which you hold your baronies from me, I am not held to you in any way.'[50] This was an argument based purely on the feudal relationship between king and prelates. Edward was not prepared to argue with the clergy on their terms, and his own case was uncompromising and simple. He must have drawn comfort from the fact that the York clergy did not take the same line as their southern brethren, but granted a tax of a fifth with little argument.[51]

Edward summoned a parliament at very short notice, in part to discuss the problem presented by the clergy. However, before it met, at Salisbury on 24 February, he acted, and placed the clergy out of his protection on 30 January. On 12 February he ordered the seizure of all lay fees, with goods and chattels, which belonged to the clergy. It was made known that the king's protection could be purchased for a sum equivalent to that which would have been paid in a tax of a fifth, had a

---

[48] *Councils and Synods*, II, ii, 1156–9. The response by the clerical proctors might have been made at the Bury St Edmunds parliament, but is more likely to have been produced at the January council.

[49] Harriss, *King, Parliament and Public Finance*, 21–4, sets out the doctrine of necessity very clearly. Winchelsey's arguments are discussed by Denton, *Winchelsey*, 105–6.

[50] Cotton, 318.

[51] Denton, *Winchelsey*, 103–4.

grant been made. The northern clergy received their protections *en bloc* on 18 February, and many of the clerks in royal service obtained theirs at the same time. Other clerks hastened to pay their fines as the king progressed across southern England towards Salisbury.[52] The work of the parliament, as far as the clergy were concerned, was probably limited to discussing the arrangements to be made for collecting the fines, and to trying to prevent any retaliation by Winchelsey. With this in view, the excommunication of royal officials was forbidden in a writ of 27 February.[53]

The main business of the Salisbury parliament, to which the clergy were not, of course, summoned, was not the question of the taxation of the church, but rather that of the king's military plans. Edward asked his magnates to go to fight overseas. A series of refusals infuriated the king, who threatened to give the lands of those who would not go to those who would. The Bury St Edmunds chronicle suggests that the magnates argued that they could not leave their own country when it was in such danger, but Walter of Guisborough has it that Roger Bigod and Humphrey de Bohun refused to consider going to Gascony on the grounds that their hereditary offices of marshal and constable obliged them to stay with the king. Bohun was not, in fact, present at this parliament, which casts some doubt on the chronicler's splendidly dramatic presentation of these events. He reported a dialogue between Bigod and the king, which culminated in Edward's outburst, 'By God, Sir Earl, either go or hang', to which Bigod replied, 'By the same oath, O king, I shall neither go nor hang'.[54]

Edward had to admit a temporary defeat, and no military summonses were issued. He remained in the south-west, however, preparing to send assistance to the beleaguered troops in Gascony. He and his officials were also busy with the collection of the fines from the clergy. Very considerable pressure was put on the church. At Canterbury, royal officials moved in to lock and seal many of the buildings of the cathedral priory as early as 27 February. By 6 March the stored grain was rotting and overheating as a result of the lack of care.[55] Winchelsey decided to go to see the king in person. On his way, he was virtually besieged at Maidstone, and his horses were confiscated. Nevertheless, he reached Salisbury. The interview with the king was predictably futile. Edward argued that even if the pope himself had lands in England, he would be entitled to take them into his hands for the

---

[52] Ibid., 113–15; *CPR 1292–1301*, 235–7.

[53] *Documents 1297–8*, 43–4.

[54] Guisborough, 289–90; *Chron. Bury St Edmunds*, 138–9; H. Rothwell, 'The Confirmation of the Charters, 1297', *EHR*, lx (1945), 25.

[55] Denton, *Winchelsey*, 111–12; *Documents 1297–8*, 42–3, 45–6.

defence of the realm. Winchelsey expressed his readiness to let the pope decide if the necessity was so serious that it justified the taxation of the clergy, but Edward was not prepared to do this without full consultation. The only concession he was ready to make was that the lands confiscated from clergy who refused to purchase protections from him might now be sown with seed.[56] The business of collecting fines from the clergy who wished to purchase the king's protection continued. On 1 March bannerets had been appointed to undertake this task, and there was so much work for them that on 20 March they were told to take on assistants.[57]

The next stage came with a new church council, summoned by Winchelsey to meet in London on 24 March. Edward was clearly alarmed at what might take place, and forbad the clergy to do anything which might harm himself, his officials, or any of those under his protection. An appeal to Rome was announced, against any action which might be taken against the king or his subjects, and this was made public when the council opened. There was clearly bitter argument. The archbishop failed to convince the clergy that they should stand firm: royal pressure and propaganda had convinced many that a grant of taxation was necessary. There were rumours that, unless the clergy submitted, all church property, spiritualities and lay fees alike, would be seized and forfeited for ever. A suggestion that a tax be granted, but that it should be strictly administered by the church, was rejected, however, and Winchelsey proposed that each man should be allowed to follow his own conscience. This preserved the principle that no grant should be made, in accordance with the papal bull *Clericis Laicos*, but the king was able to collect his money in the form of the fines paid to regain his protection. It also meant, as one chronicler noted, that the clergy departed from the council 'like wandering sheep without a shepherd'.[58]

The business of collecting the fines proceeded apace. On 2 April the exchequer was told to sell the goods that had been taken from the clergy: this would both raise money, and put more pressure on those churchmen who had not yet come to terms. Further instructions issued on 11 April stated that it did not matter if goods were sold for less than their real value, for the king needed money quickly. Those clergy who had not paid their fines 'had failed their liege lord, and their own nation, and the realm'.[59] Clergy who came forward late were not to be

[56] Denton, *Winchelsey*, 119–20; J.H. Denton, 'The Crisis of 1297 from the Evesham Chronicle', *EHR*, xciii (1978), 571–2.

[57] *Documents 1297–8*, 16, 53–4.

[58] *Councils and Synods*, II, ii, 1166–8; Denton, *Winchelsey*, 126–7; Denton, 'The Crisis of 1297 from the Evesham Chronicle', 574.

[59] *Documents 1297–8*, 16–17, 61–2, 68–9.

treated as well as those who had settled promptly with the king, and if payment was not made by 23 May, then new protections would have to be bought.[60] It is clear that in April, impressive numbers of clergy were making their peace with the king. Between February and September 1297 a total of £23,174 was received by the exchequer, a sum similar to that which a true tax would probably have raised.[61]

The laity were not put under pressure similar to the clergy, for they had granted a tax of a twelfth and eighth at Bury St Edmunds in November 1296. The king's growing financial difficulties in 1297, however, meant that every effort was made to collect revenue. On 12 March an ordinance was issued for the appointment of commissioners who were to investigate debts owed to the crown. Sheriffs, bailiffs and tax collectors were to appear before them, to give details of what money was due, and stringent procedures were laid down for them to be imprisoned and fined, should it be found that they had improperly accepted favours in return for delays in payment.[62] The measure does not seem to have brought in much revenue, and probably did much to lose the co-operation of sheriffs and their subordinates. Further steps were needed if the king's financial situation was to be improved.

At Easter, which fell in mid-April, it was decided to institute a seizure of wool. This, of course, had been attempted in 1294, but it had not been particularly successful then. Much of the wool that had been taken on that occasion had been returned to its owners when the heavy new export duties had been introduced, but that belonging to French merchants and to the Riccardi had been retained by the crown. It was then exported, but much was lost through shipwreck at sea, as was Laurence of Ludlow, the great wool merchant who had co-operated with the king in the venture. In the end, royal profits were less than £5,000.[63] In the spring of 1297, however, Edward needed large sums of money quickly, and a new prise of wool must have seemed to him to be an attractive option. The Easter prise is, unfortunately, badly documented, but it appears that it was initially intended to apply only to wool that had been purchased by foreign merchants. Then Hugh Despenser, John Droxford and other councillors decided, on their own initiative, to extend it to wealthy English merchants' wool. A proclamation was issued, asking for all wool to be taken to specified towns by 21 April, with no indication that it was then going to be seized. There must

---

[60] Ibid., 74.

[61] Denton, *Winchelsey*, 128. As is pointed out, ibid., 299, the full assessed figure for a tax of a fifth was about £42,000, but since the tax of a tenth in the previous year raised only about £12,000, the yield from the fines in 1297 was in fact impressive. For this yield, see *Documents 1297–8*, 18n.

[62] *Documents 1297–8*, 48–50.

[63] Lloyd, *English Wool Trade in the Middle Ages*, 75–6, 78–9; *Ann. Worcester*, 518.

THE YEARS OF CRISIS, 1294-8

have been suspicions, however, for some wool was removed to franchises so that it would be safe from the attention of royal officials, and at Royston, one of the collection centres, no wool had come in by the required date.

The whole business of the seizure was undertaken with far less competence than any other major measure in 1297. There was undoubtedly malpractice by officials, and Edward himself disavowed the action of his councillors. At Boston the customs officials were so puzzled by one royal letter that they returned a transcript of it to the exchequer with a request for elucidation: they had received very little wool, and orders to export it to Flanders and Brabant were far too imprecise. During May concessions were made, with favoured magnates and religious houses obtaining restoration of their wool. In the end, it seems that only about 2,333 sacks of wool were collected. The whole affair had caused much resentment, had taken up a great deal of official time, and had not achieved the expected financial goal.[64]

Perhaps because of the rebuff he had received at the Salisbury parliament, Edward was slow to issue summonses for military service in 1297. He may also have delayed until it became clear how the plans for the grand alliance were proceeding. On 15 April, however, writs were issued. About 130 magnates were asked to muster at London on 7 July; female tenants-in-chief and ecclesiastics were to send their feudal quotas. The summons was a remarkable one. No appeal was made in the conventional way to the fealty and homage owed by the magnates; they were instead 'affectionately required and requested' to muster 'for the salvation and general advantage of the realm'. It was not stated where the army was to go once it mustered, just that it was to go overseas. No mention was made of pay. In addition to this, the king asked all those with twenty pounds worth of land to attend at London: ten days previously, the sheriffs had been asked to draw up lists of such men.[65] What Edward was doing was quite unprecedented.

The muster at London was a disaster for Edward. Before it took place, many of the magnates held a meeting in the Welsh March, at Montgomery. Bigod and Bohun were present, as were the earls of Warwick and Arundel, John Hastings and Edmund Mortimer. They decided that they could not serve the king overseas, because they had spent so much already on his wars in Wales and Scotland, and because they were impoverished by the frequent taxes.[66] Roger Bigod, however,

---

[64] Ibid., 87–90; *Documents 1297–8*, 10–11, 81.

[65] *Parl. Writs*, i, 281–2.

[66] Denton, 'The Crisis of 1297 from the Evesham Chronicle', 576. Arundel used arguments of impoverishment again, probably in August 1297: *Documents 1297–8*, 141–2.

did not exclude the possibility that he might be forced to go to Flanders, or to send troops there, for when an agreement was drawn up on 9 June between himself and John Segrave, two clauses provided for Segrave's service under these circumstances.[67] The magnates in general certainly did not consider that they were in any position to refuse the king's summons. The earl of Warwick, according to the Evesham chronicle, was bribed into submission by the king, and Arundel was making efforts to raise the money he would need for the coming campaign.[68] However, when the time came for the muster, Edward asked Bigod and Bohun, in their capacities as marshal and constable, to draw up lists of those who attended, just as if it were a normal feudal levy. This they refused to do, arguing in a written reply that they had come to London in response to a royal request, not a summons. Edward promptly dismissed them, and appointed Geoffrey de Geneville and Thomas Berkeley to their offices of marshal and constable.[69]

The earls naturally looked to Archbishop Winchelsey for support. Langtoft in his chronicle described him as 'bearing down like a lion', and arguing that the king must suspend the planned expedition, as to make war without making amends for his treatment of the church would be to court disaster.[70] Edward, however, skilfully divided the opposition, and achieved a reconciliation with Winchelsey on 11 July, the date when restitution of the archbishop's lands was ordered. On 14 July, in a carefully contrived ceremony, Winchelsey took part in the swearing of fealty to the king's son Edward of Caernarfon. The earl of Warwick and John Hastings were also present: Edward had thus divided the ranks of those who had met at Montgomery. Bigod and Bohun could hardly ignore a request to perform fealty to the future king, but they only did so two days later, in the company of the aldermen and citizens of London.[71] Winchelsey's role was now transformed from that of opponent of the king into mediator. He, with other bishops, sought Edward's permission to negotiate with the recalcitrant earls. An initial meeting at Waltham was abortive, as the earls did not attend. Royal safe-conducts for a further conference at St Albans failed to reassure them, and no meeting took place.[72] The royal concession that those who went on the expedition would be paid wages did little to defuse the situation. When a meeting took place between Anthony Bek, bishop of Durham, the earl of Warwick and Geoffrey de Geneville,

[67] Denholm-Young, *Seignorial Administration in England*, 168.

[68] Denton, 'The Crisis of 1297 from the Evesham Chronicle', 576; *CPR 1292–1301*, 289.

[69] *Documents 1297–8*, 126.

[70] Langtoft, ii, 288.

[71] Denton, *Winchelsey*, 131–2; *Documents 1297–8*, 106–7.

[72] Ibid., 127.

acting for the king, and the earls at Stratford, just outside London, Humphrey de Bohun made a speech. He stressed that the king's opponents bore Edward no ill-will, but he demanded the correction of abuses and the restoration of established laws and customs. The speech was a lengthy one, but a convenient written statement of grievances, known as the Remonstrances, was drawn up.

The first complaint concerned the summons to the recent muster, which had not stated where the expedition was to go. If, as was rumoured, it was destined for Flanders, no service was owed there. In any case, Edward's subjects were too impoverished by his demands to perform any military duties. The way in which men were arbitrarily deprived of their franchises by the king was a matter for protest, as was the way in which the provisions of Magna Carta were being ignored. The argument then reverted to the proposed Flanders campaign: this, it was suggested, was hardly wise in view of the situation in Scotland. The burden of the maltolt on wool was excessive, amounting, it was claimed, to a fifth of the value of the land. The harsh application of forest law was another grievance. One version of the text then added that the various 'tallages, aids, mises and prises' might serve as a precedent for reducing the people, lay and ecclesiastics, to a state of serfdom, and the king was asked to promise that this would not happen.[73]

The document was an able one, summarizing a wide range of grievances. The terminology of 'tallages' and 'mises' has puzzled historians, for there was no tallage collected at this time, and 'mises' is a very unspecific word. It made good propaganda sense, however, to refer to tallage, for this was an arbitrary tax levied on the unfree (or on the royal demesnes), and many must have felt that a comparison between the recent taxes and tallage was a fair one. The range of royal impositions was such that use of a vague term such as 'mises' was surely justifiable. The document did not present the king with a carefully worked out constitutional case: it was primarily a protest at the weight of the burdens he had imposed on his subjects. It has been suggested that 'the language seems to be that of the smaller landowner rather than of the earl',[74] but this is surely not the case. There was no specific mention of the twenty-pound landowners, and the complaint of poverty was certainly put by the earl of Arundel, and probably Warwick as well.[75] The question of the franchises was an issue which concerned the great men, rather than the small landowners.

Edward denied that he received a text of the Remonstrances, but he

---

[73] *Documents, 1297-8*, 115-16.

[74] B. Wilkinson, *Constitutional History of England 1216-1399*, i, 196.

[75] *Documents 1297-8*, 141-2; C 81/1699, no. 102. This latter document is a request from Warwick's brother for the lifting of distraint for various debts that the earl owed.

was certainly well aware of the tenor of the arguments that Bohun put forward at Stratford in late July.[76] He was obviously not impressed, and probably considered that he had done enough to divide the ranks of his opponents. The only compromise he was prepared to envisage was the confirmation of Magna Carta and the Forest Charter, in return for the grant of a new tax. He was ready to institute a fresh prise of wool, and his thoughts even turned to the prospect of negotiating a subsidy from the clergy.

On 30 July, men were appointed to assess and collect a tax of an eighth and fifth, for which Edward claimed that he had received full consent. Another view was that it had been agreed merely by 'people (*plebe*) standing round in his chamber'.[77] In fact, the grant probably was made in parliament, which was in session between at least 8 and 22 July. However, there were no representatives present at this assembly, and the magnates present had not, it seems, received the usual summonses to attend. This was certainly no normal grant, and the fact that Edward's officials described it in some documents as a gift (*doun*) shows that they were aware that it had not been negotiated in the same manner as previous taxes.[78]

Edward did not try to pretend that the prise of wool had been approved by his subjects. An exchequer memorandum set out the problem. The king was under an obligation to pay Adolf of Nassau 30,000 marks when the English landed on the continent, and a further 25,500 marks was owed to the duke of Brabant; 20,000 marks was needed for the payment of troops, over and above what was expected to come into the exchequer. Council discussion led to the conclusion that the best way to raise the money was to seize 8,000 sacks of wool, which the crown would then export and sell. Those whose wool had been taken would eventually, it was hoped, be repaid at the full market price. This measure had little success, for records suggest that a mere 799 sacks were exported.[79] The fact that little wool was collected did not make the measure any less unpopular. Meanwhile, prises of foodstuffs were still continuing: in April collection of 13,000 quarters of grain had been demanded, and in June Edward had asked for 3,100 carcases of bacon and 1,500 of beef. In the course of 1297, at least 10,300 quarters of wheat, 6,700 quarters of oats, 2,400 quarters of barley and malt, and 1,000 quarters of beans were seized by royal officials.[80]

In instructions to the assessors of the lay tax, issued on 8 August,

---

Edward – or his officials – claimed that the clergy had made him a grant. This was simply not true, but it may be that at the time of his reconciliation with Winchelsey, the archbishop had encouraged him to think that a grant would be forthcoming.[81] A clerical council was summoned to meet at London, on 10 August, to consider the matter. Confirmation of the charters and redress of clerical grievances were promised by the king, but this was not enough. The clergy were not in a co-operative mood, and insisted that no tax would be granted unless the pope was consulted first. They must have been aware of events in France, where the clergy had asked permission to grant a tax in January 1297, and this had been conceded in the bull *Coram illo fatemur* of 28 February, though they would not yet have known of the concession of *Etsi de statu* at the end of July, which permitted the king to ask for subsidies without the need for papal consent. The fact that Edward was in urgent need of money must have been well known, and the delay that would have been involved in obtaining an answer from the pope meant that the clergy's answer to the king was tantamount to a refusal. Winchelsey made his anger with Edward very clear when he ordered the promulgation, on 1 September, of excommunications against all those who attacked church property.[82]

Edward was not prepared to consult the pope over a clerical grant, and on 19 August he prohibited the excommunications. The next day he ordered the exchequer to proceed with the levy of a tax of a fifth on all church property, or, as an alternative, a third on spiritualities. There was no pretence that any consent had been obtained, nor did Edward make a clear statement of his rights in a situation of urgent necessity. He emphasized the fact that the planned expedition to Flanders was for the honour, profit and salvation of himself and the realm, and the tax was described, with surprising honesty, as a prise. A vague promise was added that Edward would provide satisfaction to all those who aided him.[83] The levy, not surprisingly, was a failure. There is no evidence that any money was collected, and it was superseded by fresh taxes voted in the autumn. Edward was not even successful in obtaining a grant from the northern clergy, who until now had been more co-operative than the southern. When they met at York on 23 August, they refused to make any offer.[84]

Edward did not make any further provocative demands for military

<hr />

[81] Ibid., 121; Denton, *Winchelsey*, 144.

[82] *Councils and Synods*, II, ii, 1168–76; Denton, *Winchelsey*, 123–4, 145–7; Strayer, *Philip IV*, 254.

[83] Denton, *Winchelsey*, 149–51; *Documents 1297–8*, 133–5.

[84] Ibid., 152–3. There had been some earlier resistance from northern clerics: see *Documents 1297–8*, 60, 65–6.

service in late July or August 1297. Writs were issued on 28 July, under the privy seal, summoning men to Winchelsea, but the phraseology of the summons to London, which had proved so controversial, was avoided. Instead, the king simply asked all those who had agreed to serve to do so, and he invited anyone who wished, and who had the proper equipment, to come to accept his wages. The response to this summons was very limited. Returns from three counties survive, and provide the name of only one man who had agreed to go. The account for the army in Flanders suggests that, in all, only sixty-three men responded to this appeal of Edward's.[85]

Edward made determined efforts in August to justify his actions. On the 8th he asked the exchequer to appoint men 'who know how to speak to the people well' to take oaths from the tax collectors, and to put the king's case. Edward argued that he could not do more for his people than put his life at risk on their behalf, and he stressed the duty that men should have for their liege lord.[86] Then, on 12 August, a long letter justifying the royal position was issued. This provided a full account of what had taken place at the time of the muster in London. Edward pointed out that he could not defend the realm without the assistance of his subjects, and he apologized for burdening them so heavily. He pointed out that he was not using the money raised to buy lands or castles. The need to bring a quick end to the war was stressed, and Edward warned his subjects about the troubles that had occurred in the past as a result of disputes between ruler and subjects. The argument was not put in terms of the Roman law doctrine of necessity, though obviously there was an emphasis on the dangers facing the realm. What the king put to his people was realistic, if biassed, statement of the situation, with promises that once the expedition had returned, the people's grievances would be met.[87] All the indications are that the propaganda put forward by the king's opponents was more effective. The arbitrary imposition of the tax of an eighth, and the prise of wool, had provided Bigod, Bohun and their allies with new, powerful, arguments.

When the king was at Winchelsea, on 22 August, about to embark on the long-delayed expedition to Flanders, the two earls, Bigod and Bohun, with a group of bannerets and knights, appeared at the exchequer. Hereford acted as spokesman, as he had done at Stratford. Claiming to be speaking on behalf of the community of the realm, he said that there were two heads of grievance. One was stated in the

[85] Ibid., 7, 108–9.
[86] Ibid., 120–2.
[87] *Documents 1297–8*, 125–9. Harriss, *King, Parliament and Public Finance*, 63, suggests that Edward's case was couched in terms of the 'necessity' arguments, but the argument does not seem to be a strong one. See also *Documents 1297–8*, 29.

articles already presented to the king, the Remonstrances. The second arose from the new impositions of the eighth and the wool prise, which Hereford suggested had been implemented by the exchequer without the king's knowledge (an assumption which surviving correspondence shows to have been false). He pointed out that the eighth had not been properly granted, that to impose such a tax was tantamount to placing the people in a state of servitude, and was equivalent to an act of disinheritance. All present declared that the tax, and the prise of wool, were intolerable, and would not be allowed to proceed.

Edward, when told of this, wrote to the exchequer officials, instructing them to have proclamations made to the effect that the tax of an eighth would not be used as a precedent, and that there was no question of anyone being reduced to servile status. A further letter stressed that the tax, and the wool prise, had to proceed, and Edward stated – there is a very authentic note to the words – 'It seems to us that we should be as free as any man to buy wool in our land.' He wanted his subjects to be reminded of the fealty and homage they owed, and laid emphasis on the danger that he, and those with him, were about to face.[88]

Edward embarked on the *Cog St Edward* on 22 August 1297, ready to set sail for Flanders on the following day. It could be regarded as either a bold, or a foolhardy, decision to leave the country at such a moment of political crisis. There was an undoubted threat of civil war, but Edward had to choose between the prospect of the war and its consequent burdens continuing if he did not sail, and the domestic consequences of his departure. In fact, settlement of the political difficulties in England probably became easier in Edward's absence, but it was not to be achieved without much further argument and some alarms.

On 20 August 170 knights had been asked to appear before the king's son Edward, nominally in charge during his father's absence, at Rochester on 8 September. Ostensibly this was for discussions to take place, but the men were to come with horses and arms, and it looks as if this was an attempt to provide the government with an armed force to match that which Bigod and Bohun had established outside London. Further summonses to fifty-six men were issued on 28 August to attend at Rochester. The only hint that negotiations were being considered comes from a summons to four of the knights who had accompanied Bigod and Bohun to the exchequer on 22 August, in which they were asked to come before the prince on 4 September. At Rochester an appeal was apparently made, to the effect that some of the knights should stay near the coast in case of an invasion, but no doubt the real business of the assembly was to discuss the political situation.[89]

[88] *Documents 1297–8*, 137–40.
[89] *Parl. Writs*, i, 296–8.

There was certainly no spirit of compromise evident at this time. On
1 September, Hugh of Yarmouth, a royal proctor, entered Canterbury
cathedral, and went up to the great altar while Winchelsey was giving a
sermon. Hugh read out, no doubt loudly, his letters of appointment,
announced a royal appeal to Rome against Winchelsey, and forbad the
archbishop to take any action, such as excommunication, against the
king, his councillors, justices, clerks and supporters. Winchelsey
continued to preach all the while. Further appeals were made in other
dioceses, and although Winchelsey himself had not been deterred from
issuing sentences of excommunication, some prelates hesitated to do so,
or carefully made an exception of the king and his son.[90] The archbishop
of Canterbury was in no mood to attempt any work of mediation, but
the church did not represent a real threat to the government.

The events that took place in England in September and October were
not well recorded by the chroniclers, but writs of summons to various
assemblies show that this was a very busy time. The earl of Arundel,
and various others, were asked to come before Edward of Caernarfon
on 22 September. The prelates and magnates were summoned to
parliament at London on 30 September, and knights of the shire were
asked to attend on 6 October. They were to receive royal letters,
promising that the tax of an eighth would not be used as a precedent. It
was presumably hoped to obtain belated consent for the tax from
them.[91] It was not only the crown that was holding meetings. Some of
the opposition magnates gathered in Northampton in late September,
and there was, no doubt, much discussion in county courts. In Sussex,
the local assembly refused to elect representatives to attend the parliament, on the dubious grounds that they could not do so in the absence
of so many magnates in Flanders and elsewhere. At Worcester, the
county community challenged royal officials who were attempting to
collect the eighth, arguing that they would not grant the money until
they received the liberties to which they were entitled under Magna
Carta and the Forest Charter. The country was clearly in a state of high
tension. The sheriffs and others were asked to retain knights and
squires in royal service, and to muster at London.[92] Castles were being
put into a state of defence. At Tickhill, in Yorkshire, iron bars were
fitted at the bridgehead on the approach to the castle, new ropes were
provided for the drawbridge, and a new lock was fitted. The walls
were repaired, the ditches enlarged, and crossbow bolts purchased.
Thirteen crossbowmen and twenty archers were hired.[93]

[90] *Documents 1297–8*, 142–4; Denton, *Winchelsey*, 156–7; Cotton, 335–6.
[91] *Parl. Writs*, i, 56, 298–300.
[92] *CCR 1296–1302*, 129; *Parl. Writs*, i, 60; *Ann. Worcester*, 534; *Parl. Writs*, i, 299–300.
[93] SC 6/1087/17.

There is, unfortunately, no good account of events in the parliament which began at the end of September. The political situation, however, had been transformed as a result of the news of the defeat of Earl Warenne by William Wallace and the Scots, at Stirling Bridge, news which was clearly known by 24 September.[94] The defeat proved that the king's opponents had been right when they had argued that the situation in the north was so serious that he should not leave the country, but it also meant that they were under an increased obligation to settle the dispute with the crown, so that they could turn their attention to the restoration of the English position in Scotland. Yet, despite the pressure to reach a settlement, it was not easy to abandon firmly entrenched positions.

The demands made of the government in the parliament are, very probably, those expressed in a document known as *De Tallagio*. This appears to be a draft of articles which the crown's opponents wanted to see added to Magna Carta.[95] Much was drawn from the earlier Remonstrances, but the document was also a response to the attempted imposition of the eighth. The first clause stated that no tallage or aid should be taken without the consent of all, from archbishops to freemen. Prises were to be subject to the consent of those whose goods were taken, and the maltolt was to be abolished. One clause provided for the pardoning of Bigod, Bohun, John de Ferrers and all those, including the twenty-pound landholders, who had refused to go with the king to Flanders.

The prince's council, under the leadership of Reginald de Grey, could not concede these demands without making considerable modifications. They were not prepared to see new clauses added to Magna Carta, but negotiated the issue of a separate document, known as the *Confirmatio Cartarum*, on 10 October. The regency government could not itself pardon the earls and their confederates, but letters patent issued on 12 October promised that everything possible would be done to persuade the king to release the 'rancour and indignation' in which he held them. In return for this, and the confirmation of Magna Carta and the Forest Charter, a new tax of a ninth was granted on 14 October:

---

[94] *CCR 1296-1302*, 132.

[95] *Documents 1297-8*, 154-5. There has been much controversy about this document: see J.G. Edwards, '*Confirmatio Cartarum* and Baronial Grievances in 1297', *EHR*, lviii (1943), 273-300; Rothwell, 'The Confirmation of the Charters, 1297', 300-15. The *De Tallagio* appears in many later collections of statutes, but is clearly not an official document. It may be no more than a summary of the baronial demands, for the Evesham chronicle provides a text of a draft pardon to Bigod, Bohun, John de Ferrers and their associates which looks like a much fuller version of clause 5 of *De Tallagio*; see Denton, 'The Crisis of 1297 from the Evesham chronicle', 566-7, 679; *Documents 1297-8*, 155.

clearly no one was prepared to allow the infamous eighth to be collected.
The final measure taken by the authorities was the appointment, on
16 October, of men to mark out, or perambulate, to use the technical
term, the boundaries of the royal forests.[96]

The *Confirmatio Cartarum* covered much of the same ground as did *De
Tallagio*, but there were significant changes. A promise was given that
no precedent would be made of the 'aids and mises' that had been
granted, and likewise, prises would not become customary. The
phraseology used reflected very closely the final clause of one version of
the Remonstrances.[97] The document then continued to concede that
'aids, mises and prises' would not be taken in future save with 'the
common assent of all the realm, and for the common profit of the same
realm'. This rather vague formula was a substantial dilution of the
proposal in *De Tallagio*. It did not provide any clear definition of who
precisely should give their consent, and abandoned the notion of individual agreement to the taking of goods. The idea, however, that
taxation should be for the common profit of the realm was an advance,
and can be seen as pointing the way towards future attempts to control
not merely the granting of taxes, but also the way in which the money
raised was spent.[98] It is striking that no mention was made of parliament as the place where consent would be given. The final clause
abolished the forty-shilling maltolt on wool exports, but whereas *De
Tallagio* did not consider the possibility of any revival of the tax, the
Confirmatio provided that it might be taken in future, but only with
common assent. In strictly grammatical terms, it appears that it is only
the common assent of 'the greater part of the community' which was
required, but this was surely a careless piece of drafting, rather than a
careful attempt to limit the extent of the concessions being made by the
crown.[99]

De Tallagio had concluded with a clause providing for the charter –
Magna Carta, with the new additional articles – to be read out in
churches, and enforced with threats of excommunication. The *Confirmatio*, in contrast, began with clauses concerning the publication of

[96] *Documents 1297–8*, 110–13, 155–6, 158–60; *CPR 1292–1301*, 312.
[97] The version found in the bishop of Worcester's register by J.H. Denton has this
final clause: J.H. Denton, 'A Worcester Text of the Remonstrances of 1297', *Speculum*,
liii (1978), 520–1; *Documents 1297–8*, 117.
[98] Harriss, *King, Parliament and Public Finance*, 68, argues that in *Confirmatio Cartarum*,
'the magnates had left behind the notion of individual assent of *De Tallagio* and now
envisaged a form of national assent'. It is more likely that it was the regency government that wanted to avoid the very specific character of assent envisaged in *De Tallagio*,
and so produced a vaguer formula.
[99] In ibid., 425, Harriss takes a different view, suggesting that what was envisaged
was the consent of the merchants, as part of the community of the realm.

the Charters, and the excommunication of those who infringed their terms. What this meant was that the new concessions were not themselves covered by these provisions: there was no requirement for the *Confirmatio* itself to be read out. This was probably not of very great importance in practice, but it shows the way in which the government was trying to minimize the damage caused by the very considerable concessions that it was compelled to make.[100]

The agreement reached in the October parliament had, of course, been achieved in the king's absence. Edward's consent still had to be obtained. The king cannot have been pleased by the news of the concessions. There is no evidence to suggest that he had authorized anything more than the confirmation of Magna Carta and the charter of the forest, and a promise that no precedent would be made of the tax of an eighth. He delayed for three days, but had no real alternative to issuing the *Confirmatio Cartarum* in his own name, at Ghent on 5 November.[101] No changes were made to the text that had been agreed in England. At the same time a letter of pardon was issued to Bigod, Bohun, John de Ferrers and their followers, assuring them that they would not suffer in the future as a result of what had taken place.[102] That promise Edward may have kept in the letter, but he hardly did so in spirit.

The documents containing the king's agreement were brought back to England by Walter Langton, the treasurer, and publicly read out at Westminster. On 23 November orders were issued cancelling the collection of the maltolt. At the same time, there was evidence that the leopard had not really changed his spots, for writs were issued for the collection of yet another prise of foodstuffs, needed to supply the army in Flanders. No mention was made of consent: the goods were simply to be 'bought and taken'.[103] There were no protests, however, for the attitude of the public seems to have been transformed by the concessions, and by the bad news from Scotland. On 20 November a clerical council met, and a grant of a tenth was conceded with little difficulty.

---

[100] Prestwich, *War, Politics and Finance*, 260; Denton, *Winchelsey*, 167. Curiously, there was one change made to the text of Magna Carta itself when it was reissued in 1297: the rate of a baronial relief was changed from £100 to 100 marks. As the document was technically an *inspeximus*, the text should not have been altered from that of 1225, and it seems most likely that the change was simply an error, probably made because the chancery clerks used a faulty text. I owe this suggestion to Susan Reynolds, who will, I hope, elaborate the argument in a forthcoming publication.

[101] Denton, ibid., 165, plausibly suggests that Edward had been sent a copy of *De Tallagio* as well as the *Confirmatio Cartarum*.

[102] *Registrum Roberti de Winchelsey, archiepiscopi Cantuariensis, 1294–1308*, ed. R. Graham (Canterbury and York soc., 1917–51), ii, 207–9.

[103] Langtoft, ii, 306; *Documents 1297–8*, 171–3.

The papal bull *Etsi de Statu* of 31 July 1297 meant that, if a necessity existed, there was no need for the pope to be consulted about taxation. The invasion of England by the Scots provided Winchelsey with the clear evidence that there was an urgent necessity, which had been lacking previously. However, the council laid down that the tax should be collected without any lay assistance, and the burden on the lower clergy was alleviated, as they were asked to pay on an outdated, and therefore light, assessment. Winchelsey had maintained the liberty and independence of the church for which he had struggled so hard.[104] The northern clergy, in greater danger from the Scots, gladly granted a fifth. If they did not have sufficient cash, their archbishop said that they would be prepared to hand over animals and goods to make up the sums they owed.[105]

The Londoners' cause had been somewhat neglected in the debates in the October parliament, and it was not until the end of November that they began to achieve their aims. The royal warden, John le Breton, announced that the king's son, the barons of the exchequer, and Bigod and Bohun had ordered him to act as mayor. The old liberties of the city were to be revived, the Tun prison abolished, and the edicts which had protected grain-sellers from the sharp practices of city merchants repealed. The mob promptly moved on the Tun, and freed all those found inside.[106] It is interesting to see that Bigod and Bohun were still actively involved in obtaining more concessions from the government, after the *Confirmatio Cartarum* had been granted.

There was clearly some uncertainty in the minds of the magnates as to whether they really had achieved what they wanted. Bigod, Bohun and others prepared themselves for an expedition against the Scots, which was to be largely financed out of the clerical tax, but it seems likely that they refused to proceed until a further guarantee was received that the concessions would be respected. A meeting was held at York, in January 1298, under Warenne's leadership, and whatever arguments took place they were resolved when the bishop of Carlisle stood in the pulpit, flanked by Bigod and Bohun, and excommunicated anyone who might infringe Magna Carta.[107] It remained to be seen how the king would react when he returned from Flanders.

---

[104] Denton, *Winchelsey*, 173–4; *Councils and Synods*, ii, 1181.

[105] *The Registers of John le Romeyn, lord archbishop of York, 1286–1296, part II, and of Henry of Newark, lord archbishop of York, 1296–1299*, ed. W. Brown (Surtees Soc., cxxcviii, 1917), 316–17.

[106] Williams, *Medieval London*, 260–1.

[107] Guisborough, 314; Langtoft, ii, 306–8; Denton, *Winchelsey*, 183–4. What the bishop of Carlisle did was, of course, precisely what was demanded in the *Confirmatio Cartarum*, though Guisborough implies that *De Tallagio* was read out as part of the Magna Carta.

To judge by the surviving official correspondence, Edward himself was not much concerned by the events which took place in England during his absence. The war, and the negotiation of the truce, were uppermost in his mind. He returned to England on 14 March 1298, landing at Sandwich. Parliament was held at the end of the month at Westminster, but this was a select gathering, with no representatives present, and was probably concerned in the main with making plans for a campaign against the Scots. In addition, Edward set in motion a national inquiry into the abuses that had taken place in England since the start of the war with France, in particular those concerned with the management of the prises. In doing this, the king declared that he was putting into practice the promise he had made before he had sailed for Flanders, to remedy the grievances of the people. Commissions were duly set up, and the inquiry took place on a massive scale.[108]

It would be wrong to see the inquiry of 1298 as an attempt by the king to divert criticism from himself, and to direct blame towards minor officials. Edward was not so devious, and he must have been concerned by the evidence he had already received, showing that malpractice and corruption were rife. One member of the royal court had received complaints when he returned to his estates, which he duly passed on to the king. Apparently Roger de Swinnerton, when collecting the tenth of 1294, had taken more money than he should, in particular by the ingenious device of testing the coin paid over against specially selected heavy coins of his own, so that he gained 2s in every pound.[109] In June 1297 the activities of Richard le Hostage, clerk in charge of prises in Gloucestershire, came to light. He had been exacting payments, mainly from churchmen, in return for releasing them from the prise. His charges ranged from three pounds, and a gold ring, from the abbot of Gloucester, to three shillings each from some villeins at Nympsfield. It was also found, at about the same date, that the collectors of the eleventh in Wiltshire had been keeping back part of their receipts.[110] In November 1297, an exchequer official, Richard of Louth, was disgraced and dismissed, in part because of large-scale corruption involving the prise of victuals in Kent. This was discovered after John Cobham, a baron of the exchequer, refused to release a distraint on the possessions of one Juliana Box, as Louth asked him to do. Louth's insults to Cobham led to his dismissal, and judgement that he pay £500 damages. His activities were then investigated further, and the prise offences discovered. Winchelsey took an interest in the case, for Louth

[108] *Documents 1297–8*, 191–3.
[109] C. Swinnerton, 'Two ancient petitions from the Public Record Office', *The Ancestor*, vi (1903), 66–71.
[110] *Documents 1297–8*, 94–5.

was a cleric, and Juliana turned out to be his mistress. Louth was accused in the church courts of being married while in orders, of bigamy, immorality and perjury.[111] The case was an isolated one, but it may have helped to convince Edward that wide-ranging investigations were needed.

The records of the 1298 inquiry do not survive in full, but the surviving rolls reveal a pattern of widespread corruption among minor officials, with a great deal of extortion practised on the most vulnerable members of society. Prise and taxation were the main subjects of complaint. A typical case was that of Thomas of Eston, a Norfolk bailiff, who took two and a half quarters of wheat from the vicar of Burley, and handed over two of them to the crown, retaining a half. Another bailiff, John Everard, took four quarters of malt from Henry of Wycheford, and refused to give him a tally as a receipt. Another Norfolk case saw three sub-collectors of the twelfth accused of sparing a man who should have paid 2s in tax, and charging a pauper. The same men were accused of unjustly demanding, and receiving, twenty shillings in expenses from the village of Ingoldmells. In the following year, the village was charged with twenty-four shillings in this way. It is hardly surprising that there were such abuses of the system, particularly in view of the fact that in the county of Lincolnshire alone, there were almost 4,000 sub-taxers operating during the wartime period.[112] It is, however, wrong to argue that because the jurors and plaintiffs complained about specific acts of extortion, bribery and maladministration, and not about the measures themselves, that this was a true indication of public opinion.[113] No valid complaints about the taxes and prises themselves could be entertained by the courts: they were only competent to hear cases against individual officials. The inquiry of 1298 may well have helped to heal some of the wounds opened during the years from 1294 to 1297, but it could not cure the body politic.

The events of 1297 presented Edward I with perhaps the greatest challenge to his statesmanship, since the difficult days of the 1260s. He certainly displayed some political skill. His assessment of the clergy's will to resist was an accurate one: royal threats enabled him to collect in

---

[111] H. Rothwell, 'The Disgrace of Richard of Louth, 1297', *EHR*, xlviii (1933), 259–64. Denton, *Winchelsey*, 162, suggests that the part the archbishop played 'cannot have endeared him to other royal clerks, or to the king'. Edward, however, was not a man to stand by officials who let him down, and it is striking that it was not until Edward II had come to the throne that Louth dared to have himself reinstated in the exchequer.

[112] *A Lincolnshire Assize Roll for 1298*, ed. W.S. Thomson (Lincoln Record Society, 1944), 48, 50, 60–2.

[113] Ibid., cxxv.

fines what the church had refused to grant in taxation. He had the sense
not to drive Winchelsey too far, and in July 1297 his reconciliation with
the archbishop seriously weakened the earls' position. Edward was
able to divide the ranks of the magnates opposing him, detaching the
earls of Warwick and Arundel from Bigod and Bohun. The royal
manifesto of 12 August 1297 shows that the king had a real sense of the
value of propaganda. Yet no use was made of the principles of representation in the parliaments of February and July: had knights been
summoned, then the king might have been able to make his case more
effectively. In the propaganda war, it is hard not to conclude that the
king was constantly on the defensive in face of the powerful, and often
emotive, arguments of his opponents. It was characteristic of Edward
to overestimate the strength of his own position, and this he clearly did
at the end of July. He obviously felt that he had achieved success, and
that he could therefore impose new, arbitrary burdens. He even alienated Winchelsey once again with his demand for a new aid from the
clergy. The tax of an eighth, with the prise of wool, provided the earls
with the strong constitutional arguments that their case had previously
lacked.

It is not easy to identify the king's opponents in 1297, save for the
leading figures: there is a short list of those who appeared with the earls
at the exchequer, on 22 August, and the members of Bigod's own
household are known.[114] The inclusion of John de Ferrers alongside
Bigod and Bohun in *De Tallagio* was, very probably, a recognition of the
fact that Ferrers should have been an earl himself, had Edward not
been so spiteful towards his father and himself. He cannot be shown to
have played a particularly active part in the events of 1297. The fact
that few individuals can be securely identified should not be taken as
implying that there was only a limited degree of support for Bigod and
Bohun in the summer of 1297. Rather, Edward's own failure to recruit
many from outside the royal household for his Flanders campaign
shows how little backing there was for the king at this time. As Langtoft
noted, not a single earl went to Flanders with the king.[115] Bigod and
Bohun, meanwhile, were able to recruit substantial forces themselves:
Walter of Guisborough estimated them at 1,500 cavalry and a multitude of foot.[116] By September 1297, after the king had left for Flanders,
the country was on the verge of civil war, and it is unlikely that a
political settlement could have been reached had it not been for the

[114] *Documents 1297–8*, 137, 157–8. Those with the earls at the exchequer were Robert
FitzRoger, Alan la Zouche, John de Segrave, Henry Tyeys and John Lovel. All save
Tyeys were members of Bigod's household.

[115] Langtoft, ii, 292.

[116] Guisborough, 308.

news of the disaster at Stirling Bridge in Scotland, which rekindled patriotic emotions.

The crisis of 1297 was, largely, the product of wartime circumstances. Only to a limited extent did it arise from long-term discontent with Edward's government. Yet the issues raised were of far more than immediate significance, and the consequences of the events of 1297 were long-lasting. As far as the church was concerned, Winchelsey's determined leadership had proved that it was possible to resist intensive pressure from the crown with some success. The fines to buy the king's protection may have been paid, but no tax was granted. After 1297 Edward did not negotiate any more direct taxes from the clergy. Much of Winchelsey's case against the king rested on the doctrine of necessity, and it is possible to see here a contrast between the ideologies of church and state, for Edward preferred to argue in terms of the feudal duties of subjects to their liege lord. Even when he was justifying the imposition of the tax of a third or fifth in August 1297, Edward did not use the technical language of necessity, but stressed the need for all, lay and ecclesiastics, to provide aid in common, for the honour, profit and salvation of himself and the realm.[117] The arguments were not finally resolved, but Winchelsey undoubtedly did much to preserve the rights and liberties of the church.

The principle of consent to secular taxation was reinforced in the *Confirmatio Cartarum*, and even if the precise manner in which consent was to be obtained was not laid down, Edward was not again able to make any demands such as that for the eighth. The heavy maltolt on wool exports was abandoned, not to be revived until Edward III's reign. Prises could not be given up, as they were needed if wars were to be successfully fought, and the one concession made was that the name was changed to purveyance, and authorization in future was by means of letters under the great seal, rather than simply through the exchequer.[118] Edward and his councillors were not prepared to make any concessions in writing on the subject of military service, but there was no longer to be any question of feudal service overseas, nor of such novel forms of summons as that used to order men to come to the London muster.

There was probably much less difference between the underlying political attitudes of the king and the earls and knights than there was between the king and the archbishop. It is interesting, however, to see that the earls, in the Remonstrances, wrote of the 'community of the land', whereas Edward did not use the language of community in his

[117] See in particular the arguments that Edward hoped would be put by those appointed to collect the clerical tax: *Documents 1297-8*, 134-5.
[118] Prestwich, *War, Politics and Finance*, 130-1.

manifesto of 12 August. His preference was probably for the argument that the good people of the realm should do their duty towards their liege lord, but when the crown did use the term 'community' in the *Confirmatio Cartarum*, it became the community of the realm, not of the land. There is some significance in such nuances.[119] The arbitrary tendencies in Edward's rule received a reversal, and the notion of government through the consent of the community, in accordance with established liberties, was enhanced. Bigod, Bohun and their followers were not putting forward any radical new ideas.

The extent of the concessions made by the crown in 1297 should not be exaggerated. It was certainly feared that Edward would not wish to keep the promises he had made, and in many ways 1297 marked the start, not the end, of a struggle. The king's opponents had little success as far as their own personal grievances were concerned. Winchelsey was to suffer eventual exile, Bigod would be humbled. Humphrey de Bohun died in 1298, so no retaliation against him was possible. The Welsh Marchers did not see the aggressive nature of royal policy towards their liberties altered after 1297, though the Londoners did retain the liberties which they regained in the autumn of that year. Those who criticized Edward did well to be cautious. At the height of the crisis, in London, a man called William of Gloucester came to a tavern, and began abusing the king's reputation. Pointing at the decayed head of Llywelyn ap Gruffydd on a pike mounted on the Tower, he said that Edward's head should be up there, beside it. At this, John Paternoster, a goldsmith, and his friends, attacked William, and beat him to death.[120] Edward did not lose the allegiance of most of his subjects in 1297, though through his insensitivity and stubbornness, he put it to a considerable test.

---

[119] *Documents 1297–8*, 115–17, 125–9, 158–60.
[120] *Documents 1297–8*, 147. This was John Paternoster's explanation for William of Gloucester's death: it was well calculated to win the king's sympathy, but should perhaps be treated with a degree of scepticism.

Chapter 17

COUNCIL AND PARLIAMENT

The crisis of 1297 raised many questions about Edward I's rule in England. The way in which the king obtained the consent of his subjects was brought into focus, particularly by the imposition of the tax of an eighth. The magnates challenged the wisdom of the king's military strategy, as well as attacking the weight, and the unconstitutional character, of taxation and prise. Edward himself, in a letter to his Gascon subjects, acknowledged that his council had advised him against a campaign on the continent, in view of his financial difficulties.[1] In the *Confirmatio Cartarum* the king had to acknowledge that the consent of the community of the realm was required if he was to collect further taxes, and food supplies. It is time to examine more fully the role of counsel and consent in Edward's government of his realm, for although the king may appear, from a study of the events of 1297, to have been a man of strongly autocratic temperament, his reign taken as a whole saw developments of great importance in the royal council and above all in parliament.

There are difficult problems facing historians dealing with both council and parliament in this period. Neither was an established, solid institution with a clear-cut composition and well-defined function, and neither has left behind adequate records. Chroniclers were not in a position to provide detailed accounts of proceedings. In the case of the council, the only official record of a debate is a note of the unanimous opinions offered by its members, in the course of the Great Cause, on the questions of what laws should be used in the case, and whether the principle of primogeniture or proximity should apply to it.[2] There is only one unofficial account, a description of a debate over the proposed appointment of a converted Jew as a justice to investigate cases of coin-clipping. This provoked a violent and hysterical outburst from the bishop of Hereford, who threatened to resign from his position on the council. This was later considered to be evidence of his sanctity.[3]

---

[1] *Treaty Rolls*, 134.
[2] *Great Cause*, ii, 212–13, 216–17.
[3] *Acta Sanctorum, Octobris*, ed. J. Bollandus, i (Paris, Rome, 1866), 474–5.

There are a number of lists of members of the king's council. The
chancellor, treasurer, keeper of the wardrobe and justices of both
benches were all councillors, as was the steward of the household. Their
expert knowledge of affairs made it essential that they should be sworn
as royal councillors. Other experts might also sit on the council. One
such, in the later years of the reign, was Philip Martel, a doctor of civil
law, who was one of those described as being a royal *secretarius*, or
confidential adviser. His responsibilities were with diplomatic affairs,
and he had custody of the various documents produced in the course
of the negotiations with Philip IV.[4] Bishops were often councillors:
Cantilupe of Hereford was one, and Anthony Bek played a major role
in advising the king. A reference from 1295 suggests that the bishops of
London, Worcester and Winchester were all members of the council
on a regular basis, and towards the end of the reign the bishop of
Norwich was formally sworn in as a councillor.[5] Some earls were on the
council: Henry de Lacy, earl of Lincoln, and Humphrey de Bohun, earl
of Hereford, were among those summoned in September 1305. Other
important laymen on the same list were Hugh Despenser, Henry Percy,
John Hastings and John Botetourt.[6] The core of the council, however,
consisted of the officials. Prelates and lay magnates had their own affairs
to see to, and could not be expected to act as royal councillors on a
completely regular basis.[7] Edward's council was in no way like that
created in 1258 and forced on Henry III; it was essentially a ministerial
rather than a magnate body, and it was the king who determined who
should sit on it.

The councillors swore an oath to serve the king. This was a practice
which dated back to the 1230s. During the first half of Edward's reign,
it seems that the form of oath established in 1257 was used. The first
two clauses demanded loyalty and secrecy about council proceedings.
The third stated that no consent was to be given to alienations from the
ancient demesne of the crown, and the rest of the oath concerned the
proper conduct of councillors hearing judicial cases.[8] In about 1294 a
new version of the oath was drawn up. This was more elaborate,
particularly as far as the rights of the crown were concerned. Councillors
were put under oath to declare if they knew of any rights that had been
wrongly alienated, and they were under an obligation to do all they

---

[4] Cuttino, *English Diplomatic Administration*, 32–5, 54–5.

[5] *Parl. Writs*, i, 28; *Rot. Parl.*, i, 219.

[6] E 175/file 1, no. 20.

[7] B. Wilkinson, *Studies in the Constitutional History of the 13th and 14th Centuries* (Manchester, 1937), 146–50, where a fuller discussion of the composition of the council is
provided.

[8] J.F. Baldwin, *The King's Council in England during the Middle Ages* (Oxford, 1913),
343–7.

could to increase the power of the crown. Any agreements by which councillors became retainers of lords might be made only with royal permission: this was something which had not been included in the earlier oath.[9] It may be that it was the evidence yielded by the trials of the justices, after Edward's return from Gascony in 1289, which led to the inclusion of this clause: it was certainly at this time that the practice whereby justices took retaining fees from magnates and religious houses first attracted much attention.[10]

The earliest evidence for the activity of Edward's council dates from February 1274. A memorandum of decisions taken in the council shows that the business of the next parliament was discussed, and that a number of specific points concerning particular individuals were considered. For example, John de Ferrers (interestingly given the title of earl in the document) was allocated a day to appear in parliament to discuss the question of the manor of Chartley, upon which the earl of Lancaster had designs. Distraint was to be relaxed on the master of the Temple, who was also given a day for his case to be heard in parliament. Roger Clifford was to be asked why Thomas de Kenum had been fined, and meanwhile, distraint on Thomas was relaxed.[11]

There is more surviving evidence from Edward's later years. A note of the council agenda for a meeting at York, to be held after Easter 1303, lists five items of royal business. First, there were writs to be drafted about collection of the tax granted in 1301. The sheriffs of London were to be ordered to have two or three merchants appointed from every Italian banking company operating in the city to appear at the exchequer. There were writs to be sent to the collectors of a feudal aid. The fourth item was simply noted as 'About forfeited wool', and fifthly, there was a problem to be discussed about the valuation of Ralph Pippard's lands in Ireland.[12] A little later John Droxford came to York with instructions to the council from the king. His main concern was that the members should meet to discuss the provision of money and victuals for the war in Scotland. Droxford reported that the king was pleased with the idea, which the exchequer officials had suggested, that a tallage should be levied. He also wanted inquiries to deal effectively with the problem of desertion by the infantry troops with him in

---

[9] Ibid., 347–8, gives this oath in a version dating from 1307. E 159/68, m. 64, however, dated 1294, gives the same oath, the only difference being that the last clause of the 1307 version is given after clause 6 in it.

[10] Maddicott, *Law and Lordship*, 14, 16. *CDS*, ii, no. 1818, shows that in 1306 the bishop of St Andrews was interrogated as to why, when he was sworn in as a royal councillor, he had not disclosed an agreement which he had made with Robert Bruce in 1304.

[11] G.O. Sayles, *The King's Parliament of England* (1975), 68–9.

[12] E 175/file 1, no. 12.

Scotland, and there were many other matters which the clerk could not be bothered to enumerate in full.[13]

The council's activities in these later years of the reign were wide-ranging. Individual grievances were put before them by the king. When Ralph de Monthermer and his wife, the king's daughter Joan, had a case brought against them by the prior of Goldcliffe, the council was asked by Edward to work out a suitable remedy, so that the couple would not be troubled by the prior any more.[14] Questions of ecclesiastical patronage were a major concern: in 1303 the council was asked to resolve the problem created when the king had appointed John of Derby to the church of Wappenham, but another man had actually been installed. The council was asked to draft an ordinance which would enable John Bush, a royal clerk, to recover the chapel and prebend which he had lost to another at York.[15] Diplomatic matters might require the expertise of council members. In March 1302 the king expressed his pleasure over letters which had been drafted to be sent to the pope, but he explained that he wanted to scrap one which John Benstead had drawn up on his orders, as he accepted the advice of the council about it. Later, Robert Pickering, one of the council, suggested a subtle rewording of the documents which ratified the peace with the French in 1303: this followed a request that those members of the council skilled in such matters should see to the drafting work.[16]

It has been argued, by Wilkinson, that Edward I's reign witnessed very important changes in the royal council. He emphasized its acquisition of executive authority, and its growing importance as a court. In part, the argument depends on a careful reading of official terminology. Thus, in 1274, in a case concerning dower land, the parties involved were to come 'to do and receive as the king with his council shall ordain', whereas in 1290 a writ ordered an inquisition to be made promptly, 'in order that by the king's council the king may cause right to be done'. The later wording implies a greater freedom of action for the council. From about 1297, the authorization of writs by the council began to be noted. Although there are petitions addressed to the king's council dating from the 1270s, there are many more from the later years of the reign.[17] The difficulty is that the argument is, in part, *ex silentio*. The sources for the activities of the council are scanty in the first part of the reign, and the fact, for example, that the council is not recorded as authorizing writs prior to the late 1290s does not necessarily mean that

[13] Baldwin, *King's Council*, 466, gives part of this document, C 49/3/9.
[14] *Calendar of Chancery Warrants, 1244–1326*, 212.
[15] Ibid., 197, 216, 218.
[16] Ibid., 160–1, 183, 185.
[17] Wilkinson, *Studies in Constitutional History*, 121–4.

it did not do so. The record, already discussed, of the council proceedings in 1274, does not suggest that there was any very great extension in the powers and duties of the council in the course of Edward's reign. In the final years, however, the fact that the king was occupied for long periods of time with his campaigns, in Flanders and, above all, in Scotland, did mean that more business had to be delegated to the council than had been the case in the past. A letter from the treasurer, Walter Langton, to Edward in 1301, provides a further illustration of this. He reported to the king that he, with other councillors, had organized the issue of writs ordering the collection of a tax, and that new appointments of sheriffs and bailiffs had been effected. Letters had been drafted for an embassy to France. The earl of Lincoln had come to York, where the council was sitting, and declared himself well pleased with what had been done.[18]

The council was vital to Edward, providing him with the expert advice and assistance he needed if the country was to be governed effectively. Its chief importance did not lie in the extent to which it might exercise independent executive authority, but in the counsel which it gave to the king. In 1297 it was the council which devised the procedures whereby the clergy could pay fines to buy back the king's protection, and it was the same body which worked out the ordinances for the lay and clerical taxes.[19] There were many matters, great and small, which Edward did not wish to decide by himself. In 1302, for example, the earl of Lincoln and the count of Savoy, who were negotiating with the French, suggested a meeting with their opposite numbers at Arras, and asked the king for his views. This he was reluctant to give, 'because we have no one with us whom we can consult about agreeing to such business'.[20] The role of Edward's great councillors and confidants, men such as Robert Burnell, Ralph Hengham, Otto de Grandson, Anthony Bek and Walter Langton, was central to the success of the king's policies.

The council, in the sense discussed so far, did not provide a mechanism whereby Edward consulted, and obtained the consent of, his people in a broad sense. It was what would much later be termed the 'privy council'. The term 'council' was not, however, used with great precision in Edward's day, for it was also applied to much larger gatherings in which the king met with his nobles and others. Some of these meetings, but not all, were termed parliaments, and it is to such gatherings that attention must now be directed.

*   *   *

[18] SC 1/21, 68.
[19] *Documents 1297-8*, 41-2, 110-12, 133-5.
[20] Chaplais, *English Medieval Diplomatic Practice*, I, i, 200.

The development of parliament has been, and will surely continue to be, one of the most vexed questions facing historians of Edward I's reign. In the nineteenth century Stubbs was able to write, with the enviable self-assurance of his age, of Edward and the 'mark of definiteness and completeness which he so clearly impressed upon parliament'. The assembly of 1295 was 'the model parliament', and the date of its meeting 'may be accepted as fixing finally the right of shire and borough representation'.[21] Since Stubbs wrote, such views have been shown to be quite false, but research has done more to create doubts and overthrow old certainties than to establish new truths.

The question of what a parliament was under Edward I is a very thorny one. Opinions have varied, from a view that parliament had no exclusive function or specific composition, to the emphatic case argued by Richardson and Sayles that the one essential and central function of parliament was the dispensing of justice by the king or his representative.[22] This latter view was the result of the application of the logic of Occam's razor, the stripping away of every non-essential. While it is true that parliament might consist of little more than the king's council sitting hearing legal disputes, it does not follow that that was the most important element of parliamentary business. The historian of parliament should obviously be concerned to distinguish parliaments from other types of assembly. For an understanding of the government and politics of Edward's day, however, what is required is a study of all that took place in parliament, and in what would later be known as 'great councils', whether or not certain aspects are regarded as essential. The majority of meetings to be considered were, certainly, termed 'parliaments', but there were some important gatherings, such as that which conceded the grant of a tenth and sixth to the king in 1294, which the sources describe as 'councils'.[23]

The sources for parliament under Edward I present considerable problems. For the first half of the reign, until the 1290s, the official records are sadly deficient. Writs of summons to parliaments and councils were rarely enrolled, and there are few records of proceedings that survive. Even when the records become more abundant, they do not provide a full account of what took place. Although there are many references to parliament in the chronicles, there is no full, detailed

[21] Stubbs, *Constitutional History*, ii, 267; compare ibid., ii, 134, where it is argued that the 1295 assembly served 'as a pattern for all future assemblies of the nation'.

[22] Compare T.F.T. Plucknett, 'Parliament', *Historical Studies of the English Parliament*, ed. E.B. Fryde and E. Miller (Cambridge, 1970), i, 196, with the frequently expressed views of Richardson and Sayles. For one example of their opinion, see their *English Parliament in the Middle Ages*, V, 133.

[23] *Handbook of British Chronology*, 545–52, notes which assemblies were termed 'parliaments' and which 'councils'.

account of proceedings. People were certainly anxious to know what took place in parliament: the abbot of Ramsey wrote to Gilbert of Rothbury, who acted as clerk of parliament, asking for such information as he could reveal 'without danger or offence', but unfortunately the reply is not recorded.[24] Only one newsletter detailing events in parliament survives from Edward's reign.[25]

A later tract on parliament, probably written in the early 1320s, stated, 'It is a damaging and dangerous matter for the whole community of parliament and of the kingdom when the king is absent from parliament.'[26] Henry III had emphasized the principle that parliament could take place only in the king's presence, when his opponents, in the spring of 1260, tried to hold one in his absence.[27] Edward I maintained this royal monopoly. Parliament could be summoned only at the king's will, and had no independent existence of its own. There was, certainly, an assembly which resembled a full parliament, held at the start of Edward's reign, while he was on crusade, but it was not called a parliament in the sources.[28] The parliament held in the autumn of 1297 saw Edward represented by his son. In 1305 and 1306, parliaments were started in the king's absence, but special commissioners were appointed to represent him. When he fell ill during his first parliament, in 1275, the proceedings had to be brought to a halt.[29] It was the king who decided when and where parliament should be held.

The frequency of parliaments changed in the course of the reign. In the years before Edward's departure for Gascony in 1286, there was a normal pattern of two parliaments a year, one at Easter and one at Michaelmas. In 1278 an additional one was held at Gloucester in July, and during the second Welsh war, in 1282–3, there was only one, at Shrewsbury, in the autumn of 1283. The author of that curious legal tract, the *Mirror of Justices*, writing in the early 1290s, complained that parliaments were no longer held as often as in the past, and there was something to the charge.[30] In 1290 there were three parliaments, but in 1291 and 1292 there was only one English parliament each year, a reflection of Edward's preoccupation with Scottish affairs. Parliament

[24] *Chronicon Abbatiae Ramseiensis*, ed. W.D. Macray (Rolls ser., 1886), 404.
[25] Richardson and Sayles, *English Parliament in the Middle Ages*, XII, 436–7.
[26] *Parliamentary Texts of the Later Middle Ages*, ed. N. Pronay and J. Taylor (Oxford, 1980), 72, 85. The quotation is from the much debated *Modus Tenendi Parliamentum*.
[27] Treharne, *Baronial Plan of Reform*, 220–1.
[28] *Ann. Winchester*, 113.
[29] *Handbook of British Chronology*, 550–1; *Rot. Parl.*, i, 189; Richardson and Sayles, *English Parliament in the Middle Ages*, V, 136. Ibid., V, 142, surprisingly suggests that the meeting of Easter 1289 was a parliament: it seems more likely that in the one case where it is so called, the clerk made a slip.
[30] *Mirror of Justices*, ed. Whittaker and Maitland, 155.

was thereafter held reasonably often until 1302 – there were three in 1297 – but from October 1302 until February 1305 there was a remarkable hiatus, when no parliaments were held. This is evidence that parliament was not absolutely essential to the running of the country, but the number of petitions presented to parliament in 1305 suggests that considerable inconvenience had been caused by the long interval without any meetings.

The usual place for parliament to meet was, of course, Westminster, though the records rarely give any indication of which parts of the palace were employed. The great hall was used for the promulgation of the Statute of Westminster II, but the actual deliberations would have been held in much smaller rooms, such as the Painted Chamber. In 1290 the earl of Cornwall was described as 'going through the great hall towards the king's council'.[31] From 1292, however, the palace of Westminster became increasingly unsuitable. The building of St Stephen's chapel began in that year, and much work was also carried out in the Painted Chamber, rendering it temporarily unusable. In 1298 there was a major fire in the palace, which left only the exchequer, the great hall and the Painted Chamber fit for use. It was, of course, also possible to employ the monastic buildings: the chapter-house was well-suited to holding meetings, and was to become a regular location for the commons to sit.[32] However, Edward used other buildings as well. The archbishop of York's house was where parliament met in 1293 and 1305, and in 1299 parliament began at Westminster, but then moved to Stepney.[33]

For reasons of royal convenience, parliament was held on a good many occasions away from Westminster. There were meetings at Gloucester, Shrewsbury, Clipstone, Ashridge, Bury St Edmunds, Salisbury, York, Lincoln and Carlisle, while at Acton Burnell, Canterbury and Stepney sessions were completed which had begun elsewhere.[34] In many of these cases, there were convenient monastic buildings which could be used to house the meetings, but, especially if the parliament was a large one, very considerable preparations had to be made in advance, for the task of ensuring that there were enough foodstuffs, both for the royal household and for those attending parliament, was a very major one. When parliament was held at Lincoln in January 1301, the first instructions to the sheriff to provide food were issued as early as 28 October 1300. Accounts show that he was responsible for purveying 386 quarters of wheat, 810 quarters of oats, 89

---

[31] *Ann. Osney*, 304; *Rot. Parl.*, i, 17.
[32] For a discussion of the palace of Westminster in this period, see *KW*, i, 504–5.
[33] *Rot. Parl.*, i, 91; *Memoranda de Parliamento, 1305*, ed. F.W. Maitland (1893), 297.
[34] See *Handbook of British Chronology*, 45–52, for the location of parliaments.

quarters of malt, 100 oxen (10 of them live), 400 sheep (20 of them live) and 100 pigs (75 of them live). The documents also reveal an impressive consumption of 10,032 gallons of ale. Most of the county of Lincolnshire was affected by these demands, which were comparable with those made when supplies were collected for the royal armies.[35]

There is, unfortunately, no source which gives a reliable account of the seating arrangements in Edward's parliaments. The *Modus Tenendi Parliamentum*, of about 1320, described the way in which the king sat in the middle of the main bench, flanked by the two archbishops, with the other bishops ranged beyond them. Then, in due order, there sat the earls, barons and lords. At the king's right foot there sat the chancellor, the chief justice and his fellow justices, and at his left foot, the treasurer, chamberlains and barons of the exchequer.[36] This may well reflect more how the author thought parliament should be arrayed, than actual practice. A splendid sixteenth-century reconstruction of an Edwardian parliament was probably produced by the artist doing little more than deleting from the parliaments of his own day elements which he knew to be anachronistic, and inserting individuals who, he considered, should have been present in the late thirteenth century. This led him to place Llywelyn of Wales and Alexander III, king of Scots, on either side of the king, though there is no known meeting at which both were present.[37]

As parliament did not meet with unremitting regularity, and was not always held in the same place, it is not surprising that it had little administrative independence. The writs summoning men to parliament were produced by the chancery, and the records of proceedings, such as they were, were kept in the treasury. There were officials whose task it was to help organize the arrangements for parliament, and who were responsible for drawing up the records. Evidence suggests that until his death in 1290, John Kirkby had this responsibility, and that thereafter Gilbert de Rothbury, clerk of the council, took over. With Gilbert's appearance, a marked improvement in the quality and quantity of records took place.[38] The *Modus Tenendi Parliamentum* (of which Rothbury is a conceivable author) suggested that there should be two chief clerks of parliament and five subordinate ones, but this was surely a piece of wishful thinking. Additional clerks were, of course, needed sometimes, but parliament was not a regular institution, and did not possess a permanent staff. Certain royal clerks and officials

[35] R.A. Pelham, 'The Provisioning of the Lincoln Parliament of 1301', *University of Birmingham Historical Journal*, iii (1952), 16–32.

[36] *Parliamentary Texts*, ed. Pronay and Taylor, 72–3, 85–6.

[37] J.E. Powell and K. Wallis, *The House of Lords in the Middle Ages* (1968), 593.

[38] Richardson and Sayles, *The English Parliament in the Middle Ages*, VI, 532–42.

were often used to receive (that is, to give an initial hearing to) petitions; men such as the notaries John of Caen and John Bush, clerks such as John Sandale and John of Berwick, and laymen such as the household steward, Peter of Chauvent, and the warden of the Cinque Ports, Stephen of Pencester. These men, and others like them, no doubt acquired a considerable expertise in the conduct of parliamentary business, but their main duties to the crown lay elsewhere.[39]

The next problem is to determine who attended parliament. The king's councillors, and in particular the official members of the council, such as the chancellor, treasurer and the judges, were normally always present. In 1340 Earl Warenne (who had been about twenty when Edward I died) protested at the presence of such officials in parliament, saying, 'It never used to be like this: everything has been turned upside down.'[40] The earl's memory played him false, however, for an important element in the development of parliament in the thirteenth century had been the way in which its sessions coincided with those of the main law courts, the chancery and the exchequer, and the participation of the king's main officials was 'of the essence'.[41] In the parliament during which Earl Warenne performed homage to Edward I, in 1305, the prelates, earls, lords, knights, citizens and burgesses were dismissed after three weeks, but parliament remained in session, those still present being the councillors and anyone who still had business to be seen to.[42] So much were the councillors a part of parliament that it was not necessary for them always to receive a formal summons to come: if they were in regular attendance on the king, there was no need for such a procedure.[43]

The next category of the members of parliament to be considered is those who were normally sent individual writs inviting their attendance. The archbishops, bishops and earls were, of course, summoned (the Salisbury parliament of 1297, at which no churchmen were present is an exception). There was little consistency with regard to the summoning of the heads of religious houses. If representatives of

---

[39] Ibid., VI, 544–6; *Parliamentary Texts* ed. Pronay and Taylor, 73–4, 86–7. The suggestion that Rothbury may have written the *Modus* is mine: if he did so, it was at the very end of a long career.

[40] *Chroniques de London*, ed. Aungier, 90.

[41] J.E.A. Jolliffe, 'Some Factors in the Beginnings of Parliament', *Historical Studies of the English Parliament*, i, 46–69.

[42] *Memoranda de Parliamento*, ed. Maitland, 4.

[43] In exceptional circumstances, the king might order an official *not* to attend parliament. In 1302, he told Walter Langton to stay at the exchequer in York, rather than come to parliament at Westminster: SC 1/13/109. See also *CCR 1302–7*, 347, for a request that Bereford continue with the business on which he was engaged, rather than attend parliament.

the lower clergy were summoned, by including the clause known as *praemunientes* in the summonses sent to the bishops, then more abbots, notably Cistercians, were called to attend parliament than was otherwise the case. In 1295, when the *praemunientes* clause was included, thirty-seven Benedictine abbots were summoned, along with sixty-two Cistercians. That was the maximum asked to come. In later years, the numbers of abbots fell back: in 1302, for example, the tally was twenty-three Benedictines and twenty-one Cistercians. One problem, however, is that the lists of summonses drawn up by the chancery clerks do not appear to have been copied with much care. Twelve abbots who do not feature on the lists as having been summoned to the Carlisle parliament of 1307 did send proctors to represent them, and it seems unlikely that they would have done this had they not received requests to attend.[44]

The same problem of the unreliability of the lists of writs of summons applies to a consideration of the attendance of lay magnates.[45] It is clear, however, that there was no well-established pattern. If the king and his clerks had acted logically, they might have chosen to summon, say, all feudal tenants-in-chief with a specific degree of wealth, much as was suggested by the author of the *Modus Tenendi Parliamentum*.[46] Alternatively, it might have been possible to summon all holders of baronies. The paucity of evidence means that it is not possible to analyse the magnate composition of parliament in the first half of Edward's reign.[47] From the 1290s it is apparent that the government found it convenient to use the same lists to demand service both in war and in parliament. The parliamentary summonses for the final years were ultimately derived from a cancelled order, intended to assemble men to fight in Scotland in 1299. Numbers summoned varied considerably. In 1295, fifty-three lay magnates were sent writs, but by November 1296 there were only thirty-six. For the Salisbury parliament of 1297, six earls and seventy-five others were summoned, along with nine knights and four justices. By 1301 nine earls and eighty other lay magnates were in receipt of summonses, and for the last parliament of the reign, that at Carlisle

[44] J.H. Denton, 'The Clergy and Parliament in the Thirteenth and Fourteenth Centuries', *The English Parliament in the Middle Ages*, ed. R.G. Davies and J.H. Denton (Manchester, 1981), 89–91; Powell and Wallis, *House of Lords*, 219–22, 249–50.

[45] M.C. Prestwich, 'Magnate Summonses in England in the Later Years of Edward I', *Parliaments, Estates and Representation*, v (1985), 97–101, has a fuller discussion of this problem.

[46] *Parliamentary Texts*, ed. Pronay and Taylor, 68, 81.

[47] The writs for the Shrewsbury parliament of 1283 were enrolled, *Parl. Writs*, i, 15–16, but otherwise such writs were not recorded until 1295. Chronicle references to the parliaments of 1284 and 1285 make it clear that a substantial number of magnates did normally attend parliaments: Wykes, 300, 306.

in 1307, eighty-six men below the rank of earl were asked to attend.[48]

Although there were no clear rules defining who was entitled to receive an individual summons to parliament, it is obvious that the king was looking to men whose advice he valued, and whose local power and authority he could not ignore. There was something of a concentration of names of men who held 'estates on the borders near Wales and Scotland, a natural reflection of their military importance. If a man was sufficiently distinguished, he might be summoned even though he was not a tenant-in-chief, or particularly wealthy. One such was Brian FitzAlan, who was regularly asked to attend parliament, but whose lands were for the most part held from the honour of Richmond, and who, in 1297, rejected the offer of the keepership of Scotland in succession to Earl Warenne with the excuse that he was not sufficiently wealthy.[49]

The magnates, both ecclesiastical and lay, were summoned to parliament in recognition of the fealty and affection that they owed to the king. They were not, as a rule, summoned in the formal feudal language of homage, and hence there was no absolute obligation on them to attend. The one occasion when homage was involved in a summons was in 1306, when the main purpose of the meeting was to grant an aid, on the occasion of the knighting of the king's eldest son. Such an aid was a part of the recognized list of feudal obligations, and the gathering was not a true parliament. It was the one occasion when lay magnates sent proxies to represent them, though the prelates did use this technique at other times.[50]

How many magnates did come when summoned is not known for the most part, but what evidence there is suggests that attendance was, in practice, limited. When the grant was made for the collection of an aid on the occasion of the marriage of the king's daughter, in 1290, no appeal to homage was made, and there were, of the greater magnates, only six earls and six bishops present. At the Carlisle parliament of 1307, annotations made in the margin of the record suggest that out of 167 prelates and magnates, no more than fifty-seven actually attended. Six weeks after the parliament had started, writs were sent out ordering the personal attendance of the earls of Lancaster, Warwick and Angus, along with twenty-four other lay magnates. Only Warwick and twelve of the twenty-four responded to this severe demand.[51] The author of the

---

[48] The lists of those summoned are conveniently given in *Parl. Writs*, and for analysis, see Powell and Wallis, *House of Lords*, 222–57.

[49] Ibid., 226; *Documents*, ed. Stevenson, ii, 222–4.

[50] Prestwich, 'Magnate Summonses in England in the Later Years of Edward I', 99–100.

[51] J.S. Roskell, 'The Problem of the Attendance of the Lords in Medieval Parliaments', *BIHR*, xxix (1956), 156, 160–2; *Rot. Parl.*, i, 210, for Warwick's presence at Carlisle.

Modus Tenendi Parliamentum suggested a system of fines for non-attendance: £100 for earls and 100 marks for barons, but there is no evidence that any such procedure was actually adopted, though the problem was certainly a real one.[52]

Under the year 1294, the chronicler Bartholomew Cotton noted: 'In that year four knights were called from every county in England, who had powers to enter into obligations on behalf of the county, and were to do what was ordained by the king's council.'[53] Cotton had obviously obtained a copy of a writ summoning knights of the shire to Westminster, for his terminology echoes official usage closely, and he evidently thought that it was important. He was the first of many historians to stress the representative element in Edward I's parliaments, but the very fact that he thought the summons of 1294 worth mentioning arouses the suspicion that this was an abnormal, rather than a routine, procedure. Statistics can be quoted to justify this suspicion. Edward I held about fifty parliaments, but representatives can be shown to have been summoned on only some eighteen occasions in the course of the reign, and not all of those summonses were to parliaments.[54] The attendance of knights of the shire and urban representatives did, however, become more usual towards the end of Edward's reign than it had been in the early years, or indeed under Henry III, and the relative rarity of their presence does not necessarily mean that the part they had to play was unimportant.

The writs asking for representatives to come to parliaments or councils were sent to the sheriffs, who then had to arrange for men to be selected. There is, unfortunately, very little evidence to show how this process of selection took place. The statement by the sheriff of Sussex in 1297, that no election could take place in his county because of the absence of so many magnates and knights, strongly suggests that sheriffs could not simply nominate men to serve parliament. Similarly, the sheriff of Westmorland claimed, in 1306, that he could not make an election, as time was too short and all the knights and free tenants of the county were occupied on the Scottish border: this surely shows that elections were more than a mere formality.[55] The returns made by the sheriffs show that the representatives were required to have mainpernors, or guarantors, to ensure their attendance. This does not imply

[52] *Parliamentary Texts*, ed. Pronay and Taylor, 71, 83.

[53] Cotton, 254.

[54] Sayles, *King's Parliament of England*, gives slightly different figures: there are considerable problems in deciding what was a parliament and what was not, and my calculations are based on the tables in *Handbook of British Chronology*, 545–52.

[55] J.R. Maddicott, 'Parliament and the Constituencies', *English Parliament in the Middle Ages*, ed. Davies and Denton, 73. For other examples where the sheriffs were given too little time, see J.C. Holt, 'The Prehistory of Parliament', ibid., 12–15.

that attendance at parliament was necessarily an unpopular burden, unwillingly accepted. Parliament, however, was a court, and attendance at it was a serious matter. If the county court was not to be blamed should a representative not appear, then some form of guarantee had to be provided, and this was done in the form normally used in legal proceedings.[56] It was quite common for the same man to be elected on more than one occasion: of the seventy-four known knights of the shire who attended the parliament of October 1302, twenty-four were representing their county for the second time, eight for the third, two for the fourth and one for the fifth.[57]

The extent of urban representation varied considerably. In 1275, it is probable that more towns sent members than was the case at any other time in the middle ages, as the business of granting an export duty on wool and leather greatly concerned the mercantile communities of the realm. In 1295, 114 towns, excluding London, were represented in parliament: it was left to the sheriffs to decide which places in their counties should send men. In the last years of the reign, it was usual for some seventy or eighty towns to be represented. It is only in the case of London that details are known of how elections took place. There, in 1296, an initial election was made by all the aldermen, with four men from each ward, and this was followed by a second election, at which six men from each ward were present and in which the original choice of representatives was confirmed. In 1298, election was by twelve aldermen, and six men from each ward, and the same procedure was followed in 1300.[58] As with the counties, re-election of urban representatives was quite common.

There is no solid evidence to show how good attendance was on the part of the shire and borough representatives. It was usual, when these men were dismissed from parliament, for them to be given writs authorizing the payment of their expenses, and examination of these, at first sight, suggests that many failed to attend. In 1301, only twenty-five writs were enrolled, but it is clear that the chancery clerks often did not trouble to keep a record of these documents. Henry de Keighley, a Lancashire knight whose presence at the Lincoln parliament of 1301 is attested by a bill he presented, was not recorded as receiving a writ for

[56] J.S. Illsley, 'Parliamentary Elections in the Reign of Edward I', *BIHR*, xlix (1976), 28–30, discusses the question of mainpernors.
[57] J.G. Edwards, 'The Personnel of the Commons in Parliament under Edward I and Edward II', *Historical Studies of the English Parliament*, ed. Miller and Fryde, 152.
[58] M. McKisack, *The Parliamentary Representation of the English Boroughs during the Middle Ages* (Oxford, 1932), 4–23; *Calendar of Letter-Books of the City of London, C, c. 1291–1309*, ed. R.R. Sharpe (1901), 59–60. The dual election procedure of 1296 was, it seems, exceptional, and may have been the result of interference by the royal warden of London.

his expenses.[59] Later evidence certainly suggests that the shire and borough representatives were much more meticulous in attending parliaments than were the magnates.[60]

There was one more representative element in some of Edward's parliaments which needs to be considered, that of the lower clergy. The first summons of clerical representatives to a full parliament was issued in 1295, but in 1283 clerical proctors had been summoned, at the request of royal officials, to attend convocation, so that the question of the grant of a tax to the crown could be discussed.[61] In 1294 Edward summoned an ecclesiastical council to meet at Westminster, and this included two proctors from each diocese, to represent the lower clergy. It was obviously simpler to ask the clergy to appear, through representatives, at a full parliament, as was done in 1295. The writ to the bishops contained the *praemunientes* clause, which asked the dean and archdeacon of each diocese to attend parliament in person, and to have the chapter represented by one proctor, and the rest of the clergy by two, who were, all three, to have full powers, just like the representatives of the laity.[62] Proctors were again summoned, through the bishops, to the parliament at Bury St Edmunds in 1296, and they also came to parliament in 1300, 1305 and 1307. Precise details of representation varied from one diocese to another: in some cases archdeaconries sent proctors, in others entire dioceses. At the Carlisle parliament of 1307, more proctors were appointed than had been asked for.

The fact that the clergy were asked to provide full representation in parliament did not mean, of course, that they ceased holding their own councils, but from 1295 there was a royal policy of trying to integrate the clergy, by means of representation, into the general parliaments of the realm.[63] It must be stressed, however, that even in the final stages of Edward's long reign, neither clerical nor secular representatives were invariably present in parliament. They were summoned only when it was felt that they might be needed, and when they did attend, they were not necessarily present for the whole length of the session.

A study of the composition of Edward's parliaments, therefore, suggests that there were no firm rules, although by the last years of the reign the list of magnates summoned did not change very much from year to year, and representatives of shires, towns and clergy were asked

[59] *Parl. Writs*, i, 104–5; see also below, 525–6.

[60] Edwards, 'The Personnel of the Commons', 160–7.

[61] *Councils and Synods*, II, ii, 946–7.

[62] Ibid., II, ii, 1126–7, 1147–8; *Select Charters*, ed. Stubbs, 480–1.

[63] Denton, 'Clergy and Parliament', 88–108, provides a most important discussion of the role of the clergy in parliament.

to attend with increasing regularity. Parliament was still, however, summoned when the king chose, and it was he who decided who should attend. The nature of the business to be discussed frequently determined who should be summoned, and it is to that topic that the argument must now turn.

For evidence of what actually happened in parliament, it is necessary to turn to a range of sources, for the official records, the rolls of parliament, do not provide a full account of the proceedings. They consist of transcripts and notes of the petitions presented in parliament, and of records of the legal cases determined there. These were matters of which a record might be needed in future, but much business did not need to be treated in this way. The chroniclers, inadequately informed as they often were, still provide much information on the range of business conducted in parliaments. The Christ Church, Canterbury, chronicle reveals that in 1275 parliament was opened with a speech from the chief justice of Common Pleas, Roger de Seton, who explained the financial problems that faced Edward I and his realm.[64] It is likely that similar speeches from important officials were normally delivered at the start of the proceedings, although the only ones of which there is any record are those made in the assemblies gathered to hear the Great Cause in 1291.[65]

The writs of summons to parliaments are often tantalizingly imprecise, but the general tenor of the requests to the magnates to attend is that they were to be present at discussions about great affairs of state. In 1295 the earls and lay lords were asked to come, so that remedies might be provided for the dangers threatening the realm, while the prelates received a much fuller writ, setting out the principle of *quod omnes tangit* (what touches all should be approved by all), and explaining the loss of Gascony to Philip IV, with the consequent danger to England. In 1305, to give a later example, the purpose of the parliament, according to the summonses, was to deal with 'certain matters especially touching our realm of England, and the establishment of our land of Scotland'.[66]

There are many examples of the discussion of foreign affairs in parliament. In 1275 the king rejected a papal demand that he pay Peter's Pence, on the grounds that such a matter, concerning as it did 'the diadem of the realm' (the crown), required consultation with the magnates in parliament.[67] In 1303, when Flemish envoys sought

[64] Gervase of Canterbury, ii, 281.
[65] *Great Cause*, ii, 14, 16–19, 33–7.
[66] *Select Charters*, ed. Stubbs, 480–1; *Parl. Writs*, i, 374–5.
[67] Ibid., 381–2.

Edward's help against the French, they were told that if the question of
an alliance were put before a general parliament, as it should be, it was
unlikely that anyone would agree to it. In the previous year, the king
had agreed to change the place of a meeting of English and French
envoys, from Montreuil to Hesdin, but he told the earl of Lincoln and
the count of Savoy that he had been much criticized for this, as the
original venue had been discussed in parliament.[68] A newsletter from
the Carlisle parliament of 1307 shows that the marriage of Edward of
Caernarfon to Isabella of France was approved by all in parliament.[69]
Military as well as diplomatic plans were discussed. There is the
celebrated example of the debate at Salisbury in 1297, between the king
and the earl Marshal, Roger Bigod, over Edward's plans for the war,
and there is an interesting passage in Langtoft's chronicle, where he
states that 'in the third article of this parliament', in 1300, the matter of
military service against the Scots was discussed. The terminology
suggests that there may have been some formal agenda which was
followed.[70]

It was not always possible, of course, to place important policy
decisions before parliament. The decision to move against the rebellious Welsh in 1282 was reached at a council held at Devizes, rather
than in parliament, as circumstances demanded haste, and there was
no time to summon a large assembly. Nor is there evidence to suggest
that debate in parliament ever caused the king to change his mind:
Bigod certainly failed to do so in 1297. It was, perhaps, partly with the
events of 1297 in mind that the Ordainers in 1311 specified that the king
should not make war, or leave the realm, without the consent of the
baronage in parliament.[71]

Edward's legislation has been discussed in a previous chapter. This
was certainly regarded by the chroniclers as an important facet of
parliamentary business: Rishanger succinctly explained that in 1285,
'the king held parliament in London that year, and in it the statutes,
which are called "Westminster Two", were enacted'.[72] It made obvious sense for the king to promulgate statutes in parliament, for all his
most important legal advisers and other councillors would be present,
and with many magnates, and perhaps also representatives of shires
and boroughs, also there, whatever was decided would receive full
publicity. The preamble of the first statute of Westminster, of 1275,
read:

---

[68] Chaplais, *English Medieval Diplomatic Practice*, I, i, 116, 119.

[69] Richardson and Sayles, *English Parliament in the Middle Ages*, XII, 436.

[70] Langtoft, ii, 322. Rishanger, 404, refers to the *primus articulus* in this same
parliament.

[71] *Parl. Writs*, i, 282.

[72] Rishanger, 111.

These are the establishments of King Edward, son of King Henry, made at Westminster in his first general parliament after his coronation, after the close of Easter in the third year of his reign, by his council and with the assent of the archbishops, bishops, abbots, priors, earls, barons and the community of the land summoned there.[73]

It was not, however, the case that all important changes in the law could be enacted only in parliament. Maitland pointed out that in devising a writ for executors, and one against them, 'a change as momentous as any that a statute could make was made without statute and very quietly'.[74] Modifications might be made to statutes without consultations taking place in parliament, and, as happened with a statute agreed in 1305 aimed at preventing religious houses sending money abroad, legislation agreed in parliament might not be put into effect by the crown.[75] There was certainly no convention that the agreement, or even the presence, of representatives was required for legislation. The statute of Acton Burnell was agreed after parliament moved in 1283 from Shrewsbury to Robert Burnell's nearby manor of Acton Burnell, and it is most unlikely that there were many present who were not members of the royal council. No representatives appear to have been summoned to the parliaments of 1285 at which the statutes of Westminster II and Winchester were enacted.

The author of the *Mirror of Justices* considered that parliaments in his day were largely held for the purpose of granting money to the king, an activity which did not meet with his approval.[76] Grants of taxes were obviously extremely important: enough has already been said to show that the crown did not have sufficient financial resources to manage without them, particularly in times of war. They were also, or so it has been argued, highly significant from a constitutional point of view, for it was the need to obtain a full measure of consent which necessitated the presence of representatives in some parliaments and councils.

There has been much debate among historians about the nature of the king's right to ask his subjects to pay taxes. The older view saw the subsidies of Edward I's day as being derived from the feudal aids of the past. Kings were entitled to aid for the ransom of their own persons, and for the cost of knighting their eldest son, and that of the marriage of their eldest daughter. In addition, they might obtain 'gracious aids' on a voluntary basis. Consent to such taxes was initially an individual matter, but in time, a method was found for obtaining collective

---

[73] *Select Charters*, ed. Stubbs, 442.
[74] Pollock and Maitland, *History of English Law*, ii, 347; Plucknett, *Legislation of Edward I, 9–10*.
[75] Richardson and Sayles, *English Parliament in the Middle Ages*, XXV, 26–7.
[76] *Mirror of Justices*, ed. Whitaker and Maitland, 155.

agreement.[77] In a classic article, J.G. Edwards argued that the writs of summons demonstrated this. Before 1268, knights were usually asked to come to assemblies on behalf of their shires, though no specific form of authority was requested. Then, in 1268, borough representatives were asked to attend a meeting at Westminster armed with letters authorizing them to act in the name of their local community. In 1283, when representatives were summoned to attend gatherings at York and Northampton, the crown asked that they should have full powers on behalf of the communities. The term *plena potestas*, full power, was used in 1290, and in 1294 it was made clear that it was included so that the business might not remain uncompleted for want of such authority. In that year, two pairs of knights from each county were summoned to a meeting in November, one with full powers to consent to what might be ordained in parliament, the other without such powers, who were to put into effect what was decided. In 1295 this rather cumbersome device was simplified, and one pair of knights was requested from each county, with full powers to do what should be ordained by common counsel. Citizens and burgesses were to come in the same way. Edwards argued that 'there was a direct connexion between the demand for full power and the granting of taxation', and that the king asked for the representatives to be properly empowered to act, so that he could negotiate the grants of taxation he so badly needed.[78]

A more recent line of thought relates the development of a national system of taxation to concepts derived from Roman and canon law. The ruler was entitled to demand taxes for the common good when a state of necessity existed, and his subjects were bound to provide formal consent for these levies. Feudal principles would not apply: the taxes would not be paid on the knight's fee, as feudal aids were, but would be paid by all subjects, irrespective of their tenurial status. A more general form of consent was needed than anything that an assembly of tenants-in-chief could supply, and this demanded the development of representative institutions. Roman law provided the concept of *plena potestas*, to ensure that the representatives were fully qualified to make grants. They could not, according to this theory, refuse taxation, if a state of necessity existed.[79]

These summaries of the opposing theories do not do full justice to complex ideas, but neither view is very easy to equate with the realities

---

[77] S.K. Mitchell, *Taxation in Medieval England* (New Haven, 1951), 159, 201–2, 221.

[78] J.G. Edwards, 'The *Plena Potestas* of English Parliamentary Representatives', *Historical Studies of the English Parliament*, i, 136–49.

[79] For these ideas, see in particular G. Post, *Studies in Medieval Legal Thought* (Princeton, 1964), 15–22, 91–162; Harriss, *King, Parliament and Public Finance*, 3–26.

of Edward I's reign. The taxes of 1275 and 1290 do not fit in with a view that taxation could be taken only when there was a state of necessity. In both cases, the taxes were needed primarily so that the king might pay off his debts. It has been suggested of the 1275 levy that 'by convention the king could probably ask for an aid to support his expenses in securing his kingdom', but this was not the nature of the plea put forward by the chief justice on the king's behalf, and was without precedent.[80] The writs for the collection of the tax stated that the 'prelates, earls, barons, and others of our realm graciously granted to us a fifteenth of all their movable goods for the relief of our estate',[81] terminology perhaps more reminiscent of a gracious feudal aid than of the concepts of the state developed from Roman law. The tax of a thirtieth granted by the two regional assemblies in 1283 was the result of what could be considered a state of necessity, the war with Wales, but the character it had, of an alternative to active military service, does not tally with the theories of Roman Law.[82]

The taxes of the years from 1294 until the end of the reign do fit in rather more closely with the Romano-canonical ideas of necessity than do the earlier taxes, though of course Edward's attempt to collect the eighth in 1297 without the consent of representatives shows that he was certainly prepared to override the obligation to obtain the consent of his subjects. The fact that in 1300 the grant of a tax of a twentieth was made conditional upon Edward carrying out specific measures concerning the forest boundaries suggests that consent was far from being the formal acknowledgement of an obligation that it is sometimes thought to have been: in the event, Edward declined the offer of the tax.[83] The tax of 1306 does not fit the pattern precisely. In the form of assessment and collection, this tax of a thirtieth did not differ from the earlier taxes on movables, but the grant was in fact made in lieu of a normal feudal aid for the knighting of the Prince of Wales, and it was stressed that no precedent should be made of it. It was, at least in part, a feudal tax, and owed little to the concepts about necessity.[84]

There can be no doubt that the systematic use of the *plena potestas* formula in summoning representatives was ultimately derived from Roman law. It may even have been significant that in Francesco Accursi, Edward had a councillor highly skilled in such matters.[85] Use

---

[80] Ibid., 40.
[81] *Parl. Writs*, i, 224.
[82] Above, 238.
[83] Below, 524–5.
[84] D. Pasquet, *An Essay on the Origins of the House of Commons* (Cambridge, 1925), 234; below, 529–30.
[85] The elder Accursi, Francesco's father, had written on the subject of *plena potestas*: see Post, *Studies in Medieval Legal Thought*, 93.

of the formula was not, however, new in England under Edward I. In 1265, Henry III had summoned representatives of the clergy to a meeting at Winchester, 'who should have full powers'.[86] Knowledge of the formula was widespread throughout thirteenth-century Europe, and Edward I's use of it is in no way surprising. It certainly was not a purely royal device which ensured that consent, of a full and comprehensive character, would invariably be given. There are cases in France of local communities giving agents full powers, among other things, to protest against and oppose grants.[87] There is no reason to suppose that an English county community considered that in giving its representatives *plena potestas*, they were doing little more than authorizing them to agree to all that the crown might demand.

It is not clear that the adoption of the *plena potestas* form of authorizing representatives was as closely related to taxation as has usually been suggested. On one occasion, in a Scottish context, full powers were requested from those representing the community, so that assent might be given to changes in the law.[88] It is certainly true that, as J.G. Edwards pointed out, on every occasion between January 1283 and October 1297 when full powers were requested, a tax was subsequently granted.[89] However, representatives with such powers were summoned in May 1298, October 1302, February 1305 and January 1307, yet at none of these assemblies was a tax granted, or apparently even requested.[90] It is certainly inconceivable that Edward was intending to extend his system of taxation over the Dutch when he took the unusual step, in 1296, of summoning representatives from Holland to come to his parliament at Bury St Edmunds, yet they were to have *plena potestas*.[91] Nor, most surprisingly, was *plena potestas* demanded on every occasion when a tax was granted. The representatives who were asked to appear in 1306 to 'treat, ordain and consent' so that the tax of a thirtieth and twentieth might be collected, were not required to have full powers.[92] Edward's clerks, perhaps, were not as careful in drafting their writs of summons as they have often been thought, and it is hard to imagine that the county communities were much concerned with the constitutional niceties of *plena potestas*. The author of the *Modus Tenendi*

---

[86] *Select Charters*, ed. Stubbs, 406–7.

[87] E.A.R. Brown, 'Representation and Agency Law in the Later Middle Ages', *Viator*, iii (1972), 358. Professor Brown's view on p. 363 should be noted: 'In neither France nor England were representatives simply authorized to submit to the decrees of a sovereign court.'

[88] Below, 504.

[89] Edwards, 'The *Plena Potestas*', 141.

[90] *Handbook of British Chronology*, 550–2.

[91] *Treaty Rolls*, 120.

[92] *Parl. Writs*, i, 164.

Parliamentum, for what the fact is worth, did not consider *plena potestas* worth mentioning.

Taxes were not all granted in parliaments. The York and Northampton gatherings of 1283 were certainly not parliamentary in character. In 1294, the November meeting, at which the grant of a tenth and sixth was made, was probably specially summoned for that purpose, and did not have the wide-ranging character of a parliament.[93] The assembly of 1306, which granted the tax of a thirtieth and twentieth, was not summoned by means of the usual type of parliamentary writ, and is best described as a council.[94] Nor was full representation the rule. In 1294 the higher rate of tax, a sixth, was paid by the towns and ancient demesnes of the crown, but there were no burgess representatives present at Westminster when the grant was made. Consent was obtained instead by means of local negotiations, initially with London, and then with other towns. By 1297, for the tax of a ninth granted in the autumn, it proved sufficient to have the consent of London alone.[95]

The way in which taxes were granted under Edward I did not follow a pattern suggested by one particular set of concepts, either drawn from the doctrines of feudal relationships, or from Roman law. Changing circumstances in the course of the reign demanded different solutions to the problem of how to obtain consent. The business was certainly no mere formality, and it clearly involved the magnates as well as the representatives. The Hagnaby chronicler suggests that it was the earl of Gloucester who was largely responsible for successfully reducing the scale of Edward's demand for money in the autumn of 1294.[96] The Bury St Edmunds chronicle explains how, in 1296, anyone who hesitated to agree to a grant was publicly dressed down by the king, no doubt a very chastening experience. In 1300, according to Rishanger, the king skilfully persuaded the magnates, individually rather than collectively, to agree to the grant of a tax.[97] It became an established principle in the course of Edward's reign that taxes should be negotiated with the community of the realm, and by the end of the reign it was impossible for such discussions to take place without the presence of representatives.[98] The failure of the eighth of 1297 proved that taxes on movables could not be obtained if no representatives were summoned,

---

[93] Richardson and Sayles, *English Parliament in the Middle Ages*, VI, 146, 149.

[94] Prestwich, 'Magnate Summonses in England in the later years of Edward I', 99–100.

[95] Willard, *Parliamentary Taxes*, 15.

[96] BL Cotton MS Vesp. B.xi, f.36.

[97] *Chron. Bury St Edmunds*, 124–5; Rishanger, 404–5.

[98] I have discussed the concept of the community more fully in 'Parliament and the community of the realm in fourteenth century England', *Parliament and Community*, ed. A. Cosgrove and J.I. McGuire (Belfast, 1983), 5–24.

and it was this which, in time, would help to ensure that the commons were invariably summoned to parliaments.

Taxation may have been the main reason why representatives were summoned to parliaments and councils under Edward I, but it was not the only one. The question of what the knights of the shire and burgesses did in parliament, when there was no request for a grant, is not an easy one to answer. In 1283 they were, almost certainly, summoned for publicity purposes, as Prince Dafydd was to be tried in parliament.[99] There was, however, no obvious reason for summoning representatives in 1298, 1302, 1305 or 1307, and on the latter occasion, indeed, the burgesses were dismissed on the very day that the parliament opened.[100] One hypothesis is that the king wanted representatives to come to parliament, both so that he might discover what was going on at a local level in his realm, and so that they might take back to the constituencies news of what had taken place in parliament. There is no evidence, however, for this type of transmission of news or information until 1327, and there is no reason to suppose that the government was in any way dissatisfied with the normal means of distributing information, through proclamations by the sheriffs in the county courts and elsewhere. In the other direction, the petitioning procedure provided the king with an ample channel of communication whereby his subjects could make their complaints known, and there is little indication that, as yet, it was the representatives who brought petitions to parliament.[101] On occasion, the knights and burgesses might be given some specific duty to perform: in 1294, two of the knights summoned from each county had been called so that they might carry out the decisions reached in the assembly, and they were duly employed to assist in the collection of the tax that was granted.[102]

The view that there was a popular demand for representation to take place in parliament has often been dismissed. It may be, however, that there is some truth to it. In 1299 the mayor and aldermen of London appointed four men 'to prosecute the business of the city before the king and council in the parliament begun at Westminster', even though no representatives had been summoned, and in 1305 the men of Faversham sent three men on business to London, at a time when

---

[99] Above, 202.

[100] *Parl. Writs*, i, 190–1.

[101] Maddicott, 'Parliament and the Constituencies', 61–4.

[102] This was, at least, the case as far as Buckinghamshire was concerned: see D.W. Burton, 'Politics, Propaganda and Public Opinion in the Reigns of Henry III and Edward I' (Oxford D.Phil thesis, 1985), 207. Pasquet, *Origins of the House of Commons*, 186, shows that in 1295, tax collectors were also representatives in 21 out of 35 counties.

parliament was sitting, to discuss business with Roger Brabazon.[103] It was no burden to the crown to summon knights and burgesses: it was the local communities that paid their expenses, and the absence of complaints about this may imply that the system was one which the localities welcomed, even though it is not easy to see what real benefits they gained from it.

In 1280 a chancery memorandum attempted to make parliamentary procedure more efficient, so that 'the king and his council may be able to attend to the great affairs of his realm and his foreign lands without being charged with other business'.[104] Petitions were now to be sorted out, and sent to the department that was most obviously concerned. Only if they could not be easily dealt with, would they be submitted to the king. Petitioning, and the hearing of legal cases, have been stressed by Richardson and Sayles, as distinguishing parliaments from other types of assembly, despite the stress of the 1280 memorandum on the major matters of politics and diplomacy.

A strong case has been made for regarding the development of petitioning as being the most important step taken in the evolution of parliament during Edward's early years on the throne. Over sixty petitions presented in parliament in 1278 survive, and their variety of form is such as to suggest that the procedure was a fairly new one. Although only about one fifth of these petitions concerned official wrong-doing, it has been suggested that the king may have deliberately encouraged his subjects to present petitions in parliament, as a means of providing a check on his ministers, sheriffs and bailiffs.[105] Petitioning was not, of course, new, but under Henry III it does not seem that it took place in parliament. Rather, men presented their petitions at any convenient time.[106]

It may be that the arrears of complaints that built up during Edward's absence from his realm at the start of his reign, when he was returning from the crusade via Gascony, meant that it became convenient to postpone hearings until parliament met. It does not seem likely, however, that there can have been much time for hearing petitions in Edward's first parliaments, for there certainly was not enough time for the king to be able to deal even with *Quo Warranto* cases.[107] It is very likely that it was not until 1278 that large numbers of petitions

---

[103] *Calendar of London Letter Books C*, 36; F.F. Guiraud, 'Municipal Archives of Faversham A.D. 1304–24', *Archaeologia Cantiana*, xiv (1882), 190.

[104] *CCR 1279–88*, 57. My translation is from the full text, given by J.G. Edwards, 'Justice in Early English Parliaments', *Historical Studies of the English Parliament*, i, 284.

[105] Maddicott, 'Parliament and the Constituencies', 61–4.

[106] J.E.A. Jolliffe, 'Some Factors in the Beginnings of Parliament', *Historical Studies of the English Parliament*, i, 44.

[107] Sutherland, *Quo Warranto*, 20–22.

began to come before parliament. The chancery memorandum of 1280 could well imply that the problem of dealing with them was a relatively new one. It would, however, be wrong to look for any deeper motive on the king's part than a desire to resolve the grievances of his subjects. When he wished to check up on official wrong-doing, he set up the Hundred Rolls inquiry, and later, as in 1289, requested specific petitions to be brought forward. It may not even have been any special royal initiative that led to so many petitions coming to parliament; it could have been that it was the petitioners who realized that the best time to present their cases was at a time when the king had all his most important advisers around him.

Anyone could present a petition. The majority were from private individuals, though as the reign proceeded, petitions in the name of communities or groups of people became more common. Between 1290 and 1307 there were twenty-three from the shires and forty from boroughs, in addition to such general requests as that made in 1305, on behalf of all who sought payment from the crown of money due from the scrutiny of treasure of 1294, prises, arrears of wages or other debts incurred by the king.[108] Most petitions, however, were concerned with private grievances: in 1278 Elias de Tyngewyke complained that he had granted some land and a wood to Roger de la Hyde for five marks a year. Roger had felled the wood, let the land go to waste, and had not paid his rent. Elias hoped that the king might assist him in his plight. By the later years of the reign, more petitions were coming from men of no great social standing. In 1305 there was one from a prisoner in Canterbury gaol, and another from a mason who had been working at Caernarfon, who sought payment of arrears of wages. In 1306 the 'poor people of Windsor' petitioned the king in parliament, and the men of the East Riding of Yorkshire complained about the cost of crossing the Humber.[109]

As is the case with much that took place in parliament, petitioning was not an activity found only there. When Edward sought petitions against the judges and other officials whom he considered had failed him, in the autumn of 1289, they were to be brought before special commissioners, rather than parliament.[110] When Edward was at Plympton, in Devon, in April and May 1297, he heard a number of petitions from his Gascon subjects, but there was no parliament then in session.[111] As he was on his way north in 1306, Edward received many

---

[108] Maddicott, 'Parliament and the Constituencies', 69; *Rot. Parl.*, i, 165. For the scrutiny, see above, 403.

[109] *Rot. Parl.*, i, 12, 160, 164, 193, 202.

[110] Above, 340.

[111] *Rôles Gascons*, iii, clxxxiii–cxciv.

petitions from men asking to be given lands in Scotland. They were not answered promptly, if at all, but did not have to wait until parliament sat to make their requests.[112] In most cases, however, it made sense, from the point of view of both the king and his subjects, that petitions should come forward in parliament. The business was not spectacular, nor in many cases even controversial, but by encouraging his people to use parliament in this way, Edward served them well.

The dispensation of justice in parliament, by the king and his council, was described in a legal treatise of about 1290, *Fleta*, as follows: 'The king has his court in his council in his parliaments when prelates, earls, barons, magnates and others learned in the law are present. And doubts are determined there concerning judgements, new remedies are devised for wrongs newly brought to light, and there also justice is dispensed to everyone according to his deserts.'[113] The judicial business of parliament could not be undertaken elsewhere: this was, in effect, the highest court of the land. From the early days of parliaments, under Henry I I I, it made obvious sense for difficult or delicate cases to be postponed until parliament met, as only then would all the most learned, and most powerful, men be assembled together. The *Quo Warranto* inquiries provide many examples of cases where the justices were unable or unwilling to reach a conclusion, and which were postponed to be heard in parliament.[114] Clause 24 of the second statute of Westminster, of 1285, laid down that in cases where there was no agreement about the type of writ which was appropriate, the matter should be referred to the next parliament.[115] By the time that the Ordinances were drawn up, in 1311, it was possible to define the two main types of plea that came before parliament as those in which defendants claimed that they could not answer without the king, and those in which the justices were divided in their opinion.[116]

Major cases, such as that between the earls of Hereford and Gloucester in 1290, were naturally heard in parliament. The dispute between William de Vescy and John FitzThomas, affecting as it did the king's personal honour and reputation, could hardly have been left to some lower court.[117] When Nicholas de Segrave challenged John Cromwell to fight him in trial by battle in the French king's court, and deserted from the army to go to France, it was in parliament that he was tried in 1305. The hearing was, as usual, described as being before the king and

---

[112] *Documents and Records Illustrating the History of Scotland*, ed. F. Palgrave (1837), i, 301–18.

[113] *Fleta*, ed. H.G. Richardson and G.O. Sayles (Selden Soc., 1955), ii, 109.

[114] Sutherland, *Quo Warranto*, 91, 154–5.

[115] *Statutes of the Realm*, i, 83–4.

[116] *Rot. Parl.*, i, 285 (Clause 29).

[117] Above, 348–51, 353–4.

council, but in this case it is likely that the council consisted of all of those who had received individual summonses to the parliament.[118] This can be seen as a precedent for the concept of trial by peers in parliament, but that was not to emerge until Edward II's reign.[119] Rather surprisingly, although the Welsh prince, Dafydd, had been tried in parliament, Edward did not choose to bring such Scottish captives as William Wallace or Simon Fraser before parliament for trial. He perhaps considered that there was sufficient propaganda value in public executions in London, and that such rebels, as he saw them, did not merit the honour of a trial in the highest tribunal of the land.[120]

One important consequence of the judicial function of parliament was that it gave the assembly a particular status, with those in attendance being placed under a special royal protection. The most celebrated example of this dates from 1290, when the earl of Cornwall was served with a writ at the instigation of Bogo de Clare, which summoned him to appear before the archbishop of Canterbury. This was done as the earl was in Westminster Hall, during a session of parliament. The king claimed £10,000 damages, and the abbot of Westminster £1,000 (technically, Westminster lay outside the archbishop's jurisdiction). Complaints were also registered by the steward and marshal of the king's household, as they alone had the right to serve writs within the palace of Westminster.[121] In that case, the claims did not emphasize the fact that the offensive writ had been served in parliament, but the incident set a precedent for the future. Bogo de Clare was again involved in the very next parliament, when an attempt was made to serve a summons on him to appear before the archbishop of Canterbury. One of his servants forced the messenger to eat the writ, with its seal, and the offence was said to be particularly serious because it took place during parliament, within the royal verge.[122] The murderous attack on the earl of Cornwall's steward, which took place on the streets of London in 1292, was clearly regarded as being more serious, because it took place as he was on his way to parliament. It was only parliament that had this special status, and not other forms of royal councils or assemblies.

*   *   *

[118] *Rot. Parl.*, i, 172.

[119] Sayles, *King's Parliament of England*, 100–1.

[120] Below, 503, 508. Judgement had already been given against Wallace and Fraser in the Scottish parliament held by Edward at St Andrews in 1304: see Richardson and Sayles, *English Parliament in the Middle Ages*, XIII, 311.

[121] *Rot. Parl.*, i, 17.

[122] *Rot. Parl.*, i, 24–5; Richardson and Sayles, *English Parliament in the Middle Ages*, V, 132.

Edward I did not hold parliaments only in England. He held them in Gascony and in Scotland, and in Ireland they were held in his name. The Gascon parliaments have received little attention from historians. One, of which little is known, took place in March 1274. It probably had a more general character than the purely judicial meeting at St Sever in the previous October, when the case against Gaston de Béarn was heard.[123] On Edward's second visit to Gascony as king, a great parliament was held at Libourne in May and June 1289. There is a surviving record of the writs of summons sent to some forty lay lords, thirty prelates, and some mayors, jurats and consuls. There is no evidence of the presence of any representatives at this parliament, though it is by no means impossible that some may have attended. The main business appears to have been the promulgation of the ordinances lately drafted at Condom, and in addition, the hearing of many petitions.[124] Parliaments were not held in Gascony save when the king himself was there. Instead, many Gascon questions were raised in English parliaments: in 1305 a special panel of auditors of Gascon petitions sat in the parliament at Westminster.[125]

Parliaments were not introduced to Scotland by Edward I. The similarities between English and Scottish parliaments, before 1291 and the Great Cause, provide a warning to those historians who are too ready to impute some special constitutional genius to the English people. Scottish kings were quite as accustomed to calling parliaments as English ones were, and in Scottish parliaments great affairs of state were discussed, legal doubts resolved, and the grievances of the people, expressed through their petitions, met. There were no representatives summoned, as far as is known, to Scottish parliaments – but they had not attended many English ones before the 1290s.[126] The meetings held by Edward at Norham and Berwick, for the hearing of the Great Cause, were termed 'parliaments' in the official records: whether they should be termed English or Scottish parliaments is impossible to say, and it was not a question which concerned contemporaries. Then, in 1296, Edward held a parliament at Berwick, attended by 'all the bishops, earls, barons, abbots, priors, and the sovereigns of all the common people'.[127] Quite what this last phrase means is unclear, but it is likely that it implies the presence of local officials, such as bailiffs, rather than

---

[123] Trabut-Cussac, *L'administration anglaise en Gascogne*, 43–4.
[124] Ibid., 94–100.
[125] *Memoranda de Parliamento*, (1305), lviii.
[126] Barrow, *Kingship and Unity*, 126–8.
[127] *Documents*, ed. Stevenson, ii, 31. In a privy seal writ summoning councillors to this meeting, the assembly is not called a parliament, but a case was brought against the earl of Angus for hitting Hugh de Louther during the proceedings, and it was then termed a parliament: ibid., ii, 78, 81.

any formal system of representation. The 1296 parliament celebrated
what Edward must have thought was the conquest of Scotland: the
same is true of that held at St Andrews, in Fife, in 1304, when there was
a substantial attendance by Scottish magnates. Finally, a parliament
was held at Scone in 1305 by John of Brittany, in his capacity as
Edward's lieutenant.[128] Not enough is known of these Scottish assemblies to make any useful comparisons with the better-documented
English parliaments of Edward's later years.

As Edward never went to Ireland, he could not preside over any Irish
parliaments. These have been very fully studied, and no more than a
few points of comparison and contrast with English practice need be
made. Parliament was curiously periodic in Ireland: none was held
between 1282 and 1288, and none from 1303 to 1306. The business was
very similar to that of English parliaments: the judicial character is
very clear, with petitions heard and cases discussed. Legislation was
enacted, and matters of state discussed. Representatives were summoned, partly so that grants of taxation might be discussed, but also,
and this is much clearer than is the case in England, for consultation on
administrative matters, and even, in the case of the regulation of
wage-rates, legislation. They were also summoned to discuss the problem of the circulation of foreign coinage in the country in 1299, a matter
which was not apparently put before representatives in the English
parliament at this time. The special status of those attending parliament is clear, just as it was in England, and an interesting doctrine
emerged, as a result of a case in 1281, that a wrong done while
parliament was in session should be corrected in the same parliament.
Obviously, the Irish parliaments were largely modelled on those in
England, but there were interesting differences, such as the way in
which franchises, as well as counties, were represented. The different
circumstances that existed in Ireland meant that the English model
could not be followed slavishly.[129]

Parliament could have developed in many different ways in the reign of
Edward I. Although virtually all the elements of Edward's parliaments, in terms both of composition and function, can be traced back to
the parliaments of Henry III's day, it was far from obvious in the 1270s
how the institution would evolve. By 1307, although parliament was
hardly characterized by that 'definiteness and completeness' which

---

[128] Richardson and Sayles, *English Parliament in the Middle Ages*, XIII,
310–13.
[129] H.G. Richardson and G.O. Sayles, *The Irish Parliament in the Middle Ages* (Philadelphia, 1952), 57–70; Richardson and Sayles, *English Parliament in the Middle Ages*, XV,
128–47.

15. The Great Seal of Edward I, obverse and reverse.
(Durham, Dean and Chapter Muniments, 1.3 Reg. 8; 1.3. Reg. 12)

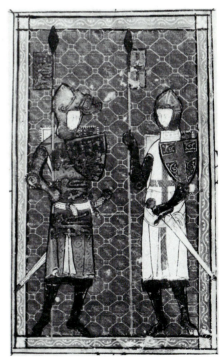

16. (*left*) Seal of Anthony Bek, bishop of Durham. (Durham, Dean and Chapter Muniments, 3.2. Pont. 15A)

17. (*right*) An earl of Lancaster, probably Edmund Crouchback, Edward I's brother, standing beside St George. (Bodleian Library, MS Douce 231, f. 1)

18. (*left*) Edward I (on the left) confronting Philip IV of France in 1297, in an informal sketch on an exchequer memoranda roll. (PRO, E 368/69, m. 54)

19. (*right*) John Balliol crossing the Channel, probably when he went to France in 1299. (British Library, Cottonian MS Julius Av, f. 4v.)

20. Edward I pointing at a request that the exchequer should observe the clauses of Magna Carta, from an exchequer memoranda roll, 1300. (PRO, E. 368/72, m. 12)

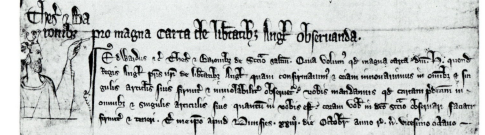

21. Examples of the new coinage (*obverse and reverse*) which began to be minted
in 1279.
That above was produced at Canterbury in 1280,
that below at Newcastle in 1281.
(Ashmolean Museum)

22. In the late 1290s, England was flooded by imitation sterling coins, often
termed pollards and crockards. That on the left was minted in Brabant, under
either Duke John I or II; that on the right in Flanders under Count Guy de
Dampierre. (Ashmolean Museum)

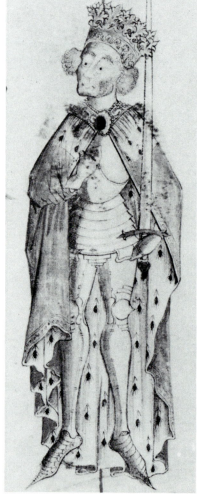

23. The coronation chair in Westminster
Abbey, containing the Stone of Destiny.
Intended in 1297 to be of bronze,
the chair was made of wood,
and was complete by 1300, when it was
decorated by Walter of Durham.

24. (*above right*) Edward I creating his son
Prince of Wales in 1301.
(British Library,
Cottonian MS Nero D. ii, f. 191v.)

25. (*right*) Edward I, as imagined by a
fifteenth-century artist.
(British Library,
Cottonian MS Julius E iv, f. 6)

Stubbs saw in it, the lines of future development had become very much clearer.

Although parliament had played a very significant part in the political struggles of the late 1250s and 1260s, it would have still been possible in the 1270s and 1280s for it to have become something much more like the French *parlement*. That body was a specialized legal tribunal, with its own expert, learned staff, attended only rarely by the king himself. It was far superior to the English parliament in terms of the records that were kept, and the professionalism of its staff, but its importance was much less, for it could never stand for the community of the realm, as the English parliament could. Had Edward not chosen to summon large numbers of magnates to his parliaments, along with representatives on occasion; had he not chosen to receive petitions, often in considerable quantity, in parliaments; then there might have appeared in England a small, specialized parliament, little more than a legal committee of the royal council, along French lines.[130]

The comparative lack of evidence about parliament in the first half of Edward's reign makes judgement on that period difficult. Representatives are only known to have been summoned to three parliaments between Edward's return to England, after the crusade, in 1274, and his departure for Gascony in 1286, and they cannot be said to have contributed much to the character of the English parliament.[131] An important innovation in this period, very probably, was the way in which petitions began to be presented in considerable numbers in parliament, although the fact that the only roll of such petitions to survive from Edward's early years on the throne is that of 1278 makes the case a hard one to prove beyond doubt. This was, of course, the age of the statutes, and it was in parliament that the bulk of Edward's legislation was promulgated. This alone made the parliaments of the period very important.

In the years after the outbreak of the war with France, in 1294, parliament's importance as the occasion for the granting of taxation became much clearer. There are more indications of political debate taking place – the disputes of the final years will be discussed in Chapter 19 – and representatives were present far more frequently than in the past. In 1295 the formula used for summoning representatives with full powers (*plena potestas*) was established in a definitive form. In the same year, Edward used the terminology of Roman law in summoning the clergy, declaring that 'what touches all, should be approved by

---

[130] For the French *parlement*, see Strayer, *Philip the Fair*, 208–36; Sayles, *King's Parliament of England*, 55n.

[131] There were representatives present in April 1275, October 1275 and September 1283: see *Handbook of British Chronology*, 545–7.

all' (*quod omnes tangit ab omnibus approbetur*).[132] The use of these phrases raises the question of the extent to which Edward's policies resulted from the application of political concepts drawn from Roman law. There is no doubt that the adoption of a system of representation in England was a part of a wider European movement, in which Roman law had an important part to play. The *plena potestas* formula was widely employed, and it would have been most surprising if the English chancery had not adopted it. The terminology of the writ of summons, however, is most unlikely to have meant that the knights of the shire regarded themselves as bound in any way by the doctrines set out by the learned canonists of the thirteenth century. In particular, it seems improbable that the knights and burgesses would have considered that they were bound by the dictates of Roman law to make grants if it was shown that a state of necessity existed, or that Edward considered that he was bound by the same dictates to summon popular representatives when he wished to collect taxes. The character of the arguments he employed in 1297 certainly is not easy to fit with such an interpretation.[133]

The doctrine of *quod omnes tangit* was only explicitly cited by Edward on one occasion, in summoning the clergy in 1295, and it is dangerous to draw wide conclusions from such slight evidence. It was a very familiar maxim, as far as the clergy were concerned, and it made sense to quote it to them, but there is no reason to go further, and suggest that Edward himself regarded it as a binding political principle. It has been suggested that use of the verbs *tangere* or *contingere* (to touch) in writs of summons to parliament implies an acceptance of the concept of *quod omnes tangit*, but the argument is not convincing.[134] Few recipients of such summonses could have been so sensitive to the use of Latin that they would be aware of the possible implications of this usage.

It was surely in the first instance the pressure of war finance, not the dictates of Roman lawyers, that worked to alter the character of Edward's parliaments and councils. The greatly increased attendance

[132] *Select Charters*, ed. Stubbs, 480. E.L.G. Stones, 'The text of the writ "Quod omnes tangit" in Stubb's *Select Charters*', *EHR*, lxxxiii (1973), 759–60, corrects the text as printed by Stubbs.

[133] I differ in my interpretation from Harriss, *King, Parliament and Public Finance*, 45–74: he lays much more stress on the concept of necessity.

[134] Post, *Studies in Medieval Legal Thought*, 233–4, where this suggestion is made. Ibid., 311–12, has some wise words of caution, in which it is noted that no canon lawyer or legist ever discussed the practice of representation in England, and that 'the Romano-canonical doctrine of consent in the maxim *quod omnes tangit* was of doubtful application in a *pays du droit coutumier*'. It is perhaps relevant to note the firm rejection of Roman law by Edward I's councillors in the course of the Great Cause: *Great Cause*, ii, 212–13.

of knights, burgesses and proctors of the lower clergy was a reflection, primarily, of Edward's growing financial difficulties in his later years. The events of 1297 showed that without proper consultation, Edward could not collect taxes. His action in demanding the tax of an eighth, without first obtaining full consent, shows that he did not feel himself to be constrained by any legal theories. Bigod and Bohun, when they appeared at the exchequer to protest about the eighth and the prise of wool, did not refer to such concepts as *quod omnes tangit*, but straightforwardly objected to the fact that Edward claimed to have obtained consent, when none had been given.[135] Practical politics made it necessary for Edward to consult his subjects in parliament, and to do so as fully as possible.

In Edward's later years, there was a growing uniformity in parliamentary practice. Parliaments were still not held at a fixed date, or in a fixed place, but the composition of the assembly did not change very much from one year to the next. In the last seven years of Edward's reign, representatives were summoned to all but one parliament, and there was much less alteration in the list of magnates who received summonses. There was a considerable improvement in record-keeping, to judge by the surviving evidence. It was still possible, between 1302 and 1305, for the king to rule effectively without calling a parliament, but the backlog of business that built up was considerable, showing how vital parliaments were. There were still anomalies: the meeting that took place in 1306 had many of the characteristics of a parliament, but, probably because it was convened so that agreement might be reached on a feudal aid, rather than a normal national tax, a different form of summons was used, and most official sources avoided calling it a parliament.[136] The division of parliament into two houses is not yet apparent, and the idea of a parliamentary peerage had not been formulated. The evolution of parliament was a long, slow process, but, both in terms of its composition and its functions, Edward I's reign saw vital precedents set for the future. By 1307, in contrast to the start of Edward's reign, it was clear that the English parliament was quite different from the French *parlement*.

In 1302 Edward claimed that 'we are allied to the good people of our realm in such manner' that he could not act without their counsel.[137] It was in parliament that the community of the realm, that intangible yet potent concept, found expression, and it was there that the king put his alliance with his subjects into effect. It was not always as comfortable

---

[135] *Documents 1297–8*, 137–8; above, 424–5.
[136] Prestwich, 'Magnate Summonses in England in the Later Years of Edward I', 99–100.
[137] Chaplais, *English Medieval Diplomatic Practice*, I, i, 200.

an alliance as Edward's phraseology suggested. There were stormy scenes and bitter disputes between the king and his subjects, as well as periods of harmony and mutual understanding. At times, as in 1297, the principles of counsel and consent were put under great pressure. The Scottish wars, which dominated Edward's last years, would place a continued strain on the relationship between the king and his subjects.

Chapter 18

THE SCOTTISH WARS, 1296–1307

Edward I was a formidable figure in his later years. His physique had deteriorated little, even in his sixties. His hair may have been white, but his glance was keen as ever, he was upright in stance, and could still mount a horse unaided. There were some signs that his physical and mental vigour were not quite what they had been. Langtoft, in his chronicle, hinted that Edward did not get up as early as he should, and that he led too luxurious a life.[1] The king occasionally admitted to forgetfulness, as when, in 1302, he asked Philip Martel to come to see him, since he had omitted to tell him about some important matters.[2] Such evidence as this does not imply that the king had lost his grip on affairs of state. There are no signs that Edward relaxed in his sixties, in the way that his grandson, Edward III, was to do. The events of 1297 would have disillusioned a lesser man, and might have caused a more sensitive one to have self-doubts, but in Edward's case, his resolve was stiffened. He was a man of immense experience and determination, in control of a highly effective bureaucracy. Age perhaps made him increasingly inflexible in his attitudes, less inclined than ever to accept compromises. It was in these final years that Edward was confronted by what turned out to be perhaps his most formidable opponents, the Scots. His tenacity of purpose meant that he would not abandon a struggle in which final success constantly eluded him. At the same time, his single-minded approach meant that possible solutions to the problems he faced were neglected in favour of more traditional methods.

The origin of the war against the Scots has already been discussed. The English invasion of 1296 can be seen both as the final move in the legal process against John Balliol, and as Edward's necessary answer to the threat posed by the alliance between the French and the Scots.[3] On 16 December 1295, Edward summoned his magnates to muster on 1 March 1296, at Newcastle upon Tyne. Balliol and the Scots nobles were asked to attend as well, but there can have been few who expected

---

[1] Langtoft, ii, 326; and see below, 560.
[2] Chaplais, *English Medieval Diplomatic Practice*, I, i, 276, where other examples are also cited.
[3] Above, 372–3.

them to appear. On 23 January Edward asked the exchequer to see to it that 1,000 men-at-arms and 60,000 infantry should assemble at Newcastle. The numbers may not have been meant literally, as armies then rarely exceeded 30,000, but Edward obviously wanted to recruit a large invasion force.[4] In February the Scots ratified their treaty with the French, and all was set for war.

The first action of the war illustrates how artificial the conflict was for some, at this stage. The border did not divide societies of a different language and character: it was, rather, an artificial political divide through a region where there were strong links across the river Tweed. At Wark on Tweed the local lord, Robert de Ros, decided for amorous reasons – he was in love with a Scottish lady – to throw in his lot with the Scots. His brother told him that he was a fool, and asked Edward, who was by now nearing Newcastle, for help. An infantry force under the command of a knight was duly sent, but when they were billeted near Wark, they were surprised by Robert de Ros with a Scottish force. A password was arranged, for without one there was no means of telling Scot from Englishman. Some of the English were killed: others overheard the password, 'Tabard', and the prearranged reply, and escaped. Wark was soon relieved by Edward: the incident was welcomed by him, for the fact that it was the Scots who opened hostilities with an attack on English soil gave him a propaganda advantage. A much more substantial Scottish force, headed by seven earls, then invaded England in the west, on Easter Monday, and attempted to take Carlisle. Although they did not succeed in this, they caused much damage in the surrounding villages.[5]

Edward himself waited, with due piety, until the Easter celebrations were over before crossing the Tweed. His army was arrayed outside the town of Berwick, on Friday, 30 March, when Edward, as was customary before battle, knighted several young men. The sailors in the English fleet mistook the activity for an attack, raised banners for an assault on the town, and unfurled their sails, moving into the harbour.

---

[4] *Documents*, ed. Stevenson, ii, 20–1, from E 159/69, m.11. Stevenson mistranscribed the sum required every week for this force as £1,000: the figure should be £5,000. Barrow, *Robert Bruce*, 294, assumes that 60,000 men were in pay, but Edward's instructions should not be taken as evidence for the actual size of the force. Unfortunately, there are no pay rolls for the 1296 host, nor indeed, any evidence of how many men the exchequer actually asked for. The total infantry wage bill for the campaign was £21,443, suggesting perhaps a force 25,000–strong at the outset of the campaign. See Prestwich, *War, Politics and Finance*, 94. There are accounts for the Irish contingent, which consisted of one earl (Ulster), eight bannerets, 26 knights, 261 hobelars (lightly armed cavalry), 27 crossbowmen and 2,549 ordinary footsoldiers: J.F. Lydon, 'An Irish Army in Scotland in 1296', *The Irish Sword*, v (1962), 184–90.

[5] Guisborough, 271–3.

The first ship ran aground, and was surrounded and burned by the gleeful Scots. The next two ships also caught fire, but their crews escaped in small boats. The rest of the fleet withdrew. When Edward heard what had happened, and saw the plumes of smoke from the burning ships, he ordered his trumpets to sound the advance. The flimsy palisade proved to be no obstacle, and the Scots stood stupefied, offering virtually no resistance. According to the English accounts only a group of Flemish merchants in the Red Hall fought to any effect. The garrison in the castle could do little save offer their surrender: their commander was retained by Edward to fight for him in the coming campaign.[6] The common people of Berwick did not fare so well. The women were allowed to leave, but the men were slaughtered in a dreadful bloodbath, which reflected Edward's anger at the way the town had resisted him, anger which was 'like that of a wild boar pursued by dogs'. The bodies 'fell like autumn leaves', and with no one left to bury them, they were thrown down wells, or tipped into the sea. Eventually, the clergy were able to plead successfully for the slaughter to cease, but not until, according to one estimate, 11,060 had been killed.[7]

The Scots were not strong enough to challenge Edward's army in open battle. Instead, a substantial raiding party was sent into Northumberland, ravaging the countryside, and allegedly burning 200 schoolboys alive in the church at Corbridge (or, by some accounts, Hexham). On their return to Scotland, the earls of Mar, Ross and Menteith, who had led this force, seized the castle of Dunbar. The earl of Dunbar was a supporter of Edward I, but he was with the king, and could do nothing to prevent his countess (or possibly his brother) opening the gates to the Scots. An English force then laid siege to the castle. Surrender was offered, but the garrison asked to be allowed to contact John Balliol, to find out what terms he would be prepared to agree to. A messenger was sent to Balliol, who was at Haddington, and advised him to attack the English during the three-day period of truce that had been agreed. When the Scots army duly approached, those within the castle unfurled their banners, and directed the customary insults at the English, calling them 'tailed dogs', and threatening them with death and the amputation of their tails (it was a well-known myth in the middle ages that all Englishmen had tails). Earl Warenne, in command of the relatively small English force, prepared his troops. The Scots mistook his manoeuvrings for flight, attacked precipitately, and were routed.[8]

---

[6] Ibid., 274–5.
[7] Rishanger, 373–4; the Hagnaby chronicle, BL Vesp. B. xi, f.40.
[8] Guisborough, 277–8; BL Vesp. B. xi, ff.40v–41.

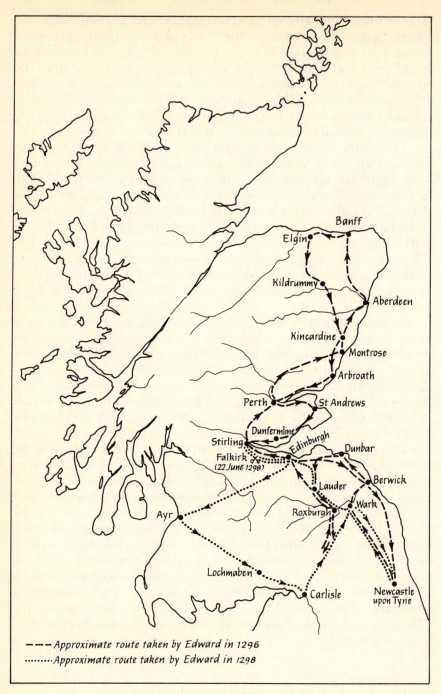

Banff
Elgin
Kildrummy
Aberdeen
Kincardine
Montrose
Arbroath
Perth
St Andrews
Dunfermline
Stirling
Edinburgh
Dunbar
Falkirk
(22 June 1298)
Lauder
Berwick
Roxburgh
Wark
Ayr
Lochmaben
Carlisle
Newcastle
upon Tyne

- - - Approximate route taken by Edward in 1296
·········· Approximate route taken by Edward in 1298

5. Edward I's Invasions of Scotland, 1296 and 1298

The English chroniclers made much of the battle of Dunbar, and a modern commentator has described it in terms of the defeat of the main feudal host of Scotland.[9] It is not clear that the engagement was, in reality, on quite so grand a scale. Patrick Graham was the only senior Scottish noble slain, and only four knights are said to have been captured. The battle was probably little more than a skirmish, involving only a portion of the main Scottish army: if the whole host had been involved, then Balliol himself would surely have taken part. What was important was that Dunbar was not relieved, and when on the day after the battle Edward himself arrived, those within the castle surrendered. This was a prime prize: three earls and many barons were taken prisoner, and sent south to captivity in England.[10] The heart was taken out of the Scottish resistance. James the Steward was prompt to surrender Roxburgh castle, and Edward was able to enjoy a military promenade through much of Scotland, in which he was virtually unopposed. Edinburgh castle surrendered after five days of siege. Stirling, a major strategic castle, was abandoned by its garrison before Edward arrived outside the walls. A triumphant English campaign saw all of Scotland conquered, as a contemporary narrative noted, in twenty-one weeks. During that time, Edward marched north to Elgin: only once in the future, in 1303, would he be able to go so far again.[11]

One reason for the failure of the Scots in 1296 was the lack of leadership shown by their king, John Balliol. He had clearly forfeited the trust of his people by 1295, when a council had been elected to take charge of affairs of state, and there was no support for him when he surrendered to Edward in 1296. Initially, Edward gave Anthony Bek and Earl Warenne the task of negotiating with Balliol, and at the end of June a treaty was proposed, by which Scotland would be granted to Edward and his heirs in perpetuity, and Balliol receive an English earldom in exchange. The plan was similar to one suggested in 1282 for Llywelyn of Wales. Edward, it seems, would have none of it, and insisted on total surrender. The documents recording Balliol's submission present some problems: the process seems to have taken place in stages between 2 July and 10 July, in Kincardine, Stracathro, Brechin and Montrose. It is not clear why the business was so protracted, but it is most likely that Edward would not be satisfied until Balliol had been completely humiliated, as he was in the final ceremony, when his coat of arms was publicly stripped from his tabard, an act which gave him

<hr />

[9] Barrow, *Robert Bruce*, 101–2.
[10] *Documents*, ed. Stevenson, ii, 26; Cotton, 311–12; Langtoft, ii, 250; the Hagnaby chronicle, BL Vesp. B. xi, f.41.
[11] *Documents*, ed. Stevenson, ii, 27–31.

his nickname of 'Toom tabard'.[12] Balliol was sent south, to custody in
the Tower of London. The Scottish regalia were also taken to England,
and the enthronement stone was removed from Scone, and presented
to Westminster Abbey. Many of the government records found at
Edinburgh were also transported south.[13]

Edward was not content simply to receive Balliol's surrender. His
progress round Scotland saw many Scottish magnates and knights
coming before him to perform fealty. At the parliament held in Berwick, at
the end of August, a very great number of fealties were formally recorded.
Many of them had probably been collected by sheriffs and English
officials in the previous weeks.[14] Arrangements were made for the
future government of Scotland. John de Warenne was put in charge as
keeper, with the fat and unpopular Hugh de Cressingham as treasurer,
and Walter of Amersham as chancellor. Two escheators were named,
and justices were appointed. Galloway was entrusted to Henry Percy.
The new administration was established at Berwick, much more
convenient for the English than Edinburgh.[15] The first steps in the
rebuilding of Berwick after the sack of 1296 were taken when the king
himself ceremonially wheeled the first barrow-load of soil, soon after
the town came into English hands. Plans for the creation of what
amounted to a new English town of Berwick were discussed in parliament, in the autumn of 1296, and in the following January a meeting of
eminent townsmen was held at Harwich, to take the project further.
Some were appointed to go north to start work. Although the earthen
rampart was not topped by Edward with a stone wall as he planned,
Berwick was comparable, as an English colonial settlement, to the new
towns established by the king in Wales.[16]

There was much delight in England at the success of this, the first of
Edward's Scottish campaigns. A number of popular songs included in
Langtoft's chronicle provide evidence of this.[17] Some were perhaps
sung by the common soldiers: one celebrated the success of 'the foot
folk' at Dunbar. Others, in French, or a mixture of French and English,

[12] Barrow, *Robert Bruce*, 102–4; E.L.G. Stones and M.N. Blount, 'The surrender of
King John of Scotland to Edward I in 1296: some new evidence', *BIHR*, xlviii (1975),
94–106; M.C. Prestwich, 'The English campaign in Scotland in 1296 and the surrender
of John Balliol: some supporting evidence', *BIHR*, xlix (1976), 135–8.

[13] *Acts of the Parliaments of Scotland*, ed. T. Thomson and C. Innes (Edinburgh,
1814–75), i, preface, 8–9; *Instrumenta*, 11–12.

[14] Barrow, *Robert Bruce*, 107–9.

[15] Langtoft, ii, 258–60; *Rotuli Scotiae*, ed. D. Macpherson and others (1814–19), i,
24–37, gives fuller details of the appointments made.

[16] Beresford, *New Towns of the Middle Ages*, 3–5; *KW*, ii, 563–4.

[17] Langtoft, ii, 234–6, 244, 248, 252, 254–8, 260–4. For discussion of these poems,
see R.M. Wilson, *The Lost Literature of Medieval England* (1952), 207–12.

may have been intended for a knightly audience, or were perhaps
translated by the chronicler. They are not easy to put into modern
English, but one has been skilfully, if loosely, rendered:

> For those Scots,
> I rate 'em as sots,
>   What a sorry shower! .
> Whose utter lack
> In the attack
>   Lost 'em at Dunbar.[18]

Some, like songs from the First World War, were borrowed from their
enemies and given new words. There was much play with the way in
which the Scots had taunted Edward at Berwick in 1296 with 'Let him
pike, let him dyke', as the English prepared their earthworks. Through
such popular literature, much of it now lost (similar songs are not
recorded from Edward's later Scottish campaigns), some information
and, no doubt, much enthusiasm for the war were spread.

   Now that it was, apparently, conquered, Scotland could be regarded
in various ways. It might be viewed as a fief which had escheated to its
overlord, or as a country gained by right of conquest. The Lanercost
chronicler even claimed that it had come to Edward by hereditary
descent from Malcolm III's daughter Matilda, Henry I's queen.[19]
According to the official record of the Great Cause, the Scots gave their
fealty to Edward as 'true and immediate lord of Scotland', but whereas
in 1295, and in the early months of 1296, the phrase 'superior lord of the
Scottish kingdom' had been added to Edward's title in documents
concerning Scottish affairs, after the fall of Berwick no mention was
made of Scotland in the royal style, which was identical both north and
south of the border.[20] The nuns of Coldstream did refer to Edward in
one document as 'king of England and Scotland', but this was not a
usage adopted by the royal chancery.[21] It is surprising, in view of the
care taken to establish Edward's position at the time of the Great
Cause, that no definitive statement was produced regarding the status
of Scotland after Balliol's forced abdication. Later, when justifying his
position to the pope, in 1301, Edward merely stated 'that the realm of
Scotland was subjected by right of ownership to our power', and
claimed that he was in possession of the country 'by right of full
dominion'. By 1305 the English were no longer calling Scotland a

---

[18] E.L.G. Stones, 'English Chroniclers and the Affairs of Scotland, 1286–1296', *The
Writing of History in the Middle Ages*, ed. R.H.C. Davis and J.M. Wallace-Hadrill
(Oxford, 1981), 337.

[19] *Chron. Lanercost*, 179–80.

[20] *Great Cause*, ii, 292; *Rotuli Scotiae*, i, 21–2.

[21] *Documents*, ed. Stevenson, ii, 32.

kingdom, or realm: it was relegated to the status of a land, like
Ireland.[22] However, it was clear in 1296, when Balliol was removed
from the throne, that Edward had no intention of reopening the issues
of the Great Cause, and awarding the vacant Scottish throne to any of
the previous claimants.

The conquest of 1296 had been deceptively easy. In 1297 the English
faced widespread rebellion in Scotland. The nature of this rebellion has
been the subject of some debate. It has been seen, on the one hand, as 'a
general resumption of resistance on a national scale', with leadership
taken, for the most part, by those who had supported the Bruce cause
during the succession dispute.[23] On the other hand, it has been described as 'the spontaneous act of middling and common folk who
found their own leaders – Wallace and Murray, not Bruce and the
Stewart'.[24] While patriotism and personal ambition must have played
a major part in inspiring the rising, irrespective of whether it is viewed
as primarily aristocratic, or popular, it is also the case that it can be
seen as the Scottish counterpart to the secular opposition that Edward
faced at home in 1297. The demands that the king made for money,
goods and, above all, men must have been deeply resented in Scotland.

Edward did not try to impose direct taxes on the English model in
Scotland, but every effort was made to raise money there for the war
against Philip IV. Hugh Cressingham sent £5,188 6s 8d to the exchequer at Westminster at the end of May, but a month later the needs of
the administration in Scotland were such that £2,000 was sent from
Westminster to the north, as a loan.[25] The prise of wool was extended
into Scotland: how much was taken is not known, but fifty-five sacks
were seized from Melrose abbey.[26] The major grievance of the Scots
was Edward's intention to recruit soldiers on a large scale for the
Flanders campaign. In a statement of their position, made in July 1297,
the bishop of Glasgow, Robert Bruce earl of Carrick, the future king,
and James the Steward claimed that they had been told 'that the king
would have seized all the middle people of Scotland to send them
overseas in his war, to their great damage and destruction'.[27] Recruiting arrangements on a large scale were certainly set up on 24 May, and

[22] *Anglo-Scottish Relations*, ed. Stones, 107–8, 120. The translation does not take
account of the significance of the term *terre d'Escoce*.

[23] Barrow, *Robert Bruce*, 113.

[24] Duncan, 'The Community of the Realm of Scotland and Robert Bruce', 193.

[25] E 405/1/11; *Documents 1297–8*, 100, 104–5; *Documents*, ed. Stevenson, ii, 206; *CDS*,
v, no. 175.

[26] *Memoranda de Parliamento, 1305*, ed. Maitland, 184. *CDS*, ii, no. 922, also refers to
the prise.

[27] *Documents*, ed. Stevenson, ii, 198. The translation does not bring out the fact that it

although little came of them, Edward was able to obtain the service of a number of Scots in his campaign in Flanders, in return for their freedom from captivity.[28] Edward's policies, as carried out by Hugh Cressingham, were a major element in causing the Scots to rise in rebellion.

The spark which set off the powder was the action of William Wallace, a man of knightly family, though not himself a knight, who killed the sheriff of Lanark in May 1297. The bishop of Glasgow, the Steward, and the earl of Carrick joined the rising, but made a poor showing when faced by English troops at Irvine, under Percy and Clifford. They offered terms, and after lengthy negotiations, eventually submitted.[29] Nevertheless, the Scots under Wallace were placing the English under increasing pressure, forcing sheriffs and other officials to abandon their posts, and even in some counties, succeeding in appointing their own men. In the north, there was a highly effective rising under Andrew Murray.[30] The English lacked firm leadership, and could not find an effective means of dealing with the many problems that faced them. Earl Warenne had been given custody of Scotland by the king, who, according to an account written much later, declared coarsely, 'When you get rid of a turd, you do a good job.'[31] The earl lacked enthusiasm, and preferred to remain south of the border. He claimed, according to Guisborough, that the Scottish climate was bad for his health.

The indecision of the English was shown in July, when Cressingham raised a force in Northumberland, and would have marched north had it not been for Percy and Clifford, who claimed to have pacified all Scotland south of the Firth of Forth, and who argued that no expedition was needed. Debate followed, and it was decided to do nothing until Warenne arrived, 'and thus the business has gone to sleep, and each of us has returned to his billet'.[32] When Brian FitzAlan was approached to take over from Warenne, early in August 1297, he protested that he did not have the resources to undertake such a task: 'In my poverty, I

---

was to the French war that it was feared men would be sent, but this is clear from ibid., ii, 193.

[28] Lewis, 'The English forces in Flanders, 1297', 313; *CDS*, ii, nos 940, 942, 948. Some of the Scots slipped away from the English in Flanders, but were rebuffed by Philip IV, as the truce was in operation: *Langtoft*, ii, 310; Barrow, *Robert Bruce*, 137.

[29] *Documents*, ed. Stevenson, ii, 192–4, 198–200; Barrow, *Robert Bruce*, 119–20. Barrow argues that Bruce did not in fact submit to the English but *CDS*, iii, no. 524, suggests that the prior of Carlisle's recollection in 1316 was that he had come to the king's peace. This evidence is hardly conclusive.

[30] Barrow, *Robert Bruce*, 121–2.

[31] *Scalacronica*, ed. J. Stevenson (Edinburgh, 1836), 123.

[32] *Documents*, ed. Stevenson, ii, 203.

could not keep the land in peace to your profit and honour, when such a
lord as the earl cannot hold it in peace with what he receives from you.'[33]

When Warenne finally moved against the Scots, he met with disaster.
He marched from Berwick to Stirling, where Wallace and Murray had
gathered their men. Half-hearted mediation by the Steward and the
earl of Lennox was unsuccessful, and the English advanced across the
bridge over the Forth, to attack Wallace. The Scots, however, caught
the English army as it was crossing, so nullifying its advantage in
numbers. Those who had gone over to the north side of the Forth were
slaughtered. Cressingham, the treasurer, was killed, and his corpse
skinned by the exultant Scots. Some of the skin was said to have been
used to make a sword-belt for Wallace. Warenne, who had overslept
that morning, so delaying the English advance, had not crossed the
bridge, and was able to make his escape, in ignominy.[34] The English in
Scotland were utterly demoralized. Those who had settled in Berwick
fled, leaving the castle garrison isolated and surrounded. One brave
man, however, succeeded in swimming across the Tweed, carrying
letters in his hair asking for help. He found Warenne at Norham, and
returned, bringing messages of hope, to the beleaguered garrison.[35]

The Scots followed up their success with a fierce raid, plundering
Northumberland, and driving many of the inhabitants south. The
accounts for Bywell noted that rents could not be collected, because the
tenants had abandoned their holdings as a result of the arson and
robbery committed by the Scots. In the end, it was winter weather, not
English resistance, which forced Wallace's men back across the border.
The reality of war had been brought home to the English in a most
savage manner, though they could have taken some satisfaction from
the fact that none of their castles had fallen to the enemy.[36]

The defeat at Stirling Bridge brought about a change of attitude and
a new sense of determination among the English. The battle was fought
on 11 September. On 23 October levies of almost 30,000 infantry were
ordered, with the muster to take place on 6 December at Newcastle. A
prise of victuals was authorized early in November. It was not easy to
mount a major expedition at short notice, particularly since the royal
household was in Flanders: the household clerks usually played a
central role in the organization of the war. It was only in December that
contracts were agreed with Warenne, Norfolk, Hereford, Warwick,

[33] *Documents*, ed. Stevenson, ii, 223–4.
[34] Guisborough, 298–303; *Chron. Lanercost*, 190. For a fuller account of the battle, see
Barrow, *Robert Bruce*, 123–5.
[35] *Documents*, ed. Stevenson, ii, 228–9, where 'feet' is an obvious mistranslation, and
'hair' intended.
[36] Guisborough, 303–7; SC6/1126/12.

Gloucester and Henry Percy for three months service. It was highly unusual for earls to accept pay in this manner, but it may be that they required this inducement in the case of winter campaigns.[37] The only action before Christmas was a successful raid into Annandale, led by Robert Clifford. When the main English army, numbering at its peak some 18,500 men, advanced early in the new year, Roxburgh and Berwick were relieved with no difficulty. Further operations, however, were halted, for victuals were short, and orders came from Edward in Flanders, asking the earls to delay until he could lead the expedition in person.[38] Edward was hardly in a position to judge the situation. He was giving the Scots time to prepare, and wasting the resources that had been assembled for the winter campaign. On the other hand, the English had scarcely distinguished themselves in the absence of his leadership, and the king's decision was entirely understandable.

The royal campaign of 1298 was to culminate in the only major battle fought by Edward since his triumph at Evesham in 1265. Unfortunately, the detailed accounts of the royal household, which undoubtedly contained a great deal of information about the campaign, have not survived, though the main outlines of it are clear enough from other sources. The king held a council at York in April, at which the campaign was discussed. The Scottish magnates had been asked to attend: their failure to do so enabled Edward to brand them as public enemies. The king was taking his usual care to ensure that the war had full legal justification. He announced that his Scottish enemies would be deprived of their lands: such a policy of expropriation was new, and offered the English a chance of acquiring estates in Scotland. The exchequer was moved from London to York, so as to simplify the administration of the campaign.[39] The army was ordered to muster at Roxburgh on 25 June: the summons was not feudal in character, but there was a willing response to the request made to the magnates to fight in accordance with the fealty they owed to the king. The cavalry forces probably numbered some 3,000. Pay rolls show that in addition, Edward had about 10,900 Welsh infantry, and 14,800 English foot in his army. The host was an impressive one.[40]

The initial stages of the march northwards from the border were frustrating, as the army passed through territory deliberately wasted

[37] *CDS*, ii, no. 956; *CPR 1292–1301*, 314; H. Gough, *Scotland in 1298* (Paisley, 1888), 64–5; Prestwich, *War, Politics and Finance*, 68–9, 73.
[38] Guisborough, 307–8, 313–15; E 101/7/8; E 101/6/35; *Chron. Lanercost*, 191.
[39] Langtoft, ii, 313; Madox, *History of the Exchequer*, ii, 9.
[40] *Parl. Writs*, i, 309–12; E 101/12/17; Prestwich, *War, Politics and Finance*, 68–9, 87, 94–5.

by the Scots. Edward chose not to enter Edinburgh, but moved westwards, camping at Temple Liston in mid-July. Anthony Bek, with his
troops, was detached to capture Dirleton and two other castles near it.
He lacked the requisite equipment, and sent John FitzMarmaduke
back to Edward to ask for help. He had an uncomfortable interview.
The king suggested that Bek was displaying too much piety, and that
FitzMarmaduke should employ the savage cruelty for which Edward
had rebuked him in the past. No material assistance was offered by
Edward, but the arrival of three ships, laden with victuals, gave Bek
and his men new heart, and the castles were duly taken.[41]

The main army, meanwhile, was suffering from a lack of food
supplies, just as Bek's forces had done. The evidence suggests that no
elaborate preparations had been made to provide supplies: specific
instructions were issued only for grain to be collected in Lincolnshire
and Yorkshire, though royal clerks were in addition sent to Lancashire
and five southern counties, and the justiciar of Ireland was asked to
arrange for food to be sent to Carlisle. The constable of Edinburgh
castle received a shipment of 100 quarters of wheat, with ten casks of
wine, and ten of salt, on 24 July, but contrary winds meant that nothing
else was brought to the port of Leith until 19 August.[42] The summary of
the wardrobe account suggests that Edward had little naval support on
this campaign, a deficiency which would have created considerable
problems in supplying the army. Only £1,551 was spent on sailors'
wages, both in fetching the king back from Flanders, and on the
Scottish expedition.[43]

According to Walter of Guisborough, among the few supplies that
did reach Edward were 200 tuns of wine. This was promptly distri-
buted among the troops. The Welsh infantry, whose morale was very
low, became drunk, and rioted. The cavalry was used to drive them off,
killing eighty. Edward was unconcerned when the danger of their
joining with the Scots was pointed out to him, declaring that both
Welsh and Scots were his enemies, and that both would be defeated.
The king decided, however, that the only thing to do was to move back
to Edinburgh, to await the arrival of more supplies. News then came
that the Scottish army was not far away, encamped at Falkirk, preparing to attack. Edward did not hesitate. He ordered his men to arm, and
asked the merchants present to come with their supplies of food. The
host marched westward, and spent an uncomfortable night in the open,
near Linlithgow. Edward himself was slightly injured by his charger,
suffering two broken ribs. The alarm felt by the English troops was soon

[41] Guisborough, 324–5.
[42] *CPR 1292–1301*, 344; *CDS*, ii, no. 997.
[43] E 372/144, wardrobe account for 26 Edward I.

gone when he mounted, and led his troops through the streets of
Linlithgow on the dawn of 22 July. The army halted so that the king
and the bishop of Durham might hear mass, for it was St Mary
Magdalen's day. As the light cleared, they could see the Scots,
prepared for battle.

William Wallace, in command of the Scottish army, adopted highly
defensive tactics, massing his troops in four heavily armoured circles,
known as schiltroms. Each one bristled with iron-tipped spears; the
formations were kept in place by means of ropes tied to stakes driven
into the ground. Edward proposed a halt for food before fighting, but it
was argued that this was dangerous, and Bigod, Bohun and the earl of
Lincoln advanced, making a detour to avoid boggy ground. They took
a western approach: Anthony Bek moved in on the east. The two
English battalions converged on the Scottish schiltroms. The Scottish
cavalry, which had not been incorporated into the defensive formations, fled. The English then prised the schiltroms open: by one
account, this was the work of the infantry, achieved by means of
archery, and even stone-throwing, but another suggests that it was an
attack from the rear, presumably by cavalry, that was decisive. The
Welsh troops had been no more than bystanders for most of the battle,
waiting, no doubt, to see which way it would go. Once it was clear that
the English had the upper hand, they joined in the rout and slaughter.[44]

The battle was hard-fought. The English payroll suggests casualties
among the English infantry approaching 2,000, and although Brian de
Jay, master of the Temple, was the only knight to be killed on the
English side, it is known that 110 horses were slain, simply among the
cavalry in Edward's pay – there were probably two or three times as
many unpaid cavalry in the English army.[45] The Scottish casualties
were evidently horrific, though the flight of the cavalry meant that
relatively few nobles or knights were killed.[46] William Wallace escaped,
but though his life was saved, his military reputation was lost.

Edward followed up his success at Falkirk with a rapid march into
Fife, where by one account, he ordered that no destruction should take
place at St Andrews, out of respect for the saint. Perth, however, was
sacked, and the army then moved south-westwards towards Ayr.
Victualling was still a problem. Bills survive for food and drink bought
on credit at Stirling, totalling over £380 in value: the king was having to

[44] Guisborough, 325–8, provides the fullest account of the battle, but see also
Rishanger, 186–8, 385–7, 415. For a modern account, Barrow, *Robert Bruce*, 144–6.
[45] *CDS*, ii, nos. 1007, 1011; Prestwich, *War, Politics and Finance*, 95.
[46] The composition of the Scottish forces, and the number of casualties, is largely
unknown, but G.W.S. Barrow, 'Lothian in the First War of Independence', *SHR*, lv
(1976), 155–7, has shown that over forty, and probably over sixty, of the free tenants of
Coldingham fought with Wallace, and that many of them were killed at Falkirk.

rely on merchants following the army, rather than on his own supply train. At Ayr, ships from Ireland were expected, but none came, and Edward was compelled to retreat through Annandale. He obtained the surrender of Lochmaben castle, and then moved south to Carlisle, which was reached in September.[47] Edward wanted to continue the fight, realizing that the battle of Falkirk had not been decisive. Political problems, however, meant that he had to abandon his plans.

The Falkirk campaign had been a remarkable achievement in view of the precarious political situation in England, in the aftermath of the crisis of 1297. Before the expedition had set out, there had been difficulties, when Bigod and Bohun asked for sound guarantees that the king would adhere to the concessions he had made in the previous autumn. They agreed to take part in the campaign only when the bishop of Durham, with the earls of Surrey, Gloucester and Lincoln, swore, on Edward's behalf, that he would implement his promises if he were victorious against the Scots. The success at Falkirk, therefore, created tension between the king and the earls, for Edward gave no sign that he would confirm the concessions. Matters became worse when Edward acceded to a request from Thomas Bisset, an Antrim magnate, for a grant of the isle of Arran. Bigod and Bohun were outraged, claiming that Edward had promised that he would not act without taking their advice. When the army reached Carlisle, the earls asked to be excused further service, pleading the exhaustion of their men.[48]

Part of their stand had clearly been taken in their capacities as marshal and constable: in October 1298 Edward asked the exchequer officials to look up the rights and duties involved in these two offices. In reply, he received an unhelpful statement of the fees due to them as contained in a version of the *Constitutio Domus Regis* dating from Henry II's reign.[49] Precisely what the earls claimed is not known, but later documents suggest that they would have demanded a range of fees, such as 2d to the marshal out of every pound paid to the infantry, and 4d a week to the constable from all merchants and whores following the army. They had a claim to certain animals captured as booty, notably those without horns, and particoloured ones. Much more important than these curious rights were such duties as the organization of sentry duty, maintaining lists of those in the army, and receiving the proffers of feudal service. The marshal was in charge of discipline in the army, and had a right to attend councils of war, or so it was claimed.[50] There

---

[47] The Hagnaby chronicle, BL Vesp. B. xi, f.47; Guisborough, 328–9; E 404/1/2.

[48] Guisborough, 324, 328–9.

[49] E 368/70, m.22d; *CDS*, v, no. 186.

[50] Prestwich, *War, Politics and Finance*, 263n, discusses the rights and duties of the marshal and constable. A translation of the treatise on the marshal, from BL Cotton

had, of course, been arguments over these claims previously, and they had been an element in the debates in 1297. It was almost inevitable that the matter should continue to cause trouble.

After Bigod and Bohun departed, Edward proceeded to distribute the estates of his Scottish enemies to his followers. Annandale and Galloway were not given away, so as not to infuriate the earls further, but many grants were made. Unfortunately, details of only a few survive, but it is known that the earl of Warwick received the estates of three important Scots. Robert de Tony was given the lands of another three, and Robert Clifford obtained Caerlaverock castle. The earl of Lincoln was granted the position and lands of James the Steward of Scotland, including the barony of Renfrew. Guisborough commented, however, that many of the grants were made 'in hope', and in very many cases the English recipients were in no position to take advantage of their king's generosity, as the Scots were still in effective possession of the lands.[51]

Edward was in no doubt that the success at Falkirk needed to be followed up with a campaign in the following year. Writs of summons were issued as early as 24 September 1298 for a muster at Carlisle in the early summer of the next year, and much more elaborate victualling arrangements were made than had been the case in 1298. However, political dissension over the question of the confirmation of the charters, together with the negotiations with the French which culminated in Edward's marriage to Philip IV's sister Margaret in September 1299, meant that no campaign took place. The English garrisons that had been left in Scotland were placed under increasing pressure from the Scots. Caerlaverock fell, and its new Scottish garrison had some initial success against the English forces at Lochmaben, until their leader was killed in a skirmish. Most serious was the plight of Stirling, where some ninety men were blockaded, facing starvation.[52]

In November 1299 Edward took a bold decision, to mount a winter campaign in Scotland. The move proved to be unwise. The king did not have the backing of the magnates, and of 16,000 infantry summoned to muster at Berwick in mid-December, only 2,500 actually appeared, to desert *en masse* within a few days. The only wages paid to cavalry noted in the accounts were those to a force of less than forty men, serving for a

---

MS Nero D. vi, is given by F. Grose, *Military Antiquities* (2nd edn, 1801), 193–7. See also above, 420.

[51] Barrow, *Robert Bruce*, 147; Bodleian Library MS Dodsworth 70, f.64; *CDS*, ii, no. 1121; *CDS*, vi, no. 188. See also M.C. Prestwich, 'Colonial Scotland', in *Scotland and England 1286–1815*, ed. R.A. Mason (Edinburgh, 1987), 8.

[52] *Parl. Writs*, i, 317–18; *CPR 1292–1301*, 388–9; *CCR 1296–1302*, 219; *CDS*, ii, no. 1101, 1119.

mere nine days, under John de St John. The Scots assembled in force, offering battle to the English, but Edward had insufficient troops to meet the challenge, and had to return south. Stirling fell to the Scots, a prime prize, commanding as it did the obvious route to the north.[53]

An earl, unfortunately not named in the 'Annals of England and Scotland', where the story is found, advised Edward strongly against a winter campaign, pointing out the dangers of pursuing the enemy into unknown territory. He recommended a summer expedition, and this was the course that Edward duly adopted in 1300.[54]

The army that Edward led into Galloway in the summer of 1300 is one of the best-documented of the period, and it is therefore worth examining its composition in some detail. The summons, issued at the end of December 1299, asked for the muster at Carlisle of the feudal service of the realm.[55] The roll recording the response to this request shows that the unpaid service of forty knights and 366 sergeants was provided, two of the latter being counted as equivalent to one knight. Service of this type was something of an anachronism, though only in the case of Hugo FitzHeyr did it become ridiculous. He was obliged by the terms of his tenure to serve with a bow and an arrow, and the record notes that as soon as he saw the Scots, he duly fired his arrow, and departed. Only three men of magnate status, the earl of Gloucester, Hugh le Despenser and John Hastings, actually performed their feudal service in person: the majority of great men appear simply to have detached some members of their retinue to do it on their behalf, even when they were themselves present on the campaign.[56] The writ of summons recognized the inadequacy of the old feudal quotas, for the magnates were asked in them to provide in addition as many men-at-arms as they felt they could. The extent of such voluntary service can only be guessed, but a comparison of the list of bannerets provided by the *Song of Caerlaverock*, with the household pay records, suggests that over sixty men with their retinues, which averaged perhaps ten or fifteen men-at-arms, fitted into this category.[57]

The royal household, of course, provided a substantial number of cavalry troops. A list of horses belonging to members of the household, with valuations, was drawn up at the start of the campaign, so as to

---

[53] Prestwich, *War, Politics and Finance*, 95; *CCR 1296–1302*, 379, 382.

[54] Rishanger, 402–3.

[55] *Parl. Writs*, i, 327.

[56] The roll is printed in *Documents and Records illustrating the History of Scotland*, ed. F. Palgrave (1837), 209–31. For some further discussion, see M.C. Prestwich, 'Cavalry Service in Early Fourteenth Century England', *War and Government in the Middle Ages*, ed. Gillingham and Holt, 147–9.

[57] Ibid., 148; Prestwich, *War, Politics and Finance*, 69–70.

simplify the task of paying compensation to anyone whose horse was killed, or died, in the course of the campaign. This shows that 522 household men were in pay. In addition, there were those temporarily retained in household service. If their numbers are added, the total of the household cavalry comes to some 850 men.[58] Among these there would have been those who possessed at least £40 worth of land, who were all invited by the king to serve him for pay.[59] Wage rates did not alter during Edward's reign: earls received eight shillings a day, bannerets four shillings, knights two shillings and men-at-arms, or sergeants, one shilling. It seems unlikely that these rates reflected the real cost of military service: a more realistic figure is suggested by agreements made by military contractors to provide the feudal service owed by ecclesiastics, which show that it cost £100 to provide five knights for forty days, or ten shillings a day each.[60] The crown did not make contracts with men for summer campaigns: the precise size of each contingent was carefully worked out, and payment made, or at least promised, by means of a bill or debenture, at fairly regular intervals.[61]

In the field, the cavalry forces were divided into four main units, which might be termed battalions or squadrons. The first was commanded by the earl of Lincoln, the second by earl Warenne, the third (consisting largely of the household men) by the king himself, and the fourth was under the nominal leadership of the king's son Edward (then aged sixteen), though in practice it was in the hands of John de St John.[62] It is not clear whether all those performing feudal service remained together, or whether, as seems more likely, they were integrated into the army as a whole. Within each battalion, there were perhaps fifteen or twenty bannerets, each in command of a retinue of knights and squires. Retinues varied in size considerably, but the accounts for this 1300 campaign suggest an average of about thirteen.[63] With each retinue, there would of course have been a few grooms and servants, and additional horses for the soldiers.

The infantry were recruited by special commissioners of array from Nottinghamshire, Derbyshire and the four most northerly counties for the 1300 campaign. A total of 16,000 men was requested, but in fact, only about 9,000 mustered at Carlisle. No Welsh were called for on this occasion. Edward wrote that 'we have given them leave to remain at

---

[58] Ibid., 52. The horse list is E 101/8/ 23.

[59] *Parl. Writs*, i, 330.

[60] Prestwich, 'Cavalry Service in Early Fourteenth Century England', 149.

[61] Prestwich, *War, Politics and Finance*, 160–1.

[62] The formation of the army is clear from the Song of Caerlaverock, printed in *The Siege of Carlaverock*, ed. Nicolas.

[63] Prestwich, *War, Politics and Finance*, 66.

home, because of all the great work which they have done in our service
in the past', but it must be suspected that he had bitter memories of
their behaviour on the Falkirk expedition.[64] The foot were organized in
units of a hundred, each commanded by a mounted sergeant. Within
these units, they were grouped in twenties. The rate of pay for an
ordinary infantryman was 2d a day. His equipment, such as it was,
would either be his own, or have been provided by his locality. The
crown was not greatly concerned to ensure that the footmen were
adequately provided with bows and arrows, or other weapons: their
real worth in battle would not be appreciated until Edward I I I's reign.
Desertion was a constant problem: in the course of August 1300, the
number of infantry in the army fell by about half.[65]

Naval support was essential for a successful campaign, not because
the Scots presented any real threat at sea, but so that supplies could be
taken to the army in reasonable quantities. In 1300, the task of obtaining ships was simplified by the fact that the Cinque Ports were obliged
to provide service when a feudal summons was issued. Edward stated
that he would be content with half the traditional number of ships,
fifty-seven, provided that those that came were manned by double
crews. In fact, thirty ships were provided by the Ports, with a total
complement of 1,106. Their period of service lasted only two weeks,
after which they were taken into pay by the crown. Some fifteen other
English vessels, of no great size, were also employed, along with two
substantial galleys, each with a crew of about fifty, provided by Simon
de Montacute. Eight Irish ships were also used. For the most part the
ships ferried supplies from Skinburness, the port for Carlisle, into
Galloway, but some transported goods across the Irish sea, and one,
the *St George* of Dartmouth, was used to carry siege engines.[66]

The task of providing sufficient supplies for the army was a major
one, eased to a certain extent in 1300 by the fact that there were some
stocks left over from the previous year. In January 7,000 quarters of
wheat, 8,000 quarters of oats, 4,300 quarters of malt and 1,000 quarters
of beans and peas were requested, largely from the east and north.
These supplies were to be taken to Berwick: 3,000 quarters of wheat,
2,000 of oats and 300 tuns of wine were to be brought to Carlisle from
Ireland. The response to these demands was, on the whole, very
satisfactory, though the quality of some of the Irish grain aroused

---

[64] Ibid., 95–6; E 159/73, m.16. See above, 481, for Falkirk.

[65] Prestwich, *War, Politics and Finance*, 105–7. The numbers of infantry employed in
the wars declined with each campaign, but their quality may have improved.

[66] Ibid., 143, 145; *Liber Quotidianus*, 271–9. The importance of the fleet to Edward is
stressed by W. Stanford Reid, 'Sea-Power in the Anglo-Scottish War, 1296–1328',
Mariner's Mirror, xlvi (1960), 7–13.

protests. Edward had stressed that 'if victuals fail on the king's planned expedition to Scotland, he will be delivered into the hands of his enemies or return dishonoured'.[67] The average price paid, or more often promised, by the royal purveyors for wheat was 4s 5d a quarter, but it was then sold to the soldiers at prices varying from 5s to 10s. This meant that whereas the total cost of purchasing victuals was £5,063, receipts from sales came to £7,290.[68] More significant than the financial costs was the immense labour that went into the collection of the supplies, with sheriffs and their underlings scouring the country for goods, organizing transport, by water wherever possible, to local collection points, from where they would be taken north, to be stored under the supervision of royal clerks at Berwick or Carlisle.

The force that mustered at Carlisle early in July 1300 was not as large as the army of 1298, but it still made an impressive sight. The poet who wrote the 'Song of Caerlaverock' described the elaborate trappings of the knights, made from richly embroidered fine cloth, and the magnificent banners displayed on the lances. The baggage train, with pack horses and waggons carrying provisions and equipment, seemed to fill the countryside. When the army encamped, there was a splendid array of tents, some white, some made of coloured cloth, their floors strewn with fresh flowers. Trees were cut down to make huts for those who were not provided with tents.[69] The poet, having described the coats of arms of the bannerets in the army, and praised their virtues, went on to consider their heroic deeds. Unfortunately, the 1300 campaign was singularly lacking in dramatic action, and all he had to describe was the siege of Caerlaverock castle, which the chronicler Langtoft sardonically, and a little unfairly, described as a poor *chastelet*, or small fortification.[70] The poet, giving his imagination a fairly free rein, recounted the successive assaults of knights and men-at-arms on the castle. None was successful: in the end, it was one of the engineers, with a siege engine, who brought about the downfall of the Scots garrison, for they could not endure the battering from the heavy stones lobbed into the courtyard, where they shattered into sharp, lethal flying fragments.[71]

According to another account of the siege, the garrison offered to

---

[67] *CPR 1292–1301*, 487–8; Prestwich, *War, Politics and Finance*, 122–4; *CDS*, v, 218.

[68] *Liber Quotidianus*, 7–15, 136.

[69] *Siege of Carlaverock*, ed. Nicolas, 2–4, 64.

[70] Langtoft, ii, 326.

[71] *Siege of Carlaverock*, ed. Nicolas, 82–6. Johnstone, *Edward of Caernarvon*, 51, assumes that the castle was undermined by the English, but the fact that a small number of miners were in Edward's army hardly proves this. The swampy character of the ground at Caerlaverock, and the fact that the castle was surrounded by a wet moat, effectively prevented mining operations.

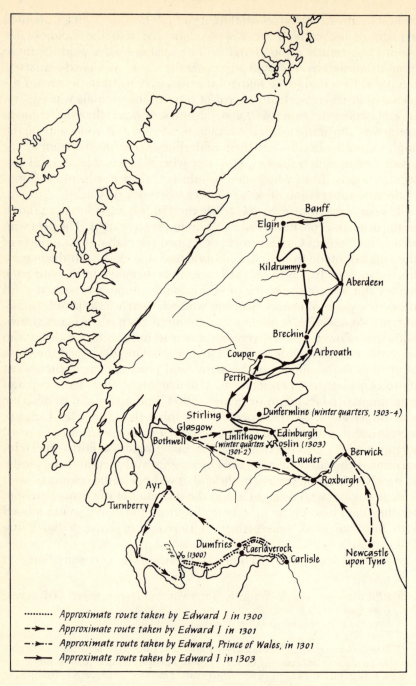

Banff

Elgin

Kildrummy

Aberdeen

Brechin

Arbroath

Coupar

Perth

Stirling

Dunfermline (winter quarters, 1303-4)

Glasgow

Linlithgow
(winter quarters
1301-2)

Edinburgh

Bothwell

×Roslin (1303)

Lauder

Berwick

Roxburgh

Ayr

Turnberry

Tree

(1300)

Dumfries

Caerlaverock

Carlisle

Newcastle
upon Tyne

.... Approximate route taken by *Edward I in 1300*
—▶— Approximate route taken by *Edward I in 1301*
—▶— Approximate route taken by *Edward, Prince of Wales, in 1301*
——▶ Approximate route taken by *Edward I in 1303*

6. Edward I's Invasions of Scotland, 1300, 1301 and 1303

surrender at the outset of the proceedings, provided that they were allowed to take all their possessions, and were not harmed in life or limb. Edward was furious, 'like a lioness whose cubs are taken from her', and ordered a full-scale attack on the castle. When a breach was forced in the walls, some of the garrison were probably hanged, but the constable and eleven others were sent to Newcastle where they were imprisoned.[72] Edward's actions contrast unfavourably with those of the Scots, who had earlier brought the starving garrison of Stirling to Berwick, where they were handed over to the English. Some of the Stirling garrison, indeed, were to form a special bodyguard for Edward.[73]

From Caerlaverock, which is not very far from the border, the great host marched westwards. Futile negotiations took place with representatives of the Scots, who demanded the return of Balliol and restoration of the lands taken from Scottish magnates. Edward was angry at such requests, and the campaign proceeded. A skirmish took place near the estuary of the Cree. A foraging party was surprised by the Scots, but in an effective counter-attack, the Scottish marshal, Robert Keith, was captured. A little later, on 8 August, the main English army reached the estuary. At low tide, some of the English archers crossed and began to engage the Scots. Edward's battalion advanced, as did Warenne's, but when the Scots began to organize themselves for battle, the king asked the earl of Hereford to withdraw the infantry who had crossed the river. They, however, thought that the earl was bringing reinforcements, and attacked the Scots with increased vigour. The king ordered his men, and Warenne's, to charge, and the Scots fled, 'like hares before greyhounds', as the chronicler put it. The greyhounds, unfortunately, were not as used to the terrain as the hares, and Scottish losses were largely confined to baggage and equipment. It was a matter of regret to the English that they had no Welsh infantry with them, for they were skilled at clambering through rough country, which was unsuited to cavalry.[74]

It was becoming increasingly difficult, as August proceeded, for Edward to keep his army together. The infantry deserted in thousands. On one occasion, a Scot who pretended to be on the English side led some 200 troops into an ambush, but the English counter-attack proved successful. Otherwise, there was little action, and many of the magnates abandoned what they rightly regarded as an increasingly

---

[72] Rishanger, 440; *CDS*, ii, no. 1162; *Chron. Lanercost*, 194. *Siege of Carlaverock*, ed. Nicolas, 86, suggests in contrast that the garrison were all spared, and that each was given a new robe by the king. The wardrobe accounts indicate no such generosity.

[73] Rishanger, 402; BL Add. MS 7966a, f.40.

[74] Rishanger, 440–2.

futile expedition. The payrolls show many retinues considerably below strength by early September. Edward was eventually persuaded to abandon the campaign, and it was a disappointed king who returned to Carlisle. In October he set out for Dumfries, with a small force, to see to the fortifications there, returning again to Carlisle early in November.[75] It was probably when he was at Dumfries that he at last agreed on a truce, to last until the following Whitsun. In the course of the negotiations, Edward apparently threatened the Scots, declaring that he proposed to lay waste to their country from sea to sea: the war was one he was determined to win.

The war was fought on the diplomatic front, as well as on the moors and hills of Scotland. The Scots had hopes of support from Philip IV of France, and from the papacy. In the aftermath of Edward I's campaign in Flanders in 1297, Philip did not abandon John Balliol as completely as the English king abandoned his Flemish allies. There was an important Scottish presence at the French court in 1298, and although Philip was cautious when presented with a demand for military aid, he made clear his support for Balliol's cause. One result of Philip's attitude was the transfer of John Balliol from English custody to a papal representative in 1299.[76] Edward I must have been nervous about the possibility of more active backing for the Scottish cause. In the autumn of 1300, two French envoys played a major part in negotiating the truce between the English and the Scots.[77]

The Scots had considerable success in arguing their case in the papal curia. In June 1299, thanks to their efforts, Boniface VIII drew up a powerful rebuke to Edward. This began with a remarkable claim that Scotland belonged to the Roman church, and was not feudally subject to the English king. Reference was made to letters, which are not known from any other source, issued by Henry III and Edward himself, which acknowledged Alexander III's assistance in the conflict with Simon de Montfort, and conceded that the Scottish king was present at Edward's coronation by grace, rather than by right. Very interestingly, this bull lent no support to Balliol's cause: he was merely referred to as 'the man to whom you are said to have committed the kingdom'.[78] The pope was obviously influenced by a very different faction among the Scots from that which had influence in the French court.

The papal bull took a remarkably long time to reach England. It was

[75] Ibid., 144–6; *Liber Quotidianus*, 195–210. Edward blamed the officials responsible for recruiting infantry, as well as the men themselves, for the desertions; *CDS*, v, no. 226.

[76] Barrow, *Robert Bruce*, 134–5; *CDS*, ii, 535–6 (this letter was written on 6 April 1299, not 1302, as the editor suggests).

[77] *Foedera*, I, ii, 924–5.

[78] *Anglo-Scottish Relations*, ed. Stones, 81–7.

probably held back by Boniface until it became clear that Edward had not given up his plans for the conquest of Scotland. It was brought to Edward by Archbishop Winchelsey, who was threatened by the pope with suspension from office should he fail to do so. Winchelsey did not relish his task. He was alarmed at the dangers of travelling through hostile Galloway, and found food supplies hard to come by. When news reached him that Edward had reached Sweetheart Abbey on his return journey, Winchelsey undertook what he considered to be a terrifying journey across the Solway estuary at low tide, through quicksands. His interview with the king was delayed for a day, and he then faced the difficult task of reading out the bull to the king and the assembled magnates, and then explaining it fully in French. He was heard out patiently, and the question of an answer was then discussed.

An initial response was easy: in such a matter, full consultation was required, and as many prelates and nobles were not there, a full answer would have to wait until parliament was assembled.[79] Nevertheless, preliminary steps were taken to answer the charges. An embassy, headed by the earl of Lincoln and Hugh Despenser, was sent to Rome in November 1300. Their main purpose was to deal with the Anglo-French dispute, but one chronicle records a letter, written in an unusually rhetorical style, which, so it is claimed, they presented to the pope. It laid stress on the homage to Edward performed by the Scots, and on the rising of 1297 against him. It does not attempt to counter the papal arguments, and reads more like propaganda produced for domestic use than a genuine letter sent to Rome.[80]

The problems facing Edward in replying to the papal bull were set out in a memorandum prepared by one of Winchelsey's officials, William of Sardinia. He presented seven possible courses of action, ranging from a full acceptance of the papal suggestion that the whole issue be submitted to the curia for judgement, to an outright refusal to make any response at all. There were problems and dangers in all possible options, and an envoy sent to Rome might, 'after clever and subtle questions put by the pope, go beyond his instructions, and perhaps say things which are prejudicial'.[81] The king went to considerable trouble in preparing his case. Cathedral and monastic archives were to be searched, to discover evidence of Edward's right to Scotland. Andrew Tange investigated the royal records, and prepared a copy of the 'Ragman Roll', the record of the acts of homage and fealty done to Edward by the Scots in 1296. Representatives from Oxford and

[79] *Ann. London*, 105–8.

[80] Rishanger, 451–3; *Great Cause*, i, 155. There is no enrolled copy of this letter in the English government records, a fact which must cast doubt on its authenticity.

[81] *Anglo-Scottish Relations*, ed. Stones, 88–95.

Cambridge, skilled in Roman law, were summoned to the Lincoln parliament, held in January 1301.[82]

At the Lincoln parliament, two replies to the pope were prepared. One took the form of a letter from the English barons, but was probably written by royal clerks. It stated the English right to superior lordship quite briefly, and rejected the idea that the king should answer the pope regarding his claims in Scotland, for the matter concerned the hereditary rights of the crown, and the dignity of the king.[83] Whether this letter was actually sent to Boniface is not known. The household accounts do not record any envoy being sent with it, and it is possible that it was decided that a document which enjoyed no support from the prelates did not carry sufficient weight. It was, however, widely circulated in England, to judge by its inclusion in a number of chronicles.[84]

The king's reply to the pope was lengthy. It provided a full historical justification for the English claim over Scotland, starting with the landing of Brutus in England, then called Albion, after the fall of Troy. The service done by one Angusel king of Scots to King Arthur at a great feast at Caerleon is among the historical 'proofs' of English overlordship that are cited. The argument concludes with Balliol's surrender of Scotland to Edward, and the homage and fealty performed by the Scots to the English king, as 'the immediate and proper lord of the realm of Scotland'. Edward argued that he could not do anything to prejudice the established fact that Scotland was his 'by reason of property and possession'. The essential purpose of the letter was not to provide a justification of Edward's claims in Scotland. Rather, it was intended to explain to the pope why it was not proper that Edward should submit any such claim to his adjudication. The letter was sent 'altogether extrajudicially', and was 'not to be treated in the form or manner of a legal plea'.[85] There was a delay in sending it, probably because it was considered worth waiting for the outcome of negotiations with French envoys. When it was clear that these had failed, the letter was entrusted to two royal emissaries, Thomas Wale and Thomas Delisle, on 15 May 1301.[86] Before anything could be achieved by these diplomatic means, Edward had embarked on another attempt to impose his will on the Scots by force.

*   *   *

---

[82] *Great Cause*, i, 154–5; BL Add. MS 7966a, f.30.

[83] *Foedera*, I, ii, 926–7; Rishanger, 208–9; Guisborough, 344–5. The letter was sealed by seven earls and sixty-four barons, but it is not clear that all were present at Lincoln, as a clerk was later sent round to have additional seals affixed to the document: Powell and Wallis, *History of the House of Lords*, 244–5.

[84] Stones, 'The mission of Thomas Wale and Thomas Delisle', 25.

[85] *Anglo-Scottish Relations*, ed. Stones, 96–109; *Foedera*, I, ii, 932–3.

[86] Stones, 'The mission of Thomas Wale and Thomas Delisle', 9.

Edward's plans for the 1301 campaign were much more ambitious than those he had adopted in the past. Rather than one army advancing into Scotland, two were to invade. The king himself would advance from Berwick, while another host, nominally under the charge of his young son Edward, but in practice commanded by the earl of Lincoln, was to march into Scotland from Carlisle. The summonses were issued in February and March, with musters fixed for 24 June. There were some 1,000 paid cavalry in the two armies, and as usual, many magnates must have provided voluntary service, even though there was no request for feudal quotas this year. There were some problems in recruiting infantry, for in mid-July commissions were set up to investigate cases where men had bribed the arrayers so that they might be allowed to remain at home. Nevertheless, some 7,500 foot mustered at Berwick, with more, to judge by the sum paid out in wages, at Carlisle.[87] The prince's army was reinforced by a substantial contingent of Irish troops under the justiciar, John Wogan.[88]

The campaign was not an eventful one, for the Scots had learned to be cautious, and to avoid battle. Edward's own army was not intended to play the major role in the campaign: it was the king's vain hope that the chief honour of defeating the Scots would be won by his son.[89] The royal host advanced from Berwick along the line of the Tweed, reaching Coldstream by 21 July. From there, they went via Kelso and Traquair to Peebles. Some units then went to Edinburgh, but the main army pushed on to Glasgow, which was reached by 23 August. There, preparations were made for an attack on Bothwell castle. This was one of the most splendid of Scottish castles, with a great circular *donjon*, very probably modelled on that at Coucy, in France. A great movable wooden siege tower, known as a belfry, was built by carpenters, and covered with thick hides as a protection against fire. This was taken, presumably dismantled, on thirty carts to Bothwell, which was besieged in September. There are, unfortunately, no narratives of the siege, but the belfry was presumably effective in giving the English entry to the castle when it was wheeled up to the walls. Bothwell was in English hands by 24 September, and Edward then moved to winter quarters at Linlithgow.[90]

The movements of the prince's army are not so easy to work out. One

---

[87] *Parl. Writs*, i, 347–59; *CPR 1292–1301*, 601–2; Prestwich, *War, Politics and Finance*, 97.

[88] J.F. Lydon, 'Irish Levies in the Scottish Wars, 1296–1302', *The Irish Sword*, v (1962), 207–17. The force consisted of 8 bannerets, 14 knights, 242 squires, 391 hobelars and 1,617 foot.

[89] *CDS*, ii, no. 1191.

[90] Details of the campaign are provided by the wardrobe account book, BL Add. MS 7966a. See in particular ff.2, 18, 116v, for the king's itinerary, and the belfry.

view has it that his march reached no further than Loch Ryan, but a victualling memorandum suggests that before he got there, he had been to Ayr and Turnberry. There is evidence that members of his force lost horses in late August and early September at both these places, while one entry in an account book suggests that Ayr was reached as early as July.[91] It seems most likely that instead of taking the coastal route, along which Edward's army had proceeded so slowly in the previous year, the prince and his men struck straight for the Firth of Clyde, probably through Nithsdale. From there they moved to attack Turnberry: the king had received the good news of the capture of the castle there by 2 September, when he gave oblations accordingly in Glasgow cathedral.[92] Instead of joining forces with his father, the prince then led his army south to Carlisle, via Loch Ryan, before joining the king at Linlithgow for the winter.[93]

Whether it had ever been intended to link the two armies up in a pincer movement is far from clear. What Edward hoped for in October was to complete a bridge over 'the Scottish Sea', by which he meant the Firth of Forth. If he had succeeded in this, 'we would have achieved such a success against our enemies, that our business in these parts would have been brought to a satisfactory and honourable conclusion in a short time.'[94] A payment made for the transport of a siege engine from Bothwell towards Stirling suggests that the king wanted to recapture Stirling castle from the Scots, but this proved impracticable so late in the year.[95] Lack of money, resulting in non-payment of troops, led to desertion on a considerable scale. Edward hoped to keep a number of magnates with him, by entering into contracts with them, and he hoped to keep a force of 3,500 infantry in pay.[96] In November, fresh levies of footsoldiers were ordered, to muster in January, but these plans were soon cancelled. A major campaign was still in prospect for 1302, as writs setting out victualling arrangements show, but by 26 January all had changed, and Edward agreed to a truce until November 1302.[97]

Lack of money, and other difficulties encountered at Linlithgow, where many of the horses died for want of fodder, contributed to Edward's decision to agree to the truce.[98] The main reasons, however,

[91] Barrow, *Robert Bruce*, 171; *CDS*, ii, no. 1233; BL Add. MS 7966a, f. 18.
[92] Ibid., f.18.
[93] Johnstone, *Edward of Caernarvon*, 77–80. This is the most satisfactory account of the campaign.
[94] E 159/75, m.7; *CDS*, v, no. 262.
[95] E 101/359/6, f.18v.
[96] E 159/75, mm.6, 10; *CDS*, ii, no. 1241.
[97] *Parl. Writs*, i, 361–2; *CCR 1296–1301*, 574; *CDS*, ii, no. 1282.
[98] Rishanger, 210; the letters calendared in *CDS*, v, nos 260–3, testify to the king's financial problems.

concerned the international situation. The mission of Thomas Delisle and Thomas Wale to the pope, bearing the letter prepared at the Lincoln parliament, had achieved little. The envoys had found three entries in papal registers which they considered useful, but their interviews with the pope, although conducted in a most friendly atmosphere, achieved nothing positive. Boniface, perhaps taking a leaf out of Edward's own book, told them that nothing final could be done without full consultation, and that this was not possible at present, particularly in view of his state of health.[99]

The Scots were, of course, also active at the papal curia. Master Baldred Bisset, with two colleagues, argued very effectively on behalf of the community of the Scottish realm. A report to Edward reveals the arguments which the Scots directed against the position that the English had adopted. The absence of any real proof for Edward's claims was castigated, and the Scots claimed that as the English had falsely stated that Edward was in full possession of Scotland, their whole case was discredited. An alternative historical narrative to Edward's was produced, which traced the history of the Scots back to an Egyptian Pharaoh's daughter, Scota, her husband Gayl, and their implausibly named son Erk. If any homage had been done by Scottish kings, it was only for lands that they held in England. Five proofs were offered to show that Scotland was free: papal privilege, common law, prescription, past history, and the evidence of muniments and texts.[100]

In the opinion of Robert Bruce's most recent biographer, 'Bisset and his colleagues carried the day at Rome'.[101] This view is based on the growing respect accorded to John Balliol by the papacy, and the release of the former king of Scots into Philip IV's hands in the summer of 1301. It does not, however, appear to be the case that Bisset had been aiming to have Balliol restored to the throne: what he had been arguing for was agreement to submit the Anglo-Scottish dispute to papal arbitration. That he did not achieve, and the position at the curia is better described in terms of a stalemate than of a Scottish success.

More important than the dealings at Rome were those with the French. The list of English negotiators who met with French envoys at Canterbury early in 1301, stands in striking contrast, in terms of power and importance, to the two knights, Wale and Delisle, who had been sent to Rome: it consisted of the earls of Surrey and Warwick, Aymer de Valence, John de St John and Hugh de Vere. It was French pressure, rather than Scottish, that achieved the release of John Balliol into Philip IV's hands, and it was through French intervention that the

---

99 Stones, 'The Mission of Thomas Wale and Thomas Delisle', 8–27.
100 *Anglo-Scottish Relations*, ed. Stones, 110–17.
101 Barrow, *Robert Bruce*, 168.

truce was agreed at the end of January 1302. The negotiations took place in France, at Asnières, with the lead probably being taken by Walter Langton on the English side, and the great lawyer Pierre Flote on the French. A private conversation between these two able and cynical men would have been interesting indeed. The negotiators could reach no agreement on the question of Balliol, who the French insisted was the rightful king of Scots, but they agreed to differ on this, and the truce was conceded.[102] Philip IV had not been prepared to send troops to assist the Scots, but he used his position skilfully to try to prevent an English victory.

One consequence of the partial recovery of Balliol's cause was the decision, at some point in the winter of 1301–2, of Robert Bruce, the future king of Scots, to come over to the English. Bruce had been on the Scottish side since 1297, although either late in 1299 or early in 1300 he resigned from his position as one of the Guardians. He was still actively opposing the English in Galloway in 1301, but then succeeded in negotiating terms with Edward. These terms are tantalizingly imprecise. Bruce and his men were not to be imprisoned. If a papal ordinance, truce or peace should adversely affect Bruce's tenure of his estates, Edward promised him compensation. The king agreed to try to maintain Bruce's inheritance intact, and granted him the wardship of the son of the earl of Mar. Then, the document recording the agreement set out what would happen if Scotland were returned to Balliol, or *le droit* (the right) reversed in a new judgement. Edward agreed that Bruce could then pursue his 'right', and offered a fair hearing in his court. If the 'right' was to be adjudicated in some other court, Edward promised assistance. These terms are open to differing interpretations. One view is that *le droit* included the Bruce claim to the Scottish throne, the other that it amounted to no more than the right to the earldom of Carrick and the family estates of the Bruces.

The ideal situation envisaged in the document is one in which Scotland was at peace in Edward's hands, and it is inconceivable that the king would have readily considered granting the Scottish crown to one who had only just come to terms with him. On the other hand, Edward may, it has been suggested, have been prepared to give Bruce backing, in the event of the French, or the papacy, restoring Balliol. It is possible that the vagueness of the text was deliberate. For Bruce, it would not have been easy to separate the various claims he had, to lands and titles, and the imprecise terminology of *le droit* might well have been seen as embracing everything from the claim to the throne of Scotland down to his right to the hereditary Bruce lands. Edward, there

---

[102] For these negotiations, see *Foedera*, I, ii, 924–5, 931, 937, 942; *Treaty Rolls*, i, 149–52.

can be little doubt, would have seen Bruce's 'right' in a more restricted light. It was only in the circumstances 'which God forbid', of Edward losing control of Scotland, that he promised to support Bruce's claims. While Edward held Scotland, all Bruce was to receive was 'his own estates, of which he is now seized in Scotland'.[103]

With the truce in force throughout the summer of 1302, no English campaign was possible. A battle of the greatest importance affecting Edward's cause did, however, take place, though not on Scottish soil. This was the defeat of the French at the hands of the Flemings, at Courtrai. After this disaster, Philip concentrated his attentions upon Flanders. He was no longer concerned to assist John Balliol, and became, at long last, ready to make a final peace with Edward I. The Scots tried hard to maintain their alliance with the French. A powerful embassy was sent to Paris, but they found, as Edmund of Lancaster had done in 1294, that Philip IV's word was not to be trusted. When the French came to terms with Edward I in 1303, Philip apparently assured the Scots that they had no need to be concerned over the fact that Scotland was not included in the treaty. It had seemed best to do things that way, and he implied that a further treaty would cover their needs, but none was forthcoming. The Scots were deserted, and Edward I was free to act.[104] Even Boniface VIII had abandoned his limited support for the Scots: in 1302 he had accused the bishop of Glasgow of stirring up trouble between England and Scotland, and he encouraged the Scottish bishops to come to terms with Edward.[105]

During the period of truce, in 1302, the English had maintained their presence in Scotland, with substantial garrisons in Berwick, Roxburgh, Jedburgh, Edinburgh, Linlithgow, Dumfries and Lochmaben provided by the crown. An experiment was tried, by which the English magnates who had been given lands in Scotland were to send a total of 113 men to serve in the castles, but this was only a partial success, as thirty-two men failed to appear. Even so, accounts suggest that in the autumn of 1302 there were probably over 1,000 men paid by the crown, holding castles in Scotland.[106] Edward was not in a financial position to build new fortifications in Scotland on the scale that he had done in

[103] The document is printed in *Anglo-Scottish Relations*, ed. Stones, 118–19, and by the same editor in *SHR*, xxxiv (1955), 122–34. It is discussed by Barrow, *Robert Bruce*, 172–4, and in a note in the second edition of this book (Edinburgh, 1976), 185. Both Stones and Barrow discount the possibility that *le droit* might mean the claim to the Scottish crown, but for an interpretation that does not preclude this, see Duncan, 'The Community of the Realm of Scotland and Robert Bruce', 195–8.

[104] *Foedera*, I, ii, 955–6. See also above, 397.

[105] *Foedera*, I, ii, 942; *CDS*, v, 287.

[106] E 101/10/5, 10; *CDS*, v, 305.

Wales, but in February 1302 James of St George was appointed to see to new defences at Linlithgow. The initial intention was to build in stone, but the instructions were changed, and the work was done in timber, at a cost of just over £900. Wooden fortifications were also put up at Selkirk, where almost £1,400 was spent in 1302, and minor works were undertaken elsewhere.[107] English control was limited to southern Scotland, and even there, it was very precarious. Once the truce ended, in the autumn of 1302, a new royal campaign was urgently required.

Edward had learned by experience that there was little point in attempting a major expedition in the winter, and so he ordered his main muster for Whitsun 1303.[108] There was much military activity before then, however. Even before the truce had ended, Edward had ordered John de Segrave and Ralph Manton, the cofferer of the wardrobe, to make a mounted foray past Stirling, as far as Kirkintilloch.[109] In January, news came that the Scots had occupied various castles and towns, and it was feared that they might invade England. Northern magnates were asked to provide Segrave, the royal lieutenant in Scotland, with assistance, and pay was promised.[110] Segrave organized a raid through territory held by the Scots, and on 24 February he, Manton and a force of knights were surprised by John Comyn of Badenoch and Simon Fraser, and defeated. Some of those captured by the Scots, including Segrave, were soon rescued, but Manton was killed by the Scots. Fraser, who had been a knight in Edward's household, rebuked him for appearing armed, rather than in clerical dress, and accused him of defrauding the king.[111] The English had been extremely fortunate that the defeat had not turned into a disaster.

Edward's army was recruited by means of a feudal summons. The quotas provided were less than in 1300, for the muster rolls show only 282 heavily armed cavalry. As usual, however, there would have been many magnates who served voluntarily, and the household provided a substantial force. By June some 450 men were in pay in the king's household, and 180 in the prince's.[112] Not so many footsoldiers were summoned as in the past, but at its peak, at the beginning of June, the army numbered some 7,500 foot.[113] The campaign of 1303 was not very eventful, for the Scots had clearly decided to avoid a pitched battle.

[107] *KW*, i, 412–14; A.J. Taylor, 'Documents concerning the King's Works at Linlithgow, 1302–3', *Studies in Scottish Antiquity presented to Stewart Cruden*, ed. D.J. Breeze (Edinburgh, 1984), 187–95.

[108] *Parl. Writs*, i, 366.

[109] *Documents*, ed. Stevenson, ii, 448.

[110] *CDS*, ii, no. 1342.

[111] Barrow, *Robert Bruce*, 178; Guisborough, 351–2; Langtoft, ii, 344–6.

[112] E 101/612/11.

[113] Prestwich, *War, Politics and Finance*, 80, 97–8.

The first major English operation was to cross the Firth of Forth. Floating bridges had been constructed at King's Lynn in the winter, and were then brought to Scotland by sea, all at a cost of £938.[114] Once the Forth was crossed, the army marched to Brechin. The castle resisted stoutly, until the constable was killed by a ricochet from a stone, hurled by one of the English siege engines. This may have been the first time that gunpowder was used in a siege in Britain, for an account records a payment for sulphur used for burning the castle, and it may be that the sulphur was used, as it was in the next year, as one of the components of an explosive mixture.[115]

From Brechin, Edward marched northwards, to the shores of the Moray Forth. There were problems on the route when supplies ran short, but the situation was saved at Aberdeen, where merchants provided the necessary victuals. In September the king turned south from Kinloss, marching to Lochindorb and then Boat of Garten. He then followed the course of the Spey north-eastwards for a time, before turning again southwards, to Kildrummy. By 5 November he had reached Dunfermline, in Fife, where he remained to spend the winter. Once Brechin had fallen, the king seems to have met with little resistance.[116]

Other forces were operating elsewhere in Scotland. Aymer de Valence was appointed as the king's lieutenant south of the Forth, and he evidently had some success, for in September he wrote to the chancellor to tell him that he was negotiating with 'the great lords of Scotland'.[117] The earl of Ulster, after lengthy negotiations, led the largest force from Ireland that came to assist the English in Scotland. At its greatest strength, it consisted of 3,457 men, transported by a very substantial fleet of 173 ships. The Irish were mainly active in the west of Scotland, capturing Rothesay castle on the Isle of Bute, and fighting the Scots near Inverkip on the Clyde.[118] Scottish resistance was being whittled away, but William Wallace was still at large, and continued raids against the Scots were needed during the winter of 1303–4. One such raid, or *chevauchée*, was led by John Segrave, Robert Clifford and William Latimer into Lothian. Great care was taken to ensure that no strangers infiltrated the company, as they might be Scottish spies. A Scottish force

[114] BL Add. MS 8835, f.22; *CDS*, ii, no. 1375; *KW*, ii, 416–17. Curiously Langtoft, ii, 348, claims the bridges were not needed.

[115] *Flores*, iii, 114; BL Add. MS 8835, f.7.

[116] Barrow, *Robert Bruce*, 179; Johnstone, *Edward of Caernarvon*, 91.

[117] *CDS*, ii, no. 1393, and see also *CDS*, iv, no. 1792.

[118] J.F. Lydon, 'Edward I, Ireland and the War in Scotland, 1303–1304', *England and Ireland in the Later Middle Ages*, ed. Lydon (Dublin, 1981), 42–61. This article provides a splendid example of the complex operations involved in organizing warfare in this period.

under Wallace and Fraser was routed, but the two leaders managed to escape.[119] Robert Bruce was active on Edward's behalf, in company with Segrave. The king begged them to continue the good work, encouraging them with a homely proverb to make the hood as well as they had made the cloak.[120] The earl of March, another major Scottish magnate on the English side, was however rebuked by the king for his lack of energy and determination.[121]

Early in 1304, at Strathord, near Perth, the majority of the Scottish leaders surrendered to the English king. John Comyn asked that Edward should maintain the laws and customs of Scotland as they were under Alexander III, and that if they needed to be changed, that this should be done by the king with the counsel and assent of the good people of the land. No ordinances made by Edward and his council should be to the prejudice of the Scots. No hostages were to be taken. Edward suggested that James the Steward, John de Soules and Ingram de Umfraville should not receive safe-conducts until Wallace was captured, and that other Scottish leaders should be commissioned to perform this task. In the end, however, neither Comyn nor Edward obtained all that they wanted. One major problem was presented by the fact that many Scottish lands had been granted to Englishmen, and the surrender terms provided the Scots with the opportunity to re-purchase their estates, at terms which varied according to the extent of their involvement with resistance to Edward. Some of the leaders were to be exiled for varying terms, some as short as six months, some as long as three years.[122] The scheme for the repurchase of lands was strikingly similar to that of the Dictum of Kenilworth of 1266, and the relative generosity shown to those who surrendered of their own volition, as against those who struggled on to the bitter end, is reminiscent of Edward's attitude in the aftermath of the fight against Simon de Montfort.[123]

Successful as the negotiations in the early months of 1304 were, resistance was not ended. Wallace was still at large, though he had little support, and a more immediate problem for Edward was presented by Stirling castle and its garrison under William Oliphant. In 1303 Edward had bypassed Stirling, because, according to Walter of Guisborough, it would, if in Scottish hands, be a strong deterrent to any who wished to desert from the English army campaigning further north.[124] Now, in

---

[119] *CDS*, ii, no. 1423; Barrow, *Robert Bruce*, 179.
[120] *CDS*, ii, no. 1465.
[121] *Documents*, ed. Stevenson, ii, 467–70.
[122] *Documents and Records*, ed. Palgrave, 276–88.
[123] Above, 57, 59.
[124] Guisborough, 357.

1304, Edward determined on a major siege of Stirling, as a show of strength. The king went from his winter quarters at Dunfermline first to St Andrews, where a parliament was held, at which Wallace, Simon Fraser and the defenders of Stirling were declared outlaws.[125] He then moved to Stirling, where the siege began in April.

The operations began, as was customary, with negotiations. William Oliphant asked to be allowed to consult his superior, John de Soules, as to whether or not he should surrender. The demand may sound reasonable, but Soules was in France, and consultation with him was hardly practicable. Oliphant prepared to resist, justifying himself in legal terms, on the grounds that he had never personally sworn fealty, or done homage, to Edward. Edward apparently then justified his own position in a lengthy speech, in which he outlined events since the death of Alexander III. These formalities over, hostilities began.[126] The English had made extensive preparations. Reginald the Engineer assembled the siege train at Berwick, and two siege engines were brought from Brechin, with one coming from Aberdeen. Ropes, lead and ammunition were collected together, and shipped to Stirling. The Prince of Wales was ordered to collect lead from the roofs of all the churches near Perth and Dunblane: it was needed to make counter-weights for the great trebuchets. Robert Bruce, now on the English side, sent his siege machines to Stirling, though there were problems in transporting the great beam of the largest one.[127] It was not only large machines that were needed. Great numbers of crossbows and ammunition, and ordinary bows and arrows, were supplied by the sheriffs of London, Lincolnshire and Northumberland, and by the mayor of Newcastle upon Tyne. Crossbowmen and workmen, particularly carpenters, were sent for. A particularly interesting item in the records is the note of the supply of cotton thread, sulphur and saltpetre, for the purpose of throwing 'greek fire' into the castle. It looks as if this was an explosive gunpowder mixture, prepared by the same Burgundian, Jean de Lamouilly, who had used sulphur at Brechin. It was, very probably, put into earthenware pots, which could be hurled into the castle.[128] The siege made a grand spectacle: an oriel window was constructed, so that the ladies of the court could watch the proceedings in safety (the queen had come to join Edward in Scotland in the winter).[129]

There was, it seems, one attempt made by a Scottish force to relieve

[125] Richardson and Sayles, *English Parliament in the Middle Ages*, XIII, 311.
[126] The fullest accounts of the siege are in *Flores*, iii, 118–20, 315–20.
[127] *CDS*, ii, nos. 1500, 1504, 1510; *Documents*, ed. Stevenson, ii, 481–5.
[128] Ibid., ii, 479–80; BL Add. MS 8835, ff.8v, 9v, 18v, 21v. For Jean de Lamouilly, see J.R.S. Phillips, *Aymer de Valence, earl of Pembroke 1307–1324* (Oxford, 1972), 111–13.
[129] BL Add. MS 8835, f.15v; *CDS*, iv, 466.

the siege, but nothing came of it, as troops under the earl of Hereford (the son of Edward's opponent of 1297) easily routed it.[130] The garrison, however, held out gallantly against the onslaught of the English siege engines, with their picturesque names, such as Segrave, Forster and Robinet. The Scots were able to take refuge in deep caves within the rock on which the castle was perched, and also kept their supplies safe there. Edward worked hard to maintain the morale of his troops, often riding close up to the walls of the castle. This habit nearly proved disastrous, when a crossbowman on the battlements fired a shot which went through the king's garments, and lodged in his saddle, but which left him unharmed. On another occasion, he was thrown from his horse when a stone hurled from the castle landed near him, but again, he was unhurt. According to the fullest chronicle account, the king decided to gain entry to the castle by constructing a great battering ram, but this achieved little. More success was gained by employing a machine called a Warwolf.[131] Documents show that this had taken a team of five master carpenters and fifty men a long time to construct, and that it was not in fact quite complete on 20 July, when the garrison offered unconditional surrender.[132] Edward, however, wanted to see how effective the new machine was, and refused to let anyone enter, or leave, the castle until it had been tried out. A modern commentator has condemned his action as 'cold-blooded cruelty', and has described it as a display of 'meanness of spirit and implacable, almost paranoic, hostility'.[133] No contemporary, however, expressed any such views, as far as is known, and Edward was not as harsh towards the garrison when they did make their way out as he could have been. The men came before the king in all humility, barefoot and with ashes on their heads, seeking mercy. 'You don't deserve my grace, but must surrender to my will', was the harsh reply, but Edward eventually succumbed to their pleas, and spared them their lives, with the single exception of the traitor who had betrayed the castle to the Scots just over four years earlier.[134]

The siege of Stirling effectively completed the conquest of Scotland, and in the summer of 1304 Edward was at long last able to return to England. William Wallace was still at liberty. He escaped capture in a skirmish in September, but eleven months later, in August 1305, he was captured by John of Menteith's men near Glasgow, as he lay with his

---

[130] A.R. Wagner, *Catalogue of English Medieval Rolls of Arms* (Harleian Soc., c, 1948), 36.

[131] *Flores*, iii, 318–19.

[132] E 101/11/15; E 101/12/25; *CDS*, ii, no. 1560.

[133] Barrow, *Robert Bruce*, 181–2.

[134] *Flores*, iii, 320.

mistress, according to Langtoft's chronicle. As Edward had hoped, it was the Scots themselves who turned Wallace in. The man who first found Wallace was promised forty marks, those with him shared sixty marks, and John of Menteith was granted land worth £100.[135] Wallace was taken to London, and a show trial took place in Westminster Hall. The accusations against him reproduced some, but not all, of the English propaganda against a man who was feared and hated to a remarkable extent. He was accused of sparing none who spoke the English language, and of slaying infants, children, widows and nuns, but the curious charge that he had organized choirs of naked Englishmen and Englishwomen to sing for him, who were then tortured, was, understandably, not produced in court. At the heart of the accusation made in court was the fact that Wallace had rebelled against Edward, his feudal lord. No account was taken of the fact that Wallace did not regard Edward in this light. In legal terms, Wallace was tried by a commission of gaol delivery, the justices being John de Segrave, Peter Malore, Ralph de Sandwich, John Bakewell and the mayor of London: there was no question of his being brought before parliament. It does not appear that Wallace was given any opportunity to answer the charges against him: it was legally sufficient in such a case for conviction to follow the rehearsal of the crimes that had been committed.

From Edward's point of view, there can have been no doubt whatsoever that Wallace was a traitor who deserved to die a traitor's death. The king may appear today to have been ungenerous in failing to recognize the obvious qualities of his victim, who had shown a great capacity for leadership. Yet Wallace had not conducted his campaigns according to the chivalric codes of the day, and there was no reason why Edward should have treated him with compassion or respect. Wallace's end was horrific. He was made to wear a crown of laurel leaves, because it was claimed that he had said that he would wear a crown at Westminster. From Westminster, he was drawn to the place of execution at Smithfield, and there he was hanged and disembowelled. He was then beheaded, and his entrails were burned. Finally, his remains were quartered. His head was placed on London bridge, and the quarters sent to Newcastle, Berwick, Stirling and Perth.[136] John de Segrave received fifteen shillings for the grisly task of escorting them northwards.[137]

In parliament in September 1305, Edward turned his attention to the question of the future government of Scotland. Nine Scots were present

---

[135] Langtoft, ii, 362; *Documents and Records*, ed. Palgrave, 295.
[136] *Ann. London*, 139–42; *Flores*, iii, 321; Barrow, *Robert Bruce*, 193–5. It is Barrow who condemns Edward as 'small and mean' in his treatment of Wallace.
[137] E 101/367/16, f.4.

to represent the community of the land of Scotland. A tenth, Patrick earl of March, failed to attend, and the king nominated John of Menteith in his place. These men met with twenty of the king's councillors, to draw up an ordinance. It was agreed that John of Brittany should be the royal lieutenant in Scotland, and guardian of the land (the document carefully avoided terming Scotland a realm). William de Bevercotes was to remain chancellor, and John Sandale chamberlain. Four pairs of justices, each pair consisting of one Englishman and one Scotsman, were appointed. Sheriffs were nominated: at Edinburgh, Jedburgh, Linlithgow and Peebles the office remained in English hands. The castles of Roxburgh and Jedburgh were entrusted to the king's lieutenant, and only Stirling and Dumbarton were put in the hands of Scotsmen.

Arrangements were made for a review of Scottish law. In terms which echoed Edward's policy in Wales, 'the laws and customs which are clearly displeasing to God and to reason' were to be corrected by John of Brittany and his council. Some matters would have to be put to the king, and these were to be submitted to a parliament to be held at Easter 1306, where the Scots would be represented by men with full powers to act on behalf of the community, just like the English knights of the shire. The custom 'of the Scots and the Brets' was, however, forbidden with no debate. This was probably a system of blood-money payments, or wergilds, of an archaic type, and it is unlikely that its abolition was resented. The last part of the ordinance dealt with the oath to be sworn by the councillors and officials in Scotland, which conspicuously avoided any phraseology that might suggest that Scotland was a kingdom. A separate memorandum noted that John of Brittany was to have a company of sixty men-at-arms, and a fee of 3,000 marks a year. Twenty-two Scots were named as members of his council.[138]

The scheme for the government of Scotland was the product of three weeks debate, and it met with Edward's thorough approval. It has also found favour with modern commentators: one of the king's sternest critics considers that the fact that Edward consulted the Scots shows that 'he had learned part of the lesson of 1296-7', and that 'it was no small achievement for this elderly, conventional, conservative, unimaginative man that he had learned anything at all'.[139] The ordinance was, however, a thoroughly limited document, which does not bear comparison with the statute of Wales of 1284, or even with the ordinances drawn up at Condom in 1289. No constructive changes to the

---

[138] *Anglo-Scottish Relations*, ed. Stones, 120-9; *Documents and Records*, ed. Palgrave, 292-3.
[139] Barrow, *Robert Bruce*, 189.

way in which Scotland was ruled were proposed, and the manner in which a kingdom was downgraded to the status of a land was little more than petty. Nothing was done in the document to introduce the very real benefits of English legal procedure to Scotland. Nor did the ordinance do anything to resolve the very real problems of the many rival claims to lands in Scotland which resulted from almost a decade of war, although shortly after it was produced Edward did announce revised terms for the redemption of lands by his former opponents in Scotland.[140] The king must have felt that, at long last, he was free of the burden of Scottish affairs.

On 10 February 1306, at Dumfries, Robert Bruce, earl of Carrick, murdered John Comyn, lord of Badenoch. This dramatic event, with hindsight so obvious in its implications, mystified Edward at first. He learned of it by 23 February, and on the next day described it as the work of 'some people who are doing their utmost to trouble the peace and quiet of the realm of Scotland'. Two Oxford friars were sent to inquire as to what had happened.[141] The reasons for Bruce's action have been extensively discussed. It seems likely that he had made a bid for the Scottish throne before the murder, and that he received some support. Comyn's death was not premeditated, but was the result of a quarrel over Bruce's plans.[142]

Resentment at the way he had been treated by Edward I must have played its part in Bruce's decision to turn against the English king. He had not received many favours from Edward since he had joined the English cause early in 1302. Like so many who served Edward he had difficulty in recovering his expenses, incurred when he had charge of Ayrshire and Lanarkshire. He also faced arguments over the rights he claimed in Annandale.[143] There is no evidence that Bruce was badly treated by Edward, but rather, he must have felt that he was not rewarded in the way that he had expected.

The first sign of discontentment came in June 1304, when Bruce made a pact with the bishop of St Andrews. The purpose was not made clear in the document, but there was, significantly, no clause saving loyalty to King Edward.[144] Bruce was asked, with two others, to advise

---

[140] *Flores*, iii, 125.

[141] E 101/365/19, f.39; *CDS*, ii, no. 1747; *CDS*, v, no. 472, pp. 199, 200.

[142] Barrow, *Robert Bruce*, 205–8; T.M. Smallwood, 'An unpublished early account of Bruce's murder of Comyn', *SHR*, liv (1975), 1–10.

[143] *CDS*, ii, nos 1588, 1658. Ibid., nos 1493, 1495, probably date from 1295, and refer to Bruce's father, termed earl of Carrick by courtesy. I am grateful to Professor G.W.S. Barrow for pointing this out to me.

[144] *Documents and Records*, ed. Palgrave, 323–6.

Edward on Scottish affairs, in the Lent parliament of 1305, but when it came to the parliament in the autumn, when the ordinance for the government of Scotland was produced, Bruce was not present, and no significant role was accorded to him in the arrangements that were made.[145] It was in character that Edward should not have rewarded Bruce on any scale: the cases of Prince Dafydd and Rhys ap Maredudd in Wales provide other examples of men who rebelled after Edward had failed to show them the appreciation they felt they deserved. Patriotic emotions no doubt had their part to play, but with more careful handling by Edward, it is very likely that Bruce would have remained a valuable ally of the English.

The rising took the English by surprise. A letter written from Berwick in March 1306 reported that Bruce held the royal castles of Dumfries and Ayr, and had taken Dalswinton and Tibbers. There was, apparently, little support for him in Galloway, but he had received the fealty of many men at Glasgow and Rutherglen. The 'wicked bishop' of Glasgow had given him absolution, and he had crossed the Forth with sixty men-at-arms. The main English-held castles were adequately supplied with victuals, 'but they will have no keepers until word comes from the king'. The letter-writer was aware that Bruce was attempting to seize the throne, but seems not to have appreciated how imminent this was.[146] Late in March Robert Bruce was formally enthroned, in two ceremonies, at Scone.[147]

Serious preparations for an English campaign began on 1 March, when clerks were authorized to collect food supplies, but it was not until 5 April that Aymer de Valence was appointed to command the troops in the east, and Henry Percy those in the west. A feudal muster was requested for 8 July.[148] Aymer de Valence had a force of 139 cavalry in pay by 15 April, and by mid-July almost 300. He also had, at one time, 1,300 infantry. This small army was reinforced by thirty men-at-arms and eight hobelars, who came to Carlisle in answer to the feudal summons, and who were promptly sent to join Aymer and his pay-master, John Sandale.[149] The main army was commanded by the Prince of Wales, and set out from Carlisle in July. Unfortunately, there are no surviving accounts to show how large this force was. As for

[145] *Memoranda de Parliamento*, 1305, ed. Maitland, 14; E.M. Barron, *The Scottish War of Independence* (2nd ed., Inverness, 1934), 164–71, provides a full discussion.
[146] *Anglo-Scottish Relations*, ed. Stones, 130–4. Some of the castles taken by Bruce were retaken fairly soon: Tibbers had an English garrison from 22 February, Dumfries from 3 March, Caerlaverock from 29 May and Durisdeer from 1 May. See E 101/369/11, f.89.
[147] Barrow, *Robert Bruce*, 212–13.
[148] *Parl. Writs*, i, 374, 377; *CDS*, ii, no. 1757.
[149] E 101/13/16. This account book is calendared in *CDS*, v, no. 492.

Edward himself, age was taking its toll. He was ill in the summer of 1306, and progressed slowly, and no doubt painfully, northwards. At Hexham one of the canons was paid 20s for his efforts to cure the king.[150] By late September, his health was on the mend: 'he is hearty and strong enough, considering his age', wrote one correspondent.[151] He had some cheering news as he travelled towards Scotland. The household accounts contain entries recording payments of up to £10 to messengers who brought news to the king of events such as the capture of Simon Fraser.[152] Edward was in no state to lead an expedition, and in October he took up winter quarters at Lanercost priory.

In previous campaigns, the English had concentrated all their efforts in one main invasion force. This time, operations took place under different commanders, in various parts of Scotland. Things began very well, when, on 19 June, Aymer de Valence routed Bruce and his men in a surprise attack at Methven, near Perth. The Scots, interestingly, covered their heraldic blazons with white cloth, so that individuals could not be recognized. This was not a war in which the chivalric conventions were to be observed.[153] From Methven, Bruce fled west, and a further engagement took place near Loch Tay. He was defeated again at Dalry, near Tyndrum, and succeeded in making his way further west, to safety, though precisely where is not known.[154] John Botetourt and John of Menteith conducted a successful siege of Dunaverty castle in Kintyre in September, but did not find Bruce himself there, as they had hoped to do.[155] They had two siege engines brought by sea from Carlisle.[156] The English forces also had considerable success elsewhere in Scotland. Simon Fraser was captured in August near Stirling, and towards the end of the month Bruce's castle at Loch Doon fell.[157] Edward's surgeon took charge of the preparation of boats and other equipment for the assault, a remarkable example of the way in which the king's servants were ready to turn their hands to any task.[158] The prince's army advanced from Carlisle, received the

---

[150] E 101/369/11, f.98.

[151] CDS, ii, no. 1832.

[152] E 101/369/11, ff.96–8; CDS, v, no. 472, p. 203.

[153] Guisborough, 368. The date of the battle is discussed by Barrow, Robert Bruce, 216n. It should be noted that it is not merely the Scottish chronicles which give the date as 19 June: Ann. London, 148, specifies the same day.

[154] The Loch Tay engagement is referred to in E 101/13/16, f.16; CDS, v, no. 492, p. 213; for that at Dalry, or Dail Righ, see Barrow, Robert Bruce, 227–8.

[155] CDS, ii, nos 1833, 1834; Guisborough, 368, where it is wrongly assumed that Neil Bruce and the new queen of Scots had taken refuge at Dunaverty: in fact, they went to Kildrummy.

[156] E 101/369/11, f.46.

[157] Political Songs, ed. Wright, 216–17; Documents and Records, ed. Palgrave, 310.

[158] E 101/369/11, f.51v.

surrender of Lochmaben, and then marched to Perth, ravaging the countryside as it went. According to one account Edward I was angry at his son's treatment of the poor. In September, the prince and his men successfully besieged Kildrummy castle. The ladies of Bruce's court, who had been sent there for safety, left the castle with the earl of Atholl before it fell, but were soon taken captive.[159]

Edward responded to the events in Scotland with unprecedented savagery. The earl of Atholl was tried and executed, despite the pleas of the queen and many magnates that he should be spared because of his noble birth. Edward's answer was to order that he should be hanged higher than the rest, though one account does state that he was spared being drawn through the streets of London.[160] Simon Fraser was also tried and executed in London, with all possible indignities. The body, and even the gallows on which he was hanged, were burned by the king's special order. Edward felt particularly strongly about Fraser, who had been a knight in his household.[161] Herbert de Morham and Thomas du Boys were also executed in London. Christopher Seton died horribly at Dumfries, and his brother at Newcastle. Neil Bruce was executed at Berwick. The list could easily be lengthened.[162]

Edward's treatment of Bruce's sister Mary and the countess of Buchan was highly unusual. The order for their custody specified that they were to be confined in secure cages, one at Roxburgh and one at Berwick. They were to be provided with food, drink and other necessities by Englishwomen: no Scots were to approach them. The cages were to be equipped with privies. One account described that for the countess of Buchan as being fashioned in the likeness of a crown, because she had played a leading part (by hereditary right) in Bruce's enthronement, and the chroniclers are clear that the cages were in the open, although Edward's memorandum said they were to be in a tower. It was initially intended that Bruce's daughter Marjorie should receive similar treatment in the Tower of London, but Edward relented in her case, presumably because she was no more than twelve years old. The use of cages was not unprecedented: in 1305 one was built for the unfortunate Owain, Dafydd ap Gruffydd's son, at Bristol, where he had been in custody since 1283. Women, however, were not normally harshly treated: a more conventional decision was that to send Bruce's queen to the royal manor at Burstwick, where she was to be kept in custody, and given servants who were on no account to be cheerful or riotous. She was fortunate in being a daughter of the earl of Ulster, a man who

---

[159] Johnstone, *Edward of Caernarvon*, 113–15; Rishanger, 230.

[160] Guisborough, 369; *Flores*, iii, 135.

[161] *Political Songs*, ed. Wright, 220–2; *Ann. London*, 148–9.

[162] Barrow, *Robert Bruce*, 228–9, discusses the executions more fully.

served Edward well.[163] Edward obviously decided to make a public spectacle of Mary Bruce and the countess of Buchan, keeping them in Scotland rather than sending them south, and the decision does him no credit. The fact that the ladies were allowed 4d a day for their sustenance, and that the cages were large affairs, with privies, hardly proves Edward's humanity. However, the king's subjects did not think to accuse him of a lack of chivalry. Rather, the implication of Guisborough's account is that the king was generous to the countess of Buchan, in not ordering her death.[164]

The war had undoubtedly reached a new level of savagery. The normal conventions did not apply, as Edward regarded the conflict as a rebellion, rather than a war between two countries. An ordinance issued at Lanercost provided for the pursuit of all those who were, or had been, against the king with hue and cry. All involved in John Comyn's death were to be drawn and hanged, and the same treatment was to be given to those who had either advised, or consented to, Bruce's action. Those taken in the war were to be hanged, or decapitated. Anyone who surrendered would be imprisoned, until further orders were received from the king, and anyone who supported Bruce and his faction was to be arrested and imprisoned. As for the ordinary people who were dragged into the war, they were to pay ransoms according to the scale of their involvement.[165] A different indication of the depth of Edward's feelings is provided by the request he submitted to the pope in November 1306, for the transfer of the abbey of Scone from its present site 'in the midst of a perverse nation'.[166]

There was, it appears, less seriousness of purpose in the English forces in the autumn and winter of 1306-7 than there had been in the past. The prince of Wales did not stay in Scotland, and twenty-two knights, many of them closely connected with the prince, left the army without permission, so as to go overseas for a tournament. Edward was angry, and ordered the seizure of their lands, but on the intervention of Queen

---

[163] *Documents and Records*, ed. Palgrave, 358-9; *Flores*, iii, 324; Rishanger, 229; Guisborough, 367.

[164] Lord Hailes wrote, in his *Annals of Scotland* (1799), ii, 11n, of Edward's ordinances, that 'to those who have no notion of any cage but one for a parrot or squirrel, hung out of a window, I despair of making this mandate intelligible'. For a more recent defence of Edward's actions, see E.L.G. Stones in *SHR*, lii (1973), 84; and for a critical view, Barrow, *Robert Bruce*, 230. The suggestion made in a note there, that Edward II regarded the punishments as savage, is not warranted, and is not included in the second edition of the book (Edinburgh, 1976). See also the additional note in the second edition, 233.

[165] *Documents and Records*, ed. Palgrave, 361-3.

[166] *Foedera*, I, ii, 1003.

Margaret, sixteen of the knights were pardoned in January 1307, and no action was taken against the others. A tournament was even planned to take place at Wark, on the Scottish border, but the idea was abandoned.[167] There was more serious business to be done.

By the winter of 1306–7, Edward probably considered that all that was needed to settle the problem of Scotland was to arrange for the judicial process of dealing with Bruce's supporters, and to grant out confiscated lands to his own followers, who had presented him with a great many requests for estates in Scotland.[168] In fact, the English were faced with an astonishing recovery by Robert Bruce.

The year began badly, however, for Bruce. In February he sent his brothers Thomas and Alexander to Galloway, but they were soon captured by Dungall MacDouall. Most in their party were promptly executed, and the heads then sent to the Prince of Wales as trophies; a gruesome touch.[169] Bruce himself had more success when he landed in Scotland, having spent the winter in either Ireland or the inner Hebrides. Aymer de Valence was sent to Ayr, and the king was irate at the absence of news. He asked Walter Langton, the treasurer, to write to Valence and the other commanders, to tell them that he had heard that they had done so badly that they dared not let him know – although in fact, Edward had heard no such news.[170] Orders went out for the recruitment of more infantry to pursue Bruce. John Botetourt led two raiding parties, one in February and one in March into Nithsdale, while Robert Clifford was operating separately to the west of the Cree. Little was achieved, though Edward must have been cheered by the news of the capture of John Wallace, William's brother, which he received on 1 April.[171]

In May, the tide turned in Bruce's favour. Aymer de Valence was routed by Bruce at Loudoun Hill, and three days later the earl of Gloucester was defeated, and forced to take refuge in Ayr castle. These were little more than skirmishes, but Edward was, not surprisingly, 'much enraged'.[172] As for the Scots, it was widely considered that Bruce's success proved that 'God is openly for him, as he has destroyed

[167] Johnstone, *Edward of Caernarvon*, 115–17; E 101/369/11, f.57, details purveyance for the Wark tournament.

[168] The petitions asking for lands are printed in *Documents and Records*, ed. Palgrave, 301–18.

[169] Barrow, *Robert Bruce*, 242; BL Add. MS 22923. f.14v.

[170] *CDS*, ii, no. 1895. No. 1896 shows that Edward suspected that Valence was being too cautious. For the problem of where Bruce spent the winter of 1306–7, see Barrow, *Robert Bruce*, 237–40.

[171] *CDS*, ii, nos 1897, 1902, 1913, 1923; E 101/13/24; E 101/370/16, f.9v.; E 101/612/21; C 47/22/3/64.

[172] Guisborough, 378; *CDS*, ii, no. 1979.

all the king's power both among the English and the Scots, and the English force is in retreat'. Popular agitators encouraged the belief that Bruce would be successful, and cited a prophecy of Merlin predicting a powerful alliance between the Welsh and the Scots, which would follow Edward's death.[173] Operations in Galloway in May and June, under John de St John, achieved little. What was needed was a major campaign against the Scots, but although the chronicles suggest that a feudal muster was to take place at Carlisle in July, there is no documentary evidence for this.[174] Some troops were certainly assembled at Carlisle, for at Whitsun Edward held a review there, at which about 400 men rode past him, decorated with leaves, a sight which made him 'much pleased and merry'.[175] The force which set out with the king for the border was probably not a large one, and it was halted on 7 July 1307 at Burgh-by-Sands, by the death of the king.[176]

Edward I failed in his Scottish wars. The task of conquering Scotland was an immense one, and failure is perhaps less surprising than the degree of success which the king achieved. His armies proved invincible in large-scale battles, as Falkirk showed, and his engineers had an impressive record in siege warfare. In 1296, and again in 1304, Edward appeared to be victorious. Before suggesting reasons for the king's ultimate failure, it is appropriate to see how it was that he achieved as much as he did.

The support of the magnates was essential in war. Apart from the arguments with Bigod and Bohun in 1298, Edward faced no hostility from the earls or other great men as far as his plans in Scotland were concerned. Many methods were used to win their co-operation. Writs of protection were granted, to safeguard the domestic interests of nobles while they were on campaign, and Edward was even prepared to suspend the action of novel disseisin where it was brought against someone present in the army.[177] Payments of debt owed to the crown were respited or pardoned, but if anyone left the campaign without leave, as some men did in 1303, the exchequer was ordered to adopt a harsh attitude towards him.[178] Many magnates were prepared to serve the king in Scotland without pay, but they did so in the expectation of other rewards. Promises were made of grants of lands in Scotland, sometimes even before they had been taken. Thus, in 1301, Aymer de

---

[173] Ibid., ii, no. 1926. For a different translation, see Barrow, *Robert Bruce*, 245.
[174] Guisborough, 378–9; *Chron. Lanercost*, 207; E 101/13/16, f.13v.
[175] *CDS*, ii, no. 1979.
[176] See below, 556–7, for Edward's death.
[177] See, for example, a memorandum drawn up in 1300 in E 101/8/4, m.2.
[178] E 159/77, m.4.

Valence was granted Bothwell a month before the castle fell. Edward, so cautious where English titles were concerned, was prepared to give his followers Scottish ones. At the end of the reign, Henry Percy was granted Bruce's earldom of Carrick, John de Hastings became earl of Menteith, and Ralph de Monthermer earl of Atholl.[179] Service in war was the best route to obtain the king's favour. Robert FitzRoger, one of those who had appeared with the earls at the exchequer in 1297 to protest against the tax of an eighth, earned Edward's gratitude by his efforts in protecting the northern Marches against the Scots.[180]

Propaganda, too, played a part in persuading men to fight. At an unofficial level, there were the horror stories that circulated about the activities of William Wallace. The crown explained the need for the campaigns in the writs of summons, and in the Feast of the Swans in 1306, on the occasion of the knighting of the Prince of Wales, chivalric impulses were carefully directed towards the coming campaign in Scotland by means of a series of oaths.[181]

It was little use recruiting magnates, and indeed also infantry, for the war, if there was no efficient administrative machinery to support the armies. The clerks of the royal wardrobe were highly experienced in performing this function, and men such as John Droxford and Ralph Manton deserve much of the credit for the English achievements in the north. It was necessary to supplement the wardrobe with a more permanent administrative structure, in particular to deal with the needs of the English garrisons. John de Weston served as paymaster at Berwick from 1298 until 1304, and Richard de Bromsgrove took charge of the victualling establishment there. At Carlisle, James de Dalilegh saw to both pay and supplies. In the final stages of the reign, John Sandale was responsible for the payment of many of the troops in Scotland, in his function as chamberlain there.[182] A great many accounts and other documents survive, giving details of the activities and concerns of these clerks. One letter is worth quoting, not because it illustrates any dramatic moment in the war, but because it reveals something of the daily worries about money, accounting and supplies. It was written at Whitsun 1307, probably by James de Dalilegh, to an unidentified recipient.

> Greetings. When I came to Dumfries, I found 400 marks there, and I am sending you 300 of them. The remaining 100 I have paid over to men of the king's household, and because I do not know how these 400 marks are being entered in the wardrobe accounts, I am sending you a list of their names. I

---

[179] Prestwich, 'Colonial Scotland', 8, 11.
[180] Prestwich, *War, Politics and Finance*, 239.
[181] Above, 121.
[182] Prestwich, *War, Politics and Finance*, 162–5, provides a fuller discussion.

will also take a list to Carlisle, to enter in the wardrobe and have them charged with the money, if it is not all to be charged to you. And could you warn those in Ayr and Rutherglen, and that neighbourhood, to have as much flour as possible ready for the arrival of the troops, and please hurry the despatch of the letters to Ireland, asking for wine and other victuals, and do not neglect this matter.[183]

The task that was performed best, after the difficulties experienced in 1298, was that of providing the armies and garrisons in Scotland with sufficient supplies. Careful estimates were made of what was needed, and, with only a few exceptions, sufficient quantities were provided. There were some problems, as when grain brought all the way by sea from the Isle of Wight proved to be rotten on arrival. On occasion, it proved necessary to turn to private victuallers for assistance, but in general, as far as the forces in Scotland were concerned, the arrangements worked well.[184] The counterpart to this success, of course, was the unpopularity of the system of purveyance in England.[185]

The administration of war was not, of course, an unqualified success in Edward's later years, and some of the difficulties that were not fully overcome suggest some reasons for the king's eventual failure in Scotland. The infantry were never very satisfactory. The numbers recruited to serve in Scotland fell with every campaign after 1298, and although smaller numbers may have meant higher quality, the crown never did much to ensure that the men were properly armed and equipped. Desertion was a constant problem, and a harsh ordinance threatening imprisonment, and recovery of any wages paid out, which was drawn up in 1303, does not seem to have been particularly effective.[186] In 1300 the king considered that his campaign was badly hampered because he did not have sufficient good-quality footsoldiers. He wrote to his leading officials, then at York, in the following terms:

As our affairs in Scotland are considerably behind hand, because of a lack of good infantry, we firmly order and charge you that you should have additional men recruited in the counties nearest to the Scottish march, beyond the number who are with us at present. Arrange for the selection of up to 10,000 foot soldiers, the best, strongest, and most experienced that can be found.[187]

It was considered that infantry were needed, if the Scots were to be pursued into the mountains and marshes, and the right sort of men were rarely available. In time, by the 1330s, there would evolve

[183] E 101/33/8/2.
[184] Prestwich, *War, Politics and Finance*, 122–35.
[185] Below, 524, 527.
[186] *Documents and Records*, ed. Palgrave, 204–5.
[187] SC1/61/63.

'mounted infantry', archers who could ride with the cavalry, but who fought on foot. Their role was presaged by the Irish hobelars in this period, but the English were not capable of completely remodelling their armies at short notice.[188]

Shortage of funds was a constant problem. The accounts do not make it possible to provide a precise calculation of the costs of the Scottish campaigns, but a reasonable estimate is that the Caerlaverock campaign of 1300 cost between £40,000 and £50,000, and that the expenditure on the war in 1303–4 amounted to £75,000 or £80,000.[189] The crown did not have such reserves available as it had in 1294–5, when over £54,000 was sent to Wales to pay for the military operations there. In 1300, only about £12,000 was sent to Scotland. The surviving wardrobe journal for the last year of the reign shows that the most that the officials had in hand at any one time was about £1,500.[190] In 1301, letters from the king to the exchequer officials stressed that the main obstacle facing him, in conducting further operations against the Scots, was a lack of cash. 'Know that we wonder greatly why you have sent us as little money, as you have sent up till now, and in particular, we are surprised that you have sent it in such small instalments.' Troops were leaving, as they were not receiving their wages, and a bridge over the Forth could not be completed for want of funds.[191] In the same year, troops at Berwick mutinied, when they discovered that they were not due to receive all of a sum of £200 sent to the town, as part of the money was destined for Jedburgh and Roxburgh.[192] The men of Winchelsea on one occasion stated that they would make no preparations for a campaign, because they had received no payments to meet the debts the king owed them. Instead, the clerks of the wardrobe had broken the tallies which provided evidence of these sums.[193] Many men, however, were prepared to continue to serve Edward in return for promises of future payment, or no wages at all, but obviously, the king's task would have been much easier had funds been more readily available. The problem lay in the collection of revenue in England, not its disbursement in Scotland, where Edward's officials did the best they could in difficult circumstances.

Edward's strategy and tactics brought rich rewards at the battles of Dunbar and Falkirk, and at the siege of Stirling. Yet the suggestion has

---

[188] For a fuller discussion of the infantry, see Prestwich, *War, Politics and Finance*, 92–113.

[189] Ibid., 175–6.

[190] Prestwich, 'The Crown and the Currency', *Numismatic Chronicle*, cxlii (1982), 58; E 101/370/16.

[191] E 159/75, mm.5d., 7; *CDS*, v, nos 260–3.

[192] *CDS*, ii, no. 1223.

[193] *CDS*, v, no. 488.

been made that the king was inadequate as a military commander: 'what he lacked was military ability. However good a tactician he may have been, he was a pitiable strategist.'[194] The criticism is harsh. In concentrating on establishing firm English control south of the Firth of Forth from 1297 to 1301, Edward was not attempting too much too fast, and although the campaigns of 1300 and 1301 yielded only limited results, they were probably effective in wearing down Scottish resistance. It is striking that the English did much better when Edward was present in Scotland than when he was not, and in comparison with Earl Warenne, the king emerges as at least a highly competent military leader, if not an imaginative or inspired one. Even in the final year of the reign, the English military performance was not disastrous, and had it not been for Edward's death in July 1307, the defeats at Loudoun Hill and Ayr might well have been avenged.

Successful conquest was much more than a matter of tactics, strategy and organization. Until 1302, and the French defeat at Courtrai, continued support for John Balliol by Philip IV made Edward's task in Scotland a hard one. Papal hostility to English claims to lordship over Scotland added to the difficulties. One reason for Edward's success in 1304 was the fact that he no longer faced such international antagonism. Thereafter, the king's political insensitivity does much to explain why the achievement of 1304 proved so fragile. The policy of granting out the lands of Scottish rebels, and then the adoption of a system permitting the Scots to repurchase their lands, at a heavy price, cannot have won Edward many friends. The system of government created in 1305 offered few, if any, benefits to the Scots. Edward's choice of John of Brittany as his lieutenant in Scotland was a bad one: John showed no enthusiasm to take up his appointment, made in the autumn of 1305, and temporary arrangements had to be made until his arrival in the north in the spring of the following year.[195]

Above all, of course, Edward misjudged Robert Bruce, and his ferocious reaction to Bruce's rebellion, far from cowing the Scots, merely stiffened their resolve. Edward's anger is easy to understand, but had he taken a different attitude, then Bruce might not have found support so easily. It was too late when Edward declared, in March 1307, that many people had been interpreting his ordinance for dealing with Bruce and his followers as 'too harsh and rigorous'.[196] Edward was, in medieval terms, an old man at the time that Bruce turned against him. Age might have brought with it greater political wisdom, and an increased sense of realism, but in Edward's case, it made a rigid

[194] H.G. Richardson, reviewing *KW*; *EHR*, lxxx (1965), 553–6.
[195] *CPR 1301–7*, 394.
[196] *CDS*, ii, no. 1909.

mind more inflexible still. Yet Edward should not be judged too harshly for the English failure in Scotland. He achieved much, and at the time of Edward's death the real triumphs for Robert Bruce still lay in the future.

Chapter 19

THE LAST YEARS, 1298–1307

In an uncharacteristically rhetorical preamble to an ordinance issued in 1306, Edward I explained how he spent sleepless nights, 'tossed about by the waves of various thoughts', deciding what was the right course of action to take. His chief care, he claimed, was the promotion of 'pleasantness and ease and quiet for our subjects dwelling in our realm, for in their quiet we have rest, and in their tranquillity we are inwardly cherished with the scent of satisfaction among the flowers of hoped-for peace'.[1] Such phraseology should not, perhaps, be taken too seriously, but it was certainly natural for a man in his sixties, a good age for the period, to hope that he might end his days with his country at peace.

The Scots, and Robert Bruce in particular, ensured that there would be no external peace in Edward's last years, and the domestic history of this period has to be seen against the backdrop of the frequent campaigns, and the heavy drain on English resources, of the Scottish war. One theme is provided by Edward's efforts to undo what his opponents had achieved with the confirmation of the charters of 1297, efforts which reached their culmination when he obtained an annulment from the pope, in 1305, of the concessions he had made.[2] These years also saw the king achieve a measure of stability only by abandoning unpopular exactions, and weakening the crown by incurring huge debts. As a result Edward was unable to translate the papal action of 1305 into any major material advantage.[3] Although these years did not see any systematic investigation of magnate liberties, along the lines of the earlier *Quo Warranto* inquiries, Edward was able to take action in individual cases, notably that of the bishop of Durham, without provoking widespread hostility.[4] These were not easy years for the king, but there was no challenge to the essential basis of his authority.

There was considerable concern in 1298 lest the King should go back

---

[1] *Statutes of the Realm*, i, 147.
[2] See in particular, H. Rothwell, 'Edward I and the Struggle for the Charters, 1297–1305', *Studies in Medieval History*, ed. Hunt, Pantin, Southern, 319–32.
[3] Prestwich, *War, Politics and Finance*, 262–81.
[4] Below, 541–6.

on the concessions that he had been compelled to make in the previous year. Whether Edward's reputation for bad faith, earned in the Barons' Wars, was still remembered, cannot be known, but there was certainly alarm lest he might declare the *Confirmatio Cartarum* invalid, on the grounds that it had been conceded in a foreign land, rather than in England. When the army for the 1298 expedition to Scotland assembled at Roxburgh, Bigod and Bohun declared that they would go no further unless Edward provided them with guarantees that the boundaries of the royal forests would be investigated, and the concessions of 1297 confirmed. The matter was temporarily settled when the bishop of Durham, and the earls of Gloucester, Lincoln and Warenne swore on the king's behalf that if victory was gained, Bohun and Bigod's demands would be met. However, despite the great success achieved at Falkirk, the king did not make the required concessions, perhaps because of the further arguments that took place with Bigod and Bohun over the distribution of lands in Scotland.[5]

The question of the Forest had not been of much importance in 1297, but it received great prominence from 1298 onwards. There is no reason to suppose that Edward had been enlarging the boundaries of the royal forest in recent years, but it was considered that an extension had occurred under Richard I and John. During Henry III's minority, the Charter of the Forest had been issued, and some disafforestation had taken place, although in some cases this was reversed after the king came of age. The scale of the Forest was a grievance, because of the special jurisdiction which applied to those areas, not necessarily wooded, which were classified as being part of the royal hunting reserves. Not only were there laws protecting game, but also many which limited the exploitation of land, with prohibitions on making clearings and grazing livestock. Foresters were among the most unpopular of all royal officials.[6] In October 1297, perambulations (or investigations) of the Forest boundaries had been ordered, and although these were not completed, half of the Forest of Dean was declared not to be royal Forest, and all of the Oxfordshire part of Bernwood was treated likewise.[7] These verdicts were ignored by the king, but they must have given rise to considerable expectations. The question of the perambulations then became, in 1298 and 1299, a test of

---

[5] Guisborough, 324, 329; see also above, 482–3. Rishanger, 186, gives the names of the earls who swore on the king's behalf as Warenne, Warwick and Gloucester. The earl of Gloucester was Ralph de Monthermer, who held the title *jure uxoris* as a result of his marriage to Joan of Acre in 1297.

[6] For a recent work on the Forest, see C.R. Young, *The Royal Forests of Medieval England*, (Leicester, 1979).

[7] *CPR 1292–1301*, 312; M. Bazeley, 'The Extent of the English Forest in the Thirteenth Century', *TRHS*, 4th ser., iv (1921), 155.

the king's good faith. The Forest was an aspect of the royal prerogative, and the issue therefore had wide implications for royal power in a more general sense. It was also easy to see, in this case, whether or not the king was keeping the promises he made.

The arguments with the church had not been concluded in 1297. Robert Winchelsey was not concerned with the question of the Forest boundaries, but *Confirmatio Cartarum* was important to him, as was the continuing question of the taxation of the clergy. A church council was held in June 1298, to discuss what Edward no doubt considered were his very moderate requests. The king's representatives asked for prayers to be said for Edward's success in the war against the Scots, and for the excommunication of the Scots who attacked the church, and disturbed the peace in England. These demands presented no problems. Edward was not so tactless as to ask the clergy for a tax: instead, he promised to manage from his own resources. He did, however, ask the clergy to promise aid in the future, should those resources prove inadequate. This promise was not made, as it was argued that papal permission would have to be given. There was also a demand from the king that he should receive the rest of the tax of a tenth, which the clergy had granted in the autumn of 1297 because of the danger from the Scots. This money the church refused to hand over, on the grounds that it could only be employed to drive the Scots out of England. An English campaign in Scotland did not fit the bill, and so payment could only be made if the pope's approval was obtained.

The council proceeded to discuss the question of *Confirmatio Cartarum*. Dates were set for the biennial publication of the excommunication decrees, which were the main means of enforcing the terms of the reissue of the Charters. Particular attention was given to the question of prises. Winchelsey pointed out that in 1297 the king had conceded that prises should not be taken without common assent, and he continued, in tones more reminiscent of *De Tallagio* than of the *Confirmatio Cartarum*, to order the excommunication of those who seized goods without the consent of the owners or their bailiffs. Severe ecclesiastical sanctions, of interdict and excommunication, would be imposed, should any clerk be imprisoned for carrying out these instructions.

Edward had attempted to take a conciliatory line with Winchelsey. He even tried the expedient, according to the Bury chronicler, of sending his son to address the clergy, for in 1297 his request for fealty to be performed to the prince had been successful. The archbishop, however, was in no mood to trust the king. Edward did not respond aggressively to the rebuff he received. He accepted what was reported from the council, and never again attempted to negotiate direct taxes with the clergy. He did not want to face concerted opposition from both laity and clergy, and was anxious to ensure the support, or at least the neutrality, of the church in any future political arguments.[8]

In 1299 the political temperature rose. When parliament was held in March, there was much argument over the proposed confirmation of the Charters, promised in 1298. The king prevaricated in a most unsatisfactory manner, but when pressed hard, announced that he would give an answer on the next day. Instead of doing so, he left London in secret. The earls, with a mob, went after him. Edward excused his conduct, saying that the foul air of London was damaging his health, and he promised that, if they returned to London, the council would give an answer. When it came, the answer was far from satisfactory. According to Walter of Guisborough, articles put to the king were conceded, but only with the addition of a clause saving the rights of the crown. What the king and council produced on 2 April was the statute known as *De Finibus Levatis*, which made it clear that the investigation of the Forest boundaries would not be allowed to curtail royal rights, and that the king was not prepared to confirm the Charter of the Forest in its entirety. The earls and their followers departed from London in high dudgeon. The council feared riots in the city, and had both the Forest Charter and Magna Carta read out in St Paul's churchyard. Initial delight turned to dismay when it became clear that the king was not keeping his word, and that he was not conceding all the demands made of him. The most important clauses of the Forest Charter were omitted.[9] On 10 April a new parliament was summoned, to meet in May, in a fresh attempt to resolve the situation. A week later, in a rather obvious move to buy political peace, a final settlement of the king's long-running dispute with London was reached, and the city's liberties were formally confirmed.[10]

Accounts of what took place in parliament in May differ. One version has the magnates infuriated by the king's peevish and empty replies, and by his transparent prevarication. Another suggests that Edward's courteous explanation, that he wished to delay the investigation of the Forest boundaries until after his marriage to the French princess Margaret, convinced the earls and barons of his sincerity.[11] Sufficient pressure was placed on the king for him to order a public proclamation, on 25 June, to announce that the perambulation of the Forest would start at Michaelmas. It would have been sooner, he claimed, most

[8] *Councils and Synods*, II, ii, 1190–98; Denton, *Winchelsey*, 188–92.

[9] Guisborough, 329–30; *Statutes of the Realm*, i, 126–30; Rothwell, 'Edward I and the Struggle for the Charters', 323–4.

[10] Williams, *Medieval London*, 261.

[11] *Chron. Bury St Edmunds*, 152; Langtoft, ii, 318.

unfairly, 'had it not been for some people, who were giving him much trouble', and he rebuked those who were claiming that he had no intention of keeping the terms of the Charters, or of allowing the Forest boundaries to be investigated.[12]

An interlude in the political wrangling occurred on 10 September 1299, when Edward married Margaret of France at Canterbury, in a ceremony conducted by Archbishop Winchelsey, who was, at least briefly, on relatively good terms with the king. The bishops of Durham, Winchester and Chester were present, as were the earls of Lincoln, Warenne, Warwick, Lancaster, Hereford and Norfolk, along with a host of other magnates. It was too much to hope, however, that even on such an occasion, there would be no arguments. There was vigorous debate as to who should receive the cloths that were used as a canopy above the newly married couple: the archbishop, the prior, the clerk who assisted the archbishop, or the clerks of the royal chapel. Edward's solution was to hand the cloth over to the earl of Lincoln, in the hope that his wise counsels might resolve the matter. After the ceremony, there was a splendid feast, with entertainment provided by a host of minstrels. The festivities took three days in all, for the feast was followed with much jousting, and other sports, with prizes given to the winners by the king.[13]

The magnificence of the wedding was only made possible because the Italian merchant banking firm of the Frescobaldi lent Edward sufficient money to buy the food for the feast.[14] Finance was a growing worry in this period. There had been no new taxes requested since the ninth was granted in the autumn of 1297, but the hope Edward had expressed, that he would be able to 'live of his own', was proving to be in vain. Figures of the debts incurred by the wardrobe show that by November 1298 there was an accumulated deficit of £38,722.[15] The Frescobaldi of Florence had come to the king's assistance when he was in the Low Countries in the winter of 1297–8, and in October 1299 the firm was granted the profits of Ireland, save for the customs, in return

---

[12] *CPR 1292–1301*, 424.

[13] Gervase of Canterbury, ii, 317–18; Rishanger, 396. It has been suggested that this wedding feast was the basis for the description of a series of theatrical scenes which took place at an English royal wedding, given by the Brabantine chronicler, Lodewijk van Velthem, but his work is so unreliable that little credence can be given to it. See above, 121.

[14] E 101/126/15.

[15] E 101/354/5. The suggestion that the king would 'live of his own' had been made in the requests Edward put to the clergy in June 1298. Its use at this time shows that the arguments put forward by B.P. Wolffe, *The Royal Demesne in English History* (1971), 47–9, need some modification, for Wolffe suggests that the concept was not employed until 1311, and then only in the context of prises.

for a loan of £11,000 to the wardrobe.[16] The Frescobaldi, however, never quite filled the place occupied by the Riccardi in the first half of the reign, and lacked either the will, or the resources, to lend on the same scale. Other Italian firms were prevailed upon to lend the crown poor-quality foreign coin, known as pollards and crockards, which they had in their possession, but the sums involved were not large. Edmund of Cornwall, the king's wealthy cousin, lent 2,000 marks in the summer of 1299: the crown's debts to him already stood at £6,560.[17] Edward and his officials could not go on borrowing when revenue was insufficient to pay off existing debts, and a financial crisis in 1299 was perhaps averted only because no major expedition set out for Scotland in that year. By 1300, the year of the Caerlaverock campaign, it was clearly necessary to try to negotiate a new tax. The scene was set for much argument in parliament, and hopes must have been high that it would prove possible to force concessions out of the king in exchange for a tax.

The parliament which was summoned to meet in London on 6 March 1300 was the fullest assembly, in terms of its composition, since 1296, for it included not only prelates and lay magnates, but also representatives of shires, boroughs and diocesan clergy. Early in the proceedings, Robert Winchelsey, on behalf of the clergy, requested the confirmation of Magna Carta. He was followed by Roger Bigod, with the same request on behalf of the baronage.[18] Separate lists of clerical and lay grievances were also presented.

The clerical articles had probably been drafted in a council held the previous autumn. For the most part, they covered familiar ground, developing points made in 1280 and 1285. Complaints about the way in which the crown exercised its rights to the custody of vacant bishoprics and churches may have been related to recent problems over the vacancy at Ely, and the articles reflected current preoccupations of the treatment of alien priories (seized by the crown during the French war, in 1295), and royal free chapels. Questions of royal interference in church courts, objections to the terms of the statute of Mortmain and some clauses of Westminster II, and similar matters, were not related to immediate problems, but were issues of long-standing concern.

---

[16] The £11,000 is referred to in *CPR 1292–1301*, 449. R.W. Kaeuper, 'The Frescobaldi of Florence and the English Crown', *Studies in Medieval and Renaissance History*, x (1973), 55, assumes that it was the total of the king's debt after account had been made with the Frescobaldi. While this is possible, the sum appears separately in the final account made with the firm, in E 372/154, and it seems more likely that it represents an actual loan. It does not appear in the accounts made by the Italians with the wardrobe, such as E 101/126/15, or E 101/126/21, perhaps because it was to be repaid in Ireland.

[17] *CPR 1292–1301*, 431, 447.

[18] Rishanger, 404.

These petitions do not seem to have been answered by the king: the clergy were not prepared to make a grant of taxation, although one source suggests that a tenth was requested from them. Edward was hardly likely to meet their requests without a *quid pro quo*.[19]

The requests made on behalf of the laity unfortunately survive only in a badly damaged text. Imprisonment, as well as excommunication, was demanded for violators of the Charters. There were complaints about purveyance, household jurisdiction, the use of the privy seal to interfere with the processes of the law, and a wide range of other matters. One very immediate issue was the recent summons of forty librate landholders to serve in Scotland, and it was argued that those who were not tenants-in-chief were not liable to perform military service.[20] The text provided the basis for royal concessions, known as the *Articuli super Cartas*, which were clearly a part of the price that Edward paid for the grant of a twentieth in this parliament.

The Articuli were very different from the concessions made by the crown in 1297. There was a much greater concern with the workings of the law, and, with the provision that sheriffs were henceforth to be elected in their counties, a new emphasis on local affairs, but one which also harked back to the early 1260s. There was to be a new procedure for the enforcement of the Charters, with three knights to be elected in each shire to hear complaints against those who did not respect their terms. Arbitrary legal proceedings, in the courts of the royal household and of the constable of Dover, were curtailed, and the privy seal was not to be used so that cases under the common law were affected. The jurisdiction of the exchequer was limited. Some earlier measures were reinforced. The statute of Winchester, on law and order, was to be read out publicly four times a year, and its terms maintained by the three knights appointed in each county to see to the maintenance of the Charters. The procedures introduced in cases of conspiracy were extended, with the possibility of procedure by plaint being added to the form of action by writ. The last clause of the *Articuli* was very different in character to the rest of the document. It provided for goldsmiths to use the hallmark of the leopard's head in future, as an indication of quality. This does not seem to have been the result of any pressure brought by the king's opponents, but was probably the work of the king's council. As an important customer of the London goldsmiths, Edward had a strong interest in maintaining the standard of their products.[21]

---

[19] *Councils and Synods*, I I, ii, 1205–18; *Ann. Worcester*, 544; Denton, *Winchelsey*, 194–9.

[20] Somerset Record Office, MS DD/AH, 186. I am grateful to Dr J.R. Maddicott for lending me a photocopy of this document, which is printed in part in *Royal Historical MSS Commission, 6th report*, appendix, 344.

[21] *Statutes of the Realm*, i, 136–41.

The *Articuli* did not go as far as the articles on which they were based. The king was not prepared to make formal concessions over military service, and so no mention was made of the summons of the forty librate men, even though such a summons was not repeated by Edward I. Although the *Articuli* allowed for actions to be brought against royal officials as private individuals, there was no provision for this to be done in their official capacity, save as far as prises were concerned. Prise offences, however, were not to be treated as offences against the Charters. It has been argued that the separation of the question of prise from that of the Charters 'must be reckoned the supreme evidence of the success of Edward's stand for the prerogative in 1300'.[22] In fact, prise offences were separate from the Charters in 1297, featuring as they did in the *Confirmatio Cartarum*, a document which was distinct from *Magna Carta* and the Forest Charter. Where the interests of the royal prerogative were clearly protected, was in the final clause, which explicitly saved royal rights. Yet, despite this saving clause, the *Articuli* can only be seen as a royal victory by perverse reasoning.[23] Substantial concessions, of a much more detailed kind than those of 1297, were forced from the king, and Edward was not able to use the savings clause to wriggle out of his obligations.

There were arguments over the precise legal form that the confirmation of the Charters should take. The earls and bishops asked that their seals should be put to the Charters, now to be reissued, but the suggestion angered the king, who declared, 'Do you think that I am a child, or a deceiver?'[24] There was what seems to have been a compromise, for the reissue was in charter form, unlike that of 1297, which was done as letters patent. A long list of witnesses gave added formality.[25]

There were further contentious issues raised in this parliament. Almost certainly, the king brought up the question of franchises, for in February he had asked the exchequer to have both Domesday Book and the charter rolls ready for discussions on that matter.[26] He perhaps hoped to use the subject as a bargaining counter, threatening to reopen the *Quo Warranto* inquiries. Then, of course, there was still the question of the Forest. On 1 April commissioners were appointed to undertake the perambulation, but the terms of appointment included a saving clause, protecting the rights of the crown. This can hardly have been welcome but nevertheless a grant of a twentieth was made, following a

---

[22] Rothwell, 'Edward I and the Struggle for the Charters', 329.
[23] Prestwich, *War, Politics and Finance*, 265–6, argues against the case put in favour of Edward by Rothwell, op. cit., 327–9.
[24] Rishanger, 405.
[25] Rothwell, op. cit., 326.
[26] E 368/71, m.28.

lengthy series of individual negotiations with the magnates.[27] The grant, however, was conditional. 'When we have secure possession of our forests, and of our liberties, often promised to us, then we will willingly give a twentieth, so that the folly of the Scots may be dealt with.'[28] Collection of a tax was, almost certainly, dependent on the king not merely agreeing to the perambulation of the forests, but also to his putting into effect the verdicts reached in the inquiries.

In spite of all the work that went into obtaining a grant in 1300, the tax was not in fact collected. Whether this was because the king decided that he was not prepared to submit to the conditions placed upon it, or because the magnates felt that he had not fulfilled those conditions properly, is not clear. The former is perhaps more likely, as there is no evidence that the exchequer began to make any preparations for the collection. Edward had gained little, and conceded much, in the parliament of 1300. In particular, nothing had been done to ease the crown's financial difficulties. The arguments were bound to continue in the following year, as the need for a tax became more desperate.

The next parliament was summoned to meet in January 1301, at Lincoln. In an unusual move, Edward asked for the same representatives of shire and borough to be returned as had attended the last parliament, a clear sign that the Lincoln assembly was intended to finish off uncompleted business.[29] The proceedings were, it appears, opened with a speech from Roger Brabazon, the chief justice of the King's Bench, who asked for a grant of a fifteenth. There was much murmuring at this, in part because so many taxes had been levied relatively recently, and in part because it was felt that the king had still not put his promises into effect.[30] A remarkable bill was put forward by a Lancashire knight of the shire, Henry of Keighley, which was then presented to the king by the magnates on behalf of the whole community.[31] It began with the demands which were by now becoming conventional, for the observance of Magna Carta and the Forest Charter. Statutes contrary to the Charters should be annulled, and the magnates ought to define the powers of justices appointed to maintain the Charters. The perambulation of the Forest should be completed, and its finding put into effect. Offences against the regulations in the

---

[27] CPR 1292–1301, 506.

[28] Ann. Worcester, 544.

[29] The suggestion that a parliament was summoned for October 1300, but then postponed, is made in Handbook of British Chronology, 550–1, and Richardson and Sayles, English Parliament in the Middle Ages, 147, but the documents on which this is based in fact date from 1302. See Prestwich, 'Magnate Summonses in the Later Years of Edward I', 99.

[30] Rishanger, 454.

[31] Parl. Writs, i, 104–5.

Articuli of 1300, about prise, should be properly dealt with. Sheriffs ought to be charged with the income from their shires, the annual farm, as in the time of Henry III, and increments recently added should be cancelled. If all this was done, then the fifteenth could be collected after Michaelmas.

Edward was forced to agree to most of the demands in Keighley's bill, though he did not approve of the idea of special auditors to hear cases of official malpractice, and stated that he would provide some other remedy. Although he conceded that statutes contrary to the Charters would be repealed, nothing was done in this way, and no further confirmation of the Charters took place. The king was angered by the bill; and showed this in 1306, when he at long last identified Keighley as the man responsible for it, and had him imprisoned.[32]

The magnates, in addition to supporting Henry of Keighley's bill, asked that the king's chief ministers should be appointed by common consent. Complaints were directed at the treasurer, Walter Langton, in particular: he was, it seems, regarded as responsible for the unpopular prises, and was alleged to have overthrown the old customs of the exchequer. Edward was furious. He replied at length, appearing in person, and accused the magnates of wishing to reduce him to a servile condition. Why, he asked, did they not each go so far as to ask for a crown for himself? Any lord, he argued, had the right to appoint his own officials, and the king should be able to do the same. Edward was prepared, however, to investigate any specific wrongs done by his officials. According to one account, the king's speech ended the matter there and then, so effectively did he shame his critics.[33] Langtoft, however, states that Edward agreed to the appointment of a committee of twenty-six, who were to determine whether the requests made in parliament were compatible with the preservation of the crown. The twenty-six refused to act, and the debates continued. It appears that a compromise of sorts was eventually agreed, which allowed the king to collect the tax of a fifteenth after Michaelmas, provided that the Charters were maintained, and the perambulation of the Forest accepted.[34]

As in 1300, the clergy had their debate with the crown in this Lincoln parliament of 1301. It was probably on this occasion that answers were given to the clerical grievances which had been presented in 1300, and were now put forward again. For the most part, the royal response was simply to repeat the replies that had been made in 1280, when many of the complaints had been first made. In many cases, it was noted that the king's answers were highly prejudicial to the interests of the church,

---

[32] Stubbs, *Constitutional History*, ii, 158n; see also E 159/79, m.40d.
[33] Rishanger, 460–1.
[34] Langtoft, ii, 330–2.

or at best inadequate. Edward hoped to obtain a grant of a fifteenth from the clergy, but this Winchelsey would not agree to, because of the papal prohibition expressed in *Clericis Laicos*. There was even a version of this bull in circulation among the English clergy that had been given a false date of February 1300, the true date being, of course, 1296. This was clearly intended to try to add additional strength to the archbishop's arguments. If the church was unwilling to make a grant, then it had no effective bargaining position. Edward, given his financial problems, would only have been prepared to make genuine concessions in return for a grant. In the absence of any promise of taxation from the church, he decided to levy the lay tax of a fifteenth on clerical temporalities, and was able to bypass Winchelsey's refusal by negotiating with the papacy for a tenth to be imposed from Rome, for three years. This was, in theory at least, a crusading tax, and the proceeds were to be divided between the crown and the papacy.[35]

The king conceded much in 1301. The grant of taxation he obtained was important, but the price he paid for it was high. It seems likely that he renounced the future use of this type of taxation, and if so, this was a step which went far beyond anything suggested in 1297.[36] The results of the perambulation of the Forest must have confirmed the king's worst fears, for in many cases land was put out of the Forest on quite inadequate evidence. The jurors of Warwickshire argued that when Henry II was crowned, there had been no royal forest in their county, or so their ancestors had said. No documentary proof was provided. The result of the proceedings was that about half of the Forest was declared to lie outside the old boundaries, and was therefore no longer subject to the special jurisdiction of the king's Forest officials.[37]

As far as prise was concerned, the terms of the *Articuli* of 1300 made it impossible to continue to operate the system as in the past, and use it to supply the army in Scotland with large quantities of victuals. Writs ordering purveyance were not sent out in 1301, but instead, officials were sent to negotiate loans of foodstuffs from the counties. Payment was to be made out of the receipts of the fifteenth. In practice, the counties all agreed to provide the quantities that the crown wanted, but in theory, the crown had relinquished power in an important sphere.[38] As far as military service was concerned, Edward did not use a summons of forty librate men after 1300, but in 1301 he attempted to summon men of that status by issuing 935 individual summonses. Although no protests at this technique are recorded, the fact that it was

[35] *Councils and Synods*, II, ii, 1206–18; Denton, *Winchelsey*, 198–204.
[36] Rishanger, 454.
[37] Bazeley, 'The Extent of the Forest', 155–7; Young, *Royal Forests*, 140.
[38] Prestwich, *War, Politics and Finance*, 131–2.

never repeated suggests that it was vigorously opposed. The absence of
any formal concessions by the king on the subject of military service
cannot be read as a royal success. The fact that in the final years of the
reign, Edward had to revert to thoroughly traditional forms of summons is testimony to the success of his opponents on this question.[39]

Only one source suggests that the arguments of 1301 may have
continued into the following year. The chronicle of the little Premon-
stratensian house of Hagnaby records the creation in parliament,
after Michaelmas, of a committee of thirty-five, under Archbishop
Winchelsey's leadership, which discussed matters of church and state.
No other evidence refers to this, and it is unlikely that, if it met, the
committee took any decisive steps.[40] Another incident, which certainly
did take place in 1302, may have had political implications, but it
remains mysterious. In August, the chancellor, John Langton, who had
held his post since Robert Burnell's death ten years before, was abruptly removed from office. A letter from someone in court reported the
matter to a colleague:

> Sire, know that at the time of writing there is no good news from the court
> that I can tell you, but there is bad news, and it is this. Sir John Langton, the
> chancellor, has been dismissed from all royal service, and the seal has been
> taken from him by the king's command, but I do not yet know why this has
> been done.[41]

It is not likely that Langton's dismissal was the result of complaints
such as those made in the Lincoln parliament of 1301 against royal
officials, for he was soon on good terms with Edward's opponent,
Winchelsey. In 1302 the ex-chancellor was able to reach an agreement
with the archbishop over a long-running dispute about a living at
Reculver in Kent.[42] Most probably, Langton's dismissal resulted from
some dispute unconnected with the central issues of national politics.

From 1301 until the end of the reign, the amount of political dissension
diminished markedly. In part, this was due to the military situation.
Most of Edward's English subjects supported his policies in Scotland.
The fact that there was no campaign in 1302 meant that the king's
demands on his subjects slackened, while the success of the 1303–4
campaign was sufficient to still any possible criticisms. The king did not
respond to Bruce's seizure of the Scottish throne in 1306 by sending

[39] Ibid., 88–90.
[40] BL Vesp. B.xi, f.53v, cited by Denton, *Winchelsey*, 208n. See also Prestwich, *War, Politics and Finance*, 90.
[41] E 101/368/18, no. 63.
[42] Denton, *Winchelsey*, 275–6.

armies north on the scale of those of 1298 or 1300, and there can have been few Englishmen who did not approve of their king's determination to defeat the new Scottish ruler.

The costs of the Scottish war, however, meant a continuing deterioration in Edward's financial position. Save for the year from November 1301 to November 1302, the accounts of the wardrobe show substantial deficits. In 1305–6, the deficit was over £13,000. After the difficulties he had faced in obtaining the grant of the fifteenth in 1301 (a tax which probably raised about £47,000), Edward and his officials were very careful about the means they adopted to raise money. In 1290, the king had been granted a feudal aid for the marriage of his daughter Joan, but he had chosen not to collect it, and had negotiated a far more lucrative fifteenth instead. On 7 November 1302 collection of the feudal aid was at long last authorized. This was a prerogative tax, to which the king was fully entitled. It was collected on the basis that each knight's fee was assessed at forty shillings. The final account shows that a total of £10,465 was due, for there were just over 5,000 knights' fees in the country. However, the yield was only £7,985, and receipt rolls suggest that only £6,832 was actually paid into the exchequer by 1307. Some went in expenses to the collectors, and there were arrears still due at the end of Edward I's reign.[43]

The next year saw another prerogative tax, tallage, revived. The idea of doing this came from the exchequer officials, and met with full royal approval.[44] The tax was payable only by those living in towns, and on the royal demesne – it was because of their liability to it that they frequently paid normal subsidies at a higher rate than the rest of the country. Tallage had been collected fairly frequently by Henry III, but never by Edward I until now. In contrast to the parliamentary subsidies, which were assessed solely on a valuation of movable goods, rents as well as movable property were the basis for the tallage. The assessment was probably over £6,000, and the tax yielded over £5,000.[45] The tallage, and the aid for the marriage of the king's daughter, were not failures, but their yields hardly compared with those of the taxes granted in parliament. Edward was entitled to a further feudal aid, in 1306, on the occasion of the knighting of his eldest son. Instead of taking this in the same way as the aid for Joan's marriage, he negotiated an agreement to take it as a tax of a thirtieth and twentieth, which was indistinguishable, in its methods of assessment and collection, from a normal parliamentary subsidy, although it

[43] J.F. Hadwin, 'The Last Royal Tallages', *EHR*, xcvi (1981), 345n.
[44] Baldwin, *King's Council*, 466, prints a council memorandum recording the king's agreement to the tallage.
[45] Ibid., 346–9.

was not granted in a conventional parliament. The assessment came to almost £35,000, and the receipt rolls show that by December 1307 about £26,500 had been collected.[46] These various forms of taxation, some more successful than others, were hardly sufficient to pay for the Scottish wars. Further resources had to be sought.

Although the *maltolt* of forty shillings on each sack of wool exported had been abolished in the autumn of 1297, the original customs duty of 6s 8d, agreed in 1275, still stood. The combined effects of the truce with the French and the fall in the level of duty payable boosted English wool exports, though not to such an extent that the customs receipts were as high as those from the *maltolt* had been. From Michaelmas 1297 to Michaelmas 1303 the duties raised an average £9,000 a year. Then, in 1303, the government decided to negotiate an increase in the customs. Early in the year agreement was reached with the foreign merchants trading in England that they would pay an additional 3s 4d, in return for various privileges, conceded by Edward in the *Carta Mercatoria*. In particular, they received protection from the attempts made in various towns, notably London, to constrict their activities and movements. Initial soundings by exchequer officials suggested that the English merchants would also be prepared to accept a similar increase in duty, and urban representatives were accordingly summoned to appear at York (the effective capital during the Scottish wars) in June. When the meeting took place, the royal request was rejected. There was, perhaps, anger at the favours granted to the foreign merchants, and it does not seem that the crown had much to offer English traders in return for the tax.[47] There is no reason to place the rejection of the proposed duties in a wider political perspective. It was, of course, contrary to the spirit of the concession of 1297 that the king should negotiate with one section of the community, on a matter which affected all, but it is unlikely that an assembly of burgesses would have based their objections on such grounds. Despite the refusal of the English merchants to pay the new duty, customs revenues from Michaelmas 1303 until Edward's death were at a much higher level than they had been in the previous six years. The new custom, paid by the foreign traders, yielded about £23,000 out of a total of some £72,000. It was not, therefore, so much the increased duties, as a boom in the wool export trade that led to this welcome increase in royal revenue.[48]

Efficient management of the coinage brought useful profits to the

---

[46] Prestwich, *War, Politics and Finance*, 179, 182; E 401/1708, 1713, 1716, 1728; above, 455.

[47] Lloyd, *English Wool Trade*, 124; SC 1/31/99. See also the summary of the *Carta Mercatoria* in Powicke, *Thirteenth Century*, 630–1.

[48] Wool customs accounts, E 356/2.

crown in this period. In 1299 the government took steps to deal with the circulation in England of inferior-quality foreign coins, known as pollards and crockards, which had been minted in deliberate imitation of English sterling pennies. Numismatic evidence suggests that they were not of very bad quality, but that they were far from uniform, and on average weighed about ten per cent less than English coin. It is not clear when the import of these coins began. It may have been in the late 1280s, when the output of English mints began to fall markedly, but the flow of them into England only became a flood after the Anglo-French truce was agreed in the autumn of 1297. One chronicler reported that Edward permitted their import as a part of the terms agreed with Philip IV. By 1299, the number of pollards and crockards in circulation in England was sufficient to affect prices, pushing them up.[49]

The first step to deal with this situation was taken in the statute of Stepney of May 1299, which was designed to prevent the import of any more pollards and crockards, and to stop the export of sterling coins. Then, at Christmas 1299, in an ordinance made by the council at York, it was decreed that henceforth pollards and crockards would only be valid as currency at half their face value, so that one pollard penny would be worth only a halfpenny. In most cases, this was less than the silver content of these foreign coins, and what the crown hoped was that payments would be made to its officials at this low valuation. Considerable profits could then be made by reminting the pollards and crockards into good sterling. This technique, which was of questionable morality, was not very successful. Some officials, failing to appreciate Edward's purpose, refused to accept pollards and crockards, and there were also difficulties in enforcing the new exchange rate. There was much confusion, and this was only resolved when, on 26 March, it was ordained that from that Easter, only sterling coins would be valid as currency in England. Pollards and crockards would have to be sold to the mints as bullion. Large-scale preparations were made for the expected increase of work at the mints. No less than 451 foreign workmen were brought over, at a cost of £1,146.[50]

The reminting process was thoroughly successful. By the end of 1300, £183,000 worth of pollards and crockards had been melted down, to be reissued as sterling. The figure for the next year was £64,750. The crown made a net profit on the operation of £8,202.[51] The mints were

---

[49] N.J. Mayhew and D.R. Walker, 'Crockards and Pollards: imitation and the problem of fineness in a silver coinage', *Edwardian Monetary Affairs (1279–1344)*, 125–9; Mate, 'Monetary Affairs in England', 62–3.

[50] Ibid., 66–7; *CCR 1296–1302*, 347, 385–6; E 159/73, m.12.

[51] E 372/152, John de Everdon's account.

then quiescent for a time, but from 1303 to the end of the reign, and beyond, a mounting tide of foreign silver was brought in. In Edward I's final year, the figure rose to £143,000. If it could be shown that this was the result of a deliberate royal policy, it would rank as a most remarkable triumph of economic management. In fact, however, it was probably the result of the highly successful English wool export trade, which boomed once the Low Countries began to recover from the French campaign of 1302. In addition, England was, it seems, benefiting from a cyclical process which affected the major currencies of north-western Europe in turn. Profits to the crown were appreciable, amounting to almost £7,000 for the years from 1304 until the end of Edward's reign. The addition of so much coinage to that already in circulation in England had its effect on prices, pushing them upwards. This did not, however, result in a marked increase in the costs facing the crown. Wage rates paid to soldiers, for example, remained static. The crown gained far more than it lost from the monetary situation in the early years of the fourteenth century.[52]

Clerical taxation provided Edward with much-needed funds in the last six years of his reign, a fact which appears initially surprising, after the fierce resistance put up by Archbishop Winchelsey to Edward's demands. However, in 1301, Boniface VIII imposed a new crusading tenth for three years. Relations between the French king, Philip IV and the papacy deteriorated rapidly, and Edward, in contrast, rose in papal estimation. He was granted half the proceeds of the tax by Boniface. There were some difficulties over the collection: after the first instalment had been paid in November 1301, Edward suspended the tax until a papal mandate was issued in March 1302, which made it quite clear that half of the receipts were to be paid to him. Further arguments on Boniface's death were resolved in Edward's favour. In all, this tax yielded almost £42,000 for the crown.[53]

The election of a Gascon, Clement V, as pope in 1305 proved very convenient for Edward. Negotiation of a new tax on the clergy was one of the main tasks of the embassy which set out from England in 1305, and Clement duly ordered the payment of a tenth for the next seven years. This was, ostensibly, a crusading tax, and it was laid down that the first year's receipts were to go to the king, the second year's to his

---

[52] For a general discussion of the implications of the monetary developments of this period, see my 'Edward I's monetary policies and their consequences', 406–16, and also M. Mate, 'High Prices in early fourteenth-century England: causes and consequences', *Economic History Review*, 2nd ser., xxviii (1975), 1–16. For a more sceptical view of the effects of monetary changes on prices, see A.R. Bridbury, 'Thirteenth Century Prices and the Money Supply', *Agricultural History Review*, xxxiii (1985), 1–20.

[53] Lunt, *Financial Relations of the Papacy with England*, 367–77; SC 1/32/37.

son Edward, and all the rest to the king, save for £2,000 a year for five years, allocated to the queen. Early in 1307 the terms were modified, and Edward conceded that a quarter of the proceeds of the tax might go to the papal curia. By the end of Hilary term 1307, £25,502 had been received by the exchequer from this tenth, and in the following term £2,996 came in. In all, therefore, papal taxes yielded some £70,000 for the crown in the last six years of Edward's reign, all with no constitutional objection possible from the English clergy.[54] Royal officials did not even have to undertake the work of collecting the money, and it was the popes, rather than the king, who incurred the anger of the English churchmen.

There were some other sources of revenue available to the crown, but none of them offered any hope of solving the financial crisis. The exploitation of vacant bishoprics could be useful: York was empty from October 1304 until March 1306, and Ely suffered two vacancies in the later years of the reign. When Archbishop Winchelsey was suspended from office, lay officials took charge of the temporalities of his see, to Edward's profit.[55] Another feudal right enabled the king to take fines, and scutage, in lieu of military service. Fines were the more profitable of these. As a result of the feudal summons of 1300, Edward raised about £2,000 in fines. From those who did not wish to serve in 1303, £1,777 was collected, and for the army of 1306, the equivalent figure was £1,881. In contrast, when collection of scutage was ordered in 1305 from those who had not served in 1300, less than £400 was raised. The reason for this discrepancy between fines and scutage was that fines were based on the new reduced quotas of military service which had come in by the mid-thirteenth century. Scutage, in contrast, was payable on the old assessment of knights' fees. Attempts by the exchequer to persuade men to pay scutage, when they had served with a reduced quota, were naturally resented.[56]

It was inevitable, given the disparity between the crown's financial resources and its income, that money would have to be borrowed. The obvious source of loans were the Italian companies of merchant bankers. From the point of view of the Italians, Edward cannot have seemed a good risk: the Riccardi had been broken as a result of their dealings with him. The king's lack of credit-worthiness was made clear early in 1298, when Thomas Paynel was trying to raise a ransom of £5,000 on behalf of John de St John, who was at that time a prisoner in France. The Italians would not lend on security provided by the king,

---

[54] Lunt, op. cit., 382–91.

[55] M. Howell, *Regalian Right in Medieval England* (1962), 242–3.

[56] Prestwich, *War, Politics and Finance*, 82, 185; H.M. Chew, 'Scutage under Edward I', *EHR*, xxxvii (1922), 332–3; E 370/1/13.

but insisted that guarantees be provided by various religious houses instead.[57]

By 1299, however, the firm of the Frescobaldi of Florence was prepared to make advances of money to Edward on a regular basis. This firm had made the most substantial contribution to forced loans of almost £30,000, taken from eleven Italian companies between 1294 and 1298, and had lent to the king when he was in Flanders. They claimed, later, that when this connection became known, their depositors had withdrawn sums totalling, by one account, about £30,000, by another, £50,000. The firm's best chances of recouping their losses was, so its members seem to have judged, to continue lending to the crown, so as to retain Edward's favour. They calculated that by 1302 they had lent £33,886, £13,250 of it since the end of the war with Philip IV. From 1303 the Frescobaldi company was paid the receipts from the new custom, paid by foreign merchants, and in the next year the old custom was handed over to them as well. They thus came to occupy the position that the Riccardi had held in the first half of Edward's reign, though their advances were never as substantial. Unfortunately, the accounts that they had made with the exchequer in 1310 do not make it possible to work out an accurate chronology for their loans, but it is likely that, in all, they lent Edward I and his son a total of about £150,000 between 1297 and 1310, of which about £125,000 was repaid. They were promised a total of £13,000 as compensation for the losses they incurred as a result of their loans to the crown, but never received much of this. Interest payments, of course, were forbidden under the terms of canon law. In 1305 it was estimated that it would take eighteen months to repay the firm out of the customs revenue, and it seems that in the last years of Edward's reign, the crown's obligation to it averaged over £15,300.[58]

Other Italian firms were much more reluctant to lend to Edward. The Ballardi of Lucca were used regularly by the great wardrobe to provide luxury goods, particularly textiles, and this firm lent a total of almost £7,500 between 1298 and the end of the reign. The Spini also lent on a small scale. When, however, John Droxford was commissioned to approach five companies for loans, in 1301, no funds were forthcoming, and in 1303 he had a similar experience, when only the Frescobaldi were prepared to make a loan.[59] The Italians faced

---

[57] M.C. Prestwich, 'Italian Merchants in late thirteenth and early fourteenth century England', *The Dawn of Modern Banking*, ed. Center for Medieval and Renaissance Studies (New Haven, 1979), 80–1.

[58] Prestwich, *War, Politics and Finance*, 209–11; Kaeuper, 'The Frescobaldi', 72; *CPR 1292–1301*, 508, 585; *CPR 1301–7*, 57–8.

[59] Prestwich, *War, Politics and Finance*, 215–16.

considerable difficulties in England in these early years of the fourteenth century. There were extreme fluctuations in the exchange rates, particularly against the florin, which could bring financial disaster.[60] It was to prevent companies leaving the country with their debts unpaid that in 1306 the leading firms in London, including the Frescobaldi, were brought before the royal council, and told that if they did this, or exported any of their belongings, all their assets would be confiscated. Security was demanded from them, to guarantee their good behaviour. The government's attitude is very understandable, for the firm of the Pullici and Rembertini had recently failed, but such an approach was hardly likely to win Edward the support of the Italian community in England.[61]

It is usually, and rightly, argued that Edward I's reign ended with the financial system in a state of near collapse. Several attempts were made, however, to keep the situation under control. In 1299 the king instructed all sheriffs and other royal officials to pay their receipts directly into the wardrobe, so bypassing the exchequer , and directing money more swiftly to where it was needed. This policy was then reversed in 1301, and the sheriffs were asked to pay their receipts into the exchequer in June, rather than at Michaelmas, in order to ease the shortage of cash. Direct payment to royal creditors, or to the wardrobe, by the sheriffs was discouraged. In subsequent years, the sheriffs reverted to coming to the exchequer at Michaelmas. When they assembled in 1304, they were told that they were to pay money over to the wardrobe only when specifically instructed to do so in a royal writ. The exchequer, under the treasurer, Walter Langton, was clearly trying to maintain effective control over crown expenditure, but this was difficult to achieve when it was the practice to authorize wardrobe expenditure by means of very large writs of *liberate*, sometimes for as much as £20,000, which were often issued long after the expenditure had in fact been incurred. In 1305, when Langton went abroad, John Droxford, as his deputy, was ordered to make specific allocations of cash to meet the needs of the royal household, and above all the wardrobe. A list of debts was to be drawn up in an attempt to introduce some order to the chaos that existed.

Such attempts were largely in vain. The incessant pressures of war meant that it was impossible to reorganize the financial system effectively. There was no means found to prevent the wardrobe officials issuing bills, or debentures, promising creditors payment at some future date, and so huge deficits were run up. There was insufficient

---

[60] M.C. Prestwich, 'Early Fourteenth-Century Exchange Rates', *Economic History Review*, 2nd ser., xxxii (1979), 471–5.
[61] E 159/79, m.34d.

time even to audit the wardrobe accounts: after 1298, none of them was approved by the exchequer and enrolled on the pipe rolls. The exchequer itself kept a record in this period of its own cash balance by means of *jornalia* rolls, but in the absence of an effective means of controlling the assignment of revenues to the wardrobe, it was impossible to work out any proper budgets, or even to check overall levels of royal expenditure.[62]

All this was bad enough, without the additional financial embarrassment of the robbery of the royal treasury at Westminster in 1303. An attempt had been made, in 1296, to break into this treasury, which was sited in the crypt beneath the abbey chapter house. The cellarer and another monk had been imprisoned, along with thirty others, for their part in the affair. Edward, however, had shown some sympathy for the monks of Westminster, and no steps seem to have been taken to avoid a fresh attempt. In 1302 Richard Pudlicote, a merchant who may have had a grudge against the king, as he had suffered imprisonment in Flanders in 1298 as surety for the king's debts, successfully stole some of the abbey's plate. He then, according to his own later confession, spent some months tunnelling through the massive stone walls of the chapter house, disguising the entrance to the tunnel by sowing hemp. He finally forced an entry to the treasury, where he spent two nights. When he made his way out, he was carrying so much silver and gold plate that some fell from his grasp, as he ran for safety. The tale is scarcely credible, and it was probably designed to exonerate the monks of Westminster, who had been the immediate suspects when the crime was discovered. Edward, as in 1296, was reluctant to see the monks of the great royal foundation of Westminster Abbey found guilty, and in the end only Pudlicote, and six laymen, were hanged. Much of the treasure was recovered.[63] The fate of some of it, however, is hinted at by the case of the stranger who came to King's Lynn in Norfolk, soon after the robbery, with 100 gold florins, six of which he sold for much less than their true value.[64] In the event, the great robbery probably did not do serious damage to the royal finances, for the treasure was more a store of valuables, to be given as presents or to be used on grand occasions, rather than a true financial reserve. The incident was, nonetheless, a blow to the credibility of the financial administration.

[62] For a fuller discussion, see M.C. Prestwich, 'Exchequer and Wardrobe in the Later Years of Edward I', *BIHR*, xlvi (1973), 1–10. See also Prestwich, *War, Politics and Finance*, 219–23. The *Jornalia* rolls, a somewhat neglected source, are in E 405/1.

[63] The robbery is fully discussed by Tout, in his *Collected Papers*, iii (Manchester, 1934), 93–115; see also his *Chapters in Medieval Administrative History*, ii, 53–8.

[64] *CPR 1301–7*, 289.

At the time of his death, Edward I was probably in debt by about £200,000. The figure of £60,000, which is often quoted, represents the sum still owed on Edward's accounts towards the end of his son's reign.[65] Indebtedness on such a scale inevitably caused problems. In 1303, for example, it proved hard to persuade workmen to assist in the war in Scotland, for they argued that they were owed so much for work at Linlithgow, that they would rather leave the country than go on working for the king.[66] Many petitions in parliament in 1305 testify to resentment at the king's failure to pay his debts. There was no one group that was notably ill-treated in comparison with any other: petitioners ranged from the royal justices to the crossbowmen and archers in the Kirkintilloch garrison.[67] This resentment, however, did not result in concerted opposition to the crown. There is no reason to suppose that Edward and his adviser had deliberately chosen to incur heavy debts, rather than burden the country with taxes as had been done between 1294 and 1297. The situation was forced on them, as a result of the costs of war and the difficulties in negotiating taxes. In political terms, it proved, at least in the short term, less costly to run up large debts than to raise huge sums in taxation. The fiscal policies of the last years of the reign proved to be a financial failure, but a political success.

There were further reasons why Edward in his final years did not face political opposition on the scale of that in 1297. In 1302 and 1305 he made agreements with Roger Bigod, earl of Norfolk, which, while they can be seen in part as the king's retaliation against a leader of the 1297 opposition, also had the effect of neutralizing the earl. In April 1302 Bigod surrendered his lands, earldom and office of marshal to Edward, and received them back entailed to his direct heirs. If he died without children, then they would all revert to the crown, rather than going to a collateral heir. In addition, Edward granted the earl lands worth £1,000 a year. According to Walter of Guisborough, and Rishanger's chronicle, this was done by Bigod so as to disinherit his brother, who was pressing him for repayment of debt: the earl was elderly and childless at the time, and it was most unlikely that he would have a direct heir.[68]

Rishanger, however, in his entry for 1305, gives a different version of the story, in which he states that the deal was Edward's revenge against

---

[65] The figure of £60,000 is Tout's: see his *Chapters in Medieval Administrative History*, ii, 125, but for the correction to some £200,000, see my *War, Politics and Finance*, 221.

[66] *CDS*, ii, no. 1412.

[67] *Memoranda de Parliamento*, ed. Maitland, 49, 169–70.

[68] Guisborough, 352; Rishanger, 215; McFarlane, *Nobility of Later Medieval England*, 262; *CPR 1301–7*, 29–31.

Bigod for the part the earl had played in plotting against the king in 1297. Edward did in fact make a further arrangement with Bigod in 1305, the terms of which were that the earl was to be pardoned all his debts to the crown, on condition that his heir should pay £20,000 upon his coming of age.[69] From the earl's point of view, this was a splendid arrangement. He still had no children, and had nothing to lose by the deal. It is less easy to see what advantage the king gained, though he must have recognized that it was highly improbable that he could ever recover the debts owed by Bigod. The two agreements, of 1302 and 1305, show that the earl had been persuaded by financial arguments to abandon his hostility to the crown.

A similar arrangement to that made with Bigod was agreed with the earl of Hereford, Humphrey de Bohun, also in 1302. Bohun was the son of Edward's opponent of 1297, and in his case, there can be no question of the king seeking revenge. The young earl married Edward's daughter, Elizabeth, in 1302. In line with the arrangements that had been agreed when the earl of Gloucester married Joan of Acre in 1290, Humphrey surrendered his lands and earldoms to the king, and received them back entailed upon himself and his bride. In contrast to what had been done in 1290, there were provisions to prevent Elizabeth disposing of the Bohun lands, should she marry again after her husband's death.[70] In so far as this marriage, and the territorial arrangements associated with it, provided a strong family link between the crown and a great earldom, they were politically important, but they were not a response to any immediate problem faced by the king.

In the absence of concerted opposition, Edward was able to limit the authority of individual holders of liberties. A complex, long-running dispute over the lordship of Gower in South Wales began in 1299, when the bishop of Llandaff brought complaints against William de Braose, lord of Gower. The issue was complicated by the grievances of William's tenants against him. The matters were brought before parliament, and arguments strongly reminiscent of the days of the *Quo Warranto* inquiries were rehearsed. An inquiry was held in 1302, but for some unknown reason, its findings were overturned. In 1304, William de Braose appeared to win a decisive advantage, for, profiting from the fact that he was serving in Scotland, he persuaded the king to confirm earlier charters, which gave him similar rights in Gower to those enjoyed by the earls of Gloucester in Glamorgan.

However, in 1305, the atmosphere changed. In the course of an

---

[69] Ibid., 317; Rishanger, 227. *Flores*, iii, 125 has the same story, but tells it of the earl of Warwick, which is clearly an error.

[70] McFarlane, *Nobility of Later Medieval England*, 261.

entirely different case, de Braose denounced a royal judge, Roger de Hegham, and the justice he provided. He was hauled before the royal council, and for his offence, he had to walk with bowed head bared, without a sword in his belt, to the exchequer to make his apologies to Hegham. He was even imprisoned for a time. A new inquiry was held into the question of the status of the lordship of Gower in 1306, at Swansea, and William de Braose's position became weaker. The issue was effectively settled when, under royal pressure, he granted two charters, one to the men of Swansea, the other to those of Gower, which limited his arbitrary authority to a marked degree.[71] This should not be seen as a part of a general policy directed against holders of franchises, a new *Quo Warranto*. Edward was taking action against a man who appeared both to be exceeding his authority, and failing to rule his liberty effectively. Edward was understandably cautious in these years when it came to creating franchises, and in 1306 he announced, after making a grant to his friend the earl of Lincoln, that no further grants involving return of writ would be made during his lifetime, save to his own children.[72]

In Ireland, too, the rights of some franchise holders were diminished during Edward's later years. Early in 1297, the former justiciar, William de Vescy, was the subject of a deal which in some ways foreshadowed that made by the king with Roger Bigod. He formally surrendered his lands to Edward, and in return was pardoned all his debts. After a few months, Kildare was restored to de Vescy, but with reversion to the crown. De Vescy's own son had died, and he had only a short time to live himself. He probably had few regrets at disinheriting distant relatives, and later in 1297, after his death, Kildare was duly taken over by the crown, to become a royal county. William de Vescy had failed the king during his period as justiciar, and owed substantial debts to the crown, much as Roger Bigod did.[73]

The treatment of another franchise holder in Ireland, Geoffrey de Geneville was very different, for he was a loyal supporter of the king. Through his wife, Geoffrey held half of Meath. The other half, held by the de Verduns, had largely lost its franchisal status in about 1280, and in 1297 it was created a separate royal county. Geoffrey and his wife, however, in the course of a lengthy series of disputes with the Dublin authorities, succeeded in maintaining their position in the liberty, centred on the

---

[71] *Glamorgan County History, iii, The Middle Ages*, ed. T.B. Pugh (Cardiff, 1971), 231–41; Davies, *Lordship and Society in the March of Wales*, 264–5; *Select Cases in the Court of King's Bench*, ed. Sayles, iii, 152–4.

[72] *Rot. Parl*, i, 211.

[73] Otway-Ruthven, *History of Medieval Ireland*, 212; *CDI 1293–1301*, nos 365, 374, 414, 481.

castle of Trim.[74] There was no systematic policy of destroying liberties, though their number was certainly whittled down by the crown.

Edward took an aggressive attitude towards the church in his later years, securing the suspension of Archbishop Winchelsey, confiscating the great liberty of Durham, and, apparently, frightening the archbishop of York to death. He considered that Winchelsey was the man primarily responsible for the criticisms of the crown made in parliament in 1301, and even, according to one account, claimed that he had been plotting deposition.[75] Winchelsey himself was certainly in determined mood. When John de Ferrers pursued his claim to the earldom of Derby in the papal courts, claiming £20,000 from the earl of Lancaster, who had possession of most of the former Derby estates, Winchelsey was appointed by Boniface VIII to judge the issue. Despite a royal writ of prohibition, the archbishop went ahead with the case, and in 1301 Thomas, earl of Lancaster, Edward's nephew, sued him in the royal courts, claiming exemplary damages of £100,000. Winchelsey was accused of weakening the law of the land, disinheriting the crown, and subverting the realm. The case was never concluded, but was frequently adjourned.[76] Winchelsey's support for John de Ferrers must have angered Edward, but the king was unable to to take decisive action against the archbishop while Boniface VIII occupied the papal throne.

Boniface VIII died in 1303, as did his succcessor, Benedict XI, in the following year. By 1305, Edward was, therefore, in a stronger position. On 1 April he summoned Winchelsey to the exchequer to answer for £6,000 of the clerical tenth, which had been granted in the autumn of 1297, and which, it was alleged he was keeping back. Winchelsey refused to attend, and the sheriff of Surrey was ordered to distrain all his lands in the county, and to ensure that he appeared on 20 June. This case, however, was dropped, perhaps as it was considered there were more suitable weapons available with which to attack the archbishop. There were disputes over Winchelsey's claims to jurisdiction over the royal free chapels at Hastings and Worcester, which added to the tension, but by the autumn of 1305, Edward at last felt able to bring political charges against the man he regarded as his chief opponent.[77]

Edward's position was decisively strengthened by the election of one of his former clerks, the Gascon Bertrand de Got, as Pope Clement V, in

---

[74] G.J. Hand, *English Law in Ireland, 1290–1324* (Cambridge, 1967), 124–30.

[75] Prestwich, *War, Politics and Finance*, 270, citing R. Twysden, *Historiae Anglicanae Scriptores Decem* (1652), 1990, 2004–5 (William Thorn's chronicle).

[76] Denton, *Winchelsey*, 205–6.

[77] Ibid., 213–18.

June 1305. He could now rely on papal support in the dispute. According to a Westminster chronicler, Winchelsey appeared before the king in the autumn of 1305. He was charged with taking action arbitrarily against royal clerks, and other offences. Winchelsey was, by this account, so overwhelmed by Edward's verbal onslaught that he submitted, and sought the king's blessing. The story is problematical, for it follows an account in which the author appears to confuse the earls of Warwick and Norfolk, which does not fit the facts for either earl, and there is no confirmation in other chronicles of this interview. The Westminster writer suggests that Edward argued that Winchelsey should be tried by the bishops, his peers, but no such trial took place.[78] Instead, Edward relied on Clement V to take appropriate action. A powerful embassy, which included the earl of Lincoln, Otto de Grandson, and Walter Langton, set out for the papal curia in October 1305. There was much business to be done with the pope, and one item was the question of Winchelsey. The archbishop was charged with plotting against the king, who, it was alleged, had only narrowly escaped losing his throne and possessions. On 2 February 1306, Clement obliged Edward by formally suspending Winchelsey from office. The bull was handed over to Winchelsey on 18 May, and on the next day he sailed from Dover, not to return to England during Edward's lifetime.[79]

Winchelsey was not the only prelate against whom Edward acted in these years. The king turned on his old friend Anthony Bek, bishop of Durham, in a complex dispute. Bek's role in 1297 had been that of peacemaker: a chronicle of Edward II's reign includes vivid memories of the way in which Bek had, apparently, rebuked both king and barons.[80] It may be that Edward resented this, and felt that Bek should have given him his whole-hearted support, but there was no immediate breakdown of relations between the two men, as is shown by grants made by Edward in 1298. The immediate cause of the trouble was the determination of Richard de Hoton, prior of the Durham cathedral convent, to maintain the independence of his house from Bishop Bek. Hoton was careful to obtain influential allies, by providing prebends for Walter Langton, John Droxford, Walter Bedwin and John Sandale, all powerful men in the royal administration. Edward's own personal devotion to the cult of St Cuthbert, and the presence of a Durham monk bearing the saint's standard on the expeditions to Scotland, prejudiced the king in the priory's favour. When Edward passed through Durham in January 1300, he confirmed various charters which secured grants of

[78] *Flores*, iii, 125–6.
[79] Denton, *Winchelsey*, 224, 234–5.
[80] 'Gesta Edwardi de Carnarvan', *Chronicles of the Reigns of Edward I and Edward II*, ed. Stubbs, ii, 38–9. Langtoft, ii, 290–2, also has a passage on Bek's peacemaking role in 1297.

lands and rights to the house, and this process was continued at
Westminster in March.[81] Once Prior Hoton's position was strengthened in this way, he took action against some of his own subordinates,
with whom he was having difficulties. Complaints about this inevitably
reached Bek, who announced his intention of conducting a visitation of
the priory. The monks, however, had a strong tradition of opposition to
visitations: Guisborough's chronicle, probably drawing on a lost
Durham source, contains a section detailing the successes they had in
resisting them in the past.[82]

On 20 May 1300 Bek appeared at the priory, with a full following,
ready to conduct the visitation.[83] There was fierce argument, and Prior
Hoton, with others, was excommunicated on Bek's behalf. The priory,
and indeed the whole castle bailey at Durham, within which the
cathedral and priory lay, were put under guard, with the gates locked.
One of the monks, Robert of Rothbury, succeeded in making his
escape, and obtained letters from the archbishop of York prohibiting
Bek and his men from taking any further action until an appeal by the
monks was heard. It was unlikely that such a *cause célèbre* as this was
fast becoming, affecting as it did one of Edward's chief councillors,
could be resolved within the ecclesiastical sphere. Both sides made
overtures to Edward, and the seriousness with which he regarded the
matter is shown by his appointment of Otto de Grandson, Walter de
Winterbourne (his confessor), John de Craucombe and the notary
John of Caen to try to settle the dispute.

Edward himself came to Durham on 18 June, and made a speech
outside the cathedral, He expressed his desire for a peaceful settlement,
on the one hand because of Bek's valuable services on the crusade, and
in the king's wars, and on the other because of the important aid offered
to his cause by St Cuthbert, thanks to the intercession of the Durham
monks. The king's offer of mediation was accepted, and on the next day
a meeting took place at the episcopal manor of Evenwood, near Bishop
Auckland. The occasion was not an easy one. Bek, according to a
distinctly hostile account, said that he would rather die than allow the
king to interfere in his liberty, Edward retorted that he was quite as
zealous in defence of a religious house founded from royal alms and
dependent on royal protection as Bek was zealous in defence of his
palatine rights. In a theatrical and effective gesture, Edward went on
his knees before his old friend Anthony Bek, and a compromise was
eventually agreed.[84]

[81] C.M. Fraser, *A History of Anthony Bek* (Oxford, 1957), 129–30.
[82] Guisborough, 349–51.
[83] For the events which follow, see in particular Fraser, *Anthony Bek*, 134ff.
[84] 'Gesta Dunelmensia', ed. R.K. Richardson (Camden Soc. Miscellany, xiii, 1924),
17–18; *Records of Anthony Bek*, ed. C.M. Fraser (Surtees Soc., clxii (1947), 72–4.

The Evenwood agreement, even though it had the stamp of Edward's authority, was soon shown to be ineffective. Bek would not hand back the priory estates he had taken over; the monks would not withdraw their case against the bishop, which they had brought at York. Each side accused the other of bad faith. The minority of monks who were opposed to Prior Hoton asked Bishop Bek to name a new prior, and he duly nominated Henry de Luceby, prior of Holy Island. Measures were then taken to install Luceby by force. Philip Darcy, constable of Durham castle, with a force of, it was claimed, 300 men from Tynedale, attacked the priory on 20 August 1300. Hoton and forty-six monks bravely refused to leave the cathedral. Conditions were extremely difficult. Food was very short. There were no latrines available, so Hoton and his men were forced to relieve themselves in the cathedral, 'which was an unheard of action by Christians up to that time'. Eventually, on 24 August, Darcy and his men dragged Hoton by force from his stall.[85] He was imprisoned in the castle, and in September, under duress, resigned his position. His friends, however, did not give up, and in December assisted him in escaping.[86] He prepared to put his case against Bek to the king at the Lincoln parliament early in 1301. What took place there is not clear, but it seems likely that Bek gave Winchelsey his full support in his arguments with the king, and that the Durham issue remained unresolved.[87]

Relations between Edward and the bishop of Durham deteriorated in 1301, when a tenant of the priory, William de Brometoft, was arrested by the constable of Durham castle, in spite of the fact that he carried royal letters of protection. The bishop's officials argued that a royal writ had no validity within the franchise of Durham. Even this did not cause a final breach, and after a meeting between Edward and Bek at Tynemouth, in June 1301, Brometoft was released, and the case postponed until the next parliament.[88] Edward was too concerned with his campaign in Scotland to press the matter. In the next year, Bek was not present in parliament, as he had gone to the papal curia, following his suspension from office by Boniface VIII. So, when Brometoft brought his case, judgement went in his favour. The royal attorney had firm words to say about the fact that liberties were inferior to the crown, and the palatinate of Durham was taken into the king's hands.

Brometoft's case provided Edward with the excuse to confiscate the liberty of Durham, but underlying the action was the problem of

[85] For a detailed account, see Durham Dean and Chapter Muniments, Loc. 7, 14 (Bereford's plea roll).
[86] 'Gesta Dunelmensia', 52; Guisborough, 347.
[87] Fraser, *Anthony Bek*, 152; and see Denton, *Winchelsey*, 161.
[88] *Records of Anthony Bek*, ed. Fraser, 85.

obtaining military service from the men of the palatinate. They took the view that they were not obliged to fight beyond the Tees to the south, or the Tyne to the north. This caused considerable trouble in the case of the ineffectual winter campaign against the Scots early in 1300, and it is striking that no Durham men featured in the pay rolls of the Caerlaverlock army of the summer of 1300.[89] The importance of Durham as a staging post and recruiting ground for the Scottish wars was obvious, and the king must have welcomed a chance to intervene directly. In Robert Clifford, he found a keeper for the palatinate of considerable military expertise.

When the palatinate was in the king's hands, full hearings into Bek's administration of Durham took place before William de Ormesby. Many officials were fined and imprisoned, although Bek himself was named as defendant in only two cases. The king had no desire to destroy the special position of Durham. He wrote that he was merely the minister and maintainer of the franchise of St Cuthbert, and was not anxious to keep it in his hands for longer than was necessary. His main concern was to establish his rights to military service. By February 1303 Bek was discussing with representatives of the county community of Durham a draft charter, proposed by the latter. In May, after Edward had brought his personal influence to bear, the bishop and the community reached agreement. The way was open for restoration of the liberty, and this was done on 8 July. The community had wanted to include a clause specifying that no service be done beyond Tyne or Tees, but this, unlike the majority of their demands, was not acceptable. Edward, no doubt remembering the way that the Evenwood settlement had been ignored, was insistent that this time there should be full observance of the agreement.[90]

The settlement of 1303 had not resolved the problems raised by the bishop's dispute with Prior Hoton. The prior brought further accusation against Bek, and in 1304 William de Bereford and Roger de Hegham were sent to investigate. The royal right to intervene in the affairs of Durham was allowed, under the terms of the aggreement of 1303. The prior and his supporters brought forward a wide range of accusations against Bek. They ranged from a failure to return books borrowed from the library, to matters which the king could take very seriously indeed. One was the case of Thomas of Bamburgh, from whom, when he tried to read out royal letters of protection at Holy Island in 1302, they had been seized, and the seals smashed. He was then dragged feet first from the church. More significant still was the imprisonment by Bek of a certain Robert le Messager, who also had

[89] Ibid., 56–7; Fraser, *Anthony Bek*, 139, 178; *Liber Quotidianus*, 241ff.
[90] Fraser, *Anthony Bek*, 183–7; *Records of Anthony Bek*, ed. Fraser, 92–3.

royal letters of protection. The bishop had announced that Robert was being punished, so that no one else might dare carry letters, within his bishopric, which were in derogation of the franchise. It was claimed that, on one occasion, a Scottish knight in Bek's service had gone so far as to declare that letters from the king, or anyone else, were valueless in Durham, as the bishop was king within his regalian liberty, just as Edward was king outwith it.[91]

Matters looked ominous for Bek. He was ordered to pay damages to Prior Hoton and the priory, but the offences against messengers bearing royal letters of protection were so serious that in December 1305 the bishopric of Durham was once again taken into the king's hands, and entrusted to Robert Clifford. It became possible for the first time to tax Durham – the thirtieth and twentieth was imposed on the palatinate – and in 1306 the military resources of Durham were mobilized for the war against Bruce.[92] Bek was able to obtain support from Clement V, his former colleague in royal service. Clement made him Patriarch of Jerusalem; as Guisborough commented, Bek was rich, and the pope poor.[93] Edward, however, was in determined mood, and took every possible step against Bek. He investigated, for example, the bishop's acquisition of some of John Balliol's lands, notably Tynedale and Barnard Castle. Although the king had earlier himself confirmed the grant of these, Bek was now unable to defend his title.[94] A newsletter from the Carlisle parliament of 1307 reported that all lands of the bishopric of Durham, held in lay fee, had been seized, because the king and his council had been told that Bek had given his support to Robert Bruce, and that without Bek's support, the new king of Scots would not be trying to continue his war against Edward.[95] The rumour was, of course, malicious, but the king may have believed it. He was clearly determined to break his old friend Bek, and it was only the death of the master he had served devotedly for so long which saved the bishop of Durham.

Edward's quarrel with Bek was a very revealing affair. It demonstrated the king's readiness to intervene in ecclesiastical affairs, and showed the surprising way in which his pious attachment to the cult of St Cuthbert could override his affection for an old friend. The importance of the military service provided by the men of Durham was evident, but much more important in Edward's eyes, no doubt, was the fact that his own royal authority had been challenged. The reported

[91] Fraser, *Anthony Bek*, 196–7; Durham, Dean and Chapter Muniments, Loc. 7, 14.
[92] Fraser, *Anthony Bek*, 199–200.
[93] Guisborough, 364.
[94] Fraser, *Anthony Bek*, 203–10.
[95] Richardson and Sayles, *English Parliament in the Middle Ages*, XII, 436.

insults to men bearing royal writs of protection, and the statements that
Bek enjoyed regal authority between Tyne and Tees, were matters
which Edward could not let pass. It is remarkable that Bek, with his
long ministerial experience, failed to realize the effect they would have
on the king. There was much that Edward was prepared to forgive in
his friends, but Anthony Bek, glorying perhaps in his own position went
too far.

There were other ways in which royal authority over the church was
increasing in the later years of Edward's reign. The increase in ecclesiastical patronage under crown control was striking. Edward was
successful in defending his existing rights, such as those to appointments at the church of St Martin's-le-Grand in London, where
Winchelsey unsuccessfully tried to conduct a visitation in 1303. When
the earldom of Cornwall came into his hands, on the death of his cousin
Edmund in 1300, Edward claimed that the church of St Buryan's was a
royal free chapel. He appointed in turn William Hamilton and Ralph
Manton, both important royal clerks, as dean, and although the
crown's position was not strong, it was successfully maintained in the
courts. At St Mary's, Hastings, the royal attempt to establish the castle
church as a royal free chapel eventually foundered in June 1307, but
before then, John of Caen, Walter of Amersham and Giles of
Audenarde, all influential men in royal service, had all benefited from
royal patronage there.[96]

Every advantage was taken of minorities of royal tenants-in-chief to
make presentations to churches: it was increasingly common for the
king to retain the right to do this, even when the wardship itself was
granted out. Acquisitions, such as that of the Bigod estates, also
increased the scope for the exercise of ecclesiastical patronage.[97]
Ingenious use was made of the king's rights during vacancies in
bishoprics and royal abbeys. By making use of the legal doctrine that
time does not run against the king, Edward and his clerks developed
techniques of making appointments to churches, long after a vacancy in
a bishopric had ended. In 1305, for example, John Droxford was
appointed to a living at Nassington, in Northamptonshire, although
the vacancy in the bishopric of Lincoln had ended in 1300. In 1306,
Walter Bedwin was appointed to the treasurership of St Peter's, York,
on a similar basis. A papal plea that the king's rights had lapsed
through the passing of time was dismissed, and it was made very clear
that the rights of the crown were at stake. The matter was regarded by

---

[96] Denton, *Winchelsey*, 285–90.

[97] P.C. Saunders, 'Royal Ecclesiastical Patronage in England, 1199–1356' (Oxford
D. Phil. thesis, 1978), 278–82. I am very much indebted to this important thesis for
information and ideas about ecclesiastical patronage.

Edward and his council as extremely important.[98] A letter written in the next year, 1307, provides a rare insight into the manoeuvrings that went on at court, as the king's clerks competed for rich livings. Someone (it is unfortunately not known who) wrote from court to Bedwin, to tell him that he had discussed with Walter Langton John Droxford's attempt to take the treasurership at York away from Bedwin, to give it to his own brother. Langton's view was that Bedwin should retain the post, as to give it up would be tantamount to depriving the king, and the church of York, of an important position.[99]

In many cases, the impetus behind royal policy on church patronage was no doubt given by the clerks who benefited from it. In one *cause célèbre* at York, however, the archbishop, Thomas Corbridge, was left in no doubt as to the strength of the king's own feelings. Edward had nominated the notary John Bush to a post, to which there was also a papal nominee. When Corbridge failed to comply with Edward's wishes, he was summoned to appear before him. No lawyer would speak on his behalf, and the unfortunate archbishop was sentenced to lose his temporalities. A later story had it that the king joked when Corbridge attempted to defend himself: 'Our father the archbishop has a lion's heart: soon he will have a sheep's tail.' According to the chronicler Walter of Guisborough, Corbridge was so shaken by the treatment he received that he promptly succumbed to illness and died.[100]

In the autumn of 1305, with Scotland apparently settled, and his domestic opponents of the past no longer presenting any threat, Edward felt in a strong enough position to go back on his earlier concessions. The embassy which set out for the papal curia in October 1305 was charged, among other matters, with persuading Clement V to absolve Edward from certain promises. On 29 December, the pope duly issued a bull, revoking the concessions the king had made. They were described as 'varied and harmful, relating to the forests and other rights belonging of old to the crown and the honour of your royalty'.[101] The bull seems superficially straightforward, but it is not in fact clear precisely what it referred to. It certainly annulled the *Confirmatio Cartarum* of 1297, though it wrongly suggests that sentences of excommunication were ordered against any who infringed the terms of that document. The *Articuli Super Cartas* of 1300 were not

[98] Ibid., 291–2; A. Deeley, 'Papal Provision and Royal Rights of Patronage in the Early Fourteenth Century', *EHR*, xliii (1928), 511; *CPR 1301–7*, 380, 467.

[99] E 101/368/18/61.

[100] Saunders, 'Royal Ecclesiastical Patronage', 324; B. Smalley, *English Friars and Antiquity in the Early Fourteenth Century* (Oxford, 1960), 161, 323; Guisborough, 358–9.

[101] *Foedera*, I, ii, 978, translated by B. Wilkinson, *Constitutional History of England*, i (Oxford, 1948), 230.

mentioned in the bull, and despite the very specific mention of the Forest, it does not appear that the pope explicitly cancelled the concessions Edward had made in 1301 with regard to the Forest boundaries. However, when the London annalist recorded the way in which the bull was read out at St Paul's, he described it as absolving the king from his oath regarding the Forest, and from the terms of the perambulation. In an ordinace of 1306, the king related the papal action to the question of the disafforestation that had taken place.[102] It is unlikely that Edward and his councillors seriously intended to sweep away all the concessions that had been made, but it is very clear that they did intend to reverse the action taken in 1301, which had so reduced the boundaries of the royal Forest.

Edward had shown the strength of his feelings on the question of the Forest in 1305, when in an ordinance, he accepted the disafforestation that had taken place as a result of the perambulation of 1301, but laid down that those people who had now been placed outside the Forest boundaries would no longer be allowed to exercise any rights of common within them. Now, in 1306, he was able to reverse the disafforestations. At the same time, it was made clear that proper legal procedures were to be adopted by the foresters, and procedures against corrupt officials were set out. Those who returned to the Forest, as a result of readjustment of the boundaries, were once more to be permitted to exercise their rights of common. Edward was careful to try to ensure that the conduct of his foresters would not become a matter of grievance in the future, and the ordinance is a mixture of a return to the past, and of valuable change.[103]

The papal bull, absolving Edward from his promises, did not affect royal policy in other respects. There were no attempts to reimpose the arbitrary taxes of 1297, or to summon twenty-pound landholders to campaign with the king. There was no new prise of wool, although of course prises of foodstuffs for the armies in Scotland still continued. Edward had learned caution, and as a result, was not the subject of much criticism in these years. The same, however, was not true of the treasurer, Walter Langton. He attracted hostility, and perhaps thus diverted attention from the king himself.

The first indications of antagonism towards Langton can be discerned in 1300, when Edward had to make elaborate arrangements for the auditing of Langton's accounts for the time when he had been keeper of the wardrobe. It was feared that Langton's enemies might be

[102] *Statutes of the Realm*, i, 149; *Ann. London*, 146; and see also *Flores*, iii, 130. The question is discussed more fully by Denton, *Winchelsey*, 229–31, 237–8.
[103] *Statutes of the Realm*, i, 144, 149; Young, *Royal Forests of Medieval England*, 141.

able to make political capital should Langton, in his capacity as treasurer, supervise the auditing of his own accounts, as keeper of the wardrobe, and so a special commission had to be set up to do the job.[104] In 1301 Langton came under attack at the Lincoln parliament, when his dismissal was demanded. This Edward would not do, and the matter went no further. However, an accusation against Langton brought by a knight, John Lovetot, proved to be a serious embarrassment to the treasurer. Lovetot, whose father was a close friend of Langton, produced charges of such implausibility that it is hard to imagine anyone inventing them. Langton had, it was said, made Lovetot's stepmother his mistress, and with her aid, strangled his (Lovetot's) father. In addition, Lovetot accused Langton of simony, pluralism, sale of papal constitutions, and of performing homage to the devil. The accusations were put to the papal curia, and in October 1301 Langton had to go to Rome in order to clear himself: the charges were sufficiently serious, and the tale sufficiently circumstantial for Boniface VIII to suspend Langton from his episcopal office in March 1302. He came home to England, but returned to Rome in 1303 to hear the verdict of the commission which had been appointed to look into his case. He was found to be entirely blameless: Edward, and the clergy of his diocese of Coventry and Lichfield, had provided impressive testimonials. The case had arisen out of the complex relationship of Langton with the Lovetot family, which cannot be fully disentangled, but clearly gossip had spread because of Langton's important position in government.[105]

In 1305 Walter Langton was the cause of an embarrassing dispute between Edward and his son, the prince of Wales. According to one account, this began when Langton rebuked the prince for breaking into one of his woods.[106] Edward gave Langton his full support in the quarrel, and forbad his son to appear before him. The prince was to receive nothing towards the costs of his household: it may be that his extravagance was an element in the dispute, as well as the contempt he had shown to a royal minister. The young heir to the throne remained in the vicinity of the court, staying a few miles away. The estrangement between father and son lasted from June until October, when at the feast of St Edward, a reconciliation took place. It was probably the need to proceed with negotiations for the marriage of the prince with Isabella of France that finally caused Edward to come to terms with his son. When Edward of Caernarfon came to the throne in 1307, Langton paid

[104] Tout, *Chapters in Medieval Administrative History*, ii, 91, and note.
[105] A. Beardwood, 'The Trial of Walter Langton, bishop of Lichfield, 1307–1312', *Transactions of the American Philosophical Society*, n.s. liv (1964), 7–8.
[106] *Ann. London*, 138.

the price for this quarrel of 1305, for he was soon arrested and imprisoned.[107]

Langton faced further problems at the Carlisle parliament of 1307, when John de Ferrers accused him of champerty, or supporting a plaintiff in the courts in return for a share of the profits of successful litigation. Given the prominence accorded to John in the crisis of 1297, it is very tempting to see this as a political move. However, Ferrers had a good case, as a result of complex land transactions concerning the manor of Newbottle in Northamptonshire, in which Langton had become involved. Ferrers had the support of the prince of Wales, but this was of little avail, for although Langton admitted to champerty, he produced a letter of pardon from the king. Ferrers argued that the document was a forgery, concocted without the king's knowledge. It was certainly strange that Edward had, apparently, given verbal instructions for the pardon to be drawn up, to the chancellor, William Hamilton, but that the document was not in fact issued until over a month after Hamilton's death.[108] Whatever the truth of the matter, Langton's position was far too well entrenched under Edward I for attacks such as that initiated by Ferrers to have any chance of success.

Edward's second queen, Margaret of France, described Walter Langton as 'the king's right eye'.[109] As in the case of Robert Burnell earlier, it is not easy to document the relationship between king and minister. In one remarkable instance, however, it seems that Edward deliberately made Langton bear the responsibility for an unpopular appointment. In October 1304, Edward wrote to Langton, approving of the treasurer's decision to have up to twenty pike caught (a curious example of the intrusion of domestic business into state affairs), and went on to explain that, while he was quite happy to see Bamburgh castle handed over to Isabella de Vescy, this was not to be done by royal command. The appointment was to be made 'by your ordinance and your authority'. Hostility must have been anticipated, both because Isabella was a woman, and because she was an alien, and Edward obviously did not want to be criticized.[110] In a different context, however, Edward wanted Langton to receive the credit for an act of clemency which in fact was the king's own doing. When the

---

[107] The quarrel between the king and his son is fully described by Johnstone, *Edward of Caernarvon*, 96–102. See also the roll of Edward's correspondence, *Letters of Edward, Prince of Wales, 1304–5*, ed. H. Johnstone (Roxburghe Club, 1931); *Select Cases in the Court of King's Bench*, iii, 153.

[108] Beardwood, 'The Trial of Walter Langton', 14–15.

[109] Ibid., 8n., citing *The Liber Epistolaris of Richard de Bury*, ed. N. Denholm-Young (Roxburghe Club, 1950), 317.

[110] M.C. Prestwich, 'Isabella de Vescy and the Custody of Bamburgh Castle', *BIHR*, xliv (1971), 148–50.

imprisonment of Henry de Keighley was ordered in 1306, Edward gave instructions that he should be well treated, and not put in irons, and that this should appear to be at Langton's orders.[111] Edward was consistently loyal towards Langton, who, as Guisborough explained, he had picked out, and promoted from being a poor clerk to a bishopric.[112] Just as in Burnell's case, Edward was unmoved by accusations of personal immorality levied against Langton, and the king's attitude towards him contrasts notably with his behaviour towards William March, the chancellor John Langton, Jean de Grailly, or all those dismissed from office in, or shortly after, 1289.

The last parliament of Edward's reign was held at Carlisle, and began in January 1307.[113] There appears to have been surprisingly little discussion of Scottish affairs: the main issues examined were the projected marriage of the prince of Wales to Isabella of France, the question of the exactions of the papal tax collector, William Testa, and the problem of papal demands in general. The proceedings were very lengthy, for it was not possible to do much until 12 March, when the king, and cardinal Peter of Sabina, arrived. The cardinal's main mission was the negotiation of the French marriage, but advantage was taken of his presence, and he was persuaded to excommunicate the murderers of John Comyn. On the next day, relations with France were discussed. Edward insisted that Philip IV had not fulfilled the peace terms, as Gascony had not been fully returned. The question of the status of the castle of Mauléon particularly exercised the king, but he was eventually reassured by the cardinal that the castellan would not hand the stronghold over to the French.[114]

The main debates were about ecclesiastical matters. There was much discussion of the demands made by the papacy. A petition put forward on behalf of the earls, barons and the community of the land raised such issues as the provision of clerks, often foreigners, to benefices by the papacy, the treatment of intestacy, first fruits, appropriation of alms, and St Peter's Pence. William Testa, the recently appointed papal tax-collector, was a particular object of attack, and following his appearance in parliament, it was agreed that his exactions should cease, though once the proceedings at Carlisle were over, he was allowed to resume his operations, subject to various restrictions. A

[111] Stubbs, *Constitutional History*, ii, 158n.
[112] Guisborough, 382.
[113] For discussion of this parliament, see Richardson and Sayles, *English Parliament in the Middle Ages*, XII, 425–36; Powell and Wallis, *House of Lords in the Middle Ages*, 249–63.
[114] Guisborough, 371.

curious letter, allegedly written by one Peter, son of Cassiodorus, was used in the discussions. According to Guisborough, it appeared suddenly, descending as if sent from heaven, and was at once read out. It is hard to imagine what the audience made of its allusions to Nebuchadnezzar, the Pharaoh, and Sodom and Gomorrah, but the attacks on papal provisions and financial exactions were clear enough. Langtoft's chronicle states that the clergy proposed a statute, which was rejected by the laity.[115] The statute which was promulgated at this parliament was one which had been prepared in 1305, following protests at the way in which religious orders send money from England to their mother houses abroad. This had presumably been held back, as Edward had been anxious to persuade the pope to take action against Winchelsey. There were now no such obstacles.[116]

It was while the Carlisle parliament was in session that Edward quarrelled once again with his son, the prince of Wales. The king took exception to the young prince's relationship with his Gascon favourite, Piers Gaveston. Although this was almost certainly of a homosexual character, the sources do not suggest that this was at issue: what Edward took exception to, was his son's demand that his friend be granted either the county of Ponthieu or the earldom of Cornwall. The king, still a powerful man despite his years, tore out handfuls of his son's hair, and ordered Gaveston into exile.[117]

There is a great contrast between the atmosphere of the Carlisle parliament of 1307, and the parliaments of 1300 and 1301. The attentions of those who spoke on behalf of the community of the realm in 1307 were directed to providing what has been well described as 'a vigorous defence of the English church and the rights of English patrons and benefactors'.[118] The questions of prise, taxation and military service no longer dominated proceedings. They were not, however, forgotten. As a result of complaints made at Carlisle, Edward promised to pay for goods taken in the course of the prises imposed in the course of the French war, and to restore the money seized during the scrutiny of the churches in 1294.[119] There had not been a royal victory over the opposition: the situation was, rather, one of truce. There was, no doubt, a sense that there was little point in attempting to obtain further concessions while Edward was still alive. His son would be a much less formidable monarch, as many must have realized. Events after Edward's

---

[115] Guisborough, 371–74; W.E. Lunt, 'William Testa and the Parliament of Carlisle', *EHR*, xli (1926), 332–57; Langtoft, ii, 376.

[116] *Rot. Parl.*, 217–18.

[117] Johnstone, *Edward of Caernarvon*, 122–4.

[118] Denton, *Winchelsey*, 242.

[119] Ibid., 239; E 159/80, mm.14d, 18, 49.

death showed that the old arguments were still very much alive. The question of prises, customs duties, misuse of the privy seal, the jurisdiction of the household and the part played by the Frescobaldi bankers were all important in the debates of Edward II's early years. The statute of Stamford of 1309 was largely a reissue of the *Articuli Super Cartas* of 1300, and many of the clauses of the ordinances of 1311 related to matters which had first arisen under Edward I.[120]

The last years of Edward's reign were not easy ones in the overseas dominions of Gascony and Ireland. Gascony was in a state of considerable disorder, following the Anglo-French war and the lengthy occupation of part of the duchy by the French, which lasted until 1303. When John de Havering took up the office of seneschal of Gascony in 1305, he had considerable difficulty in putting down private wars, between the Sire d'Albret and the Sire de Caumont, and between the count of Foix and the count of Armagnac. Royal revenues had suffered badly during the period of hostilities, and, it seems, many royal rights of jurisdiction had been usurped. There was no lack of awareness of the problems on Edward's part: the many Gascon petitions heard in parliament in 1305 testify to his continued concern with Gascon affairs.[121] In 1306, the position of Gascony was changed, however, for on 7 April 1306 the duchy of Aquitaine, with the isle of Oléron and the Agenais, was formally granted to the heir to the throne, Edward prince of Wales. This was done so as to provide the young Edward with an appropriate landed endowment at a time when his marriage with Isabella of France was being actively negotiated, and perhaps in part to give the prince a semi-independent responsibility, like that Edward I had received from Henry III in 1254. It was not, however, until early in 1307 that Gascony was formally entrusted to the prince's officials, and Edward I's own death meant that the project was, effectively, stillborn.[122]

In Ireland, the English administration was facing increasing difficulties. Edward I's demands for men, materials and above all money for the Scottish war may not have seemed excessive when seen from the English headquarters, but they were onerous indeed viewed from Dublin. An exchequer receipt roll records the payment in 1305 of £11,267 of Irish revenues to the royal wardrobe, a huge sum, which represented over two years income for the Dublin government. The Irish, naturally, took advantage of the absence of magnates fighting in

[120] Prestwich, *War, Politics and Finance*, 274–5.

[121] *Rôles Gascons*, iii, clxxv-clxxxi; Trabut-Cussac, *L'administration anglaise en Gascogne*, 110–37, provides a full discussion of this period in Gascony. For the petitions in parliament, see *Memoranda de Parliamento, 1305*, ed. Maitland, 321–7.

[122] *CPR 1301–7*, 424; Trabut-Cussac, *L'administration anglaise en Gascogne*, 132–7.

Scotland and rose in revolt. Those of the Leinster mountains even threatened the neighbourhood of Dublin itself. In 1305 the murder of the leading members of the O'Connor family, of Offaly, by Peter de Bermingham, led to chaos in south Leinster. In the same year, the seneschal of Wexford was killed by the Irish. The government, under John Wogan, responded as best it could, sending an armed force in 1306 against the Irish of the Leinster mountains at a cost of about £2,000. The situation, however, was becoming more and more difficult, and it is easy to understand why William de Walhope offered to exchange lands in Ireland, worth £30, for lands in Scotland worth only about £20.[123] The effects in Gascony and Ireland of Edward's wars were more serious still than they were in England.

The years from 1298 until Edward's death in 1307 were not constructive ones, in the way that the 1270s and 1280s had been. Nor did political argument threaten to deteriorate into civil war, as in 1297. It is not easy to discern any central thrust to royal policy at this period, beyond a determination to keep the war against the Scots going. The action taken over the palatinate of Durham, and the Marcher lordship of Gower, did not form a part of a general policy of reducing the power of the holders of liberties. The king's success in obtaining a papal bull annulling his concessions cannot be seen as the cornerstone of Edward's triumph over his political opponents, for the bull was used only in the limited context of the question of the forest boundaries. It is unlikely that there was a conscious decision to incur heavy debts, rather than impose a further burden of taxation: government policy drifted in that direction as a result of the problems involved in obtaining grants of taxation. The frequent purveyance of large quantities of food supplies for the armies continued to be an unpopular burden on the country. Edward was, undoubtedly, concerned to maintain his royal rights to the best of his ability, but the policies that were adopted, in his relations with the magnates, in financial matters, and with regard to the church, were pragmatic and empirical. The system of government and administration was maintained, but there was not the same drive and enthusiasm that was evident in Edward's early years on the throne.

The task that Edward I left for his son was a very considerable one. The political conflicts, rather than being settled, were in a state of truce. The financial situation was extremely difficult, with a heavy burden of debt. Above all, of course, there was the uncompleted war in Scotland. Had Edward died in 1305, when Scotland appeared to be settled, his achievements would have appeared much more solid. By 1307, the

[123] Lydon, 'Edward I, Ireland and the War in Scotland', 55–7; Otway-Ruthven, *History of Medieval Ireland*, 218–19; *CDS*, ii, no. 1969.

outlook was beginning to look bleak. The many difficulties that Edward II faced in his first years on the throne help to show how important Edward I's own personality had been in maintaining stability in the first years of the fourteenth century.

Chapter 20

EPILOGUE

Edward I died on 7 July 1307, at Burgh-by-Sands, a few miles north-west of Carlisle. His health had been poor for some time. In the summer of 1306, he had been ill during the long journey northwards.[1] At the end of September he and his entourage arrived at Lanercost priory, not far from Carlisle. It was intended that they should move on fairly soon to the Cistercian monastery of Holme Cultram, but further illness meant that Edward stayed at Lanercost until 4 March 1307. There are full records of royal expenditure there. Carpenters worked on the king's and queen's chambers: glass windows were fitted, and a chimney constructed. Much food was provided for the royal household. Wine was brought from Newcastle, spices and wax from York. Goods were brought by sea from Boston to Newcastle, and then by cart across to Lanercost. Oxen and pigs were collected together to provide meat. All this was normal enough: no monastic house had sufficient resources to provide for the king's household. What is unusual in these accounts is the quantity and range of medicines that are listed, testifying to the constant worry over Edward's health. The list contains many exotic items. There was an electuary, or cordial, made with amber, jacith, musk, pearls, gold and silver; sugar rosettes made with pearls and coral; Damascus rose water, pomegranate wine, herbal baths, and a range of ointments. The precise nature of the king's illness is not, of course, evident from this, but he was clearly having trouble with his legs, for a special ointment was made for them on six occasions, and some leather leggings were also provided for him. His neck was also causing him discomfort, for a plaster was made for it.[2] Whatever Edward was suffering from, it was lingering and painful.

The spring seems to have brought some improvement to the king's health. He was well enough to attend parliament at Carlisle for a time, and to enjoy a review of his troops at Whitsun, though in May one of his doctors, Peter the Surgeon, was sent to York to buy a fresh supply of

[1] Above, 507.
[2] J.R.H. Moorman, 'Edward I at Lanercost Priory 1306–7', *EHR*, lxvii (1952), 161–74.

medicines for him.[3] Edward was certainly not in a fit state to campaign in Scotland, but his determination was such that, on 3 July, he rode out from Carlisle. He was suffering from dysentery, and progress amounted to a bare two miles a day. He spent the night of 6 July at Burgh-by-Sands, and when his servants came to lift him from his bed the next morning, so that he could eat, he died in their arms.[4]

Tales were told, of course, about the instructions Edward gave on his deathbed. According to a song, written not much later, he asked that his heart be taken to the Holy Land, along with four score knights who were to fight against the heathen.[5] The most celebrated story is that he called his son Edward to his side, and made him swear that on his death, 'he would have his body boiled in a large cauldron until the flesh should be separated from the bones; that he would have the flesh buried, and the bones preserved; and that every time the Scots should rebel against him, he would summon his people, and carry with him the bones of his father; for he believed most firmly, that as long as his bones should be carried against the Scots, those Scots would never be victorious.'[6] There is no contemporary warrant for this tale, which was recorded by Froissart in the late fourteenth century; it reflects Edward's later reputation, rather than recording a genuine deathbed scene. More plausible, perhaps, is the account in the *Brut* chronicle, which suggests that Edward charged the earls of Lincoln and Warwick, along with Aymer de Valence and Robert Clifford, with seeing to the welfare of Edward of Caernarfon. In particular, they were not to permit the return of the young Edward's favourite, Piers Gaveston, from the exile into which Edward I had sent him.[7]

The king's death appears to have caught the royal officials by surprise, and their first instinct was to keep it secret, lest the Scots should be encouraged by the news.[8] On the day after the sad event, letters were sent to the queen, Edward of Caernarfon and the earl of Lincoln, presumably to tell them what had happened. The journal of the royal household gives no other indication of the king's death, and continued to be written up until 17 July.[9] In London, the chancellor went on sealing routine writs in Edward's name until 25 July, and it was not until 18 August that writs under the great seal were issued bearing the

---

[3] Above, 511; E 101/370/16, f.13.

[4] Guisborough, 379.

[5] *Political Songs*, ed. Wright, 247.

[6] *Chronicles of England, France, Spain ... by Sir John Froissart*, translated by T. Johnes (1839), 38.

[7] *The Brut*, ed. F.W.D. Brie (Early English Text Soc., original series, cxxxi, 1906), i, 202–3.

[8] Guisborough, 379.

[9] E 101/370/16.

name of the new king.[10] It was as if Edward had reigned for so long that men could not believe that he had died.

Edward's corpse was brought south, and placed on a bier in Waltham Abbey, where vigils were kept, and frequent masses said for his soul. It was not until about 18 October that the body was taken to London, where it was placed first in the monastery of Holy Trinity, and then in St Paul's, before being carried to its last resting place, Westminster Abbey. The funeral service, on 27 October, was conducted, fittingly, by Edward's old friend, and recent adversary, Anthony Bek, bishop of Durham and patriarch of Jerusalem.[11] The eulogy written by John of London very probably incorporates material from the funeral oration. Edward was compared with past heroes, legendary and historical, from Brutus to Richard I: his triumphs were stressed, and the grief of his people set out.[12]

The service in Westminster Abbey was not the only one held for Edward I. In late July Pope Clement V had solemn exequies performed in Poitiers cathedral for his former master: these were the first such exequies held for a king in the papal curia.[13] A collection of sermons in a manuscript at Rome preserves, as models for use on similar occasions, orations in honour of Edward which were probably given on this occasion. The praise of Edward was predictable: the strength of his rule, his sense of justice, his clemency, were stressed, as was his crusade and his successes against his enemies. Interestingly, these sermons made considerable use of the Book of Maccabees, with such quotations as: 'In his acts he was like a lion, and like a lion's whelp roaring for his prey.' Maccabees was an obvious, yet unusual choice, which might be connected to the use of scenes from the life of Judas Maccabeus which featured on the walls of the Painted Chamber at Westminster.[14]

There are no simple judgements to be made on Edward I. An assessment of his personality presents great problems. It is hard to know how far documents issued in the king's name truly reflect his own view: they may have been the work of his ministers or clerks, and issued without specific consultation with Edward himself. It is similarly hard to determine to what extent the concept of the great castles in Wales was

[10] *Foedera*, I, ii, 1018; *CPR 1307–13*, 1.

[11] *Flores*, iii, 330.

[12] *Chronicles of the Reigns of Edward I and II*, ii, 3–21.

[13] W. Ullmann, 'The Curial Exequies for Edward I and Edward III', *Ecclesiastical History Review*, vi (1955), 26, 30–2.

[14] MS Rome, Angelica 158, ff.156–8. I am extremely grateful to Dr David d'Avray for sending me his transcripts of this material, the existence of which I was quite unaware. He also drew my attention to the relevance of these sermons to Ullmann's article, cited in note 13.

Edward's own, and to what extent Master James of St George's. There are, in addition, difficulties that arise from the very different way in which contemporaries thought about personality. Their minds were not cluttered with psychological concepts, and it did not even occur to them to ask if the king was clever or stupid, original or derivative, or even whether he had powers of leadership, in the sense that they would be understood today. They found character hard to describe: John of London, in his eulogy of Edward, was forced to adapt Peter of Blois's analysis of Henry II, to fit Edward I as he knew him.[15] There were, however, criteria which were applied by contemporaries. Arthurian literature provided definitions of kingly behaviour in terms of the chivalric virtues of courage, loyalty, generosity and piety. Further, by the late thirteenth century, clear theories had been developed, according to which *rex inutilis*, a worthless king, might be deposed, and there was little difficulty involved in defining tyrannical behaviour on the part of a ruler.[16]

Edward met most of the contemporary requirements for a king. His physical presence alone commanded respect. He did not lack courage, or piety, and he was loyal to those who proved worthy of his trust. His generosity, however, was limited: although he was very heavily in debt at the time of his death, he had husbanded the resources of the crown with care.[17] Documentary evidence shows that he had a violent temper, but this was not viewed as a fault by his subjects, even though many had reason to fear Edward's anger. For some at least, Edward represented an ideal of kingship. The romance of Havelock the Dane, written in the late thirteenth century, in part draws on the author's view of Edward when the hero is described.[18] The artist who drew the magnificent Windmill Psalter flattered Edward by comparing him with Solomon, when he placed a scene of the Judgement of Solomon within a splendid letter E.[19] Yet Edward did not go uncriticized. The author of the Song of Lewes, discussing him at an early stage of his career, perceptively saw that he could be both the brave lion, and the duplicitous leopard.[20] The widespread view that the outbreak of war with France in 1294 was the result of the king's misguided lust for a French

---

[15] *Chronicles of the Reigns of Edward I and Edward II*, ii, 4–6.

[16] E. Peters, *The Shadow King* (New Haven, 1970), provides a discussion of deposition theory up to the early fourteenth century.

[17] For a brief discussion of Edward's patronage policies, see M.C. Prestwich, 'Royal Patronage under Edward I', *Thirteenth Century England: I*, ed. Coss and Lloyd, 41–52.

[18] D. Staines, 'Havelock the Dane: a thirteenth-century handbook for princes', *Speculum*, li (1976), 602–23.

[19] A. Bennett, 'The Windmill Psalter: the historiated letter E of Psalm One', *Journal of the Warburg and Courtauld Institutes*, xliii (1980), 52–67.

[20] Above, 24.

princess suggests that many Englishmen did not regard Edward's judgement as infallible.[21] In 1297, the leaders of opposition to royal policy were careful not to allow their propaganda to degenerate into personal attacks on the king, but concentrated instead on the effects of his policies. In the final years of the reign, however, the chronicler Langtoft, no doubt echoing popular opinion, began to compare the king adversely with his legendary predecessor, King Arthur. He implied that Edward feasted too much in the evenings, and rose too late in the mornings; that he gave his trust to criminals; showed too much compassion to his enemies; acted according to his will, rather than taking proper counsel; and failed to make a proper distribution to his supporters of the lands that he conquered.[22]

An examination of the various aspects of Edward's career, and of the various periods into which it can be divided, can provide a multitude of arguments, some in his favour, some against him. His conduct during the period from 1258 until the battle of Evesham in 1265 can be explained in terms of his youth, and the difficulties he faced in equating his position as heir to the throne with his sympathy for some of the ideals of Earl Simon de Montfort and the baronial reformers. If he failed to show political consistency, with his various changes of side, he did at least learn much in a hard school, and he acquired the loyalty of a small group of men who were to serve him well for many years. Few, however, could have anticipated the success of his rule in his prime, in the 1270s and 1280s, on the basis of his early career.

Edward's reign was of prime importance in law and administration. In the 1270s he and his officials, notably Robert Burnell, developed many of the techniques initiated in the period of baronial ascendancy, and gave a new vigour and determination to government policy. The process began with the massive inquiry of 1274–5 which yielded the Hundred Rolls, and was continued in the series of statutes which began with Westminster I in 1275. The development of legislation by statute may not have been consciously deliberate, but it transformed the process of legal change. Edward's statutes did not represent the imposition of arbitrary notions from above, but were produced in response to known grievances, or to problems which came up in courts. It is a mistake to try to see in the legislation of this period any fundamental principle, beyond that of correcting wrongs, and improving the efficiency of royal justice. It certainly was not intended to transform the fabric of society, even though some measures did have such an effect in time. The king and his advisers were hardly conscious of the likely long-term implications of such measures as *De Donis Conditionalibus*. Nor was the

---

[21] Above, 380.
[22] Langtoft, ii, 326.

story of the law one of consistent success under Edward. The reign saw the virtual demise of the system of judicial eyres under an ever increasing weight of business, but there was no really effective replacement for them devised. The maintenance of law and order posed increasing problems in the later years, and while it would be wrong to write in terms of a complete breakdown of law and order, it is clear that the pressures of war from the mid-1290s aggravated an already difficult situation. Few criminals were brought to book, and of those who were, many received pardons for good service on the king's campaigns.

There was no administrative revolution under Edward I, but the great increase in the quantity of records produced by the busy clerks in the king's household, the chancery, and the exchequer, indicates how important this reign was. Experiments, such as that of putting the crown's estates in the hands of three stewards in the late 1270s, came to nothing, but there was much steady work done to improve the bureaucratic machine. There were important changes in the exchequer in the mid-1280s, and the increasing sophistication of the household accounts shows that there was much work done there as well. The financial situation was never easy, but the tasks facing Edward's officials were facilitated by the grant in 1275 of the custom of 6s 8d on every sack of wool exported from the realm, while the development of credit mechanisms, using above all the Italian firm of the Riccardi, gave a new measure of flexibility to the royal administration.

Matters became much more difficult in the 1290s. The substantial cash reserve which Edward had available in 1294 was soon dissipated on the costly war with France, and expenditure increasingly outran income, despite the heavy additional customs dues and the many direct taxes that were imposed. The immense task of administering and financing the king's wars largely fell to the household department of the wardrobe. In the absence of a proper budgetary system, and of a method of controlling crown expenditure through the exchequer, there was a state of considerable confusion by the final years of the reign. The increasingly long delays in drawing up the final accounts for the wardrobe provide good evidence of this: from 1298, none of the accounts of this department proved acceptable to the exchequer auditors. An attempt made in 1305 to set cash limits on household expenditure foundered. The many accounts which survive from this period at the end of the reign provide a vivid impression of the frantic efforts of the royal clerks to maintain the immense military efforts in Scotland, but they also suggest that the administrative and financial resources of the realm were being stretched further than their real capability.

The political world of medieval England was a small one, in which what really mattered were the relations between the king and a handful

of magnates, lay and ecclesiastical. Edward did not use the techniques
of persuasion and patronage with any real ease: his preferred style was
one of confrontation and compulsion. He was reluctant to make lavish
grants, either of lands or of titles, particularly within his realm of
England.[23] The *Quo Warranto* proceedings in the first half of the reign,
even though they became bogged down in legal technicalities and
delays, demonstrated a new aggressiveness towards magnate privileges. He was ready to threaten men into obedience, by demanding that
they pay long-standing debts owed to the crown. The methods he used
to acquire land were unscrupulous and unworthy. His relationship
with Gilbert de Clare, earl of Gloucester, was a stormy one, and he did
much to antagonize the two leaders of the lay opposition in 1297, the
earls of Norfolk and Hereford. The chronicler Langtoft noted the lack of
co-operation Edward received from the earls, notably in the Flanders
expedition of 1297.[24] Yet it would be quite wrong to see the king and the
lay nobles as being constantly at loggerheads. There were some
magnates, such as the earl of Lincoln, who were loyal to Edward
throughout. The problems that faced Edward in 1297 were primarily
the result of the demands made by the king on his subjects in time of
war, and were not caused by a clash of opposing ideologies. Edward's
management of the lay magnates was not subtle, but for the most part it
proved very effective.

Edward had many arguments with Archbishop Pecham, and still
more with his successor at Canterbury, Robert Winchelsey. Again, it
would be a mistake to assume that the secular power was set on a
collision course with the spiritual. There was, certainly, a grey area of
overlap between the authority of church and state, and it was the task of
each to establish its rights as they were understood, but this does not
mean that there was no fundamental consensus. The papal prohibition
on the clergy paying taxes to the lay power, expressed in the bull *Clericis
Laicos* of 1296, certainly created a new strain, but it was the product of
wartime conditions, and once a truce had been made between Edward
I and Philip IV of France in the autumn of 1297, a *modus vivendi* was not
too hard to achieve, even though Edward certainly continued a personal
vendetta against Archbishop Winchelsey. Improved relations with the
papacy meant that Edward was in fact able to receive substantial sums
in taxation from the English clergy, in the form of a share of crusading
taxes.

[23] The classic statement of Edward's relationship with the greater magnates is by
K.B. McFarlane, 'Had Edward I a "Policy" towards the Earls?', in his *Nobility of Later
Medieval England*, 248–67. See also M.C. Prestwich, 'Royal Patronage under Edward I',
Thirteenth Century England 1, 41–52.
[24] Langtoft, ii, 296.

Edward's reign saw the attendance of representatives of shires, boroughs and lower clergy in parliament become more frequent, although their presence was certainly in no way essential. The use of certain phrases, notably 'quod omnes tangit ab omnibus approbetur' (what touches all should be approved by all) might suggest that the king had a genuine belief in the principles of full consultation and representation, but in practice, it was particular circumstances which drove Edward to seek a wider degree of support in parliament than could be provided by the magnates alone. The needs of war, above all, necessitated the frequent levy of taxes, and the best method of raising money, the subsidies collected on an assessment of movable wealth, involved the consent of representatives. This owed something to ideas derived from Roman law, but practical necessity was the main driving force. The development, from an early stage in the reign, of the practice of presenting petitions in parliament, was an important step in establishing links between crown and populace, which in many ways were of more practical value than the system of representation.

On several occasions, notably in 1297, Edward expressed his concern for his poorer subjects. He argued, for example, that they should be protected from arbitrary prises.[25] There is no reason to doubt the genuine character of his worries about the way in which his demands might press most heavily on those least able to bear them. Throughout his reign, he was anxious to ensure that his officials should not use their positions to oppress the poor, and his decision, in 1298, to set up an inquiry into the abuses that had taken place during the period of the French war was typical of his style of kingship. At the same time, as the careers of Robert Burnell and, above all, Walter Langton show, the king could forgive much in the case of officials he valued and trusted.

Edward I was a man of action, and it would be wrong to expect him to have had a consistent and clear philosophy of government. Alongside the belief in the value of consultation with his subjects, and his conception of his duty to protect the poor, there was a determined sense of his own rights and authority. He was resolute that lost royal rights should be recovered, and bitterly resented what he regarded as undue interference in his affairs. The speech he made in 1301, as reported by Langtoft, in which he compared the magnates' right to appoint their own household servants with his own right to nominate state officials, has the ring of truth about it.[26] This was the same Edward as the man who declared, when the practice of compulsory purchase was criticized in 1297, that he was as free as any man to buy wool in England.[27] To

---

[25] *Documents 1297–8*, 75.
[26] Langtoft, ii, 330.
[27] *Documents, 1297–8*, 140.

talk in terms of constitutional monarchs in this period is anachronistic: Edward asked for, and accepted, advice when he wanted, but he also considered that his subjects 'should naturally have regard for, and do their duty towards their lord with a good will, as good and loyal men ought and are obliged to do towards their liege lord'.[28]

Edward's military career was a notable one. In personal terms, it demonstrates his single-minded persistence. On his crusade, he showed a far greater determination to carry his plans through, than did any of the other leaders who had vowed to go to the East. A similar determination was evident in the course of the war with the French in the 1290s, and in the Scottish campaigns of the last years of Edward's life. The same determination, however, could lead Edward to persist in policies long after it had become clear that they had no real chance of success. That was certainly the case with the crusade, and again in 1297, when he insisted on carrying through his plan to campaign in the Low Countries, despite the inadequate size of his army, and the lack of sufficient support from his allies.

Edward's wars were not fought in a spirit of careless adventurism, but in defence of what he regarded as his lawful rights. He was in no doubt as to the justice of his claims to feudal suzerainty over the princes of Gwynedd, or of his superior lordship over the realm of Scotland, but lacked the capacity to appreciate the effects his demands might have on others. He placed the Welsh princes, and the Scottish leaders, in a position where they had little option, as they saw it, but to have recourse to arms, even though this had not been Edward's intention. Once war had begun, the English did not achieve their successes as a result of any brilliant strokes of generalship, either in tactical or strategic terms. Rather, Edward was able to organize the resources of his country on a new scale, putting armies of up to 30,000 into the field, a most impressive number for the period. Much attention was paid to the question of providing adequate supplies, and proper transport. The household accounts provide impressive evidence of the energy and efficiency of Edward's war machine. It was not the case, as has sometimes been suggested, that this period saw the transformation of an old-fashioned feudal host into a more modern paid army, but the manner in which Edward was able to deploy the resources of the whole country in support of his military efforts was something new.

Success in Wales was, perhaps, not surprising, in view of the disparity of resources between the two sides, and the fact that Edward's campaign marked the culmination of a process of conquest which had begun in the eleventh century. Philip IV of France was a much more formidable adversary than Llywelyn of Wales, and the English did well

---

[28] Ibid., 122.

to achieve the condition of stalemate that led to the agreement of the truce in the autumn of 1297. Scotland posed major problems for Edward, but it should not be forgotten that by the time that Stirling fell in 1304, the English had, apparently, succeeded in their aims. Edward, however, lacked the political skill to hold what he had gained, and did not have the flexibility of mind to appreciate the way in which the military requirements in the north changed, as the Scots responded to the threat presented by the English armies.

There can be few men who die happy in the knowledge that they have achieved all they set out to do. Edward's own conception of his life's purpose must have changed with the years, but it is striking that he did not come near to achieving the goals he set himself in his prime. The crusade was dear to him, and Edward had seen clearly that peace had to be obtained in Europe if the reconquest of the kingdom of Jerusalem from Mamluk rule was to take place. His efforts to achieve this peace in the 1280s were noble, but ultimately ineffectual. The rivalries of such rulers as the kings of Aragon and Naples could not easily be settled by an English king, and as the events of the 1290s showed, it was impossible for Edward to avoid becoming enmeshed in a conflict he did not want, against an aggressive, self-confident French monarchy. The dream of the crusade faded, and Edward's wide horizons narrowed.

At his coronation, Edward had stressed the importance of the recovery and maintenance of the rights of the crown. He had seen the crown reduced in power and prestige in the late 1250s and early 1260s, and in many ways he was extremely successful in restoring royal authority. The *Quo Warranto* inquiries may not have resulted in the recovery of many royal rights, but they testified to the very different attitude of Edward and his officials compared to that of his father, Henry III.[29] In a wide variety of ways, from the exercise of justice to the collection of food supplies for royal armies, the crown was more active, with its influence extending deeper into the social fabric, than in the past. Edward had more money at his disposal, and was able to deploy much greater military power than had been available to his predecessors. His magnificent chain of castles in north Wales far exceeded any previous royal building programme. One simple indication of Edward's power is that, although rebellion was threatened in 1297, none of his English subjects took up arms against him in armed insurrection. That was not something that could be said of any of his predecessors since the Conquest – or even before that.

Yet was the crown in fact so much stronger at Edward's death than it had been at his accession? He left behind him a very difficult legacy.

[29] For Henry III's policy, see in particular Carpenter, 'King, Magnates and Society: the Personal Rule of King Henry III', *Speculum*, lx (1985), 49–52.

The administration was in a state of some confusion, above all in the vital household department of the wardrobe. There was a massive burden of unpaid debts. There was no substantial body of earls devoted to the king and the crown, for Edward had done nothing to increase the number of earldoms, and the concentration of power in the hands of members of the royal family was not to prove beneficial, as the career of Thomas of Lancaster, Edward II's cousin, son of Edmund of Lancaster, was to show.[30] Edward I had struggled to reverse the concessions he had been forced to agree to in 1297, but although he was able to obtain a papal annulment in 1305, it was only on the issue of the royal forest that he was able to do much to turn the clock back. Very many problems had not been resolved, and were to surface again in the early years of Edward II's reign. There was, above all, the unfinished war against Robert Bruce and the Scots. Monarchy was still a very personal matter in this period, and Edward II was not the man to hold on to what his father had achieved. No strengthening of the institutions of the crown could sufficiently compensate for such a lack of personal ability as that which Edward I's heir was to display.

Edward I was finally laid to rest in Westminster Abbey, in a remarkable tomb, apposite in its size and severity. It was made from polished Purbeck marble, unadorned by any sculpture. It must have been intended that it should have been finished with an effigy of the king, to match those of Henry III and Eleanor of Castile, but the temporary wooden figure which lay on the coffin during the funeral service was never replaced by a proper statue. The tomb was certainly treated with proper respect for the rest of the medieval period, with frequent orders to the exchequer to pay for the wax candles which were kept burning around it.[31] The celebrated inscription, *Edwardus Primus Scotorum Malleus hic est, 1308. Pactum Serva*, was almost certainly added later, probably in the sixteenth century.

Edward's body was left undisturbed until 2 May 1774, when the tomb was opened in the presence of the dean of Westminster and a number of learned antiquaries. The lid was easily raised, for it had not been cemented into place. Within the great tomb was a coffin, also of Purbeck marble, which was also opened with no difficulty. The investigators seem to have been overawed by what they were doing,

[30] Thomas of Lancaster, by 1311, held the earldoms of Lancaster, Leicester, Derby, Lincoln and Salisbury.

[31] J. Ayloffe, 'An Account of the Body of King Edward the First, as it appeared on opening his Tomb in the year 1774', *Archaeologia*, iii (1786), 386, 398–412. It was once supposed that the wax that was paid for by the crown was used to renew the cloths around the corpse, but this is most unlikely.

for although they pulled back the outer wrapper of the corpse, and removed the covering over the face, they did not carry out a full investigation of the remains. The corpse was evidently in excellent condition, the flesh shrunken but intact.

The chin and lips were intire, but without any beard; and a sinking, or dip, between the chin and under-lip, was very conspicuous. Both the lips were prominent; the nose short, as if shrunk; but the apertures of the nostrils were visible. There was an unusual fall, or cavity, on that part of the bridge of the nose which separates the orbits of the eyes; and some globular substance, possibly the fleshy part of the eye-balls, was movable in their sockets under the envelope.[32]

The corpse was richly dressed, with a red silk tunic, and an elaborately decorated stole. There was also a mantle of red satin, and the lower part of the body was covered with cloth of gold. In the right hand there was a sceptre with a cross, in the left, one surmounted by a dove. On the head was an open crown. The only measurement taken proved that Edward was indeed a tall man, precisely six feet two inches in height.[33] The solemnity of the occasion was somewhat marred by the fact that it proved necessary that one noted antiquary present should undergo 'a search for the embezzlement of a finger of the great Plantagenet'.[34]

It would be wrong to leave Edward with this macabre scene of the open coffin, pored over by eighteenth-century scholars. There is no one moment, however, which fully encapsulates the man and his career. Perhaps he would have wished to be remembered riding out from the security of the walls of Acre to attack the infidels, or possibly leading his army through the woods of north Wales, against Prince Llywelyn. He should also be remembered presiding in parliament, seeing to the promulgation of statutes, or browbeating those who were not sufficiently ready to bend to his will. There was also the domestic Edward, more shadowy to the historian, with his beloved queen, Eleanor, and his children, especially his headstrong daughters. Edward was a formidable king; his reign, with both its successes and its disappointments, a great one.

[32] Ibid., 381.
[33] Ibid., 383–5.
[34] *Transactions of the Bristol and Gloucestershire Archaeological Society*, iv (1879–80), 234.

Appendix

FINANCIAL TABLES

A. Tax Assessments

The figures given in the following table have to be treated with considerable caution. They represent assessments, rather than the actual yield of taxes, and while in the case of the lay taxes, the amount received by the crown was usually not far short of the assessed figure, there was a greater gulf in the case of the taxes paid by the clergy. For the lay taxes, a new assessment was made on each occasion, but the clerical taxes were based, until 1291, on the valuation made by the bishop of Norwich in 1254, which put the annual worth of clerical income at about £102,000, considerably less than the real figure. In 1291 a new assessment was made on the orders of Pope Nicholas IV, and this produced a figure of about £210,000. In 1297, however, the taxes conceded by the clergy in the autumn were to be collected with spiritualities valued according to the 1254 assessment.[1]

[1] The lay taxes on movables are tabulated in Prestwich, *War, Politics and Finance*, 179; for the clerical taxes, see Lunt, *Financial Relations of the Papacy with England*, 260–1, 346–55; Deighton, 'Clerical Taxation by Consent', *EHR*, lxviii (1953), 161–92; Denton, *Winchelsey*, 299–301. My figures differ in some particulars from those given by Denton.

Year	Nature of tax	Assessment
1275	Lay 15th	£81,954
1279	Canterbury clergy, triennial 15th	c. £16,000
1280	York clergy, biennial 10th	c. £4,000
1283	Lay 30th	£47,765
1283	Canterbury clergy, biennial 20th	c. £8,000
1286	York clergy, triennial 30th	c. £2,000
1290	Lay 15th	£116,346
1290	Canterbury and York clergy, 10th	c. £10,000
1294	Canterbury and York clergy, moiety	£105,000
1294	Lay 10th and 6th	£81,838
1295	Lay 11th and 7th	£52,870
1295	Clerical 10th	£21,000
1296	Lay 12th and 8th	£38,870
1297	Clerical fine of 5th	£42,000
1297	Lay 9th	£34,419
1297	Canterbury clergy, 10th	c. £16,000
1297	York clergy, 5th	£10,800[2]
1301	Lay 15th	£49,755
1301	Papal triennial 10th on the clergy	£63,000[3]
1302	Feudal aid	£10,465
1303	Tallage	c. £6,000[4]
1305	Papal biennial 10th on the clergy	£42,000
1306	Lay 30th and 20th	£34,777

B. Wardrobe Receipts and Expenses

(See table overleaf.) The dates of these accounts ran from 20 November to 19 November, following Edward I's regnal year.[5]

[2] E 372/155B.

[3] Lunt, *Financial Relations of the Papacy with England*, 380–1, put the annual yield of this tax at £21,000, but the king only received two thirds of the total, which is why Denton, *Winchelsey*, gives an annual figure of £14,000.

[4] For the feudal aid and the tallage, see Hadwin, 'The Last Royal Tallages', *EHR*, xcvi (1981), 345, 349.

[5] The 1272–4 account ran from 4 November. The figures in the table are taken from Tout, *Chapters in the Administrative History of Medieval England*, v, 76–83, unless otherwise indicated.

Date	Receipts from Exchequer	Total	Expenses
1272–4	£200	£31,457	£32,808
1274–5	£4,089	£17,816	£17,727
1275–6	£3,000	£16,221	£16,258
1276–7	–	£35,713	£35,776
1277–8	£50	£19,316	£19,302
1278–9	£4,066	£30,920	£30,922
1279–80	£6,861	£23,942	£23,608
1280–2	£20,072	£50,942	£51,088
1282–4	£23,694	£101,952	£100,178[6]
1284–5	£23,000	£40,698	£41,176
1285–6	£15,000	£35,413	£40,090
1286–8	£43,319	£77,339	£76,677
1288–90		£140,900	£134,260
1290–91		£62,045	£41,578[7]
1291–2	£30,000	£33,154	£47,641
1292–3	£19,651	£34,878	£40,698
1293–4	£53,387	£65,801	£67,827[8]
1294–5	£115,820	£124,792	£138,255
1295–6	£64,546	£105,324	£83,648
1296–7	£75,524	£106,356	£119,519
1297–8	£30,814	£39,826	£78,549
1299–1300	£49,048	£58,155	£64,105[9]
1300–01	£39,031	£47,550	£77,291[10]
1301–02	£43,316	£72,969	£61,949[11]
1302–03	£43,589	£52,195	£64,036[12]
1303–04			£68,958
1305–06	£50,010	£64,128	£77,318

[6] There is also a wardrobe account for the Welsh war, which ran from 22 March 1282 until 20 November 1284. This shows receipts from the exchequer of £6,373; total receipts of £102,641; and total expenditure of £90,248.

[7] E 372/138. This figure was omitted by Tout, and is reached by adding the 'normal' expenses, of £38,652 and the £2,925 spent in Scotland.

[8] E 372/144.

[9] Calculated from *Liber Quotidianus*.

[10] E 101/360/25 and E 101/371/21/70 give slightly different figures: receipts from exchequer, £39,031; total receipts, £46,768; expenditure, £77,171.

[11] E 101/360/25, a draft version of the account.

[12] E 101/364/14, a draft version of the account.

GENEALOGICAL TABLES

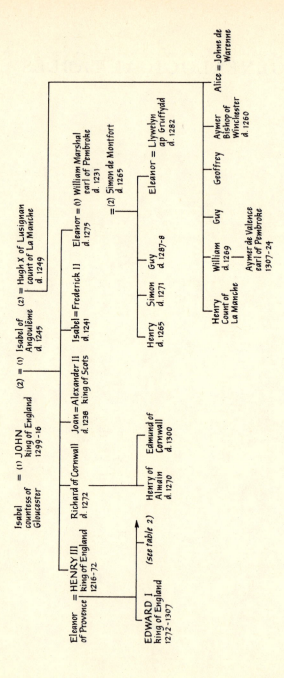

1. The English Royal Family (1)

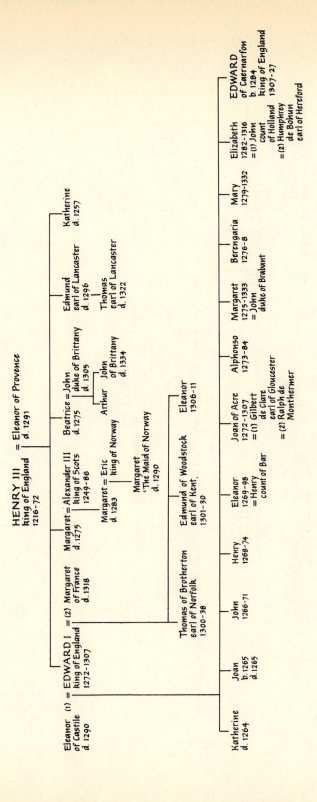

2. The English Royal Family (2)

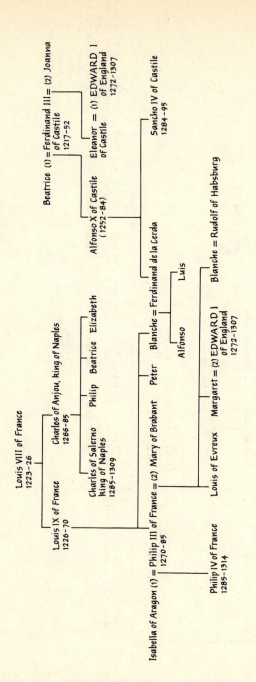

3. The Royal Houses of France, Naples and Castile (simplified)

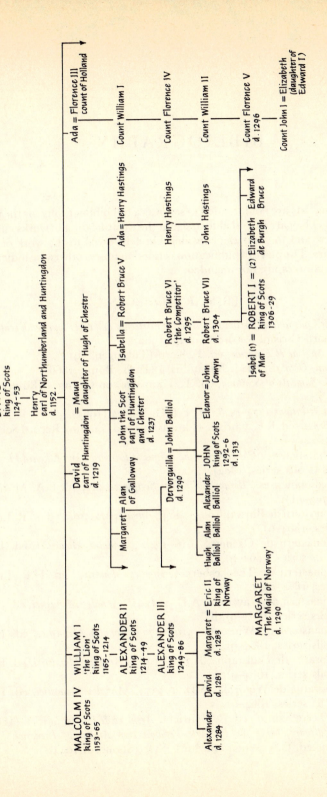

4. The Succession to the Scottish Throne

BIBLIOGRAPHY

The following lists are not intended to serve as a full bibliography for the reign of Edward I. They are intended to assist in the identification of works cited in the footnotes, and to show the considerable debt owed to the work of very many scholars. The place of publication is London unless otherwise indicated. Manuscript sources are not included.

I. PRIMARY SOURCES

Accounts of the Constable of Bristol Castle in the thirteenth and early fourteenth centuries, ed. M. Sharp (Bristol Record Society, 1982).

Acta Imperii Angliae et Franciae, ed. F. Kern (Tübingen, 1911).

Acta Sanctorum, Octobris, ed. J. Bollandus, i (Paris, Rome, 1866).

Acts of the Parliaments of Scotland, ed. T. Thomson and C. Innes (Edinburgh, 1814–75), i.

Anglo Scottish Relations 1174–1328, ed. E.L.G. Stones (1965).

Annales Cestrienses, ed. R.C. Christie (Lancashire and Cheshire Record Society, xiv, 1886).

'Annales Londonienses', *Chronicles of the Reigns of Edward I and Edward II*, i, ed. W. Stubbs (Rolls series, 1882).

'Annales Mediolanenses', *Rerum Italicarum Scriptores*, xiv, ed. L.A. Muratori (Milan, 1723–51).

'Annales Monasterii de Burton, 1004–1263', *Annales Monastici*, ed. H.R. Luard (Rolls series, 1864–9), i.

'Annales Monasterii de Oseneia, 1016–1347', *Annales Monastici*, ed. H.R. Luard (Rolls series, 1864–9), iv.

'Annales Monasterii de Theokesberia', *Annales Monastici*, ed. H.R. Luard (Rolls series, 1864–9), i.

'Annales Monasterii de Waverleia, A.D. 1–1291', *Annales Monastici*, ed. H.R. Luard (Rolls series, 1864–9), ii.

'Annales Monasterii de Wintonia, 519–1277', *Annales Monastici*, ed. H.R. Luard (Rolls series, 1864–9), ii.

'Annales Prioratus de Dunstaplia, A.D. 1–1297', *Annales Monastici*, ed. H.R. Luard (Rolls series, 1864–9), iii.

'Annales Prioratus de Wigornia, A.D. 1–1377', *Annales Monastici*, ed. H.R. Luard (Rolls series, 1864–9), iv.

'Annales de Terre Sainte', ed. R. Röhricht, *Archives de l'orient latin*, ii (1884).

The Art of Falconry, being the De Arte Venandi cum Avibus of Frederick II of Hohenstaufen, ed. C.A. Wood and F.M. Fyfe (Stanford, 1943).

Bartholomaei de Cotton, Historia Anglicana (A.D. 449–1298), ed. H.R. Luard (Rolls series, 1859).

Book of Prests, 1294–5, ed. E.B. Fryde (Oxford, 1962).

Brenhinedd y Saesson, ed. T. Jones (Cardiff, 1971).

The Brut, ed. F.W.D. Brie (Early English Text Society, original series, cxxxi, 1906), i.

Calendar of Ancient Correspondence concerning Wales, ed. J.G. Edwards (Cardiff, 1935).

Calendar of Ancient Petitions relating to Wales, ed. W. Rees (Cardiff, 1975).

Calendar of Chancery Rolls Various, 1277–1326 (1912).

Calendar of Chancery Warrants, 1244–1326 (1927).

Calendar of Charter Rolls (1903–).

Calendar of Close Rolls (1892–).

Calendar of Documents relating to Ireland, ed. H.S. Sweetman, 5 vols (1877–86).

Calendar of Documents relating to Scotland, i–iv, ed. J. Bain (1881–8); v, ed. G.G. Simpson and J.D. Galbraith (Edinburgh, 1986).

Calendar of Fine Rolls (1911–).

Calendar of Letter-Books of the City of London, C, c. 1291–1309, ed. R.R. Sharpe (1901).

Calendar of Liberate Rolls (1916–).

Calendar of Papal Registers, Papal Letters, i, 1198–1304 (1893).

Calendar of Patent Rolls (1891–).

Cartulaire Générale de l'ordre des Hospitaliers de St Jean de Jerusalem en terre sainte, ed. J. Delaville le Roulx (Paris, 1894–1906).

Chronica Johannis de Oxenedes, ed. H. Ellis (Rolls series, 1859).

The Chronicle of Bury St Edmunds, 1212–1301, ed. A. Gransden (1964).

The Chronicle of Pierre de Langtoft, ed. T. Wright, ii (Rolls series, 1868).

The Chronicle of Walter of Guisborough, ed. H. Rothwell (Camden Society, lxxxix, 1957).

The Chronicle of William de Rishanger of the Barons' Wars, ed. J.O. Halliwell (Camden Society, 1840).

Chronicles of England, France, Spain, and the adjoining Countries, by Sir John Froissart, translated T. Johnes (1839).

Chronicles of the Reigns of Edward I and Edward II, ed. W. Stubbs, 2 vols (Rolls series, 1882–3).

Chronicon Abbatiae Ramseiensis, ed. W.D. Macray (Rolls series, 1886).

'Chronicon Haniense', *Monumenta Germaniae Historica, Scriptores*, xxv (Hannover, 1880).

Chronicon de Lanercost, ed. J. Stevenson (Maitland Club, 1839).

'Chronicon Parmense', ed. L.A. Muratori, *Rerum Italicarum Scriptores*, ix (Milan, 1723–51).

Chronicon Petroburgense, ed. T. Stapleton (Camden Society, 1849).

'Chronicon vulgo dictum Chronicon Thomae Wykes, 1066–1289', *Annales Monastici*, ed. H.R. Luard (Rolls series, 1864–9), iv.

Chroniques de London, ed. G.J. Aungier (Camden Society, 1844).

Close Rolls, Henry III (1902–38).

'I conti dell' ambasciate al Chan di Persia nel mccxcii', ed. C. Desimoni, *Atti delle Societa Ligure di storia Patria*, xiii (1879).

Councils and Synods, II, 1205–1313, ed. F.M. Powicke and C.R. Cheney (Oxford, 1964).

The Court and Household of Eleanor of Castile in 1290, ed. J.C. Parsons (Toronto, 1977).

Crown Pleas of the Wiltshire Eyre 1249, ed. C.A.F. Meekings (Wiltshire Archaeological and Natural History Society, Records Branch, 1961).

'De controvertia Bonifacium inter et Philippum Pulchrum agitata', ed. K. de Lettenhove, *Patrologia cursus completus, series Latina*, ed. J.P. Migne, clxxxv (Paris, 1860).

'Document pour servir à l'histoire des relations de la France avec l'Angleterre sous le règne de Philippe le Bel', ed. F. Funck-Brentano, *Revue Historique*, xxxix (1889).

Documents on the Affairs of Ireland before the King's Council, ed. G.O. Sayles (Dublin, 1979).

Documents of the baronial movement of reform and rebellion, 1258–1267, selected R.F. Treharne, ed. I.J. Sanders (Oxford, 1973).

Documents Illustrating the Crisis of 1297–8 in England, ed. M.C. Prestwich (Camden Society, 4th series, xxiv, 1980).

Documents Illustrative of the History of Scotland, ed. J. Stevenson, 2 vols (1870).

Documents and Records Illustrating the History of Scotland, i, ed. F. Palgrave (1837).

Dubois, Pierre, *De Recuperatione Terrae Sanctae*, ed. C.V. Langlois (Paris, 1891).

Early Compotus Rolls of the Priory of Worcester, ed. J.M. Wilson and C. Gordon (Worcestershire Historical Society, 1908).

Early Huntingdonshire Lay Subsidy Rolls, ed. J.A. Raftis and M.P. Hogan (Toronto, 1976).

Early Yorkshire Charters, vii, ed. C.T. Clay (Yorkshire Archaeological Society, 1947).

Edward I and the Throne of Scotland, 1290–1296. An Edition of the Record Sources for the Great Cause, 2 vols, ed. E.L.G. Stones and G.G. Simpson (Oxford, 1978).

The Estate Book of Henry de Bray, ed. D. Willis (Camden Society, 3rd series, xxvii, 1916).

L'Estoire de Eracles Empereur', *Receuil des Historiens des Croisades* (Paris, 1841–1906) *Historiens Occidentaux*, ii.

Feudal Aids, 1284–1431, i. (1899).

Fleta, ed. H.G. Richardson and G.O. Sayles, ii (Selden Society, 1955); iv, ed. G.O. Sayles (Selden Society, xcix, 1983).

Flores Historiarum, ed. H.R. Luard, 3 vols (Rolls series, 1890).

Foedera, Conventiones, Litterae, et Acta Publica, I.ii, ed. T. Rymer (Record Commission ed., 1816).

Formulary E, Scottish Letters and Brieves 1286–1424, ed. A.A.M. Duncan (University of Glasgow, Scottish History Department, Occasional Papers, 1976).

Gascon Register A, ed. G.P. Cuttino, 3 vols (1975–6).

Gesta dei per Francos, ed. J. Bongars (Hannover, 1611).

'Gesta Dunelmensia', ed. R.K. Richardson (Camden Society Miscellany, xiii, 1924).

'Gestes des Chiprois', *Receuil des Historiens des Croisades* (Paris, 1841–1906), *Documents Armeniens*, ii.

Historiae Anglicanae Scriptores Decem, ed. R. Twysden (1652).

Historiae Anglicanae Scriptores Varii, ed. J. Sparke (1724).

Historia de Rebus Gestis Glastoniensibus, ed. T. Hearn (1727).

Historical Manuscripts Commission, Report on the Manuscripts of Lord Middleton (1911).

Historical Manuscripts Commission, 6th Report (1877).

Historical Manuscripts Commission, Report on Various Collections, i (1901).

The Historical Works of Gervase of Canterbury, ed. W. Stubbs, 2 vols (Rolls series, 1880).

Ibn al-Furat, Ayyubids, Mamlukes and Crusaders, edited and translated by U. and M.C. Lyons, introduction by J.S.C. Riley-Smith (Cambridge, 1971).

'Johannis Longi Chronica S. Bertini', *Monumenta Germaniae historica, Scriptores*, xxv (Hannover, 1880).

Lancashire Lay Subsidies, i, *1216–1307*, ed. J.A.C. Vincent (Lancashire and Cheshire Record Society, xxvii, 1893).

The Ledger Book of Vale Royal Abbey, ed. J. Brownbill (Lancashire and Cheshire Record Society, lxviii, 1914).

Letters of Edward, Prince of Wales, 1304–5, ed. H. Johnstone (Roxburghe Club, 1931).

Lettres des rois, reines et autres personnages, ed. M. Champollion-Figeac, i (Paris, 1839).

'Lettres du roi Edouard I à Robert de Bavent, King's Yeoman sur des questions de venerie', ed. F.J. Tanquerey, *Bulletin of the John Rylands Library*, xxiii (1939).

Liber de Antiquis Legibus: Cronica maiorum et vicecomitum Londoniarum, ed. T. Stapleton (Camden Society, 1846).

The Liber Epistolaris of Richard de Bury, ed. N. Denholm-Young (Roxburghe Club, 1950).

Liber Quotidianus Contrarotulatoris Garderobiae, 1299–1300, ed. J. Topham et al. (1787).

A Lincolnshire Assize Roll for 1298, ed. W.S. Thomson (Lincolnshire Record Society, xxxvi, 1944).

List of Welsh Entries in the Memoranda Rolls, 1282–1343, ed. N.M. Fryde (Cardiff, 1974).

Littere Wallie, ed. J.G. Edwards (Cardiff, 1940).

Lodewijk van Velthem, Voortzetting van den Spiegel Historiael (1284–1311), ed. H. Van de Linden and W. de Vreese (Brussels, 1906).

The London Eyre of 1276, ed. M. Weinbaum (London Record Society, xii, 1976).

Makrizi, Histoire des Sultans Mamlouks, ed. M. Quatremère (Paris, 1837).

Matthaei Parisiensis, Monachi Sancti Albani, Chronica Majora, ed. H.R. Luard, 7 vols (Rolls series, 1872–83).

Memoranda de Parliamento, 1305, ed. F.W. Maitland (Rolls series, 1893).

'Memoriale Potestatum Regiensium', *Rerum Italicarum Scriptores*, viii, ed. L.A. Muratori (Milan, 1723–51).

'Menkonis Chronicon', *Monumenta Germaniae Historica, Scriptores*, xxiii (Hannover, 1873).

The Merioneth Lay Subsidy Roll, 1292–3, ed. K. Williams-Jones (Cardiff, 1976).

The Metrical Chronicle of Robert of Gloucester, ed. W.A. Wright, 2 vols (Rolls series, 1887).

The Mirror of Justices, ed. W.J. Whittaker and F.W. Maitland (Selden Society, 1893).

Moamin et Ghatif, traités de fauconnerie et des chiens de chasse, ed. H. Tjernfeld (Stockholm and Paris, 1945).

Nicholai Triveti Annales, ed. T. Hog (1845).

Parliamentary Texts of the Later Middle Ages, ed. N. Pronay and J. Taylor (Oxford, 1980).

Parliamentary Writs and Writs of Military Summons, ed. F. Palgrave, 2 vols in 4 (Record Commission, 1827–34).

Placita Parlamentaria, ed. G. Ryley (1661).

Placita de Quo Warranto, ed. W. Illingworth, 2 vols (Record Commission, 1818).

'Plea rolls of the Reign of Edward I', ed. G. Wrottesley, *Staffordshire Record Society, Collections for a History of Staffordshire*, vii.

The Pleas of the Court of King's Bench, Trinity Term, 25 Edward I, ed. W.P.W. Phillimore (British Record Society, 1898).

The Political Songs of England, ed. T. Wright (Camden Society, 1839).

'Ptolemaei Lucensis, Historia Ecclesiastica', ed. L.A. Muratori, *Rerum Italicarum Scriptores*, xi (Milan, 1723–51).

Radulphi de Hengham Summae, ed. W.H. Dunham (Cambridge, 1932).

Receuil des Historiens des Croisades, Lois, ii (Paris, 1843).

Receuil des lettres Anglo-Francaises, 1265–1399, ed. F. Tanquerey (Paris, 1916).

Receuils d'actes relatifs à l'administration des rois d'Angleterre en Guienne, ed. C. Bémont (Paris, 1914).

Records of Anthony Bek, ed. C.M. Fraser (Surtees Society, clxii, 1947).

Records of the Wardrobe and Household 1285–1286, ed. B.F. and C.R. Byerly (1977).

Records of the Wardrobe and Household 1286–1289, ed. B.F. and C.R. Byerly (1986).

The Registers of John le Romeyn, lord archbishop of York, 1286–1296, part II, and of Henry of Newark, lord archbishop of York, 1296–1299, ed. W. Brown (Surtees Society, cxxviii, 1917).

The Registers of John de Sandale and Rigaud de Asserio, bishops of Winchester, 1316–23, ed. F.J. Baigent (Hants Record Society, 1897).

Les Registres de Clement IV (1265–68), ed. E. Jordan (Paris, 1945).

Les Registres de Gregoire X et Jean XXI, ed. J. Guiraud and L. Cadier (Paris, 1892–1906).

Les Registres de Nicholas IV, ed. E. Langlois (Paris, 1886–1905).

Registrum Epistolarum Johannis Peckham, ed. C.T. Martin, 3 vols (Rolls Series, 1882–4).

Registrum Roberti de Winchelsey, archiepiscopi Cantuariensis, 1294–1308, ed. R. Graham (Canterbury and York Society, 1917–51).

Registrum vulgariter nuncupatum 'The Record of Caernarvon', ed. H. Ellis (1838).

Report of Manuscripts in Various Collections, Historical Manuscripts Commission, i (1901).

Rôles Gascons, ed. F. Michel and C. Bémont, 3 vols. (Paris, 1885–1906).

Rotuli Hundredorum, 2 vols (Record Commission, 1812–18).

Rotuli Parliamentorum, i (Record Commission, 1783).

Rotuli Scotiae, ed. D. Macpherson et al., i (1814).

Royal and other historical letters illustrative of the reign of Henry III, 2 vols., ed. W.W. Shirley (Rolls series, 1862–6).

Royal Justice and the Medieval English Countryside, ed. A.R. deWindt and E.B. deWindt, 2 vols (Toronto, 1981).

Scalacronica by Sir Thomas Grey of Heton, Knight, ed. J. Stevenson (Maitland Club, 1836).

Scotland in 1298, ed. H. Gough (Paisley, 1888).

Select Cases before the King's Council, 1243–1482, ed. I.S. Leadham and J.F. Baldwin (Selden Society, xxxv, 1918).

Select Cases in the Court of King's Bench, i–iv, vii, ed. G.O. Sayles (Selden Society, 1936, 1938, 1939, 1957, 1971).

Select Cases of Procedure without writ, ed. G.O. Sayles and H.G. Richardson (Selden Society, lx, 1940).

Select Charters, ed. W. Stubbs (9th edn, Oxford, 1921).

Select Pleas in Manorial and Other Courts, ed. F.W. Maitland (Selden Society, i. 1889).

Select Pleas, Starrs, and other Records from the Exchequer of the Jews, 1220–1284, ed. J.M. Rigg (Selden Society, xv, 1901).

The Siege of Carlaverock, ed. N.H. Nicolas (1828).

The Song of Lewes, ed. C.L. Kingsford (1890).

State Trials of the Reign of Edward I, 1289–93, ed. T.F. Tout and H. Johnstone (Camden Society, 3rd series, ix, 1906).

Statutes of the Realm i (Record Commission, 1810).

The Survey of the County of York taken by John de Kirkby, ed. R.H. Skaife (Surtees Society, xlix, 1867).

Treaty Rolls, i, *1234–1325*, ed. P. Chaplais (1955).

The War of Saint-Sardos, (1322–1325), ed. P. Chaplais (Camden Society, 3rd series, lxxxvii, 1957).

The Welsh Assize Roll, 1277–1284, ed. J. Conway Davies (Cardiff, 1940).

II. SECONDARY SOURCES

ABRAHAMS, B.L., *The Expulsion of the Jews from England in 1290* (1895).

ALTSCHUL, M., *A Baronial Family in Medieval England: The Clares, 1217–1314* (Baltimore, 1965).

AVENT, R., *Cestell Tywysogion Gwynedd, Castles of the Princes of Gwynedd* (Cardiff, 1983).

AYLOFFE, J., 'An Account of the Body of King Edward the First, as it appeared on opening his Tomb in the year 1774', *Archaeologia*, iii (1786).

BALDWIN, J.F., *The King's Council in England during the Middle Ages* (Oxford, 1913).

BARKER, J.R.V., *The Tournament in England, 1100–1400* (Woodbridge, 1986).

BARLOW, F., 'The King's Evil', *EHR*, xcv (1980).

BARRACLOUGH, G., 'Edward I and Adolf of Nassau', *Cambridge Historical Journal*, vi (1940).

BARRON, E.M., *The Scottish War of Independence* (2nd edn, Inverness, 1934).

BARROW, G.W.S., *Kingship and Unity: Scotland 1000–1306* (1981).

——, 'Lothian in the First War of Independence', *SHR*, lv (1976).

——, *Robert Bruce and the Community of the Realm of Scotland* (1965).

BAZELEY, M., 'The Extent of the English Forest in the Thirteenth Century', *TRHS*, 4th series, iv (1921).

BEAN, J.M.W., *The Decline of English Feudalism* (Manchester, 1968).

BEARDWOOD, A., 'The Trial of Walter Langton, bishop of Lichfield, 1307–1312', *Transactions of the American Philosophical Society*, new series liv (1964).

BEEBE, B., 'Edward I and the Crusades' (University of St Andrews Ph.D. thesis, 1971).

——, 'The English Baronage and the Crusade of 1270', *BIHR*, xlviii (1975).

BÉMONT, C., *Simon de Montfort*, translated by E.F. Jacob (Oxford, 1930).

BENNETT, A., 'The Windmill Psalter: the historiated letter E of Psalm One', *Journal of the Warburg and Courtauld Institutes*, xliii (1980).

BERESFORD, M.W., *New Towns of the Middle Ages* (1967).

BILES, M., 'The Indomitable Belle: Eleanor of Provence', *Seven Studies in Medieval English History and Other Historical Essays Presented to Harold S. Snellgrove* (Jackson, Mississippi, 1983).

BINSKI, P., *The Painted Chamber at Westminster* (1986).

BLAAUW, W.H., *The Barons' War* (2nd edn, 1871).

BLACK, J.G., 'Edward I and Gascony in 1300', *EHR*, xvii (1902).

BLOCH, M., *Les Rois Thaumaturges* (Paris, 1924).

BOWERS, R.H., 'From Rolls to Riches: King's Clerks and Moneylending in Thirteenth Century England', *Speculum*, lviii (1983).

——, 'English merchants and the Anglo-Flemish Economic War', *Seven Studies in Medieval English History and Other Historical Essays Presented to Harold S. Snellgrove* (Jackson, Mississippi, 1983).

BRAND, P.A., 'The Control of Mortmain Legislation in England, 1200–1300', *Legal Records and the Historian*, ed. J.H. Baker (1980).

——, 'Edward I and the Judges: the "State Trials" of 1289–93', *Thirteenth Century England I*, ed. P.R. Coss and S.D. Lloyd (Woodbridge, 1986), 31–40.

——, 'Hengham Magna: a thirteenth-century English common law treatise and its composition', *The Irish Jurist*, xi (1976).

——, ' "Quo Warranto" law in the reign of Edward I: a hitherto undiscovered opinion of Chief Justice Hengham', *The Irish Jurist*, new series xiv (1979).

BRETT-JAMES, N.G., 'John de Drokensford, Bishop of Bath and Wells', *Transactions of the London and Middlesex Archaeological Society*, new series x (1951).

BRIDBURY, A.R., 'Thirteenth Century Prices and the Money Supply', *Agricultural History Review*, xxxiii (1985).

BRIEGER, P., *English Art 1216–1307* (Oxford, 1957).

BROOKS, F.W., 'The Cinque Ports' Feud with Yarmouth', *Mariners' Mirror*, xix (1933).

BROWN, E.A.R., 'Death and the Human Body in the Later Middle Ages: the legislation of Boniface VIII on the division of the corpse', *Viator*, xii (1981).

——, 'Representation and Agency Law in the Later Middle Ages', *Viator*, iii (1972).

BROWN, R.A., *English Castles* (3rd edn, 1976).

BROWN, R.A., COLVIN, H.M., TAYLOR, A.J., *The History of the King's Works*, i, *The Middle Ages* (1963).

BULLOCK-DAVIES, C., *Menestrallorum Multitudo* (Cardiff, 1978).

BURTON, D.W., 'Politics, Propaganda and Public Opinion in the Reigns of Henry III and Edward I' (Oxford University D.Phil. thesis, 1985).

CAM, H.M., *The Hundred and the Hundred Rolls* (London, 1930).

——, *Studies in the Hundred Rolls: some aspects of thirteenth-century administration* (Oxford, 1921).

CARPENTER, D.A., 'King, Magnates, and Society: the Personal Rule of King Henry III, 1234–1258', *Speculum*, lx (1985).

——, 'The Lord Edward's Oath to aid and counsel Simon de Montfort, 15 October 1259', *BIHR*, lviii (1985).

——, 'Simon de Montfort and the Mise of Lewes', *BIHR*, lviii (1985).

——, 'What Happened in 1258?', *War and Government in the Middle Ages*, ed. J.B. Gillingham and J.C. Holt (Woodbridge, 1984).

CHABOT, J.B., 'Histoire du Patriarche Mar Jabalaha III', *Revue de l'Orient Latin*, xi (1894).

——, 'Notes sur les relations du roi Argoun avec l'occident' *Revue de l'orient Latin*, xi (1894).

CHAMBERS, E.K., *Arthur of Britain* (1927).

CHAPLAIS, P., *English Medieval Diplomatic Practice*, I, i, ii (1982).

——, *Essays in Medieval Diplomacy and Administration* (1981).

——, 'Some Private Letters of Edward I', *EHR*, lxxvii (1962).

CHEW, H.M., *The English Ecclesiastical Tenants in Chief and Knight Service* (Oxford, 1932).

——, 'Scutage under Edward I', *EHR*, xxxvii (1922).

CLANCHY, M.T., *England and its Rulers 1066–1272* (Glasgow, 1983).

——, *From Memory to Written Record* (1979).

——, 'The Franchise of Return of Writs', *TRHS*, 5th series, xvii (1967).

——, 'Moderni in education and government in England', *Speculum*, l (1975).

CLIFFORD, E.R., *A Knight of Great Renown* (Chicago, 1961).

COKAYNE, G.E., *Complete Peerage of England, Scotland, Ireland, Great Britain and the United Kingdom*, ed. V. Gibbs and others, 12 vols (1912–59).

COSS, P.R., 'Sir Geoffrey de Langley and the Crisis of the Knightly Class in thirteenth-century England', *Past and Present*, lxviii (1975).

COULSON, C.L.H., 'Rendability and Castellation in Medieval France', *Château Gaillard*, vi (1972).

COX D.C., 'Peace-Keeping without Frankpledge: Shropshire Claims in 1307', *Transactions of the Shropshire Archaeological Society*, lx (1975–7).

COX, E.L., *The Eagles of Savoy* (Princeton, 1974).

CUTTINO, G.P., 'A chancellor of the Lord Edward', *BIHR*, xlx (1977).

——, *English Diplomatic Administration 1259–1339* (2nd edn, Oxford, 1971).

DALRYMPLE, D, (LORD HAILES), *Annals of Scotland from the Accession of Malcolm III surnamed Canmore to the Restoration of James I* (1799).

DAVIES, R.R., 'Colonial Wales', *Past and Present*, lxv (1974).

——, *Conquest, Coexistence and Change: Wales 1063–1415* (Oxford, 1987).

——, 'Law and national identity in thirteenth century Wales', *Welsh Society and Nationhood*, ed. R.R. Davies, R.A. Griffiths, I.G. Jones and K.O. Morgan (Cardiff, 1984).

——, 'Llywelyn ap Gruffydd, Prince of Wales', *Journal of the Merioneth Historical and Record Society*, ix (1983).

——, *Lordship and Society in the March of Wales, 1282–1400* (Oxford, 1978).

——, 'The survival of the bloodfeud in Medieval Wales', *History*, liv (1969).

DEELEY, A., 'Papal Provision and Royal Rights of Patronage in the Early Fourteenth Century', *EHR*, xliii (1928).

DEIGHTON, H.S., 'Clerical Taxation by Consent, 1272–1301', *EHR*, lxviii (1953).

DENHOLM-YOUNG, N., 'Edward I and the Sale of the Isle of Wight', *EHR*, xliv (1929).

——, *History and Heraldry* (Oxford, 1965).

——, *Richard of Cornwall* (Oxford, 1947).

——, *Seigneurial Administration* (Oxford, 1937).

——, 'The Tournament in the Thirteenth Century', *Studies in Medieval History presented to F.M. Powicke*, ed. R.W. Hunt, W.A. Pantin, R.W. Southern (Oxford, 1948).

DENTON, J.H., 'The Clergy and Parliament in the Thirteenth and Fourteenth Centuries', *The English Parliament in the Middle Ages*, ed. R.G. Davies and J.H. Denton (Manchester, 1981).

——, 'The Crisis of 1297 from the Evesham Chronicle', *EHR*, xciii (1978).

——, *English Royal Free Chapels 1100–1300* (Manchester, 1970).

——, *Robert Winchelsey and the Crown 1294–1313* (Cambridge, 1980).

——, 'A Worcester Text of the Remonstrances of 1297', *Speculum*, liii (1978).

DE STURLER, J., 'Deux comptes "enrolés" de Robert de Segre, receveur et agent payeuer d'Edouard Ier, roi d'Angleterre, aux Pays-Bas (1294–1296)', *Bulletin de la commission royale d'histoire*, cxxv (1960).

——, 'Le paiement à Bruxelles des allies franc-comtois d'Edouard Ier, roi d'Angleterre (Mai 1297)', *Cahiers Bruxellois*, v (1960).

——, *Les relations politiques et les échanges commerciaux entre le duché de Brabant et l'Angleterre au moyen âge* (Paris, 1936).

DICKINSON, W.C., *Scotland from the earliest times to 1603*, 3rd edn revised by A.A.M. Duncan (Oxford, 1977).

Dictionary of National Biography, ed. L. Stephen (1885–1900).

DOUIE, D., *Archbishop Pecham* (Oxford, 1952).

DUNCAN, A.A.M., 'The Community of the Realm of Scotland and Robert Bruce', *SHR*, xlv (1966).

EDWARDS, J.G., 'The Battle of Maes Moydog and the Welsh Campaign of 1294–5' *EHR*, xxxix (1924).

——, '*Confirmatio Cartarum* and Baronial Grievances in 1297', *EHR*, lviii (1943).

——, 'Justice in Early English Parliaments', *Historical Studies of the English Parliament*, i, ed. E.B. Fryde and E. Miller (Cambridge, 1970).

——, 'Madog ap Llywelyn, the Welsh Leader in 1294–5', *Bulletin of the Board of Celtic Studies*, xiii (1950).

——, 'The Personnel of the Commons in Parliament under Edward I and Edward II', *Historical Studies of the English Parliament*, i, ed. E.B. Fryde and E. Miller (Cambridge, 1970).

——, 'The *Plena Potestas* of English Parliamentary Representatives', *Historical Studies of the English Parliament*, i, ed. E.B. Fryde and E. Miller (Cambridge, 1970).

——, 'The site of the Battle of "Meismeidoc", 1295 (Note)', *EHR*, xlvi (1931).

——, 'The Treason of Thomas Turberville, 1295', *Studies in Medieval History presented to F.M. Powicke*, ed. R.W. Hunt, W.A. Pantin, R.W. Southern (Oxford, 1948).

ELMAN, P., 'The Economic Causes of the Expulsion of the Jews in 1290', *Economic History Review*, vii (1936).

FAIRBANK, F.R., 'The Last Earl of Warenne and Surrey', *Yorkshire Archaeological Journal*, xix (1907).

FARMER, D.L., 'Some Grain Price Movements in Thirteenth Century England', *Economic History Review*, 2nd series, x (1957).

——, 'Some Livestock Price Movements in Thirteenth-Century England', *Economic History Review*, 2nd series, xii (1969).

FAVIER, J., *Philippe le Bel* (Paris, 1978).

FAWTIER, R., *L'Europe occidentale de 1270 à 1380* (Paris, 1940).

FRAME, R., *Colonial Ireland 1169–1369* (Dublin, 1981).

——, 'Ireland and the Barons' War', *Thirteenth Century England I*, ed. P.R. Coss and S.D. Lloyd (Woodbridge, 1986).

FRASER, C.M., *A History of Anthony Bek* (Oxford, 1957).

FREEMAN, A.Z., 'A Moat Defensive; the coast defense scheme of 1295', *Speculum*, xlii (1967).

FRYDE, N.M., 'A royal enquiry into abuses by Queen Eleanor's ministers in north-east Wales, 1291–2', *Welsh History Review*, v (1970–1).

GALBRAITH, V.H., 'Statutes of Edward I: Huntington Library MS H.M. 25782', *Essays in Medieval History presented to Bertie Wilkinson*, ed. M.R. Powicke and T.A Sandquist (Toronto, 1969).

GARDELLES, J., *Les Châteaux du Moyen Age dans la France du sud-ouest: la Gascogne Anglaise de 1216 à 1327* (Geneva, 1972).

GILLINGHAM, J.B., 'Richard I and the Science of War in the Middle Ages', *War and Government in the Middle Ages*, ed. J.B. Gillingham and J.C. Holt (Woodbridge, 1984).

Glamorgan County History, iii, *The Middle Ages*, ed. T.B. Pugh (Cardiff, 1971).

GRANSDEN, A., *Historical Writing in England, c.550–c.1307* (1974).

GRASSI, J.L., 'The clerical dynasties from Howdenshire, Nottinghamshire and Lindsey in the royal administration' (Oxford University, D.Phil. thesis, 1959).

GRAVES, E.B., 'Circumspecte Agatis', *EHR*, xliii (1928).

GREEN, M.A.E., *Lives of the Princesses of England* (1850).

GRIFFITHS, J., 'Documents relating to the rebellion of Madoc, 1294–5', *Bulletin of the Board of Celtic Studies*, viii (1935–7).

——, 'The revolt of Madog ap Llywelyn, 1294–5', *Transactions of the Caernarvonshire Historical Society* (1955).

GRIFFITHS, R.A., *The Principality of Wales in the Later Middle Ages*, i (Cardiff, 1972).

——, 'The revolt of Rhys ap Maredudd', *Welsh History Review*, iii (1966–7).

GROSE, F., *Military Antiquities* (2nd edn, 1801).

GUIRAUD, F.F., 'Municipal Archives of Faversham A.D. 1304–24', *Archaeologia Cantiana*, xiv (1882).

GWYNN, A., 'Edward I and the proposed purchase of English law for the Irish, c.1276–80', *TRHS*, 5th series, x (1960).

HADWIN, J.F., 'The Last Royal Tallages', *EHR*, xcvi (1981).

——, 'The Medieval Lay Subsidies and Economic History', *Economic History Review*, 2nd series, xxxvi (1983).

HAND, J.G., *English Law in Ireland, 1290–1324* (Cambridge, 1967).

——, 'The Opinions of the Paris Lawyers upon the Scottish Succession c.1292', *The Irish Jurist*, new series v (1970).

Handbook of British Chronology, 3rd edn, ed. E.B. Fryde, D.E. Greenway, S. Porter, I. Roy (1986).

HARDING, A., 'Early Trailbaston Proceedings from the Lincoln roll of 1305', *Medieval Legal Records*, ed. R.F. Hunnisett and J.B. Post (1978).

——, 'The Origins of the Crime of Conspiracy', *TRHS*, 5th series, xxxiii (1983).

——, 'Plaints and Bills in the History of English Law, mainly in the period 1250–1350', *Legal History Studies*, ed. D. Jenkins (Cardiff, 1972).

HARRISS, G.L., *King, Parliament and Public Finance in Medieval England to 1369* (Oxford, 1975).

HASKINS, G.L., and KANTOROWICZ, E., 'A Diplomatic Mission of Francis Accursius and his Oration before Pope Nicholas III', *EHR*, lviii (1943).

HIGOUNET, C., 'Bastides et Frontières', *Le Moyen Age*, liv (1948).

HILL, G., *A History of Cyprus*, ii (1948).

HILL, M.C., *The King's Messengers, 1199–1377* (1961).

HILLGARTH, J.N., *The Spanish Kingdoms* (1976).

A History of the Crusades, ed. K.M. Setton *et al.*, ii, *The Later Crusades*, ed. R.L. Wolff and H.W. Hazard (Philadelphia, 1962).

HOLT, J.C., 'The Prehistory of Parliament', *The English Parliament in the Middle Ages*, ed. R.G. Davies and J.H. Denton (Manchester. 1981).

HOOPER, D., and WHYLD, K., *The Oxford Companion to Chess* (Oxford, 1984).

HOWARTH, H.H., *History of the Mongols*, iii (1888).

HOWELL, M., *Regalian Right in Medieval England* (1962).

HUGHES, U.W., 'A Biographical Sketch of Robert Burnell, with materials from his life' (Oxford University B.Litt. thesis, 1936).

HURNARD, N.D., 'Did Edward I reverse Henry II's policy upon Seisin?', *EHR*, lxix (1954).

——, *The King's Pardon for Homicide* (Oxford, 1969).

ILLSLEY, J.S., 'Parliamentary Elections in the Reign of Edward I', *BIHR*, xlix (1976).

Itinerary of Edward I, part 1: 1272–1290 (List and Index society, ciii, 1974).

JACOB, E.F., *Studies in the period of Baronial Reform and Rebellion, 1258–1267* (Oxford, 1925).

JENKINSON, C.H., 'The First Parliament of Edward I', *EHR*, xxv (1910).

JOHNS, C.N., *Criccieth Castle* (Official Guide, 1970).

JOHNSON, C., 'The System of Account in the Wardrobe of Edward I', *TRHS*, 4th series, vi (1923).

JOHNSTONE, H., 'Archbishop Pecham and the council of Lambeth of 1281', *Essays in Medieval History presented to T.F. Tout*, ed. A.G. Little and F.M. Powicke (Manchester, 1925).

——, *Edward of Carnarvon 1284–1307* (Manchester, 1946).

——, 'The County of Ponthieu, 1279–1307', *EHR*, xxix (1914).

——, 'Wardrobe and Household of Henry, son of Edward I', *Bulletin of the John Rylands Library*, vii (1922–3).

JOLIFFE, J.E.A., 'Some Factors in the beginning of Parliament', *Historical Studies of the English Parliament*, i, ed. E.B. Fryde and E. Miller (Cambridge, 1970).

JONES, W.R., 'The Court of the Verge: the Jurisdiction of the Steward and Marshal of the Household in Later Medieval England', *Journal of British Studies*, x (1970–1).

JORDAN, W.C., *Louis IX and the Challenge of the Crusade* (Princeton, 1979).

KAEUPER, R.W., *Bankers to the Crown: the Riccardi of Lucca and Edward I* (Princeton, 1973).

——, 'The Frescobaldi of Florence and the English Crown', *Studies in Medieval and Renaissance History*, x (1973).

——, 'Law and Order in Fourteenth-Century England: the evidence of special commissions of oyer and terminer', *Speculum*, liv (1979).

KEEN, M.H., *Chivalry* (New Haven and London, 1984).

KERN, F., 'Edouard I von England und Peter von Aragon', *Mitteilungen des Instituts fur Osterreichische Geschichtsforschung*, xxx (1909).

KINGSFORD, C.L., 'John de Benstede and his Missions for Edward I, *Essays in History presented to R.L. Poole*, ed. H.W.C. Davis (Oxford, 1927).

KIRALFY, A.K., *The Action on the Case* (1951).

KNOWLES, C.H., 'Provision for the Families of the Montfortians disinherited after the Battle of Evesham', *Thirteenth Century England 1*, ed. P.R. Coss and S.D. Lloyd (Woodbridge, 1986).

——, 'The Resettlement of England after the Barons' War, 1264–67', *TRHS*, 5th series, xxxii (1982).

KOHLER, C., 'Deux projects de croisade en terre-sainte composée à la fin du xiiie siècle et au début du xive', *Revue de l'Orient Latin*, x (1903–4).

KOHLER, C., and LANGLOIS, C.V., 'Lettres inédits concernant les croisades (1275–1307), *Bibliothèque de l'école des chartes*, lii (1891).

KOSMINSKY, E.A., *Studies in the Agrarian History of England in the Thirteenth Century* (Oxford, 1956).

LABARGE, M.W., *Gascony, England's First Colony, 1204–1453* (1978).

LANGLOIS, C.V., 'Project for Taxation presented to Edward I', *EHR*, iv (1889).

LAPSLEY, G.T., 'John de Warenne and the Quo Warranto proceedings in 1279', *Cambridge Historical Journal*, ii (1926–7).

LAWTON, R.P., 'Henry de Lacy, Earl of Lincoln (1272–1311), as *locum tenens et capitaneus* in the duchy of Aquitaine' (London University Ph.D, thesis, 1974).

LÉONARD, E.G., *Les Angevins de Naples* (Paris, 1954).

LEWIS, A., 'Roger Leyburn and the Pacification of England, 1265–7' *EHR*, liv (1939).

LEWIS, A.W., *Royal Succession in Capetian France: Studies in familial order and the state* (Cambridge, Mass., 1981).

LEWIS, E.A., *The Medieval Boroughs of Snowdonia* (1912).

LEWIS, N.B., 'The English Forces in Flanders, August–November 1297', *Studies in Medieval History presented to F.M. Powicke*, ed. R.W. Hunt, W.A. Pantin, R.W. Southern (Oxford, 1948).

LINEHAN, P.A., 'A fourteenth century history of Anglo-Scottish relations in a Spanish Manuscript', *BIHR*, xlviii (1975).

LLOYD, J.E., *A History of Wales* (2nd edn, London, 1922).

LLOYD, S.D., 'English Society and the Crusades, 1216–1307', (Oxford University D.Phil. thesis, 1983).

——, 'Gilbert de Clare, Richard of Cornwall and the Lord Edward's Crusade', *Nottingham Medieval Studies*, xxxi (1986).

——, 'The Lord Edward's Crusade, 1270–2: its setting and significance', *War and Government in the Middle Ages*, ed. J.B. Gillingham and J.C. Holt (Woodbridge, 1984).

LLOYD, T.H., *The English Wool Trade in the Middle Ages* (Cambridge, 1977).

——, *The Movement of Wool Prices in Medieval England* (*Economic History Review Supplement no. 6*, 1973).

LODGE, E.C., *Gascony under English Rule* (1926).

LOGAN, F.D., *Excommunication and the Secular Arm in Medieval England* (Toronto, 1968).

LOOMIS, R.S., 'Edward I, Arthurian Enthusiast', *Speculum*, xxviii (1953).

LUBIMENKO, I., *Jean de Bretagne, comte de Richmond. Sa vie et son activité en Angleterre, en Ecosse et en France (1266–1334)* (Lille, 1908).

LUNT, W.E., *Financial Relations of the Papacy with England to 1327* (Cambridge, Mass., 1939).

——, 'William Testa and the Parliament of Carlisle', *EHR*, xli (1926).

LYDON, J.F., 'Edward I, Ireland and the War in Scotland, 1303–1304', *England and Ireland in the Later Middle Ages*, ed. J.F. Lydon (Dublin, 1981).

——, 'Irish Levies in the Scottish Wars, 1296–1302', *The Irish Sword*, v (1962).

LYON, B.D., 'Un compte de l'échiquier relatif aux relations d'Edouard I d'Angleterre avec le duc Jean II de Brabant', *Bulletin de la commission royale d'histoire*, cxx (1955).

MCFARLANE, K.B., *The Nobility of Later Medieval England* (Oxford, 1973).

MCINTOSH, M.K., *Autonomy and Community: The Royal Manor of Havering 1200–1500* (Cambridge, 1986).

MCKISACK, M., *The Parliamentary Representation of the English Boroughs during the Middle Ages* (Oxford, 1932).

MCLEAN, N., 'An Eastern Embassy to Europe in the years 1287–8', *EHR*, xiv (1899).

MADDICOTT, J.R., 'Edward I and the Lessons of Baronial Reform: Local Government, 1258–80', *Thirteenth Century England 1*, ed. P.R. Coss and S.D. Lloyd (Woodbridge, 1986).

——, *The English Peasantry and the Demands of the Crown 1294–1341* (*Past and Present Supplement*, 1975).

——, *Law and Lordship: Royal Justices as retainers in thirteenth- and fourteenth-century England* (*Past and Present Supplement*, 1978).

——, 'The Mise of Lewes, 1264', *EHR*, xcviii (1983).

——, 'Parliament and the Constituencies', *The English Parliament in the Middle Ages*, ed. R.G. Davies and J.H. Denton (Manchester, 1981).

MADOX, T., *The History and Antiquities of the Exchequer* (1769).

MAITLAND, F.W., 'The "Praerogativa Regis"', *EHR*, vi (1891).

MATE, M., 'High Prices in early fourteenth-century England: causes and consequences', *Economic History Review*, 2nd series, xxviii (1975).

——, 'The Impact of War on the Economy of Canterbury Cathedral Priory, 1294–1340', *Speculum*, lvii (1982).

——, 'Monetary Policies in England, 1272–1307', *British Numismatic Journal*, xli (1972).

MAYHEW, N.J., and WALKER, D.R., 'Crockards and Pollards: imitation and the problem of fineness in a silver coinage', *Edwardian Monetary Affairs (1279–1344)*, ed. N.J. Mayhew (British Archaeological Reports, 1977).

MEEKINGS, C.A.F., *Studies in Thirteenth-Century Justice and Administration* (1982).

MILLER, E., 'War, taxation and the English economy in the late thirteenth and early fourteenth centuries', in *War and Economic Development*, ed. J.M. Winter (1975).

MILLS, M.H., '"Adventus Vicecomitum", 1272–1307', *EHR*, xxxviii (1923).
——, 'Exchequer Agenda and Estimate of Revenue, Easter Term 1284', *EHR*, xl (1925).
MITCHELL, S.K., *Taxation in Medieval England* (New Haven, 1951).
MOORMAN, J.R.H., 'Edward I at Lanercost Priory, 1306–7', *EHR*, lxviii (1952).
MORGAN, R., 'The Barony of Powys, 1275–1360', *Welsh History Review*, x (1980–1).
MORRIS, J.E., *The Welsh Wars of Edward I* (Oxford, 1901).

NICHOLSON, R., *Scotland: The Later Middle Ages* (Edinburgh, 1974).
NEILSON, G., 'Bruce *versus* Balliol', *SHR*, xvi (1919).

ORME, N., *From Childhood to Chivalry* (1984).
ORPEN, G.H., *Ireland under the Normans*, iii, *1216–1333* (Oxford, 1920).
OTWAY-RUTHVEN, J., 'The Constitutional Position of the Great Lordships of South Wales', *TRHS*, 5th series, viii (1958).
——, *A History of Medieval Ireland* (1968).

PAINTER, S., *The Reign of King John* (Baltimore, 1949).
PALMER, R.C., *The County Courts of Medieval England 1150–1350* (Princeton, 1982).
PARSONS, J.C., 'The Year of Eleanor of Castile's Birth and her Children by Edward I', *Medieval Studies*, xlvi (1984).
PASQUET, D., *An Essay on the Origins of the House of Commons* (Cambridge, 1925).
PELHAM, R.A., 'The Provisioning of the Lincoln Parliament of 1301', *University of Birmingham Historical Journal*, iii (1952).
PETERS, E., *The Shadow King* (New Haven, 1970).
PHILLIPS, J.R.S., *Aymer de Valence, earl of Pembroke 1307–1324* (Oxford, 1972).
PLUCKNETT, T.F.T., *Legislation of Edward I* (Oxford, 1949).
——, 'Parliament', *Historical Studies of the English Parliament*, i, ed. E.B. Fryde and E. Miller (Cambridge, 1970).
POLLOCK, F., and MAITLAND, F.W., *History of English Law*, 2 vols (2nd edn, Cambridge, 1898).
POOLE, A.L., *From Domesday Book to Magna Carta, 1087–1216* (Oxford, 1955).
——, *Obligations of Society in the XII and XIII centuries* (Oxford, 1946).
POST, G., *Studies in Medieval Legal Thought* (Princeton, 1964).
POST, J.B., 'Ravishment of Women and the Statute of Westminster', *Legal Records and the Historian*, ed. J.H. Baker (1978).
POWICKE, F.M., 'Edward I in Fact and Fiction', *Fritz Saxl Memorial Essays*, ed. D.J. Gordon (1957).
——, *Henry III and the Lord Edward*, 2 vols (Oxford, 1947).
——, *The Thirteenth Century, 1216–1307* (2nd edn, Oxford, 1962).
POWICKE, M.R., *Military Obligation in Medieval England* (Oxford, 1962).
POWELL, J.E., and WALLIS, K., *The House of Lords in the Middle Ages* (1968).
PRESTWICH, J.O., 'The Military Household of the Norman Kings', *EHR*, xcvi (1981).

PRESTWICH, M.C., 'Cavalry Service in Early Fourteenth Century England', *War and Government in the Middle Ages*, ed. J.B. Gillingham and J.C. Holt (Woodbridge, 1984).

——, 'Colonial Scotland', *Scotland and England 1286–1815*, ed. R.A. Mason (Edinburgh, 1987).

——, 'The Crown and the Currency. The Circulation of Money in late thirteenth- and early fourteenth-century England', *Numismatic Chronicle*, cxlii (1982).

——, 'Early Fourteenth-Century Exchange Rates', *Economic History Review*, 2nd series, xxxii (1979).

——, 'Edward I's Monetary Policies and their Consequences', *Economic History Review*, 2nd series, xii (1969).

——, 'Edward I's Wars and their Financing, 1294–1307', (Oxford University D.Phil. thesis, 1968).

——, 'The English Campaign in Scotland in 1296 and the surrender of John Balliol: some supporting evidence', *BIHR*, xlix (1976).

——, 'Exchequer and Wardrobe in the Later Years of Edward I', *BIHR*, xlvi (1973).

——, 'Isabella de Vescy and the Custody of Bamburgh Castle', *BIHR*, xliv (1971).

——, 'Italian Bankers in late thirteenth and early fourteenth century England', *The Dawn of Modern Banking*, ed. Center for Medieval and Renaissance Studies (New Haven, 1979).

——, 'Magnate Summonses in England in the Later Years of Edward I', *Parliaments, Estates and Representation*, v (1985).

——, 'A New Account of the Welsh Campaign of 1294–5', *Welsh History Review*, vi (1973–4).

——, 'Parliament and the community of the realm in fourteenth century England', *Parliament and Community*, ed. A. Cosgrove and J.I. McGuire (Belfast, 1983).

——, 'The Piety of Edward I', *England in the Thirteenth Century*, ed. W.M. Ormrod (Harlaxton, 1985).

——, 'Royal Patronage under Edward I', *Thirteenth Century England 1*, ed. P.R. Coss and S.D. Lloyd (Woodbridge, 1986).

——, *The Three Edwards: war and state in England 1272–1377* (1980).

——, *War, Politics and Finance under Edward I* (1972).

PUGH, R.B., *Imprisonment in Medieval England* (Cambridge, 1968).

——, *London Trailbaston Trials* (1975).

PURCELL, M., *Papal Crusading Policy 1244–1291* (Leyden, 1975).

RHODES, W.E., 'Edmund earl of Lancaster', *EHR*, x (1895).

RICHARDSON, H.G., 'The Coronation of Edward I', *BIHR*, xv (1937–8).

——, 'Early Coronation Records', *BIHR*, xiii (1935–6).

——, 'The English Coronation Oath', *Speculum*, xxiv (1949).

——, *The English Jewry under the Angevin Kings* (1960).

——, Review of *The History of the King's Works*, *EHR*, lxxx (1965).

RICHARDSON, H.G., and SAYLES, G.O., *The English Parliament in the Middle Ages* (1981).

——, *The Governance of Medieval England* (Edinburgh, 1963).

——, *The Irish Parliament in the Middle Ages* (Philadelphia, 1952).

RIDGEWAY, H.W., 'The Lord Edward and the Provisions of Oxford (1258): a Study in Faction', *Thirteenth Century England 1*, ed. P.R. Coss and S.D. Lloyd (Woodbridge, 1986).

——, 'The Politics of the English Royal Court, 1247–65, with special reference to the role of the aliens' (Oxford University D.Phil. thesis, 1984).

RODERICK, A.J., 'The Four Cantreds: a study in administration', *Bulletin of the Board of Celtic Studies*, x (1940).

RÖHRICHT, R., 'Etudes sur les derniers temps du royaume de Jérusalem. A. La croisade du Prince Edouard d'Angleterre (1270–1274), *Archives de l'Orient Latin*, i (1881).

——, 'Etudes sur les derniers temps du royaume de Jérusalem. C. Les combats du Sultan Baibars', *Archives de l'Orient Latin*, ii (1884).

ROSKELL, J.S., 'The Problem of the Attendance of the Lords in Medieval Parliaments', *BIHR*, xxix (1956).

ROTH, C., *History of the Jews in England* (Oxford, 1941).

ROTHWELL, H., 'The Confirmation of the Charters, 1297', *EHR*, lx (1945).

——, 'The Disgrace of Richard of Louth, 1297', *EHR*, xlviii (1933).

——, 'Edward I's case against Philip the Fair over Gascony', *EHR*, xlii (1927).

——, 'Edward I and the Struggle for the Charters, 1297–1305', *Studies in Medieval History presented to F.M. Powicke*, ed. R.W. Hunt, W.A. Pantin, R.W. Southern (Oxford, 1948).

ROUND, J.H., *The King's Sergeants and Officers of State* (1911).

RUNCIMAN, S., *The Sicilian Vespers* (Harmondsworth, 1960).

RYAN, J.D., 'Nicholas IV and the Evolution of the Eastern Missionary Effort', *Archivum Historiae Pontificum*, xix (1981).

SALT, M.C.L., 'List of English Embassies to France, 1272–1307', *EHR*, xliv (1929).

SALZMAN, L.F., *Edward I* (1968).

SAUNDERS, P.C., 'Royal Ecclesiastical Patronage in England, 1199–1356' (Oxford University D.Phil. thesis, 1978).

SAYLES, G.O., 'The dissolution of a guild at York in 1306', *EHR*, lv (1940).

——, *The King's Parliament of England* (1975).

——, 'Medieval Judges as Legal Consultants', *Law Quarterly Review*, liv (1940).

SCHEIN, S., 'Gesta Dei per Mongolos 1300. The genesis of a non-event', *EHR*, xciv (1979).

SIMPSON, A.B.W., *An Introduction to the History of the Land Law* (Oxford, 1961).

SIMPSON, G.G., 'The Claim of Florence count of Holland to the Scottish Throne, 1291–2', *SHR*, xxxvi (1957).

——, 'The *Familia* of Roger de Quincy, earl of Winchester and Constable of Scotland', *Essays on the Nobility of Medieval Scotland*, ed. K.J. Stringer (Edinburgh, 1985).

SIMPSON, W.D., *Castles in England and Wales* (1969).

SMALLEY, B., *English Friars and Antiquity in the Early Fourteenth Century* (Oxford, 1960).

SMITH, J. BEVERLEY, 'The Legal Position of Wales in the Middle Ages', *Law Making and Law Makers*, ed. A. Harding (1980).

——, 'Edward II and the allegiance of Wales', *Welsh History Review*, viii (1976–7).

——, 'The Origins of the Revolt of Rhys ap Maredudd', *Bulletin of the Board of Celtic Studies*, xxi (1964–6).

SMITH, L. BEVERLEY, 'The death of Llywelyn ap Gruffydd: the narratives reconsidered', *Welsh History Review*, xi (1982).

——, 'The Gravamina of the Community of Gwynedd against Llywelyn ap Gryffudd', *Bulletin of the Board of Celtic Studies*, xxxi (1984).

——, 'The Statute of Wales, 1284', *Welsh History Review*, x (1980–1).

SOMERVILLE, R., *History of the Duchy of Lancaster*, i (1953).

SPITZER, A.L., 'The Legal Careers of Thomas of Weyland and Gilbert of Thornton', *Journal of Legal History*, vi (1985).

SPUFFORD, P., *Handbook of Medieval Exchange* (1986).

SPULER, B., *History of the Mongols* (Berkeley and Los Angeles, 1972).

STAINES, D., 'Havelock the Dane: a thirteenth century handbook for princes', *Speculum*, li (1976).

STANILAND, K., 'Welcome, Royal Babe! The Birth of Thomas of Brotherton in 1300', *Costume*, (1985).

STELL, G., 'The Balliol Family and the Great Cause of 1291–2', *Essays on the Nobility of Medieval Scotland*, ed. K.J. Stringer (Edinburgh, 1985).

STEPHENSON, D., *The Governance of Gwynedd* (Cardiff, 1984).

——, *The Last Prince of Wales* (Buckingham, 1983).

——, 'Llywelyn ap Gruffydd and the struggle for the principality of Wales, 1258–1282', *Transactions of the Honourable Society of Cymmrodorion* (1983).

STEWART BROWN, R., 'The end of the Norman earldom of Chester', *EHR*, xxxv (1920).

STONES, E.L.G., 'English Chroniclers and the Affairs of Scotland, 1286–1296', *The Writing of History in the Middle Ages*, ed. R.H.C. Davis and J.M. Wallace-Hadrill (Oxford, 1981).

——, 'The mission of Thomas Wale and Thomas Delisle from Edward I to Boniface VIII in 1301', *Nottingham Medieval Studies*, xxvii (1982).

——, 'The Text of the Writ "Quod Omnes Tangit" in Stubbs's Select Charters', *EHR*, lxxxiii (1973).

STONES, E.L.G., and BLOUNT, M.N., 'The Surrender of King John of Scotland to Edward I in 1296: some new evidence', *BIHR*, xlviii (1975).

STRAYER, J.R., 'The Costs and Profits of War: the Anglo-French conflict of 1294–1303', *The Medieval City*, ed. H.A. Miskimin, D. Herlihy, A.L. Udovitch (New Haven, 1977).

——, *Medieval Statecraft and the Perspectives of History* (Princeton, 1971).

——, *The Reign of Philip the Fair* (Princeton, 1980).

STUBBS, W., *The Constitutional History of England*, ii (4th edn, Oxford, 1906).

——, *Seventeen lectures on the Study of Medieval and Modern History* (Oxford, 1887).

STUDD, J.R., 'A Catalogue of the Acts of the Lord Edward, 1254–1272' (Leeds University Ph.D. thesis, 1971).

——, 'The Lord Edward's lordship of Chester, 1254–72', *Transactions of the Historic Society of Lancashire and Cheshire*, 128 (1979).

——, 'The Lord Edward and King Henry III, *BIHR*, l (1977).

SUTHERLAND, D.W., *The Assize of Novel Disseisin* (Oxford, 1973).

——, *Quo Warranto Proceedings in the Reign of Edward I, 1278–1294* (Oxford, 1963).

SUMMERSON, H.R.T., 'The early development of Peine Forte et Dure', *Law, Litigants and the Legal Profession*, ed. E.W. Ives and A.H. Manchester (1983).

SWIFT, F.D., 'Marriage Alliance of the Infanta Pedro of Aragon and Edward I of England', *EHR*, v (1890).

SWINNERTON, C., 'Two ancient petitions from the Public Record Office', *The Ancestor*, vi (1903).

TAYLOR, A.J., 'The castle of St-Georges d'Esperanche', *Antiquaries Journal*, xxxiii (1953).

——, 'Castle-Building in Wales in the later thirteenth century: the prelude to construction', *Studies in Building History*, ed. E.M. Jope (1961).

——, 'Documents concerning the King's Works at Linlithgow, 1302–3', *Studies in Scottish Antiquity presented to Stewart Cruden*, ed. D.J. Breeze (Edinburgh, 1984).

——, 'The Earliest Burgesses of Flint and Rhuddlan', *Flintshire Historical Society Publications*, xxvii (1975–6).

——, 'Edward I and the Shrine of St Thomas of Canterbury', *Journal of the British Archaeological Association*, cxxxii (1979).

——, 'A fragment of a *dona* account of 1284', *Bulletin of the Board of Celtic Studies*, xxvii (1976–8).

——, 'Master James of St George', *EHR*, lxv (1950).

——, *Rhuddlan Castle* (Official Guide, 1956).

——, 'Royal Alms and Oblations in the Later Thirteenth Century', *Tribute to an Antiquary: essays presented to Marc Fitch*, ed. F.G. Emmison and R. Stephens (1976).

——, 'Some notes on the Savoyards in north Wales, 1277–1300, with special reference to the Savoyard element in the construction of Harlech castle', *Genava*, new series, xi (1963).

——, *Studies in Castles and Castle-Building* (1985).

——, 'Who was "John Penardd, leader of the men of Gwynedd"?', *EHR*, xci (1976).

THORPE, L., 'Mastre Richard, a thirteenth-century translator of the "de Re Militari" of Vegetius', *Scriptorium*, vi (1952).

TOUT, T.F., *Chapters in the Administrative History of Medieval England*, ii, vi (Manchester, 1920, 1933).

——, *Collected Papers*, iii (Manchester, 1934).

——, 'Communitas bacheleriae Anglie', *EHR*, xvii (1902).

——, *The Place of Edward II in English History* (Manchester, 1914).

TRABUT-CUSSAC, J.P., *L'administration anglaise en Gascogne sous Henry III et Edouard I de 1254 à 1307* (Paris, 1972).

——, 'Bastides ou Forteresses?', *Le Moyen Age*, lx (1954).

——, 'Date, fondation et identification de la bastide de Baa', *Revue Historique de Bordeaux*, new series, x (1961).

——, 'Le financement de la croisade Anglaise de 1270', *Bibliothèque de l'école des Chartes*, cxix (1961).

——, 'Itinéraire d'Edouard I en France, 1286–89', *BIHR*, xxv (1952).

——, 'Un rôle de lettres patentes émanées du prince Edouard pendant son premier séjour en Gascogne (Mai–Octobre 1254)', in *Receuil des travaux offert à M. Clovis Brunel* (Paris, 1955).

TRAUTZ, F., *Die Könige von England und das Reich, 1272–1377* (Heidelberg, 1961).

TREHARNE, R.F., *The Baronial Plan of Reform* (Manchester, 1932).

TURNER, T.H., 'Unpublished notices of the times of Edward I', *Archaeological Journal*, viii (1851).

ULLMANN, W., 'The Curial Exequies for Edward I and Edward III', *Ecclesiastical History Review*, vi (1955).

VALE, J., *Edward III and Chivalry* (1983).

VALE, M.G.A., 'The Gascon Nobility and the Anglo-French War, 1294–8', *War and Government in the Middle Ages*, ed. J.B. Gillingham and J.C. Holt (Woodbridge, 1984).

Victoria County History, A History of the County of Cheshire, ed. B.E. Harris, iii (1980).

VINOGRADOFF, P., 'Ralph of Hengham as Chief Justice of the Common Pleas', *Essays in Medieval History presented to T.F. Tout*, ed. A.G. Little and F.M. Powicke (Manchester, 1925).

WAGNER, A.R., *Catalogue of English Medieval Rolls of Arms* (Harleian Society, 1948).

WALKER, R.F., 'The Hagnaby Chronicle and the Battle of Maes Moydog', *Welsh History Review*, viii (1976–7).

WARREN, W.L., *Henry II* (1973).

WATERS, W.H., *The Edwardian Settlement of North Wales* (1935).

WAUGH, S.L., 'The Fiscal Uses of Royal Wardships in the Reign of Edward I', *Thirteenth Century England 1*, ed. P.R. Coss and S.D. Lloyd (Woodbridge, 1986).

WILKINSON, B., *Constitutional History of England 1216–1399*, i (1948).

——, *Studies in the Constitutional History of the 13th and 14th centuries* (Manchester, 1937).

WILLARD, J.F., 'An Exchequer Reform under Edward I', *The Crusades and other Historical Essays presented to Dana C. Munro*, ed. L.J. Paetow (New York, 1928).

——, *Parliamentary Taxes on Personal Property, 1290 to 1334* (Cambridge, Mass., 1934).

WILLIAMS, G.A., *Medieval London from Commune to Capital* (1963).

WILSON, R.M., *The Lost Literature of Medieval England* (1952).

WOLFFE, B.P., *The Royal Demesne in English History* (1971).

YOUNG, C.R., *The Royal Forests of Medieval England* (Leicester, 1979).

ZUCKERMAN, C. 'The ending of French interference in the papal financial system in 1297: a neglected episode', *Viator*, xi (1980).

INDEX

Hexham (Northumb.), 471, 507

Hobelars, 514

Hohenstaufen family, 318

Holderness (Humberside), 36, 104

Holebrook, Richard de, 102–3, 234

Holland, 129, 388–9, 391, 456; counts of, *see* Florence, John

Holmcoltram (Cumbria), 141, 556

Holt (Clwyd), 216

Holy Island (Northumb.), 365, 543

Honorius IV, pope, 323–4, 327–8

Hope (Clwyd), 183, 189, 217, 229

Hopton, Walter de, 186, 340–1

Horses, 75, 111, 162–3, 177, 197, 229, 494; valuation list, 484–5

Hospitallers, 77, 80–1, 234

Hostage, Richard le, 431

Hotham, William de, abp of Dublin, 313, 325, 328, 387, 393

Hoton, Richard de, 541–4

Household, Edward's as prince, 7, 15, 23, 26, 68–9; as k., 134ff; accounts, 479, 492, 507; clerks, 138–45, 478, 561; in Flanders, 478; jurisdiction, 165–8, 462, 523, 553; knights, 59, 134–5, 147–54, 176, 484–5; Ordinance (1279), 135, 143, 145–6, 168; *see also* Edward I; Wardrobe

Huelgas, las (Spain), 10

Hugh, k. of Cyprus, 66, 76–7

Hugh, Little St, of Lincoln, 345

Hull, *see* Kingston upon Hull

Hulton, Vincent de, 201

Humber, river, 99, 460

Hundred Rolls, 92–8, 106, 235, 258, 262, 291, 301, 460, 560

Hungary, k. of, 330

Huntercombe, Walter de, 362

Hunting, 6–7, 115, 117, 161, 186

Huntingdonshire, 262, 272, 283, 289, 410

Huntington (Powys), 42

Huxloe Hundred (Northants), 95

Hyde (Hants), abt of, 276

Hyde, Roger de la, 460

Hythe (Kent), 383

Infantry, 180, 198, 498, 513; recruitment, 407, 470, 484–5, 493; Welsh, 480–1, 485–6, 489; *and see* desertion

Ingoldsmells (Lincs), 432

Inquiries, into crown rights (1255), 93; in shires (1258), 29, 93; of 1279, 235–6; Kirkby's Quest, 236–7, 243, 266; in Gascony, 301, 303, 311; of 1298, 431–2, 563; *see also* Hundred Rolls

Inverkip (Strathclyde), 499

Ipswich, 165

Ireland, 22, 47–8, 188, 246, 299, 402, 438, 476, 510, 513; under Edward as prince, 11–14, 19–20, 26, 40, 52; Edward's rule of, as

k., 353–4, 553; franchises, 263, 539–40; law, 288; parliament, 464; profits from, 521, 553; troops from, 493, 499; victuals from, 19, 179, 198–9, 225, 228, 231, 480, 482, 486, 553

Irfon Bridge (Powys), 193

Irvine (Strathclyde), 477

Isabel of Fife, countess of Buchan, 109, 508–9

Isabella, countess of Aumale, 62

Isabella, qu. of Edward II, 395, 398, 452, 549–50, 553

Isabella, qu. of King John, 21

Iscennen, commote of, 204

Italian bankers, 36, 100, 137, 179, 219, 244–5, 249, 278, 332, 344–5, 390, 403, 438, 533–5; *see also* Ballardi, Frescobaldi, Riccardi

Jaffa (Israel), 66

Jaime, señor of Gerica, 152, 155

James II, k. of Aragon, 326, 389

James, k. of Majorca, 323–4

James, Master, *see* St George

James, Steward of Scotland, 359, 473, 476–8, 483, 500

Jardin, Eustace de, 152

Jay, Brian de, Master of the Temple, 481

Jeanne of Dammartin, 123, 126, 316

Jeanne of Navarre, 305, 315

Jeanne, qu. of Philip IV, 379

Jedburgh (Borders), 374, 497, 504, 514

Jerusalem, 66–7, 76–7, 79, 81, 85, 328, 331, 545, 565

Jesmond, Adam of, 68

Jews, 101, 188, 245, 250, 436; debts to, 35, 62, 65, 104, 125, 155; expelled from Gascony, 306, 345; expelled from England, 343–6; receipts from, 38, 80

Joan of Acre, dau. of Edward I, 79, 126–9, 312, 317, 343, 348–51, 439, 538

Joan, dau. of Edward I (d. 1265), 126

John, k. of England, 8, 12, 22, 115, 132, 228, 314, 398, 407, 518

John, count of Holland, 128–9

John, duke of Brabant, 163, 317, 333, 387, 400, 422

John, duke of Brittany (d. 1305), 235, 275

John of Brittany (e. of Richmond), 127, 132, 298, 381–2, 385, 464, 504, 515

John, s. of Edward I, 82, 126

Joinville, Jean de (brother of Geoffrey de Geneville), 108

Jülich, margrave of, 392

Justices, 102, 153, 537; trial of, 89–93, 460

Justiciar, post of, 25

Kalavun, sultan of Egypt, 329

Katherine, dau. of Edward I, 125–6

Katzenellenbogen, count of, 387

Keighley, Henry de, 449, 525–6, 551

Keith, Robert, 489